P9-DVS-102

BOEING

BOEING 747 B
HB-IGA

BOEING

PLANEMAKER TO THE WORLD

ROBERT REDDING & BILL YENNE

Crescent Books
A Division of Crown Publishers, Inc.
A Bison Book

17 Sherwood Place
Greenwich, Conn. 06830
U.S.A.

This 1983 Edition is published by
Crescent Books, distributed by
Crown Publishers Inc.

Printed in Hong Kong

ISBN 0-517-422700

HGFEDCBA

Reprinted 1984

Half-title page: The **P-26 Peashooter**, which made its appearance in 1932, was the US Army Air Corps' first all-metal monoplane fighter and probably Boeing's most famous fighter. In its day it was the fastest fighter in service and though outclassed by the time of World War II, it gave a good account of itself in the war's first week.

Title spread: Boeing built the world's biggest building in order to assemble the world's biggest jetliner. Boeing's **Model 747** is the overwhelming choice of major carriers flying long-distance international routes and can be seen at any major airport in the world.

Below: This billboard appeared near **Boeing Field** around 1941 at a time Boeing was pioneering its multi-engined aircraft. By this time the company that had started in a boathouse on Lake Union was one of the world leaders in the field of four-engine aircraft.

CONTENTS

Charts and Production Closeups

BOEING AND THE NORTHWEST

The Boeing Company, together with its subsidiaries, is one of America's major aerospace firms, the largest manufacturer of transport aircraft in the Western world and the largest non-agricultural employer in the Northwestern United States. Boeing exerts a powerful and unique influence on that area of the Northwest around the city of Seattle, providing fully ten percent of the jobs in the area. There is a saying in the Northwest that sums up Boeing's importance: 'As goes Boeing, so go I.' It is significant that this notion permeates the thinking of an entire region.

Boeing's principal business is conducted through four divisional 'Companies,' Boeing Commercial Airplane Company, Boeing Aerospace Company, Boeing Military Airplane Company and Boeing Vertol Company. Of Boeing's roughly one hundred thousand employees, half (49.5 percent) are employed by the Boeing Commercial Airplane Company, 17.8 percent are employed by the Boeing Military Airplane Company, 17.2 percent are employed by Boeing Aerospace, 4.6 percent are employed by Boeing Vertol while 6.4 percent are employed in Boeing's Computer Service Company.

Boeing was born in Seattle, and continues to maintain its corporate headquarters there, with many of its important activities in or very near to Seattle. Three quarters (74.9 percent) of Boeing's employees work in the Seattle area, compared to 15.4

Below: **Boeing Field** circa 1983, looking south toward Mount Rainier, with examples of all of Boeing's 707 through 767 airframes visible in the foreground.

percent in Wichita, headquarters of Boeing Military Airplane Company, and 4.6 percent near Philadelphia, the headquarters of Boeing Vertol.

William E Boeing began building aircraft in 1915 on the shores of Lake Union in the center of Seattle, and on 15 July 1916 Pacific Aero Products was incorporated. In April 1917 the company name was changed to The Boeing Airplane Company and the company moved to the present headquarters site in the southern part of the city adjacent to the Seattle/King County Airport (Boeing Field). The headquarters site centers on Plant 2, the famous factory complex which has presided over the construction of many of Boeing's most famous aircraft from the *Monomail* through the B-17 to the B-52. Today the Plant 2 complex houses the corporate headquarters, the wind tunnel, the E-3A (Airborne Warning and Control System, or AWACS) Program, the E-4A & B Advanced Airborne Command Post Program, the Minuteman Missile Modification Program, sheet metal and line gear operations for the Fabrication Division as well as the Roland Missile Program. Adjacent to Plant 2 are the Customer Training Center and the Thompson Tract, which is the site of new program engine buildup. Down the road a short distance is the Boeing Developmental Center, site of Military Airplane Development Management, the Minuteman Program, the Army Systems Division, the Short Range Attack Missile (SRAM) Program and the MX Missile Program. Across the street (East Marginal Way South) at Boeing Field is the Boeing Flight Center and the final delivery point for all commercial aircraft, except the 747 and 767.

In the course of the expansion of the Company during World War II a new plant was built in Renton at the southern tip of Lake Washington. Today Renton is the headquarters site of the Boeing Commercial Airplane Company and the manufacturing site for 707, 727, 737, 757 and E-3A (AWACS) aircraft. Renton is also the headquarters of Boeing Marine Systems and, because of the close proximity to Lake Washington, the manufacturing site for Marine Systems' military hydrofoils and commercial Jetfoils.

In 1966, with the go-ahead for the 747 Program, Boeing acquired 780 acres adjacent to Paine Field in Everett, 30 miles north of Seattle, on which to construct the 747 manufacturing complex. Included in the complex is the world's largest building in volume. Originally containing 200 million cubic feet, the building was enlarged in the early 1980s to 285 million to accommodate production of the 767 jetliner. As a result, major portions of manufacturing, sub-assembly and final assembly for both aircraft are housed under one roof. As the 767 Program evolves into the 777 Program, this development may take place at the huge Everett site. About another 30 miles north from Everett at Tulalip, Boeing has located its Hazardous Testing Site.

South of the Seattle/Renton area at Kent are the Boeing Space Center and the Spares Support Center. The Boeing Space Center houses the headquarters of the Boeing Aerospace Company, engineering and high technology aspects of Boeing Computer

Below: An open house at **Boeing Field** circa 1955, with all of Boeing's major military aircraft of the previous two decades: a B-17, a B-29, a B-47, a KC-97, the then brand-new B-52A and the XB-52 in the background.

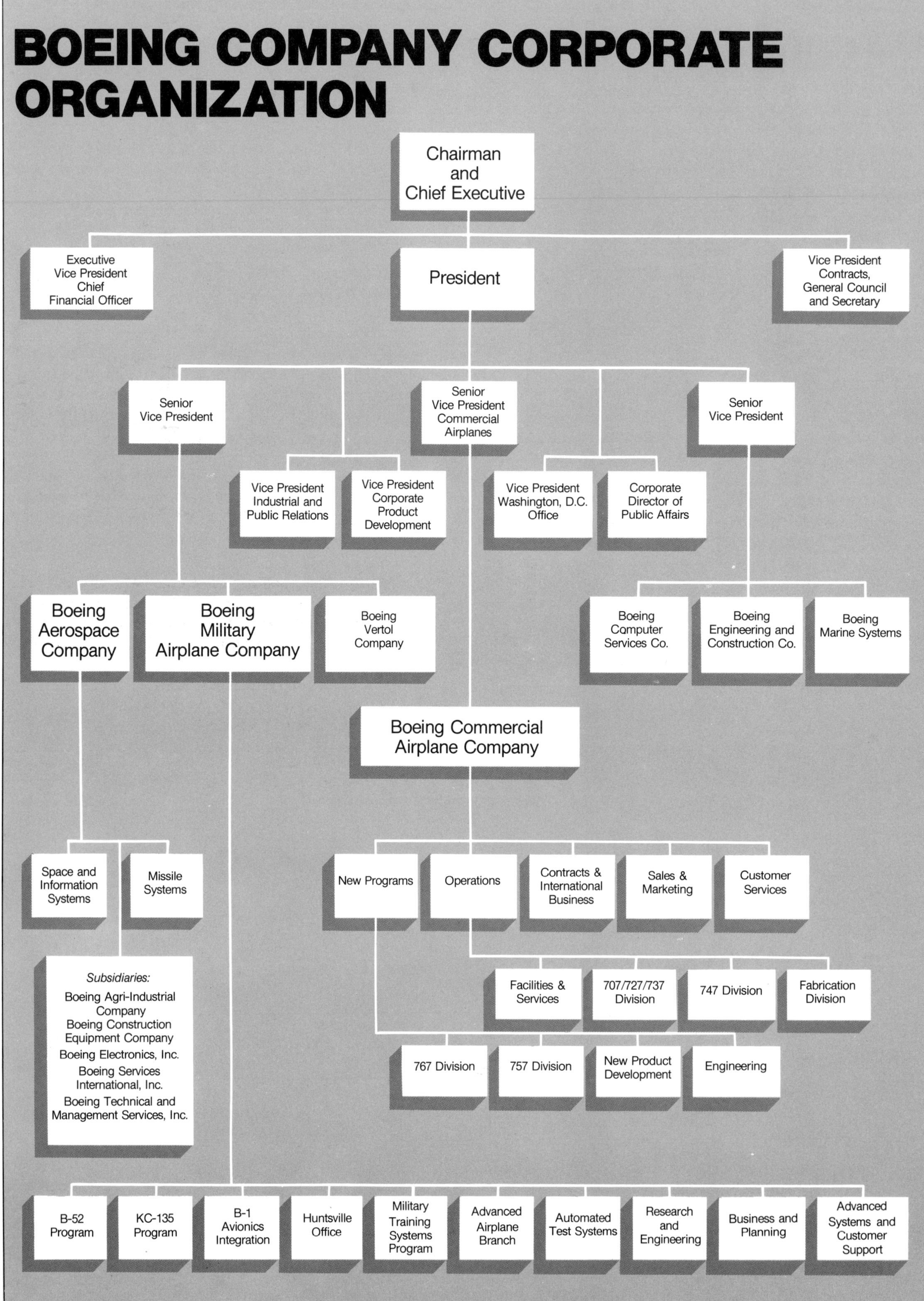

BOEING COMPANY CORPORATE ORGANIZATION
Chairman and Chief Executive
Executive Vice President Chief Financial Officer
President
Vice President Contracts, General Council and Secretary
Senior Vice President
Senior Vice President Commercial Airplanes
Senior Vice President
Vice President Industrial and Public Relations
Vice President Corporate Product Development
Vice President Washington, D.C. Office
Corporate Director of Public Affairs
Boeing Aerospace Company
Boeing Military Airplane Company
Boeing Vertol Company
Boeing Computer Services Co.
Boeing Engineering and Construction Co.
Boeing Marine Systems
Boeing Commercial Airplane Company
Space and Information Systems
Missile Systems
New Programs
Operations
Contracts & International Business
Sales & Marketing
Customer Services
Subsidiaries:
Boeing Agri-Industrial Company
Boeing Construction Equipment Company
Boeing Electronics, Inc.
Boeing Services International, Inc.
Boeing Technical and Management Services, Inc.
Facilities & Services
707/727/737 Division
747 Division
Fabrication Division
767 Division
757 Division
New Product Development
Engineering
B-52 Program
KC-135 Program
B-1 Avionics Integration
Huntsville Office
Military Training Systems Program
Advanced Airplane Branch
Automated Test Systems
Research and Engineering
Business and Planning
Advanced Systems and Customer Support

Above: Boeing's **Renton** facility at the foot of Lake Washington is the site of the Boeing Commercial Airplane Company headquarters as well as the Boeing Marine Systems headquarters. The jetliner models 707, 727, 737 and 757 are all produced here.

Services, Missile and Space programs management, Product Development and the Air Launched Cruise Missile (ALCM) Program. The Spares Support Center houses the Boeing Computer Services Company, Boeing Surplus Sales and a warehouse complex. The Boeing Employment Center, and the Boeing Engineering and Construction Company are based at Southcenter, while the Fabrication and Spares divisions of the Boeing Commercial Airplane Company are located still farther south at Auburn.

Boeing's principal locations outside the Seattle area at Wichita and Philadelphia were acquired in 1934 and 1960 respectively. In 1934 Boeing bought the Stearman Aircraft Company of Wichita which became the Wichita Division of Boeing in 1939. After World War II Boeing's military operations were gradually concentrated in Wichita. Boeing acquired the Vertol Aircraft Company (formerly Piasecki Aircraft Corporation) in 1960 as the Boeing Vertol Division. In 1972 the Division became the Boeing Vertol Company.

Boeing is today the largest manufacturer of commercial jetliners in the Western world, outdistancing McDonnell Douglas and Lockheed combined. While Boeing was rolling out its quiet

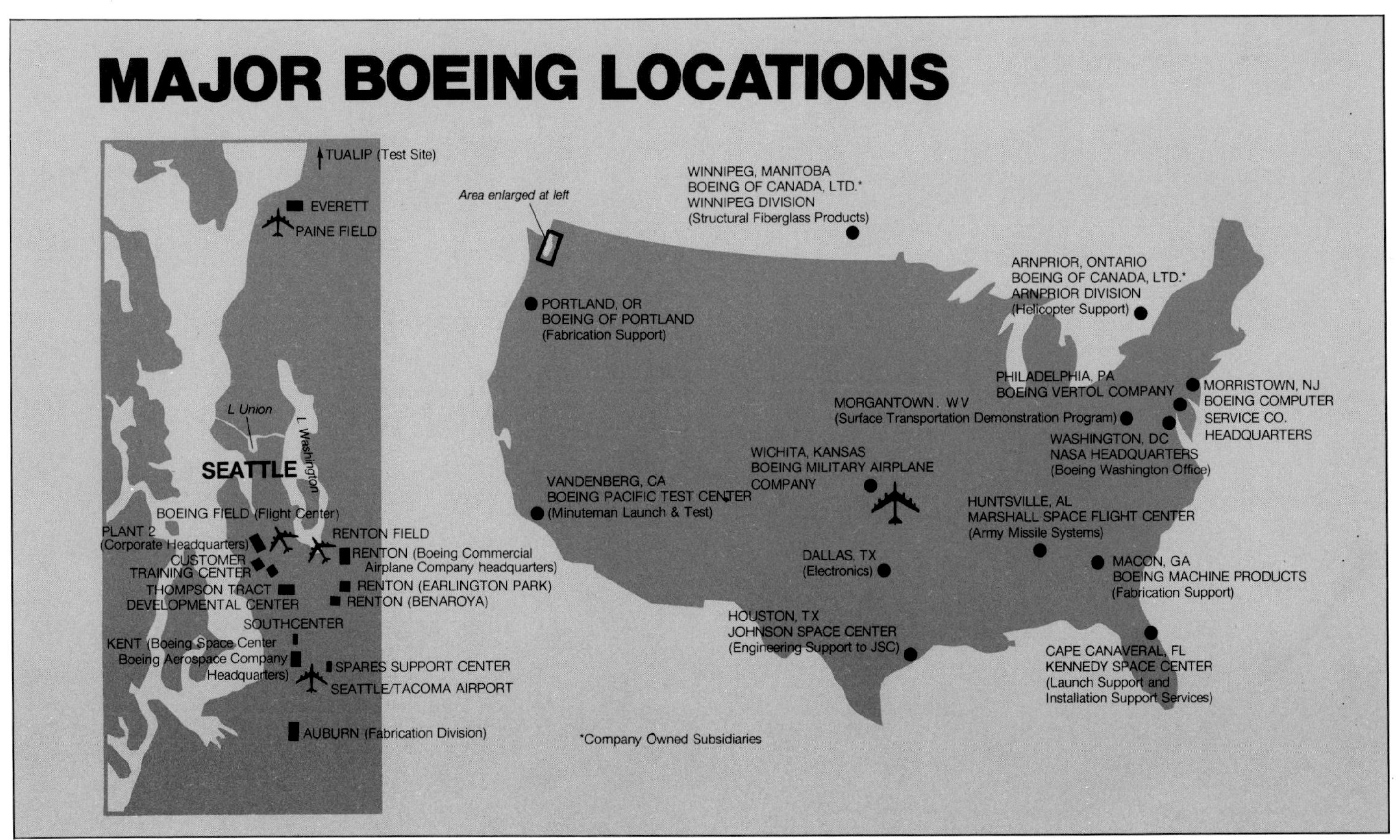

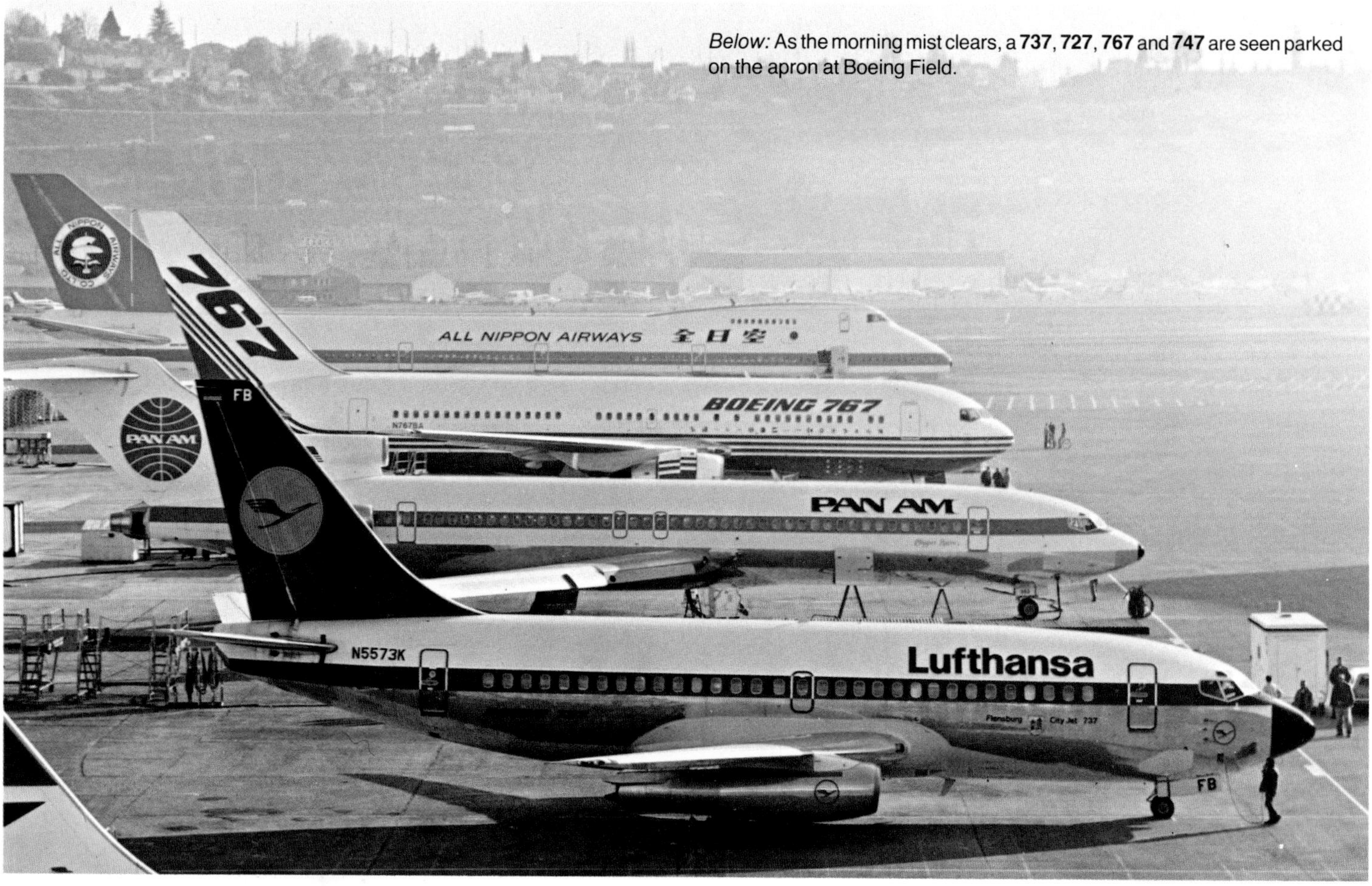
ALL NIPPON AIRWAYS
767
BOEING 767
PAN AM
N5573K
Lufthansa
FB

Below: As the morning mist clears, a **737**, **727**, **767** and **747** are seen parked on the apron at Boeing Field.

BOEING SALES AND AVERAGE ANNUAL EMPLOYMENT

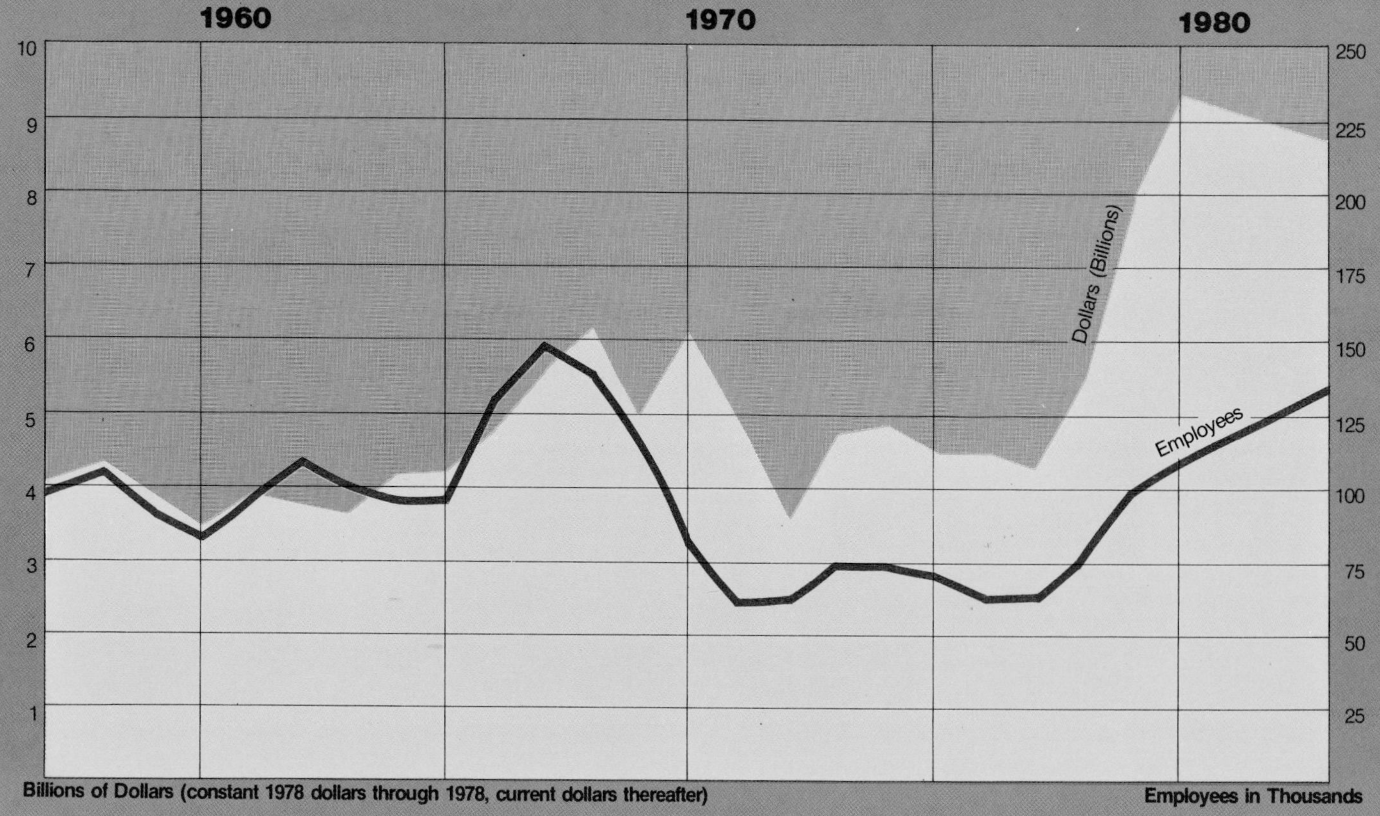
1960
1970
1980
10
9
8
7
6
5
4
3
2
1
250
225
200
175
150
125
100
75
50
25
Dollars (Billions)
Employees
Billions of Dollars (constant 1978 dollars through 1978, current dollars thereafter)
Employees in Thousands

and fuel efficient 757 and 767 in the early 1980s, McDonnell Douglas had nothing on the horizon to succeed or complement its DC-9 and DC-10, and Lockheed was announcing the closing of its L-1011 assembly line. Boeing's principal competition in the 1980s and 1990s is seen to be Airbus Industries, a European consortium based in Toulouse, France. While in the early 1980s Airbus moved ahead of McDonnell Douglas and Lockheed in worldwide sales volume with its popular A300, it has yet even to approach Boeing. Of the jetliners presently in service with the world's airlines (excluding Aeroflot of the USSR), Boeing enjoys a comfortable market share in excess of 60 percent.

Boeing's family tree reads like a Who's Who of American aircraft history. The Model 314 Clipper was a household word on the transpacific and transatlantic airways in the years before the war, while during World War II the B-17 and B-29 were certainly among the dozen or even half dozen most important and famous of the thousands of aircraft types that served. Today planes like the 707, 727 and certainly the 747 are household words among the millions who fly on business and pleasure.

Many other companies and regions have profited from Boeing's success. In the 757 Program, for example, Boeing has awarded sub-contracts to the value of some $2,000,000,000 to 1400 companies for the production of major and minor components. US companies have received the largest share but not all. Manufacturers in Australia, Canada, England, Northern Ireland, Japan and Spain are also involved.

When the giant superjet, the 747, was in production, about 50 percent of the work (by value) was subcontracted to other firms. Approximately 1500 primary suppliers and 15,000 secondary suppliers, located in 47 states of the USA and six foreign countries, could thank Boeing for at least a portion of their income.

The airplane business fluctuates. Some years are better than others, and knowing this, Boeing has diversified even beyond the areas already mentioned. Among other projects the company has undertaken recently is a study of backaches. Much of the company's work comes through competitive bidding. Recently a $200,000 NASA contract to see how supersonic transport technology could be applied to combat aircraft was won. For Boeing this is not a large contract but the point was not so much the money involved as the contact with a new opportunity. Eventually jobs may be the fruit of the contract, jobs not only for Seattle and the Northwest, but for the United States as a whole and for other countries.

While Boeing owes its success to a variety of factors, what it all seems to boil down to is the Company's reputation for building sound, dependable, thoroughly thought out, high quality products. Each member of the Boeing Jetliner family, for example, is thoughtfully designed for a specific market. The 737 is designed to serve short feeder routes, the 727 and now the 757 for intermediate distances, and the 747 and 767 for long distance intercontinental flights. As one airline executive put it, Boeing is always coming up with the right plane, at the right price, and at the right time.

William Boeing once wrote, 'Our task is to keep everlastingly at research and experiment, to adapt our laboratories to production as soon as practicable, to let no new improvement in flying and flying equipment pass us by.'

They are words for any company to live by.

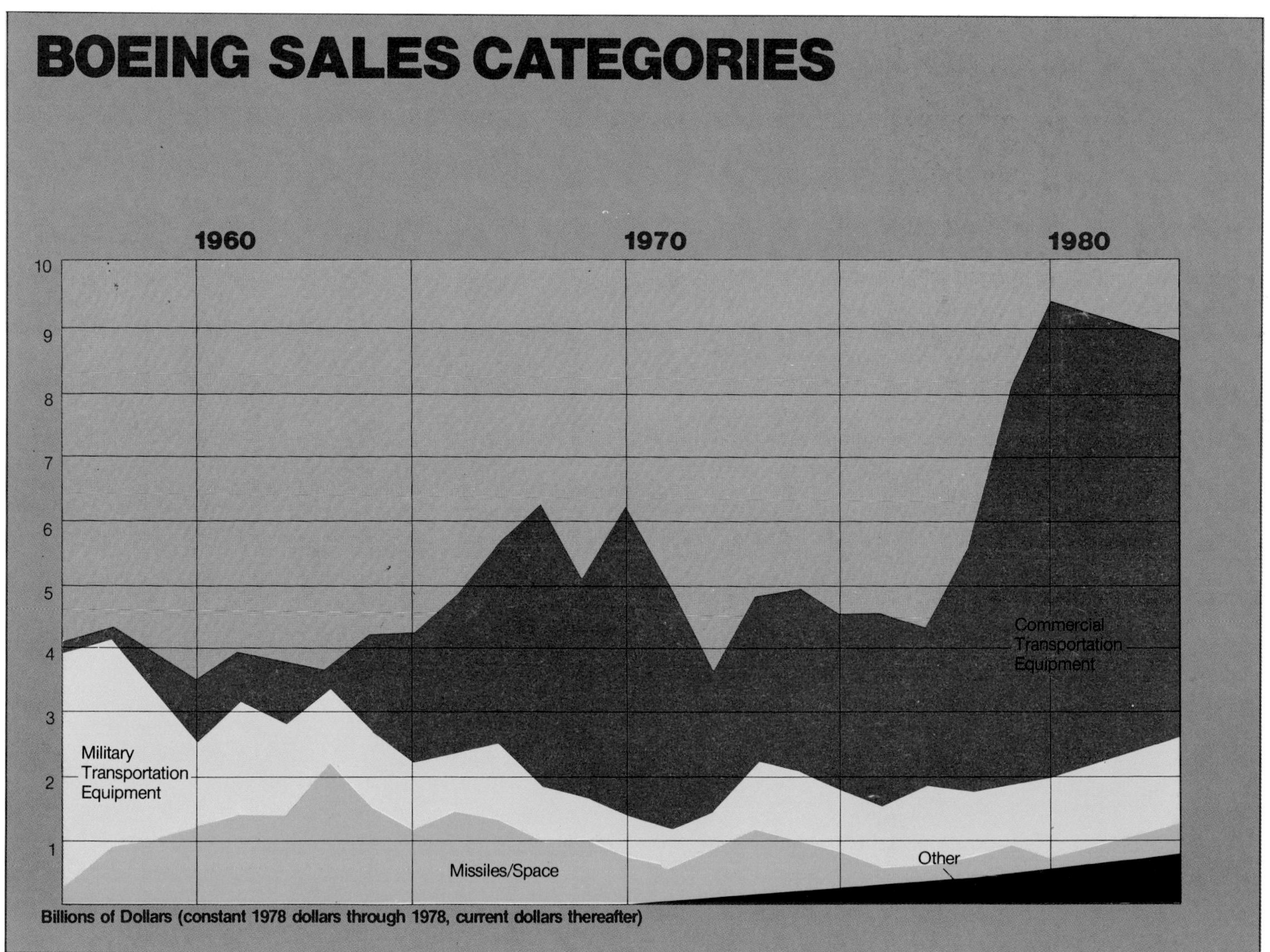

THE EARLY YEARS

On 4 July 1914, a barnstormer named Terah Maroney was hired to put on a flying exhibition as part of the Independence Day festivities in Seattle, Washington. Having put on a display of acrobatics in his Curtiss seaplane, Maroney landed and offered to take up passengers. A lumber company owner named William Edward Boeing stepped up and allowed as how he would like to take a ride. What happened in the next 30 minutes changed the course of aviation history and the history of the Northwest as well. William E Boeing had caught the flying bug. He was never to recover. During the ensuing two decades Bill Boeing built one of the most successful aircraft manufacturing companies in the country as well as being a founding partner in the air passenger service that would become United Airlines, today the largest airline in the world.

Bill Boeing had a tenacious mind, one that viewed the world as a place full of opportunities. In addition to his timber interests, he owned a furniture factory and a boat yard. They were successful, and aircraft, he reasoned, had potential. Public opinion would not have agreed with Boeing's optimism. Flying was considered a dangerous game, a plaything for stuntmen and thrill seekers. During the years since Orville and Wilbur Wright first took a heavier-than-air craft aloft at Kitty Hawk, in 1903, flying had not advanced far into the public consciousness as a means of transportation. Though Louis Bleriot had flown across the English Channel on 25 July 1909, aircraft were not taken seriously. Even when so serious a man as Alexander Graham Bell, inventor of the telephone, experimented with flight, public opinion still catered to the flamboyant. When another American,

Right: The **B & W**, the first Boeing plane, is launched from Boeing's factory on the shores of Lake Union. The plane, whose profile resembled that of the seaplane Bill Boeing had purchased earlier from Glenn Martin, was supposed to make its maiden flight on 29 June 1916 with Herb Munter at the controls. For some reason Munter was late in arriving for the event, so Boeing himself climbed into the rear cockpit and took his Model 1 aloft. When he brought the plane back down, Munter was the first to greet him. When asked how the flight had gone, Boeing responded by telling the small group of workers assembled at the Lake Union plant that they were at last in the airplane business.

PRODUCTION CLOSE-UP:

BOEING AIRCRAFT 1916-1935

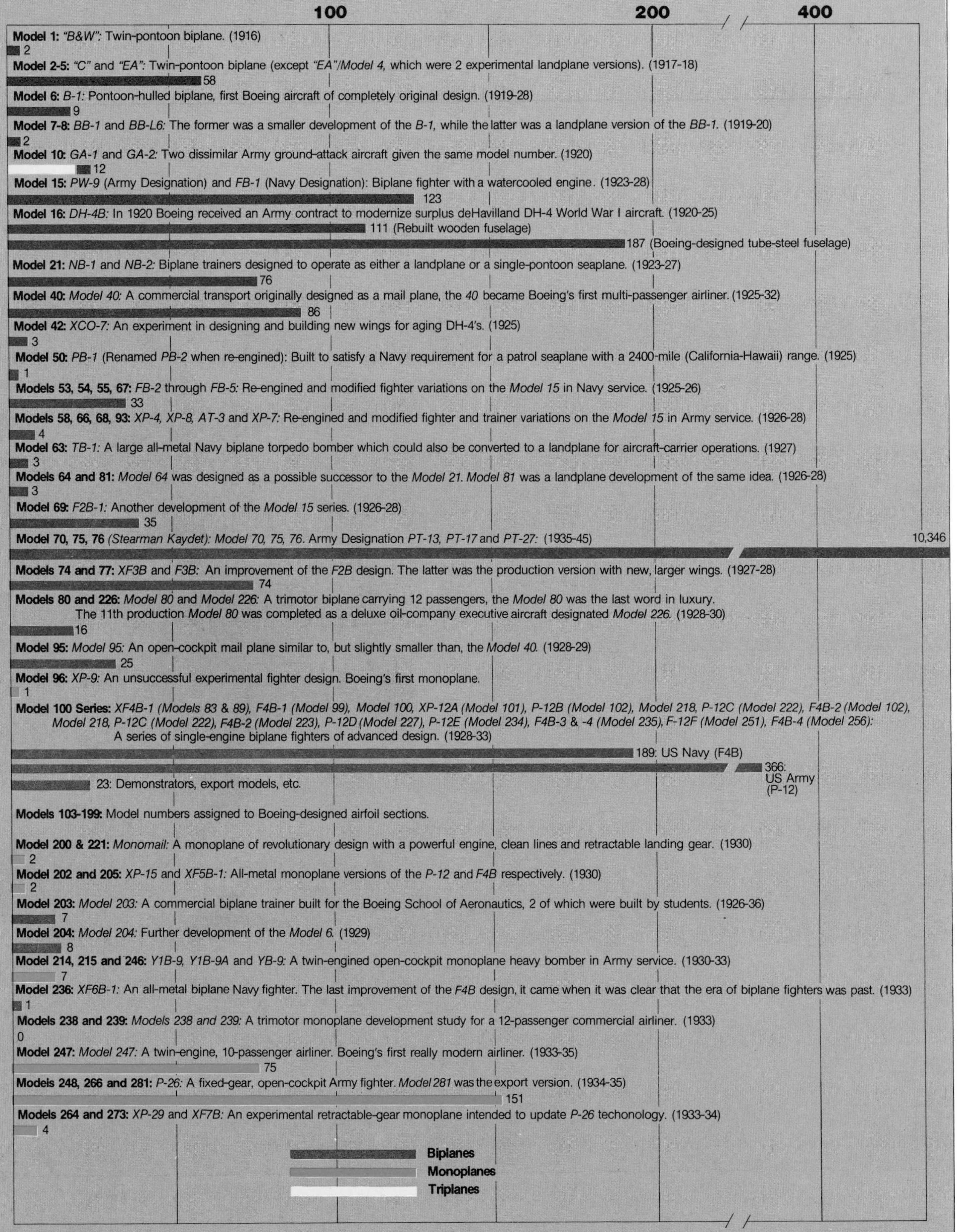

100 200 400

Model 1: *"B&W":* Twin-pontoon biplane. (1916)
2

Model 2-5: *"C"* and *"EA":* Twin-pontoon biplane (except *"EA"/Model 4,* which were 2 experimental landplane versions). (1917-18)
58

Model 6: *B-1:* Pontoon-hulled biplane, first Boeing aircraft of completely original design. (1919-28)
9

Model 7-8: *BB-1* and *BB-L6:* The former was a smaller development of the *B-1,* while the latter was a landplane version of the *BB-1.* (1919-20)
2

Model 10: *GA-1* and *GA-2:* Two dissimilar Army ground-attack aircraft given the same model number. (1920)
12

Model 15: *PW-9* (Army Designation) and *FB-1* (Navy Designation): Biplane fighter with a watercooled engine. (1923-28)
123

Model 16: *DH-4B:* In 1920 Boeing received an Army contract to modernize surplus deHavilland DH-4 World War I aircraft. (1920-25)
111 (Rebuilt wooden fuselage)
187 (Boeing-designed tube-steel fuselage)

Model 21: *NB-1* and *NB-2:* Biplane trainers designed to operate as either a landplane or a single-pontoon seaplane. (1923-27)
76

Model 40: *Model 40:* A commercial transport originally designed as a mail plane, the *40* became Boeing's first multi-passenger airliner. (1925-32)
86

Model 42: *XCO-7:* An experiment in designing and building new wings for aging DH-4's. (1925)
3

Model 50: *PB-1* (Renamed *PB-2* when re-engined): Built to satisfy a Navy requirement for a patrol seaplane with a 2400-mile (California-Hawaii) range. (1925)
1

Models 53, 54, 55, 67: *FB-2* through *FB-5:* Re-engined and modified fighter variations on the *Model 15* in Navy service. (1925-26)
33

Models 58, 66, 68, 93: *XP-4, XP-8, AT-3* and *XP-7:* Re-engined and modified fighter and trainer variations on the *Model 15* in Army service. (1926-28)
4

Model 63: *TB-1:* A large all-metal Navy biplane torpedo bomber which could also be converted to a landplane for aircraft-carrier operations. (1927)
3

Models 64 and 81: *Model 64* was designed as a possible successor to the *Model 21. Model 81* was a landplane development of the same idea. (1926-28)
3

Model 69: *F2B-1:* Another development of the *Model 15* series. (1926-28)
35

Model 70, 75, 76 *(Stearman Kaydet): Model 70, 75, 76.* Army Designation *PT-13, PT-17* and *PT-27:* (1935-45)
10,346

Models 74 and 77: *XF3B* and *F3B:* An improvement of the *F2B* design. The latter was the production version with new, larger wings. (1927-28)
74

Models 80 and 226: *Model 80* and *Model 226:* A trimotor biplane carrying 12 passengers, the *Model 80* was the last word in luxury. The 11th production *Model 80* was completed as a deluxe oil-company executive aircraft designated *Model 226.* (1928-30)
16

Model 95: *Model 95:* An open-cockpit mail plane similar to, but slightly smaller than, the *Model 40.* (1928-29)
25

Model 96: *XP-9:* An unsuccessful experimental fighter design. Boeing's first monoplane.
1

Model 100 Series: *XF4B-1 (Models 83 & 89), F4B-1 (Model 99), Model 100, XP-12A (Model 101), P-12B (Model 102), Model 218, P-12C (Model 222), F4B-2 (Model 102), Model 218, P-12C (Model 222), F4B-2 (Model 223), P-12D (Model 227), P-12E (Model 234), F4B-3 & -4 (Model 235), F-12F (Model 251), F4B-4 (Model 256):* A series of single-engine biplane fighters of advanced design. (1928-33)
189: US Navy (F4B)
366: US Army (P-12)
23: Demonstrators, export models, etc.

Models 103-199: Model numbers assigned to Boeing-designed airfoil sections.

Model 200 & 221: *Monomail:* A monoplane of revolutionary design with a powerful engine, clean lines and retractable landing gear. (1930)
2

Model 202 and 205: *XP-15* and *XF5B-1:* All-metal monoplane versions of the *P-12* and *F4B* respectively. (1930)
2

Model 203: *Model 203:* A commercial biplane trainer built for the Boeing School of Aeronautics, 2 of which were built by students. (1926-36)
7

Model 204: *Model 204:* Further development of the *Model 6.* (1929)
8

Model 214, 215 and 246: *Y1B-9, Y1B-9A* and *YB-9:* A twin-engined open-cockpit monoplane heavy bomber in Army service. (1930-33)
7

Model 236: *XF6B-1:* An all-metal biplane Navy fighter. The last improvement of the *F4B* design, it came when it was clear that the era of biplane fighters was past. (1933)
1

Models 238 and 239: *Models 238 and 239:* A trimotor monoplane development study for a 12-passenger commercial airliner. (1933)
0

Model 247: *Model 247:* A twin-engine, 10-passenger airliner. Boeing's first really modern airliner. (1933-35)
75

Models 248, 266 and 281: *P-26:* A fixed-gear, open-cockpit Army fighter. *Model 281* was the export version. (1934-35)
151

Models 264 and 273: *XP-29* and *XF7B:* An experimental retractable-gear monoplane intended to update *P-26* techonology. (1933-34)
4

Biplanes
Monoplanes
Triplanes

Above: The twin-pontooned **B & W** during taxiing trials on Lake Union.

Glenn Curtiss, remained aloft for two hours and fifty-one minutes in 1910, flying was still a curiosity.

However, Boeing had met Navy Commander Conrad Westervelt in Seattle. Westervelt was stationed at the Naval shipyards in Bremerton, across Puget Sound. The two men hit it off from the start. They went boating together on Boeing's yacht, and among the many topics discussed was that of aviation, in which both were deeply interested. Prompted by this interest, Boeing finally took his first airplane ride. He and Westervelt both went aloft with Terah Maroney in a Curtiss seaplane with a pusher type engine. The excursions convinced Boeing that he should build his own plane, and he had the means to do so. To Westervelt's astonishment, Boeing asked him to design the aircraft, which was to be a seaplane. Westervelt had had no experience in aircraft design. Few people did. Testing facilities were just as scarce. There was only one wind tunnel in existence capable of such a large job, and that was at the Massachusetts Institute of Technology, some 3000 miles away. Nor were aircraft engineers plentiful. Aeronautics was not exactly a hot item in the university curriculum. But Westervelt accepted the challenge. He contacted the right people, learned from them what he could, and designed what came to be named the B & W, after the initials of the two originators.

The B & W was a utility aircraft, accommodating two, seated in tandem. It was powered by a Hall-Scott A-5, water-cooled, 125 horsepower (hp) engine, and the wingspan was 52 feet. The length, overall, was 27 feet 6 inches. The aircraft was designated, simply Model 1. The B & W was built in two different locations. The fuselage was put together in a hangar on Seattle's Lake Union. The wings and floats were assembled at the Heath Shipyard, on Puget Sound's Elliot Bay. Boeing had purchased the shipyard primarily as a repair shop for his yacht, but he quickly changed it into a factory. There were few aircraft technicians, so carpenters, shipwrights and cabinet makers from Boeing's furniture factory were employed. Ed Heath, a man familiar with boats, supervised the construction of the pontoons.

In the meantime, Boeing had taken flying lessons at Glenn Martin's school in Los Angeles. He returned to Seattle in October 1915, after purchasing a ten thousand dollar seaplane

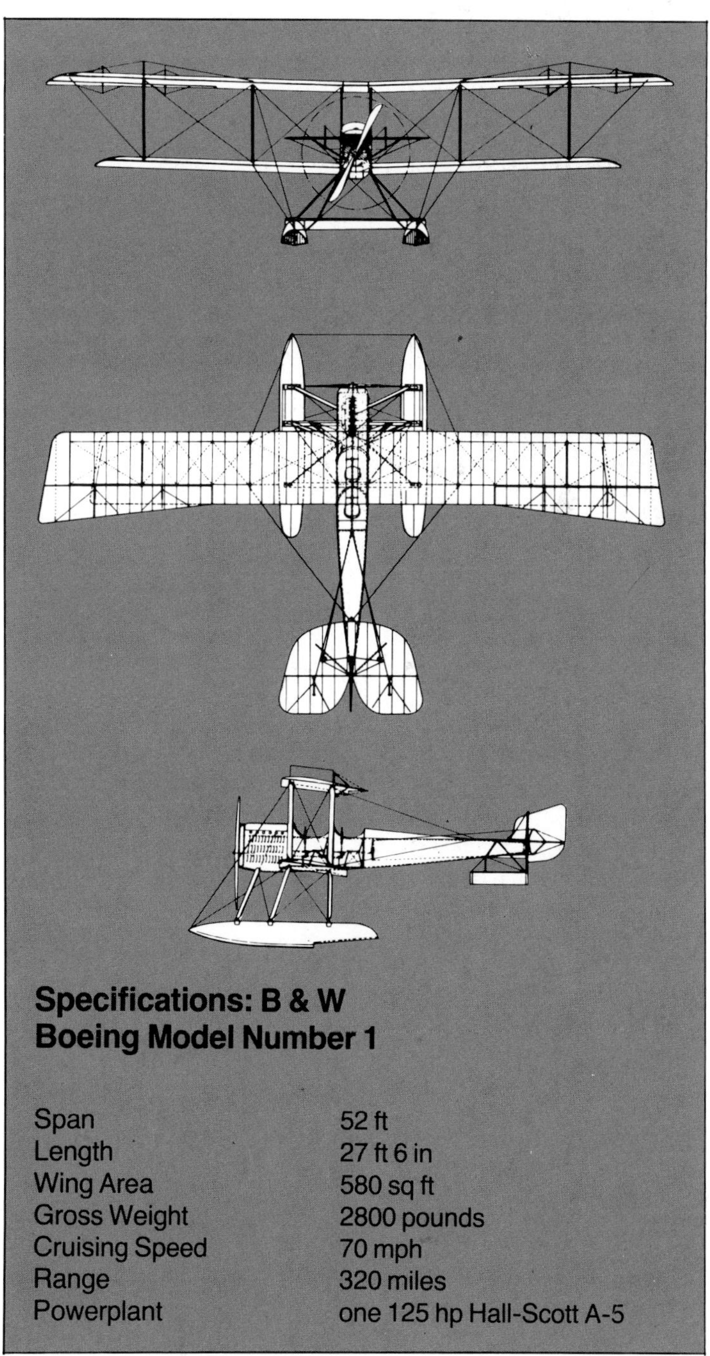

Specifications: B & W
Boeing Model Number 1

Span	52 ft
Length	27 ft 6 in
Wing Area	580 sq ft
Gross Weight	2800 pounds
Cruising Speed	70 mph
Range	320 miles
Powerplant	one 125 hp Hall-Scott A-5

Below: The **EA**, Boeing Model 4, was the landplane version of the Model C (model numbers 2, 3 and 5). The US Army ordered a pair of EAs as trainers with side-by-side seating and a 90hp Curtiss OX-5 engine.

Specifications: Model C/EA
Boeing Model Numbers 2-5

Span	43 ft 10 in
Length	27 ft
Wing Area	495 sq ft
Gross Weight	2395 pounds
Cruising Speed	65 mph
Service Ceiling	6500 ft
Range	200 miles
Powerplant	one 100 hp Hall-Scott A-7A
Capacity	1 passenger

from Martin. Floyd Smith, his instructor, went to Seattle to uncrate and assemble the plane. Aircraft were shipped in crates, hence the expression 'crate,' meaning aircraft, which came into popular use during World War I.

Herb Munter, a 22-year-old mechanic, who had built and flown his own planes, was hired to fly the Martin. Munter, an expert at improvization, shaped his own aircraft from wood and home-sewn fabrics. The engines usually sat just behind the cockpit, and would, said Munter laconically, replace the pilot in case of a head-on crash. Munter was the first of Boeing's employees in the aircraft business, the first of thousands, though the 34-year-old timberman had not thought that far ahead yet.

Work on the B & Ws had progressed to a point, where in June 1916, the first of the pair was ready. It was named *Bluebill*, and Boeing himself tested it. This was a crucial moment. Though Westervelt had designed it, the plane was Boeing's baby.

The engine sputtered into action and as Bill Boeing floated down Lake Union, the eyes of his factory workers followed his progress. He revved the engine, and zipped over the lake's placid surface. In moments, he was airborne, and a feeling of relief brought a smile. Bill Boeing had a good airplane, and he knew it. Munter tried the B & W next, and gave an affirmative report. That was all Boeing needed to hear. He contacted the Navy, asking for a chance to show his plane. Once more, much was on the line. If the Navy liked the B & Ws, there might be a contract for more, meaning that he was in the airplane business to stay.

The Navy liked the plane, but it had a tendency to tilt while airborne. Though the matter was corrected in a couple of hours, the final decision was no. That was a disappointment to Boeing, but, by then, he was hooked. He was able to make good airplanes, and he knew it and he was determined to prove it to others as well.

Prior to the Navy tests, Boeing lost his partner Commander Westervelt to World War I. Although America had not yet joined the war, Westervelt had been ordered to the east coast and Boeing was on his own. On 15 July 1916, the Pacific Aero Products Company was incorporated with Boeing as president, and his cousin, E N Gott, vice president.

After the failure of the B & W to bring contracts, Boeing hired T Wong, a brilliant Chinese designer. Wong developed the Model C, a twin-float ship. Boeing was proud of his product, calling it the first 'all-Boeing' design, because his B & W had borrowed some wing data from Martin. Herb Munter, however, didn't like the plane. He felt the rudder was too small, and there was no horizontal stabilizer. Against his better judgment, he took the

William Edward Boeing was born in Detroit on 1 October 1881, the son of a wealthy lumberman. He was educated in the United States and in Switzerland and entered Yale Sheffield School of Science in the class of 1904. He then spent five years learning the timber business and indulging in his hobby of aeronautics and flying.

On 15 July 1916 Boeing incorporated his small biplane-manufacturing operation as Pacific Aero Products, and a few months later he changed the name to Boeing Airplane Company. By 1928 his company had become one of the nation's largest aircraft builders, the success of which can be attributed to Boeing's belief in the importance of research and experimentation. In his desire to strengthen the aircraft industry, he effected the formation of the United Aircraft and Transport Corporation and became the firm's first chairman. The new company included the Boeing Airplane Company, Pratt & Whitney, Chance Vought, Hamilton Propeller Co and Boeing Air Transport. In 1934 the government ordered the corporation split up on the grounds it was a monopoly.

Boeing retired as chairman of the company in 1934. His only association thereafter was during World War II, when he returned in an advisory capacity.

When William Boeing died on 28 September 1956 his company was a world leader in the production of multi-engine aircraft, and had entered the field of commercial jet transportation. Boeing was active in the aviation industry for only 18 years, but few men in United States' history have contributed so greatly to the development of a single industry.

Below: The famous '**Red Barn**,' seen here on 8 June 1917, was the first Boeing company headquarters building on the present site south of downtown Seattle. Because Boeing was manufacturing aircraft for the war effort, military guards were stationed outside.

plane up, and nearly crashed. The plane proved unstable, and only skilful piloting landed it safely. He refused to fly it again until a larger rudder had been installed. On 9 April 1917 Munter again lofted the Model C into the sky. This time, he brought better news to Boeing. The plane was airworthy, and the twin pontoons felt good in rough water.

Boeing immediately headed east to drum up Navy interest. Two Model Cs were crated and shipped to the Naval Air Station, Pensacola, Florida. Herb Munter and another pilot, Claude Berlin, were handed the responsible task of impressing the critical eyes of the inspectors. The importance of their mission was not lost on them. Success could mean an order for more. However, the Navy was no pushover. The B & W, a good plane, had been turned down, and so could the C. It was a chancy business!

The two pilots came through with more than just flying colors. Boeing received an order for 50 Model Cs, to be used as trainers. Things were falling into place, and the president of Pacific Aero Products Company was satisfied. But in the midst of success came another setback. T Wong, the Chinese designer, resigned.

Unable to find good engineers in the east, Boeing returned to Seattle, and now his genius came to the fore. He knew how to pick good men, and once he had them, he knew how to delegate authority. He wanted ideas men, but the ideas had to be practical enough to turn into reality. It was good to dream, but the dream had to be based on firm foundations.

At the University of Washington, he consulted with Professor C C Moore, and on his recommendation hired two engineering seniors. One was Clairmont Egtvedt, who had failed his military fitness requirements and was out of the running for wartime service. Boeing put him in charge of calculating stresses, something that appealed to Egtvedt. He was to remain with the Boeing company for nearly 50 years. He was its president on two different occasions, and during World War II, he became known as the 'father of the four-engined bomber.' The other student was Philip G Johnson, who turned out to be an organizational expert. He was ambitious and capable, and by 1920 he was a superintendent. In 1921 he was made vice-president, and in 1926, president. He was just 31 years old. Bill Boeing had chosen his men well.

In those early days of the aircraft industry, airplanes designed by one company were often built by rivals on government contract. With America's entry into World War I Boeing accepted a contract from the Navy to build 50 Curtiss HS-2L flying boats. Business, at this point, was firm.

During the war, the orders came in, but the men of the Boeing Airplane Company, as the organization was renamed in April 1917, were not necessarily happy about the cause. Nobody liked

Clairmont L Egtvedt was born on a farm near Stoughton, Wisconsin, on 18 October 1892. He received his degree in mechanical engineering from the University of Washington and joined the Boeing Company as a draftsman in 1917, following his graduation. Within a year 'Claire' Egtvedt was chief experimental engineer and soon after, chief engineer. America was then in World War I and Boeing was building trainers for the air force. These were aviation's early days and Egtvedt's time was consumed by testing glues, woods and varnishes as well as metals.

In 1926 Egtvedt was named general manager and vice-president, and in 1933 he became president. During this period he guided Boeing to the forefront of the revolution that produced large bombers, the Model 314 flying boats and Stratoliners with the first pressurized cabins used in civilian flights. Egtvedt also developed the B-17, and it was this plane that earned him his reputation as 'father' of the four-engined bomber.

Egtvedt was elected chairman of the company in 1939. When company president Phil Johnson died in 1944, Egtvedt resumed the presidency for a year until William Allen took over. Egtvedt retired in 1966. He died on 25 April 1975, closing a career which had helped to change the face of aviation across the world, to bring a company to leadership in an industry, to win wars and to shrink distances on the globe.

Below: On the banks of the **Duwamish River**. In 1917 Boeing moved the Pacific Aero Company south to its present site and changed the company name to the Boeing Airplane Company. The Red Barn can be seen directly below.

Left: **Edward Hubbard** was an army pilot instructor at Rockwell Field, San Diego, California, during World War I, and from 1917 to 1920 he worked for the Boeing Company as an experimental pilot. Following the first-ever international mail flight to Vancouver in 1919, Hubbard began an airmail service between Seattle and Victoria, BC, operating by private contract. For the next five years he worked under the name Seattle-Victoria Air Mail Line, flying between 25,000 and 50,000 pounds of mail annually.

He did not live to see the growth of another of his ideas, United Airlines, the largest airline in the western world. The day after its formation, on 18 December 1928, he died in Salt Lake City, where he was vice-president in charge of operations of the Boeing company and, unknown to the many who flew with him, a millionaire.

Below: Dateline Seattle, 2 March 1919, Eddie Hubbard (left) and Bill Boeing (center) climb aboard a **Model C** mailplane for what would become the first international airmail flight to take off from the United States. The two aviators began with a pouch of US mail under dark overcast skies, and ran into a heavy snowstorm en route. With visibility down to nearly zero, they made a landing at Anacortes, Washington, where they spent the night. The next day, the storm past, they continued on their way, landing at the Royal Vancouver Yacht Club Basin. They picked up a pouch of Canadian mail and three hours later were parked on Lake Union in Seattle.

Above: The **B-1** used by Eddie Hubbard for most of his mail flights.

war. Egtvedt, for one, looked forward to the time when Boeing could design a commercial aircraft. He believed the real future lay in commercial endeavors, rather than with the military.

After the Armistice was signed in November 1918, there were cuts in military spending, and hundreds of surplus military aircraft flooded the civilian market. The Navy canceled half its order for the Curtiss HS-2Ls, and the Boeing Airplane Company, along with the aircraft industry as a whole, went into a slump.

Bill Boeing fought back. He was still very much a timberman, and he was involved in related industries. He returned to making furniture and cabinets. He also experimented with Sea-Sleds, in vogue then. He took on any job that would keep his employees working. Nevertheless, in 1920, the company lost $300,000.

While the company concentrated on non-aircraft activities such as furniture making, the airplane side was not dormant. Having made a moderate success of its Model C (Boeing Models 2 through 5), the company in 1919 began development of its next series of aircraft. With the myriad of lakes and rivers of the Northwest in mind, the Boeing engineers began work on a small commercial flying boat that could serve the area carrying passengers and mail. The plane was the B-1 (Model 6), powered by a 200hp Hall-Scott L-6 pusher type engine. Two variations on the B-1 followed. First there was the BB-1 (Model 7), essentially a smaller (45 feet 6 inches versus 50 feet 3 inches span), shorter (27 feet 8 inches versus 31 feet 3 inches) B-1 with a 130hp Hall-Scott L-4. Finally, there was the BB-L6 (Model 8), a still smaller land plane with a front mounted 214hp Hall-Scott L-6.

Neither variation on the B-1 went past the single prototype stage and it was not until the resurgence of interest in aviation generated by Lindbergh's 1927 Paris flight that the B-1 itself began to sell. Nonetheless, pilot Eddie Hubbard was to use his re-engined B-1 (it had a war surplus 400hp Liberty) with great success for over eight years on his Seattle to Victoria international air mail run.

Specifications: B-1
Boeing Model Number 7

Span	50 ft 3 in
Length	31 ft 3 in
Wing Area	492 sq ft
Gross Weight	3850 pounds
Cruising Speed	80 mph
Service Ceiling	13,000 ft
Range	400 miles
Powerplant	one 200 hp Hall-Scott L-6
Capacity	1 passenger

Despite these successes in design, the Boeing Airplane Company was not doing well. The furniture department was not bringing in the hoped-for revenue, and experiments with Sea-Sleds were scrapped. Boeing was digging into his own pocket to meet payrolls, but he told his executives that unless something positive happened, the company would fold. It was a roller-coaster situation, one that was common to the airplane industry of the time. Chicken on Sunday, feathers on Monday. This, said the chief, has to stop. Men were laid off. J W Miller, head of engineering, departed, leaving only two engineers on the staff, Claire Egtvedt and Louis Marsh. The horizon was not exactly golden.

Then the company received a military contract to rebuild a number of Liberty-engined wartime De Havilland DH-4 aircraft. Though the contract was happily received, there was, also, a feeling that the Boeing Airplane Company should be designing and building its own planes. Claire Egtvedt felt so strongly about this that, along with Louis Marsh, he went to see the company's president to stress his point. Bill Boeing kept on top of his many interests from an office in the Hoge Building in downtown Seattle.

'We are in the business to build airplanes, not sidewalks,' he told his boss. 'If you want planes you'll have to hire designers.' Bill Boeing agreed, and gave Egtvedt the go-ahead. The young engineer had already decided that what was needed was a plane to interest the Army. Military contracts were the largest contracts, and it paid to favor their interest. He began plans on a Boeing pursuit plane that would become the PW-9, but the work was kept secret. When the time was right, he would let the right people know.

The DH-4 modernization contract in hand, Boeing next received a direct boost from the Army Air Service. General Billy Mitchell, then assistant to the chief, believed that a large air force was necessary for future security. Boeing was awarded a contract to build 20 Army designed planes called the GAX, for Ground Attack, Experimental. They were to be triplanes, with a pair of Liberty engines, a 20mm cannon, and eight machine guns. The cockpits were to be heavily armored to provide protection from ground fire.

This was all to the good, and Boeing's skilled production staff went to work with a will. The men were no longer the uninitiated craftsmen who had worked on the B & W. These were men who had built hundreds of aircraft for military use and knew their way around an airplane.

However, the military changed its mind about the GAX, and altered the order from 20 to 10. Yet, even as the order was halved, another order came through to build three GA-2s, which the Army redesigned from a twin-engine triplane GAX into a single-engined biplane.

The GAX, in all its phases, proved too clumsy for an attack plane. The armored cockpits were difficult to see from, and met with general disfavor among the Army pilots. It was such a chore to fly the planes that commanding officers threatened their men with a tour of duty on the GAX if they stepped out of line.

Eventually, the GAX was phased out, and once again the chicken and feathers pattern loomed on the Boeing Airplane Company's economic horizon. Plenty of work one month, little of it the next. Ed Gott, still vice-president, grumbled that he didn't like what was going on. The military was the largest customer, and you had to build to their designs. If you submitted your own design, you did not necessarily get to build the plane. Another company, such as Curtiss, might underbid and get the

Left: The Boeing 26-foot **Standard Sea-sled** was fitted with two 6-cylinder Model C-6 Van Blerck engines. Moments after this picture was taken, in Boston at 4:30 am on 9 July 1914, the boat left on a run for Bar Harbor, Maine. The total running time was 8 hours 20 minutes for 230 miles in open water, or an average speed at sea of over 25mph. Pictured in the foreground are John A Murray, C B Page and C F Chapman, with Holly MacRae aft at the steering wheel. The picture shows the position of extra seats in the forward cockpit.

Below: The **BB-1** (Model 7), a smaller three-seat version of the B-1 (Model 6), made its first flight on 7 January 1920, only 11 days after the first flight of the B-1. It was powered by a 130hp Hall-Scott L-4 engine. The BB-L6 (Model 8), a three-seat landplane version, made its first flight on 24 May.

Below left: Boeing's only triplane was built to satisfy an Army requirement for an armored ground-attack aircraft under the designation GAX (Ground Attack Experimental). Ten of the planes, redesignated **GA-1** when delivered, were built under an early post-war policy whereby the Army designed its own aircraft and contracted for their manufacture. Boeing employee Charlie Thompson is seen here at Camp Lewis with one of the first GA-1s.

Below: The heavily armed and armored **GA-2** was the result of a redesign of the cumbersome GA-1. Despite the redesign, the aircraft proved itself in flight testing to be impractical and the program was abandoned.

Specifications: GA-1
Boeing Model Number 10

Span	65 ft 6 in
Length	33 ft 8 in
Wing Area	1016 sq ft
Gross Weight	10,426 pounds
Bomb Capacity	250 pounds
Top Speed	105 mph
Cruising Speed	95 mph
Range	350 miles
Service Ceiling	9600 ft
Powerplant	two 435 hp Liberty 12A
Armament	eight 0.3 in Lewis machine guns and one 37 mm Baldwin cannon

Specifications: GA-2
Boeing Model Number 10

Span	54 ft
Length	36 ft 9 in
Wing Area	851 sq ft
Gross Weight	8691 pounds
Top Speed	113 mph
Cruising Speed	100 mph
Range	200 miles
Service Ceiling	12,000 ft
Powerplant	one 750 hp Army Engineering Division W-18
Armament	six 0.3 in Lewis machine guns and one 37 mm Baldwin cannon

Top: The crackup of an **MB-3** at Camp Lewis in June 1922 went a long way toward convincing Bill Boeing (standing, far right) that the idea of the much superior PW-9, then under consideration within the company, was worth exploring.

Above: **Edgar N Gott** was born in Detroit, Michigan, in 1887 and received a BS in chemical engineering from the University of Michigan in 1909. Eventually migrating to Tacoma, he entered the lumber business, where he met Bill Boeing. He became general manager of the Boeing Company in 1917 and served as president from 1923-25. He went on to become a vice-president of Fokker Aircraft Corporation from 1925-26. After leaving Fokker, he served as president of Keystone Aircraft and later as vice-president of Consolidated Aircraft.

work. This was one of the reasons Claire Egtvedt was keeping his pursuit design under wraps. Airplane construction was a new and highly competitive field, and ideas were 'borrowed' without conscience. It was a case of survival of the fittest.

Despite Gott's feelings about government methods of awarding contracts, it worked in favor of Boeing. The company was awarded a contract to build 200 MB-3 pursuit planes, designed by the Thomas Morse Company. Their bid for the job was $1,448,000, which was lower even than the bid submitted by Thomas Morse, the designer. Gott was alarmed by this. How could Boeing bid so low and come out ahead? The answer was simple: Bill Boeing, always the timberman, had large holdings of spruce in the state of Washington. Spruce was essential in the construction of aircraft, and who could get it more cheaply than the man who owned the rights to vast forests?

The MB-3 contract proved a financial success, and Boeing Airplane Company ended the year 1922 in the black. The employees received a Christmas bonus, and feelings were high. It looked as if the plant would remain in business.

On 23 April 1923, the Boeing Model 15, Claire Egtvedt's new pursuit plane, Army designation PW-9 (Pursuit, Water cooled), was tested by Frank Tyndall. He liked it, but cautioned that the stability could be better. Stability was the bugbear haunting manufacturers of the time. It was a trial and error matter, because aircraft construction was still new in the world. Nobody knew very much yet.

The day after Tyndall's trial, he ground looped the PW-9, damaging the propeller. Because tests were due to take place at McCook Field in a couple of weeks, there was no time for detailed repairs. The propeller was repaired, and the plane shipped. The results for the Boeing Airplane Company were not good.

General Mason Patrick, procurement officer for the Air Service, told Egtvedt the PW-9 didn't match the performance of the Curtiss PW-8. Another propeller was substituted, and the PW-9 performed better, but still not well enough for General Patrick. In addition, the General told Egtvedt that Boeing's plant was not large enough to handle big orders. Egtvedt held his tongue diplomatically, but he would have liked to remind the General that the Boeing plant was turning out hundreds of

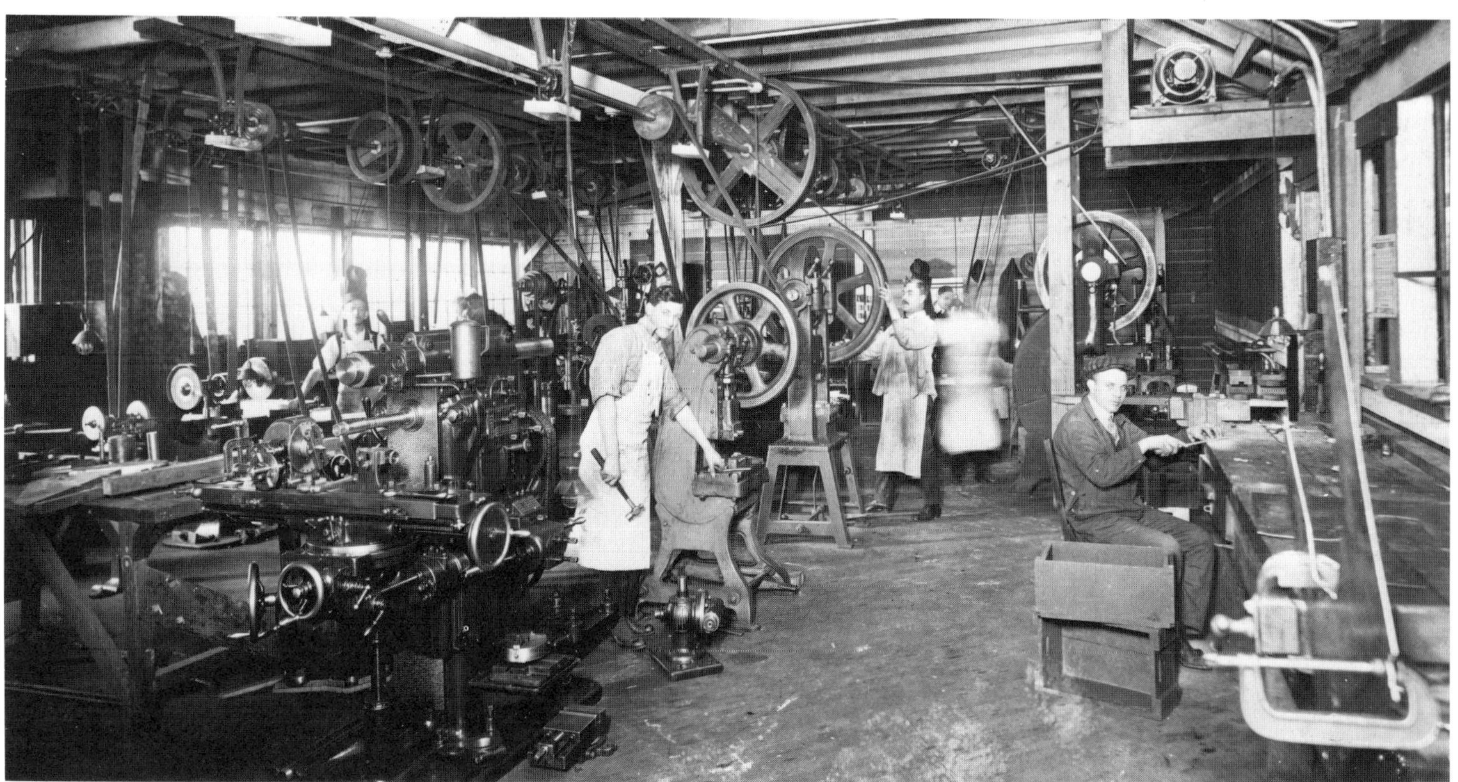

MB-3s and DH-4s. The upshot of the McCook tests was an order for the PW-9 being tested, and two more. No great shakes, but it was something.

During the course of his dealings with the Army, Egtvedt was invited to watch an aerial bombing. Two obsolete battleships, the *New Jersey* and the *Virginia*, were to undergo the test. The young executive witnessed an eye-opening drama from the deck of the *St Mihiel*, a transport standing off from the field of action. Both battleships were sunk with direct hits from bombing aircraft. This result would have far-reaching effects on military thinking. It also started Egtvedt down a long trail of experimentation. Bombers? What about them? Egtvedt was impressed by what had seen, and he began what was to be a life-long relationship with an aircraft which would be called, in full development, the Flying Fortress.

While Egtvedt was tending to business in the east, another trainer was being readied back at the plant in Seattle. It was the NB-1 (Model 21), and was aimed at the Navy. Eddie Hubbard tested it, and declared the plane the best ever. However, in the competition for contracts at the Naval Air Station, Pensacola, the Navy could not make up its mind. Other entries by Martin and Huff Deland were also good. No conclusion was drawn, and the matter was left dangling, like a stranded kite. The winter of 1923–24 proved to be a slow one. Again the specter of closing loomed on the horizon. But in the spring of 1924, the Navy finally declared Boeing the winner of the competition. The company was awarded a contract to build 49 NB-1s, together with its companion the NB-2. The planes would be used as trainers.

On top of this success, the Post Office authorized an experimental design for an air mail plane. It was to be constructed with a plywood body, and a Liberty engine. Success breeds success, and next the Air Service sent word that it approved Egtvedt's PW-9. 'Drives as easy as a car,' declared the approving pilots. The Army was impressed with the welded steel tube fuselage, a major improvement over the MB-3, and accordingly ordered an additional series of rebuilt DH-4s that incorporated a steel tube fuselage.

Things were once more on the upswing. Then, bad news: the Navy NB-1 was having problems. Planes were crashing. Engi-

Above: The **Boeing machine shop** as seen in January 1918.

Below: The **NB-1**, like its successor the NB-2, was a Navy trainer designed to function as either a landplane or a seaplane.

Specifications: NB-1 and NB-2
Boeing Model Number 21

Span	36 ft 10 in
Length	28 ft 9 in
Wing Area	344 sq ft
Gross Weight	2837 pounds (NB-1)
Bomb Capacity	3037 pounds (NB-2)
Top Speed	99.5 mph
Range	300 miles
Service Ceiling	10,200 ft
Powerplant	one 200 hp Wright J-4 (NB-1)
Armament	one 0.3 in Browning machine gun in rear cockpit of gunnery trainers

Below: A **PW-9 (Model 15)** in Boeing markings prior to being transferred to the Army.

neers decided the plane needed a different kind of wing, and another was developed. Again, Eddie Hubbard took the plane up. It crashed, but Hubbard escaped uninjured. The Navy complained loudly, and Phil Johnson explained that Boeing would have to keep experimenting. Nobody knew all the answers. Finally, the body of the NB was lengthened, and the plane flew nicely. No crashes. However, it proved *too* stable. It could not be made to spin. It would have to spin, said Navy inspectors, because the trainees have to know about spinning. An adjustment was made to the elevators, and the Navy accepted it in January 1926. The NB was considered suitable for training purposes – but no stunting was allowed.

Some big changes were taking place in the Boeing Airplane Company at this time. Ed Gott resigned after a dispute with Bill Boeing. Phil Johnson was named president, and Claire Egtvedt became vice president and chief engineer. Boeing himself assumed the chairmanship.

There was a big change in government supervision of the airways as well. President Calvin Coolidge had created the Morrow Board to study the growing aviation industry. Its report moved Congress into passing the Aviation Five-Year Program, and the Army Air Service was re-named the Army Air Corps. The Board also gave industry proprietary rights to the planes it designed, a matter that should have pleased Ed Gott, now an executive for Fokker in the US. The Air Commerce Act was passed to encourage civil aeronautics, and the Post Office turned the air mail service over to private operators. The Boeing Airplane Company now had 500 employees, and 50 engineers. They were kept busy with another order for 40 PW-9C pursuits, with a 435hp Curtiss engine.

Meanwhile the Navy began to order PW-9s. They began with ten Model 15s which were designated FB-1 in Navy nomenclature, followed by a pair of FB-2s for aircraft carrier use. Because of design changes, the Boeing model number for the FB-2 was 53. Three FB-3s (Model 55) with Packard engines and an FB-4 (Model 54) followed. In October 1926 a Navy FB-3 set world speed records for pursuit planes at the National Air Races in Philadelphia. Such triumphs brought the attention that the company would need to survive. Publicity was an important ingredient in the survival mixture.

Between 1923 and 1928 Boeing built 113 Model 15s (as PW-9) for the Army and 10 Model 15s (as FB-1) for the Navy. In 1926 an Army PW-9A was built as an advanced trainer and designated by the Army as AT-3, being given the Boeing model number 68. For the AT-3, the 435hp Curtiss was replaced by a 180hp Wright E engine.

In addition to the six variations in the Model 53–55 series, the Navy ordered 27 Packard-powered Model 67s, which were designated FB-5. Subsequent to its order of FB-5s, the Navy decided to discontinue use of aircraft with liquid-cooled engines aboard carriers, so they experimentally re-engined their FB-5s with a Pratt & Whitney 425hp air-cooled Wasp engine. This plane was then redesignated FB-6.

In May of 1924 the Army's complicated 1919 nomenclature for aircraft was scrapped in favor of a more simplified system. Under the old system a pursuit plane might have had one of five different prefix designations. PA stood for Pursuit, Air-cooled engine; PG for Pursuit, Ground attack; PN for Pursuit, Night; OS for Pursuit, Special alert and of course PW for Pursuit, Water-cooled engine. One is uncertain what horrible grief might have come to the Army's official giver of numbers should an aircraft with a PN prefix be found flying in the daytime with an air-cooled engine. After 1924, all pursuit planes, except those already in production like the PW-9 (which would retain their old nomenclature), were simply given the prefix P. Initial experimental prototypes of any series would continue also to be given an X for experimental, however.

Boeing's first Army contract under the new nomenclature was its Model 58 in 1926. The plane, designated XP-4 by the Army, was actually an outgrowth of the PW-9. It had a basic PW-9 airframe with longer wings and, for high altitude operations, the engine was fitted with a turbo-supercharger. The last PW-9, a PW-9D, was experimentally equipped with a 600hp Curtiss V-1570 as Boeing Model 93, and redesignated XP-7. Another stepchild of the PW-9 was Boeing's Model 66 which had an experimental inverted Packard engine and which was purchased by

Below: A Navy **FB-5 (Model 67)** designed for aircraft-carrier operation is seen here in September 1926 at the time of the first test flights.

Above: The **FB-4 (Model 54)**, seen here at the time of its delivery in January 1926, was equipped with a 400hp Wright P-1 radial engine. It was the lightest of the FB series and was redesignated FB-6 when retrofitted with a 425hp Pratt & Whitney R-1340B Wasp radial engine.

Specifications: PW-9C
Boeing Model Number 15

Span	32 ft
Length	23 ft 5 in
Wing Area	252 sq ft
Gross Weight	3170 pounds
Bomb Capacity	244 pounds
Top Speed	163 mph
Cruising Speed	142 mph
Range	390 miles
Service Ceiling	21,000 ft
Powerplant	one 435 hp Curtiss D-12C
Armament	two 0.3 in Browning machine guns, or one 0.3 in Browning plus one 0.5 in Browning

Specifications: FB-5
Boeing Model Number 67

Span	32 ft
Length	23 ft 9 in
Wing Area	241 sq ft
Gross Weight	3249 pounds (landplane) 3593 pounds (seaplane)
Top Speed	176 mph
Range	420 miles
Service Ceiling	22,000 ft (landplane) 17,800 ft (seaplane)
Powerplant	one 520 hp Packard 2A-1500
Armament	two 0.3 in Browning machine guns, or one 0.3 in Browning plus one 0.5 in Browning

Above: The **PB-1**, nicknamed the 'Flying Dreadnought,' is seen here during trials in August 1925. The PB-1 was the largest aircraft Boeing had built up to that time. To reduce weight the hull was constructed of aluminum below the water line and wood above.

Specifications: PB-1
Boeing Model Number 50

Span	87 ft 6 in
Length	59 ft 4 in
Wing Area	1801 sq ft
Gross Weight	23,500 lb
Bomb Capacity	2000 lb
Top Speed	112 mph
Cruising Speed	94 mph
Range	2450 miles
Service Ceiling	9000 ft
Powerplant	two 800 hp Packard 2A-2500
Armament	three 0.3 in Browning machine guns

The single prototype became the PB-2 when re-engined with the 800 hp Pratt & Whitney Hornet radials.

Specifications: F2B-1
Boeing Model Number 69

Span	30 ft 1 in
Length	23 ft
Wing Area	242 sq ft
Gross Weight	2804 pounds
Bomb Capacity	125 pounds
Top Speed	160 mph
Cruising Speed	132 mph
Range	358 miles
Service Ceiling	21,200 ft
Powerplant	one 425 hp Pratt & Whitney Wasp
Armament	one 0.3 in and one 0.5 in Browning machine gun

Specifications: XP-9
Boeing Model Number 96

Span	36 ft 6 in
Length	25 ft 2 in
Wing Area	210 sq ft
Gross Weight	3623 pounds
Bomb Capacity	125 pounds
Top Speed	213 mph
Cruising Speed	180 mph
Range	425 miles
Service Ceiling	26,800 ft
Powerplant	one 600 hp Curtiss Conqueror SV-1570-15 with F2A superchargers
Armament	two 0.3 in Browning machine guns

Above: The Army-designed **XP-9** was Boeing's first monoplane. With its unorthodox wing structure, dreaded by test pilots, it was probably the worst plane ever built by Boeing.

Below: The Navy **F2B-1**, seen here in September 1927 prior to its first delivery, was an outgrowth of the FB-4 and FB-6 experiments as well as Boeing's experience with the Army XP-8.

the Army as XP-8. Only a single prototype of each of these three models was built.

The XP-9 (Model 96), Boeing's first monoplane, was designed at Army request and built with the single wing fixed to the fuselage directly ahead of the cockpit. On the single prototype, this configuration was shown to restrict the pilot's vision so severely (the test pilot called it a menace) that the whole design concept was swiftly scrapped.

While it was building the various derivatives of the Model 15 pursuit plane for both services, Boeing was also undertaking a couple of quite different projects for the Navy. In 1925 the Navy requested a flying boat capable of flying the 2400 miles from the US mainland to Hawaii non-stop. The result was Boeing's Model 50, Navy designation PB-1 (Patrol, Bomber). The PB-1, with an 87 feet 6 inches wingspan, was the largest aircraft yet built by Boeing. The Navy later redesignated the single PB-1 as PB-2 when they replaced the two liquid-cooled 800hp Packard engines with a pair of Pratt & Whitney Hornet air-cooled radials. In 1927 the Navy ordered three Boeing Model 63s, which were designated TB-1 for Torpedo, Bomber. The TB-1 was a twin pontoon seaplane designed to be used as either a reconnaissance aircraft or as a torpedo bomber with the torpedo slung under the fuselage between the pontoons. The versatile TB-1 was also designed to operate with wheels from the deck of an aircraft carrier.

While the PW-9s evolved into the P-4, P-7 and P-8 in Army service, their twin brothers, the Navy FBs, were spawning further developments. The F2B-1 (in Navy nomenclature FB was the equivalent of F1B), Boeing's Model 69, was a carrier-based fighter incorporating the use of the 425hp Pratt & Whitney Wasp that had been tested in the FB-6. The Navy bought the XF2B-1 prototype and 32 production F2B-1s between 1926 and 1928. Boeing exported two of the planes as Model 69B. In 1927 Model 74, a further improved F2B, was presented under the designation XF3B-1. After initial flight tests, the plane was sent back to Boeing for redesigning. The result was the Model 77 (F3B-1) with larger wings and greatly enhanced high altitude performance. In 1928 the Navy received 73 F3Bs.

A lesson learned was a lesson never forgotten. Mistakes flushed out in designs were not slipped into a lower drawer. They marched side by side with successes, and this mating of information was to serve well in the coming years. This policy was one of the great strengths of the company.

Left: **F3B-1** fighters prepare to take off from the flight deck of the USS *Saratoga* (CV-3) circa 1929. In addition to its service as a carrier-based fighter, the F3B could also operate as a seaplane and be catapulted from the decks of battleships or cruisers.

Above: The **TB-1** torpedo bomber was designed as a replacement for the Martin T3M. A large aircraft, its wings could be folded for storage aboard aircraft carriers. The bombardier's position can be seen on the bottom of the plane below the cockpit.

Specifications: F3B-1
Boeing Model Number 77

Span	33 ft
Length	24 ft 10 in
Wing Area	275 sq ft
Gross Weight	2945 pounds
Bomb Capacity	125 pounds
Top Speed	156 mph
Cruising Speed	131 mph
Range	340 miles
Service Ceiling	21,500 ft
Powerplant	one 450 hp Pratt & Whitney Wasp
Armament	one 0.3 in and one 0.5 in Browning machine gun

Specifications: TB-1
Boeing Model Number 63

Span	55 ft
Length	40 ft 10 in
Wing Area	868 sq ft
Gross Weight	9786 pounds
Bomb Capacity	one 1740 pound torpedo
Top Speed	115 mph
Cruising Speed	100 mph
Range	878 miles
Service Ceiling	12,500 ft
Powerplant	one 730 hp Packard 3A-2500
Armament	two 0.3 in Browning machine guns

In 1928 eight improved versions of the B-1 flying boat (Model 6), Boeing's first flying boat, that had made its initial lift off from the waters of Lake Union nine years before were built. Improved structural innovations and more power were built into the B-1, and the resulting plane was called the Model 204. One of these was a dual-control ship, the 204A, especially engineered for Bill Boeing himself. Four of the eight constructed were built by Boeing-Canada, and were called Model C-204 *Thunderbirds*.

While Boeing was being blessed with continued success in designing and building military aircraft, Claire Egtvedt had been toying with the idea of starting a passenger service in the Northwest. A route connecting Seattle, Vancouver and Victoria might be expected to pay off. It might have paid handsomely had there not come a knock on the door from Eddie Hubbard. Hubbard, who had earlier operated an air mail route through the same airspace, appeared in Egtvedt's office. He was excited about a new proposal. The Post Office department was about to let its air mail run from Chicago to San Francisco go into private hands. The stipulation was that the successful bidder would have to furnish 25 planes by 1 July 1927. Hubbard was certain that the Boeing Airplane Company could compete successfully.

Egtvedt was doubtful. He pointed out the hazards of the night flying which would be necessary. Hubbard countered with a proposal for setting up searchlights every 25 miles. For every doubt Hubbard had a solution, and as he argued for his idea, Egtvedt's doubts diminished. After all, Eddie was an experienced airman, and Egtvedt listened with respect. It was decided to present the idea to Bill Boeing, and they went to the Hoge Building together. To their dismay, Boeing was not for the idea. He had the same doubts as Claire Egtvedt, and remained adamant – at first. After the men left his office, he mulled the plan over. That night he talked to his wife about it, and she suggested that Hubbard was right.

The next morning he called Egtvedt, and gave the green light. Twenty-five Model 40 airplanes quickly went into production. The Model 40 had been designed, and a prototype built, for a Post Office competition two years earlier. The Post Office had bought the prototype and nothing more, so the Model 40 program sat on the shelf for two years. The 40s were powered with a 420hp Pratt & Whitney air-cooled engine, and had an all-steel frame. They were capable of carrying two passengers, and a thousand pounds of mail.

Specifications: Model 204
Boeing Model Number 204

Span	39 ft 8 in
Length	32 ft 7 in
Wing Area	470 sq ft
Gross Weight	4940 pounds
Cruising Speed	95 mph
Service Ceiling	9000 ft
Range	350 miles
Powerplant	one 410 hp Pratt & Whitney Wasp
Capacity	4 passengers

Specifications: Model 203A
Boeing Model Number 203A

Span	34 ft
Length	24 ft 4 in
Gross Weight	2625 pounds
Cruising Speed	92 mph
Range	400 miles
Powerplant	one 165 hp Wright Whirlwind

Below: The **Model 203** was built exclusively for use by the Boeing School of Aeronautics, the flying-school division of Boeing Air Transport established at the Oakland, California, Municipal Airport on 16 September 1929 to provide training for BAT personnel. The school was acquired as part of BAT by United Airlines in 1934 and its activities were suspended 1 August 1942, by which time 2801 students from around the world had graduated.

Above: The **Model 204** was the ultimate fisherman's plane. The dedicated fisherman could climb into a 204 after a busy week at the office, be whisked to a remote and unspoiled lake in the far reaches of British Columbia or the Cascades and catch a creelfull of rainbow trout, literally a few steps from the flying boat.

Above: In 1929 Boeing carried out its earliest air-to-air refueling experiments using a Boeing **Model 95** mail plane known as the *Hornet Shuttle* as a receiver and a Boeing **Model 40B** as tanker. In these tests a trailing hose was extended from the tanker and the two airplanes were flown into position so a receiver crew member could grasp the nozzle and fit it into the fuel-tank filler pipe. The men pictured were company and Army fliers who accomplished a transcontinental flight from Oakland to New York with aerial refueling over Elko, Nevada, Cheyenne, Wyoming, Omaha and Cleveland, Ohio.

Far right: Three view of a Boeing **Model 40**.

Below: A **40B-4** in Pacific Air Transport (the Boeing System) markings parked in front of the company administration building on Boeing Field in May 1930.

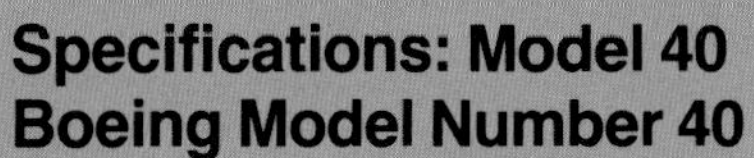

Specifications: Model 40
Boeing Model Number 40

Span	44 ft 2 in
Length	33 ft 2 in
Wing Area	547 sq ft
Gross Weight	5495 pounds
Cruising Speed	135 mph
Service Ceiling	15,800 ft
Range	700 miles
Powerplant	one 400 hp Liberty
Capacity	2 passengers (but principally a mail plane)

Specifications: Model 40B-4
Boeing Model Number 40B-4

Span	44 ft 2 in
Length	33 ft 3 in
Wing Area	545 sq ft
Gross Weight	6075 pounds
Cruising Speed	125 mph
Service Ceiling	16,100 ft
Range	535 miles
Powerplant	one 525 hp Pratt & Whitney Hornet
Capacity	2 passengers

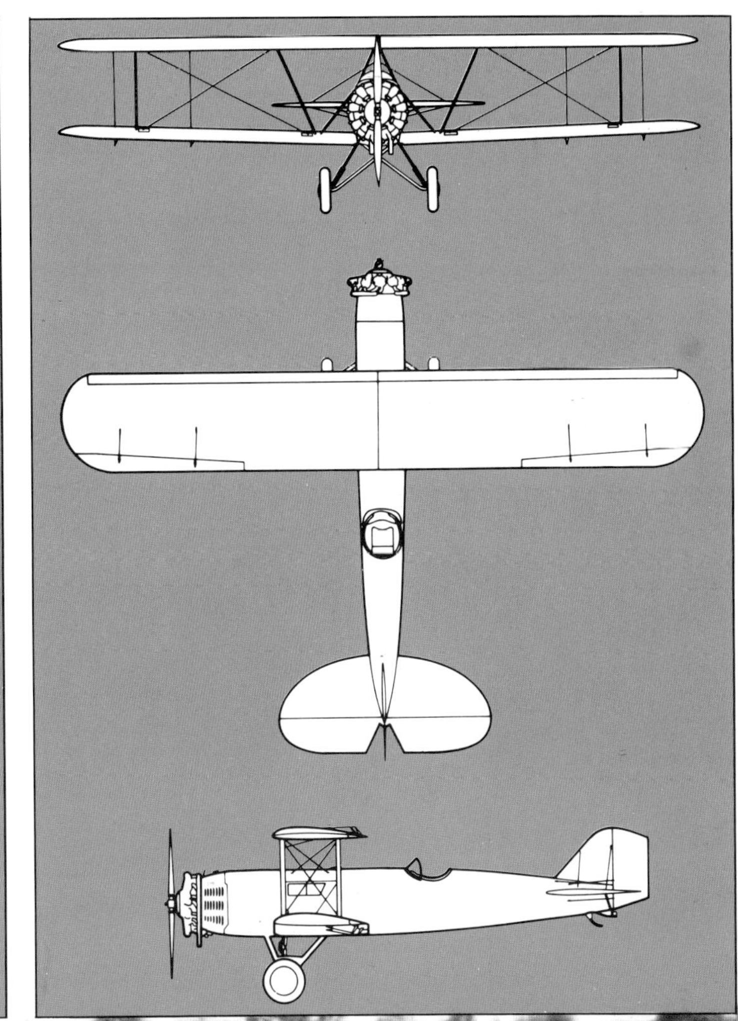

On 1 July 1927, they were lined up, ready to go. The mail contract, bid under the name of Edward Hubbard and Boeing Airplane Company, was won easily – so easily, in fact, that the Post Office officials frowned. The bid, they felt, was too low – an opinion shared by others. But the new operators were successful. The lighter Wasp engine enabled them to carry the two paying passengers, and that made the difference. During the first year of operation 1863 passengers paid $400 each to fly the route.

This was a time of great expansion among airline companies. The Ford Motor Company developed an all-metal trimotor airplane, which carried 15 passengers. Pilots affectionately called it the 'tin goose,' and it was widely used by both the military and civilians. Commander Richard Byrd was to fly a Ford Trimotor in his triumphant flight over the South Pole in November 1929. The Curtiss Condor appeared in 1929, carrying 18 passengers. It was soundproofed, and the cabin was heated, something new in passenger comfort. European air companies had also been moving ahead for some time in the civilian transportation market. The German Junkers F-13, an all-metal, low-wing monoplane produced early in 1919, was called the 'father of world civil aviation.' The Fokker F-3, another development, carried five passengers, and was popular in Europe in the 1920s. A Farman Goliath had the distinction of carrying the first international civilian passengers on a flight from Paris to London on 8 February 1919. The Europeans were ahead in the passenger business, but that did not deter Bill Boeing. With the success of the Model 40, he thought a larger plane should be created. The result was the Model 80, which was delivered to Boeing Air Transport in August 1928. BAT was the wholly-owned subsidiary set up by Boeing to carry passengers and mail.

The Model 80 had room for 12 passengers in a heated cabin with hot and cold running water. There was forced air ventilation, individual reading lamps, and leather upholstery. The pilot and co-pilot sat in a forward cabin, closed off from passengers. They kept on top of weather conditions by using a two-way radio system, developed in part by Western Electric.

The 80 was so successful that the 80A was a natural successor. This large trimotored craft was powered by larger Pratt & Whitney Hornet engines. The same luxury appeared in the cabin, but there was more. It had been noticed that occasionally passengers needed attention, especially in rough skies, so registered nurses were employed as flight attendants and box lunches were also served.

The Boeing Airplane Company was now on firm financial ground, an established business, a force to be reckoned with in the fiercely competitive world of airplane manufacture. This was only the beginning. Officials of the company, including Bill Boeing, Claire Egtvedt and Phil Johnson, knew that air travel

Below: The **Model 80B**, seen here in July 1930, was a variation on the 80A designed with an open cockpit because pilots liked the feel of wind in their faces.

Right: The **Model 80s** operated by the Boeing system were the last word in luxury. There were leather upholstered seats, reading lamps and the first-ever airline stewardesses.

had only started. A door had been opened, and through it interested observers saw vast skies of promise. Flying in the 1920s and 1930s was not, however, fully integrated into the American consciousness. The rich could afford to fly, the adventurous took wing and business people saw the advantage of swift travel. The man in the street, meanwhile, still preferred train and boat, and, increasingly, private automobile.

Questions lay unsolved in the public's mind. Was air travel safe? Could it not cost a bit less? A passenger paid up to $900 for passage across the States. Was flying not still more of a plaything than a serious mode of travel? There was another problem, too. Once an airplane reached its final destination, that did not necessarily mean the passenger's journey was over. It was often necessary to transfer to a train or a car. That was a nuisance. Airports had not yet been established in sufficient numbers to accommodate trunk lines and air taxi services. There was one more problem, and this was admitted by the air industry as serious. Airplanes were noisy, and made the skeptical nervous. Soundproofing was still more idea than fact. Noise kept passengers away, so something would have to be done about noise! With commercial airplane sales an on-and-off matter, manufacturers suffered. In order to survive, Boeing and other companies continued to go after military orders. Uncle Sam was a valuable customer.

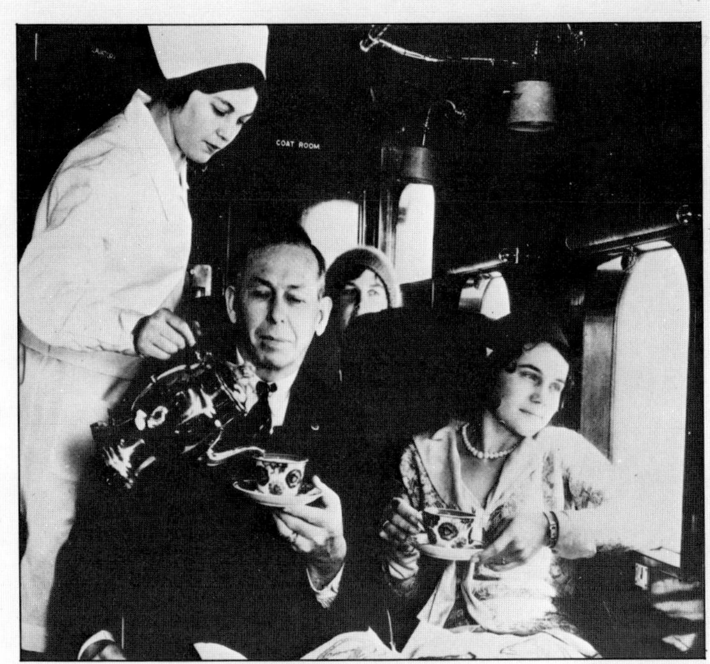

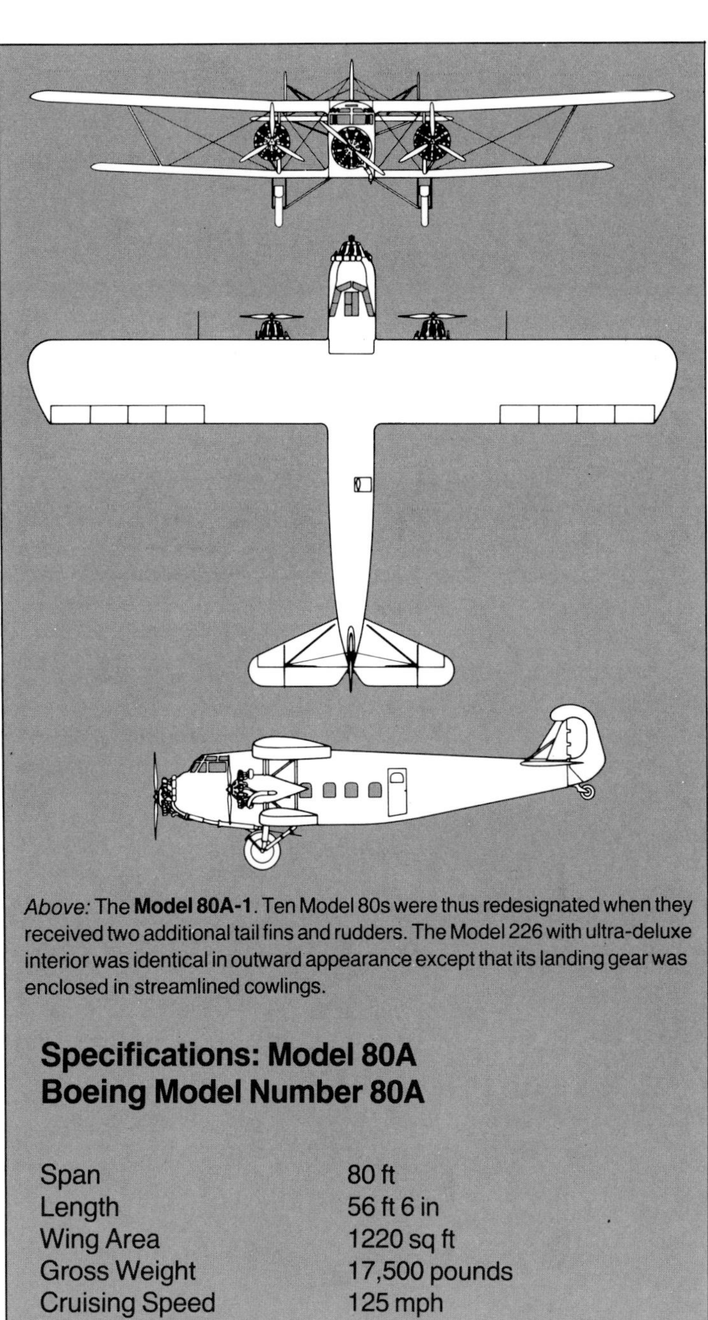

Above: The **Model 80A-1**. Ten Model 80s were thus redesignated when they received two additional tail fins and rudders. The Model 226 with ultra-deluxe interior was identical in outward appearance except that its landing gear was enclosed in streamlined cowlings.

Specifications: Model 80A
Boeing Model Number 80A

Span	80 ft
Length	56 ft 6 in
Wing Area	1220 sq ft
Gross Weight	17,500 pounds
Cruising Speed	125 mph
Service Ceiling	14,000 ft
Range	460 miles
Powerplant	three 525 hp Pratt & Whitney Hornets
Capacity	18 passengers

Specifications: Model 80
Boeing Model Number 80

Span	80 ft
Length	54 ft 11 in
Wing Area	1220 sq ft
Gross Weight	15,276 pounds
Cruising Speed	115 mph
Service Ceiling	14,000 ft
Range	545 miles
Powerplant	three 425 hp Pratt & Whitney Wasps
Capacity	12 pasengers

Above: A **Model 80A** parked on the east side of Boeing Field in August 1929.

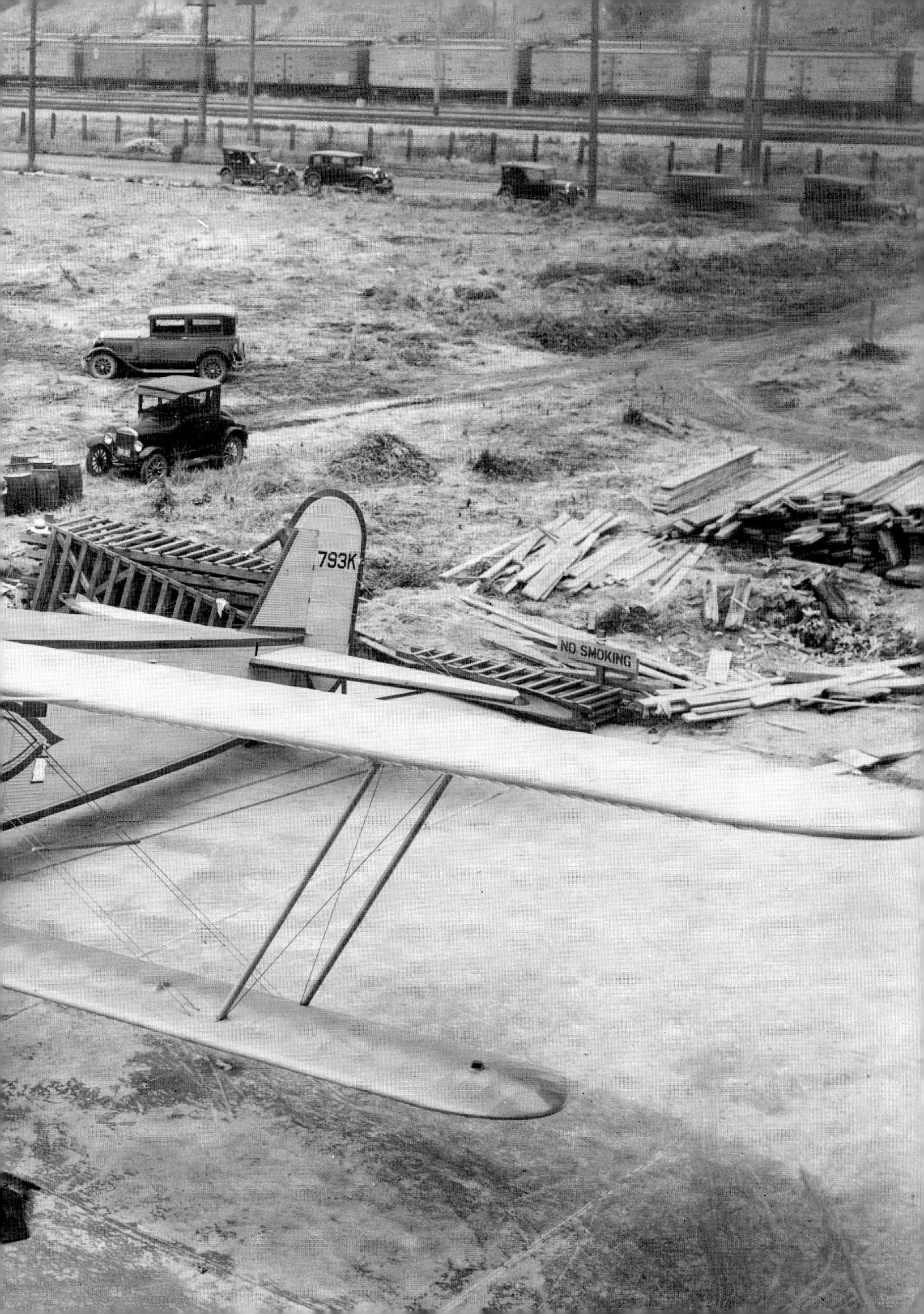
793K
NO SMOKING

Above: This **Model 377 Stratocruiser** served Pan American World Airways as the *Clipper Southern Cross*.

Boeing Model 367, had been developed. This large military transport was an offspring of the B-29 bomber and utilized the same wings and tail. It was the direct forerunner of the Model 377, the Stratocruiser, destined to be Boeing's next commercial airplane.

William Allen realized that Boeing's next venture into commercial aircraft would have to be something special. It would have to be big: very big. It would be fast, safe, and comfortable. The Pullman characteristics must prevail to attract passengers.

The Model 377 Stratocruiser was the airliner counterpart of the C-97, and the first commercial Boeing airplane produced since the 314 Clipper. Using adaptations of the proven C-97 airframe, and four 3500hp Pratt & Whitney Wasp Major engines the competitive advantages offered by the Stratocruiser were long range and passenger comfort.

In the midst of a postwar recession in the aircraft industry, Boeing decided to gamble its own money on the 377. It would be a big gamble, perhaps the largest ever, but William Allen ordered 50 of the Stratocruisers. At the same time he warned his sales force to sell the new airplane or Boeing would go broke! Boeing products were well known, and had a good reputation, but there was a hitch. The Stratocruisers cost over one million dollars each. Would customers buy at that price? The salesmen, and Boeing's reputation, had a job to do.

They were successful. On 28 November 1945 Pan American Airways placed an order for 20 Stratocruisers. The $24,500,000 contract was the largest ever given for commercial airplanes, but Juan Trippe, still president of Pan Am, had faith in the Boeing product. They had given him the efficient and graceful Clippers, and he planned on following the precedent by calling the new 377s Strato-Clippers.

Pan American Airways, however, couldn't afford to gamble on its planes – not to the tune of millions – but it held an ace. Officials knew that a C-97 AAF transport had, on 9 January 1945, flown from Seattle to Washington, DC in six hours and four minutes. The average speed was 383mph, with spurts to 400. That was speed, and fast time cut down on overhead. The C-97 was mother to the Stratocruiser and what one could do, so could the other. It was the simple logic of heredity, and Pan Am's reasoning helped pull Boeing out of trouble once more.

The Stratocruiser fuselage design was its own. It was a two-deck, figure eight shape, sometimes called the 'double-bubble.' Its wing, the Boeing-invented '117' airfoil, was considered the fastest wing of its time. Aerodynamic improvement over brute

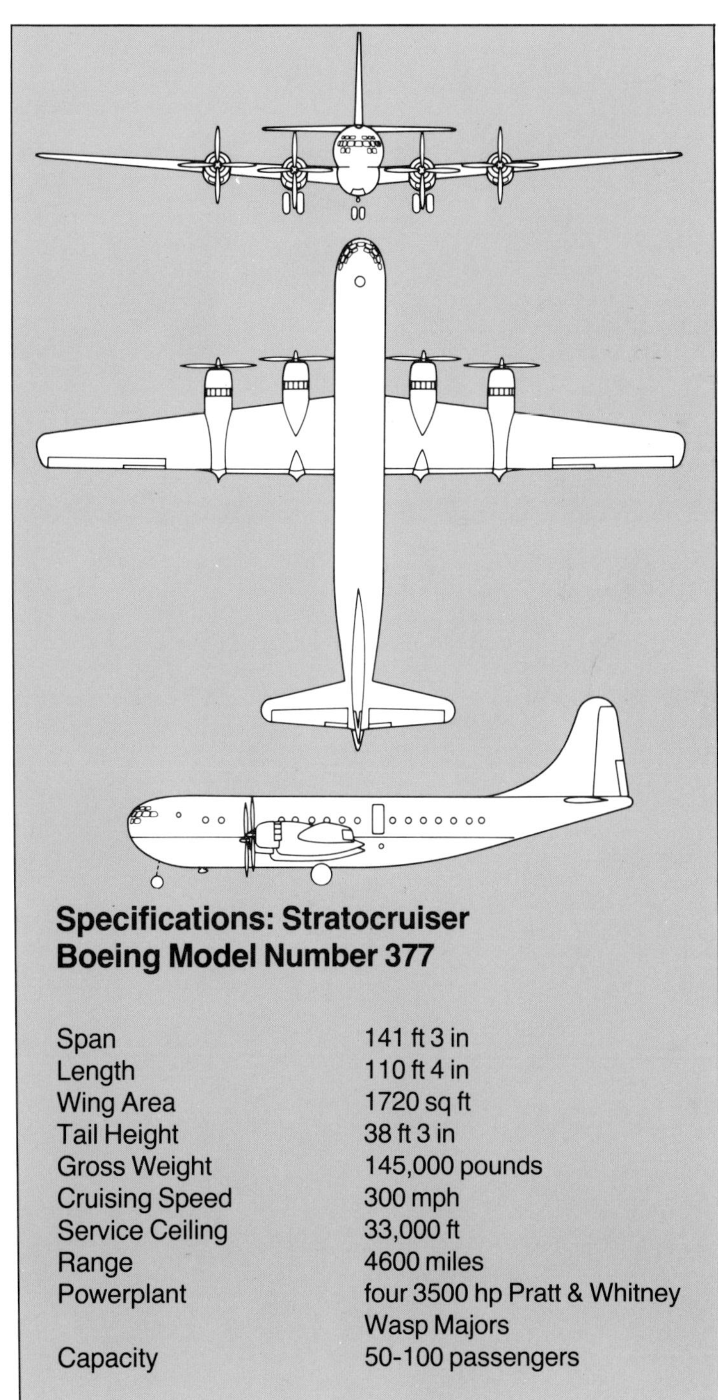

Specifications: Stratocruiser Boeing Model Number 377

Span	141 ft 3 in
Length	110 ft 4 in
Wing Area	1720 sq ft
Tail Height	38 ft 3 in
Gross Weight	145,000 pounds
Cruising Speed	300 mph
Service Ceiling	33,000 ft
Range	4600 miles
Powerplant	four 3500 hp Pratt & Whitney Wasp Majors
Capacity	50-100 passengers

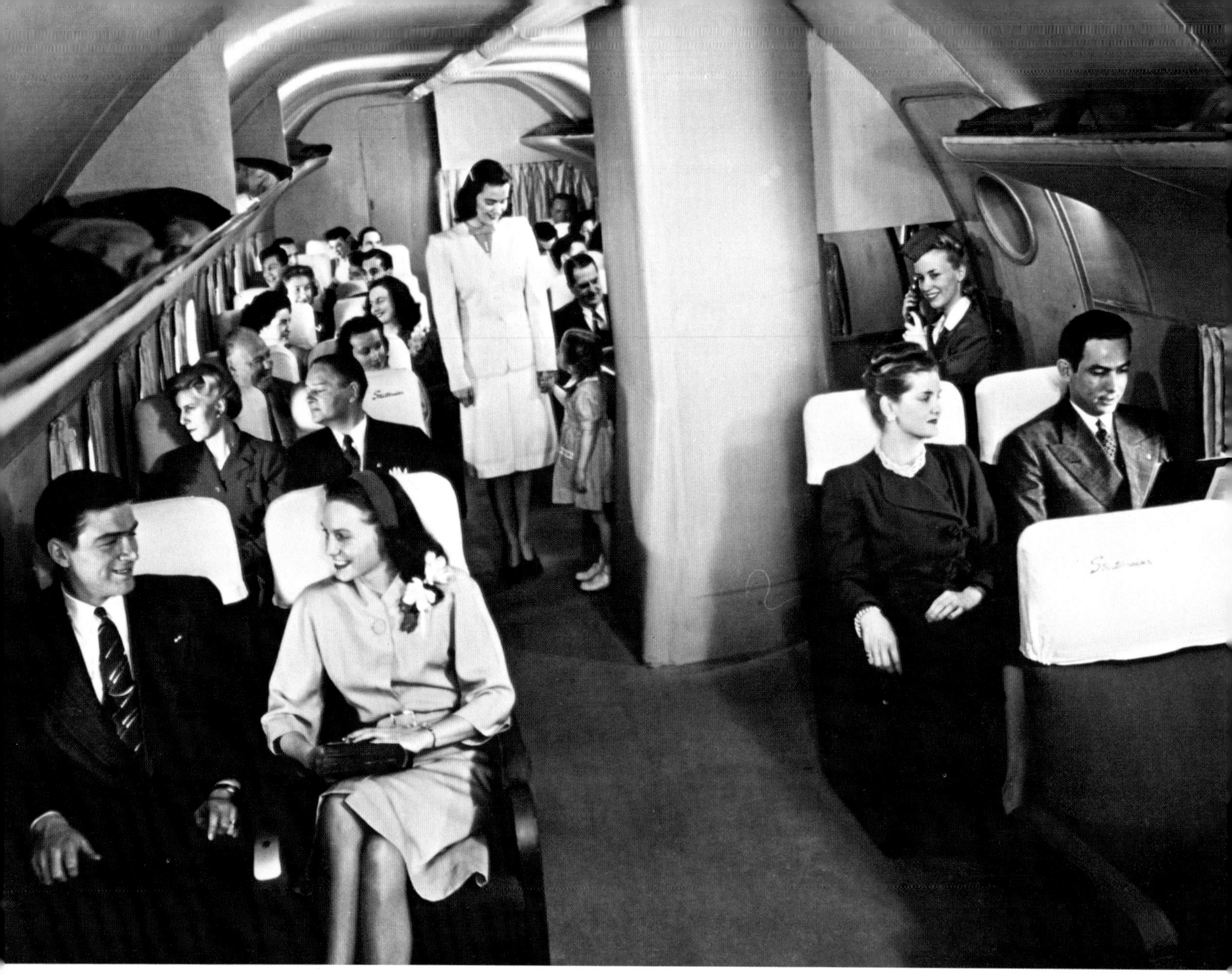

Above: Passengers relax in the air-conditioned comfort of the Stratocruiser's spacious cabin. The **Stratocruiser** could accommodate as many as 100 passengers, but then, as now, passengers were more comfortable when there were fewer seats.

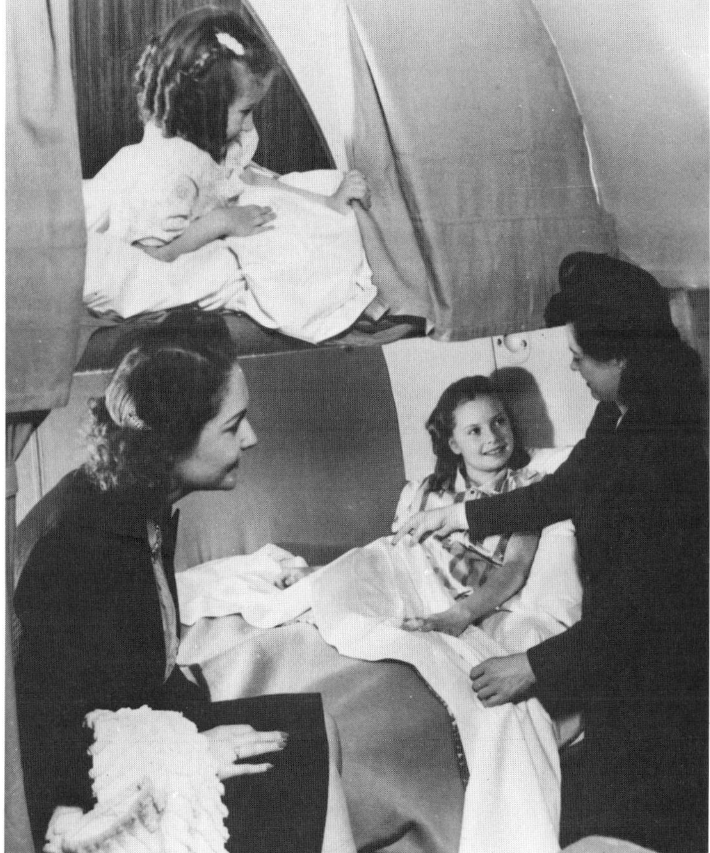

Left: Bedtime in the clouds. The **377** was the last Boeing production airliner to offer Pullman-style berths.

engine power was nothing new to Boeing, who realized the importance of aerodynamics with the *Monomail* of the early 1930s.

Another important feature of the Stratocruiser was its wide cabin. It allowed extra room for passengers, who relieved the monotony of long flights by walking around. Passengers could descend to the lower deck via a circular staircase. There was a lounge on the lower deck, which sat 14 comfortably and where drinks were served. A nominal charge was set on the drinks, but talk was free and, according to those who were there, it was plentiful.

Two important additions helped increase passenger comfort on the Stratocruiser. They were air conditioning and altitude conditioning. At high altitudes, these features eased discomfort. Clean air, warmed to the proper temperature, was injected into the cabin. Supercharging equipment kept the air at the proper pressure, while the plane was cruising above the country's highest mountain peaks. Rapid changes in altitude could be effected with little or no change in cabin pressure. Soundproofing, as with the Stratoliner, reduced engine roar to a distant thrum. The interior of the Stratocruiser could be altered and equipped

Above: The gleaming **Stratocruiser** prototype, with Boeing markings, passes high over the Cascades.

to suit the needs of the purchasers. The standard version of the long-range ship was equipped to handle 75 seats. Fifty-six of these could be turned into berths, similar to the upper and lower berths of Pullman accommodations. Nineteen sleeper-seats provided night-time comfort for remaining passengers. The dressing rooms were arranged to provide ample space, and were tastefully decorated. When all available space was taken by seats, as many as 114 passengers were carried. A galley was located to the rear of the main deck, completely equipped for food preparation. It was considered to be as efficient as any modern kitchen. Because of all the luxury of first class accommodations, it was only natural that the nickname 'Statuscruiser' was soon given to Boeing's latest product.

Boeing, always eager to find the best design possible, which meant one that combined safety with performance, put in 4,000,000 engineering hours on the Stratocruiser. Though Pan Am ordered its ships in late 1945, the prototype did not fly until July 1947. The first 377s were delivered to Pan Am on 31 January 1949, a little over three years from the date ordered.

Pan Am, itself always conscious of safety, did not object. Boeing test-flew three of the 377s to cure imperfections. They put the trio through 250,000 miles of 'torture flights,' flying the big ships through every difficulty possible, while studying stress and performance. When Pan Am got the airplanes, their executives knew they could depend on them.

The 377s were built for easy maintenance and low-cost operation. They carried passengers for one cent per mile less than competitors, a fact airline accountants took into consideration. And engine mounts were designed so that powerplants could be changed quickly, a fact not lost on maintenance crews.

Although the safety record was excellent overall, several Stratocruisers were lost. Pan American Airways lost the *Good Hope* in the jungles of Brazil, and the *Clipper Romance of the Skies* went unromantically to its doom in the Pacific. Captain Richard Ogg landed his *Clipper Sovereign of the Skies* close to a Pacific weather ship. The seven crew members and all passengers were saved, but the airplane was lost. The great majority of the Stratocruisers, though, survived to end up in the junk dealer's yard, a sad end for a great skycruiser.

President William Allen's gamble paid off. Fifty-six Stratocruisers were sold and their ultimate performance was remarkable. As of March 1955, they had carried 3,199,219 passengers, crossed the Pacific and Atlantic 27,678 times and made 3597 transcontinental flights. In addition, they round-tripped to South America 822 times, bringing the total mileage for the Stratocruisers to 169,859,579!

The last of the 56 Stratocruisers was delivered to BOAC in May 1950. Wellwood Beall went along, and when he returned he had news for Boeing executives. Great Britain's jet-propelled De Havilland DH-106 Comet was making a hit. If Boeing wanted to remain competitive in the commercial airplane field, the next step was to design its own jet. Boeing designers went to work, for a new age in airliners had arrived, and Boeing certainly meant to catch up.

THE WAR YEARS

In May 1934, when the Boeing Airplane Company was surviving on military contracts, Claire Egtvedt received a letter from General Conger Pratt. General Pratt was Chief of the Air Corps Materiel Division. The letter requested Egtvedt to be present at a meeting to be held on 14 May at Wright Field. C A Van Dusen, a representative from the Martin Company, would also be present.

Leonard 'Jake' Harmon, an aide to Pratt, presented an exciting plan. He had long been an advocate of General Billy Mitchell's progressive ideas about the United States building a superior Air Force. Though Mitchell's ideas had fallen into disfavor, (airplanes, declared Navy brass, will never replace dreadnoughts), minds were changing.

'I want a big bomber,' said Harmon, in effect. 'It should have a span of 150 feet, and gross 60,000 pounds. It should have a range of 5000 miles in order to protect not only US coastlines, but those of Hawaii and Alaska, too.' These were still experimental times in the aircraft industry. Efficiency was equated with size. The bigger the better.

Both Egtvedt and Van Dusen were invited to submit plans for this mammoth by 15 June. The project was called XBLR-1, Experimental Bomber, Long-Range, No. 1. This was shortened to 'Project A,' and was top secret. Boeing designers went to work eagerly. Hard times still clutched the company's pursestrings, and any work meant paychecks. Midnight oil burned and the plans for Project A were submitted on time. Notice was eventually

Above: The giant **XB-15** was the largest landplane bomber in the world when it made its first flight on 15 October 1937.

Far left: The **XB-15's flight deck**, offering more than ample working space for the crew, resembled the interior of a large motor yacht. The double doors in the center lead to the bombardier's station in the nose.

PRODUCTION CLOSE-UP

BOEING MILITARY AIRCRAFT 1937-1946

1000 2000 3000 4000 5000 6000 7000

Model X90 (Stearman Model No.): *XBT-17:* An experimental USAAF basic trainer. (1942)
1

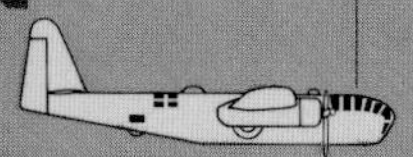

Model X100 (Stearman Model No.): *XA-21:* An experimental USAAF attack bomber. (1939)
1

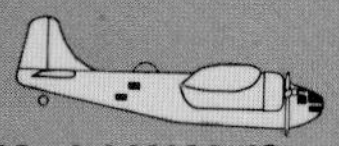

Model X120 (Stearman Model No.): *XAT-15:* An experimental USAAF advanced trainer. (1941)
2

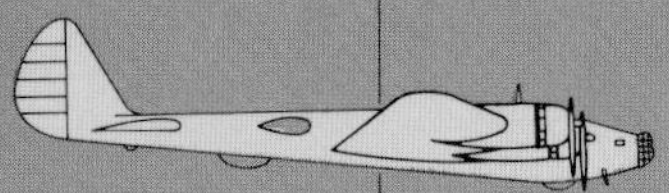

Model 294: *XB-15:* A four-engine USAAF experimental heavy bomber. (1937)
1

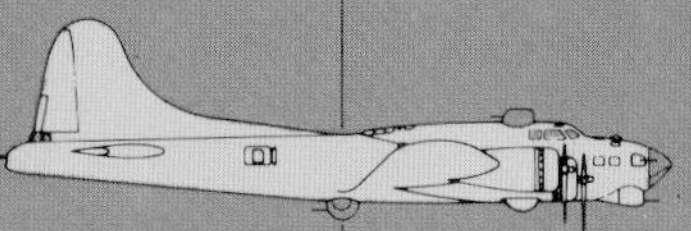

Model 299: *B-17 Flying Fortress:* A four-engine USAAF heavy bomber. (1935-45)
6981

5745 (Produced by Vega and Douglas)

Model 320: *VPB:* An unproduced design for a very large six-engine US Navy flying boat-patrol bomber, half again larger than the *Model 314.*
0

Models 316, 322, 333, 334 and 341: Experimental designs for a long-range bomber to replace the *B-17* (1939-42). (Model 316 was designated *B-20* by the USAAF). The project eventually led to the *B-29* (Model 345).
0

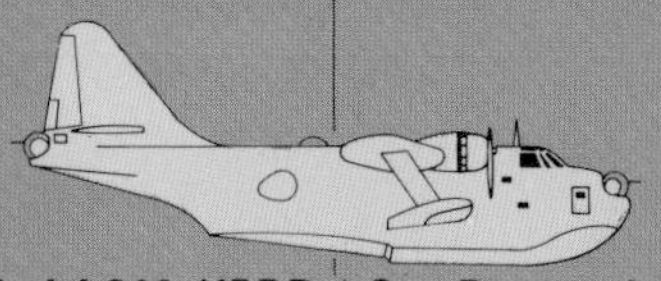

Model 344: *XPBB-1 Sea Ranger:* A two-engine experimental US Navy Seaplane patrol bomber. (1942)
1

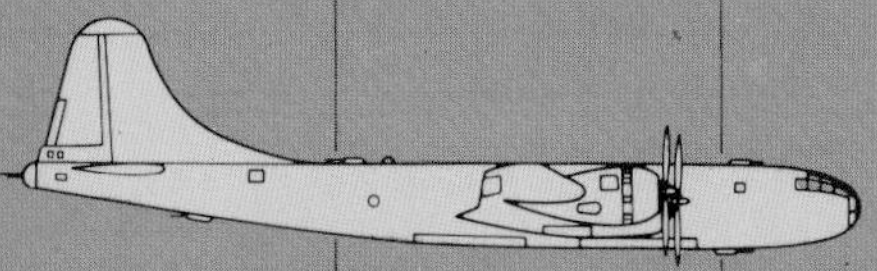

Model 345: *B-29 Superfortress:* A four-engine USAAF heavy bomber. (1942-45)
3049

1204 (Produced by Martin and Bell)

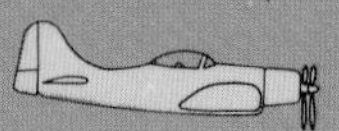

Model 400: *XF8B:* An advanced experimental long-range US Navy Fighter. The last in a long series of Boeing Navy fighters. (1944-45)
3

received that Boeing had been awarded the contract. This meant $600,000, and hard times eased their grip a little. Jack Kylstra was made project engineer and work went ahead on what Boeing called their Model 294. The Army, meanwhile, had changed its designation from XBLR-1 to XB-15.

It took nearly three and one-half years to finish the giant. One of the problems was the XB-15's sheer size. Nobody at Boeing had worked on an airplane so large before, and it became an experimental project for the work force as well as the engineers. Special tools had to be designed in order to make parts. A total of 670,000 man-hours went into its construction, and many of those hours were spent in testing components to destruction. Each section underwent thorough examination. A complete wing panel, for example, was weighted with lead far exceeding requirements. But technicians wanted to know the ultimate breaking-point and kept adding lead weights until the wing broke.

The bomber was so large that it was necessary to build it in sections. It was started in Seattle's Plant No. 1, but later barged up the Duwamish River to Plant No. 2, which was bigger and offered more space. When the sections had all been put together, the finished airplane was rolled across the street, Marginal Way, to Boeing Field.

The XB-15 was first flown on 15 October 1937 by Eddie Allen. He learned that the four 850hp Pratt & Whitney Twin Wasp radial engines were not going to make the XB-15 a speedy aircraft. It was simply too heavy, the design having outdistanced available powerplant technology.

Those who flew in the XB-15 were impressed by its size. Private R F Fowler of the 31st Bombardment Squadron, claimed that it would be necessary to establish radio communication between engines. This tongue-in-cheek remark was prompted by the fact that the wings contained passageways, enabling crewmen to make minor engine repairs while underway.

Its size brought other innovations. The endurance potential was far beyond that of a single crew, so bunks were installed to permit the carrying of two watches, nautical style. There was a kitchenette, complete with a hot plate, coffee pot, soup heater and a dry-ice box. Because many of its accessories were electrical, two auxiliary generators, driven by gasoline engines, were installed in the fuselage. This was a first for airplanes, and they helped deliver 110 volts through seven miles of wiring. The spacious living and working quarters were heated, ventilated and soundproofed.

This was also the first Boeing military design with a flight deck instead of a cockpit. The flight deck was roomier, and was equipped with the latest technology. The fittings included an automatic pilot, controls for de-icing and a fire protection system. An aerodynamic improvement was the installation of large wing flaps to reduce landing speed.

The Army accepted the XB-15 prototype in March 1938, but it was to be the only one built. Although the B-17 (Model 299) had by then become the center of attention, it did not mean the end of the big ship. 'Grandpappy,' as the XB-15 was called, flew to Chile in February 1939, with a load of emergency supplies for earthquake victims. Piloted by Caleb Haynes, the big plane made the 3000 mile journey with two stops for fuel. Pilot Haynes flew the distance nonstop on the return, however, proving that Grandpappy's long-range potential was there. In that same year, 1939, skippered once again by Haynes, the XB-15 broke records by climbing to a height of 8200 feet with a load of 31,205 pounds. The load, plus the hefty 43,000 pounds of airplane, was a notable feat, though a little beyond the recommended gross of 70,706 pounds. Grandpappy was also notable for endurance, and could remain aloft for 24 hours before landing. Had there been air-to-air refueling on a practical basis, the XB-15 could have broken more records.

Most airplanes are usually described in the feminine gender; like ships they are called she. Not Grandpappy. Because of its very size the XB-15 presented an undeniable masculinity, hence the nickname.

Though never used as a bomber, the XB-15 served in support of the Sixth Army in the South Pacific during World War II. Designated as the XC-105, Grandpappy carried troops and cargo into hostile skies for the duration. Perhaps the XB-15's most significant contribution to aviation was its usefulness as a test bed. The Army tested anti-drag cowlings, as well as various engines and electrical systems. Grandpappy also contributed its wing design to Boeing's Model 314 flying boat and its electrical system to the B-29.

A very important factor in building the XB-15 was the learning experience for Boeing. The company learned a lot about building big airplanes, and the experience put them far ahead of the competition.

In August 1934, not long after design work on the XB-15 began, Boeing received another letter from Wright Field. The Army was interested in developing yet another bomber concept. This one would carry a bomb load of 2000 pounds, with a range of 1020 miles, but with a *desired* range of 2200 miles. The required top speed would be 200mph, but the desired top speed was 250mph. It was to carry a crew of four to six men. Companies were invited to submit bids, and the successful bidder would build 220 airplanes!

This prize was worth going after, and Boeing entered a bid, though there was a tough stipulation: a flying bomber would have to be ready by August 1935. This meant company money would have to be spent, because there would be no financial aid from the military. None of the airplane builders of the mid-1930s were burdened with cash, but Claire Egtvedt went to the company's board of directors, which was, fortunately, composed of people who thought, as he did, that this was an important contract. He was voted an appropriation of $275,000 for the project.

The Army's plans for this newest concept called for 'multiple engines,' but multiple usually meant two. Boeing designers had been developing a wing capable of carrying four engines so Egtvedt phoned Wright Field, and asked if four engines would be accepted. The Army didn't mind. It was Boeing's money, anyway.

Specifications: XB-15
Boeing Model Number 294

Span	149 ft
Length	87 ft 7 in
Wing Area	2780 sq ft
Tail Height	18 ft 1 in
Gross Weight	70,706 pounds
Bomb Capacity	8,000 pounds
Top Speed	200 mph
Cruising Speed	152 mph
Ferry Range	5130 miles
Service Ceiling	18,900 ft
Powerplant	four 850 hp Pratt & Whitney R-1830-11 Twin Wasps
Defensive Armament	four 0.3 in and two 0.5 in machine guns

Above: The **XB-15** is prepared for the installation of the horizontal and vertical stabilizers.

Below: The rollout of the **XB-17**. Though there were to be numerous detail changes over the next 12,000 B-17s, the famous Flying Fortress profile was more than evident in this first glimpse in front of the hangar at Plant 1.

Four-engine bombers were not new. Four engines were then being planned in the XB-15 development. Up to then, however, additional engines were employed mainly to get more weight into the air. Boeing's idea was to give better performance, once the aircraft was aloft.

The new bomber was Boeing model number 299, and was conceived as a purely defensive weapon. This meant it was to protect the coastlines of the United States from foreign warships. When newsmen saw the Model 299 in flight for the first time they dubbed it 'a veritable flying fortress.' This was a nickname that would prove significant during World War II.

In size and configuration, the Model 299 was halfway between the Model 247 transport and the XB-15 bomber. Bombs were carried internally, and defensive weaponry consisted of machine guns installed in four streamlined blisters. The blisters were

Specifications: XB-17* Flying Fortress
Boeing Model Number 299

Span	103 ft 9 in
Length	68 ft 9 in
Wing Area	1420 sq ft
Tail Height	18 ft 4 in
Gross Weight	32,432 pounds
Bomb Capacity	4800 pounds
Top Speed	236 mph
Cruising Speed	140 mph
Ferry Range	3010 miles
Service Ceiling	24,620 ft
Powerplant	four 750 hp Pratt & Whitney R-1690-E Hornets
Defensive Armament	five 0.3 in machine guns

*XB-17 was the unofficial designation of the Boeing-owned Model 299 prototype

placed on the back and belly of the fuselage, and one on either side about midships. A fifth gun protruded from the nose cone, and all of the guns could be either .30 or .50 caliber. Power for this fortress was provided by four 750hp Pratt & Whitney Hornet engines.

A year was not a very long time in which to design and build any airplane, but the 299 prototype was rushed to completion and first flown by Les Tower on 28 July 1935. After a series of shake-down flights, it was ferried to Wright Field on 20 August. Les Tower made the trip nonstop in nine hours. The new airplane averaged 232mph for the 2100 mile journey from Seattle, an unheard of speed. Boeing executives were hopeful, but other giants in the business were competing for the lucrative contract. Martin was showing a twin-engine ship, the B-12, and Douglas was flexing its muscles with another, the B-18.

Lieutenant Don Putt, who was assigned to test the 299 for the Army, recalled later, 'We thought it was one of the best ships that ever came across the board. Our inspection boys practically tore it apart, and I don't think there was a plane that ever went through with a better record.'

On 30 October, with Army test pilot Major Pete Hill in the cockpit, the 299 took off. The controls were inadvertently left in locked position, and the big plane spun into the ground. Control locks, which kept the rudder and flaps in place to prevent damage from the wind when the aircraft was on the ground, were not yet well known, so it was not uncommon for even experienced pilots to overlook them. Hill was killed, and Les Tower, along with a Boeing representative, died of burns later. The rest of the crew, including Lieutenant Don Putt, escaped, but the accident knocked Boeing out of the competition. Douglas's B-18 won the contract.

In spite of the accident, the Army had liked the way the 299 had performed. The accident had not been a fault of the airplane, but a tragic oversight. General Henry 'Hap' Arnold, of the Army Air Corps, gave permission on 17 January 1936 for Boeing to build 13 airplanes. In addition, an order was placed for a static test model, bringing the order up to 14 Model 299Bs.

The Army gave the Model 299B the designation YB-17, with the designation changing to Y1B-17 on 20 November as the planes were being purchased with 'F-1' funds. Boeing went into

Near right: A pair of **B-17Es** can be recognized by their faceted plexiglass noses. Later B-17Es were equipped with the ball turret that was standard equipment on the F and G models.

Above right: The **B-17C** was the first to be equipped with the 'bathtub' style gun fairing in the ventral position.

Below: The early **B-17s** were sent to Wright Field, Ohio, for evaluation by the Army Air Corps.

Specifications: B-17C Flying Fortress (RAF Fortress I) Boeing Model Number 299H

Span	103 ft 9 in
Length	67 ft 11 in
Wing Area	1420 sq ft
Tail Height	15 ft 5 in
Gross Weight	39,065 pounds
Bomb Capacity	4800 pounds
Top Speed	300 mph
Cruising Speed	227 mph
Ferry Range	3400 miles
Service Ceiling	36,000 ft
Powerplant	four 1200 hp Wright R-1820-65
Defensive Armament	seven machine guns, typically one 0.3 in and six 0.5 in

Specifications: B-17E Flying Fortress (RAF Fortress IIA) Boeing Model Number 299-0

Span	103 ft 9 in
Length	75 ft 10 in
Wing Area	1420 sq ft
Tail Height	19 ft 2 in
Gross Weight	40,260 pounds
Bomb Capacity	4200 pounds
Top Speed	318 mph
Cruising Speed	226 mph
Ferry Range	3300 miles
Service Ceiling	35,000 ft
Powerplant	four 1200 hp Wright R-1820-65
Defensive Armament	eight 0.5 in machine guns in turrets and waist positions and one 0.3 in in the nose

immediate production, and the first Y1B-17 was flown on 2 December 1936, a little over two years from the invitation to bid. The major change over the original Model 299 was the substitution of Wright Cyclone engines for the Hornets. The Wrights yielded 930hp, against the Hornets' 750.

Shortly after the first Y1B-17s went into service, the Army delivered specifications for the static test airplane, the fourteenth. It was to be a high-altitude bomber, with turbo-supercharged engines. This was delivered as the Y1B-17A and first flew in April 1939. This in turn resulted in a production order for 39 more slightly improved planes, which were called the B-17B. These were all delivered by March 1940. The B-17B featured 1200hp Wright Cyclone engines, and a redesigned nose. There was a navigator's blister above the cockpit, and constant-speed full feathering propellers. This model also introduced larger flaps and rudder.

The United States was aware it could become involved in World War II long before the Japanese attacked Pearl Harbor. German U-boats had been sinking Allied freighters off the east coast for some time. US Coast Guard escorts were assigned to the nearly helpless cargo ships, but German Wolf Packs lurked deep in international waters, where the Coast Guard had no authority, and picked off their targets. It was a ghastly slaughter, and it brought death so close that Washington, DC could not miss it. This arrogant nose-thumbing by the Axis served as a warning and led the United States to begin preparations for World War II much sooner than might otherwise have been the case. President Franklin D Roosevelt did not wait for the Japanese to attack Pearl Harbor before increasing the forces of defense.

As the war in Europe gathered momentum, the 'Arsenal of Democracy' went to work. The Boeing Airplane Company was to be among the most important of the bomber manufacturers. Long before the US entered the war, the B-17 was on the way though it had inadequacies. These were not fully realized, however, until the B-17 came under actual combat conditions. Twenty B-17Cs were delivered to Britain's Royal Air Force, as Fortress Mark Is, in 1941. The RAF took them into combat, but the results were disappointing. Though the supercharged engines were efficient enough at high altitudes, the Browning machine guns froze up in the frigid atmosphere, and German fighters attacked from the rear, a blind spot. Eight bombers were lost in a short time, and instead of Flying Fortresses, the B-17s earned the less-confident nickname Flying Coffins.

Boeing had expected that changes would be needed, went back to the drawing board and came up with the B-17D. The electrical system was revised and self-sealing fuel tanks were added. More protective armor was added for the crew, and firepower increased. Cowl flaps opened the way for better engine cooling.

Most of the USAAF B-17Ds were delivered to the 19th Bombardment Group in the Philippines where they were caught largely off guard when the Japanese attacked Clark Field on 8 December 1941 (at the same time as their 7 December attack on

Leslie R Tower was born in Polson, Montana, in 1903. He saw his first 'flying machine' at the age of eight and thereupon dedicated his life to aviation. As soon as he graduated from high school he went to Seattle to study engineering at the University of Washington. After a year there, he joined the army as a flying cadet and served at Brooks and Kelly Fields before returning to his studies. In 1925 he joined the Boeing Aircraft Company as a draftsman. In 1927 he became chief test pilot for Boeing. Every plane developed by the company until 1935, from tiny pursuits to the giant Boeing 299 bomber, was taken on its first flight by Tower.

In addition to testing the new designs, Tower often ferried new military planes to Wright Field, Ohio, or Bolling Field in Anacostia, DC, as well as to west coast fields. He went as far as Japan, Spain and Brazil to demonstrate Boeing planes. He was in Spain with Major Erik Nelson demonstrating a Boeing ship in 1935 when he was recalled to test the bomber in which his career was brought to a premature end. He was severely injured in the wreck of the Army's newest Flying Fortress at Dayton, Ohio, in October, with another pilot at the controls. Tower died on 19 November 1935 after a hopeless fight against complications which resulted.

Les Tower was recognized as possibly the finest test pilot in the world. His record of eight years as chief pilot for Boeing without a single crackup is without equal.

Below: The **XB-17** prototype.

Pearl Harbor across the International Date Line in Hawaii). The aircraft that survived fought a valiant rear guard action as the Japanese advanced. They were, however, hampered by the same lack of defensive armament (particularly the absence of a tail gun) that had caused the British so much grief earlier against the Germans. Only one of the B-17Ds, nicknamed 'The Swoose' survived the campaign, returning to the States via Australia in 1942.

The tremendous stamina of the Boeing planes grew into legend. Many returned from raids with hundreds of bullet and flak holes in their bodies. Engines were shot out of action, wings and tail surfaces shattered, men killed and wounded, and yet the Fortress staggered home. Not all made it to safety, however, and a total of 4750 were lost. This of course reflects the B-17s large share of the fighting over Europe, Africa and, to a lesser extent, the Pacific.

The B-17's reputation as a powerful weapon grew after each encounter, whether in the Pacific or Europe.

On 14 December 1941, a B-17D commanded by Lieutenant Hewitt T Wheless, of the 19th Bombardment Group, was sent to attack a Japanese transport. The 19th BG had retreated from Clark Field under enemy pressure and were now stationed at Del Monte on Luzon, still in the Philippines. There were three Fortresses in the squadron that sallied out to sink the transport. Wheless became separated from the others in low clouds, so he continued alone. He found the freighter and was getting ready to drop his bombs, when a force of 18 Japanese fighters dropped on him.

There followed a short, fierce battle that left one US airman dead and three Japanese fighters destroyed. The bombs were released on target, but the Japanese kept coming. The Fortress crew fought back until their guns jammed or ran out of ammunition. There was nothing they could do now but wait in grim silence. Lieutenant Wheless turned the bomber toward Del Monte.

The number one engine was dead and the radio out of commission. One fuel tank had been ripped apart, and the oxygen system shot away. The B-17s were not pressurized, and crews wore oxygen masks at high altitudes. However, in this case Wheless was flying low, and oxygen was not needed. In addition to the rest of the damage, the tail wheel was missing and the tires were flat. Two-thirds of the control cables had been damaged, and the fuselage was riddled with holes. Despite all this, the B-17D thrummed along on three engines, while the surviving crewmen waited. After 20 minutes more of Japanese attack, the enemy guns were quiet, out of ammunition. The Japanese pilots flew close for a look at this dauntless bomber, and later reported it as a 'four engined fighter.'

Below: War and peace. **B-17Bs** share the floor of Plant 2 with **Stratoliners** in this photograph taken in November 1939, ten weeks after the outbreak of the war in Europe.

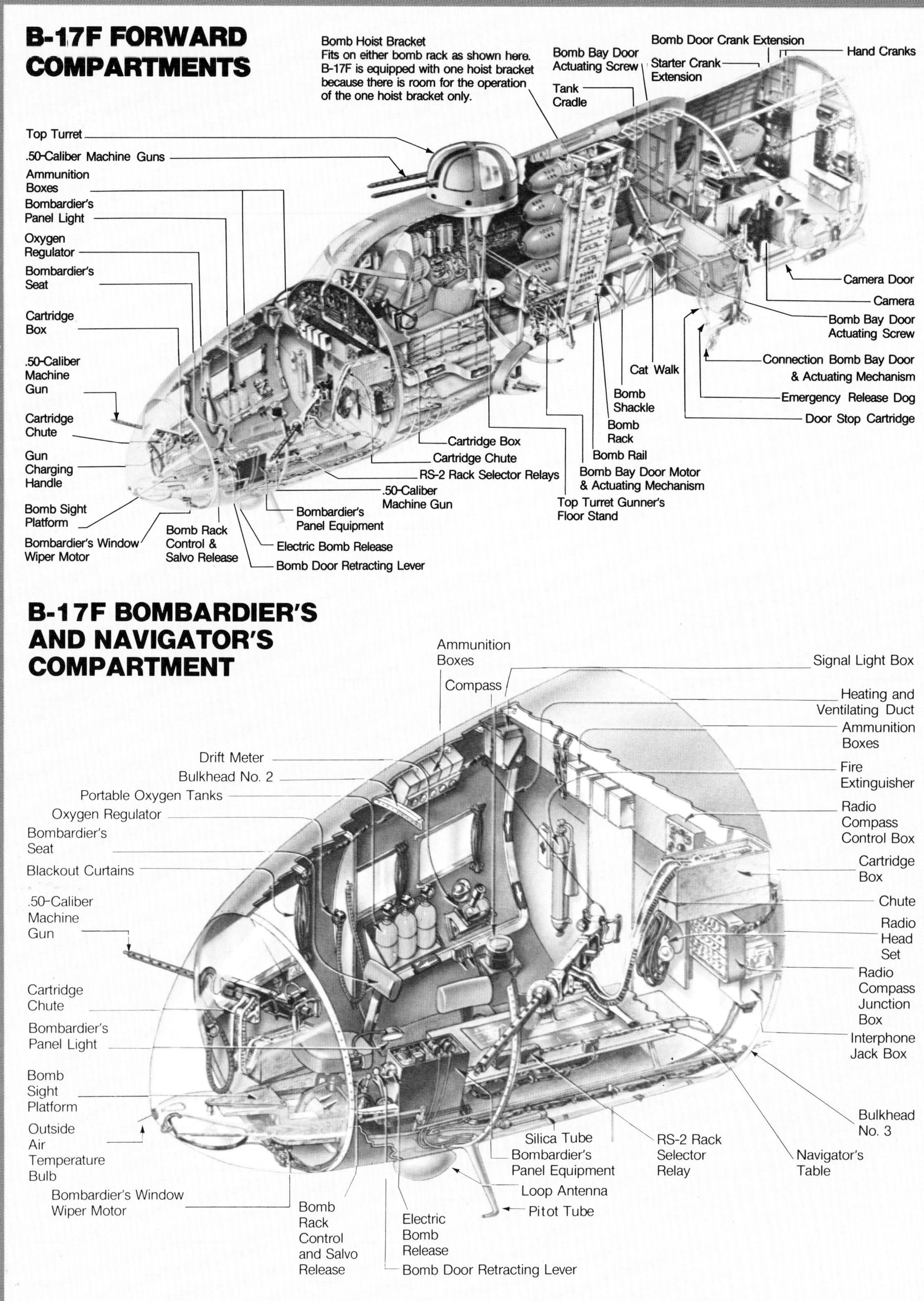
B-17F FORWARD COMPARTMENTS
Bomb Hoist Bracket
Fits on either bomb rack as shown here. B-17F is equipped with one hoist bracket because there is room for the operation of the one hoist bracket only.
Bomb Bay Door Actuating Screw
Tank Cradle
Bomb Door Crank Extension
Starter Crank Extension
Hand Cranks
Top Turret
.50-Caliber Machine Guns
Ammunition Boxes
Bombardier's Panel Light
Oxygen Regulator
Bombardier's Seat
Cartridge Box
.50-Caliber Machine Gun
Cartridge Chute
Gun Charging Handle
Bomb Sight Platform
Bombardier's Window Wiper Motor
Bomb Rack Control & Salvo Release
Electric Bomb Release
Bomb Door Retracting Lever
Bombardier's Panel Equipment
.50-Caliber Machine Gun
RS-2 Rack Selector Relays
Cartridge Chute
Cartridge Box
Top Turret Gunner's Floor Stand
Bomb Bay Door Motor & Actuating Mechanism
Bomb Rail
Bomb Rack
Bomb Shackle
Cat Walk
Camera Door
Camera
Bomb Bay Door Actuating Screw
Connection Bomb Bay Door & Actuating Mechanism
Emergency Release Dog
Door Stop Cartridge
B-17F BOMBARDIER'S AND NAVIGATOR'S COMPARTMENT
Ammunition Boxes
Compass
Signal Light Box
Heating and Ventilating Duct
Ammunition Boxes
Fire Extinguisher
Radio Compass Control Box
Cartridge Box
Chute
Radio Head Set
Radio Compass Junction Box
Interphone Jack Box
Bulkhead No. 3
Navigator's Table
RS-2 Rack Selector Relay
Silica Tube
Bombardier's Panel Equipment
Loop Antenna
Pitot Tube
Bomb Door Retracting Lever
Electric Bomb Release
Bomb Rack Control and Salvo Release
Bombardier's Window Wiper Motor
Outside Air Temperature Bulb
Bomb Sight Platform
Bombardier's Panel Light
Cartridge Chute
.50-Caliber Machine Gun
Blackout Curtains
Bombardier's Seat
Oxygen Regulator
Portable Oxygen Tanks
Bulkhead No. 2
Drift Meter

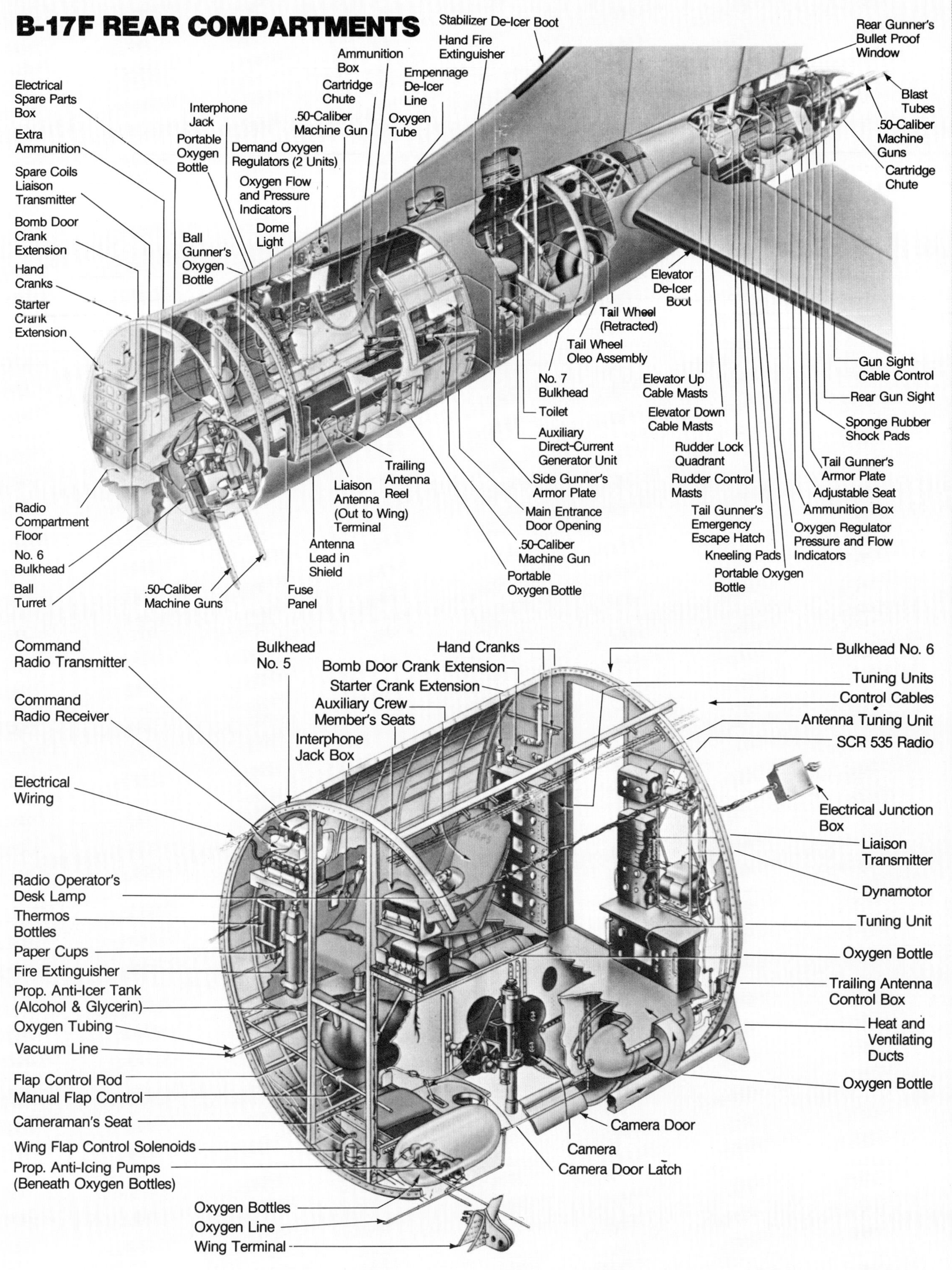

B-17F REAR COMPARTMENTS
Stabilizer De-Icer Boot
Hand Fire Extinguisher
Rear Gunner's Bullet Proof Window
Ammunition Box
Empennage De-Icer Line
Electrical Spare Parts Box
Cartridge Chute
Interphone Jack
.50-Caliber Machine Gun
Oxygen Tube
Blast Tubes
Extra Ammunition
Portable Oxygen Bottle
Demand Oxygen Regulators (2 Units)
.50-Caliber Machine Guns
Spare Coils Liaison Transmitter
Oxygen Flow and Pressure Indicators
Cartridge Chute
Bomb Door Crank Extension
Dome Light
Ball Gunner's Oxygen Bottle
Hand Cranks
Elevator De-Icer Boot
Starter Crank Extension
Tail Wheel (Retracted)
Tail Wheel Oleo Assembly
Gun Sight Cable Control
No. 7 Bulkhead
Elevator Up Cable Masts
Rear Gun Sight
Toilet
Elevator Down Cable Masts
Sponge Rubber Shock Pads
Auxiliary Direct-Current Generator Unit
Rudder Lock Quadrant
Tail Gunner's Armor Plate
Trailing Antenna Reel
Side Gunner's Armor Plate
Rudder Control Masts
Adjustable Seat
Liaison Antenna (Out to Wing) Terminal
Main Entrance Door Opening
Tail Gunner's Emergency Escape Hatch
Ammunition Box
Radio Compartment Floor
Oxygen Regulator Pressure and Flow Indicators
Antenna Lead in Shield
.50-Caliber Machine Gun
Kneeling Pads
No. 6 Bulkhead
Portable Oxygen Bottle
Portable Oxygen Bottle
Ball Turret
.50-Caliber Machine Guns
Fuse Panel
Command Radio Transmitter
Bulkhead No. 5
Hand Cranks
Bulkhead No. 6
Bomb Door Crank Extension
Starter Crank Extension
Tuning Units
Command Radio Receiver
Auxiliary Crew Member's Seats
Control Cables
Antenna Tuning Unit
Interphone Jack Box
SCR 535 Radio
Electrical Wiring
Electrical Junction Box
Liaison Transmitter
Radio Operator's Desk Lamp
Dynamotor
Thermos Bottles
Tuning Unit
Paper Cups
Oxygen Bottle
Fire Extinguisher
Prop. Anti-Icer Tank (Alcohol & Glycerin)
Trailing Antenna Control Box
Oxygen Tubing
Heat and Ventilating Ducts
Vacuum Line
Flap Control Rod
Oxygen Bottle
Manual Flap Control
Cameraman's Seat
Camera Door
Wing Flap Control Solenoids
Camera
Prop. Anti-Icing Pumps (Beneath Oxygen Bottles)
Camera Door Latch
Oxygen Bottles
Oxygen Line
Wing Terminal
B-17F RADIO COMPARTMENT

PRODUCTION CLOSE-UP (Model 299)

B-17 FLYING FORTRESS

1000 2000 3000 4000

XB-17-B-17A

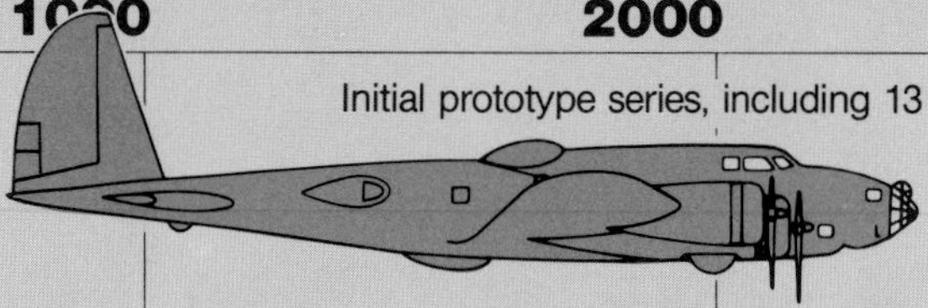

15

Initial prototype series, including 13 *Y1B-17's.*

B-17B-D

119

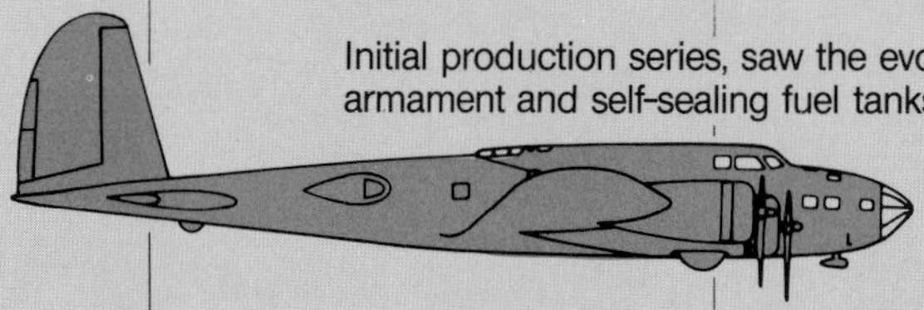

Initial production series, saw the evolution of a redesigned nose and the addition of armament and self-sealing fuel tanks. 20 were transferred to Britain as *Fortress Mk I.*

B-17E

512

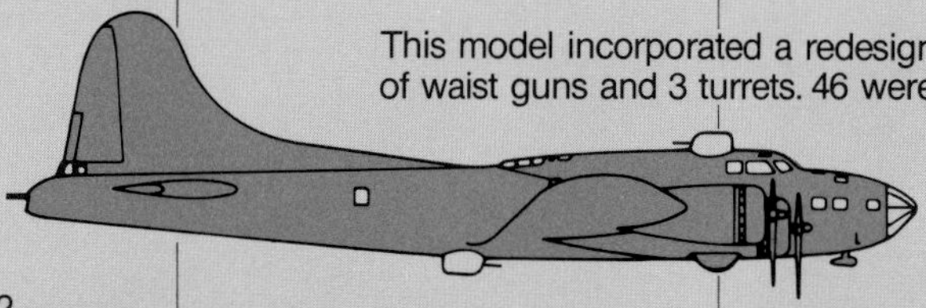

This model incorporated a redesigned rear fuselage and vertical tail surface, the addition of waist guns and 3 turrets. 46 were transferred to Britain as *Fortress MkIIA.*

B-17F

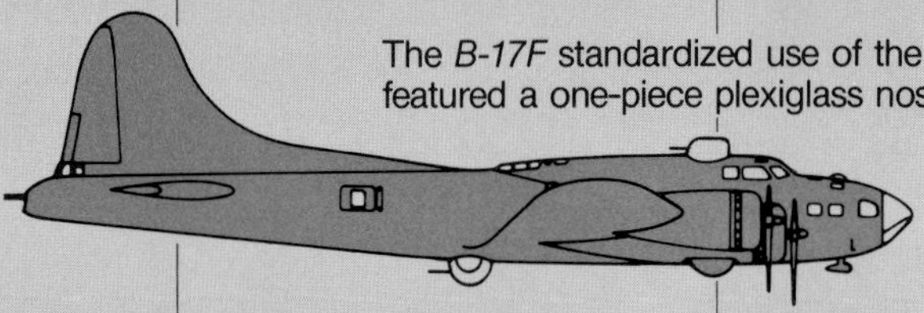

The *B-17F* standardized use of the Bendix ball turret introduced in later *B-17Es* and featured a one-piece plexiglass nose. 19 were transferred to Britain as *Fortress Mk II.*

2300 (Produced by Boeing/Seattle plant)

605 (Produced by Douglas)

500 (Produced by Vega)

B-17G

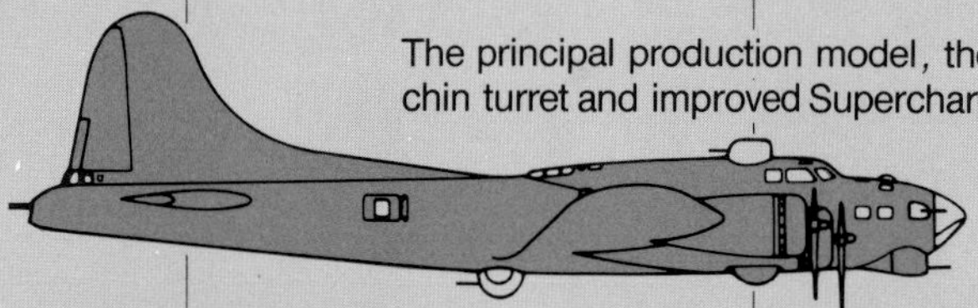

The principal production model, the *G* model was like the *F,* but with the addition of a chin turret and improved Superchargers. 112 were transferred to Britain as *Fortress Mk III.*

4035 (Produced by Boeing/Seattle plant)

2395 (Produced by Douglas)

2250 (Produced by Vega)

Other military aircraft designations with B-17 (Model 299) Airframes.

B-17H: Airborne lifeboat conversions of *B-17G.* 130 were planned, but only 12 were actually converted.

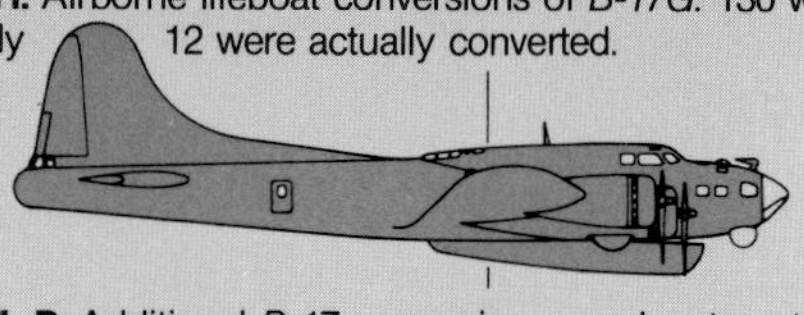

B-17L-P: Additional *B-17* conversions, used as target drones, target drone directors, etc.

XB-38: A single *B-17E* re-engined with 4 Allison liquid-cooled engines.

B-40: 25 *B-17Fs* equipped with a greatly increased number of machine guns, including additional dorsal & ventral turrets on some. The *B-40* saw limited service with the 8th AF as a long-range escort for bomber formations over Europe.

BQ-7: 25 used *B-17Es* & *Fs* were modified as radio-controlled bombs under Project Castor. Carrying up to 20,000 lbs of high explosives each, 11 one-way missions were flown against German targets before the project was cancelled because of the unreliability of the radio-control mechanism.

C-108: Four transport conversions from *B-17Es and Fs* including General MacArthur's personal executive transport "Bataan."

F-9: 29 *B-17Fs* and 9 *B-17Gs* converted to photo-reconnaissance versions with the addition of cameras in the nose, bomb bay and rear fuselage. In 1945 they were redesignated *FB-17F and G* and in 1948 they were redesignated again as *RB-17F and G.*

PB: 32 *B-17Gs* in US Navy service with APS-20 search radar added and defensive armament removed. An additional 17 *B-17Gs* became *PB-1Gs* in US Coast Guard Service.

Above: A Seattle-built **B-17F** with the one-piece plexiglass nose and ventral ball turret that became standard on the F model. The ball turret had first been introduced on the B-17E, but the one-piece nose was the feature that most distinguished the B-17F from its predecessor.

Lieutenant Wheless kept the ship on course, but gas was leaking from punctured tanks, and he realized the plane would run out of fuel before reaching home base. He changed course for Cagayan on Mindanao, but as he approached the airfield he saw it was covered with barricades. There was no way to avoid them, and not enough fuel left to reach another base, so the Fortress plowed across the field, coming to an abrupt halt tipped up on its nose. The crewmen leaped to safety, and the danger was over. They later counted over 1000 bullet holes in their ship.

Even before America was at war with Japan, Boeing had made radical improvements to the B-17D design. The next variant, the B-17E, which first flew on 5 September 1941, featured a major redesign of the rear fuselage and tail which considerably changed the outward appearance of the aircraft. The fuselage and tail surfaces were increased in size, which gave better control and stability in high altitude bombing. The B-17E was some six feet longer than the earlier models. The larger tail permitted the fitting of a pair of .50 caliber machine guns in that long-neglected position. Power operated turrets were also fitted in the dorsal and ventral positions and additional armor plate was carried. With all these changes the B-17E was considerably heavier than the original Model 299. During the next hectic months 512 B-17Es were built, 46 of which were delivered to Britain as Fortress IIAs.

Initially, the ventral turret was operated by periscope from below the waist hatches. This proved awkward in combat so the turret was replaced by the unique Sperry ball turret, an innovation that was to be maintained on later model B-17s.

In the summer of 1942 the first B-17Es arrived in Britain manned by American crews. These Fortresses were bristling with armament, quite different than earlier versions. The Es struck first on 17 August 1942. Their target was Rouen, a rail center northwest of Paris. Twelve Forts poured destruction on freight yards, trains, and round houses. Despite RAF experience of heavy losses in daylight raids in the early months of the war, the American leaders were still convinced that the Flying Fortresses could defend themselves against daytime fighter attack while bombing far more accurately than was possible at night. Although both these claims were later to come into question, on this occasion the B-17s came over at 25,000 feet, plastered their targets effectively and then returned safely to England.

The B-17F was introduced in April 1942 with a Wright Cyclone GR-1820-97 engine delivering 1380hp at 25,000 feet. In addition to the new engines and the now institutionalized ventral ball

Specifications: B-17F Flying Fortress (RAF Fortress II) Boeing Model Number 299P

Span	103 ft 9 in
Length	74 ft 9 in
Wing Area	1420 sq ft
Tail Height	19 ft 2 in
Gross Weight	65,000 pounds
Bomb Capacity	9600 pounds
Top Speed	299 mph
Cruising Speed	200 mph
Ferry Range	3500 miles
Service Ceiling	37,500 ft
Powerplant	four 1200 hp Wright R-1820-65/97
Defensive Armament	nine 0.5 in machine guns

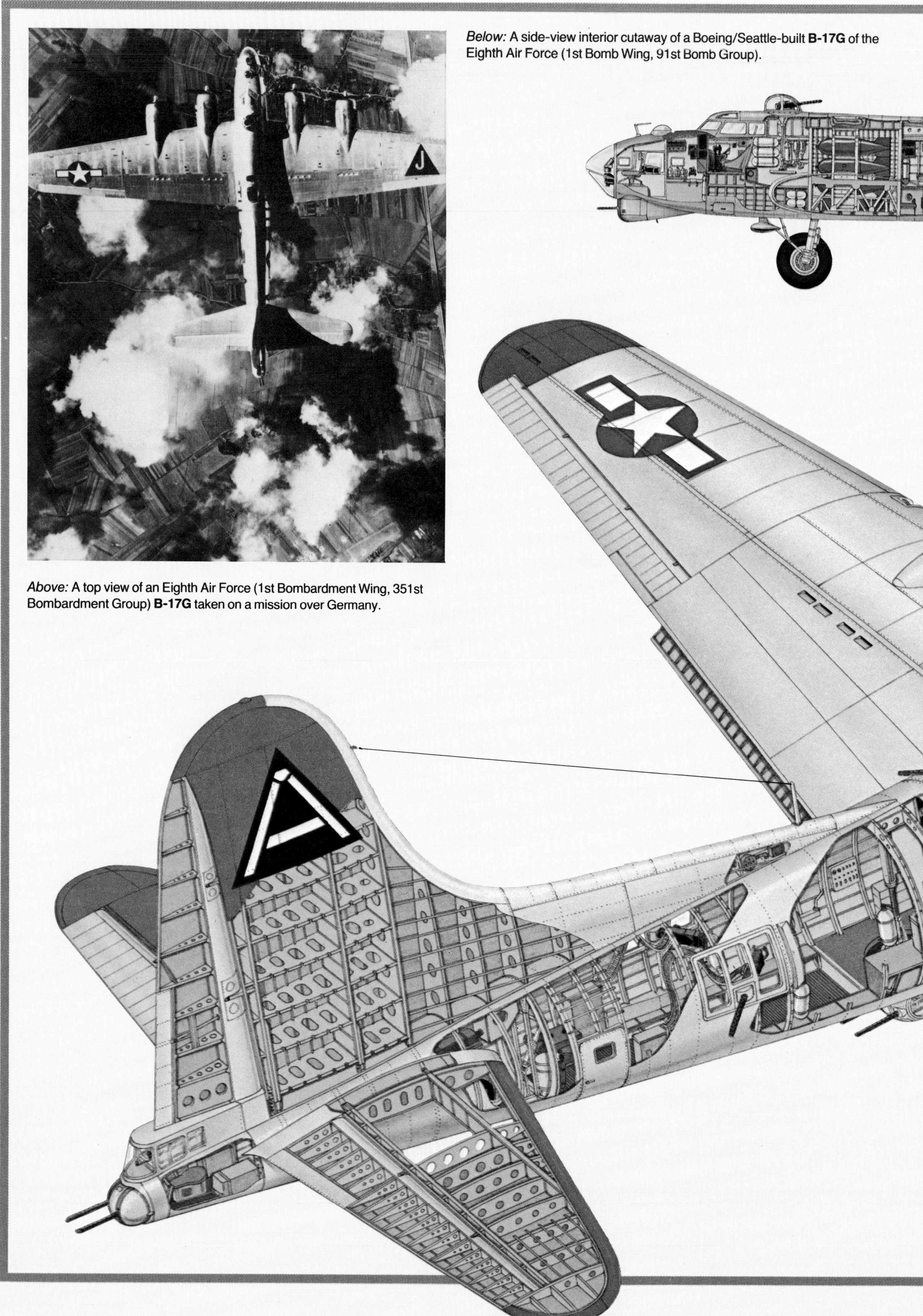

Below: A side-view interior cutaway of a Boeing/Seattle-built **B-17G** of the Eighth Air Force (1st Bomb Wing, 91st Bomb Group).

Above: A top view of an Eighth Air Force (1st Bombardment Wing, 351st Bombardment Group) **B-17G** taken on a mission over Germany.

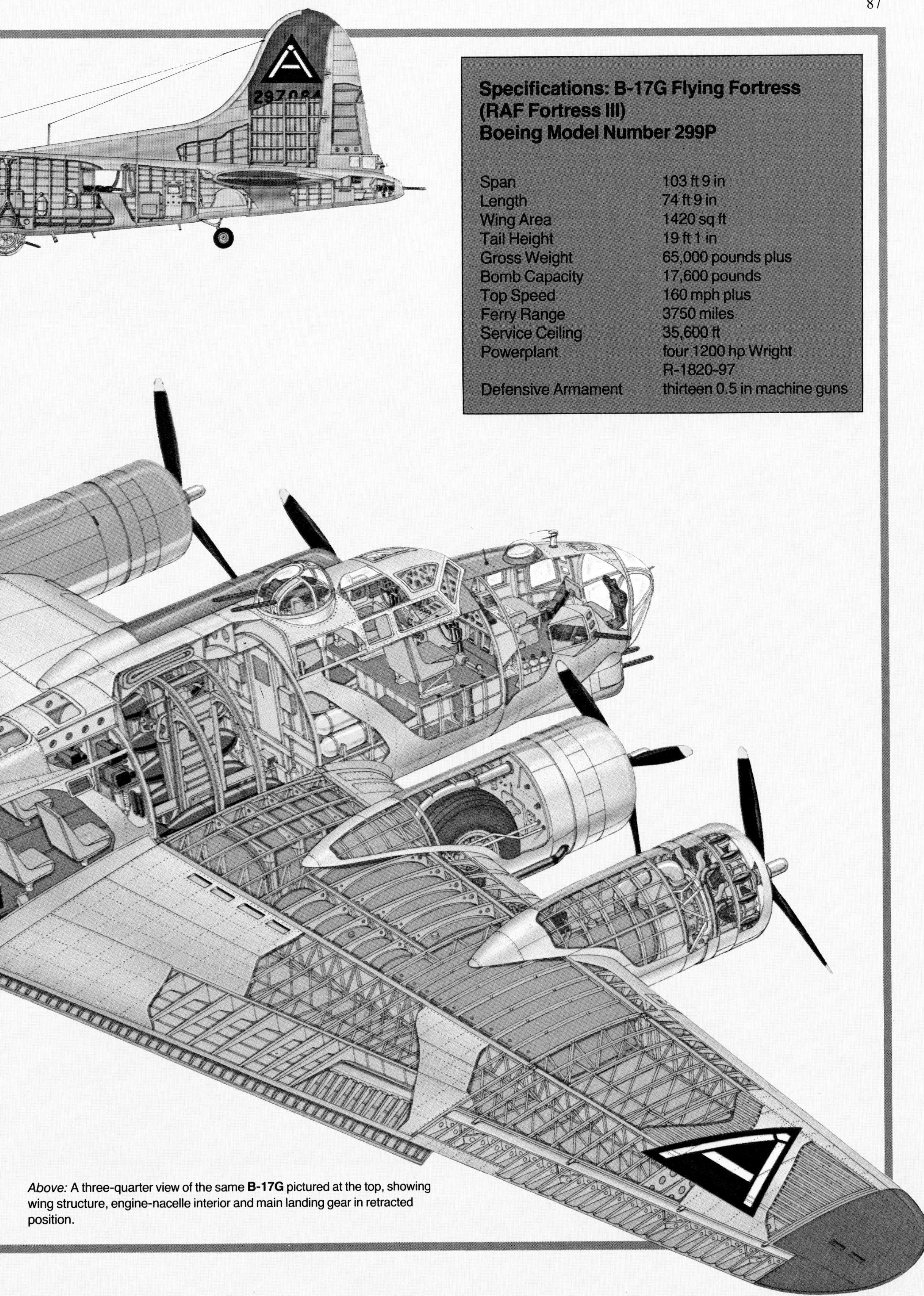

Specifications: B-17G Flying Fortress (RAF Fortress III) Boeing Model Number 299P

Span	103 ft 9 in
Length	74 ft 9 in
Wing Area	1420 sq ft
Tail Height	19 ft 1 in
Gross Weight	65,000 pounds plus
Bomb Capacity	17,600 pounds
Top Speed	160 mph plus
Ferry Range	3750 miles
Service Ceiling	35,600 ft
Powerplant	four 1200 hp Wright R-1820-97
Defensive Armament	thirteen 0.5 in machine guns

Above: A three-quarter view of the same **B-17G** pictured at the top, showing wing structure, engine-nacelle interior and main landing gear in retracted position.

Above: Eighth Air Force (1st Bomb Wing, 91st Bomb Group) **B-17Gs** in camouflage colors on their way to a target in Occupied Europe.

Below: The **B-17G** 'front office.'

turret, the F incorporated a one-piece molded plexiglass nose. The faceted nose of earlier models had inhibited visibility, making the one-piece nose a welcome improvement. The gross weight limit of the F was greatly increased over the E and extra 1100 gallon fuel cells, known as 'Tokyo Tanks' were added, extending the range considerably. It had been planned to have some of the B-17E production taken over by other manufacturers with surplus production capacity, but the B-17F superseded the E before the plan could be implemented. Over the course of the 15 months the F was in production, however, 605 Fs were built by the Douglas factories and another 500 by Vega. Boeing itself was to build a staggering 2300 in Seattle.

In May 1943 one B-17E was experimentally fitted with four 1425hp Allison V-1710-89 twelve cylinder liquid-cooled engines and redesignated XB-38. The idea was to determine whether the more powerful engines would increase the overall performance of the Model 299 airframe sufficiently to make it worthwhile to consider building a production series of B-38As. Performance was increased, but the single XB-38 was destroyed by fire in June before the tests were completed. With the Allison engines in great demand for the P-38 and P-40 fighters and the coming on line of the B-17F, it was considered less than prudent to divert precious production capability to an untested project, so the B-38 program was scrapped.

Meanwhile the B-17Es and Fs were swelling the ranks of the Eighth Air Force in England as a major part of the Allied Combined Bomber Offensive against targets in occupied Europe. The USAAF was given the daylight precision bombing role, while the RAF conducted area bombing by night. In flying to and from their targets it became evident that, despite their defensive armament, the bombers needed fighter escorts. The targets were generally beyond the range of Allied fighters so the German fighters found themselves free to attack the bombers without having to fight their way through a protective screen of fighters.

Below: The **B-17** gained a well-deserved reputation for being able to suffer severe damage and still limp back to base.

While longer range fighters were being developed, an interim idea evolved to take the basic B-17/Model 299 airframe, which certainly had the required range, and adapt it as a flying gun platform. Vega converted a B-17F and the result was designated XB-40. Twenty YB-40s followed. Though the specific armament varied from plane to plane, the result was a true 'flying fortress.' There were as many as 30 automatic weapons ranging from .50 caliber machine guns in multiple turrets to 20mm and in some cases 40mm cannons mounted in the waist positions. The first mission to be flown with a YB-40 escort was against St Nazaire in May 1943, and there were others to follow. It soon became evident that while the B-40s could keep up with the bomb laden B-17s on the way to the target, they could not, with the weight of all their guns and ammunition, match the speed and altitude of the empty B-17s on their way home. The project was deemed a failure and although four TB-40s would see service stateside as crew trainers, the program was scrapped in August 1943.

One innovation of the B-40 program was deemed successful however, and was incorporated into the later B-17Fs and the new B-17Gs that went into production in July 1943. That innovation was the Bendix power-operated chin turret. The B-17G was essentially similar to the B-17F except for the chin turret and a few other more minor armament modifications. The B-17G went on to be produced in larger numbers than any other model of any Boeing-designed aircraft before or since. In total 8680 B-17Gs were produced against less than half that for all other variants combined. Of the total, 4035 Gs were produced by Boeing with the rest coming off the Douglas and Vega lines, bringing the total B-17s of all variants to 12,731.

At the time Pearl Harbor was bombed, Boeing was producing B-17s at the rate of 60 a month. A year and a half later, as the B-17G was coming on line, production had more than quadrupled. The Boeing/Douglas/Vega pool went on to hit a peak B-17 production month in March 1944, when 578 B-17Gs rolled off the lines. After that, Boeing's contribution to the pool declined as emphasis was put on B-29 production.

Although the B-17 opened its campaign over occupied Europe in August 1942 with the attack on Rouen already mentioned, it was not until 27 January 1943 that a target in Germany, the port of Wilhelmshaven, was attacked. By the summer of 1943 the Eighth Air Force had begun to make deep-penetration daylight raids over Germany in considerable strength, giving the B-17s their most difficult assignment to that date. Although the Fortresses inflicted serious damage on German industry in these attacks, their losses became very severe as the German defenses increased their skill. Typical of this period were the particularly important and bloody attacks on Regensburg and Schweinfurt on 17 August. On 14 October Schweinfurt was visited again, this time by 291 Forts. After this raid 60 B-17s were missing, another 17 were critically shot up and many more were damaged.

Such losses could not be tolerated and, for a time, the Eighth Air Force limited its attacks to targets closer to home. However, with the introduction of the long-range escort version of the P-51 Mustang fighter at the end of 1943, the B-17s were able to resume their battle over Germany with growing success. The increase in Allied strength was such that, on Christmas Eve 1944, some 2000 American bombers were sent on missions over Germany. Of these, 1400 were B-17s. The Allies were well able to repeat this

Top: **'Aluminum Overcast'** was the term applied to the vast number of natural-metal finish B-17s that appeared over German targets in the last year of the war. This B-17G, individually named *Aluminum Overcast,* flew with the 1st Bombardment Wing of the Eighth Air Force and has been preserved in flying condition.

Left: An armada of Eighth Air Force (1st Bombardment Wing, 381st Bomb Group) **B-17Gs** with fighter escort leave England for their targets.

Above: After the war the USAF found little need for the USAAF's gallant bombers. A dozen B-17Gs, however, served the USAF as **B-17H** search and rescue aircraft.

Left: The arsenal of democracy. **B-17Gs** in the final phase of assembly on the floor of Plant 2.

performance, and such large numbers in the end ground Germany's resources to bits. Hitler had reason to fear the Flying Fortress.

These gallant ships and their crews served on the European front until 25 April 1945. On that day, 307 of them flew a final bombing mission. They attacked the Skoda armament factory and did their worst, or best, depending on point of view. American crews by this time were experts at the deadly work of dropping bombs. Six of the big ships were lost on the raid, however, so a price was paid.

The role played by the B-17 as part of the awesome Allied air armada that undertook the destruction of the war-making capability of the German Reich was tremendous. Of the more than one and one half million tons of bombs dropped on European targets by the USAAF, 640,036 fell from B17s compared to 452,508 tons dropped by Consolidated B-24 Liberators and 463,544 by all other aircraft combined.

After the war was over in both Europe and the Pacific, most B-17s went into the scrap heap, but not all.

It was fitting that the airplane would survive which prompted General Ira C Eaker to say, 'The B-17, I think, was the best combat plane ever built.' General Eaker was instrumental in developing offensive bombing tactics during the most critical period of the war and he knew his airplanes. The United States Air Force's first Chief of Staff, General Carl A 'Tooey' Spaatz, echoed Eaker's words when he said, 'I'd rather have the B-17 than any other.'

So the Flying Fortress did not perish outright. Foreign air forces, including those of Brazil and Israel, bought some. The Israeli Air Force took Fortresses into action during its 1948 War of Independence. Some B-17s were 'civilianized' by the Danish airline DDL, and flown as passenger/cargo carriers.

There were other uses. B-17s carrying underslung lifeboats which could be dropped by parachute were put to use with the designation B-17H (PB-1G in Coast Guard service). The Navy converted others for action in anti-submarine and weather reconnaissance work. Some Forts remained in military service as VIP transports and trainers. More were converted to radio-controlled drones, serving as targets. The last B-17 in US military service, a QB-17 drone, was destroyed in 1960. It was an incident touched with irony, because the destroying weapon was a Boeing developed Bomarc missile.

Below: After the war most of the **B-17Gs** that escaped the scrapyard ultimately had all their turrets deleted. The *Virgin's Delight* is preserved at the Castle Air Museum on the grounds of Castle AFB near Merced, California. Boeing KC-135 Stratotankers can be seen in the background.

Above: **The five thousandth B-17** was a Seattle-built G which was autographed by everybody who worked on it.

Below: The 'village' on the roof of **Plant 2** as photographed in 1945, after aerial photographs of the site were permitted. The 'roads' across Boeing Field, still visible in this photograph, were allowed to deteriorate later in the war as air attack became less likely.

The success of the B-17 and the enormous numbers of them produced were no accident. In 1939 Phil Johnson had been brought back into the company as president. Under his leadership and organizational ability, Boeing met the challenge of wartime production. To handle the enormous increase, thousands of workers were added to the payroll. Security was a constant worry. War jitters panicked sensible men, and every Japanese-American became suspect of spying. The Aleutian Islands were, after all, under attack, and enemy submarines had been sighted off the west coast with one shelling oil tanks near Santa Barbara, California.

To accommodate wartime production, the Boeing plants grew to an enormous 1,500,000 square feet of space, over 26 acres. If one Japanese submarine shell could cause trouble, a dozen would create a tangle it would take months to clear. Nor was there any doubt a raid was possible. The Boeing plants were on the Duwamish River, which flowed into Puget Sound, so close the fog horns could be heard on thick nights. And Puget Sound was deep enough to allow submarines access. There was also the threat of Japanese pilots flying long-distance one-way missions from a carrier and dropping destruction by the ton.

To prevent this, or at least to confuse the enemy, an ingenious marvel of camouflage was created. The Army Engineers, Passive Defense Division, were the instigators. They created a village over the roof-tops of Boeing's Seattle plants. From the air, the factory area looked for all the world like a small town. And who would bother about a helpless little town?

It was a huge task, covering a 26 acre site. Houses were made from canvas with painted windows. Trees up to twelve feet tall, shrubs and grass, were created from a million and a half feet of chicken wire covered with feathers and spun glass. They were colored whatever hue was necessary to lend an aspect of reality. Roads and streets were shaped with more canvas, covered with burlap. Where 'roads' crossed Boeing Field, which was directly across the street from the factories, they were made of dirt soaked with oil.

There were 53 houses in 'town,' 24 garages, a corner service station, three greenhouses, and a store. There were three main streets, with numerous automobiles, and a cow grazing in a pasture. It was a real cow, eating real grass. There were even street signs with names like 'Synthetic Street,' and 'Burlap Blvd.' Two of the buildings, however, were genuine. They housed anti-aircraft guns with crews. Those who flew over the area in Army air transports recall that the camouflage was perfect, even at low levels, though it did seem weird to land on a country road. Occasionally, a pilot new to the area became confused, and had to be led down by another airplane.

The entire village was treated with a fire-retardent chemical as a precaution. There were, in addition, 67 sprinklers and 100 fire hydrants. One million board feet of lumber had gone into the construction of the village, an invitation to disaster by fire.

Security personnel were everywhere, in around-the-clock service. These included a company of Army Military Guards from the 41st Division as well as civilians. Among the civilian security people were women. Women were found to be especially good at such duties as traffic control, pass checking, and searching cars – and lunch pails – for pilferage. They were sharply dressed in blue-gray gabardine uniforms, but carried no firearms. Their duties did not take them to areas of possible violence, such as remote areas of the plants, where there were few, if any, people. But the women took their work seriously, and there was never a lack of applications. Being a guard was considered a top job.

It was a far cry from an occasion during World War I when E M Gott, General Manager, sent a typed letter to I M Ortman, Purchasing Agent, directing him to have a talk with the day watchman. The watchman was not showing enough authority at the gate. He should ensure that 'suspicious characters do not loiter in the vicinity of the gate or fence.'

Despite precautions, there were leaks. In order to obtain access to the B-29 assembly lines, it was necessary to get a special pass. The work was kept under wraps, secret, nobody other than workers directly involved knew a B-29 was in the making.

Top company brass were surprised, therefore, when a twelve-year-old boy from Wyoming wrote asking for more information on the B-29. He then proceeded to list amazing details about the hush-hush project, and made suggestions as to what information he would like to have. The leak was attributed to loose talk, and nothing was ever done to the boy.

There was little sabotage, however. A B-29 wing section was deeply slashed, but it had been done by an irate employee, not a saboteur. Some industrial diamonds were missing, but subsequent investigation turned them up at the home of another

Below: A stroll on Synthetic Street.

worker. The elaborate security system seemed to be working well.

However, not all systems are perfect. Though Boeing personnel managers made every effort to screen prospective employees, weeding out suspicious characters, some got by. The war had drawn Army contingents to many Alaskan towns. The Territory was considered vulnerable to Japanese air attacks, and defenses were bolstered. It happened that the Army contingent in Ketchikan closed the red-light district. The girls were sent to Seattle, where eventually, they found their way to Boeing payrolls. Alas for patriotism! The girls had to be fired, when it was learned that making arrangements for off-duty liaisons took precedence over building airplanes. All in all, though, Boeing security was very good.

The Seattle plants were awesome in their efficiency. Around-the-clock shifts involved a total of 40,000 men and women. The acres of overhanging fluorescent lights, the cavernous assembly halls whose floors were covered with gleaming metal wings, gave the scene a surrealistic atmosphere. The din of chattering rivet guns and clanking power tools added to the confusion. Yet it was here, in a larger-than-life setting, that the B-17 and B-29 were built, two airplanes which hastened the end of a terrible war.

Below: A shift change at **Plant 2** circa 1942.

Above: A **B-29** outside the big Renton plant at the foot of Lake Washington, where the majority of the B-29s were built.

Below: Technicians check out the engines of a **B-29** at the Boeing Field dispersal site.

Above: One of the first **B-29 Superfortresses** in formation with a **B-17G,** the last production model of the Flying Fortress. The early B-29s and B-17Gs were painted in camouflage colors but spent most of their careers in natural metal finish.

As first-hand combat experience and new technology brought improvements to the B-17, these improvements were extended to Boeing's second great World War II bomber, the B-29 Superfortress.

The story of the B-29, like that of the B-17, starts in the 1930s. In 1938 Claire Egtvedt and Ed Wells paid a visit to Wright Field. Colonel Oliver Echols, an Air Corps engineering chief, was an admirer of the Flying Fortress and Consolidated's B-24 Liberator as well. 'The trouble is,' said Echols in essence, 'we need airplanes with a longer range. Our present bombers can fly 3000 miles. We want one that will go four or five thousand.' There was no money, however, from the military for preliminary plans. Congress felt that larger bombers would show the world an untoward 'aggressiveness.' It might spark suspicions in unfriendly countries, and set off conflicts. In 1938, Congress did not want war. The Great Depression, which had laid the nation flat economically, was trouble enough. When Egtvedt returned to Seattle, he did not worry about money. Instead, he put designers to work on a superbomber study. Ed Wells was to oversee the project. 'Get the drag down,' he told engineers. 'It's the only way we can give Echols the distance he wants. The rivets must be flush, gun turrets cannot protrude, nacelles have to be skin tight.'

By late 1939, however, official opinion had changed and a specification for a long-range bomber was drawn up. Boeing had continued with unofficial design work on the long-range bomber idea and was thus well prepared to respond when the specification was issued to a number of aircraft manufacturing companies in February 1940. What was required was a bomber with 5333 miles range and an all-round performance considerably superior to the B-17 in speed and payload. The initial design had to be ready in one month. A revised design was submitted in April and after further work and consideration an official contract to produce prototype XB-29s was issued in September 1940.

What was wanted, Boeing concluded from the original specification, was an airplane with no more drag than a B-17, even though twice as large. It would have to have flight and landing performances never before achieved. Though Boeing had had experience in big planes like the XB-15, the Clippers, and the Stratocruisers, the new aircraft was in a class by itself, presenting problems never encountered.

One of the results of the experimentation that followed was a new wing for what was to be the XB-29, Boeing Model 345. Enormous wing flaps were originated, larger in themselves than the wings of many fighter planes, the biggest ever put on an air-

plane. They did the job, providing hoped-for lift and performance, yet keeping landing speed acceptably low. Drag was reduced to a minimum, and the resultant wing became known as the '117' wing.

An ingenious 'three bubble' system of pressurization for the crew spaces was developed. The pilots' cabin and the waist gunner's section were pressurized, and the two compartments were connected by a pressurized tunnel. The tunnel overrode the two bomb bays. The tail gunner's area was pressurized on its own.

There were two bomb bays. One was forward of the wing, and the other aft. This meant that one bay could not be emptied before the other, without throwing the bomber temporarily out of trim, its center of gravity having shifted. So an alternating system of dropping bombs was invented by the engineers to release the bombs first from one bay then the other. In this way, the center of gravity was maintained, and the bomber kept level flight.

With customary thoroughness, Boeing tested its work the hard way. A fantastic structural testing program was developed for this special airplane. Included were tests to destruction in which major sections of the XB-29 were torn to pieces. Changes were made because of these 'torture tests,' and no alternations were

Above: Boeing people not only built the bombers, they went overseas to supervise their servicing. **Ken Hamner** was a Boeing service rep with the Fifteenth Air Force in Italy in 1944.

Below: A veteran of the Battle of Kansas: a Wichita-built **B-29** goes to war.

Below: Eddie Allen's namesake, the **B-29** *Eddie Allen* of the 40th BG, 20th Bomber Command, nears the target on the 3 November 1944 raid on Rangoon, Burma.

required in the basic structure after the Model 345 was completed. The engineers had done their work well.

Even before the first XB-29 had been thoroughly tested, the Army ordered 990 of them. Ten were to be delivered in 1942, 450 in 1943 and 530 in 1944. It was an unprecedented act of faith, but Echols, who authorized the contract, had that faith.

There was to be a hitch, however. Competing builders tried to convince Echols that the B-29 would have too much drag. They knew little about the '117' airfoil, which had been kept secret. Don Putt, the Army man who had tested the military's first B-17, was sent to Seattle to meet with Wellwood Beall and other officials. After reviewing what had been done with the wing, plus the other anti-drag features, Putt convinced Echols to go ahead with the program. However, the Army did require a large number of detail changes throughout the design process. Particularly important was the decision made in late 1941 to fit a remote control gun-aiming system based around a General Electric computer. This involved considerable changes to the aircraft's electrical system and an increase in weight.

The Boeing work force expanded dramatically to handle production. In addition to the Renton plant near Seattle, other companies were asked to build what had now become the B-29. Bell erected buildings in Marietta, Georgia, expressly for the purpose. Martin did the same in Omaha, Nebraska. Mass production of the world's largest bomber was underway, and, as yet, the B-29 had not been flown!

On 21 September 1942 Eddie Allen, Boeing's chief test pilot, took the first one aloft. He liked what the big airplane did. It was as far ahead of its contemporaries, as the Boeing B-9 had been in 1931. It handled well, was fast, and though there were minor problems, he landed and said briefly, 'She flies.'

There followed a series of flight tests with Allen and others at the controls. Then, on 18 February 1943, an engine on the second prototype XB-29 that he was testing caught on fire over Lake Washington. Allen headed for an emergency landing on Boeing Field, but the stricken bomber lost altitude rapidly and crashed into the four-storied Frye meat-packing plant on Seattle's south side, killing all those aboard.

The Boeing Airplane Company lost eleven of the most experienced Superfortress program personnel. Once again the B-29 program faltered, but General Arnold, Chief of Staff of the Army Air Force, was by now committed to them. He had arranged with Chinese leader Chiang Kai-shek to build a number of bases inside Chinese borders specifically to handle the B-29s. There was no turning back now. Boeing stepped up production, and by early 1943, there were 25,000 employees in the Wichita plant and another 33,000 in Renton.

In such a large undertaking, there were bound to be problems. Boeing was obviously not the only company involved in producing war products, and vital materials were being used in great quantities. Parts for the B-29s stopped coming, and work slowed down. There were particular problems with the supply of engines. General Arnold had promised the first bombers would leave for China by 10 March 1944. He sent General Orval Cook, military production chief, to Kansas to confer with Earl Schaefer, top man at the plant.

On investigation, Cook learned that each B-29 needed much final work before passing inspection. One of the foremen took him through a typical round of 'touch up' work. Everything from correcting crossed-up switches to recalibrating fuel gauges had to be done. Nothing was left to chance. Every switch, knob, dial and lever was manually checked to see if it responded properly. It was a time-consuming task, and technicians were in short supply.

General Arnold had a war to fight, and when he learned that the 10 March deadline could not be met, he said very definitely that he wanted the first batch of B-29s in the air by 15 April, no excuses. Thus began the 'Battle of Kansas.'

Six hundred specialists were flown in from Seattle, and they worked steadily for four weeks to get the B-29s ready for flight.

Edmund T 'Eddie' Allen was born on 4 January 1896 in Chicago, Illinois. In 1917, after he had completed his first year at the University of Illinois, he enlisted in the Infantry, but changed to the aviation branch and enlisted in the Signal Corps. Following his training, he was sent to England to learn how the British tested their planes, which led him into the test-pilot field.

Allen returned to McCook Field, Ohio, before the armistice and later resigned from the army to become the first test pilot of the National Advisory Committee for Aeronautics at Langley Field. In 1920 he entered MIT for two years' study of aeronautical engineering. In 1923 he began test piloting for various airplane manufacturers. He became a civilian test pilot at McCook Field and in 1925 a pilot of the Post Office airmail service. When Boeing Air Transport took over the Chicago-San Francisco airmail service in 1927, Allen became one of their leading pilots, and by 1929 he was one of the nation's top consulting test pilots.

Allen test flew Boeing's B-17, the B-15 and the Clipper. He was Boeing's best test pilot and he knew more about the infinite mechanical complexities of the giant airplanes than any other man. In 1939 he became head of Boeing's Research Division and directed the planning and testing that led to the B-29.

Below: On **18 February 1943**, Allen took off in the second prototype XB-29 (its three-bladed props visible here) for engine tests. Twenty minutes after takeoff, he notified Boeing Field that he was coming in with a wing on fire. Moments later, the plane hit the Frye Packing Plant.

W J Yenne, a welder working at the nearby Todd Shipyard, saw the plane moments after the crash. He remembered seeing a huge plane, unlike the familiar B-17, on the building 'like a hen on her nest.' Soon the windows were glowing orange as the flames spread, then the building was swallowed in billowing smoke.

It was an all-out battle, and the technicians won. Late in March 1944, the first one was flown to India by Colonel Leonard 'Jake' Harman. It was turned over to the 20th Bomber Command, which was led by General K B Wolfe. This unit had been formed some months previously but because of the shortage of B-29s its training had been less extensive than had been planned.

Other B-29s followed Harman's to India but more trouble waited. Engines overheated in the 120 degree heat and several aircraft crashed. Word was sent back to the States about the problem and baffles were designed and fitted to allow cool air to flow back over the engines. In addition, top cowl flaps, originally fixed, could be adjusted from the cockpit.

An immediate ferrying operation began to supply the Chinese bases from which the bombers would conduct operations. It was an urgent matter, and the B-29s themselves and other aircraft were pressed into service.

It was necessary to cross the Himalayas between Burma and China (fliers called it 'flying the Hump') and the cold air at altitudes of 25,000 feet could cause carburetors to freeze. It was a serious problem, until an enlisted man, Sergeant Leonard Egyed, developed a method of keeping them warm, and efficiency smoothed out.

The first two B-29s to surmount the Hump arrived safely on 24 April 1944. They landed at Chengtu, 1000 miles from their starting point, on an airfield made ready by 75,000 Chinese laborers. Chiang Kai-shek had kept his word although facilities were far from perfect.

On the 26 April Major Charles E Hansen took off for Chengtu. As he crossed over the Hump, he was challenged by a dozen Japanese Nakajima Ki-43 fighters (Allied code name Oscar). For the first few moments, the fighters flew along with the Superfortress, looking it over. Later writings by Japanese pilots called the B-29s 'monstrous bulls,' and 'stupendous giants.' As, indeed, they were. After their look, the Japanese opened fire, and the gun crews of the B-29 returned the greeting with a fusillade of .50 caliber bullets. Due to inexperience, things did not go well for the Americans, and several guns jammed. The Oscars had their own way with the 'monstrous bull,' until the tail gunner, whose guns were still working, shot one down. Pilot Hansen climbed to 18,000 feet and the Japanese declined to follow. After they disappeared, Hansen continued to Chengtu, landing with, it was learned, surprisingly little damage. News of the fight spread throughout the B-29 bomber commands, and was greeted with cheers. The big ship had had its baptism of fire, and had proven worthy.

On 5 June 1944 the B-29 made its first actual bombing mission. Some 98 planes steered for Bangkok to blow up railroad yards. The planes flew in a loose formation, the better to use radar bomb aiming, but accuracy was poor. Damage was minimal. Japanese fighters and antiaircraft guns defended the territory but no B-29s were lost to enemy action. Fourteen had turned back at the outset because of mechanical trouble, one had crashed on take off and two were forced to ditch in the Bay of Bengal as a result of bad weather.

Above: **Dorothy Bennett** at work in a B-29.

Though the raid on Bangkok was nothing to crow about, it did serve well in the experience department. The crews of the ditched bombers were rescued and reported that the B-29s 'ditched well.' Crews gained valuable insights in handling the giants; pilots sharpened their skills, gunners improved their aim. It had, on balance, been a worthwhile sortie.

On 14 June the 20th Bomber Command sent 75 B-29s against the Imperial Iron and Steel Works at Yawata, on the Japanese island of Kyushu. This was the first raid on Japan since General Jimmy Doolittle's daring B-25 attack from the aircraft carrier *Hornet* two years before. Each B-29 carried two tons of explosives and several news correspondents and photographers.

From the beginning there were problems. Seven B-29s were unable to get airborne, and one that did crashed. Four more returned because of engine trouble, but the remaining squadrons continued. They arrived over the target after midnight, and, under harassment from Japanese fighters and antiaircraft fire, made their runs. Many, unable to locate their target by sight, unloaded their bombs by radar. Once again, accuracy was poor and damage minimal. Several planes jettisoned their explosives because of mechanical difficulties, and the bombs went off harmlessly in the countryside.

Before the B-29s returned to Chengtu, seven more were lost, six to accident and one to enemy fire, the first B-29 so lost. Fifty-five men were listed as missing after this first strike against Japan. The United States hailed the raid as a victory, but the Japanese newspapers belittled it.

Although many important lessons were learned from this and later raids from Indian and Chinese bases, supply problems made these B-29 operations far less effective than had been hoped.

Below: Security was intense, with three different services guarding the **XB-29** as it was barged up the Duwamish on 21 July 1942.

Above. The **YB-52**.

running into trouble because, with turboprop propulsion, the performance could not exceed that of the new B-36 by a significant degree.

It is interesting to note that, at the same time the Boeing engineers were evolving a swept wing turboprop based ultimately on the B-29, Russian engineers of the Tupolev design bureau were developing a swept wing turboprop based on the B-29. Their aircraft, the Tu-95 (later NATO codename 'Bear') was developed out of their experience producing the Tu-4, which was virtually a bootlegged copy of B-29s that had made forced landings in Russian territory during World War II. The career of the Tu-95 has closely paralleled that of the B-52, and today it is the mainstay of the Soviet equivalent of SAC, the *Dalnaya Aviatsiya* or Long Range Aviation.

Ed Wells and George Schairer argued for an all-jet aircraft. After all, the B-47, their all-jet medium bomber, was proving to be a success on her early test flights. Colonel Pete Warden of Wright Field, long a Boeing advocate, managed to get them an OK to try a jet design. 'But,' he told them, 'keep the turboprop in mind.' In October 1948 plans for the new airplane were submitted to officials at Wright Field. The bomber now had a 20 degree sweepback and it was to be powered by Pratt & Whitney jet engines. The gross weight stood at 300,000 pounds, speed 500mph.

Pete Warden looked the plan over with a critical eye, and was doubtful. 'Give it more speed,' he advised in effect. 'You need a faster wing, something like the B-47.' It was Friday, and the end of the work-week, so the Boeing engineers that had come along for the presentation returned to their hotel for a talk. Top men were present, including Ed Wells, George Schairer, Bob Withington and Vaughn Blumenthal from the aerodynamics department. Art Carlsen and Maynard Pennell represented preliminary design.

They worked all weekend, revising the plans for their Model 464-49, which they now called the Stratofortress. They gave the bomber more sweep, angling the wings back 35 degrees like those of the B-47. They added two more engines, making a total of eight, two to a pod. It was known that Pratt & Whitney was experimenting at that time with a more powerful jet engine, the J57, which the Boeing men proposed to incorporate into the Stratofortress, which now weighed 330,000 pounds but whose range outdistanced the B-47 and whose speed was more than 600mph.

To make their new concept more eye-appealing and graphic, the planners built a balsa wood model, and took it to Wright Field for a Monday meeting with the military brass. The results pleased the officers. They read the 33 page report and studied the clean lines of the balsa model. Based on what they read and saw, Boeing was authorized to build two prototypes of the Model 464, given the Air Force designation B-52. Thus was history shaped over a weekend in a hotel room, for the B-52 was destined to make much history in the years to come.

With its contract in hand, Boeing got set to build the two prototypes, the XB-52 and YB-52. They were equipped with eight P&W J57 engines (as had been Convair's failed YB-60) and each was able to develop 10,000 pounds of thrust. That made them 10 times more powerful than the B-29. The B-52s could fly higher than the B-47s and required only five crewmen – as against the Convair B-36's 22.

Left: Like a scene from an early 50s spy movie, the **YB-52**, draped in acres of shroud, was rolled out of Plant 2 on a cold, rainy November night in 1951. East Marginal Way (right) was closed for the event. Thirty years later some aspects of the B-52 were still classified.

Above: The third Wichita-built **B-52G** is refueled by Boeing **KC-135A** Stratotanker.

The first prototype to lift from Boeing Field was the YB-52. In the cockpit were test pilot Tex Johnson and co-pilot Lieutenant Colonel Guy Townsend. It was 15 April 1952.

A crowd had gathered for the event, and as the J57s wound up, they split the air with an eerie wail. As one reporter put it, 'the sound was like a piercing cry.' It made the audience jittery, causing a mechanic to mutter, 'Tex Johnson will chop off the engines if they don't sound right to him.'

But all was well in the cockpit, and the YB-52 lifted off at 11.09 a.m. She flew for two hours and 51 minutes, anxiously observed by George Schairer and Wellwood Beall from the ground. Their design, the result of an inspired weekend four years before, had become a beautiful reality.

The YB-52 cut through the sky smoothly and the test went well. After Johnson landed he said, 'The airplane functioned very satisfactorily with no trouble at all with basic systems. Its performance appears to be just what was predicted by Boeing engineers.' Then he added, 'It landed just like any airplane.'

The other prototype, the XB-52, made its first flight on 2 October 1952. The same two pilots took her through two hours and 42 minutes of tests. After landing, they reported no serious problems, and the B-52 bomber was 'in.'

Representatives of the Air Force were at both test flights, but they were as much observers as critics. The Air Force had already signed a contract for 13 B-52As in February of 1951 even before the prototypes flew. The big bombers were needed and the military had faith in the Boeing product. The Cold War with Russia had intensified and nobody knew for sure which way it would go. The US was also deeply involved in the Korean War, which was seen as part of the effort to resist Soviet communism.

The size of the Air Force's new long-range bomber was striking. Its tail stood 48 feet in the air, nearly five stories high. The wings spanned 185 feet and the body was 156 feet 6 inches long. The wing area of 4000 square feet was larger than a good-sized house. In fact, this latest Boeing aircraft was so large that the 'world's biggest doorway' was built into a new hangar just to accommodate it.

The terrific noise, noted on the first test flight of the YB-52, was causing problems. Flaps installed between engines were cracking. Consequently the largest noise suppressors yet invented were added. The fuel load of 29,645 gallons (more in later models) was so heavy that outrigger wheels were pressed hard against the ground. Indeed, the plane was so hefty that it sagged both in the air and on the ground. Because of this, the problem of reinforcement against sag became an on-going engineering battle. Engineering won, but the present day B-52 is a different airplane structurally than its prototypes. Extended tests were made on the structure of a B-52G, one of the last models. An entire airplane, except for engines, instruments, wiring and other accessories, was subjected to Boeing's famous 'torture test.' It was systematically destroyed while several thousand gauges and instruments recorded the stresses and strains on different components from wings to empennage. The testing lasted for approximately nine months, and as a result major structural changes made it virtually a new bomber.

The B-52A, nominally the first production model, but actually a flight test model, was flown in August 1954. It and all successive Model 464s differed from the prototypes in having adopted a traditional flight deck with the pilot and co-pilot seated side-by-side, as in a commercial airliner. Below were the bombardier and radar operator, while a gunner occupied a separately pressurized compartment in the tail. The compartment could be jettisoned if necessary, but until that fateful moment, the gunner was in charge of four .50 caliber machine guns.

PRODUCTION CLOSE-UP (Model 464)

B-52 STRATOFORTRESS

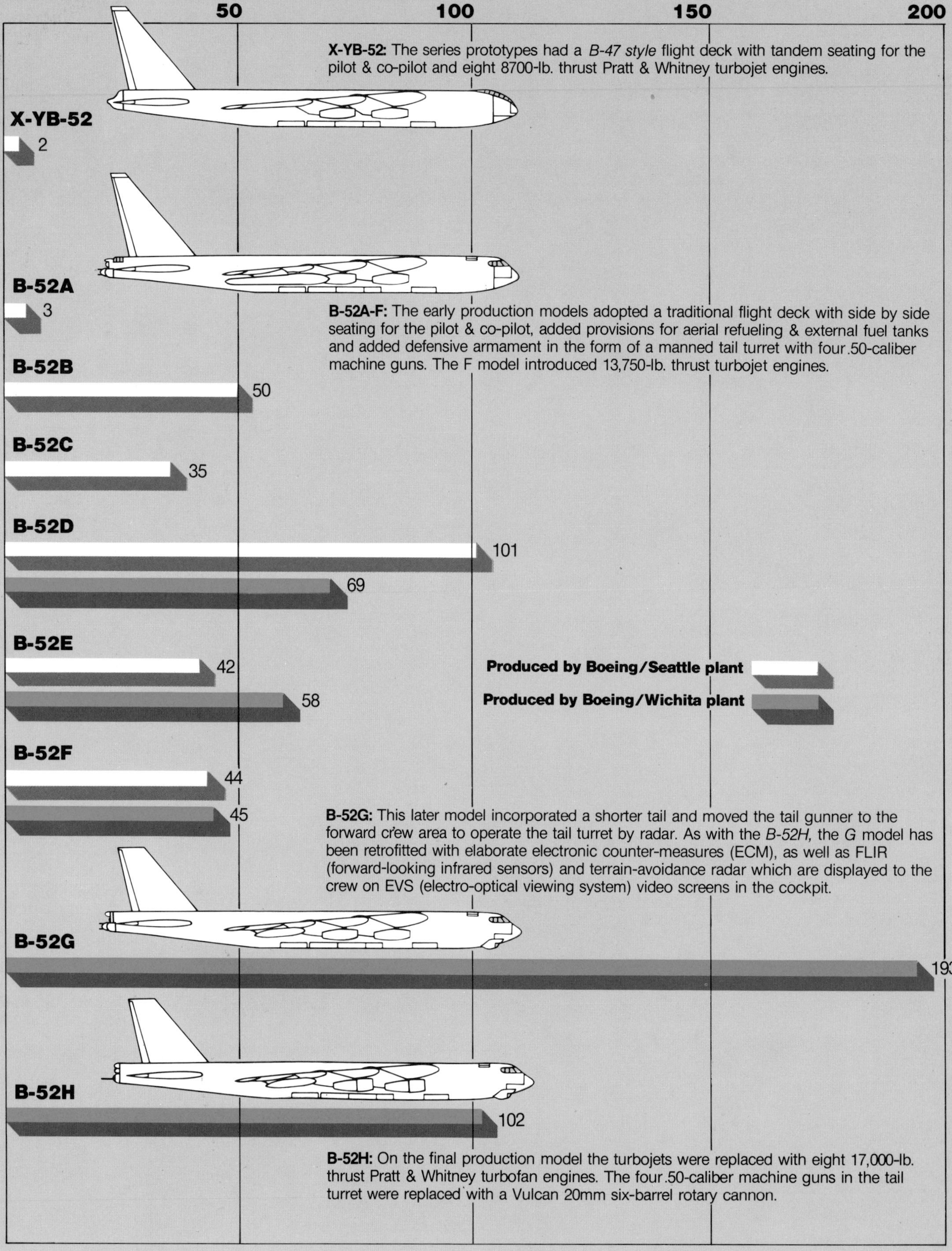

50 100 150 200

X-YB-52: The series prototypes had a *B-47 style* flight deck with tandem seating for the pilot & co-pilot and eight 8700-lb. thrust Pratt & Whitney turbojet engines.

X-YB-52
2

B-52A
3

B-52A-F: The early production models adopted a traditional flight deck with side by side seating for the pilot & co-pilot, added provisions for aerial refueling & external fuel tanks and added defensive armament in the form of a manned tail turret with four .50-caliber machine guns. The F model introduced 13,750-lb. thrust turbojet engines.

B-52B
50

B-52C
35

B-52D
101
69

B-52E
42
58

Produced by Boeing/Seattle plant

Produced by Boeing/Wichita plant

B-52F
44
45

B-52G: This later model incorporated a shorter tail and moved the tail gunner to the forward crew area to operate the tail turret by radar. As with the *B-52H,* the *G* model has been retrofitted with elaborate electronic counter-measures (ECM), as well as FLIR (forward-looking infrared sensors) and terrain-avoidance radar which are displayed to the crew on EVS (electro-optical viewing system) video screens in the cockpit.

B-52G
193

B-52H
102

B-52H: On the final production model the turbojets were replaced with eight 17,000-lb. thrust Pratt & Whitney turbofan engines. The four .50-caliber machine guns in the tail turret were replaced with a Vulcan 20mm six-barrel rotary cannon.

The fuel capacity of the B-52A had been increased by the addition of 1000 gallon drop tanks under each wing. Provision had also been made for flying boom refueling, which greatly increased the range. Pratt & Whitney J57-P-9Ws replaced earlier engines, yielding a thrust of more than 9000 pounds each, and the gross weight of the airplane reached a staggering 415,000 pounds.

Even before the 3 flight test B-52As first flew, the Air Force issued a contract for 50 B-52Bs. Photo-reconnaissance or electronic capsules could be installed in the bomb bay. Twenty-seven were built with the capsules and designated RB-52B.

Next off the line were 35 B-52Cs also with J57-P-29W turbojets. Quite similar to the B-52B, the Cs were also to serve dual purposes, but were built to higher load factors, grossing 450,000 pounds. Fuel capacity had been increased to 3000 gallons by installing larger drop tanks.

The next version, the B-52D, was to be used only as a bomber. Because of the winding down of the B-47 program and their desire to have strategic aircraft produced inland rather than near a coastline, the Air Force chose Wichita as the primary source of production. The first of 69 Wichita-built B-52Ds and 58 B-52Es rolled out in December 1955. Seattle, however, still rolled out 101 B-52Ds and 42 B-52Es from its production lines. Seattle's direct involvement with manufacturing the B-52 ended with the 'F' model. Forty-four were built in Seattle, and another 45 in Wichita. One of the principal changes over earlier models was

Above: The installation of **Pratt & Whitney J57 engines** on a B-52 assembly line.

Specifications: B-52D Stratofortress Boeing Model Number 464

Span	185 ft
Length	157 ft 7 in
Wing Area	4000 sq ft
Tail Height	48 ft 4½ in
Gross Weight	450,000 pounds
Bomb Capacity	54,000 pounds conventional explosives, or four free-fall nuclear weapons
Top Speed	585 mph
Ferry Range	7500 miles
Service Ceiling	50,000 ft
Powerplant	eight 10,000 pound thrust Pratt & Whitney J47-29W Turbojets
Defensive Armament	four 0.5 in machine guns in tail turret

Below: A **B-52D** of Strategic Air Command's 43rd Strategic Wing (Third Air Division) at Andersen AFB, Guam, in August 1979. The black-bottomed B-52Ds, with their enlarged bomb bay, flew frequent missions from Guam against targets in Southeast Asia throughout most of the Vietnam War years.

Above: Boeing test pilot **Chuck Fisher's B-52H** during its final approach into Blytheville AFB, 700 miles after it lost its tail to clear-air turbulence.

the engine. Eight P&W J57-43W turbojet engines gave the B-52F over 13,750 pounds of thrust for each engine. As the B-52 increased in weight because of added structural metal, larger fuel tanks and other innovations, the engines provided more power. Pratt & Whitney kept pace.

Significant innovations were first seen in the B-52G. In this version, the gunner was moved from the tail to a forward position with other crewmen for greater team efficiency. He monitored a television screen in his forward position which was fed images by a scanning camera. Enemy fighters could be fired on by remote control. The armament remained unchanged – 4 deadly .50 caliber machine guns.

The B-52G's exterior appearance was also modified by decreasing the height of the tail. One of the most important improvements was a redesigned wing in which wing fuel bladders were eliminated in favor of integral tanks, which reduced overall weight and opened the way by strengthening the wing, to the mounting of two supersonic AGM-28 Hound Dog missiles. Hound Dogs were long-range air-to-surface weapons, among the first of their kind. The AGM-28 was a 9600 pound, winged missile, powered by an underslung turbojet. It had a range of 690 miles and its mission was to increase the range of strategic bombers. The missile flew on, after firing, as the bomber turned away in what was called a stand-off situation. The missile continued to the target, but the bomber would be spared the danger.

The B-52H was fitted with eight 17,000 pound thrust P&W TF-33-P-1/3 turbofan engines, increasing the unrefueled range by 30 percent over the G. The .50 caliber machine guns were replaced by a six-barreled 20mm Vulcan gun, capable of virtually shredding any would-be attackers.

From its inception the B-52 has been an outstanding aircraft, most notably for its range. On 18 January 1957, three B-52s landed at March AFB, California after flying nonstop (with inflight refueling) around the world in 45 hours, 19 minutes. They averaged over 530mph during the 24,325 mile flight from Castle AFB, also in California. This cut the previous record in half, a record set by another Boeing bomber, the B-50A, 'Lucky Lady II.'

On 10 January 1962 a B-52H took off from Kadena AB, Okinawa and flew *unrefueled*, nonstop, the 12,532 miles to Madrid, setting a world distance record.

As recently as November 1981, SAC B-52s, taking part in a Rapid Deployment Force exercise codenamed operation 'Bright Star' flew nonstop to a bombing range south of Cairo, dropped their bombs and returned to their home bases in North Dakota. Earlier, in March 1980, a B-52 from K I Sawyer AFB in Michigan flew nonstop around the world in 45 hours, repeating the feat of the three B-52s in 1957. Thus the B-52 proved to the world time and again that it had the right stuff.

Even this excellent bird has had its moments of stress. In 1964 a B-52H was being tested for low-level flying performance over the Rockies. A Boeing crew was taking the bomber through a variety of tests, of structural design in high turbulence. Cruising at an altitude of 500 feet, moderate turbulence was encountered and it was decided to discontinue low-level trials. The B-52H climbed to 14,300 feet, finding smooth air, but after several minutes rough turbulence suddenly rocked the ship. It was jabbed from the side severely, then tossed up and down. The crew noted high vertical G-forces and lateral motion of the airplane. It was as if the plane had been shoved to the right by a heavy blow. The aircraft came through the encounter, but almost all of the tail fin had been ripped off!

In the words of pilot Chuck Fisher, 'I gave orders to prepare to abandon the airplane, because I didn't think we were going to keep it together. We didn't know what was damaged, but control was difficult. We cut our speed to 225 knots, and dropped to about 5000 feet. Everybody was ready, should the need come to leave the ship. We figured we'd put a little more altitude between us and the ground, so we climbed to 16,000 feet very slowly. We kept trying to figure out the reason for our control problem. We had all eight engines, and all leading edges, but the plane would suddenly pitch or tuck in response to control. When this happened, control was very marginal and we didn't hold out much hope for getting it in in a landable condition. But we headed for Wichita.

'As soon as we got into a range where we could rendezvous with another airplane, Dale Felix came up in a fighter, and reported our damage. Most of our vertical fin was gone, but the horizontal stabilizer was intact. There was a chance.

'Because of the heavy population around Wichita, we decided to divert to Blytheville. We proceeded with a KC-135 and a T-33 escorting us. Arriving at Blytheville, we lowered our landing gear, experiencing yaw, but only during transition from up to down. The landing was not my best one, but the airplane was drifting left off the runway, and the only way to stop it was to get

it on the ground. Our weight at touchdown was 250,000 pounds, and we were going at 158 knots. We stopped at 5000 feet, and we were safe. So was the airplane.'

There have been close calls of another nature. In January 1961 two 24-megaton thermonuclear bombs came loose from a B-52 over Goldsboro, North Carolina. One of them was found in a marsh; five of its six interlocking safety devices had failed. Part of the second bomb was never found.

In 1966 a B-52 crashed into another airplane off the coast of Spain and four nuclear bombs fell. One was found intact on the ground. Two exploded on impact, and the last was pulled from the sea after a four month search. As a result of this accident, 5000 barrels of contaminated Spanish soil were shipped to South Carolina. Total cost of the tragedy, 50 million dollars.

The B-52's service record can be broken into three parts, the first part being the decade from 1955 to 1965 when it was the high flying cutting edge of SAC's nuclear deterrent force, constantly patroling the skies, waiting to be called upon to take part in a nuclear counterstrike against the Soviet Union. The final part is the period from 1973 when upgraded B-52s have shared the

Above: B-52s of the 93rd Bomb Wing depart Castle AFB on their 1957 **nonstop round-the-world flight**.

Below: **B-52s** share the flight line at Boeing's Wichita plant with their little brothers, the **B-47s**.

nuclear deterrent roles with land-based and submarine-based ballistic missiles. In between, the B-52 went to war.

The war in Southeast Asia began for the B-52 on 18 June 1965 when 27 stateside based B-52Fs flying from Andersen AFB on Guam struck Vietcong positions in South Vietnam. The missions were code named 'Arc Light,' and they were to continue until the US withdrawal from Vietnam. The controversial Arc Light carpet bombing raids were flown pretty much continuously from Andersen AFB, and later also from U Tapao Royal Thai Air Base, 12 to 14 hours closer to the target than Guam. The big bombers would come in at very high altitude from which they could be neither seen nor heard on the ground and drop their bombs by radar on preselected Vietcong targets in South Vietnam. They would then begin the long haul back to Andersen or the shorter one to U Tapao without having seen their targets or

Above: A Wichita-built **B-52F** drops 750-pound general-purpose bombs against a Vietcong target. When the B-52s went to war in 1965, they kept the natural-metal finish with the previously white undersurfaces painted gloss black for night operations.

Above: By October 1966 the **B-52Ds** with the three-tone camouflage system and black bottom and tail were replacing the silver Fs in the skies over Vietnam. The era of natural-metal Air Force bombers that began with the B-17Gs around 1944 was over.

Above: During 'Linebacker II' B-52s like this B-52D took off from **Andersen AFB** as frequently as three an hour, around the clock.

Above: Loading **general-purpose bombs** onto a B-52D at U Tapao AB, in Thailand.

Above: Armorers use a hoist to position bombs on one of a B-52D's **external weapons pylons**.

Above: A Guam-based **B-52D** unloads its bombs over the target.

the enemy below. A year after the beginning of Arc Light, they were averaging 8000 tons of bombs a month and though their results against the guerrilla targets were often hard to determine, intelligence reports generally stated that the B-52s were the weapon that the Vietcong feared most.

Arc Light constituted day-in day-out drudgery for the B-52 crews. They lived for up to six months at a time in sticky heat, flying long, boring missions against an unseen enemy. The planes themselves were designed for strategic missions. Indeed they came from a long line of strategic bombers. They found themselves, however, flying routine tactical support missions.

But in December 1972 all that changed. The US was finally trying to disengage itself from an increasingly unpopular war. American diplomats were at the Paris Peace Talks trying to negotiate a settlement that could allow them to withdraw, and North Vietnam was dragging its feet.

It was decided at the highest levels of the US Government that North Vietnam must be forced to negotiate. SAC was ordered to prepare to undertake massive strategic bombing raids over North Vietnam, striking the capital of Hanoi and the major port city of Haiphong.

In what has since been called their finest hour, the B-52s finally went to war as strategic bombers in the operation codenamed 'Linebacker II.' All the B-52Ds in SAC's arsenal, except those already at U Tapao, were flown out to Andersen where they were supplemented by additional B-52Gs. The battle plan

Below: A B 52D drops 1000- and 750-pound bombs on a target 25 miles from Bien Hoa AB, Vietnam, on 1 December 1966.

called for a series of nighttime raids over a three night period with over 80 aircraft from both bases taking part the first night and that number growing to nearly 100 by the third night.

On 18 December wave upon wave of the big planes lumbered off the two fields. Navy and Air Force fighter bombers had preceded them, and Boeing KC-135 tankers were standing by to top off B-52 fuel tanks enroute. The North Vietnamese had assembled an awesome concoction of SAM missiles and anti-aircraft defenses in the Hanoi-Haiphong area, and the B-52s found the going tough. After three days the aerial armada was suffering losses at the unacceptable rate of 7 percent. In World War II, when a B-17 went down, there were three or four coming off the assembly line to replace it. In SE Asia when a B-52 went down, that was it, there was no longer an assembly line. The enemy, however, was suffering as well. When the decision was made to continue the raids past the third night and to go after the SAM sites that had proved so costly, the loss rate went down to a very acceptable zero percent for the next three nights.

Captain David R Rusch, a Boeing KC-135 tanker pilot with the 99th Air Refueling Squadron based at U Tapao airbase in Thailand, flew in support of the final operations of Linebacker II. Except for 24 hours during Christmas, there was constant activity over North Vietnam during the raids.

Circling the Tonkin Gulf, Captain Rusch had this view of the second night's raid: 'The B-52s came in high over the gulf, as the Navy aircraft went down after antiaircraft artillery sites, which opened fire as they were attacked. Then came SAM calls over the radio, and attack planes went in to hit the missile launchers. I

Left: The **manned tail turret with four 50-caliber machine guns** common to B-52A through F. *Below:* The **20mm Vulcan cannon** in the tail turret of the B-52H. When the B-52D retires, it will mark the end of manned turrets in the USAF, an end to the gut-wrenching rides in the 'roller-coastering tall tails.' The B-52 tail gunner has had his guns armed and ready for nearly 30 years, but it was only during 'Linebacker II' in December 1972 that they actually looked through their sights at a 'live' MiG and squeezed the trigger. There were two confirmed kills of MiG-21s, by SSgt Samuel Turner on the 18th and by A1C Albert Moore on the 24th, both of them from the manned tail turret of a B-52D. Three 'probables' were also claimed.

saw the B-52s begin their bomb runs, when suddenly the whole sky lit up. A B-52 had taken a direct hit from a SAM. Although the B-52s were protected by fighters, and had their own superb electronic jamming equipment, the North Vietnamese found a way to determine the bomber's altitude. One or two MiGs would dart through the formation, not shooting at anybody, but just up there to determine the altitude, which the pilot would radio to the ground. Then the North Vietnamese would fire several missiles timed to go off about that altitude and hope for a lucky hit, which they occasionally scored.'

At the end of 11 days of bombing, the overall loss rate was down to 2 percent, North Vietnamese air defenses had been all but wiped out and Le Duc Tho and the North Vietnamese team at the Paris Peace Talks were back at the negotiating table.

The last B-52H rolled off the assembly line at Wichita on 26 October 1962. Since then the Stratofortress has seen itself outlive a whole lineage of would-be successors. First there was the Convair (formerly Consolidated-Vultee, later General Dynamics) B-58, the supersonic high altitude bomber of the late 1950s. Then there was the huge Mach 3 Rockwell (formerly North American) B-70 of the middle 1960s that never got past the flight test stage. Finally there was the Rockwell B-1A in the mid 1970s which, though it died a political death, was considered to be no more of an improvement over the B-52 than the Boeing 462 had been over the B-36.

It is a compliment of the highest order to the men who developed the B-52 that their design was so sound and forward looking as to allow it to extend its service life into its fourth decade. It has survived far past the point at which an aircraft brought on line in the mid 50s should have been expected to be phased out. In fact, it is generally accepted that when the B-1B, the much improved offspring of the B-1A, comes on line in the mid 80s it will operate side by side with updated B-52s.

Updating, and the flexible systems that allow updating, are indeed the underlying reasons for the B-52's continued success. Today the B-52 fleet within SAC has been simplified to just three models, the D, G and H. (The D is on the point of retirement.) When it was decided to commit B-52s to combat in SE Asia in 1965, it was almost exclusively the B-52F that went into service. Simultaneously, SAC initiated a project called 'Big Belly' in which the bomb bay capacity of B-52Ds was dramatically increased. Gradually the Fs were pulled out, mothballed and replaced with Ds. Before the Big Belly program, B-52s generally could carry 27 500-pound conventional bombs in their bays. Afterward, with the expanded bomb bay and two underwing pylons, the B-52D's bomb carrying capacity quadrupled.

While the B-52D became SAC's principal bombing platform for conventional high explosive or 'iron' bombs, the more advanced G and H have been designated as the principal carriers of nuclear weapons in the form of internally carried gravity weapons (bombs), or the underwing mounted Boeing Short Range Attack Missile (SRAM), successor to the earlier Hound Dog. As the B-52s ply the uncertain skies of the 1980s and 90s, they will gradually become the launch platform for yet another Boeing product – the Air Launched Cruise Missile (ALCM).

All three in-service B-52 models have been structurally strengthened and have been retrofitted with advanced electronics. In an important change of tactics necessitated by advances in radar and surface to air missiles (SAMs) that have made traditional high altitude strategic bombing impractical, bombers have had to switch to practicing extremely low-level bombing runs to allow them to come in under the enemy's radar. To permit this, B-52s have been equipped with ACR (Advanced Capability Terrain Avoidance Radar) that allows the giant bombers to fly, hugging the lay of the land, at 300 feet (500 for B-52D) for extended periods. In addition to ACR, B-52s are equipped with Phase VI (Phase V on B-52D) Electronic Counter Measures (ECM) which allow them to counter or defend themselves against enemy radar and radar-guided missiles fired from either the ground or hostile aircraft.

The newer and more advanced B-52s, the G and H, have received the more advanced electronics packages. Most important is the AN/ASQ-152 Electro-optical Viewing System (EVS). The EVS consists of two steerable cameras, one a TV

B-52G MAJOR INTERNAL SYSTEMS

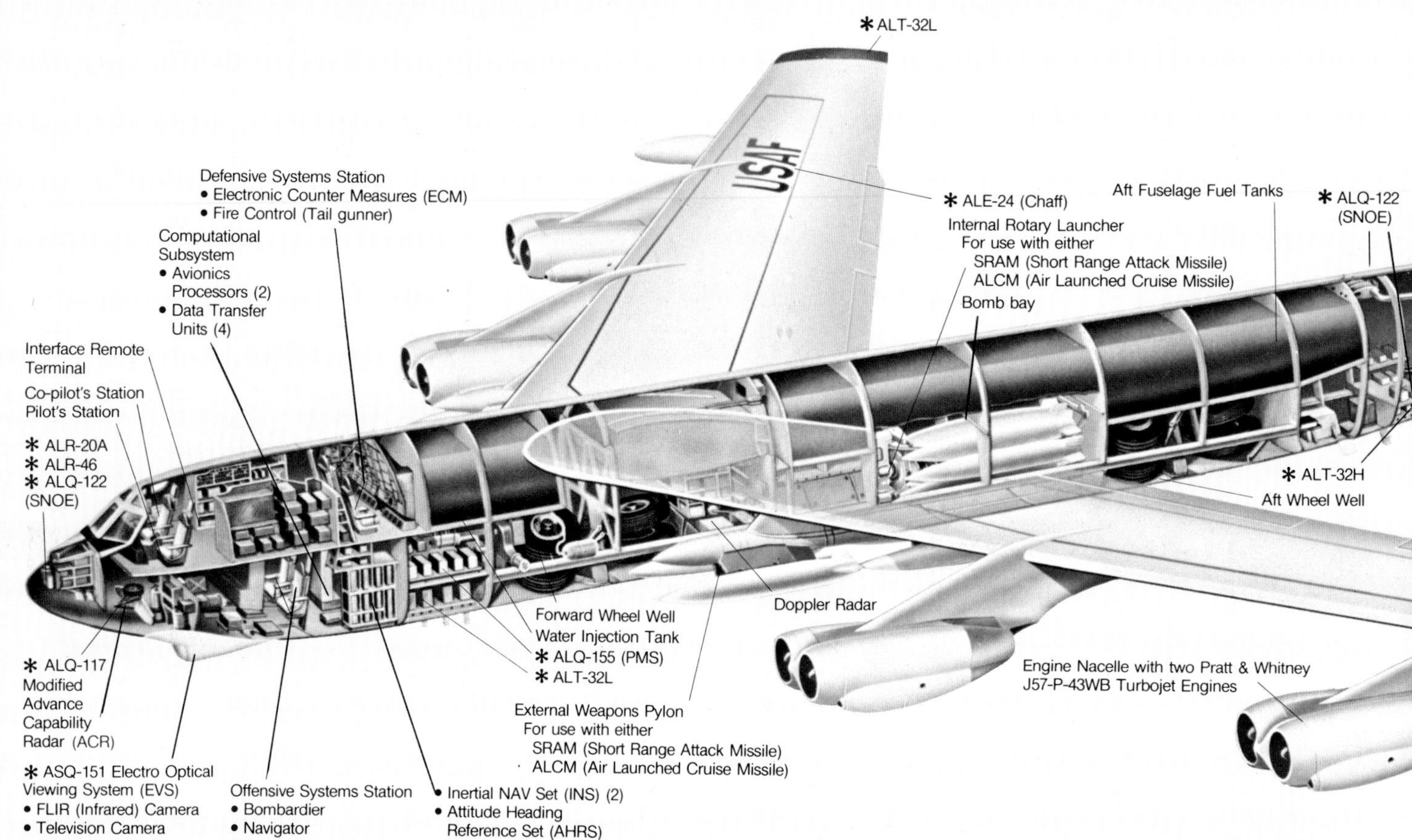

Above: The appearance of the nose of the B-52G and H, the youngest of the B-52 fleet, has been completely transformed. Visible under the chin are the **Hughes AAQ-6 forward-looking infrared sensor (FLIR)** and **Westinghouse AVQ-22 low-light television (LLTV)** cameras with their covers in the closed position. The FLIR sensors provide a daylight-type image at night and during periods of low visibility due to fog or storms. The LLTV cameras provide a clear image during daylight and even under starlight. The combination permits low-altitude operations in all visibility conditions.

Above: **The flight-deck interior** of the B-52G and H has been transformed by the addition of the green electro-optical viewing system displays. The EVS displays are the terminal for both FLIR and LLTV as well as the Advanced Capability Terrain-Avoidance Radar System (ACR). The displays also provide the pilot with such information as air speed, radar altitude, artificial horizon (with horizontal reference line) and heading error. In the foreground, the B-52's eight throttle levers are visible. The B-52 is the only jet flying with eight engines.

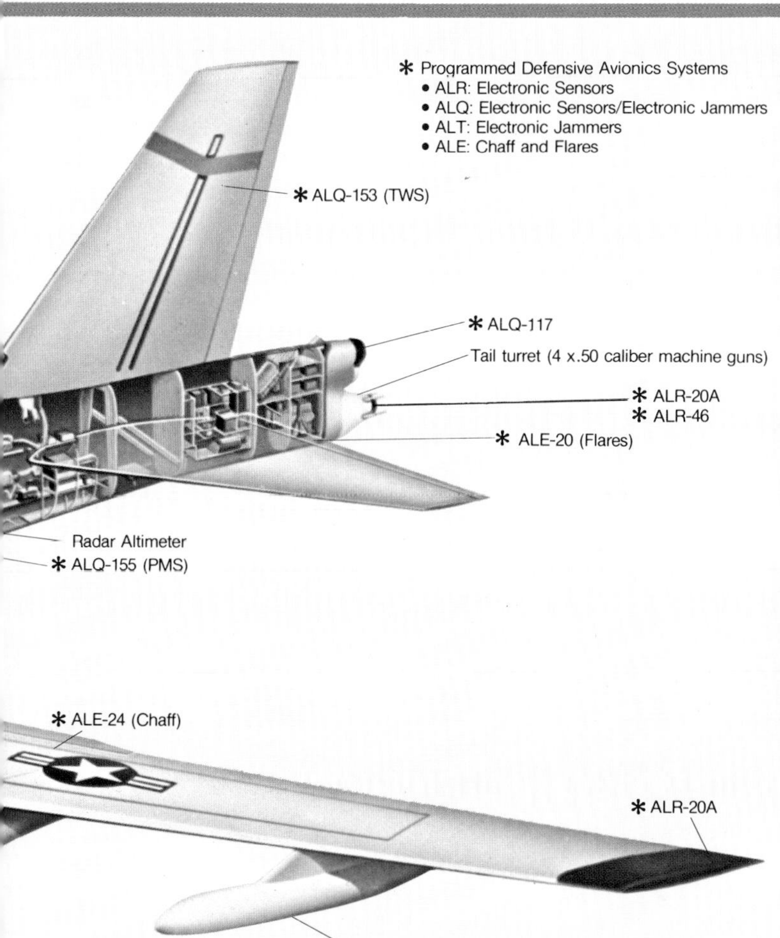

Specifications: B-52G Stratofortress Boeing Model Number 464

Span	185 ft
Length	160 ft 11 in
Wing Area	4000 sq ft
Tail Height	40 ft 8 in
Gross Weight	488,000 pounds
Bomb Capacity	13,500 pounds (conventional), or eight nuclear bombs, or twenty SRAM
Top Speed	595 mph
Ferry Range	8400 miles
Service Ceiling	55,000 ft
Powerplant	eight 13,750 pound thrust Pratt & Whitney J57-P-43WB Turbojets
Defensive Armament	four 0.5 in machine guns in tail turret

Left: A **cutaway drawing of a B-52G** in its original natural-metal finish showing its major internal systems, particularly the **Defensive Avionics Systems** and the position of **Boeing SRAM missiles**, on the external weapons pylons and within the bomb bay.

Below: A **B-52G** of the 328th Bomb Squadron (93rd Bomb Wing) based at Castle AFB in California. The 93rd Bomb Wing was the first to receive B-52s in 1955.

camera, the other infrared (FLIR), mounted side by side under the chin of the aircraft. The cameras are in turn connected to three video screen monitors on the flight deck. There is one each for the pilot, co-pilot and navigator.

In broad daylight, the TV camera shows the viewer exactly what he can see out the front window. In times of low and marginal visibility, the FLIR camera shows the viewer exactly what he could see out the front window if it were broad daylight. In addition to the visual picture (and the reason for viewing the screen rather than looking out the window), the EVS gives the pilot all the critical data he needs to fly the aircraft. Like the Head Up Display (HUD) now being used in fighters that projects instrument data on the front of the canopy so that the pilot does not have to look down during a dogfight, the EVS allows the B-52 pilot to fly the aircraft while looking in only one place. While the TV or FLIR shows him visually what is outside, numbers on the top of the screen give him his airspeed, heading and time to go on the mission. An altitude indicator is on the right, while the artificial horizon is in the center.

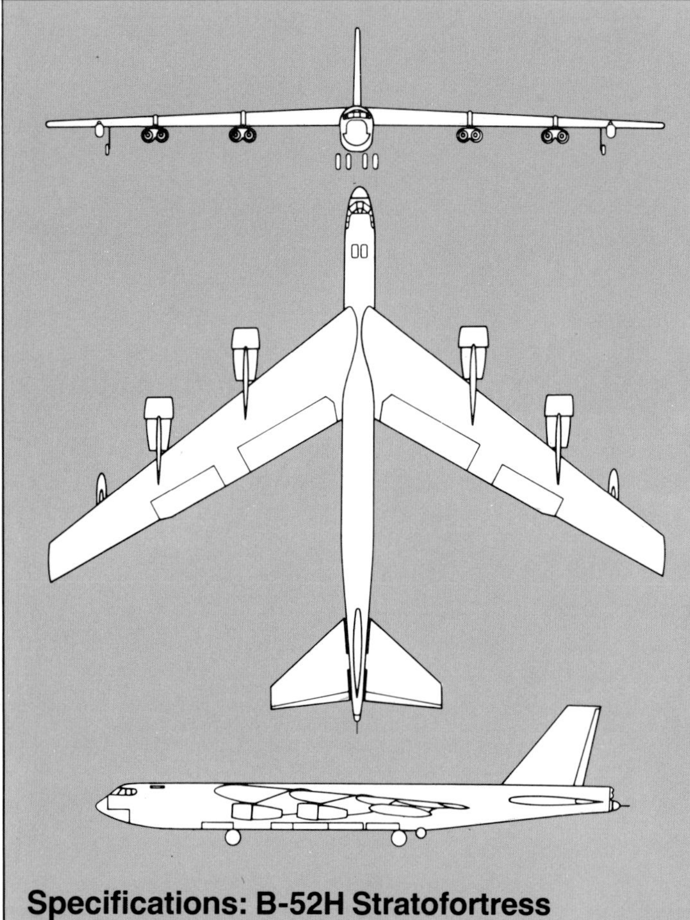

Specifications: B-52H Stratofortress
Boeing Model Number 464

Span	185 ft
Length	160 ft 11 in
Wing Area	4000 sq ft
Tail Height	40 ft 8 in
Gross Weight	488,000 pounds
Bomb Capacity	13,500 pounds (conventional), or eight nuclear bombs or twenty SRAM
Top Speed	650 mph
Ferry Range	11,000 miles plus
Service Ceiling	55,000 ft
Powerplant	eight 17,000 pound thrust Pratt & Whitney TF33 Turbofans
Defensive Armament	one six barrelled 20 mm Vulcan cannon in tail turret

In addition to flight information, the EVS monitor, via the terrain avoidance radar, 'paints' the terrain profile in the form of a graph across the screen. The graph is constantly changing so that the pilots' graphic perception of the terrain is constantly updated. This is critical when flying a mission in bad weather at 500mph, 300 feet off the ground.

Further planned and scheduled improvements will allow the B-52 systems to serve until the end of the century. Many newer electronic and weapons systems are under consideration as is a possible re-engining with larger, jumbo-jet type turbofan engines, such as the 47,800-pound thrust Pratt & Whitney JT9D-7R4D that is now being used on the 767 Airliner. One B-52 has in fact been flown with the huge General Electric XTF-39 turbofan engine.

In the early stages of the B-52 development Boeing was also working, as has been noted, on turboprop designs. In the late 1940s some authorities felt that turboprops might ultimately prove superior to pure jets because the combination seemed to offer a solution to the drag problems encountered by jet engines at high speed. However, by 1948 the idea had been rendered largely obsolete by advancing wing and engine technology. This ensured the demise of the Boeing Model 474, an unproduced four-engine turboprop design that was a parallel development to the Model 462 which turned into the 464/B-52 program. The progress of the B-52 also put an end to a development of the 474, the larger swept-wing Boeing Model 479. The Air Force issued a contract for the 479 on 1 July 1948 and gave it the designation XB-55. It was to have six Pratt & Whitney J-40 engines arranged in the same pylon arrangement as the B-47 and some of the structural design was similar to that of the B-52. The success of the B-52 led to the abandonment of this program, however.

No sooner had jet bombers succeeded piston engine bombers than the Air Force began to set its sights on a supersonic bomber. Supersonic flight, long a mysterious theory, was now a reality, and both the United States and the USSR were building supersonic fighters. In order to compete with supersonic interceptors, it was reasoned, one needed a supersonic bomber. The idea was that a supersonic bomber would replace the B-52 as the B-52 had the B-47. Boeing first began work on a supersonic bomber design in 1951. The original conception of a supersonic bomber revolved around the Model 450-65 which was a variation on the B-47. The Model 450-65 design was similar in profile to the B-47, with shorter, broader wings and the engines buried in the wing.

Eventually Boeing evolved a series of designs for a sleek Mach 2 aircraft which they proudly designated Model 701. In its various metamorphoses, the 701 (which the Air Force had designated XB-59) had a swept, canard and even a delta wing configuration. Ultimately, Boeing lost the supersonic sweepstakes to Convair's B-58 Hustler, of which over one hundred went into SAC inventory as supersonic replacements for the B-52s. In the mid-1960s the B-58 itself came by a potential successor in North American's gigantic B-70, which flew at three times the speed of sound.

Finally, both the B-58 which had made it into production, and the B-70 which never got past the prototype stage, fell victim to much the same kind of changing Air Force requirements that had earlier killed the B-47. In the end, both planes were replaced by updated versions of the B-52, the plane that they had been supposed to replace.

We have already seen that even as the last KC-97 was being rolled out, production of its Boeing successor the C-135 Stratolifter/KC-135 Stratotanker was just beginning. For reasons of corporate security this new jet program had been camouflaged under the Stratofreighter model number 367 at first. The Model 367-80 or 'Dash Eighty' as it came to be known around the drafting tables at Boeing, would be the immediate prototype for both the Model 707 jetliner and the Model 717.

The C-135/KC-135 story is still unfolding today but there were no assurances at first that the 717 would arouse Air Force interest. The KC-97G was doing well, but military orders would be important if the $15 million price tag for the new ship was to be paid. Both William Allen and Wellwood Beall campaigned for Air Force orders, but without results. As work on the Dash Eighty progressed, and more money was pumped into the enterprise, the Boeing company faced another difficult period. Layoffs threatened the work force and stockholders were not going to take such a huge loss happily.

In the spring of 1954, however, Boeing's luck changed. The Strategic Air Command let it be known that a jet tanker was going to be needed and Air Force interest in the 717 accordingly increased. Air Force Secretary Harold Talbot was impressed with the airplane, but no decision to buy was made.

On 14 May 1954, the 367-80 prototype was rolled out of the Renton plant. Air Force representatives were present for the roll-out, and liked what they saw. On 15 July the prototype made its first flight, and shortly thereafter, on 5 August, the Air Force announced it would purchase a limited number of the jet tanker/transports. Boeing was in business.

The 717 had only a single large cargo door and, because the fuel tanks were located in the lower portion of the two-deck body and in the wings, this allowed an unobstructed upper deck for passengers and cargo. In tanker versions the flying boom, now a telescoping, streamlined apparatus, operated from the lower deck. The crew consisted of the pilot, co-pilot, navigator and boom operator.

The first production Stratotanker rolled out on 18 July 1956 at Renton, and its test flight took place on 31 August. As R L Loesch, Senior Experimental Test Pilot for Boeing, said, 'The KC-135 should be one of the best-liked airplanes in the Air Force. I would predict that any difficulty that arises will not be in getting pilots in the KC-135s, but in keeping them out.'

The new jet fitted into its refueling duties with ease. It is still in service. It can operate at altitudes up to 40,000 feet and cruises at 530mph, a comfortable match for the jets it refuels. Its principal strategic mission lies in refueling long-range bombers. For this reason, the active duty tanker fleet is owned and managed by SAC. Another 128, flown by National Guard and Reserve forces, support SAC missions.

The KC-135 is a powerful airplane. Four turbojets, mounted under the 35-degree swept wings, thrust it skyward at weights grossing 297,000 pounds. All internal fuel, save for 1200 gallons, can be pumped through the flying boom, and time spent during the transfer of fuel is not critical. A KC-135, piloted by Colonel K H Kalberer, and a B-52, skippered by Captain W W Leesburg, once kept in transfer position for an even 60 minutes, while 10,000 pounds of fuel were transferred. After the test, Captain Leesburg reported that the two airplanes could have gone on indefinitely.

KC-135s were used extensively in the Vietnam War, demonstrating that the tactics of air war had changed for all time. Combat aircraft were no longer limited by onboard fuel. Fighter pilots, knowing a Stratotanker could be tapped for more fuel, could spend more time in a combat area. Far-flung bomber targets were brought within reach thanks to KC-135 refueling facilities.

Through the years, the C-135/Model 717 became the true workhorse of the Air Force, a real jack of all trades. Beginning with C-135A there have been more designation variations of this plane than with any other aircraft in USAF service, taking the alphabetic nomenclature system up to RC-135W. It will likely be the first aircraft to go past Z. The overwhelming majority of C-135s though, have been KC-135 Stratotankers. Most of these, 724, were KC-135As, while 17 KC-135Bs were built and three KC-135As were converted to KC-135R (sometimes referred to as RC-135R) reconnaissance/tanker aircraft. A number (classified, but probably in excess of 40) of KC-135As were also modified to carry JP-7 fuel for the SR-71 strategic reconnaissance aircraft. These were redesignated KC-135Q.

Of the others, 53 were built as transports, 18 C-135As, 30 C-135Bs and 5 VC-135s. An additional 11 were completed as

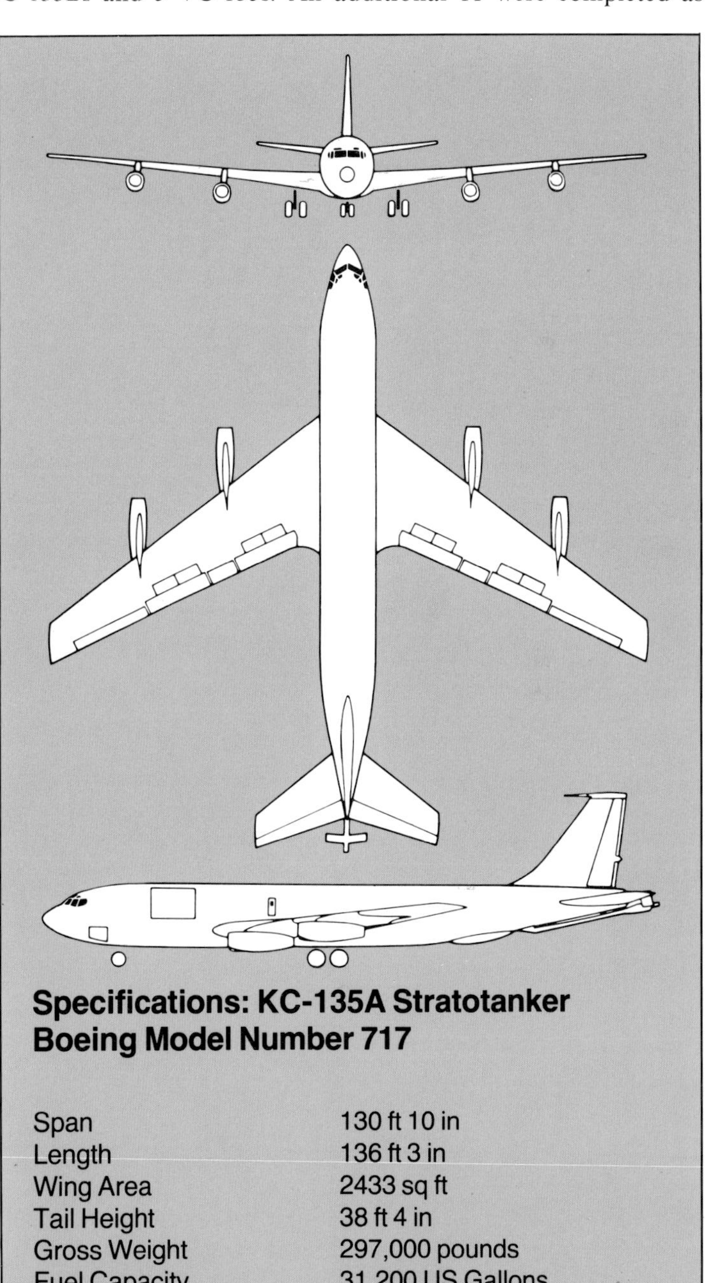

Specifications: KC-135A Stratotanker
Boeing Model Number 717

Span	130 ft 10 in
Length	136 ft 3 in
Wing Area	2433 sq ft
Tail Height	38 ft 4 in
Gross Weight	297,000 pounds
Fuel Capacity	31,200 US Gallons
Cruising Speed	600 mph
Ferry Range	5000 miles
Service Ceiling	41,000 ft
Powerplant	four 13,750 pound thrust Pratt & Whitney J57 Turbojet

Above right: A receiving aircraft's view of the **KC-135** refueling boom. The linkup between the two planes can take place in just a few minutes; thereafter the two can remain linked for close to an hour. In this view the boom operator's window can be clearly seen just forward of the boom root.

Top: A SAC **KC-135** of the 93rd Air Refueling Squadron based at Castle AFB in California.

WC-135B weather reconnaissance aircraft. The remaining C-135 designations include EC-135A, B, J, K and L electronic reconnaissance and flying command post aircraft, many of which are conversions from other C-135s. Because conversions are continually taking place, and because much of the electronic gear and many of the aircraft missions are classified, it is not always certain which aircraft are designated as which, and when. The same is true of JC-135, JKC-135, NC-135 and NKC-135 aircraft which are used for various types of classified and unclassified testing of assorted electronic devices and laser weapons.

Finally, there were 14 RC-135A and B reconnaissance and photo-reconnaissance aircraft built in the mid-1960s under the Boeing model number 739. These had a distinctive large radome in the nose and have since been upgraded and redesignated RC-135D, G, M, W etc.

Boeing's KC-135 became an important part of the Air Force. The last of them was delivered in 1965, and a year later its Boeing predecessor, the last active-duty KC-97, was phased out – nearly 24 years after it was originally conceived. The present-day KC-135 expects an even longer life than the KC-97. Like its teammate, the B-52, it will see use until the close of the 20th century.

Specifications: C-135B Stratolifter
Boeing Model Number 717

Span	130 ft 10 in
Length	136 ft 6 in
Wing Area	2433 sq ft
Tail Height	41 ft 8 in
Gross Weight	275,000 pounds
Cargo Capacity	60,000 pounds
Cruising Speed	600 mph
Ferry Range	5000 miles
Service Ceiling	41,000 ft
Powerplant	four 18,000 pound thrust Pratt & Whitney TF-33-P5 Turbofans

While the 717 model number was assigned to the military and the 707 model was reserved for commercial programs, the USAF has adapted the slightly larger 707 airframe for a couple of unique functions.

Designated VC-137A (later re-engined with TF33P turbofan engines and redesignated VC-137B), three Model 707s were acquired in 1959 for use as VIP transports. Five VC-137s, now including VC-137Cs, are operated by the 89th Military Airlift Wing based at Andrews Air Force Base near Washington. One of the VC-137Cs, when used as the VIP transport of the President of the United States, is designated 'Air Force One.' The interiors of the VC-137s are fitted out with offices, sleeping quarters and the complicated communications equipment required by the President and his entourage whether they are flying to Europe for a summit conference or to Iowa for a political rally.

The Air Force is also obtaining Model 707s as Airborne Warning And Control System (AWACS) aircraft. Originally designated EC-137, the AWACS aircraft are now given the designation E-3A.

The idea for an AWACS aircraft goes back to 1963, but the theory behind it is as old as radar. Normal ground-based radar has an inherent blind area near the ground where surface features

Above: This **EC-135C (Boeing Model 717)** began life as a **KC-135B** tanker but had its refueling boom removed when it was converted into an airborne command post. Now identical in outward appearance to a standard C-135B in matt-gray finish, this plane confirms that you really do need a detailed listing to tell 135s apart. Aircraft may be modified and subsequently redesignated on more than one occasion.

such as trees and hills interfere with the radar's ability to 'see.' Hence the term 'flying under the radar' is used to refer to an aircraft flying low to the ground to avoid detection by enemy radar. The AWACS incorporates a new technology in radar called 'look down radar' which is able to look into the blind spot near the ground and separate targets from the kind of ground clutter that confuses conventional radar.

The most distinctive feature of the E-3A is its unique 'skunk-striped' Westinghouse rotodome. The rotodome, perched over the rear fuselage, measures 30 feet across and is six feet thick. It rotates at 6rpm while in operation, but is rotated at $\frac{1}{4}$rpm while not operating, to prevent the bearing lubricant from congealing. The active ingredients of the rotodome are the AN/APY-1 surveillance radar, IFF (Identification, Friend or Foe), and data link fighter-control (TADIL-C) antennae.

While the 707 airframe is produced (as are all 707 airframes) by the Boeing Commercial Airplane Company, the responsibility for the E-3A AWACS part of the program falls to Boeing Aerospace. They received an Air Force contract in July 1970 to flight test two competing radar systems, which included one designed by Hughes Aircraft, in addition to the Westinghouse system that eventually was adopted. After the radar was proven, there came the System Integration Demonstration (SID) phase of the AWACS evaluation. The SID was followed by a series of Initial Operational Test and Evaluation (IOT&E) flights. These testing programs complete, the decision was made in April 1975 to begin production of the E-3A. All the test aircraft were refurbished and delivered as operational systems, the first one being delivered on 23 March 1977.

All of the USAF E-3A aircraft are assigned to the 552nd AWACS Wing at Tinker AFB in Oklahoma, but serve temporary duty all over the world from Okinawa to Iceland. They play a critical role in North American and Western European air defense. When tensions heated up in the Middle East in the early 1980s with the fall of the Shah of Iran and the Iran-Iraq war, Saudi Arabia asked for and received assistance from the United States in the form of several USAF E-3As to be based in Saudi Arabia to keep track of Iranian aircraft. The Saudi Air Force has since decided that they would like to purchase E-3s of their own. This has aroused an angry response from the Israelis who feel that Saudi E-3s could be used to track Israeli aircraft for hostile Arab countries.

In December 1978 the NATO Defense Planning Council, made up of the defense ministers of member nations, gave the go-ahead for acquisition of a fleet of 18 E-3 AWACS for the NATO airborne early warning requirement. Boeing Aerospace is leading an international team of American, Canadian and German firms to develop the electronics and support package for the NATO E-3A. The NATO AWACS program contract was signed in 1980, and deliveries began in early 1982.

In addition to the VC-137s and E-3s for the USAF and NATO, 707 airframes have been acquired by several foreign Air Forces as military transports and tankers. The Canadian Armed Forces use five 707s (designated CC-137) of which two have been converted for use as hose and drogue tankers. The Federal German Luftwaffe has acquired 707s for use as transports, while the Imperial Iranian Air Force (before it became the Islamic Iranian Air Force) received 14 707s, some of which were completed as tankers. It is worth noting that Iran's Air Force was the only one to purchase a tanker version of the 747. The IIAF had also ordered a number of E-3s, but the order was terminated when the Shah's government was overthrown in 1979.

Specifications: VC-137C Air Force One
Boeing Model Number 707

Span	145 ft 9 in
Length	152 ft 11 in
Wing Area	3050 sq ft
Tail Height	42 ft 5 in
Gross Weight	328,000 pounds
Cruising Speed	626 mph
Service Ceiling	38,500 ft
Range	7000 miles
Powerplant	four 13,000 pound thrust Pratt & Whitney TF33-P Turbofans

Specifications: E-3A Sentry (AWACS)
(Formerly EC-137 D)
Boeing Model Number 707

Span	145 ft 9 in
Length	152 ft 11 in
Tail Height	41 ft 4 in
Gross Weight	325,000 pounds
Cruising Speed	600 mph
Service Ceiling	29,000 ft plus
Mission Endurance	11 hours plus (unrefuelled)
Powerplant	four 21,000 pound thrust Pratt & Whitney TF33-PW Turbofans

Above: A **KC-135A (Model 717)** in the high-visibility orange markings common in the late 50s and early 60s.

Above: This **VC-137 (Model 707)**, tail number 27000, has served as *Air Force I*, the US president's personal transport, since 1972.

Above: An Imperial Iranian Air Force **Model 707** tanker refuels an IIAF **747**. Canada and Iran operate 707 tankers, while the IIAF has the only 747 tankers.

Below: Twelve **KC-135Fs** were supplied to France to serve its strategic bomber force. They have since been modified to use the probe-and-drogue method of refueling (not shown here).

Above: The US Air Force **E-3A Sentry (Model 707)** Airborne Warning And Control System (AWACS) aircraft is the most advanced radar aircraft in the world.

Right: Avionics equipment in the **E-3A** includes surveillance radar, navigation, communications, data processing, identification and displays.

Above: One of 19 **T-43A** crew trainers (Model 737) supplied to the USAF Air Training Command. Fifteen remain with ATC while four now serve the Air National Guard.

Above: The plane that might have been. Boeing's **'C-5A'** design strongly resembled the later 747 but incorporated the same high wing as the winning Lockheed C-5A design.

While it had been a common practice during and shortly after World War II for commercial airliners all to lead to military variations, Boeing's commercially successful 700 family has seen little military service. The 717 has been a significant exception of course, because the 717 designation was specifically earmarked for the military. The 707, as has been shown, is in service in VIP transport and AWACS roles while of the others, 19 Model 737s were purchased as crew navigation trainers and given the designation T-43A (*see* page 185).

The story of Boeing's Jumbo Jet, the Model 747, presents a variation on this theme. It was born as a result of a USAF requirement for a very large transport for oversized cargo. Boeing failed to win this contract but put the experience to good use with the 747. The story has now come full circle and Boeing is proposing the 747 for military use.

The project (originally designated CX-HLS) would eventually evolve into the C-5A project, and the resulting aircraft would be the biggest airplane in the world. Boeing, Douglas and Lockheed all submitted designs and in September 1965, Lockheed was given the contract. While the Air Force generally felt that Boeing's design was superior, it was regarded as too costly. Though the Lockheed bid was lower, design flaws and cost overruns have made the Lockheed C-5A one of the most costly aircraft in USAF service.

Specifications: T-43A
Boeing Model Number 737

Span	93 ft
Length	100 ft
Wing Area	980 sq ft
Tail Height	37 ft
Gross Weight	115,500 pounds
Cruising Speed	575 mph
Service Ceiling	35,000 ft
Range	2995 miles
Powerplant	two 14,500 pound thrust Pratt & Whitney JT8D-9 Turbofans
Capacity	twelve students (or four advanced students) and three instructors

The Boeing-Lockheed C-5 controversy was to rear its head again 17 years later. At the onset of the 1980s the Military Airlift Command of the Air Force found itself with a Rapid Deployment Force to support. Rapid deployment of forces means deployment by transport aircraft, and the RDF requirement for outsize airlift capacity (*big* transport planes) outstrips the capacity of MAC's 70-odd Lockheed C-5As. In 1982 Congress was faced with the dilemma of whether to ask Lockheed to gear up its long-dismantled production lines to produce a line of new C-5Bs, or whether, as Boeing has suggested and Senator Henry Jackson of Washington State has proposed, simply to go into the used-airplane market and buy the Air Force already existing 747 cargo planes. The advantage to the C-5 design is that its cargo area is larger, large enough to handle the Army's bulkiest equipment such as the new M-1 Abrams Main Battle Tank; and that both ends of the aircraft open so that equipment can be driven on one end and off the other. The C-5A or B can also land on short semi-improvised runways in remote or front line areas. The 747, on the other hand, can carry almost anything that the C-5 can and a greater volume. The 747 can also fly farther and faster than the C-5 and has a far better maintenance record. The principal advantages of the 747 as far as Congress is concerned are that the used 747s are immediately available at a fixed cost that is much lower than the estimated cost of the C-5B, which would not come on line for years.

Some 747 aircraft are presently in service with the USAF with the designation E-4A and E-4B. They serve as Airborne Command Post Aircraft, successors to the older EC-135s. Airborne command posts add the flexibility of movement and altitude to the functions performed by command posts situated on the ground. They serve as a communications hub from which a commander can communicate with superiors and subordinates and direct the forces under his control. The E-4 Airborne Command Post aircraft is a modified 747 equipped with extensive electronics which would be the critical communication link between national command authorities and the nation's strategic retaliatory forces during and following an attack upon the United States.

The E-4s would be used by the National Command Authorities and by the Commander-in-Chief of the Strategic Air Command to direct USAF strategic forces during a nuclear conflict. One E-4 is always kept on the alert at Andrews AFB near Washington DC for use by the President of the United States as his airborne command post in case of an attack. They can be used to order the

firing of intercontinental ballistic missiles if ground control centers become inoperative.

Boeing built and delivered to the US Air Force three 747-200s which were modified to an interim E-4A configuration by E-Systems, Inc, of Dallas, Texas. These interim systems utilize older command, control and communication equipment from EC-135s. Boeing has since developed an advanced version, the E-4B, which entered service in January 1980. The E-4B is able to operate in a nuclear environment where nuclear explosions usually disrupt currently used communications equipment.

Following competitive bidding Boeing Aerospace Company was awarded a contract in June 1980 to modify one of the existing E-4A systems to the improved E-4B configuration. A second E-4A/E-4B modification was added to the program in December 1980. Plans call for the Air Force to modify a third system and to acquire two additional 747-200 airplanes and equip them as E-4Bs to make up a fleet of six advanced command posts.

The E-4 will replace the EC-135, which is much smaller. The principal advantages of the E-4B over the EC-135 are improved communications capability, increased protection from nuclear bursts, greater endurance and more room to accommodate battle staff and new equipment. The E-4 is designed for missions as long as 72 hours while carrying nearly three times the payload of the EC-135.

The aircraft's main deck is divided into six functional areas: the command work area, conference room, briefing room, battle-

Above: An **E-4A (Model 747)** is refueled by a **KC-135 (Model 717)**. The first E-4As were supplied to the USAF in 1974 to support the National Emergency Airborne Command Post (NEACP, known as 'kneecap') and serve as the presidential airborne command post. Eventually the E-4As will all be converted to E-4Bs and assume all of the airborne command-post functions of NEACP and SAC.

Specifications: E-4A/B Airborne Command Post Boeing Model Number 747

Span	195 ft 8 in
Length	231 ft 10 in
Wing Area	5500 sq ft
Tail Height	63 ft 5 in
Gross Weight	803,000 pounds
Cruising Speed	600 mph
Service Ceiling	45,000 ft
Unrefuelled Endurance	14 hours plus
Mission Endurance	72 hours plus
Powerplant	four 52,500 pound thrust General Electric CF6-50E Turbofans

Above: The **E-4B (Model 747)** differs from the E-4A in outward appearance by the addition of the radomes at the rear of the upper deck.

Below: One of 18 **E-3As** supplied to NATO is seen with an F-16 fighter, one of the planes that it would control in the event of a war in Europe. Originally given NATO markings, these E-3s will eventually wear the national markings of Luxembourg, which ironically has no other air force (OTAN is NATO in French).

Below: USAF **E-3As** are prepped for delivery at the south end of Boeing Field. Visible top left is the **Red Barn**, Boeing's first headquarters building, now being restored as a museum (see p 17).

staff work area, communications control center and rest area. The flight deck houses the cockpit, navigation station and flight-crew rest area. Cargo areas beneath the main deck house communications and power supply equipment, spares and on-board maintenance facilities. Equipment on the E-4B includes thermal shielding, advanced command and control electronics, a 1200-KVA generator which is the largest power generation system ever flown, and both SHF (super high frequency) and VLF/LF (very low frequency/low frequency) communications systems. The VLF system requires trailing wire antennae up to five miles in length. In all, the E-4B carries 13 external communications systems employing 50 antennae. To cool this large array of equipment, it has an air conditioning system with an output up to 8000 cubic feet of air per minute.

The total program for equipping all six command post aircraft is expected to be completed in the mid-1980s. The E-4B program is under direction of the Electronic Systems Division of the US Air Force Systems Command. The E-4 Airborne Command Posts are based at Offutt Air Force Base, Nebraska, headquarters for the Strategic Air Command, which is the operating command.

Right: Boeing's **YC-14** short-field transport takes off during tests at Edwards AFB, California. Using new technology such as Upper Surface Blowing, the YC-14 was one of two planes considered to replace the USAF C-130 Hercules transport.

Below: The second prototype **YC-14** in camouflage colors.

In November of 1972, Boeing and McDonnell Douglas were selected to build prototype aircraft as part of the US Air Force's Advanced Medium STOL (Short Take Off and Landing) Transport (AMST) program competition. The military requirement was for a transport that could operate from short semi-prepared fields, yet still have the cruising capability of a modern jet transport. Each company built a pair of aircraft. The McDonnell Douglas entry was powered by four 16,000-pound thrust UAC JT8D-17 turbofan engines and was designated YC-15A. Boeing's Model 953, designated YC-14A, was powered by a pair of 50,000-pound thrust GE CF6-50D turbofans, mounted above and forward of the high wing. The YC-14A was the first large aircraft to employ the concept of Upper Surface Blowing (USB). USB uses the thrust of the engines to blow high speed air over the wing and flaps, creating powered lift. The high positioning of the wing and engines also minimizes the possibility that the YC-14 would be damaged by debris and dirt on remote landing strips. The YC-14 is capable of lifting 27,000 pounds or 150 troops from 2000 foot runways and 69,000 pounds from normal runways. The aircraft also utilizes an advanced electronic flight control system and high flotation, lever type rough field landing gear.

The first YC-14 flew on 9 August 1976, with the second prototype following on 21 October. Funding for the AMST program was deleted from the 1979 budget, though there is a possibility that it will be revived. Boeing leased its two prototypes back from the Air Force for continued testing, but they were later mothballed by the Air Force at the Air Force Logistics Command Military Aircraft Storage and Disposition Center at Davis Monthan AFB near Tuçson, Arizona. One of the mothballed YC-14s was later put on display at the Pima County Air Museum just outside the Davis Monthan complex.

While the YC-14 may never fly again, much of the technology that it helped pioneer almost certainly will. The small supercritical wing and the utilization of Upper Surface Blowing to create lift are innovations which will likely be seen in both military and commercial transport aircraft of the future. Because of the need of the Military Airlift Command to support both the Rapid Deployment Force as well as regular forces in remote areas, the need for STOL aircraft is great. The commercial advantages of a STOL type aircraft in hauling freight to and from remote or short runways have not been fully explored, but the prospects are promising.

Toward this end, Boeing has become involved in NASA's Quiet Short-haul Research Aircraft (QSRA) program. The test-bed is a De Havilland C-8A Buffalo light military aircraft lent to NASA by the US Army and modified by Boeing to incorporate the technology of Upper Surface Blowing. NASA testing, taking place at the Ames Research Center near San Francisco, is aimed at studying Upper Surface Blowing, and at developing criteria for certification of future transports using the technology pioneered in the YC-14.

In 1981, Boeing received a contract to apply the supersonic transport (SST) technology that they were working on to a supersonic military fighter aircraft. Boeing had won the NASA contract in four-way competition with Grumman, Rockwell and McDonnell Douglas, the latter also winning a study contract. Concepts will be developed for a European theater tactical aircraft with a 500 mile combat radius and a Middle-East theater fighter with a 1500 mile radius.

Boeing's fighter will have vectorable nozzles on its underwing pod-mounted engines. The vectorable nozzles can be moved to change the direction of thrust, improving performance of the aircraft from short landing fields, in effect giving it STOL characteristics. The new fighter would also incorporate low aspect ratio wings blended into the fuselage, with variable-camber control surfaces and vortex lift. The latter involves controlling the flow of air over the wings with special leading-edge devices, to enhance high angle of attack performance. The plane would be equipped with variable cycle engines that would be efficient under a range of operating conditions. The recessed weapon carriage would be such that it would permit supersonic operation of the aircraft with weapons attached. Furthermore the weapons could be launched when the aircraft was travelling at supersonic speed.

Boeing has indicated that these studies will be used as a point of departure in the development of a 'larger, longer-range combat airplane' (a bomber). Technology that will probably appear in both aircraft includes weight saving nonmetallic composites and specially formed and bonded titanium structures, as well as active controls (automatically responding to changing loads) and digital avionics for improved control response.

Specifications: YC-14
Advanced Medium STOL Transport
Boeing Model Number 953

Span	129 ft
Length	132 ft
Wing Area	1762 sq ft
Tail Height	48 ft 4 in
Gross Weight	216,000 pounds
Gross Weight (STOL)	170,000 pounds
Top Speed	547 mph
Cruising Speed	460 mph
Ferry Range	2990 miles
STOL Range	460 miles
Service Ceiling	45,000 ft
Powerplant	two 50,000 pound thrust General Electric CF6-50 Turbofans

THE JET AGE

The first commercial jet airplane in the world was the British De Havilland DH-106 Comet. Powered by four De Havilland Ghost turbojets which were buried deep in the wings, this advanced concept of manned flight flew first in the summer of 1946. Tests were successful, and the British Overseas Airways Corporation, BOAC, placed an order for 16.

The Ghosts provided 4450 pounds of thrust each, giving unprecedented power and speed to the Comet, a swept-wing introduction to the Jet Age. Though passenger seating was limited to 36 at first, the Comet cruised at 490mph, beating its nearest competitor, the Boeing Stratocruiser, by 190mph. Its range was only 1750 miles, but this was a limitation that could be improved,

Above: A **707-120** in Trans World Airlines markings. TWA received its first 707 on 20 January 1959 and has ordered 15 707-120s and 123 707s of all types.

Right: The **367-80 *Dash Eighty*** after being redesignated 707 and re-engined, on its way to being turned over to the Smithsonian Institution.

as jet engine efficiency increased with more study. On 2 May 1952, the Comet I left London Airport, making a successful flight to Johannesburg, and the world took notice.

In August 1952 the Comet I started operations between London and Ceylon, cutting flying time by 12 hours. Several months later, Comets were reaching Singapore in 25 hours, against the two and a half days it took for piston-engined aircraft. Jet aviation was on the way to solid respectability, as other European airlines, notably Air France, put Comets to work.

Then tragedy struck. In January 1954 a Comet disintegrated over the Mediterranean, killing all passengers and crew. The Comets were grounded, and extensive examinations were conducted. No lethal weaknesses were discovered. In March the jets were returned to service, but fate was aiming another blow. Two weeks later, a second Comet broke up over the Mediterranean near Rome. The flying world that had been excited about the new airplane was stunned. Again, the Comets were grounded.

Diligent searching yielded pieces of the wreckage. It was discovered that metal fatigue (a previously unknown phenomenon) around the square-cut windows resulted in a weakening of the fuselage structure that could have caused the crash. It was also possible that the engines, deep in the wings, caused problems that led to the twin deaths of the world's first jet-propelled commercial aircraft. Although the Comets' problems were solved by improvements in design and maintenance, other manufacturers had a clear opportunity to catch the Comet's lead.

Wellwood Beall had seen the first Comet himself, and alerted Boeing executives. He felt that if Boeing were to survive in the commercial field, the company must think about jets. The company had the technology, based on B-47 experience, and Beall knew that a commercial jet could be built.

In spite of the excitement caused by the Comet's appearance, jets did not immediately catch on in the US. Pan American, American Airlines and other carriers knew that pistons worked. Maybe the internal combustion engine did not get the speed of jets, but they had been proven. They were safe, and as for capability, Douglas's DC-6 flew coast to coast easily, and both United and American Airlines liked them. In April 1951 the company introduced the DC-6B. It seated 102 passengers, cruised at 315mph, and was thought by many to be the finest piston-engined airplane ever built. In 1951 Lockheed also introduced its L-1049 Super Constellation. Powered by four 2700hp Cyclone engines and carrying 66 passengers, this graceful airplane went into service with Eastern Air Lines in December 1951, and performed well.

Boeing's own Stratocruiser (Model 377) had evolved into a sound and comfortable airliner, but by comparison to the likes of the DC-6 and the Constellation, it was a sales failure. Boeing realized that in order to compete in the fierce and expanding world market, they would have to build a better airplane and that airplane would have to be a turbojet with sufficient range to cross the North Atlantic. The crucial decision was taken at a board of directors meeting in April 1952.

The B-47 program was underway and the Boeing engineers went to work on a design for the jet transport which would ultimately be designated 707. For reasons of corporate secrecy, as we noted in the last chapter, the project was disguised as a variant of the Model 367/C-97 military transport, the military equivalent of the Model 377 Stratocruiser. Because the program designation was Model 367-80, the new jet transport prototype acquired the nickname 'Dash Eighty.'

The fuselage was longer than that of the C-97 or the Stratocruiser with a more pointed nose, and did not show the 'double bubble' of the original 367. Early drawing-board versions of the 707, including Models 367-40 to 367-70, differed in the location of engines and landing gear. Aerodynamically, the Dash Eighty was closer to the B-47 than the piston driven C-97. One of the early studies considered placing four Pratt & Whitney JT3 engines in double nacelles like those on the B-47, one pod under each wing. In the final version, though, each of the four engines

Above and below: The ***Dash Eighty*** as originally configured.

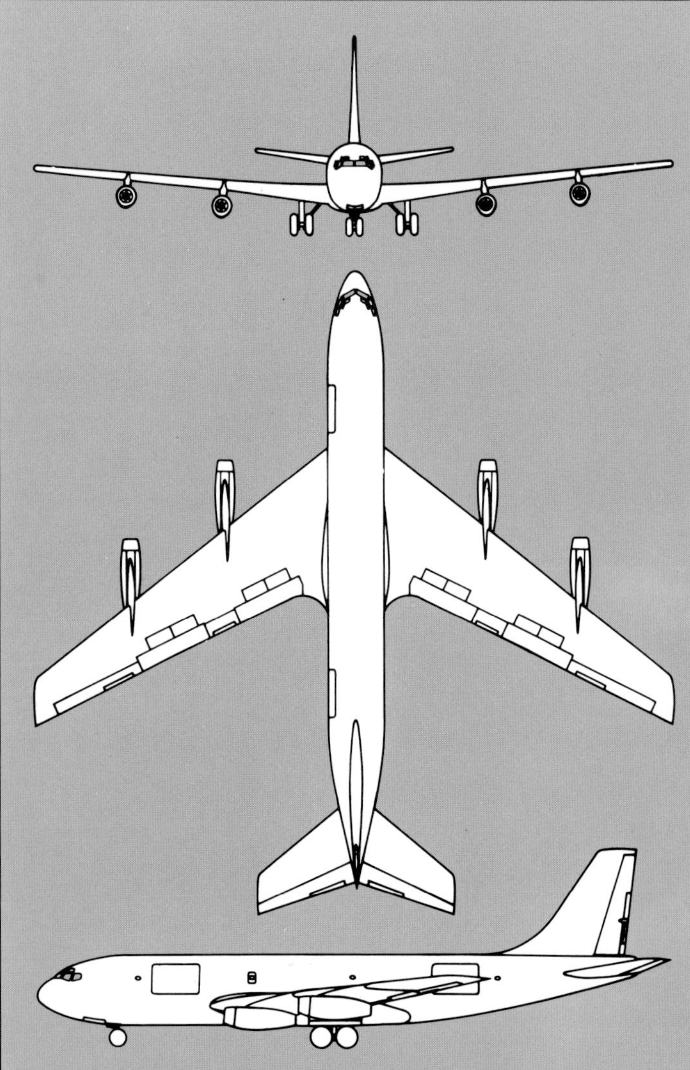

Specifications: 707/717 Prototype Boeing Model Number 367-80

Span	130 ft
Length	128 ft
Wing Area	2402 sq ft
Tail Height	38 ft 4 in
Gross Weight	160,000 pounds
Cruising Speed	600 mph
Service Ceiling	42,000 ft
Range	2000 miles
Powerplant	four 11,000 pound thrust Pratt & Whitney JT3P Turbojets

was housed in a single nacelle. Four such nacelles gave a structural advantage, through better weight distribution. An entirely new type of tricycle landing gear was adopted. The main wheels retracted inward from the center wing stub, nesting in recesses in the lower fuselage.

Boeing pumped its own money into the Dash Eighty prototype. Though Wellwood Beall and others tried to interest Pan American and United Air Lines in signing advance orders, they had no luck. Most airline executives, aware of the Comet's fate, were still wary. There were other doubts. For example, could airline pilots, schooled in piston-engined aircraft, make the transition to an airplane whose speed approached that of sound? And how about the 'little old lady in the street?' Could she adjust to that terrific increase in speed? And furthermore, an awful thought, because of the increased seating in these powerful airplanes, a crash would be catastrophic.

The work was kept secret, though William Allen admitted in a September 1952 magazine article that 'The company has for some time been engaged in a company-financed project which will enable us to demonstrate a prototype jet airplane of a new design for both armed services and commercial airlines in the summer of 1954.'

The American jet transport era began when the 367-80 first flew on 15 July 1954. With four P&W JT3 powerplants, the swept-wing prototype reached speeds of 600mph.

On 1 September 1954, the Air Force contracted with Boeing for 29 tanker versions of the Dash Eighty which were given the Boeing model number 717. Nevertheless, sales of the commercial transport version, the 707, were not immediately forthcoming and Boeing executives began to ponder the possibility that they might have a white elephant on their hands. They were also worried about Douglas's new DC-8, a jet powered transport, equipped like the 707, with P&W JT3s.

There now began what came to be known as the 'great Boeing-Douglas jet transport sales race.' Sales began to break for Boeing. Juan Trippe, president of Pan American World Airways, became interested in the 707. Always in the vanguard, he pursuaded Pan Am to invest $296,000,000 in the jet. The order was placed on 13 October 1955, and at $5,500,000 per plane, was the largest order for commercial aircraft ever placed, but Trippe had confidence in Boeing. 'People thought we were crazy,' he admitted later, but airline history was being made as the 707's success was to prove.

After Pan Am's purchase, United Air Lines announced it would buy 30 DC-8s, and Bill Allen told his staff to work harder. They did, and on 8 November 1955, American Airlines bought 30 707s.

Specifications: Boeing Model 707-120

Span	130 ft 10 in
Length	145 ft 1 in
Wing Area	2433 sq ft
Tail Height	41 ft 8 in
Gross Weight	248,000 pounds
Cruising Speed	600 mph
Service Ceiling	41,000 ft
Range	3000 miles
Powerplant	four 13,500 pound thrust Pratt & Whitney JT3C-6 Turbojets
Capacity	181 passengers

At the same time Pan Am purchased the 707s, however, the company also placed an order with Douglas for 25 DC-8s. Boeing went into production at once, and delivered the first 707-120, the production model, to Pan Am on 15 August 1958, three months ahead of schedule.

In the following months, Continental, Braniff and Sabena of Belgium ordered more 707s. Trans World Airways, Air France and Quantas also invested in the sleek turbojet. The 707's performance was impressive and helped sales. It could cross the Atlantic in six and a half hours, and could carry as many passengers as the *Queen Mary* could in the same amount of time. Even so, Eastern Airlines, KLM of Holland and Scandinavian Airways System (SAS) committed themselves to DC-8s.

The 707's advantage over the DC-8, however, was timing. It appeared nearly a year before the DC-8. This by no means undercuts the importance of the DC-8. Together, the two airplanes pointed the way to a new era in air travel. After the appearance of the DC-8 and the 707, the world of flying was forever transformed.

Airline people learned through the American transports that customers everywhere enjoyed the luxury of the skyliners. The 707's interior had been developed by Walter Dorwin Teague Associates, and was called a 'penthouse in the sky' by news people. 'It's like flying ten miles a minute in my easy chair,' said a passenger. The 707 had the longest, widest cabin ever seen on a commercial transport, measuring 12 feet 4 inches wide, and 100 feet in length. More than 100 windows studded the fuselage, allowing even aisle passengers 'windows of their own.' The many windows lent the interior a sense of spaciousness, and a feeling of freedom. Sliding shades effectively cut out light for those wishing to nap, and in some of the 707s there were as many as three lounges where restless passengers could snack, have a drink, or simply strike up a conversation. Galleys located in both forward and aft positions contributed to passenger wellbeing, for electric ovens and refrigerators made it possible to serve meals of a wide variety.

The 707 catered to owners, as well as passengers. The airplane's seating configuration could be all first class, all tourist or any combination desired. This was a point looked upon favorably by operators whose business took them to many places in the world with varied and unpredictable requirements.

Flying high and fast, the 707 soared above the weather. Even in rare disturbances, which could not be avoided, the 707's swept-back wings provided an easy, springy ride, with none of the jolts and bumps encountered in earlier aircraft.

The air conditioning was the finest and most complete ever provided in an airplane. Outside air was drawn in and automatically heated or cooled as needed. It was filtered, humidity-controlled, and even deodorized for passenger comfort. At 40,000 feet cruising altitude, cabin equivalent altitude was 7000 feet. Sea-level cabin pressure was maintained to an actual altitude of 22,500 feet.

Airline operators were learning, to their relief, that pilots trained in the piston-engine era could be switched to jets with additional training. Boeing and other manufacturers were equipped to provide that training. Thus skilful pilots continued their careers into the jet age, and everybody, operators and passengers alike, was better off.

Pan American began the new era with its first transatlantic 707 flight on 26 October 1958. In six weeks company 707-120s carried 12,168 passengers across the sea. At first only two 707s

Specifications: Boeing Model 720 (707-220)

Span	130 ft 10 in
Length	136 ft 9 in
Wing Area	2433 sq ft
Tail Height	41 ft 8 in
Gross Weight	230,000 pounds
Cruising Speed	600 mph
Service Ceiling	41,000 ft
Range	3000 miles
Powerplant	four 12,500 pound thrust Pratt & Whitney JT3C-7 Turbojets
Capacity	167 passengers

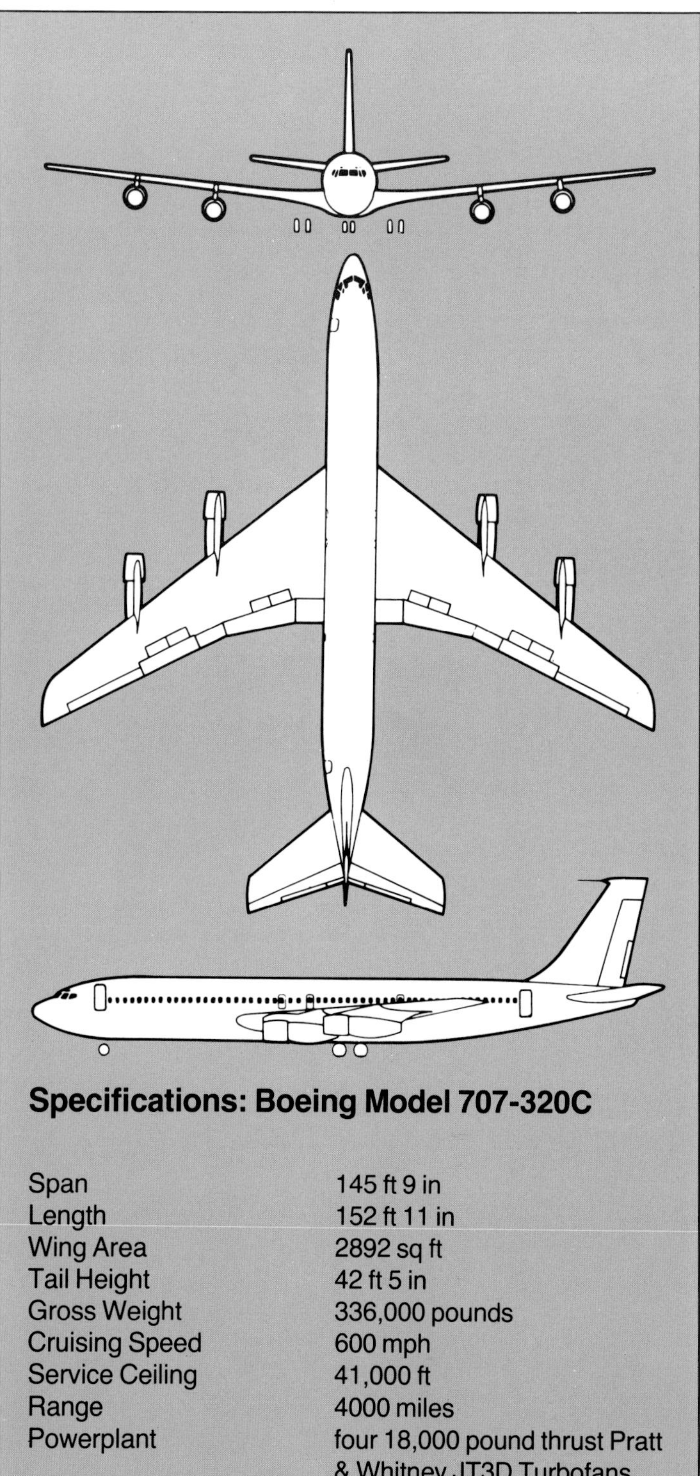

Specifications: Boeing Model 707-320C

Span	145 ft 9 in
Length	152 ft 11 in
Wing Area	2892 sq ft
Tail Height	42 ft 5 in
Gross Weight	336,000 pounds
Cruising Speed	600 mph
Service Ceiling	41,000 ft
Range	4000 miles
Powerplant	four 18,000 pound thrust Pratt & Whitney JT3D Turbofans
Capacity	219 passengers or 96,800 pounds of cargo

AMERICAN AIRLINES

AMERICAN TRANS

Left: **707s** under construction on the floor of Plant 2. Note the B-52 and the *Dash Eighty* being re-engined in the far background.

Right: Kayo II, the **720-023** used by the Los Angeles Dodgers baseball club to transport the team to away-from-home games.

Below: An American Trans Air **720** preparing for takeoff.

Bottom left: The cargo door of the **707-320C** Convertible measures 7½ feet by 11 feet, is designed to accept up to 5693 cubic feet of containerized cargo or shipping pallets.

Bottom right: The Boeing **Model 707-320** Intercontinental made its maiden flight on 11 January 1959.

Above: A Pan Am **707-321B**. Pan Am was the 707's 'launch customer,' the customer that made the 707 program possible. Pan Am has ordered 128 707s since 1955.

Specifications: Boeing Model 707-320

Span	142 ft 5 in
Length	152 ft 11 in
Wing Area	2892 sq ft
Tail Height	41 ft 8 in
Gross Weight	316,000 pounds
Cruising Speed	600 mph
Service Ceiling	41,000 ft
Range	4200 miles
Powerplant	four 15,800 pound thrust Pratt & Whitney JT4A Turbojets
Capacity	189 passengers

were available, but daily service across the Atlantic was maintained. The tremendous capacity for work demonstrated by the 707s began to show. The two airplanes replaced six piston-engined aircraft that had previously carried passengers to Paris.

On 10 December 1958 Pan Am began jet service between New York and Miami, under lease to National Airlines. The cash registers rang like fire alarms, one report happily put it. Thousands purchased tickets for Florida, or to warm, overseas destinations, leaving winter behind.

The number of jet routes increased, as more airlines bought this stunning transport. American Airlines put 707-120s into transcontinental service on 25 January 1959. It was the first cross-country jet travel in the US. Continental Airlines and Western Airlines were also quick to put the 707 into action.

Transatlantic records were still being set. Flight engineers aboard 707s watched for shifts in the jet-stream, that eastward blowing, high velocity, high altitude wind. Flying toward Europe, the 707s capitalized on the added push of the jet-stream between the 29,000 and 37,000 foot altitudes. On 12 December 1959, a 707 averaged 626mph on a New York–London flight, crossing the mighty Atlantic in 5 hours and 41 minutes. Homeward bound 707s ducked under the full force of the jet stream. Though sometimes bucked by strong headwinds, the big airplane bored ahead, still remaining above the worst of lower-level storms.

The first 707s on Pan Am's transatlantic flights were fitted with 109 passenger seats, 44 first class forward, and 65 economy seats aft. Economy became a popular feature of jet travel. People could enjoy the thrill of a new adventure and visit exotic destinations at an affordable price. Passenger service soared. By 12 October 1959 1,000,000 passengers had been carried by Boeing's entry into the Jet Age.

An important factor in making profits for airline operators was cargo. A study conducted by Stanley E Brewer, Professor of Transportation at the University of Washington, was revealing. The study, sponsored by Boeing, noted that air cargo had 'a greater potential in the international market than in the domestic, because of the longer distances to cover, and the slower speed of competing forms of transportation in the international market.'

Professor Brewer's findings were on the mark. During the first 15 days of December 1958, 707s carried 117,291 pounds of mail and cargo to Paris. This averaged 7819 pounds per flight, a figure comparable to the combined capabilities of both a Stratocruiser and a DC-7. During this same period, 707s carried 85,928 pounds of cargo and mail to London, averaging 7161 pounds per flight.

Airline officials were delighted, as profits climbed. Investment in the 707s had been deep, at $5,500,000 per airplane, and corporate wisdom was at stake. Things were turning out well. Flight crews were also pleased with these maintenance-free wonders. The 707s, as a group, clocked 987 hours of scheduled service, and

280 hours of training flights during one six week period without a hitch.

However, the 707 did have problems, some of them serious. In spite of elaborate testing with passenger safety the primary goal, a Pan Am 707-120 suddenly went crazy during a transatlantic flight in early February 1959. Captain W Waldo Lynch, the pilot, was conversing with passengers in the cabin when the ship whipped into a downward spiral. Lynch sprawled on the deck, but managed to crawl to the cockpit. Captain S T Peters, the co-pilot, was wrestling with the wheel, which was locked in a hard right position. Between the two men, the 707 was leveled off, but not before it fell from 29,000 feet to 6000. Disaster had been averted, and the ailing 707 made a safe landing at Gander, Newfoundland. Examination showed that the autopilot had been at fault.

On 1 March 1962 an American Airlines 707-120B crashed at the New York Idlewilde International Airport. All 87 passengers and 8 crew members were killed. The CAB reported that the yaw, sideslip and roll, observed by witnesses just before the crash, probably resulted because of a malfunction of yaw damper. This was created by an exposed wire short-circuiting in the servo unit. Investigation revealed that a workman had used tweezers for positioning the eight-wire bundle within the unit. The wires were damaged by pinching, and, in time, two of them separated, resulting in tragedy.

In neither the headlong plunge of the -120, nor the fatal crash of the -120B had there been any structural failure in the airplanes. The fault lay in equipment manufactured by outside contractors.

In 1960 the Boeing jets were given a dramatic opportunity to show the world what they could do. Africa's Congo was in bloody rebellion, and thousands fled their homes. Between 9 and 28 July, Sabena Belgian World Airlines flew over 15,000 men, women and children to safety. Using its five 707 Intercontinentals, the airline mounted a ceaseless ferrying operation between the main airports of the Congo and Brussels. On one trip, 303 passengers were carried nonstop from Leopoldville, a 4000 mile flight. The airplane was in the air for more than seven hours. Altogether, the Sabena 707s made 62 round trips, carrying more than 250 passengers on each flight.

Boeing was doing well with its 707, selling to both civilian and military markets, but company executives did not linger over the triumph. The 707 was a great airplane, and everybody knew it, but it was only the beginning. The next design to come off the boards was a short-to-medium range airplane with the model number 720. It was not so heavy as the 707, having been built specifically for the less lengthy air routes of the world. A shorter body, new full-span leading-edge flaps, lighter structure, a new inboard wing profile and less fuel capacity were the principal changes over the 707. Maximum speed was raised to Mach 0.9, nine-tenths the speed of sound, but cruising speed was kept at 600mph. Field length requirements were also shortened, a boon for out-of-the-way areas where field conditions were not practical for big jets.

United Air Lines became the first customer for this new member of Boeing's jet family, when the company signed a contract in November 1957. The first 720s went into service on 5 July 1960 over the Chicago–New York/Washington routes.

The most significant change in the basic 707 design arrived with the very long range 707-320 Intercontinental. It was equipped with four JT4A turbojets. The 707-420 Intercontinental, twin to the -320, except for power, was fitted with Rolls-Royce Conway Mk 508 Turbofan engines, which developed 17,500 pounds of thrust.

The -320 and -420 were also eight feet five inches longer than the -120, and had 11 feet seven inches more wingspan. Beginning in August 1959, the Intercontinentals went into service over the longest air routes in the world. The fuel capacity of 23,815 gallons gave these airplanes a range of nearly 5000 miles, with a full passenger payload – 189 for each.

An improved Intercontinental, the 707-320B, was ordered by Pan American, along with Air France and TWA. The -320Bs were to become, by a large margin, the longest range jets in commercial service. The main change over the -320 was in the engines and high-lift flaps. Four 18,000-pound thrust P&W JT3D turbofans extended the range of the -320B to 6000 miles with a maximum load. As in the original 320, 189 passengers could be carried.

Because cargo had become so important, the 707-320C convertible cargo/passenger airplane was the next development in the 707 series. The -320C retained all the major systems and components of the -320B Intercontinental, but included a strengthened structure to allow for heavier loading. A large 7 feet by 11 feet cargo door made it easier to handle pallets as well. Although conversion of a 'C-Jet' was (and is) possible in a few hours, most airlines preferred to use the plane in a single service, converting to passenger or cargo configuration only if unusual demand called for it. Where cargo and passengers share importance, the -320C accommodates cargo pallets in the forward main deck, and passenger seating in the aft cabin. Some versions of the -320C were ordered strictly as freighters, with plugged windows and no conversion features. A complete cycle of loading and unloading a 90,000 pound palletized payload can be accomplished in less than one hour.

An additional innovation aboard the -320C Intercontinental is its ability to carry its own cargo handling equipment. It is stored in a lower deck compartment, and offers independence from outside cargo handling facilities. There are three cargo compartments: a full upper main deck, with 8000 cubic feet of space, and two lower decks totaling 1712 cubic feet.

While the 707 was making its mark as a long range carrier, Boeing had, by the late 1950s, discovered that there was a substantial market for a medium range jetliner that would be as economical on the short to medium distance routes as the 707 was on transcontinental and transoceanic routes.

When Jack Steiner was appointed project engineer for what was to become the 727 in 1958, the choice had not been haphazard. There were other competent people on Boeing's engineering staff, but Steiner's ability had been proven by front-line experience. He had contributed to the Model 314 Flying Boats, the KC-135 tankers, and the latest success, the 707.

Steiner's first problem was deciding how many engines to use. Would there be two, three or four, and should they be jets or turboprops? France's slick Caravelle was proving that twin jets, rear-mounted on the fuselage, were practical, but on the other hand, the Vickers Viscount V-700, powered by four Rolls-Royce turboprop engines, was a successful airplane, too.

Competition was on the rise in the short-to-medium range market. Boeing had not been the only airframe builder to anticipate the need. Lockheed's solution was its Electra, powered by four Allison 501 turboprops. Douglas, Boeing's competent long-time adversary in the marketplace, was planning its DC-9.

At the start, Boeing thought a scaled down 707 with four engines would be best, but Steiner opted for an airplane with either two or three engines. There was a reason for this. After consulting with a number of airline people, he noted that inexpensive operation was the factor of prime interest. Low operating costs were the common denominator. Yet, United Air Lines wanted an airplane with four engines to provide what was considered an adequate margin of safety. If one engine malfunctioned, there were to be three left. Counter to this, American Airlines

Below: An Eastern Airlines **727-200**. Eastern was one of the first customers for the 727 and has ordered 88 727s of all types.

Bottom left: An Alaska Airlines **727-100**.

Bottom right: A **727-200**. The -200 is 20 feet longer than the 727-100.

believed two engines were enough. In the middle stood Eastern Airlines, with a very clear preference for a trijet pushing a Caravelle type fuselage.

The solution to the dilemma lay in developing a trijet. Steiner's reasoning was this: United would go for three engines if they were powerful enough, so two would provide the margin of safety expected – it would also mean considerable savings for the company by eliminating a fourth engine. American Airlines would probably go for three engines if operating costs were reasonable and Eastern, of course, had already called for three. Steiner's problem was to prove that a trijet could be inexpensive to operate. As he saw it, Boeing had to come up with an airplane that would:

1. Reduce operating costs, but retain efficiency.
2. Increase speed spread, particularly on the low speed end, to make the airplane suitable for fast service into smaller airfields.
3. Obtain a significant increase in the fatigue life of the airplane structure.
4. Gain equipment reliability compatible with short-to-medium ranges.
5. Operate with lower weather minimums.

It was a perplexing situation, one which called for more study. Developing a trijet was going to cost money, too, perhaps too much. However, Boeing was not a newcomer to spending its own money. The famed Dash Eighty, prototype for both the 707 and KC-135 (717), had been designed and built with in-house funds. To look more deeply into 727 problems, Bruce Connelly, head of the Transport Division, authorized a committee to make a study. Steiner headed the committee.

What he learned was not encouraging. Customers would have to pay up to three and one half million dollars for even a twin engine airplane. The turboprop Viscounts were selling for a little over one and one quarter million; turboprop Electras were priced at 2.1 million, and even the Boeing 720, twice the size of the projected 727, was going for three and a half.

By the spring of 1959, the idea of building a trijet was fading. Engineering opinion remained split over two or four engines. Three engines were barely in the running, though Steiner still thought they were feasible. Fortunately, he had the backing of Ed Wells, vice president of engineering. Wells believed that the 727, as envisioned by Steiner, was a sound bet. Maynard Pennell, chief engineer, also saw possibilities.

Specifications: Boeing Model 727-100

Span	108 ft
Length	133 ft 2 in
Wing Area	1650 sq ft
Tail Height	34 ft
Gross Weight	170,000 pounds
Cruising Speed	600 mph
Service Ceiling	42,000 ft
Range	2500 miles
Powerplant	three 14,000 pound thrust Pratt & Whitney JT8D-7 or 14,500 pound thrust D-9 Turbofans
Capacity	131 passengers, or 46,000 pounds cargo (727-100C/QC)

In July 1959 Steiner presented his designs to Boeing's chief executives. President William Allen was interested, but the price for a prototype with two or four engines was 130 million. The company was not yet breaking even on its 707 investment and that did not help arouse enthusiasm for a new, costly project. Taking everything into consideration, company purse strings were drawn tight.

Jack Steiner was stubborn, though, and he refused to let his 727 die. He went to England in order to look over the Rolls-Royce engines being built for the Trident. The same engine, he learned, could be used on the Boeing trijet, too. Rolls-Royce would be happy to provide them when he was ready, and Steiner returned to America.

There was bad news waiting. Boeing was in financial trouble. The 707 was yet to keep its promise, and losses were very heavy. Further, since Douglas and Convair were both building short-to-medium jets, the market place would be crowded, and Boeing was reluctant to compete. The DC-9 was the largest threat, with Boeing projections forecasting it would cut into 720 sales, and casting more doubt on the feasibility of the expensive 727. President Allen pointed out that operators were apparently happy with Lockheed's turboprop, the Electra. Would they want another jet?

In spite of financial problems and stiff competition, there was enough interest in the 727 to allow design work to go ahead. Over 150 designs were drawn for wing placement and fuselage configuration. Thousands of hours of wind tunnel tests were made on a variety of models. The venerable Dash Eighty (for it was venerable by now), was put to work testing flaps and engines. The 727 had to be designed so it could land on La Guardia Field's 4860 foot runway, an Eastern Airlines requirement. For a fast-flying jet transport, such a short landing space was considered impossible, but out of that requirement came the triple-slotted trailing edge flaps, along with the leading edge flaps and slats. These innovations created an 'umbrella,' with 25 percent more wing, enabling the 727 to land at very low speeds. In the air, the flaps and slats were retracted, streamlining the wing for the sake of speed. Because of this startling use of flaps on both leading and trailing edges, the 727 was to become known as the 'airplane whose wing comes apart.'

A unique T-shaped tail sprouted from the rear of the fuselage. To quote Steiner in regard to this: 'To achieve the difficult economic capabilities of the turboprop Electra, the 727 had to climb fast, fly fast, and descend fast. One of the advantages of the "T" tail was that it permitted deployment of wing spoilers without airplane vibration, leading to a very high useable rate of descent.'

As the aerodynamic problems of wing, tail and body were being solved, engines were still in question. Steiner had convinced the company that three engines were adequate, but now the problem was how to place them. Should there be two engines in the wing, and one aft? Or should there be three engines aft?

Steiner was for the three aft-mounted engines. He had found a way to cluster them that would actually cut down on drag. His team also showed that it would be cheaper to place them in a tight group. The engine systems would be better co-ordinated than if two were in the wing, and another far to the rear. A side benefit of rear engines would be that landing and taking off would seem quieter in the front cabin, though, once in flight, that slight edge would be lost.

The final decision on engine placement showed two aft-mounted engines, each in an individual pod, one on either side of the fuselage. The third, enclosed in a cowling, was suspended from a beam at the rear of the fuselage. An air duct led to it from the base of the vertical fin. Thrust ripped out of a nozzle in the end of the tail.

So there it was: the drawing board prototype of the 727 showed an airplane with less wing than the 707, and less sweep. It would be powered by Pratt & Whitney JT8 turbofan engines, instead of Rolls-Royce. The substitution was made at the request of Eastern Airlines, and Boeing did not quibble. Customers got what they wanted. As it happened, the JT8s were quickly designed and installed without the usual thorough testing both Pratt & Whitney and Boeing demanded. Consequently, the prototype 727 had engine problems, but they were solved during the testing period.

The 727's internal design was made with passenger comfort in mind. Six abreast seating was so arranged that there was no feeling of being crowded. Lighting and interior decor lent an air of spaciousness to the main cabin.

It was now time to meet once again with the Board of Directors. The 727's design was in hand. It was February 1960 and Steiner had been on the project for nearly two years. He had done his best. The next hour or so would tell the story.

The meeting was not an easy one. President Allen was concerned about labor costs. In France, where the Caravelle was built, labor costs were 40 percent lower than those in the United States. In Britain, home of the Trident, labor was 50 percent lower. These were significant differences. Tooling costs for the 727 would also be high, hitting the $100 million level.

The fact that the airline industry was suffering a slump was not lost on the Board either. TWA was in financial trouble, and would not be purchasing new airplanes – as far as it knew. American Airlines was holding to the Lockheed Electra. United Air Lines wished for something the company called 'Airplane X,' and nobody knew for sure if the 727 was that airplane, though discussions with United had taken place. Eastern had not made any commitments yet.

Allen, however, wanted the company to start making money. He knew that a lot of effort by a lot of good men had gone into the 727's design. It was a good airplane, a 'pilot's airplane.' So he compromised. Before any money would be appropriated for a prototype, there would have to be a guarantee of one *billion* dollars in orders! Could the 727, still on the drawing boards, sell that much? It was a mighty question, a billion dollar question. Allen set a deadline of 7 December. If the billion dollars in sales was not there, the 727 program would be shelved.

Though not all that could be hoped for, the proposition was better than nothing. The public relations and sales forces went to work – and gave a good account of themselves. By 30 November, the day before Allen's deadline, contracts had been signed for 80 Model 727s. Eastern Airlines had overcome its reserve and ordered 40. They were the first customers. Next, United Air Lines signed for 40 more, with 20 of them on option. They were apparently convinced that the 727 would meet 'Airplane X' requirements. The two contracts totaled $420 million, and though the figure was not the billion Allen had wanted, it was heartening. On the basis of two large companies buying, it was reasonable to expect that more sales would follow. The 727 program went into high gear.

Roll-out took place in Renton, on 27 November 1962, and presented the world with a breathtaking sight. The 727's high T tail was clearly unconventional with its horizontal stabilizer and elevators on top and the third engine air scoop at the base of the vertical stabilizer. Witnesses were impressed, and noted the old saying about airplanes that if they looked good they were good. The 727 looked good.

Costs for the prototype were a walloping $150 million, 20 million more than originally estimated. One of the reasons for the escalation was the intensive testing. Ed Wells and George Schairer, with typical Boeing thoroughness, had ordered an airframe solely for the purpose of loading to destruction to test the structure. A second airframe was employed in metal fatigue tests, and a third was especially equipped to measure and confirm flight loadings under every condition.

Bill Allen had not flinched because of rising costs. In a speech made in March 1964 he said, 'A substantial portion of the increased costs of the 727 were deliberate. The development programs were enlarged with greater testing – static, fatigue, flight. On the long pull, I think that was good.'

Evidently, TWA thought so too, because the company managed to scrape up $700 million despite financial difficulties. The money went for 727s even *before* the airplane's November 1962 roll-out.

The Boeing 727 took off for the first time from Renton's 5000 foot runway on 9 February 1963. It was 11.33 a.m. The prototype's test pilot was S L 'Lew' Wallick, co-pilot R L 'Dix' Loesch, and M K Shulenberger sat at the flight engineer's panel. They were all old Boeing hands. As the brand new airplane lifted, she shot up so suddenly that, as one observer put it, 'I thought somebody up there had yanked her into the sky.'

The yellow-backed airplane cruised smoothly out of sight, her silver underbelly gleaming, contrails of jet exhaust streaming behind. Two hours later, Wallick set her down at Paine Field near Everett, Washington, where Boeing had leased a flight testing facility. The sleek prototype used very little runway, an important plus. She had been designed to land and take off on short runways. Subsequent tests showed that she could brake to a stop in as little as 700 feet.

Lew Wallick's remarks as he left the cockpit were music to Boeing executive ears. 'The control systems are better than expected,' he said. 'I think they are well advanced over previous airplanes. It feels good.' Then he made a prediction. 'I think airline pilots are really going to like this one.' He was proved correct.

Dix Loesch was also enthusiastic. 'The entire period of flying was very smooth,' he told reporters.

William Allen, president of Boeing, was also at the Paine Field landing. He had bet millions of company dollars on the success of Boeing's new short-to-medium range transport, and he was happy. 'I confidently assume that our people have developed another great aircraft,' he said in a short speech. 'It should prove to be a major source of business for a number of years ahead.'

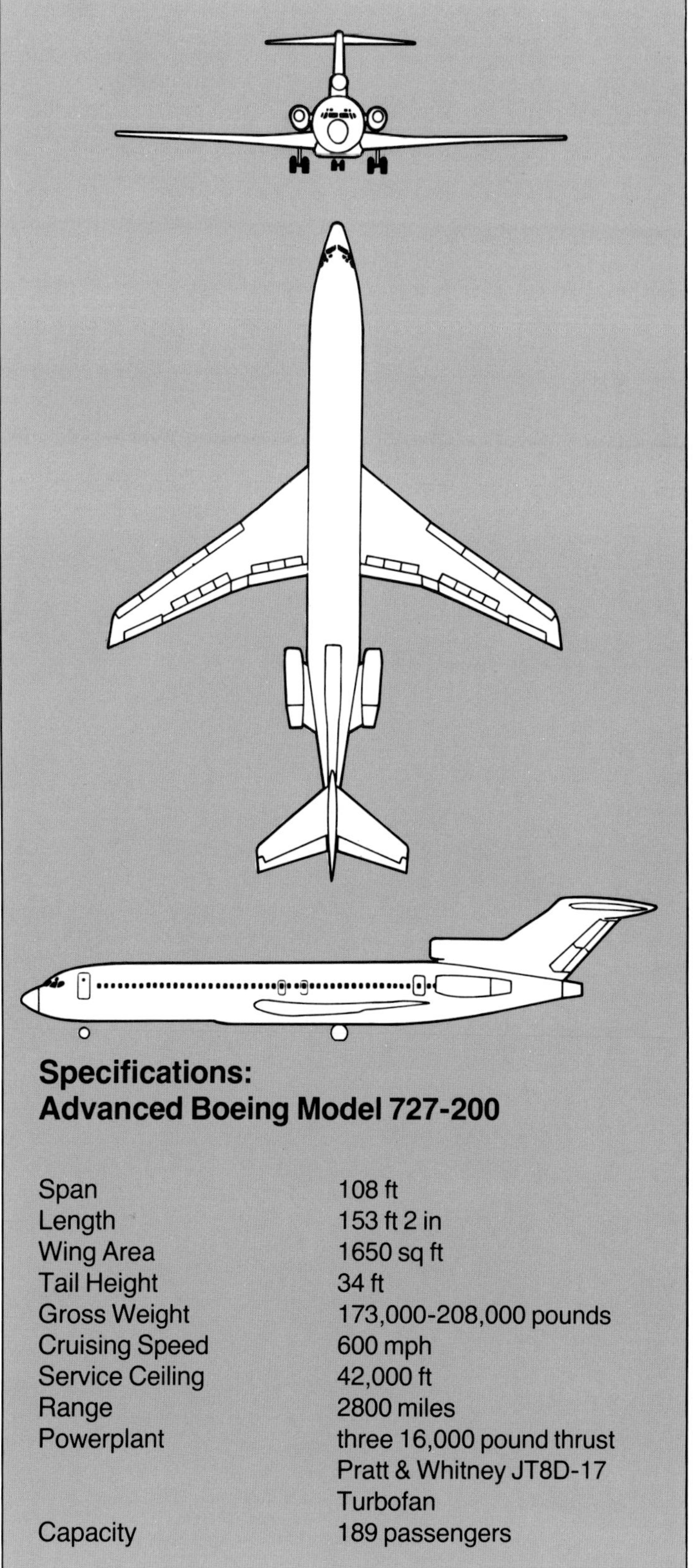

Specifications:
Advanced Boeing Model 727-200

Span	108 ft
Length	153 ft 2 in
Wing Area	1650 sq ft
Tail Height	34 ft
Gross Weight	173,000-208,000 pounds
Cruising Speed	600 mph
Service Ceiling	42,000 ft
Range	2800 miles
Powerplant	three 16,000 pound thrust Pratt & Whitney JT8D-17 Turbofan
Capacity	189 passengers

He, too, was correct. As of 1982, some 1831 727s had been sold. This was more than any other single commercial jet transport.

'I have had a few dreams in my life,' Allen said once, 'one of them was to have a large airline customer call me up, and instead of giving me hell, tell me he was really delighted with an outstanding airplane. That has happened with the 727.'

On 3 November, nearly a year after roll-out, the 727 started on a tour of the world. President Allen was aboard, along with other top executives. He wanted to fly in the airplane that had cost so much and meant so much financially to the company. Though he left the ship in Japan, the 727 continued its world flight, touching 44 cities in 26 countries. It landed at airfields not equipped for

Above: A Delta Air Lines **727-200** in flight. Atlanta-based Delta Air Lines, one of the largest and most successful domestic carriers in the United States, owns 116 727s.

DELTA
BOEING 727

Below: Trans Australia Airlines was instrumental in showing the Boeing Company the potential for the 727-200. Shown here is the first of TAA's dozen 727-200s to be painted in the new TAA livery at the company's Tullamarine facility.

jets, and made stops within 1500 feet of touchdown, proving that its triple-slotted wings could do the job they were meant to do. The airplane was so well built that mechanics and technicians brought along for trouble-shooting had little to do but enjoy the trip – all 76,000 miles of it.

Orders rushed to the home office from all over the globe. Australia's Ansett ANA and Trans Australia became customers, seeing in the 727 an excellent medium for bush as well as inter-city flights. Japan's All-Nippon Airways dropped their Trident orders for the 727, and Japan Air Lines also signed purchase contracts. Back home in the United States, Northwest Orient Airlines and National Airlines placed orders. Allen's one billion dollar figure had been well met.

After the world tour, another 727 made a spectacular entry into the Latin American market. High altitude landing for jets was not considered feasible until the 727 landed at La Paz, Bolivia, whose airport was 13,358 feet above sea level. It was the first jet to do so.

Production was in full swing even before the world tour took place, and Boeing made deliveries without delay. United received five on 29 December 1963, Eastern received two and American Airlines one. Crew training began at once.

Eastern was first to operate a 727. On 1 February 1964, the company established services connecting Miami, Washington, and Philadelphia. United followed on 6 February on its San Francisco–Denver route. American was next, establishing the 727 on its New York–Chicago run, and TWA was fourth, starting operations with the new Boeing jet on 1 June 1964. Four major airlines had commenced 727 service within a span of four months.

More orders arrived. Lufthansa, the German airline, bought 12. The company initiated service on the Hamburg–Dusseldorf–London route on 16 April 1964. Called *Europa Jets*, these were the first 727s exported to Europe.

As sales mounted and more pilots flew the 727s, reports came back to Boeing. It was, indeed, a 'pilot's airplane,' as Lew Wallick, the test pilot, had predicted.

Among its many attributes, the 727 was the first Boeing commercial airplane to be equipped with an auxiliary power unit, APU. It is a small gas turbine capable of supplying electrical and pneumatic power, as well as air-conditioning, when the main engines are shut off. The APU, along with integral aft boarding stairs, makes the airplane essentially independent of ground power facilities. This was important to airlines operating in areas where airport services were not adequate.

The success of the convertible cargo/passenger airplane in the 707 series made itself felt in the developing 727. The basic 727, the -100 series, had maximum seating for 131, but in July 1964 the 727-100C appeared. The floor and the undercarriage had been strengthened to take additional weight. The -100C was similar to the 707-320C, and was convertible to either passenger or cargo service within a few hours.

The next modification was an outgrowth of an idea advanced by United Air Lines. It was called the 'Quick Change,' or, simply, QC. Unlike the 727C, the QC's conversion could be accomplished in a short time by using palletized seats and galleys, with a full set of pallet rollers in the floor. At the end of a passenger flight, the seats and galleys can be detached from locks, and rolled out through the cargo door into a waiting storage van. Cargo pallets can then be rolled directly into the airplane and locked into place. The entire procedure takes less than an hour. Thus passengers can be carried by day, cargo by night.

With an eye on military sales, Boeing offered the US Air Force a -100C in 1965. Designated 727M, it was so designed that it could be employed as a general transport, a paratroop carrier, an ambulance or a tanker. Though versatile, it did not attract orders. However, the 727 did find its way into military service. In 1976, the Belgian Air Force acquired Sabena's series of -100s, and converted them for military use.

By late 1964 it became apparent that certain air routes had need of a higher capacity, medium range jet transport. An obvious answer was a larger 727. It would be basically the same trijet, but with a longer body to accommodate more passengers. The 727-200 was born, a -100 with an additional 20 foot extension to the cabin. The result was a passenger capacity of 189 people and range up to 1500 miles. Northeast Airlines put the new -200 to work quickly. On 14 December 1965 the company introduced the airplane on its New York–Miami route. Air France was the first foreign buyer, putting the 727-200 into service on 15 April 1968.

The success of the 727 escalated, as more attracted the attention of domestic and world airlines. On 29 November 1973, the 1000th 727 rolled out the Renton factory doors, making this the first time any commercial airliner had reached such a production figure. Number 1000 was delivered to Delta Air Lines on 4 January 1974.

Certain specifications from Trans Australia Airlines and Ansett ANA (Australian National Airlines) led to the Advanced 727-200, though Boeing had already seen the need prior to

Above: A detail of the interior of a **727's three-man cockpit**, with its three throttles and one of each gauge for each of three engines.

receiving the requests. The Advanced 727 featured more powerful engines and structural changes, which included thicker wing skins, stronger main landing gear and heavier nose gear. Up to 2400 more gallons of fuel could be carried in extra tanks, increasing the range by more than 1000 miles.

As part of a continuing effort to reduce noise levels in all its aircraft, Boeing fitted the Advanced 727 with 'Quiet Nacelles,' making it one of the quietest jets in the air. The body was the same width as that of a 707, 12 feet 4 inches, allowing six-abreast seating. Thus, the Advanced 727-200 can haul more people over heavily traveled air routes than other aircraft with narrow fuselages. This meant increased earnings for airline executives, whose job it was to make a profit.

According to Jack Steiner, in an article appearing in *Jet Age*, the 727 had led two lives. The first began in 1963, on initial delivery. The second began in the 1970s with the Advanced model. No other jetliner had, up to then, such a capability for changing configuration. This ability extended the 727's life, and forecasts predict sales of 1831. Once again, Boeing proved itself in the market place. What the customer wanted, the customer got. Bill Allen's billion dollar gamble was a gamble no more.

In addition to having been America's first certified commercial trijet, the 727 was the first airliner to have the now-common triple-slotted flap system for superior takeoff and landing performance. The 727 was also the first Boeing jetliner with completely powered flight controls. All flight controls are hydraulically powered with dual units, except for the horizontal stabilizer, which is trimmed electrically. It was the first commercial airplane to win a medal of honor. In late 1972 a Royal Air Maroc Airlines 727, with King Hassan aboard, was strafed by three jet fighters manned by dissident Moroccan Air Force officers. The 727 pilot radioed the attackers saying that the king had been killed in the first attacks, and the firing ceased. The king in fact was unharmed. The 727 was later decorated with the Head of the Order of the Throne, for taking severe punishment and yet landing safely. Boeing sent technicians to repair the damage caused by bullets, and the 727 continued in service.

The 727 was the first jetliner to use an engine specifically designed for it, the P&W JT8D turbofan. It was the first to use the 'jet mixing' principle for quieter operation. Because the engine had the lowest jet exit velocity of any engine when it was introduced, it also created the lowest noise level from the tailpipe. As part of now standard testing procedures the 727 was the first airplane to be subjected to Boeing's brutal fatigue testing and static airframe testing prior to flight. The $30 million test program was designed to ensure that no redesign of production models would be necessary. During fatigue testing, for instance, the airframe demonstrated a useful life of more than 20 years of normal service.

Yet another service provided by Boeing for all its airplanes is the in-field repair unit. When a 727 plowed into a moose on the Cordova, Alaska runway, there was extensive damage to the nose wheel and the undersides of the airplane. It was then that the 'diplomats with tool boxes,' as they are called, came into action. A team of experts arrived in hours from Seattle to assess the damage. They got an idea of what was needed, then returned to Seattle, 1300 miles away. Five days later a crew of company specialists arrived in Cordova, made the repairs, then flew the 727 to Seattle for final testing. The airplane was returned to service a few days after that.

Anytime, anywhere, a Boeing customer asks for help, he gets it. Boeing repair crews have served from London to Bombay, from Tokyo to Beirut, and from Honolulu to Karachi.

This special service unit keeps detailed records of all its repair jobs, and compiles thick technical documents. It also shares what it learns. When a non-Boeing airplane overshot a San Francisco runway and was dunked in the bay, technicians were able to shorten repair time by borrowing Boeing records of a similar accident. Boeing does not play the role of a dog-in-the-manger. Though fiercely competitive in the marketplace, the company provides a helping hand where needed.

Above: An American Airlines **727-35** of the 727-100 series. American has a fleet of over 150 727s which it operates on nearly all of its short feeder routes.

Upper right: A United Air Lines **727-222A** of the 727-200 series in flight over snow-capped mountains. United was the launch customer for the 727 and now operates well over 200 of the durable trijets.

Right and far right: The **727 assembly line at Renton**, with 737s in the background. A total of 1832 727s will have been built when the assembly line closes in late 1984. The 727 could not continue in production with a three-man crew and older, less fuel-efficient engines in an era of high-bypass ratio turbofans. They are gradually being replaced on this line by 757s.

UNITED
N7255U

The Model 737, smallest of the Boeing jets, was conceived in 1964. Company executives had been concerned about the Douglas DC-9, and the British Aircraft Corporation's BAC-111 cutting into the short-range market. It was thought that another airplane should be developed to meet this double threat. The 727, Boeing's hope for the short-to-medium range market, was in danger of losing sales to the DC-9, which had entered service with Delta Air Lines in December 1965. Boeing wasn't a company that willingly let the competition take over, and the race was on. The old competition between Boeing and Douglas had never died. Sometimes it slept, but it was awake and kicking again.

President Allen agreed that a new airplane could be the answer to the DC-9, and BAC-111, but he wanted assurance. As he had with the 727, Allen wanted pre-construction sales figures. Sell at least eighty 737s, he said in effect, and the green light will shine. Boeing could not possibly tackle the enormous expense of designing, testing and manufacturing a new airplane without commitments.

With that in mind, engineers went to work. There was the problem of engines. Some thought three engines in the rear, as with the 727, would be feasible. Some of the original two-engine designs when the company was exploring 727 possibilities had been sound, however, and Joe Sutter, chief of technology, pointed out that twin engines in the wings would be enough if the engines were large. The twin engine version won.

Then a cockpit controversy divided opinion. Should the crew consist of two or three? United Air Lines and Western opted for three-man crews (pilot, co-pilot and flight engineer). Others preferred two-man cockpits, pointing out that the DC-9 and the BAC-111, carried only two. Less payroll meant more profit for the operator. Boeing decided to leave it up to the customer. While there are now 737s with three in the cockpit, the large majority are equipped for two.

It was decided to use the same upper fuselage as earlier jets in the Boeing family. This would provide for six-abreast seating. Douglas's DC-9 seated only five, a point in favor of the 737 Douglas was ahead in its design, though, and would reach buyers

Below: An Air California **737-200** taxis to the terminal gate at San Francisco International Airport after a flight from Los Angeles. Air Cal operates 10 daily flights between the two cities, one of the busiest air corridors in the world. Air Cal is one of two major airlines whose primary function is operating intra-California commuter flights.

Above: Lufthansa was the **737** launch customer, seeing the need for a small short-range jet to funnel passengers between its principal air hub in Frankfurt and other points within Germany and neighboring countries. Lufthansa now operates over 30 737-200s and a half dozen 737-200C Convertible passenger/cargo planes.

Near right: A **737-200C** belonging to Federal Express, a courier service that offers overnight package delivery throughout most of the United States and Canada.

Far right: British Airways operates 19 **737s** on domestic and short-distance international routes.

Below: An Angola Airlines **737-200**. The 737 has been immensely popular with smaller Third World nations because it is economical and because most of their passenger routes are relatively short and have relatively low passenger density. In addition to simply selling airplanes, Boeing offers a wide range of services. These services, which the smaller airlines often take advantage of, include pilot training, route planning, graphic design for the markings and colors of the aircraft and interior design. Boeing can also even provide designs for the flight attendants' uniforms.

Specifications: Boeing Model 737-100

Span	93 ft
Length	94 ft
Wing Area	980 sq ft
Tail Height	37 ft
Gross Weight	111,000 pounds
Cruising Speed	575 mph
Service Ceiling	35,000 ft
Range	2140 miles
Powerplant	two 14,000 pound thrust Pratt & Whitney JT8D-7 or 14,500 pound thrust JT8D-9 Turbofans
Capacity	107 passengers

first, so Boeing came up with competitive innovations to make its newest design attractive. The 737 would, for example, carry more seats, and thus earn more profit.

Competition was fierce. In order to keep an edge, Douglas brought out another version of the DC-9, while the 737 was still an untried prototype. This was the more powerful DC-9-10, with P&W JT8D-1 turbofans. Continuing improvements on the basic DC-9, Douglas next brought out its DC-9-30, 15 feet longer than the original airplane. It entered service with Eastern Air Lines on shuttle operations on 1 February 1967, when Boeing was yet to take its prototype aloft.

The sales race was hot between the two firms but because Douglas was in the sky first, it began to look as if Douglas had won. There was a positive side to an apparent set-back. As Jack Steiner said, 'The 737 was the product of competitive sources. Because of this competition, all airplanes improved.'

In February 1965, Boeing made two important announcements. First, Lufthansa had contracted to purchase 21 of the 737-100s, making it the only Boeing airliner ever sold to a foreign buyer before an American purchase was made. It was a key sale, one that would attract the attention of European operators. Boeing had beaten BAC's One-Eleven to the Lufthansa sale, much to BAC's disappointment, but Lufthansa saw only good sense in buying the 737-100. It had 'commonality' with the 707, 720 and the 727s, sharing many features of the earlier aircraft. The other announcement Boeing made was its decision to go ahead with the 737. It would be built in a new factory near Plant 2, but, warned President Allen, domestic sales were important to the airplane's success. The American market must buy, because, with its aggressive thrust, it was the most sustaining.

Boeing did not have long to wait after the Lufthansa sale. United Air Lines called for the 737, but wanted a larger airplane, so Boeing lengthened the fuselage by six feet. Passenger capacity was raised from 107 to 119. The longer version was designated 737-200, as those of original design had been designated 737-100.

United's order was for 40, but the company did not stop there. In addition, United purchased twenty 727QCs, and took an additional 25 on lease. The order, in aggregate, totaled nearly half a billion dollars, setting another record for commercial airplane negotiations. However, United did not leave Douglas out, and purchased nine DC-8s at the same time.

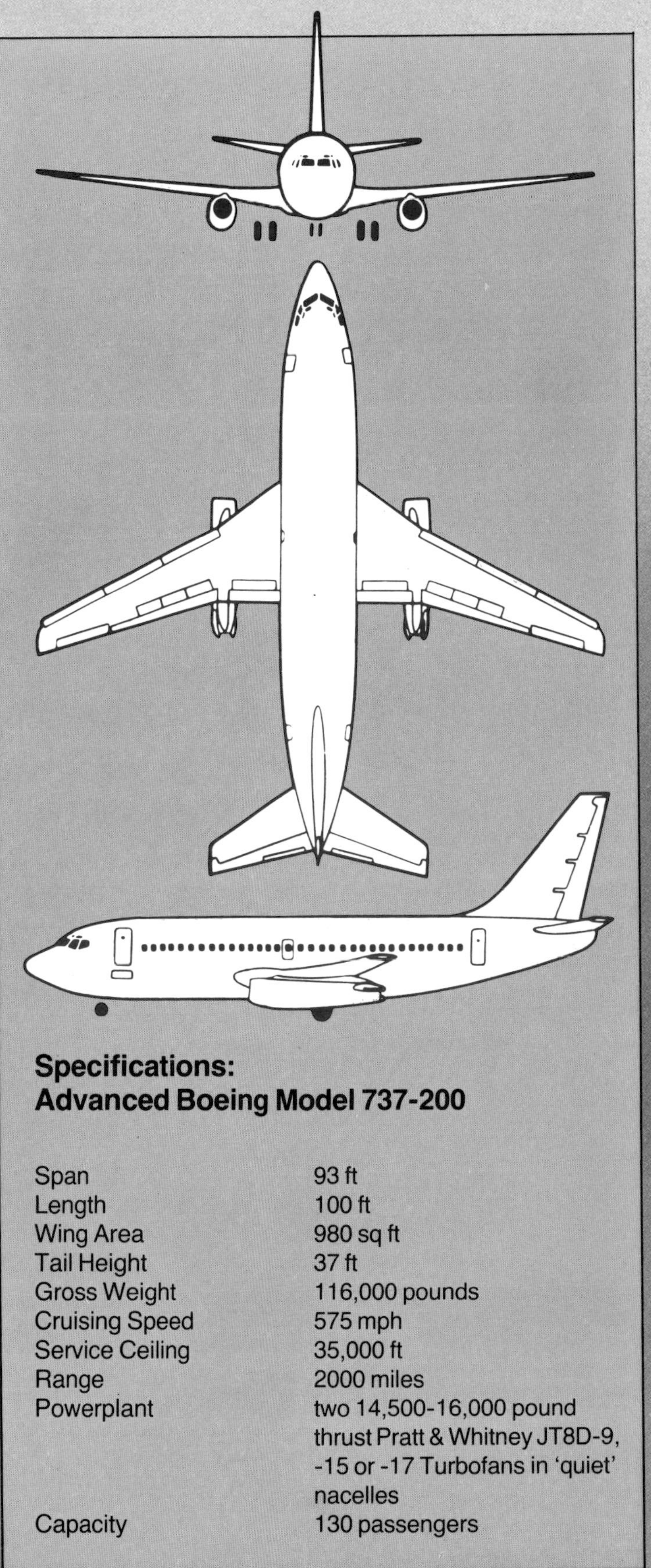

Specifications: Advanced Boeing Model 737-200

Span	93 ft
Length	100 ft
Wing Area	980 sq ft
Tail Height	37 ft
Gross Weight	116,000 pounds
Cruising Speed	575 mph
Service Ceiling	35,000 ft
Range	2000 miles
Powerplant	two 14,500-16,000 pound thrust Pratt & Whitney JT8D-9, -15 or -17 Turbofans in 'quiet' nacelles
Capacity	130 passengers

The prototype 737-100 rolled out on 9 April 1967, and the first 737-200 flew first on 8 August. There followed a period of intense testing. The 737 was encountering more drag than had been expected, and some redesign work was necessary. Despite this, Boeing promised its customers delivery on schedule. Six 737s were flown for a total of 1300 hours, and both the -100 and -200, received FAA certification in December. For the first time, certification also included approval for automatic approaches in bad weather under Category II conditions. These were defined as 100 foot ceilings and 1200 foot forward visibility.

The 737-100 entered Lufthansa service on 10 February 1968. United's inaugural flight followed with the -200s on 28 April. The Boeing Baby rapidly became a favorite with both passengers and operators, providing a smooth, comfortable ride at low costs. Both models were powered by P&W JT8D turbofan engines. Both versions were fitted with APU, auxiliary power units. High-lift flaps and leading edge devices similar to those on the 727 ensured excellent low-speed performance. The 737 was also equipped with an electronically controlled cabin pressurization system. It automatically maintained proper cabin pressure at all altitudes.

As before, Boeing offered -100C and -200C versions for cargo/passenger conversion, and the company also adopted the 'Quick Change,' QC, ability of the 727. It takes only a couple of hours to change configuration on the QC, but the C version became the choice of airline operators for mixed traffic. The first of the 727-200C convertibles was delivered to Wien Consolidated Airlines of Fairbanks, Alaska on 30 October 1968.

In May 1971 the Advanced 737 was introduced. This version came with automatic wheel brakes, more powerful engines and a greater fuel capacity. In all the Advanced 737 had a 15 percent improvement in payload/range over its younger brother.

Another innovation was the optional gravel field kit. This allowed the 737 to operate into more remote strips which had never before been usable by jets. Because it has the same fuselage, the 737 can handle the same cargo pallets as the 707 and 727, and such interchangeability was noted by airline operators – that, and the fact that the 737 could land in 4000 feet.

The 737 was to become a popular airplane, because of its dependability and versatile internal configuration. It became a

Above: One of Canadian Pacific Air's two dozen **737-200s**. CP Air is an outgrowth of the Canadian Pacific Railroad and operates scheduled services to Europe and the Far East.

Specifications: Boeing Model 737-300

Span	94 ft 10 in
Length	109 ft 7 in
Tail Height	37 ft
Gross Weight	130,000 pounds
Cruising Speed	575 mph
Service Ceiling	35,000 ft
Range	1322 miles
Powerplant	two 20,000 pound thrust CFM International CFM56-3 Turbofans
Capacity	121-149 passengers

holiday cruise ship on weekends and a cargo-hauling workhorse during the week. In August 1976 one British Airways 737-200C flew for 19 hours out of 24, while the rest of the 14 airplane fleet flew for 14 hours. It was the kind of reliability operators loved.

The 737 also refuted its stated short-haul limitations. In March 1982 an Advanced 737-200 set a twin jet transport distance record by flying nonstop from New York City to Athens, Greece. It was a distance of 4965 miles. The long-distance record for twin jets had previously been held by a Grumman Gulfstream II, which flew 4866 miles from Honolulu to Washington, DC.

The 737s (in all models) are currently rolling out of the factory at the rate of 7 a month. The 737 seems to grow in popularity every year. Uprated engines, better use of interior space, ease of maintenance (the engines can be reached from ground level) and continually improved electronic instruments have made the Boeing Baby the most productive and economical airplane of its class. For most of the shorter routes of the world, no other plane can match it. This is borne out by the fact that 112 airline operators have ordered this fine ship, more than have taken any of its competitors.

Above: A Bahamasair **737-200** over one of the islands that make up this popular tourist destination. This plane was the first of any type that Bahamasair ordered from Boeing. The airline placed its order on 7 February 1980 and received the aircraft on 8 January the following year.

On 26 March 1981 the go-ahead was given for the 737-300, a re-engined, lengthened version of the basic 737. Designed for the newly available high bypass CFM56-3 engine with a 20,000 pound thrust (developed by CFM International), the -300 will be more efficient and quieter. The -300 has been lengthened 104 inches to accommodate up to 21 more passengers, and the -300's fuel burn per seat will be significantly reduced over the -200, and it will have lower direct operating costs. On a typical 500 mile trip, the -300 will burn from 18 to 20 percent less fuel per seat, putting it in the same class as Boeing's new-generation 757 jetliners. Roll-out is expected in January 1984, and certification and first delivery are planned for November of that year.

The 737-300 will retain 80 percent commonality with the -200, and will be integrated into the same production line in Renton. Modifications will include: strengthened wing to accommodate more engine weight; heavier wheels, tires and brakes; revised wing leading-edge slats and tailoring of the aft flaps in the area of the engine exhaust for improved performance.

There have been advance orders for the -300, both US Air and Southwest Airlines ordering 10 and Orion of the UK five, with more orders to come. Able to carry up to 132 passengers in an all-tourist class configuration, the -300 is a practical airplane for both small and large operators.

In 1973 a military version of the 737 was ordered by the US Air Force. This was the first new Boeing fixed-wing aircraft sale to the military since the KC-135 program ended in 1966. Designated the T-43A, the airplanes are used as navigation trainers. Nineteen -200s were converted for the Air Force, replacing the older Convair T-29s (*see* page 156).

There are 19 stations inside the T-43A: 12 are for navigation students, four are for proficiency training and three are for the instructors. The student training compartment is equipped with advanced avionics gear identical to that in Air Force operational aircraft. This includes Doppler and mapping radar; LORAN (Long range navigation); VOR (VHF Omnirange) and TACAN (tactical air navigation) radio systems. There are facilities for inertial navigation training, as well as radar altimeter and all basic communications equipment. Five periscope sextants are spaced along the length of the training compartment for use in celestial navigation studies.

Most of the T-43A trainers were based at Mather Air Force Base, California, where the Air Force also trains Navy and Marine navigators. A number have now been turned over to the Air National Guard. The airplane is powered by two 16,000-pound thrust P&W JT8D-9 turbofans, with a range of about 3000 miles. Fuel capacity is 5961 gallons. Some changes appear from the basis 737, including strengthening of the floor to support the heavy consoles. Some windows and two fuselage doors were also removed. Other than those, the T-43A retains the original 737-200 configuration.

Some 'firsts' and facts about the 737. There are 138,666 feet of wire in the average 737, more than 26 miles of it. A fully loaded 737 can climb at the rate of 2895 feet per minute – faster than express elevators in tall buildings. The Boeing twinjet is engaged in more routine operations from gravel fields than any other jetliner, but has the lowest damage ratio. It was the world's first twinjet with six-abreast seating. There are 92,000 parts in the 737-200.

There have been many nicknames attributed to the Boeing 737, including the Boeing Baby, which, as one operator puts it, shows the public's affection for this tidy airplane. The chief pilot of an African airline has said, 'You don't fly a 737 – you have an affair with it.'

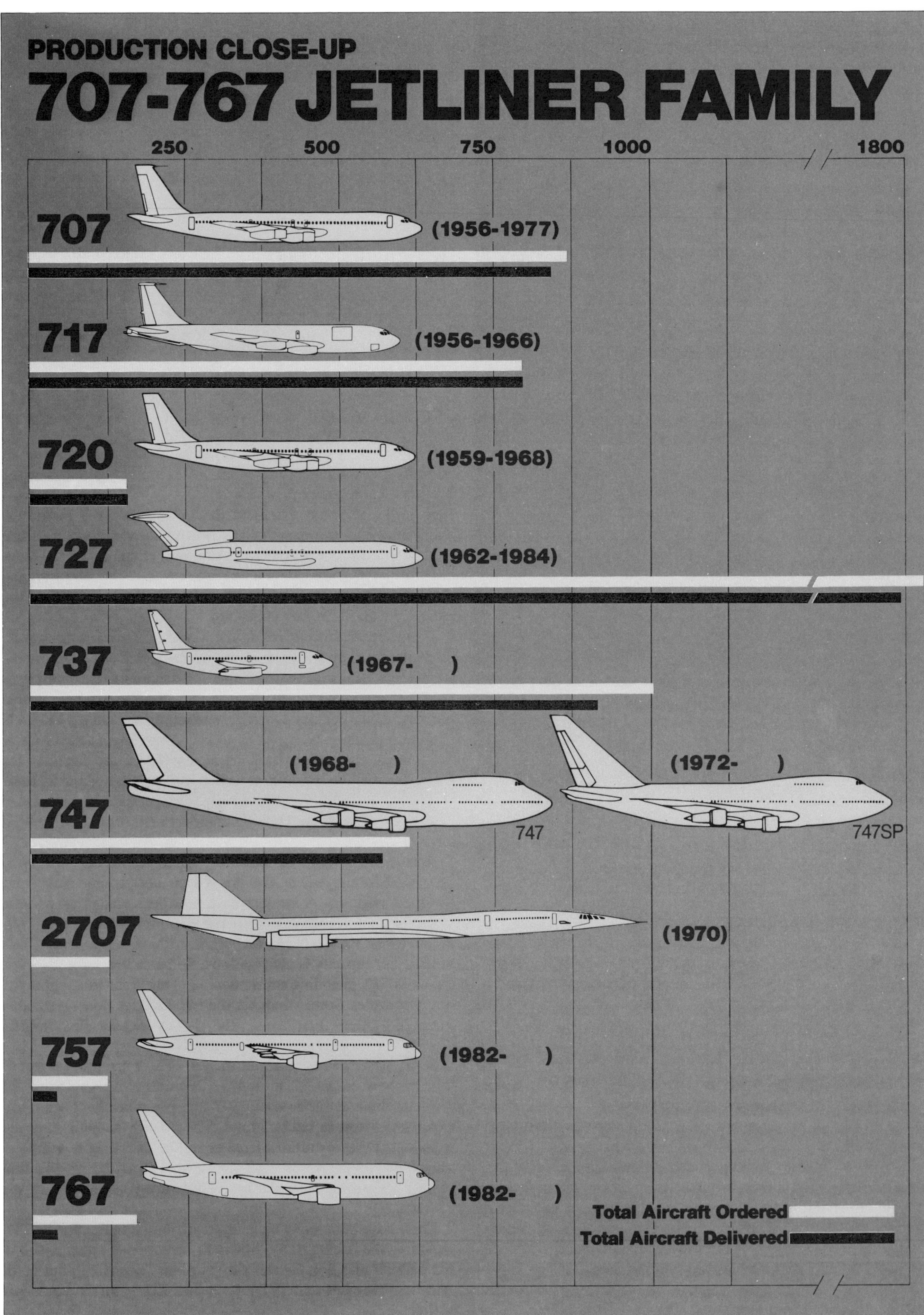
PRODUCTION CLOSE-UP
707-767 JETLINER FAMILY
250
500
750
1000
1800
707
(1956-1977)
717
(1956-1966)
720
(1959-1968)
727
(1962-1984)
737
(1967-)
747
(1968-)
(1972-)
747
747SP
2707
(1970)
757
(1982-)
767
(1982-)
Total Aircraft Ordered
Total Aircraft Delivered

In November 1955, Boeing and North American Aviation were awarded study contracts by the Department of Defense for Weapons System 110-A. It was to be a supersonic bomber with the Air Force designation B-70. It would be capable of Mach 3 speeds, or over 2000mph. Artists' impressions of the design show a tapered body, a long gooseneck and Delta wings. As one observer put it, the airplane had the appearance of being 'supersonic just sitting still.'

Designs submitted by both Boeing and North American were not satisfactory, and the Air Force requested both companies to continue the study. Though Boeing worked hard, North American won the contest. However, the B-70 program was cut back by the DOD in 1960, and eventually cancelled when a change in weapons policy took place, as we have seen.

Though Boeing lost the B-70 contract, the company once again came out ahead in experience. Lessons learned designing the B-70 were applied to something already under consideration, a supersonic transport, the SST.

Before the SST, however, came the TFX (Tactical Fighter Experimental). During the summer of 1961, the Department of Defense let it be known that designs would be accepted for the new airplane, which was to be designated F-111.

Boeing went after the contract. The Bomarc missile program was nearing completion, and it was important to acquire the additional income the TFX would bring.

In December 1961 six leading aircraft manufacturers submitted proposals to the DOD. After evaluation, the DOD narrowed the competition down to Boeing and General Dynamics (together with the Grumman Aircraft Engineering Corporation). Though it was rumored for a time that Boeing had won the contract, it was finally awarded to General Dynamics. After some serious teething problems the F-111 has come to be a successful airplane, and General Dynamics has rolled out over 500 of them.

As with the B-70, Boeing took the loss financially, but chalked up a gain in the experience department. Lessons learned in designing the TFX served Boeing's next project, the SST, called SCAT by NASA, for Supersonic Commercial Air Transport. Boeing had set up an SST study group in 1958. The company had already had several years of preliminary investigation, including design work on the B-70 and TFX, by the time it was ready to enter the project in earnest.

In June 1963, President John F Kennedy, recognizing the implications of Pan American's expressed intention to purchase the British-French Concorde SST, advocated that the United States enter the SST program. In August the FAA issued requests for proposals from major industry firms. In January 1964 Boeing submitted its ideas, amid some stiff competition. Lockheed and North American were also bidding, and were respected as tough adversaries. In May North American was eliminated, and Lockheed and Boeing were left in the running, but they were asked to design larger versions of the SST with lower seat-mile costs.

Boeing and Lockheed were given separate NASA contracts to evaluate four types of supersonic aircraft: the four were called SCAT 14, 15, 16, and 17. SCAT 16 would be an airplane with a variable-sweep arrow wing, and SCAT 17's design showed a delta wing with small, finlike canard control surfaces well forward of the wing.

After consideration, Boeing submitted plans for SCAT 16, the variable wing design. By now, the company had spent $20 million on the SST, and nothing was certain yet. However, there was something new in financing. The federal government assumed participation on a fund-sharing basis, not a normal policy, but the SST was important enough to warrant partnership. The Soviet government had spent money building its SST, the Tu-144, and both the British and French governments had invested in the Concorde. Such an airplane was too expensive for private financing.

The SST program continued on a month-to-month basis until July 1965, when President Lyndon Johnson announced an 18 month competitive phase. A year later, Boeing submitted plans for a mock-up, and was granted a contract to go ahead. General Electric was awarded a contract to develop the powerplants.

In May 1967 Boeing was given the green light to build two prototypes. However, Boeing did not feel quite ready, and asked

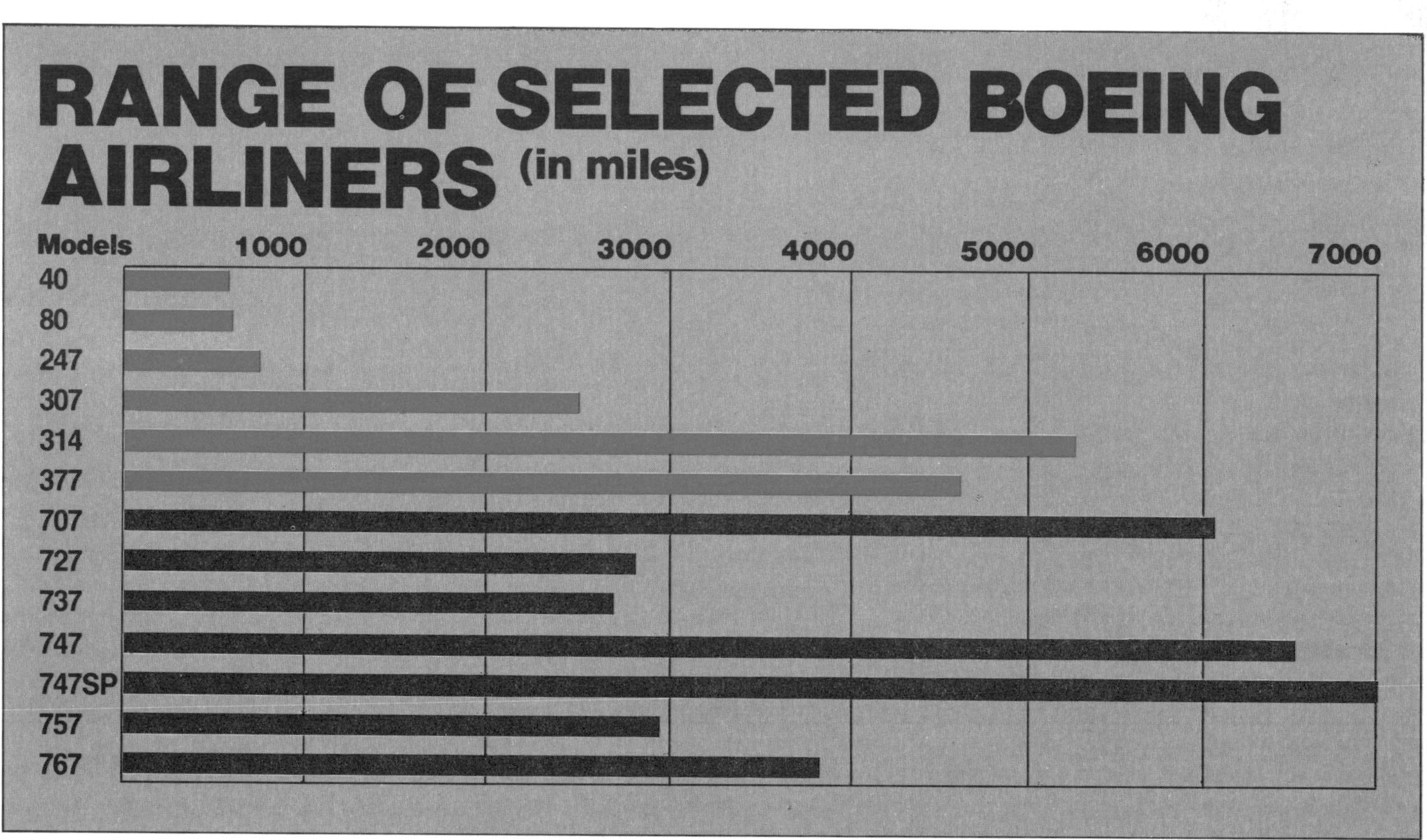

Above: The full-scale mockup of Boeing's **Model 2707-300** supersonic transport inside the Boeing developmental center in the Plant 2 complex. The mockup was complete with interior detail including all of the passenger seats in the five-abreast seating arrangement.

for an extension for further configuration development. By January 1969 the company had completed its design changes, and was ready to begin the prototype. Governmental approval had to come first, however. In September 1969 President Richard Nixon granted that approval, thus becoming the third US President involved in the SST program.

The prototype SST was to be 286 feet long, 50 feet tall, and have a wingspan of over 141 feet. The leading edge of the wing would be swept back 50 degrees. The airplane would be constructed of titanium and weigh 635,000 pounds fully loaded. For power, there would be four GE4 engines of more than 60,000 pounds thrust each. The airplane was to cruise at altitudes above 60,000 feet and would travel at Mach 2.7, or more than 1800mph.

Boeing had by now contacted airlines throughout the world about its SST, now designated Model 2707. Many were interested in buying. Pan Am opted for 15, TWA 12, United Air Lines 6, Japan Air Lines 5. Altogether, 26 operators ordered 122 of the supersonic transports. It was considered the way future air travel would turn, and airlines caught short would fall behind.

But problems arose. By 1970 such questions from the public as to why the government was subsidizing what was essentially a private venture with taxpayers' money were being asked. Who needed an SST? Subsonic jets were fast enough. The government replied that its spending of taxpayers' money was not a grant, it would be paid back. Indeed, as soon as the 500th SST was sold, the government would net a one-billion dollar profit. As to who needed it, the government responded by saying that those who flew wanted it, because of time saved in long-distance travel. SSTs, it was argued, were inevitable. The Russians and the French and British would have them.

The Anglo-French prototype, 001, flew on 2 March 1969. Both British Airways and Air France put commercial models to work simultaneously in January 1976. The Russian Tupolev version, which paralleled the Concorde so closely that espionage was suspected, did not fare so well. It flew first on 31 December 1968, but suffered problems. A second Tu-144 was built, but this crashed at the Paris Air Show in 1973. After some changes, the Tu-144 was reintroduced, but it was withdrawn after the completion of over a hundred operational flights. A fatal crash was thought to be the cause of withdrawal.

Public controversy in the United States continued. There were doubts that the SST was the wave of the future, and would not the SST create high sound levels disturbing millions of people?

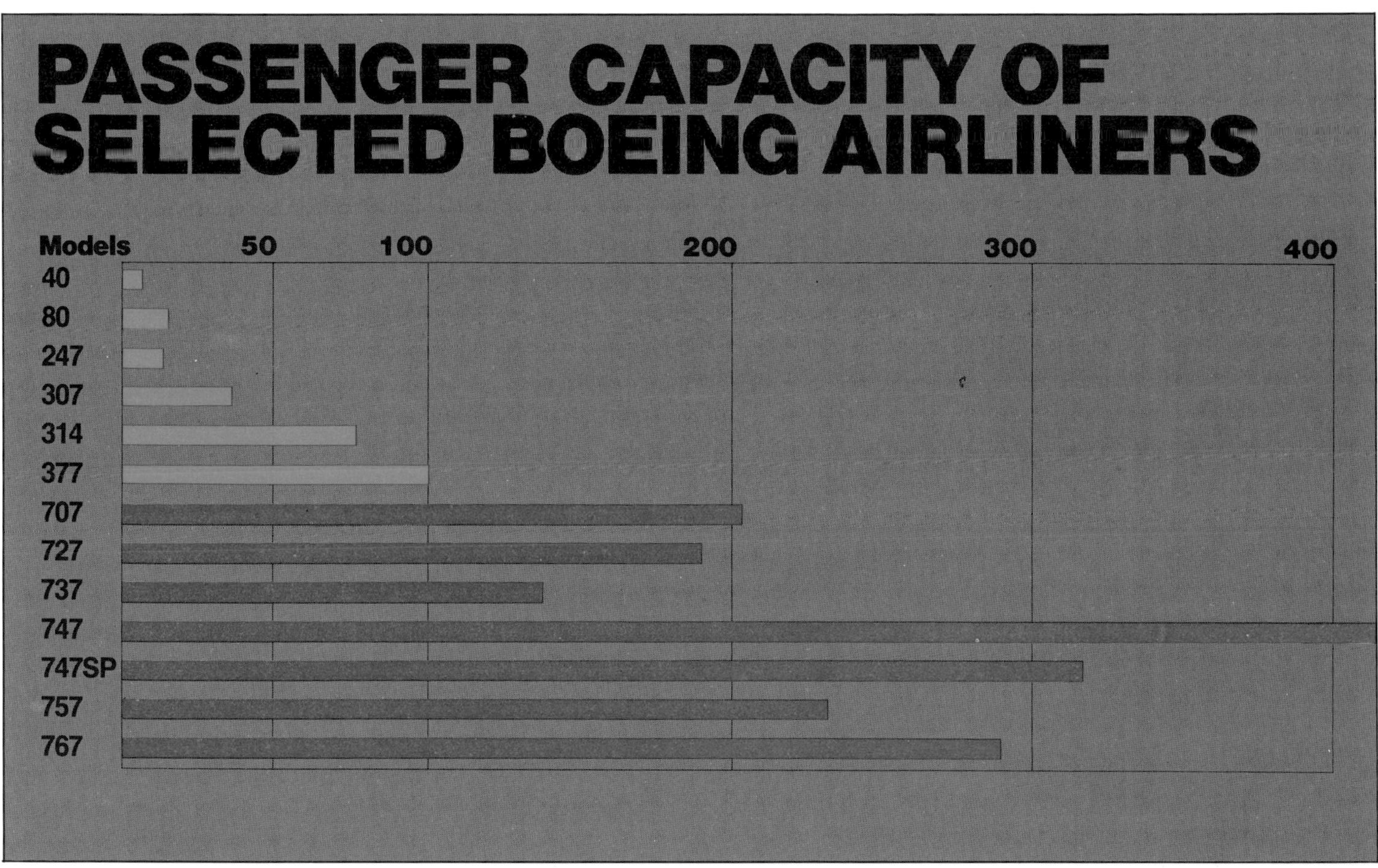

By March 1971 engineering on the Boeing Model 2707 prototype was virtually completed. The program was proceeding on schedule and within costs, the major problems were well in hand, metal was being cut and 15 percent of the first airframe had been completed. Political forces, however, were coming into play back in Washington, and on 24 March the government voted to terminate the program. As provided in the contract, Boeing's share of program costs was refunded, but thousands of Boeing workers were laid off and the American hopes for a supersonic transport were dashed.

It was a serious blow to Boeing, coming as it did at the same time as the serious early difficulties of the 747 program. The airplane market had collapsed during the 1969 recession. Boeing's earnings dropped 73 billion dollars in one year.

Specifications: Boeing Model 2707-300

Span	141 ft 8 in
Length	268 ft 8 in (296 ft*)
Wing Area	8497 sq ft
Tail Height	50 ft 1 in
Gross Weight	635,000 pounds
Cruising Speed	1890 mph
Service Ceiling	60,000 ft
Range	5000 miles
Powerplant	four 60,000 pound thrust General Electric GE4/J5P Turbojets
Capacity	250-321* passengers

*A 'stretched' version of the 2707 Supersonic Transport was already being planned when the program was cancelled

In 1968 Thornton Arnold Wilson (today known universally as 'T' Wilson) had succeeded Bill Allen as company president. Wilson was an engineer and saw the solutions to the company's problems in engineering terms. The only way to save Boeing was to reduce costs drastically, and that meant layoffs. Boeing's work force of 105,000 was cut to 38,000. Engineers were seen pumping gas. Former Boeing employees spread across the Northwest like spilled ink, trickling into and seriously affecting job markets as far away as Montana.

Wilson's painful surgery saved the company, and the dreadful loss of the SST program turned out to be a blessing in disguise. With the dramatic increase in oil prices as a result of the Arab oil embargo of 1973, cost per mile formulae for all aircraft, especially the thirsty SSTs, were rendered obsolete. Though a functional design, the Anglo French Concorde would never be commercially successful. It would continue to see service with British Airways and Air France, the national airlines of the two countries whose governments bankrolled it, but it would never prove to be anything but a lossmaker for them. Interest on the part of various airlines such as Pan Am, Iran Air, Singapore Airlines and the now defunct Braniff, waned for various reasons, and the two original operators remain the sole users of the Concorde.

Boeing's 2707, while larger, faster by over 400mph and of greater range than the Concorde, probably would have shared a fate similar to the Concorde, but without the resources of a national airline available to keep it flying for purely prestige reasons. The supersonic transport is, however, like many aircraft that have gone before it, an idea ahead of its time. It is entirely likely that a commercially viable SST will fly before the end of the century. It will benefit by the mistakes of the Concorde and it will benefit from advances in engine technology unknown during the development of the Concorde and the 2707 in the late 1960s. Boeing, while scrapping the project, never burned all the files, so it is indeed possible that the first commercially viable SST will be a Boeing.

Above: A United Air Lines **747-100** at San Francisco International Airport. United, itself once part of Boeing, operates nearly 400 Boeing aircraft, more than any other airline. However, it flies fewer than 20 747s, most of them on transcontinental flights and flights connecting Hawaii with the US mainland.

In the early summer of 1964, the US Air Force invited Lockheed, Douglas, and Boeing to submit designs for a large military transport. It would carry up to 750 troops over very long ranges. Called at first the CX-HLS, the designation was later changed to C-5A. Boeing's president, William Allen, felt that the company should go after the contract. Boeing had two other major projects on the boards already, the SST and, in the Aerospace Division, a manned orbital laboratory, MOL. The latter two were Boeing probes into the latest challenges, supersonic travel and deep space, but a contract for the C-5A was pragmatic, a foot-on-the-ground venture. Boeing could build transports. It had become famous because of them.

While the design of the C-5A was taking shape, Boeing investigators went abroad to examine the airline industry. Experience was telling the company that the time was coming for another new airplane, perhaps a superjet. The investigating team went to Europe, Japan and Australia, finding that experience had not led them astray. The world market would be ready for a

Above: With its pilot grinning from the cockpit, the Canadian Pacific Air **747-200B** *Empress of Asia* crosses the Canadian Rockies en route to the Far East.

superjet by the mid-1970s, if not sooner. Traffic was increasing by 15 percent a year, and the studies found that future airliners would have to seat up to 375 passengers if the congestion was to be relieved. The time for designing the new airplane was at hand because Boeing knew airplanes designed to fit a market should be ready at least four years ahead of time.

The C-5A plans were submitted to the Air Force, and Boeing waited. Rumors floated back to the company. Boeing was high on the technical side, Lockheed low on price by 250 million. Tense days followed. Boeing was deeply involved in the 737 program and money was scarce. A military contract would mean money in the bank.

When the news came that Lockheed had won the C-5A contract, the news was not greeted with cheers. To further the gloom, the International Association of Machinists had gone on strike at Boeing. It had always been company policy to base promotions on a merit rating system. The union wanted seniority to be the primary criterion. The longer a man or woman worked for the company, the better the chance for promotion in spite of ability. The company and the Union locked horns over the issue. The matter was finally resolved when a joint resolution was reached in which the employee merit system would continue as policy for an additional six months while the matter was given more study. In the meantime, work on money-earning projects went begging, not a boon to the company treasury.

There were grumbles in the industry about Lockheed's winning the C-5A contract with such an enormous underbid. Two hundred and fifty million dollars pretty well knocked out any competition. Could Lockheed really build a super transport for the price? As we have seen, Lockheed's C-5A Galaxy, while eventually a good airplane, was wracked with serious development problems and huge cost overruns.

Though Boeing had been hurt by the loss, the company did not brood. Sales for the 707, 720, 727 and the new 737 were picking up, and it was easy to regain the old enthusiasm. Now that the company was freed of the C-5A responsibility, thoughts turned to a giant commercial transport in earnest. If the one failed, perhaps the other would be successful.

At first a stretched 707 was considered, but the idea was abandoned in favor of an all-new concept. Joe Sutter, chief of technology, an engineer who had helped develop the 737, was asked to design such a plane. Using the advantage gained in designing the big C-5A, some startling results appeared: using the engines that were to have powered the C-5A, the superjet could promise a 25 percent reduction in fuel consumption. Improved leading edge and trailing edge flaps, coupled with further high-lift studies employed in the C-5A research, would enable the giant to land at existing world airports, an important feature if the aircraft were to reach for big sales.

In October 1965, Sutter was made chief engineer on the 747 Project. In consultation with Pan American World Airways it was decided to build an airplane for fast service, reaching speeds over 600mph. In that case, there would be more sweep to the wings, and there would have to be very powerful engines, the most powerful ever developed.

Both Pratt & Whitney and General Electric had competed for the C-5A power plants. General Electric had won. Its TF39, with 41,100 pounds of thrust, is considered to be the first turbofan suitable for wide-body jets. P&W's loss, however, was actually to become a gain. Boeing asked that the P&W JT9D engines be perfected for the 747.

Altogether, P&W had spent six years on the JT9D bypass turbofan. The company built a special factory just to assemble it because all new tools and methods of fitting the parts together were necessary. Its eight-foot diameter inlet was twice the size of 707 long range turbofans. However, it was only 128 inches in length. The engine weighed 8470 pounds and was capable of generating from 43,500 to 53,000 pounds of thrust. That's about 87,000 horsepower at the lower end of the scale.

In order to test the engine in actual use, P&W leased a B-52 from the Air Force. After extensive modification to reinforce the wing, the huge engine was mounted in the place of two J57s. In the trials that followed, the TJ9D took the B-52 nine miles up into the sky, much more altitude than expected.

There was debate on the fuselage design. It was thought that the developing SST would capture most of the passenger traffic, so planning the 747 fuselage required careful study. Maritime container shipping had proved successful, and Boeing designers felt that the basic 747 would be a freighter with container capability. In line with this thinking, a body was developed that would comfortably hold two 8 foot by 8 foot containers side by side. This was the origin of the 'wide body,' which at first had little to do with passengers or their comfort.

The airplane that came off the drawing boards had a configuration, however, that would take either passengers or freight, or a combination. Of course the SST would be cancelled and there was accordingly no intrusion by it into the passenger market. The final version of the 747 fuselage had three decks. The flight deck, on a level above the main deck, permitted straight-in loading through a hinged nose door in freighter and convertible models. Behind the flight deck on some passenger models there is a luxurious lounge, reached by a stairway from the main deck. The main deck allowed ten-abreast seating. It could also be used for freight or a combination of freight and passengers. Below the main deck was space for 26 containers, capable of holding 16½ tons of baggage, mail, and cargo.

The first-class passenger cabin was forward in the nose. The 747-100s, as the first production Superjets were designated, seated 58 first-class passengers, and 304 economy class. There were three galleys aboard, and food caterers had to think big in order to serve the large number of passengers. The average crew on a 747 consists of the captain, the first officer, flight engineer, a steward, and ten hostesses.

While the planning was going ahead, the then chief executive of Boeing, Bill Allen, and Pan Am's Juan Trippe were negotiating. Trippe was looking for a big airplane that would save from 30–35 percent per seat-mile. This meant lower fares and cargo rates, giving Pan Am a considerable edge over the competition. Trippe was a man of action. He was aware that Boeing was chary of the development costs of such an airliner – at least 500 million dollars. So on 13 April 1966 he signed a contract for $525 million. This was for 25 airplanes, two freighters, and the others to carry from 350 to 400 passengers. On the basis of another record order, Boeing's financial worries vanished. William Allen gave the go-ahead to build the largest commercial airplane ever.

In June 1966, three months after the 747 program was launched, 780 acres of land were purchased next to Paine Field, Everett, Washington. For such a huge airplane, a special manufacturing complex was needed. It included the world's largest building by volume. Originally measured at 200 million cubic feet, the building has recently been enlarged to 285 million cubic feet in order to accommodate production of Boeing's new 767 airliner. As a result, major portions of manufacturing, subassembly and final assembly functions for both aircraft are housed under one roof.

Also at the site is an area for cleaning, sealing and painting the airplane sections before they go into final assembly. The structural static test area is inside the huge complex, too, but the structural fatigue-test area lies outside the factory.

In addition, there are warehouses, a service building, several office buildings and a cafeteria. Paint hangars and a field-support building are located on the preflight apron adjoining Paine Field.

The site also includes a 15 million gallon holding basin to catch surface runoff water. A five mile railroad spur, the second steepest standard guage section in the USA, was built to bring in construction steel for the buildings and production parts and subassemblies for fabricating the aircraft.

Before production actually began, Boeing devoted 14,000 hours of wind tunnel testing to a variety of models. It spent 10 million engineering man hours on the project. Everything about the 747 was big from the very beginning. Four years of continuous testing in areas ranging from metals selection to systems operation preceded the first superjet. It was not born overnight.

The 747 Division of the Boeing Commercial Airplane Company (a wing of the corporate Boeing Company) was established. John Steiner was made vice president in charge of production development. The new division was made directly responsible for designing, developing, and manufacturing the 747, a formidable responsibility.

The first production operations at the new Everett plant began in January 1967. The buildings were occupied in stages throughout the year as each was completed. Activation of the mammoth assembly plant began on 1 May 1967, just over a year after the 747 program was announced. Actual assembly of the first airplane started in September of the same year. Later that year, components for the first nose section arrived at Everett from Boeing's Wichita, Kansas division. Because the job was so big, Boeing signed contracts with other industry-related firms to make a variety of parts. Without outside help, the 747 production would have suffered. Concurrently with the nose section, other components manufactured by major contractors arrived, and the job was under way.

While parts for the 747 were taking shape, another aspect of the project reached a satisfactory conclusion. This was the 'selling'

Below: Scandinavian Airlines 747-200B *Dan Viking* was the fifth of the jumbo jets to be built for SAS but had the distinction of being the **500th Boeing 747** to be built. The *Dan Viking* is a 'Combi' model able to carry mixed loads of passengers and freight on the main deck. SAS received its first 747 on 27 February 1971 and now operates a half dozen of the big jets, that number equally divided between the 200B model and the 200B 'Combi.'

of the Class III 747 mock-up on 12 January 1968. The mock-up was a full-scale airplane, minus engines, seats and one wing. Its purpose was to verify engineering drawings, determine assembly crew sizes and the tooling needed, set instruments for flight testing and check out specific airline cabin and cockpit arrangements. The 'buyers' were two Boeing men, the chief of the Model 747 mock-up engineering, and the chief of mock-up quality control. Their acceptance meant that crews could start on non-structural items such as wiring, panel-making, tubing and pumps. The wing and body sections were already under construction.

The first wing assembly was removed from the assembly jig in March 1968. The wing weighed 28,000 pounds, or ten times the gross weight of Boeing's first plane, the B&W.

Production moved ahead swiftly, and on 30 September 1968 the first 747 Superjet made its world debut in a roll out ceremony at the Everett plant. By January 1969 the prototype 747's major systems had been activated, and its landing gear and flight controls operationally tested. Compass calibration, fueling and engine tests came next. After that, there was nothing to keep the 747 from its big moment, the first flight.

According to *Boeing Magazine* for March 1969, this is what happened. It was 9 February, and the weather was not great, somewhere between bad and uncertain. Shortly after 11.00 a.m., however, the overcast thinned and lifted. Three men were in the 747's cockpit. They were pilot Jack Waddell, co-pilot Brien Wygle and flight engineer Jess Wallick. One of them mentioned it would be nice if there were less people on the runway. Large crowds of newspeople and photographers, company executives and employees were present to see the largest transport in the world make its maiden flight. 'Like flying in Africa,' observed another of the cockpit crew, 'you have to chase the wildlife off the runway first.'

The people moved back, though, and pilot Jack Waddell eased the throttles forward. Co-pilot Brien Wygle called out speeds as this giant of the air began to gather momentum. Flight engineer Jess Wallick kept his eyes glued to the gauges. The Boeing Model 747 superjet gained speed. The nose lifted. After 4300 feet, less than half the Paine Field runway, the main gear left the concrete. The take-off speed was 164mph. At 11.34 a.m., quietly and almost serenely, the age of spacious jets began.

'The engines,' reported one witness, 'made no more noise than a stiff breeze through a forest.' Pratt & Whitney had developed the JT9D high bypass turbofan with community noise concerns in mind. A giant step toward quieter airliners had been taken.

Above: To manufacture the world's largest jetliner, the 747, Boeing built near **Everett, Washington**, the largest building in the world. The building, enlarged in 1980 to 291 million cubic feet, encloses all major portions of manufacturing and final assembly for the 747, and recently for the 767. The four large colored doors seen here are each seven stories high. In the foreground, the new 747s are prepared for final delivery. Boeing began building the 747 at the Everett plant in 1967 and the first 767 was rolled out in 1981.

Left: The flight line at **Paine Field**, adjacent to the big Everett complex. The Everett flight line is like a United Nations of airlines, with dozens of carriers from every continent having been represented here.

Below: A **747 forward fuselage section** is joined to the rest of the fuselage.

Waddell accelerated the airplane to 184mph, and climbed nearer to the overcast at 2000ft. He then circled back over the airport and began his climb to the 15,500 feet test altitude. Snuggled close to the big airplane, and appearing, to one man, 'Like a flea about to jump on the 747's back,' was a North American F-86 chase plane. Its pilot's job was to conduct external studies of the superjet's operation.

After putting the 747 through a series of sideslips and other tests, including one simulating a loss of hydraulic systems, Waddell headed for home. At 12.50 p.m. the superjet touched down at Paine Field in a perfect landing. Waddell used light braking and thrust reversers to bring the plane to a stop, again using about half the runway. He then rolled on to make way for the chase plane coming down behind him. The 747's landing speed was 150mph, without full flaps.

Led by a string of official cars and buses, the 747 taxied into the Boeing ramp, and the engines were shut down. A few minutes later, the crew, their business suits still unwrinkled, emerged from the forward passenger door to be greeted by well-wishers. 'Look at 'em' said an East Coast newsman, 'they just flew the world's largest commercial jetliner, and they seem about as ruffled as my stockbroker.'

That may have been true, but Jack Waddell was all pilot. He had learned to fly PBYs during World War II, and after the war he earned a master's degree in aeronautical engineering at Cornell University. After five years as an engineering test pilot for North American Aviation, he joined Boeing in 1957.

Shortly before taking the world's largest commercial airplane up, he was interviewed. The interviewer caught him laid up with a badly swollen ankle. 'How do you feel about flying an untried aircraft?' he was asked. 'Safer than staying at home,' replied Waddell, with a nod at his ankle. 'How did that happen?' 'Jogging,' replied Waddell with a grin.

He made no secret about his enthusiasm for the 747, after the flight. 'It's a pilot's dream,' he said. 'I'd call it a two-finger airplane.' He curled his forefinger and thumb as if gripping a control wheel. 'The plane,' he said, 'has a very light, responsive touch: two fingers.'

Above: The company-owned **747-100 prototype** dubbed *City of Everett*, in the colors representative of Boeing-owned aircraft of 1969, and sporting the insignia of all those airlines which had placed orders for the big jet.

Below: A Middle East Airlines (Lebanon) 747-200B lifts off from **Paine Field**.

The business of testing the prototype now began. After ten hours of flying time, the 747 was taken to Seattle for more trials. Not long after, a second 747 joined it. The 747 testing program was to be the most extensive ever undertaken in commercial aviation history. In addition to laboratory tests of parts and components, the program included the assignment of five Superjets to a $28 million, year-long Boeing and Federal Aviation Administration flight testing program. By the end of the year, the five jets had logged more than 1400 hours of flight time in 1013 trips aloft. Finally satisfied that the 747 was a reliable aircraft, the FAA gave certification on 30 December 1969.

Yet, there had been problems. One of these was the 'ovalizing' of the large JT9D engines. They changed shape after running under loads. Pratt & Whitney studied the problem and engineered a structure that held its shape under the terrific stresses. In the meantime, airframes were lining up waiting for re-designed engines. By mid-October 1969, 22 airframes were idle at the Everett plant, 17 of these without engines. Subcontractors were so efficient that, regardless of a lack of engines, components arrived and airframes were completed.

Because of the engine problem, Pan Am was worried about delivery schedules. The company had millions tied up in the 747. Boeing, proud of its record of delivery-on-time, did not let Pan Am down. The company received its first superjet on time. Boeing people fully realized the importance of getting their products to customers when they said they would, and they were committed to delivery schedules.

When Boeing delivered two 747s to Pan Am for pilot training, Pan Am's new president, Najeeb Halaby (Juan Trippe had retired), took one up for a test of his own. Halaby was a jet pilot, qualified for transports. Aboard were Pan Am and Boeing officials, who were in for the ride of their lives. In the words of Robert Daly, who wrote *An American Saga*, a history of Pan Am, Halaby 'Wrung the 747 out like a fighter plane: dives, stalls, violent pull-ups that made the whole plane shudder and shake, the huge wings flapping 12 feet up and down. His conclusion: this was the safest, most comfortable, most magnificently-built plane in history.'

His findings were not mere chance. As with the 727 before it, the 747 had endured severe tests to destruction. Static testing, using one of the non-flying airframes, verified the strength of the entire frame. In one test, the 747 wing tips were deflected upward 26 feet before structural failure occurred.

Fatigue testing made use of the other non-flying airframe, and duplicated the stresses experienced in day-to-day airline flying. It was a task for which Boeing was well qualified. The fatigue-test program took the airframe through the equivalent of 20,000 airline flights, or 60,000 hours. Following this, fail-safe testing with the structure cracked or sawed through in 28 critical places, put the equivalent of 12,000 additional hours in airline flights on the structure. Boeing wanted to make certain that the 747 would continue to operate safely, even after damage. As always, it was safety first with Boeing.

After the five 747s completed their tests with the FAA and Boeing, four of them were refurbished and delivered to waiting airlines for service. The fifth 747, the first one to fly, remains in flight-test status with Boeing. It is used for checking out modifications which lead to production improvements.

On 3 June 1969, the prototype flew 5160 miles across the Atlantic for the Paris Air Show. The flight proved that the giant airliner was capable of world-wide travel. There was no distance too great for the 747 to cover. Airlines took notice.

On 21 January 1970, Pan Am inaugurated its first transatlantic flight with the Superjet. It was a grand occasion, with many people attending. The pilot started the JT9Ds for the New York–London flight, then chopped them off. One of the engines was overheating. There was a 24 hour delay, but on 22 January, the 747 taxied out once more. Again, the engine overheated, and the flight was delayed. Despite the embarrassment Pan Am was not to be thwarted and the company substituted another 747. This one took off, and the age of the 'jumbo jet' arrived.

The 747 rose swiftly in public esteem. Airlines were buying them as fast as they came off the assembly line, peaking out at seven airplanes a month. But the 1973 oil crisis brought soaring fuel prices, rising fares and a decline in airline traffic. Airline

Above: **Boeing's jumbo jets** have proven extremely popular for national airlines such as Alitalia who fly long-distance routes, particularly the North America – Europe run. Alitalia flies 14 747s of various types.

operators were hesitant about purchasing jumbo jets. Boeing survived another lean time, by introducing new models of its superjet, and by mid-1979 production had risen again to seven per month. It remained at seven throughout 1980, leveling off at five per month for 1981. One a month was forecast for 1983. It may be that three, five, or even seven superjets roll out each month, but it actually takes two years to assemble each one.

Each member of the Boeing 747 family of airliners takes years to build because much goes into them, and big is the watchword. There are three decks, and the main deck is 20 feet wide. This permits, in addition to the seats, two 20-inch aisles to extend for the entire 185 foot length of the cabin. Side walls of the cabin are nearly vertical, and the 8-foot 4-inch high ceiling is flat. Centerline galley and washroom installations divide the cabin into five separate compartments. The 747 has 10 double-width doors, five on each side of the cabin. Several are used for passenger boarding, others for airplane servicing, but all can be used for emergency evacuation if necessary.

To carry all of this safely, the airplane has a 16-wheel main landing gear, four units of four wheels each, and a two-wheel nose gear. These allow even distribution of loads on airport aprons and runways. The airplane can be landed with only one main gear unit on each side extended.

The 747-100 has led to a variety of commercial versions, with all but the 747SP having the same external dimensions.

The 747-100B carries a typical load of 452 passengers and baggage a distance of more than 4500 miles. First versions used four P&W JT9D-3 engines with 43,500 pounds of thrust each, though there was an option available for the JT9D-3W engines with 45,000 pounds thrust. Later versions employed the JT9D-7 series, providing up to 50,000 pounds thrust, or GE's CF6-50 engines.

Above: The configuration of the **inboard landing lights** on the 747 is visible here as the big bird touches down.

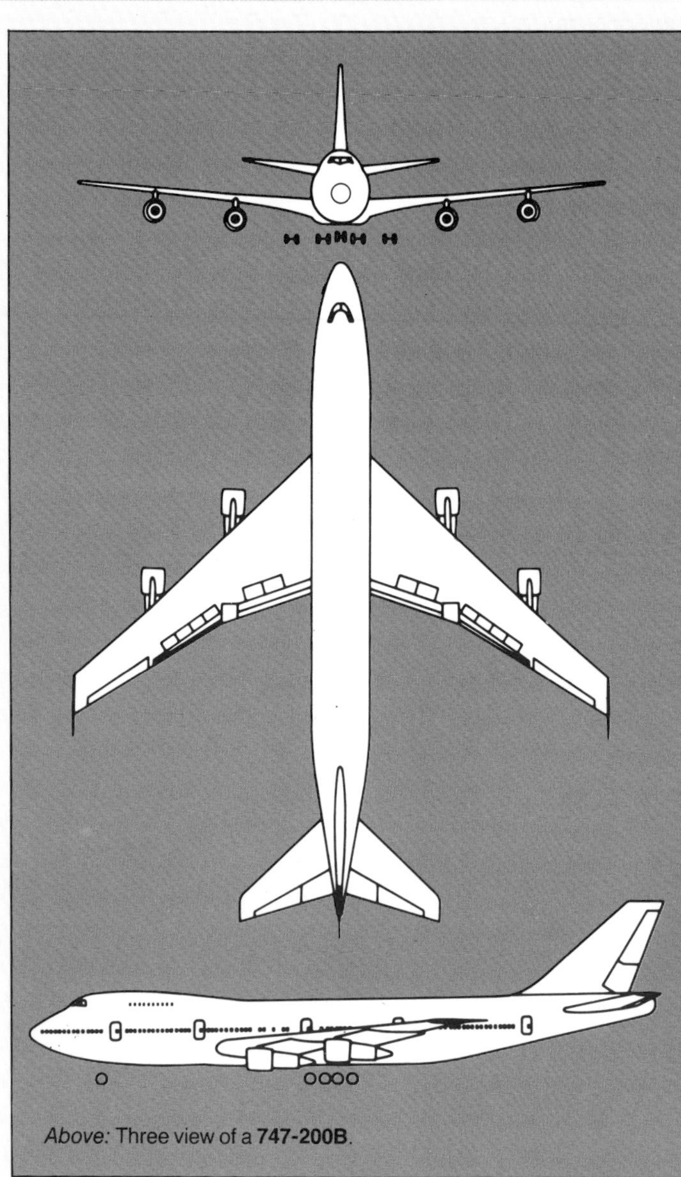

Above: Three view of a **747-200B**.

Specifications: Boeing Model 747

Span	195 ft 8 in
Length	231 ft 10 in
Wing Area	5500 sq ft
Tail Height	63 ft 6 in
Gross Weight	710,000-735,000 pounds (747-100/-1000SR) 775,000-833,000 pounds (747-200/-200C/-200F)
Cruising Speed	600 mph
Service Ceiling	40,000 ft
Range	5677 miles (747-100) 6563 miles (747-200B) 5009 miles (747-200F)
Powerplant	four Turbofans, either 43,500-53,000 pound thrust Pratt & Whitney JT9D, or 52,500 pound thrust General Electric CF6-50E or 50,100 pound thrust Rolls-Royce RB211-524B
Capacity	The basic 747 accommodates 350-450 passengers or up to 270,000 pounds of cargo or mixtures of both (with various seating rearrangements and especially with the new Stretched Upper Deck version, 747SUD, up to 500 passengers can be accommodated)

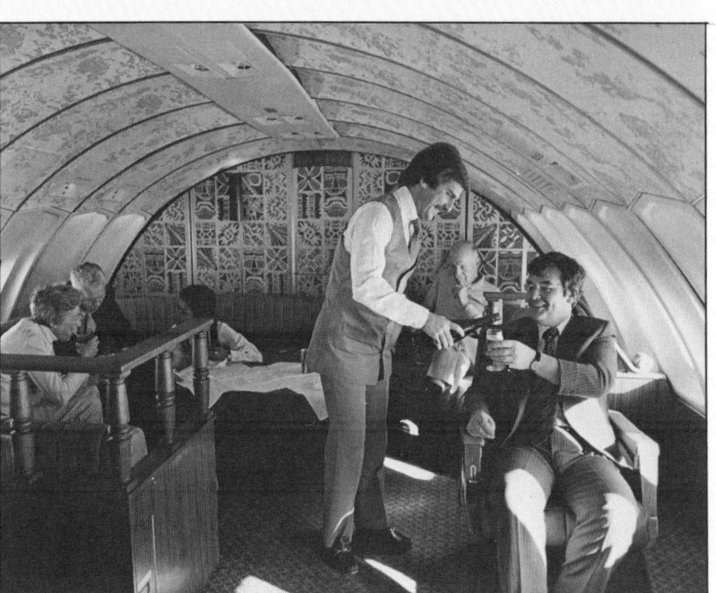

Above: A passenger enjoys a glass of champagne in the **upper-deck lounge** of a Hawaii-bound United Air Lines 747. Many airlines opt to install additional seating in the upper deck.

Left: The **staircase** which connects the first-class galley with the upper-deck lounge. In some aircraft it is a spiral staircase.

Right: The typical **747 flight deck**.

Below: A cutaway of a **747-200 'Combi'** that allows for a combination of passenger seating and cargo on the main deck. This example has a spiral staircase leading to an upper deck with seats installed.

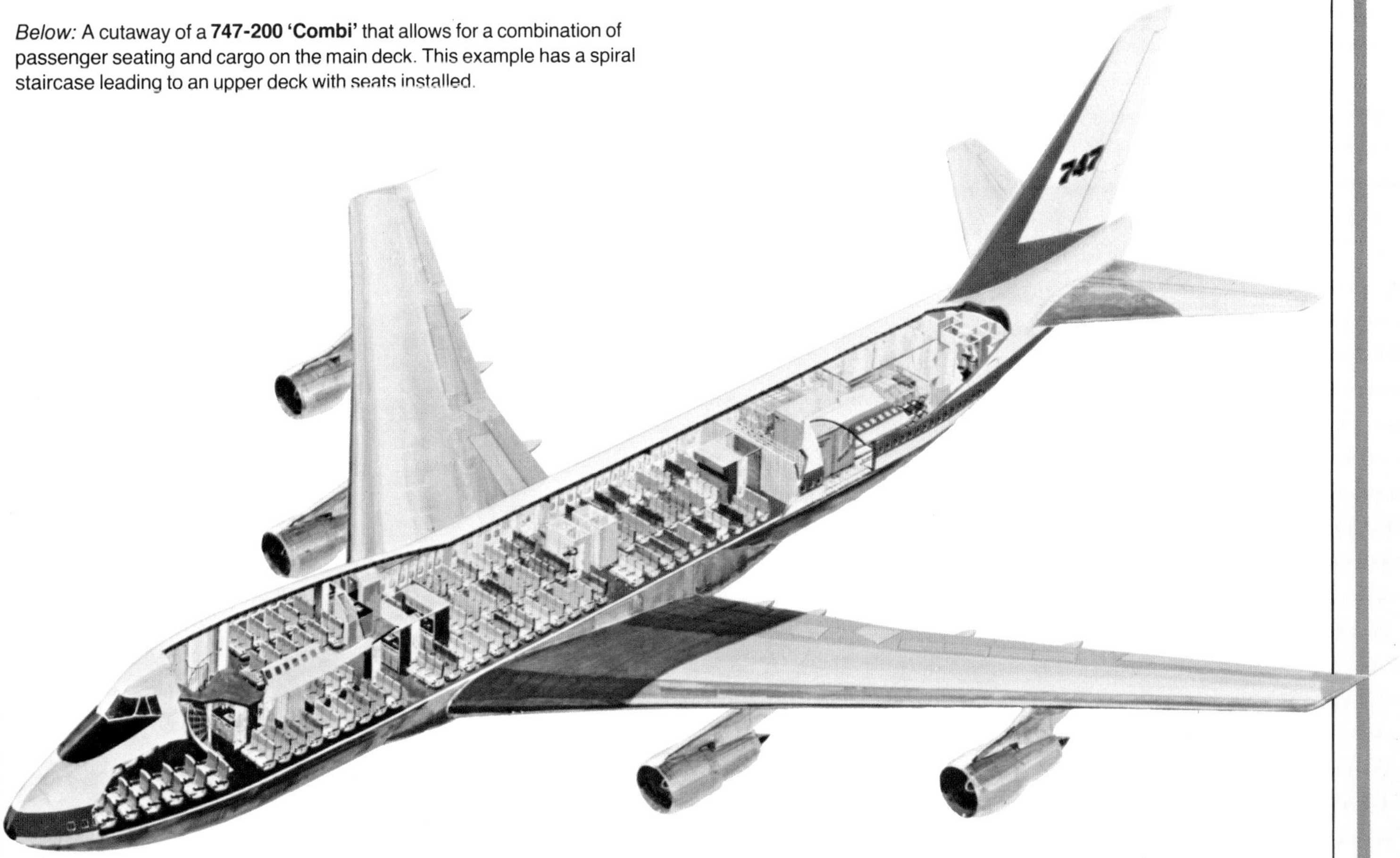

Right: The capacious interior of the **747-200F freighter**, looking forward to the hinged nose. This aircraft has a typical cargo capacity of 135 tons with 18,560 cubic feet of cargo space available on the main deck and 5190 cubic feet available on the lower deck for containerized cargo.

Far right: A **747-200F** operated by Air Afrique, the Ivory Coast based airline founded by and serving 11 former French African colonies. This aircraft, delivered on 3 October 1980, was Air Afrique's first Boeing purchase.

Left: A Pratt & Whitney powered **747-200F** freighter operated by Cargolux, an all-freight line based in Luxembourg. This plane, *City of Luxembourg*, and her sister ship are the heaviest aircraft in service in the world, weighing in at 416 tons.

Below: A Rolls-Royce engined British Airways **747-200F**. British Airways' more than 30 747s use the British-made Rolls-Royce RB211 turbofan engines.

Above: One of three **747SPs** ordered by CAAC, the airline of the People's Republic of China, in 1972.

The 747SR (Short Range option on the 747-100B) was designed specifically to fill the need for high-capacity transports on routes as short as 200 miles. The 747SR was structurally strengthened to permit it to make twice as many landings in 20 years of short-range flights, yet retain its long-range capability. Components of the 747SR and the basic 747 have 99 percent commonality, and flight characteristics are identical. Gross weight can vary from 520,000 pounds at take-off on short-range flights, to 750,000 pounds for long-range flights.

The 747-200B is an 833,000 pound gross weight passenger plane that can carry a standard 452 passenger load more than 5000 miles non-stop. It is powered by Pratt & Whitney, General Electric or Rolls-Royce engines delivering up to 54,000 pounds of thrust. The 747 Combi, an option on the 747-200B, can be operated in either all-passenger or combination passenger/cargo configurations. It offers airlines an economical means of adapting to the variations in seasonal markets and charter flights. It is equipped with a side cargo door on the main deck, permitting cargo loading in the aft section, while passengers board in the forward section. Main deck cargo capability in this combination arrangement can be either 6 or 12 pallets.

The 747-200C, convertible, was first ordered by World Airways, one of the largest charter air carriers in the world. The -200C is capable of transporting 500 passengers in 10-abreast economy seating, or a cargo payload of up to 250,000 pounds. A typical all-passenger flight would carry 380 persons and their luggage in a mixed-class configuration 5800 miles. A typical North Atlantic non-stop cargo load would be 180,000 pounds. The 747C, as the airplane is commonly called, has a swing-up nose for cargo loading. It also carries integral mechanical cargo loading and handling machinery.

The 747-200F freighter can carry a maximum payload of about 250,000 pounds for more than 3000 miles. It will carry more than 200,000 pounds over 4000 miles, or well beyond the transatlantic range. Maximum gross take-off weight is 833,000 pounds. The freighter and convertible 747s have a mechanized cargo handling system on the main deck. The nose swings up (as in the 747C) so pallets or 8 foot by 8 foot containers can be loaded straight in on the power-driven cargo system. Two men, one at the nose and one in the interior of the airplane, can complete the unloading and loading cycle in 60 minutes.

The seventh derivative of the basic 747 was the 747SP (Special Performance), which was designed to fly higher, faster and farther than any other airplane in its class. It is 47 feet shorter than the standard model, and is suited for air routes where passenger traffic requires an airliner with a capacity between that of a 707 and a full-size 747.

The first 747SP was rolled out of the Boeing 747 Division factory in Everett, Washington, on 19 May 1975. It first flew on 4 July in a test flight that the pilot described as the most ambitious test series ever attempted on the first flight of a Boeing jetliner. The fourth 747SP, and the first to be fitted with a full passenger interior, went on a world demonstration tour in late 1975. The first four airplanes made up the test group for certification, and then became part of the Pan American World Airways fleet. Certification for commercial service came on 4 February 1976.

Pan Am received its first 747SP on 5 March 1976, and put it into non-stop service between Los Angeles and Tokyo, and New York and Tokyo. The latter was the longest scheduled non-stop route until Pan Am itself went one better and began a flight between San Francisco and Sydney, Australia. This service, started in December 1976, covers 7197 miles. Proving its long-range ability even more, a 747SP being delivered to South African Airways flew non-stop from Paine Field to Capetown. It was a 10,290 mile flight, and it was made in 17 hours 22 minutes.

Although the 747SP is shorter than the standard 747, it has the same cabin width, and the usual three decks. The upper deck has a capacity of 32 passengers, but because the 747SP is shorter, overall seating capacity is reduced by 110.

The 747SP differs from earlier 747s in several other respects. It has a lighter weight structure in parts of the wing, fuselage and landing gear. It also has a taller tail, with double-hinged rudder for control equalling that of the other 747s. It has a horizontal stabilizer wider than those on the earlier models, and it carries new trailing-edge flaps. Cruising altitude is from 4000 to 6000 feet higher than any other wide-body jetliner, providing passengers with a smoother ride. A welcome feature to operators and pilots alike is the 747SP's ability to overfly slower air traffic on congested routes. The -SP's speed has reached Mach 0.97 in tests, without experiencing flutter. It normally cruises at over 600mph.

As we have seen, the 747 has been pressed into duty in special applications for the Air Force. The E-4 Airborne Command Post, a modified Boeing 747 aircraft equipped with extensive electronics, would be the critical communication link in the event of an attack on the United States. Another 747 has been acquired by NASA for use as a carrier for the Space Shuttle. While more like an airplane than any spacecraft before it, the Space Shuttle Orbiter does not have the air-breathing engines necessary for powered flight within the atmosphere. It glides to a landing, and when necessary must be transported back to its launch pad for reuse.

NASA bought a 747-100 from American Airlines on 18 July 1974, and Boeing modified it for its piggyback role. The shuttle-carrier is capable of ferrying the Orbiter from its landing site at Edwards Air Force Base in California back to the Kennedy Space Center launching pad in Florida. It can also carry the Orbiter from secondary landing sites in the Pacific back to Kennedy.

Design work for the transformation of the passenger carrying -100 into the Orbiter transporter began in April 1974. Actual modification started on 2 August 1976, and was officially completed on 14 January 1977. The Rockwell International Corporation's Space Division was the prime contractor for the job, and Boeing turned the shuttle-carrier over to them.

During a series of tests that followed the arrival of the shuttle-carrier at Edwards Air Force Base, the 747 and the Orbiter proved themselves. There were 13 747/Orbiter flights in this series. Five were with the Orbiter unmanned, and systems inactive. Three were with the Orbiter manned and electrically powered, but still attached to the 747. During the remaining five missions, the Orbiter was released from the back of the 747 at altitudes above 20,000 feet for unpowered glide landings at Edwards. These missions proved the Orbiter's ability to land safely after space flights.

The modified 747-100 is equipped to carry the Orbiter atop its fuselage attached by struts at three points on the Orbiter. One is forward, two are aft. The attach points match socket fittings built into the Orbiter for attachment to its external take-off fuel tank. Among the modifications needed to fit the 747 for its new duty was the addition of horizontal stabilizer tip fins, each measuring 10 feet by 20 feet. These fixed-position fins give the aircraft added aerodynamic stability when it is carrying the Orbiter. The aircraft's longitudinal trim system was also modified to counteract a nose-up tendency caused by downwash off the Orbiter wing onto the 747's horizontal stabilizer. Modifications were also made in the cockpit for controls and displays necessary for air-launching and ferry missions. Under a separate contract the 747's P&W JT9D-3A engines were converted to the JT9D-7AH, increasing take-off thrust from 43,500 pounds to 46,950 pounds. In all, the modifications added 11,500 pounds to the plane's weight, but as the world has seen, the conversion was a great success.

In addition to the two special versions required by the Air Force and NASA, Boeing listened to its commercial customers.

Above: Three of Trans World Airlines' 18 747s are the **747SP** version.

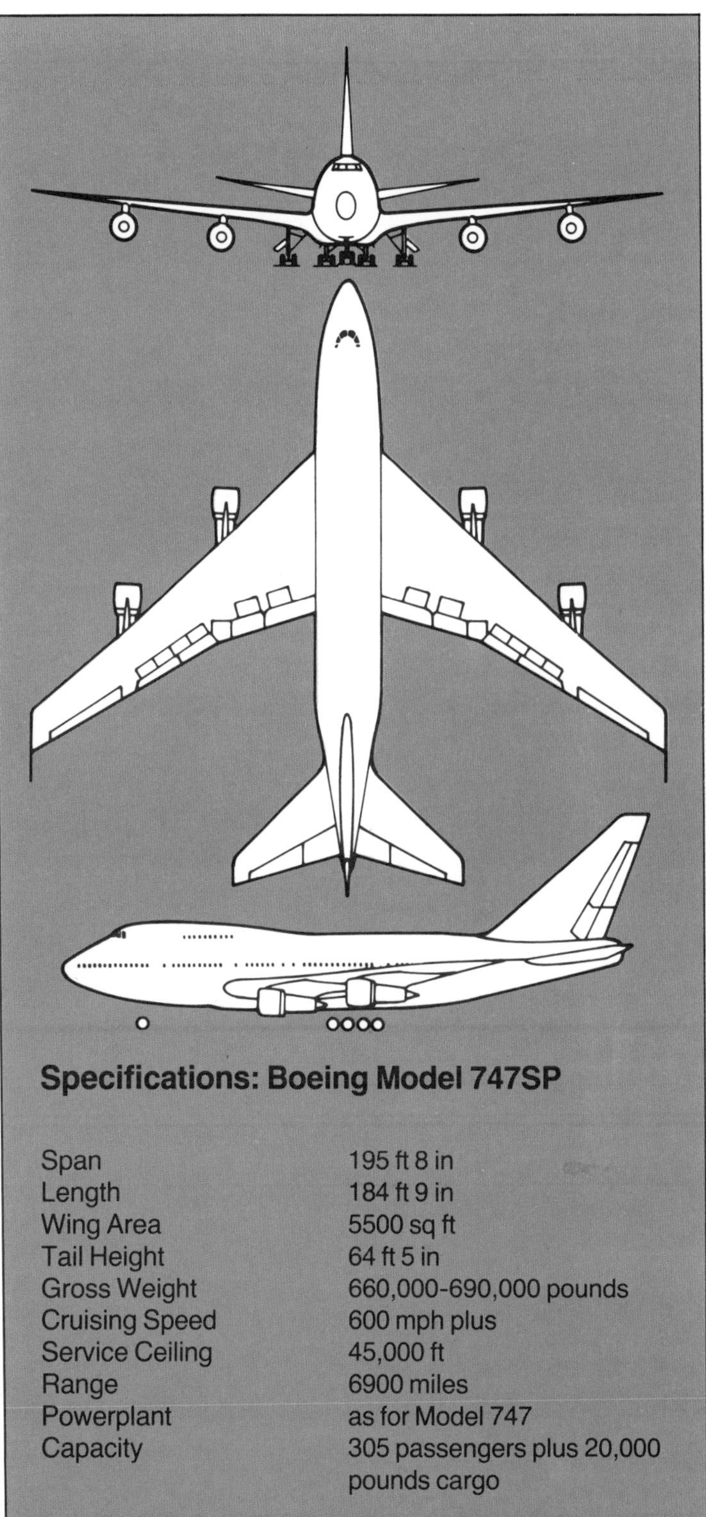

Specifications: Boeing Model 747SP

Span	195 ft 8 in
Length	184 ft 9 in
Wing Area	5500 sq ft
Tail Height	64 ft 5 in
Gross Weight	660,000-690,000 pounds
Cruising Speed	600 mph plus
Service Ceiling	45,000 ft
Range	6900 miles
Powerplant	as for Model 747
Capacity	305 passengers plus 20,000 pounds cargo

Above: **NASA's 747-100** with specially modified tail surfaces lifts off with the space shuttle *Enterprise* aboard.

Above: The **space shuttle** is mounted aboard the 747 mother ship in a specially designed gantry.

Below: Air India invites the passenger to travel like a maharaja aboard its 11-plane **747-200B** fleet with specially painted window frames.

Above: A mockup of the **747's 280-inch extended upper deck** in Boeing's Everett facility.

As with all of its airplanes, the 747 customer received his special needs. When Philippine Airlines wanted sleeping accommodation, 14 'Skybeds,' full-length beds, were built in, reminiscent of the famed Boeing Clippers of the 1930s and 1940s.

Though the 747 was designed with every thought for passenger safety, accidents happen. In late June 1982, a British Airways 747 went into a five-mile plunge, as a result of ash-clogged engines. The airplane, carrying 224 passengers and a crew of 16, was flying from Kuala Lumpur, Malaysia, to Perth, Australia, when it ran into a thick cloud of ash that had spewed from Mount Galunggung, 180 miles southeast of Jakarta. The engines choked off, and the giant airliner fell 25,000 feet before the pilots were able to start the engines once more. Despite 'sandblasted' windows hampering visibility, the pilot, Captain Eric Moody, managed to land at Jakarta. Except for a bad scare, nobody was injured.

The 747 Superjet is super in more ways than being big: by 1982, it had carried 370,000,000 people, nearly twice the population of the United States. The combined fleet of 747s flies 2.7 million miles a day. These figures indicate amazing reliability.

The 747 has a list of astonishing features. When the 747 is fully pressurized, nearly a ton of air is added to the weight. The Wright brother's first flight at Kitty Hawk could have been performed within the length of the 225 foot fuselage. The wing area of a 747 is 5500 square feet, larger than a basketball court. The lower-lobe baggage and cargo handling system can load or unload 85,000 pounds of baggage, the equivalent of 3400 pieces, in less than seven minutes. The power required to light the main 747 manufacturing building at Everett is enough to light up more than 32,000 average American homes. The tail height of the 747 is equivalent to that of a six-story building. Smaller than an office file drawer and about as light as a standard electric typewriter, the navigation system for the Boeing 747 can provide completely automatic guidance to any point on Earth with no outside contact.

A 747 freighter, certified to have the heaviest weight of any aircraft ever built, was delivered to Cargolux, the Luxembourg-based all-cargo airline. The aircraft has a take-off weight of 833,000 pounds, over 416 tons! This allows Cargolux to carry additional fuel for greater range, or a payload consisting of over 250,000 pounds of cargo.

In the early 1980s, as a result of record interest rates and escalating fuel prices, demand for 747s slackened. It is also indicative, to a certain degree, of market saturation. As of 1982, Boeing had put almost six hundred 747s into service around the world with 64 operators. The need for a 500-passenger aircraft, while significant, is finite.

A major development for the 747 in the early 80s occurred when Swissair purchased five of the superjets with extended upper decks. In the new layout (Boeing designation 747-300), as many as 69 passengers can be accommodated on the longer upper deck, increasing passenger seating by 44 over any seating arrangement then in service. The 747-300 exemplified Boeing's continuing efforts to come up with ways to increase airplane productivity by adding payload capacity. When the first 747 entered service the upper deck was certified for only eight passengers.

With the onset of the 1980s, production of 747s became marked more and more by special variants such as the 747-300, and production levels of 747s began to decline in favor of the superjet's new Everett roommate, the 767. Designed as the first all-new Boeing design since the 747, the 767 will share the Everett manufacturing complex, and will be Boeing's flagship of the 80s as the 747 was in the 1970s.

BOEING VERTOL

About the year 1500 the great artist and engineer Leonardo da Vinci planned a helicopter. His drawing shows an airscrew type machine with a helical wing. When rotated, the wing would have lifted the machine – in theory, at least. However, Leonardo never followed through on his concept, and the idea remained a dream.

Man tinkered with the idea of vertical lift throughout the years. In 1809, Englishman George Cayley published a design for a model helicopter. It worked on the principle of two contra-rotating air screws, and was the subject of much popular attention in Great Britain, for a time. Cayley's model has been the prototype for subsequent experiments in helicopter invention.

In the early 1930s, another inventor, Igor Sikorsky, started design work on helicopters. By 1938 he had produced the Vought-Sikorsky VS-300. Fitted with cyclic pitch control, his machine used a single rotor for lift, the torque being counteracted by two small tail rotors. Tethered to the ground, the VS-300 made a tentative ascent on 14 September 1939. Its first free flight came on 13 May 1940, and it was this flight that ushered the first practical single-rotor helicopter into the airways of the world.

Helicopter development continued under such names as Sikorsky, Bell, Hughes, Hiller, Piasecki and Kaman. Frank Piasecki and a group of young engineers, formed the P-V Engineering Forum in the early 1940s. This organization designed and built the PV-2, which flew first on 11 April 1943. It was the second US helicopter to be flown publicly. The P-V Engineering Forum also developed the PV-3 for the Navy in 1944. It flew on 6 March 1945 and became known as the 'Dog Ship.' Only one PV-3 was manufactured.

In 1946, the company changed its name to the Piasecki Helicopter Corporation. As such, the company designed and built the world's first tandem-rotor helicopter, the XHRP-1. It flew first on 3 November 1946, and two more were sold to the Navy. It was promptly dubbed the 'Banana,' because of its shape. In spite of this shape the XHRP-1 was a success, and the Navy ordered 20 more. Officially called the 'Rescuer,' the less-formal nickname stuck, and is still applied to helicopters with long bodies.

In the late 1950s Piasecki and other helicopter manufacturers were breaking away from piston-driven powerplants and experimenting with turbine engines. The Kaman Aircraft Corporation made its first experiments with a Boeing 520 gas turbine while Piasecki developed the turbine powered YH-16 for the USAF in 1955 and in 1957 delivered the H-21, each with two turbines to the Army. A new era was beginning. During this period also the

Piasecki company became the Vertol Corporation. In 1960 Boeing purchased the business and it became the Vertol Division of the Boeing Company.

On taking over Boeing enlarged the main plant and manufacturing facilities which were located on a 300 acre site in Delaware County, just outside of Philadelphia, Pennsylvania. The complex, today known as Boeing Center, is situated about three miles from the Philadelphia International Airport. Over 2,000,000 square feet of covered area are devoted to the manufacture of helicopters and aircraft assemblies. This huge area includes a 1,250,000-square-foot manufacturing room, engineering and office complexes, and a whirl tower for testing rotor blades. Boeing Vertol has one of the largest wind tunnels in the United States. The company's Flight Test Center is located at the Greater Wilmington Delaware Airport, 25 miles south of Boeing Center. It is situated on an 8.4 acre site, and consists of two buildings, which house computers and automatic data acquisition equipment to monitor helicopter flights. The Test Center is designed to handle the simultaneous flight testing of four helicopters.

In 1972 Boeing's Vertol Division became the Boeing Vertol Company. Since that time, the company has delivered over 2500 tandem-rotor helicopters (in which the company specializes) to the US military services and many foreign nations.

In April 1958 the turbine powered Model 107 made its appearance, and has reached a wide market throughout the world. The first of the 25 passenger Vertol 107-II helicopters was completed for commercial service by New York Airways, in 1961. It replaced the older Vertol 44s, which had gone into service under the Piasecki name in 1956. By 1965, two 107-IIs were transporting a record 44,000 passengers monthly. Also in 1965, Kawasaki

Specifications: CH-46E Sea Knight
Boeing Vertol Model Number 107

Rotor Diameter (each)	51 ft
Fuselage Length	44 ft 10 in
Maximum Weight	23,300 pounds
Top Speed	166 mph
Cruising Speed	150 mph
Range	230 miles plus
Powerplant	two 1870 shp General Electric T58-16

Specifications: CH-113
Boeing Vertol Model Number 107-II

Rotor Diameter (each)	50 ft
Fuselage Length	44 ft 7 in
Maximum Weight	22,000 pounds
Top Speed	168 mph
Cruising Speed	153 mph
Range	750 miles
Powerplant	two 1400 shp General Electric GECT-58-140

Below and opposite: Exterior and interior views of a USMC **CH-46E Sea Knight** helicopter aboard a helicopter carrier.

Above: A US Army **CH-47 Chinook** of the 1st Air Cavalry Division dumps drums of riot-control gas on suspected Vietcong positions during Operation Pershing near Binh Dinh, Vietnam, in July 1967.

Below: A US Army **CH-47** landing to pick up troops in Vietnam.

Heavy Industries of Japan acquired worldwide marketing rights (except for military versions in North America) and continues to produce these helicopters under the designation KV-107/II.

The US Army ordered ten Model 107s in July 1958 under the designation YCH-1A. The first one flew 13 months later, but by that time the Army was more interested in the Vertol Model 114, and the original order was reduced to three.

In 1961, a special version of the Model 107 won a US Navy design competition for a Marine Corps assault transport helicopter. With the primary mission of deploying large numbers of combat-equipped Marines to remote areas, the Sea Knight became operational with squadrons of the Fleet Marine Corps in early 1965. It was originally designated HRB-1 but this was changed to CH-46A.

The CH-46D, a later version, carried a crew of three and up to 25 troops. It could fly 4000 pounds of equipment over a radius of 115 miles at 150mph. This ability was more than twice that of the helicopters it replaced. The CH-46D is essentially similar to the CH-46A, but incorporates 1400shp (shaft horsepower) General Electric T58-GE-10 turboshaft engines. A later version for the Marines added a more advanced avionics package and was designated CH-46F. Some 273 of the USMC Sea Knights are being retrofitted with 1870shp T58-GE-16 turboshafts, and will be redesignated CH-46E. Other CH-46E improvements will

Specifications: CH-47A Chinook
Boeing Vertol Model Number 114

Main Rotor Diameter (each)	59 ft 1¼ in
Fuselage Length	51 ft
Maximum Weight	33,000 pounds
Top Speed	175 mph
Cruising Speed	155 mph
Range	962 miles
Powerplant	two 2200 shp Avco Lycoming T55-L-5

Specifications: CH-47C Chinook
Boeing Vertol Model Number 234

Main Rotor Diameter (each)	60 ft
Fuselage Length	51 ft
Maximum Weight	50,000 pounds
Top Speed	195 mph
Cruising Speed	170 mph
Range	250 miles
Powerplant	two 3750 shp Avco Lycoming T55-L-11A

Specifications: International Military Chinook
Boeing Vertol Model Number 414

Main Rotor Diameter (each)	60 ft
Fuselage Length	51 ft
Maximum Weight	50,000 pounds
Powerplant	two 4500 shp Avco Lycoming T55-L-712

include pilot and co-pilot crash attenuating seats, crash and combat-resistant fuel systems and an improved rescue system. The program is scheduled for completion in 1983.

Another program was launched in 1975 to replace metal rotor blades in the entire US Navy/Marine H-46 helicopter fleet. The more structurally reliable fiberglass blades are to be used. Approximately 2600 fiberglass blades will be replaced during a ten year period.

The Safety, Reliability and Maintainability (SR&M) Program commenced in December 1980. This program will extend the life of another 368 H-46 helicopters. The program includes 29 individual changes, the major changes being complete aircraft rewiring to the current state-of-the-art technology, and an advanced flight control system.

In January 1964 the US Navy ordered another series of Sea Knights, which it designated UH-46A. Its primary duty was in replenishment of combat ships. Since 1964 additional orders for the Model 107 have been placed by the Royal Canadian Air Force, where it is known as the CH-113 Labrador. It is also employed by the Canadian Army as the CH-113 Voyager. The Royal Swedish Navy and Air Force both ordered the 107 using the designation HKP-4, for both services.

The Boeing Vertol Model 114 is a larger, more powerful version of the Model 107. It was originally evaluated by the US Army under the designation YHC-1B in September 1961. It was selected as the Army's Battlefield Mobility helicopter and deliveries began in May 1967 under the designation CH-47A Chinook. Since then the Army has received 354 CH-47As, 108 CH-47Bs and 270 CH-47Cs.

During the Vietnam War, the helicopter matured as a gunship and deployment vessel for combat troops. Wartime exigencies brought out the good and bad points of helicopter transports, but the lessons learned were learned the hard way. Some 5000 helicopters of all types were lost during counter-insurgency (COIN) campaigns. Despite the losses helicopters proved their value and the US military forces are now the largest users of rotor aircraft in the world, with some 9000 machines. This compares to the Soviet Union with 6000 machines.

Because helicopters are often vulnerable to ground fire, a version of the Chinook was built in 1965 with improved protection. Called the Armed/Armored Chinook, it carried a heavy arsenal and enough armor to protect the crew and vital parts against ground fire. A grenade launcher was placed in the nose, and was turret mounted, controlled by the pilot. The flanks were protected by four gunners, two on each side of the cabin, using either 7.62mm or .50 caliber machine guns on flexible mounts. Another gunner was stationed aft on the rear loading ramp. A new type of steel armor plate was built into crew seats and other steel plates were positioned to deflect hostile bullets from different vital areas of the aircraft. Over a ton of steel plate was installed, assuring a high degree of survivability. This version served in Vietnam.

More recently a CH-47 Modernization Program has begun which will result in 436 of the earlier version CH-47A/B/Cs being upgraded and redesignated CH-47D. This new version will extend the life, increase the operational capabilities and lower the operating costs of the Army's medium-lift helicopter fleet. The CH-47 Modernization Program meets these goals at the lowest possible cost. At present, 28 aircraft have been contracted for with the Army, with 24 in the DOD FY 1983 budget request. Production is planned to continue into the early 1990s.

Modernization of the first CH-47D aircraft has been completed with the initial flight taking place on 26 February 1982, 13 days ahead of schedule. Before undergoing the modernization process, this aircraft had compiled a 2600 flight hour record as a CH-47A. As a completely modernized aircraft, the new CH-47D was delivered to the US Army on 20 May 1982, 11 days ahead of schedule.

The Modernization Program began in 1976 when, after four years of extensive study and review, the Army signed a research and development contract to build three CH-47D model prototypes. These aircraft have since successfully completed an extensive 1500-hour flight test program. During this program, they demonstrated that the CH-47D met or exceeded all of its reliability, availability and maintainability characteristics, as well as providing improved operational capabilities.

These improved operational capabilities were brought about by several new components and systems which have been incorporated into the D model, including improved transmissions with 7500shp rating; redundant and improved electrical systems; fiberglass rotor blades; Avco-Lycoming T55-L-712 engines with emergency power; modularized hydraulic systems; triple cargo hook suspension system; advanced flight control system; improved avionics; aircraft survivability equipment; single point pressure refueling; night vision goggle compatibility and a T62-T-2B auxiliary power unit.

The CH-47 Modernization Program involves more than just the installation of new components and systems. Each aircraft

Specifications:
Model 234 Commercial Chinook
Boeing Vertol Model Number 234

Main Rotor Diameter (each)	60 ft
Fuselage Length	52 ft 1 in
Maximum Weight	51,000 pounds
Top Speed	195 mph
Cruising Speed	170 mph
Range	852 miles
Powerplant	two 3750 shp Avco Lycoming T55-L-11C

Above: Boeing's **Model 234 Commercial Chinook** helicopter began service with British Airways Helicopters during 1981, supporting oil exploration and development activities in the North Sea. Currently, BAH operates five daily round-trip flights to the Shell/Esso Brent platform (seen here), 270 nautical miles offshore. Six of the 44-seat helicopters are used to transport oil workers to offshore platforms from Aberdeen, Scotland. The 234, the helicopter of choice for North Sea oilmen, is now also in service with Norway's Helikopter Service A/S, operating out of Stavanger, Norway. Helikopter Service will shuttle oil-company personnel between their Forus heliport, near Stavanger, and the offshore oil platforms in the Ekofisk and Valhall fields some 170 nautical miles offshore.

Upon entering the Boeing 234, the passenger steps into a comfortable interior whose standup head room, seating, overhead baggage bins, galley service and stereo headphones make it strikingly similar to the interior found on many contemporary jetliners.

Above: The **Chinook HC Mk 1** used by Britain's Royal Air Force is similar to the US Army CH-47C. Several Chinooks were sent to the Falklands in 1982 but only one saw service. The others went down with the container ship *Atlantic Conveyor* which was sunk before they were deployed.

Top right: The Boeing Vertol **Model 179** commercial version of the unsuccessful YUH-61A Army helicopter is still in service with the Vertol Company.

Second from top, right: The **CH-47D** is the result of an extensive modernization program of the US Army's CH-47A/B/C fleet. While the program is costly, the result is a virtually new aircraft (hence the redesignation) which is a more cost-effective means of obtaining new helicopters.

Third from top, right: The Boeing Vertol **Model 347** first flown in 1970 was a CH-47A which was experimentally retrofitted with 340-square-foot wings.

Right: The Bell-Boeing **TiltRotor XV-15** proposal. This aircraft could hover like a helicopter but would operate with airplane-like speed and range.

is cleaned, stripped to its frame and then separated into sections. When finished, a new aircraft will be available for the Army's use, regardless of its prior history. Each of the three prototypes had logged over 2500 flight hours and was involved in combat operations in Vietnam leading to varying degrees of fuselage damage.

The D model has a maximum gross weight rating of 50,000 pounds, with an empty weight of 23,189 pounds. It can also be used for external load lifting with its center cargo hook rated at 26,000 pounds, while both its forward and aft cargo hooks can move loads as large as 25,000 pounds. This leads to improved operational flexibility which supports the Army field commander's ability to conduct combat operations.

Examples abound of the types of missions only the CH-47D can perform. It can transport the M198 howitzer, the Army's new 155mm artillery piece. It is capable of lifting, with its center cargo hoist, a D5 Caterpillar bulldozer (gross weight 24,750 pounds). It enhances the Army's resupply capability by being able to lift Milvans (Army supply containers) at speeds up to 138 knots, two or three times current capability. It can also carry up to seven fuel blivets (each weighing 3500 pounds when fully loaded) in a single mission.

When compared to the model A Chinook, the CH-47D offers more than a 100 percent increase in performance when operated in a standard European climate. It also offers a 68 percent increase in performance capability when compared to both A and B models when operated in a hot climate.

By modernizing the Chinook fleet the Army will meet its medium-lift helicopter requirements, while saving over $1 billion in development and operating costs. Fleet modernization, rather than designing and developing a new helicopter, has cut the time to field an advanced medium lift helicopter.

Since Boeing Chinook helicopters were introduced in the early 1960s, almost 1000 have been sold in 14 countries. During this period, they have logged more than 1.6 million hours of flight time. While the majority have gone to the US Army as CH-47s, a number have been acquired by the armed services of Canada, Spain, Italy, Iran, Libya, Morocco, Australia, Thailand, Argentina, Tanzania, Greece, Austria, Germany, South Korea, Turkey, Egypt, South Vietnam (before it became part of reunified Vietnam) and the United Kingdom.

Currently production is under way on an order for 33 military Chinooks for the Royal Air Force. First going into service in August 1980 under the RAF designation HCMk I, it incorporates such features as fiberglass blades, triple cargo hooks and an advanced flight control system, all of which will be standard on the US Army CH-47D. A single British Chinook saw action in the Falklands in 1982. The similar international military Chinook, Vertol Model 414, is also going into service with the Spanish Army's Transport Battalion, BHELTRA-V. The first of the Spanish 414s, powered by Avco-Lycoming T55-L-712 engines, was delivered in June 1982.

The Chinook has a combat-proven record of achieving rapid deployment of men and materiel. It can transport up to 44 combat personnel to new positions in minutes, carry up to 14 tons with its three-hook system or accommodate up to 24 litters for medevac operations.

In addition to its combat service, the Chinook has been an important vehicle in rescue and relief missions. Chinooks have proven especially valuable in moving people and goods to and from remote areas made even more inaccessible by the ravages of natural disasters. In the early 1970s US Army CH-47Cs rescued people stranded on a mountainside in Huaraz, Peru after a disastrous earthquake made the town inaccessible. A few years later, US Army Chinooks were again put into service in the aftermath of earthquakes in Guatemala and Nicaragua. Spanish Army Chinooks were also used during the mid-70s for disaster relief, rescuing thousands of people that had been stranded by flood waters in rural areas. The US Army used some of its CH-47Bs to lift cars and trucks stranded by the eruption of Mount St Helens in May 1980. When President Jimmy Carter made an inspection of the disaster site, he and his entourage were aboard Army Chinooks.

Above: The fuselage of Vertol's **Heavy-Lift Helicopter (HLH)** (Boeing Vertol Model 301). The prototype, designated XCH-62A, was powered by three 8079shp XT701 turboshaft engines.

Just as Kawasaki in Japan obtained a manufacturing license for the Model 107, so has the Agusta Group of Cascina Costa, Italy been licensed by Vertol to manufacture the Chinook. The Agusta Group has Chinook sales and service contracts throughout the world as well as in Italy. While Boeing Vertol has licensed foreign firms to manufacture its products abroad, it has itself obtained a license to market the German Messerschmitt-Bölkow-Blohm Bo-105 executive and utility helicopter in Canada, Mexico and the United States.

In November 1978 the Boeing Vertol Company introduced its first commercial Model 234 Chinook, which was ordered by British Airways Helicopters, Ltd. BAH ordered three and has since placed orders for three more.

There are two versions of the 234. The 234LR (Long Range) is a passenger carrier and the other, the 234UT (Utility), is a cargo carrier. The 44-seat 234LR features the most restful and attractive helicopter interior ever developed. Major features

include stand-up headroom, a refreshment galley, a lavatory and in-flight music. There are large jumbo-jet type overhead baggage bins, and 727 style windows. The lighting is soft and there is carpeting on the deck.

The 234 was certified for passenger operations by the FAA on 19 June 1981. It was certified to a maximum gross take-off weight of 48,500 pounds, and for full day/night IFR (bad weather) operations. Approval for British passenger service was received when the Civil Aviation Authority issued its Airworthiness Approval Note on 26 June 1981.

The 234 began scheduled passenger service with BAH on 1 July 1981, and is currently used in transporting workers to off-shore oil platforms in the North Sea. Nearly 41,500 passengers were carried during its first seven months of service, such service made possible by its bad-weather capabilities, substantial fuel reserves and a cruising speed of 135 knots. It has a 574 nautical mile flight range. It is powered by twin Avco Lycoming AL5512 engines, each delivering a continuous rating of 2975shp. Should one of the powerplants fail, its twin can be boosted to an emergency rating of 4355shp to bring the 234 safely home. For flights over the stormy North Sea, passengers would not have it any other way. The engines are podded and are easily accessible for maintenance.

The Utility 234 was certified by the FAA on 2 October 1981. It was approved for a maximum gross weight of 51,000 pounds for external lift missions, giving it an external lift capacity of 14 tons for altitudes up to 12,000 feet. It is particularly useful in logging operations and in mining efforts far from the beaten path in high mountains or deep jungles. The 234 Utility is powered with the same Lycoming engines as the passenger ship.

In response to a US Army competition aimed at producing a successor to the ubiquitous Bell UH-1 Huey assault/transport helicopter, Boeing Vertol developed the YUH-61A which was flown in competition with Sikorsky's YUH-60A. The competition and flight testing concluded in December 1976, with Sikorsky being declared the winner. The YUH-61A was a twin engined advanced technology helicopter with a unique hingeless rotor system with a lightweight titanium hub and four fiberglass rotor blades. The prototype could accommodate up to 20 troops or mixtures of troops and materiel.

Vertol's parallel development of the commercial version, Model 179, ended at the same time with again a single prototype. This machine remains in company service and can carry 14–20 passengers.

For the future, Boeing Vertol has plans for a BV-234-68, which is a stretched version of the 234. If British Airways Helicopters gives the green light, the machine could be ready by 1985. The BV-234-68 would have two 5000shp T64/T5A engines, and a gross weight of 51,500 pounds. At a cruising speed of 160mph, with 68 passengers, its range is calculated at 345 miles.

The BV-234-68 will be an improvement insofar as passenger and cargo capacity are concerned, but Boeing Vertol plans to beat even that. The company's proposed BV-307, seating 225, makes its older brothers seem small. The BV-307 would be operational by 1989.

The company was recently awarded a contract to continue such heavy lift helicopter (HLH) studies. Forging ahead on all fronts, commercial and military, Boeing Vertol is following in its parent company's footsteps. Where the latest developments are, there, too, is Boeing Vertol. When better helicopters are in the sky, Boeing will have representatives among them.

Specifications: YUH-61A
Boeing Vertol Model Number 179

Main Rotor Diameter	49 ft
Fuselage Length	51 ft 9 in
Maximum Weight	18,700 pounds
Top Speed	195 mph
Cruising Speed	190 mph
Range	300 miles plus
Powerplant	two 1500 shp General Electric T700-GE-700

Specifications: Commercial Model 179
Boeing Vertol Model Number 179

Main Rotor Diameter	49 ft
Fuselage Length	51 ft 9 in
Maximum Weight	18,700 pounds
Top Speed	220 mph
Cruising Speed	200 mph
Range	475 miles
Powerplant	two General Electric GE-CT7-1

THE OTHER BOEING

The Boeing Company has passed through many changes since it began in 1916, but its primary aim has been to build airplanes. This is now closely partnered with the manufacture of missiles for national defense, and with inventing spaceships for probing the universe. There is another Boeing, though, one that investigates such terrestrial activities as computer technology, automated transit systems, agriculture, and even ships that fly.

As early as 1910, Bill Boeing showed his interest in boats when he purchased the E W Heath Shipyard in Seattle. Though his primary interest in the yard was to build a yacht for himself, the shipyard became a part of the Boeing airplane factory and Boeing's interest in boats remained.

In 1919 three years after the first flight of Boeing's first airplane, he became involved in developing the Hickham Sea Sled. The venture failed, but Boeing in the meantime became acquainted with Professor Frederick Kirsten of the University of Washington. Kirsten was interested in designing a cycloidal propeller and joined Boeing to form a company, K-B Engineering, to develop the idea. A sports boat, the M-879, was constructed to test the propeller, and it was launched in August 1922. According to eyewitnesses, the M-879 was provided 'substantial forward propul-

Right: The US Navy **PHM-2 Hydrofoil Missileship** built by Boeing Marine Systems at Renton was delivered to the Navy in 1972. The PHM-2 and her four sister ships are nearly 133 feet long, 28 feet wide and are powered by two Mercedes-Benz 8V331 diesels driving two Aerojet waterjets when hullborne and one GE LM2500 gas turbine with one waterjet when foilborne. The PHMs have a speed in excess of 40 knots when foilborne and a range of over 1200 nautical miles if hullborne. (The range is cut in half if the foils are deployed for the entire distance.) They carry a 21-man crew and are armed with eight Harpoon missiles and a 76mm rapid-fire gun.

Below: The *Bima Samudera* is a **Model 929 Jetfoil** built for the government of the Republic of Indonesia and delivered in 1982.

sion,' by its cycloidal propeller. The propeller also enabled the boat to turn on its own axis. The boat moved easily in shallow water, a forerunner of today's marine jet engines.

However, the project proved too costly for it to go into commercial production. Boat and prop would also be too expensive to maintain, and after sinking $150,000 into the venture, Boeing wrote off the K-B experiment in 1927.

Several Boeing officials were enthusiastic about the cycloidal propeller idea, though, and tinkered with the idea of using them instead of wings in a modified PW-9 pursuit aircraft. The propeller, it was believed, would give the airplane the ability to take off and land vertically. In effect, they were thinking 'vertol.' The company contracted Army and Navy engineers with their radical idea, but there was no money for such a project, and the matter was shelved. Had experiments taken place, Sikorsky, the helicopter pioneer, might have come in second.

In 1959 the Boeing company's interest in boats was renewed, when hydrofoil research began. Research culminated in 1960, with the completion of a hydroplane test craft. Constructed mainly of mahogony plywood, the boat was nicknamed 'Aquajet.' From above it looked like a giant lobster, with two prows reaching forward, each with a cockpit and instrument compartment. The open center was used like a wind tunnel for preliminary hydrodynamic testing.

Specifications: Jetfoil
Boeing Model Number 929

Cruising speed	42-45 knots
Weight	115 long tons
Length	90 ft
Beam	30 ft
Powerplant	two Allison 501-KF turbines, with two Rockedyne PJ-20 waterjet pumps. Engines rated at 3800 hp each
Crew	Two-six, depending on need

In 1962 Boeing Marine Systems (BMS), built another experimental boat, the *Little Squirt*. It was a company-financed vessel, built to prove the feasibility of waterjet propulsion, a system later used on all Boeing hydrofoils. *Little Squirt* demonstrated that hydrofoils have a 50 knot capability, an important quality. Speed was one of the requisites if hydrofoils were to compete with boats of conventional and proven capabilities.

It is generally agreed that airplanes belong in the air, boats on water, but it is different with hydrofoils. They seem to fly over the waves on waterborne wing-like structures. Attached to the hull by a system of struts, the foils lift the boat several feet above the surface, using water in the same way as airplane wings generate lift, allowing the boat to travel with its main bulk unaffected by water resistance.

There are two basic types of hydrofoil boats. On one, the foils ride on or near the surface of the water, following its contours, rising and dipping with the waves. At times this can let passengers in for a rough ride. A number of vessels using this type of foil are currently in use, mainly in Europe and Asia.

The other hydrofoil operates with its foils fully submerged. Being completely under water, this hydrofoil is unaffected by waves and other surface turbulence. The result is a smooth ride, even in rough water. BMS builds several different types of vessels with completely submerged foils.

Working on Navy contracts, BMS has experimented with a variety of hydrofoils. In 1965 the Navy awarded a contract to Boeing to build a hydrofoil gunboat. Named *Tucumcari* after the city in New Mexico, it was the first of its kind in naval history. Designated PGH-2, for Patrol Gunboat Hydrofoil-2, the *Tucumcari* was launched in July 1967, and 'flew' first in October. The vessel did not have a conventional propeller, but used Boeing's waterjet system of propulsion. Water was drawn through the craft's rear foil struts into a pump, then jetted through nozzles under the stern. There were no lubrication problems and no complicated transmission system as is required on propeller craft. A 3100shp gas turbine supplied the foil-borne power, while a second waterjet pump, powered by a 150bhp diesel, drove the ship during slower hull-borne operations.

The *Tucumcari* was 74.6 feet long, with a 19.5 foot beam, and was capable of speeds over 50 knots. It displaced approximately 60 tons, and the hull and superstructure were aluminum. The foils and struts were of corrosion-resistant steel. This swift little ship, a relative of the World War II PT-Boats, was manned by one officer and 12 crewmen. She had a short, but noble, history. After serving in the coastal waters off Vietnam, she was assigned to the Navy's Amphibious Force at Little Creek, Virginia. She became the prototype for the Patrol Hydrofoil Missileship (PHM). In the fall of 1972, the *Tucumcari* ran aground in the Caribbean and was decommissioned.

In November 1971 BMS was awarded a contract to design the Patrol Hydrofoil Missileship. With years of experience to draw on, BMS produced a satisfactory plan, and the company was awarded a construction contract.

On 9 November 1974, the first missileship, *Pegasus*, was launched. Designated PHM-1 by the Navy, she made her first 'flight' on 25 February 1975. In October that year, *Pegasus* made a record sailing from Seattle to San Diego in 31 hours and 21 minutes, averaging 37 knots. As the ship was 131.2 feet long, with a beam of 28.2 feet, and a displacement of 239.6 long tons, such speed was to be noted. It was, and a contract for five more PHMs was granted. Named after the constellations, as was the first, they are the *Hercules*, PHM-2, *Taurus*, PHM-3; *Aquila*, PHM-4; *Aries*, PHM-5 and *Gemini*, PHM-6.

Fully submerged foils and advanced automatic control systems give PHM the missile platform stability and ride comfort in heavy seas usually found only in large ships. A powerful offensive armament makes the PHM an effective weapons system for strike, patrol and surveillance missions. Waterjet systems, pioneered by Boeing, speed the craft along, when flying on its foils, or when traveling on its hull. The foil-borne system consists of a single Aerojet Liquid Rocket Company waterjet capable of pumping approximately 90,000 gallons per minute.

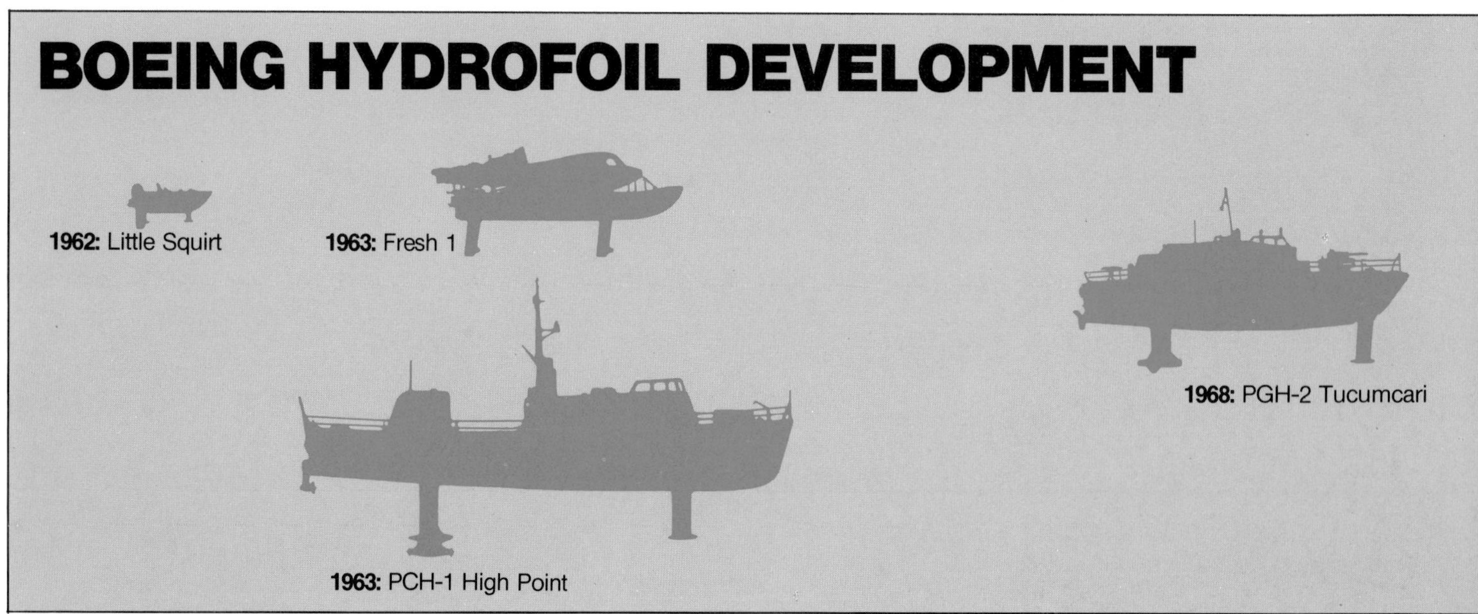

It is driven by a General Electric LM 2500 marine gas turbine. When hull borne the ship is powered by two 30,000gpm Aerojet waterjets. Each is driven by a Mercedes-Benz 8V331 diesel engine. Foil-borne cruising speed is in excess of 40 knots. The ship can be operated by as few as six officers and men on any watch, but berthing is provided for 24. The normal crew is 21, four officers and 17 enlisted personnel.

Boeing is not excluding the commercial possibilities of hydrofoils, and BMS has developed the *Jetfoil.* Hailed as a new dimension in marine transportation, the *Jetfoil* hydrofoil for commercial passenger use was announced in October 1972. The first one, Model 929-100, was launched 29 March 1974. Jetfoil service was initiated on 25 April 1975 by Far East Hydrofoil Ltd between Hong Kong and Macao.

The Jetfoil combines fully submerged, computer-controlled steel foils on an all-aluminum hull. Ride quality is unmatched by any other marine craft, assuring all passengers an unobstructed view, smooth and serene, even in rough seas. Environmentally, the Jetfoil claims kudos, too. Because only narrow struts pierce the water when foil borne, there is almost no wake. The Jetfoil is so well constructed that it had no problem finding certification in such diverse countries as the US, China, Venezuela, Belgium, Japan and Britain.

The ship has a 30-foot wide cabin, which allows for two decks with large seats. The standard configuration Jetfoil, the Model 929-100, can carry up to 250 passengers and provide space for luggage and galleys. Design flexibility permits variations according to what the customer needs, and as many as 350 seats can be provided.

Jetfoils are now in use throughout the world, from China to the Republic of Indonesia, making a total fleet of 18 vessels. A derivative, HMS *Speedy* (Model 929-115) was built for the British Royal Navy for North Sea patrols. Though the US has not used this remarkable design yet, it seems likely that the foreign market will expand.

In the spring of 1950, Lloyd Hull tested a Kenworth truck using a Model 502 175hp Boeing-developed gas turbine. Truckers who saw the twin-stacked vehicle were curious. They liked the engine, because the 502 weighed only 200 pounds. A standard diesel engine could weigh up to 2500 pounds. By any trucker's definition, that difference meant profits in the payload cargo. Development of the 502 continued, but *Boeing Magazine* for July 1951 revealed that the gas turbine seemed destined for a military rather than a commercial career. Pinpointing it further, the 502 was being tested on Navy boats in Lake Washington, adjacent to Seattle.

Improved 502s in the 240 330hp range were tested on everything military from tanks to helicopters to hydrofoils to pumps. A 520 series was developed by Boeing's Industrial Products Division, producing up to 600hp. Still another model was able to net 550hp. It might be pointed out here that Boeing had reserved model numbers 500–599 for industrial non-aircraft products. Models 502, 520, 540, 551 and 553 were gas turbine engines.

There were many firsts for Boeing gas turbines. They included the world's first turbine and twin turbine helicopters, first turbine highway truck, first turbine locomotive, commercial boat, earth-moving tractor, racing car, minesweeper and landing craft.

The market for the Boeing turbine seemed assured, but in 1969 the business was phased out. Competitors were making good products, and Boeing decided not to compete. The company decided that the money used on gas turbine development could be better employed on new airplanes and aerospace research. So Boeing bowed out.

With the swift proliferation of computers throughout the world, Boeing set up the Boeing Computer Service, BCS, in 1970. Its purpose was twofold: to fulfill the data processing requirements of The Boeing Company and to offer advanced information processing services to commercial and government markets. It currently services more than 2500 customers in the US, Canada, and Britain. To transmit data reliably and economically, BCS operates one of the largest privately managed telecommunications networks in the world. Major data centers are located in Philadelphia, Wichita, Vienna (Virginia) near Washington, DC, and two in the Seattle metropolitan area at Bellevue and Kent.

The people of BCS provide computer support services for business, scientific, engineering, industrial and government uses, as well as nationwide consulting, educational and other training services.

Ten years after its inception, the number of BCS commercial customers had risen to over 2500, including a substantial number of very large corporations. Because of increased demand for commercial data processing services in the fields of financial management and design engineering, BCS is emphasizing products relevant to these activities. Under one such contract, electronic funds transfer services are being provided to a con-

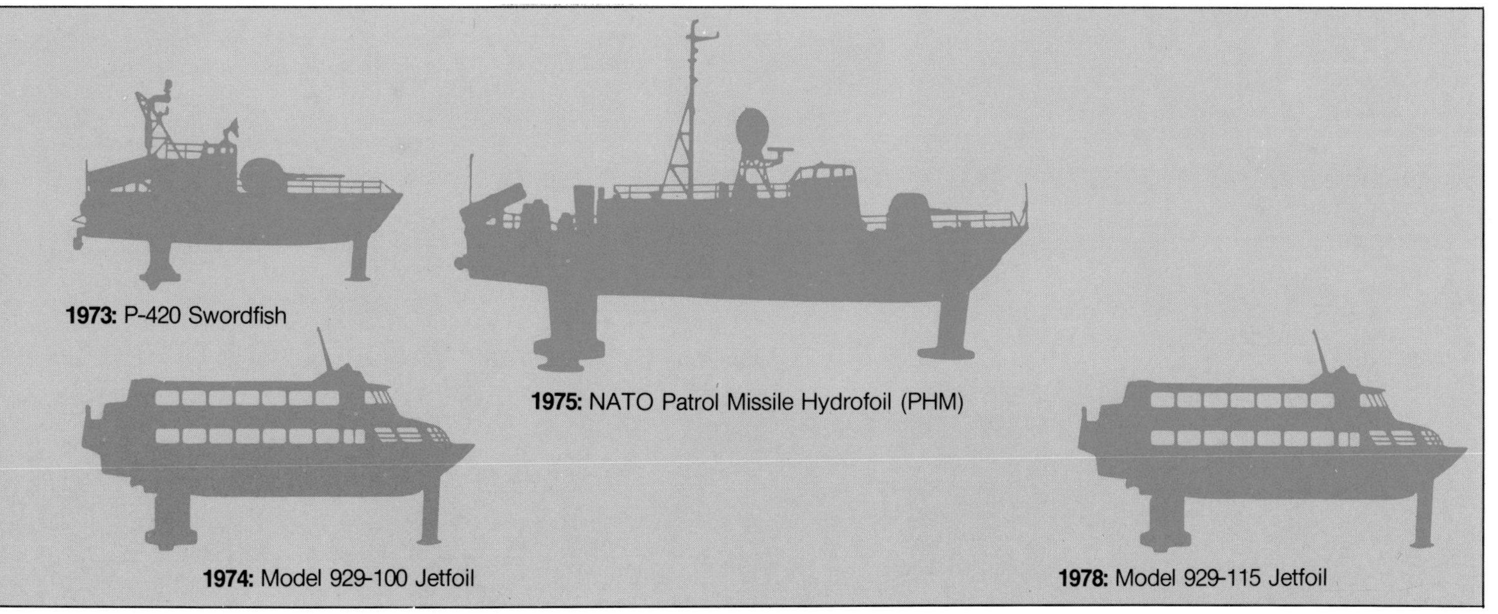

1973: P-420 Swordfish

1975: NATO Patrol Missile Hydrofoil (PHM)

1974: Model 929-100 Jetfoil

1978: Model 929-115 Jetfoil

Above: A **Model 929** jetfoil in service with Sealink on the English Channel.

Above right: The US Navy's **PHM-3** during trials on Puget Sound in 1982.

sortium of 22 mutual savings banks in New York City. Under another contract, BCS provides computer software and large scale data processing to 41 banks in the midwest.

In addition to its many major corporate customers, ranging from IBM's Federal Systems Division to the Exxon Product Research Company, BCS provides computer support for the Federal Energy Center in Richland, Washington and NASA's Marshall Space Flight Center in Huntsville, Alabama. The US General Accounting Office selected BCS to design and operate a consolidated computer system for use in managing assignments, finance and personnel.

BCS computers are now integrated into nearly every step of aircraft design and production at Boeing's aircraft divisions. They aided in the design and production of the new 757 and 767 aircraft, and then went on to provide computer support for the flight certification programs. Such certification can be accomplished quickly, because of new computing programs developed by BCS software engineers. The system verifies the validity of test conditions inflight.

In 1974, the Boeing Engineering and Construction organization was formed. The purpose was to use Boeing's engineering experience in exploring the tasks of producing energy and improving the environment.

Today, BEC is working with government agencies, utility composites and other companies on a variety of assignments. Projects include the development of wind, nuclear and solar power generating systems; energy control systems; the recovery of energy from waste; off-shore oil production and water systems management. In addition to all this BEC has become involved in construction and design.

The accomplishments of BEC have been many. The company manufactures centrifuge machines for nuclear fuel enrichment.

Below: Boeing's **Standard Light Rail Vehicle** in service with the Municipal Railway in San Francisco.

The design and construction of a fuel-enrichment facility for the Department of Energy in Oak Ridge, Tennessee was undertaken by BEC and two other contractors.

BEC has also taken a world lead in the design and development of large wind energy systems. In August 1977 the company was awarded a contract to design a wind turbine system, specifically tailored for unattended, remote operation. The contract called for the construction, installation and testing of three machines. The MOD-2 wind turbine is the largest ever built. Power production starts at a wind speed of 14mph with an automatic shutdown at 45mph. The MOD-2 utilizes a two-blade steel rotor that measures 300 feet from tip to tip. The rotor is mounted to the nacelle, a 37 foot long boxcar-shaped structure that houses the drive train, turbine-generator, electronics and other equipment. The nacelle is rotated by a mechanism that always keeps the rotor pointing into the wind. The whole arrangement is perched atop a 200-foot tall tubular steel tower.

The first three MOD-2 units, located near Goldendale, Washington, are part of the Bonneville Power Administration's power network. Ground was broken in May 1980, and all three units were synchronized with BPA a year later.

With the MOD-2 in successful operation, the future seems assured for megawatt-size wind machines as an important factor in the world's energy mix. Others are interested in the system and among them is the Pacific Gas and Electric Company of San Francisco. Boeing made its first commercial sale to PG&E in 1980. Another MOD-2 had been installed in Medicine Bow, Wyoming, under a program funded by the Federal Department of the Interior.

BOECON, a Boeing general construction subsidiary which has focused in part on nuclear power plants, is gradually expanding into the areas of water pumping stations and coal-fired electric power plants.

Solar energy projects have included the conceptual design of a commercial size plant that will utilize the sun's rays to generate power which would operate an evaporator to clean polluted water and make it potable for a small Texas town. Two advanced heliostats (sun-tracking mirrors) have been completed and successfully tested at a New Mexico test site.

Near Colorado Springs BEC has constructed a pair of Brine Concentrators that process 576,000 gallons of water daily, returning 98 percent of it for reuse in a coal-fired power plant. Work is now underway on similar projects in New Mexico, Nevada and Texas.

Boeing Services International (BSI), Incorporated provides services that benefit a variety of customers and programs. BSI was formed in 1972 as a wholly owned subsidiary of The Boeing Company to devote its total skill and resources to facilities operations and maintenance and technical support activities. BSI was a natural outgrowth of The Boeing Company's Field Operations and Support Division, which managed large government programs and supported launch operations for the nation's manned and unmanned space programs.

From this experience, the company developed a large manpower pool whose skills range through such diverse catagories as facilities operations and maintenance, spares support, systems installation and checkout, test operations, heavy equipment and vehicle maintenance, fire protection, supply, transport, aerospace ground systems operations and administration.

Below: The US Department of Energy's **Solar Test Facility** at Albuquerque, New Mexico. The spot of light on the tower is a 13-foot diameter cavity receiver designed and built by BEC and tested here at the Albuquerque facility. During the three months of testing, an increasing number of computer-controlled reflectors called heliostats was focused on the receiver. The receiver is designed to transfer the intense heat of the concentrated sunlight to a working fluid (in this case air) which in turn drives a turbine to produce electricity. Power levels reached the design condition of one megawatt, with a gas outlet temperature of 1500 degrees Fahrenheit.

Specifications: MOD-2 Wind Turbine

Rotor Diameter	300 ft
Tower Height	200 ft
Tower Diameter	21 ft (base) 10 ft (main shaft)
Rotor Orientation	Upwind
Rotor Airfoil	NACA 230XX
Rotor Tip Speed	275 ft/second
Rotor Speed	17.5 rpm
Rotor Tip Length (controllable)	45 ft
Rated Power	2.5 Megawatts
Average Annual Output	7.4 million kilowatt hrs
Generator Type	Synchronous
Pitch and Yaw Control	Hydraulic
Electronic Control	Microprocessor

Below: The Boeing **MOD-2** wind farm. Three giant wind turbines at the Goodnoe Hills near the Columbia River Gorge (upper left) in Washington State are now working together for the first time in the only multi-megawatt wind-turbine cluster in the US. To date they have produced more than two million kilowatt hours of electricity. The 2500 kilowatt MOD-2 wind turbines were designed and built by BEC under a program sponsored by the US Department of Energy and managed by NASA's Lewis Research Center. The output of the three machines, enough to provide electricity to 2000 average homes, is being fed into the Northwest power grid operated by the Bonneville Power Administration. The 350-foot-tall machines (from ground to tip of vertically extended blade), about one-third of a mile apart, are designed to begin producing power in winds of 14mph. They reach rated output in winds of 28mph, and when the wind exceeds 45mph, the blades automatically feather, shutting down the system.

The **MOD-5**, now in the detail design phase, represents the third generation of multi-megawatt machines. Analysis indicates that this machine will offer up to a 25 percent reduction in the cost of electricity compared to the MOD-2 under similar conditions.

Overseas, BSI provides support services ranging from traffic management and food services to communications and vehicle maintenance for eight major US military installations in Turkey and at USAF bases in Spain.

In October 1979 BSI was awarded a third European base maintenance contract at Hellenikon Air Base at Athens, and Iraklion on the island of Crete, together with five smaller sites in Greece. Boeing sells its support services by demonstrating that a private contractor can save money for the government. At a typical military installation, for example, turning over service functions to BSI can reduce manpower costs by as much as 25 percent. This also permits uniformed personnel to devote more of their time to combat-related duties.

Early in 1971 diversification was a watchword among many American corporations. Boeing was no different and in that year the company moved into the surface transportation field. Boeing Vertol was selected as systems manager for the Federal Government's Urban Rapid Rail Vehicle and Systems Program. One type was designed using traditional technology, whereas the other was an Advanced Concept Train (ACT) car for demonstrating the next generation of rapid transit cars. The 'current technology' train, designated SOAC, and consisting of two cars, was demonstrated on transit systems in New York, Boston, Cleveland, Chicago and Philadelphia.

Boeing Vertol also received contracts to build Light Rail Vehicles (LRV) for Boston and San Francisco. In both instances they were designed to replace existing streetcars on established routes. Vertol, the maker of helicopters, found itself blessed with the distinction of building the first streetcars to have been built in the United States in 20 years.

The two LRV contracts called for 175 cars to be delivered to the Massachusetts Bay Transportation Authority (MBTA), and 100 cars for the San Francisco Municipal Railway (MUNI). San Francisco, the city where the century-old cable cars 'climb half way to the stars,' was in the midst of a sort of transit revolution. The Bay Area Rapid Transit (BART) subway system was, after

years of bickering and delay, finally nearing completion and it was time to upgrade the city's streetcar system. BART is, in reality, more of a commuter railroad than a city transit system. With most of its stations located outside of the city limits and only one line actually running through the city, BART's primary function is to bring commuters to their jobs in downtown San Francisco. MUNI is San Francisco's real transit system, operating streetcars, buses and cable cars on hundreds of lines throughout the city. The excavation of Market Street, the city's transit hub, for installation of BART, provided MUNI with an opportunity to do something that they had wanted to do for many years. This was to put their streetcars underground along congested Market Street. The process was haunted by problems, not the least of which being that Market Street was a construction site for ten years, with many of the businesses located there abandoning it for adjacent streets. BART's problems could fill volumes, but MUNI's Vertol LRV had its share, among the most embarrassing of which were that initially the LRV's wheels were the wrong size for the tracks.

MBTA had problems too, but in November 1979 a settlement was reached resolving all outstanding disputes, claims and counter claims. In April 1980 the final MUNI LRVs were delivered, and after many teething troubles, the MUNI Metro, as the MUNI LRV system is called, is functioning according to plan and Market Street is slowly being revitalized.

Though the Boeing Vertol Company has withdrawn from the manufacturing of surface transportation vehicles after the costly experiments in Boston and San Francisco, in 1980 it received subcontracts from Kawasaki Heavy Industries to install equipment on LRVs and other rail transit cars for use in Philadelphia.

The Boeing Aerospace Company also became involved in ground transportation. A number of cities are looking for entirely new methods of transportation. Many major metropolitan governments are preparing to install a form of automated transit called Downtown People Movers in their central business districts. The project is being funded by the US Department of Transportation.

At present, there is only one automated transit system in operation in an urban setting. This is the People Mover at Morgantown, West Virginia. It was developed by BAC for the Department of Transportation's Urban Mass Transportation Administration (UMTA) and West Virginia University. It emerged from a long development and testing program to enter passenger service in October 1975. By 1979 expansion of the Morgantown People Mover's system was completed. It is 3.3 miles long, with a total of 8.7 miles of single-lane guideway, five passenger stations, and 73 vehicles.

The MPM system employs driverless vehicles which operate entirely under computer control. The cars cruise at up to 30mph, and being rubber-tired, they are virtually noiseless. They carry 21 passengers each, and can function in both good and bad weather. Though not yet perfected, the Downtown People Mover's program has attracted the attention of Los Angeles, Detroit, Miami, and St Paul. Such transportation seems to be the answer to smog problems, because it is electrically powered.

By 1977 the system was operating at an availability (reliability) rate of close to 100 percent and university students were being whisked from campus to campus in less than 10 minutes. Carrying some 17,000 passengers a day, it has demonstrated that automated guideway systems are now ready to serve cities much larger than Morgantown. The expanded MPM system is expected to have a ridership of six million passengers a year.

Operating statistics compiled at Morgantown indicate that such a system can achieve a lower cost per passenger-mile than today's urban bus systems. Its vehicles operate under the control of computers rather than drivers, and their movement is dictated strictly by passenger needs. This eliminates one of the principal causes of today's mounting transit deficits: manned buses traveling their routes nearly empty during off-peak hours. In the US the average load factor for buses is 18 percent; that is, the average bus runs 82 percent empty. Present load factor for the expanded Morgantown system is 33 percent.

Though Morgantown is generally viewed as the prototype for the coming forms of urban automated transit, it was preceded into public service by a similar system developed by Boeing and Kobe Steel of Japan for the International Ocean Exposition on the Japanese island of Okinawa, the 1975 World's Fair.

The Okinawa system, derived from Morgantown technology, linked major exhibits at the exposition with the main entrances to the site. During the fair's six-month run, the system's 16 vehicles carried more than four million riders. For its final six weeks of operation, the system maintained an availability of 99.5 percent.

Though future roles of the automated transit function will be determined by the nation's major cities, the idea has been proven in Morgantown. If People Movers succeed, they will owe their existence to this first successful experiment.

Specifications: Standard Light Rail Vehicle

Length	73 ft
Seating Capacity	68 persons
Peak Capacity	190 persons
Car Weight	69,000 pounds
Max Acceleration Rate	3.1 mph per second
Max Deceleration Rate	6 mph per second
Propulsion System	D/C traction motors at 230 hp

Turning its attention even farther from the sky than transit systems, the Boeing Aerospace Company leased 100,000 acres of land near Boardman, Oregon in the early 1960s. Until BAC came to the scene, the land was considered fit only for sagebrush and jackrabbits. The vast deserts of eastern Oregon and Washington State surprise tourists since both states are known more for mountains and evergreen forests.

Though the land was leased for testing rockets and jet engines, Boeing engineers did some thinking. A pump was installed to bring water from the Columbia River to a small section of the 100,000 acre site. Beginning in 1972 potatoes were harvested. By 1975, 8300 acres were considered prime farmland, proving that the Oregon desert could successfully be made to bloom.

Other companies, following Boeing's lead, have moved into the Boardman area, and have placed nearly ten times as much land under irrigation as the area which Boeing developed. Costs were high, about $1.5 million per 1200 acres, the minimum size for an economically feasible farming venture, and only larger combines can afford it.

By the end of 1975, Boeing had met its initial objective in demonstrating desert farming was feasible. An agricultural industry had been started. BAC decided to withdraw from direct involvement in farming, but not from its commitment to developing the region. The Boeing Agri-Industrial Company was formed to handle the business, and it sub-leases to qualified farmers and to agriculturally related industries. About one percent of the nation's potato crop is raised in the region. When potatoes are rotated with wheat, most of the wheat is shipped to the Orient where it is made into noodles.

BOEING AEROSPACE

The Boeing Aerospace Company (BAC) is an operating organization of The Boeing Company, responsible for much of Boeing's military and space efforts. It was created in December 1972 by 'T' Wilson, Boeing's chairman and chief executive officer, and was an outgrowth of the Boeing Aerospace Group. When formed in 1972, BAC employed about 20,000 persons who worked on such programs as Minuteman, Short Range Attack Missile (SRAM), the Subsonic Cruise Armed Decoy (SCAD) and various military applications of commercial airplanes, such as the Airborne Warning and Control Systems (AWACS) and Advanced Airborne Military Command Post aircraft. In the space segment of the organization, BAC was engaged in construction of the S-1C, the first stage of the Apollo Saturn V moonrocket, and the Lunar Rover, the buglike surface vehicle used on the moon by the Apollo astronauts. Much of the diversification effort of The Boeing Company was also originally placed within BAC. This included advanced surface transportation systems such as the Morgantown Personal Rapid Transit (PRT) program; the Jetfoil and Patrol Hydrofoil Missileship (PHM) ventures and the land irrigation program on the rocket and engine testing site near Boardman, Oregon. In addition to these Washington-based projects, BAC also performs work at the Kennedy Space Center in Florida, and Houston.

In its brief history, BAC has completed such successful work as the Mariner 10 spacecraft which explored Venus and Mercury; a number of small scientific satellites; Burner II and IIA booster programs; the Compass Cope remotely piloted vehicles; Apollo and Skylab related work and the 747 Space Shuttle Carrier Aircraft. Much of the firm's diversification efforts have been spun-off to other newly formed company organizations such as Boeing Marine Systems and Boeing Engineering and Construction. Some, such as advanced surface transportation and the Boardman project, still remain within the aerospace company.

BAC now has its headquarters at the Boeing Space Center built in February 1964 in Kent, south of Seattle, Washington. This 432-acre center also houses BAC's system of highly sophisti-

Below: The **Boeing Space Center** in Kent, Washington, 15 miles south of downtown Seattle, is the headquarters of the Boeing Aerospace Company.

cated laboratories and many of its spacecraft manufacturing facilities.

Minuteman, AWACS, the Airborne Command Post, the Morgantown PRT and SRAM still are part of BAC's product line. Additionally, the company has gained new customers and developed new products with the creation of such equipment as the Roland surface-to-air missile for the Army, and the Applications Explorer Missions' Heat Capacity Mapping Mission (HCMM) and Stratospheric Aerosol Gas Experiment (SAGE) base modules. It is also marketing a mobile asphalt plant under a subsidiary, the Boeing Construction and Equipment Corporation. BAC is engaged in development work for the MX Intercontinental Ballistic Missile system, Air Launched Cruise Missile, space shuttle Inertial Upper Stage, Multiple Launch Rocket System (MLRS) and solar power satellites. It also conducts logistics and support operations throughout the world.

In the late 1950s a visible change had taken place within the airplane industry. Airframe and engine manufacturers continued to astonish the world with improved technology, but there was an exciting newcomer to the field, and that was space. According to John Rae in his study, *Climb to Greatness, The American Aircraft Industry 1920–1960*, 'Aerospace was not just a fancy word for airplane, this was the age of missiles and space craft.'

In June 1945 Boeing entered the space age when the company commenced work on their model series 600–602, the Air Force's GAPA (Ground-to-Air-Pilotless Aircraft.) They were remotely controlled supersonic missiles, designed to intercept aircraft flying up to 700mph at altitudes from 6000 to 80,000 feet. GAPA could reach speeds of 1500mph with ramjet engines, and were equipped with a beam-riding guidance system. In November 1949

Above: The **IM-99 Bomarc** Interceptor Missile was designed and deployed at a time when attacks on the US by manned bombers were still a perceived threat.

Specifications:
IM-99B Bomarc Interceptor Missile
Boeing Model Number 631

Wingspan	18 ft 2 in
Overall Length	45 ft
Height	10 ft 2 in
Fuselage Diameter	35 in
Width of Horizontal Tailplane	10 ft 6 in
Powerplants	solid fuel rocket takeoff (Thiokol), 50,000 pounds thrust. Two ramjet engines for cruise (Marquardt), 12,000 pound thrust each
Armament	nuclear warhead
Speed	Mach 2 plus
Operating Altitude	sea-level to 80,000 ft
Range	more than 400 miles
Reaction time	from alert to launch, less than one minute

a GAPA reached an altitude of 59,000 feet, the highest flight for supersonic ramjet propulsion up to then.

After 100 experimental flights, the GAPA program was cancelled, however, but in the meantime Boeing had gained valuable experience in missile technology. When the company was awarded a contract in 1949 to develop its Model 621, the F-99 (later redesignated IM-99) Bomarc interceptor missile, it was ready. The name Bomarc derived from the first two letters in Boeing, and the initials of the Michigan Aeronautical Research Center, which contributed research data for the new missile. In 1951 the development contract was extended by the Air Force, and Boeing's mission was to manufacture a weapon capable of finding and destroying high-speed enemy bombers and missiles. Contact was to take place far from Bomarc's launch sites.

A primitive Bomarc was test-fired in September 1952, and on 24 February 1955, a completely instrumented test version demonstrated operational capabilities. Its two ramjet engines gave it a 200 mile range, far enough from the launch site to satisfy the Air Force.

The first production Bomarc, the IM-99A (Boeing Model 624), was rolled out on 30 December 1957. As production increased the Bomarcs were housed on a constant combat-readiness basis. Upon receiving an alert signal, the shelter roof slid back and the Bomarc was raised on its erector arm to the vertical launching position. The erector then descended, and the missile was fired. The entire process was carried out automatically in 30 seconds.

During practice firings, direct hits were scored on supersonic Regulus II drones, and a radio controlled, pilotless QB-47E jet bomber. On 3 March 1961 an IM-99B (Boeing Model 631), an improved Bomarc, made its first full-range flight, winging over the Gulf of Mexico for more than 400 miles, a considerable improvement over the IM-99A's range. On this test, the IM-99B intercepted a target at an altitude of more than 80,000 feet. The IM-99B used a solid fuel rocket engine, enabling more space to be given to ramjet fuel, which contributed significantly to the increased range.

The Bomarc IM-99A was phased out of operation during 1964, and the last Model B was produced in 1962. The IM-99Bs were eventually retired from service as technology moved beyond them, and more sophisticated missiles appeared. All Bomarc bases were closed in the early 1970s, bringing to an end an important era in missile evolution.

The Bomarc, which was able to deliver effective defense coverage to about 500,000 square miles, was guided by radio command from land-based air defense control centers. In all 570 Bomarcs were produced, including 269 IM-99As with liquid fuel and 301 IM-99Bs with solid fuel.

The Short Range Attack Missile (SRAM), another Boeing product, was developed under a contract awarded in October 1966. After a series of tests, during which a SRAM was fired from the B-52G and B-52H as well as General Dynamics' FB-111, a production contract was issued on 12 January 1971.

The SRAM has two functions: it can attack defensive installations, allowing its parent aircraft, the B-52 or FB-111, to penetrate primary targets. SRAM can on the other hand strike primary targets inside enemy lines. The missile provides the Strategic Air Command a capability never attained before. It can be launched from high or low altitudes, at subsonic or supersonic speed. It can hit targets ahead of the launching aircraft, or can turn in flight to strike objectives to the side or even behind the aircraft.

This versatile missile is 14 feet long, with a diameter of 17.5 inches. It is powered by a Lockheed LPC-415 two-stage solid fuel rocket, with another as a cruising engine. It carries a W-69 nuclear warhead, with an explosive yield of 200 kilotons. Its performance is remarkable in that it reaches speeds of Mach 3, with a hundred mile range. It was designed to destroy last-ditch enemy defenses, especially surface-to-air missile sites. A B-52 can carry eight internally, and 12 under its wings in clusters of six. The F-111 carries two internally and four under its wings.

On 30 July 1975 Boeing delivered its 1500th, and final, SRAM. By the end of the program, the missile had exceeded contract requirements in range, accuracy and reliability. Many people were involved in manufacturing SRAM. There were seven major companies among the 60 primary subcontractors.

In July 1960 Boeing signed a $247 million contract with the Air Force to continue the development of the silo-based Minuteman ICBM (named after the heroes of the Revolutionary War). Boeing had already completed two years of research on this missile for which the company received high praise. Brigadier General Don Coupland, commander of the AF Ballistic Missiles Center said, 'The company's on-schedule efforts have been important factors in the success of the Minuteman development program.'

The general also commented on the success of the first silo-launch tests at Edwards AFB. The tests, he said, saved the taxpayer some $20 million dollars. Eight Minuteman missiles were launched without a hitch.

Since 1962, the Minuteman ICBM system has been America's primary deterrent to nuclear aggression. It was nicknamed 'the instant missile,' because it is constantly ready for immediate firing. Supporting those missiles is a US Air Force/Industry team dedicated to maintaining Minuteman as an effective preventative to large scale conflict. The Boeing Company assists the Air Force in training Minuteman crews, though the missile is so designed as to eliminate the need for skilled manpower in the field. Boeing also keeps the Minuteman up-to-date as strategic requirements demand. They can be upgraded readily and at a comparatively low cost.

Deployment of the Minuteman is mainly in the midwest. Less than three years after production began, 800 Minuteman I missiles nested in underground silos were on the alert with SAC wings located in Montana, South Dakota, North Dakota, Missouri and a three-state complex centered at Warren AFB, Wyoming.

An improvement program called 'Force Modernization,' was started in 1964. It called for replacing Minuteman I missiles with Minuteman II and III. The missile silos were also upgraded.

Another wing, centered at Grand Forks, North Dakota, and armed with the larger and more powerful Minuteman II, became operational in December 1965. Minuteman II is also deployed in another 50 missile squadron near Malmstrom AFB, Montana. When this squadron installation was completed during the first half of 1967, the Minuteman force had achieved its goal of 1000 missiles.

The improvements in Minuteman II are greater range and accuracy and an upgraded guidance system. It can deliver a heavier payload over greater distances. Minuteman III incorporates all the II improvements, and carries three independently targeted warheads, a very important advance. The Minuteman missile uses a special truck-tractor for transporting it between various Air Force bases, and the last of these, also built by Boeing, went to the Air Force in February 1982. In addition to its instant readiness, great efficiency and accuracy, the Minuteman missile was attractive to the Air Force because it was cheaper to build than its predecessors, the Atlas and Titan.

The Minuteman system is a vital part of the US strategic triad. This is a combination of land-based ICBMs, submarine-launched missiles, and the manned strategic bomber. An aggressor seeking to overcome this force must be able to mobilize enormous resources in both offensive and defensive weapons. This triad forms America's deterrent to nuclear attack. With the Minuteman and B-52, Boeing has made a significant contribution to that triad.

One of the most dramatic and deadly of the Boeing missiles is the ALCM, the Air Launched Cruise Missile. Conceived as a weapon to be carried by the B-52 and the Rockwell International B-1 supersonic bomber, the first test flight took place in 1976, from a B-52. The Boeing Aerospace Company was responsible for the ALCM on which development began in 1974, after the SCAD (Subsonic Cruise Armed Decoy)

Specifications: Minuteman ICBM Series

Diameter	6 ft (at widest point)
Length	Minuteman I (LGM-30A) 54 ft Minuteman I (LGM-30B) 55.9 ft Minuteman II (LGM-30F) 59.8 ft Minuteman III (LGM-30G) 59.8 ft
Gross Weight	Minuteman I 65,000 pounds Minuteman II 70,000 pounds Minuteman III 78,000 pounds
Speed	15,000 mph
Range	6000 miles
Powerplant	three solid-fuel rocket engines
Reaction Time	instantaneous
Armament	nuclear warhead

Right: A Boeing **Minuteman ICBM** hurtles skyward.

Specifications: AGM-86B ALCM Boeing Model Number 641

Length	20 ft 9 in
Height (fin deployed)	4 ft
Wingspan (deployed)	12 ft
Weight	3000 pounds
Range	more than 1500 miles
Speed	subsonic (about Mach 0.7)
Propulsion	one Williams International F-107-WR-100, 600 pound thrust turbofan
Guidance	inertial guidance, plus terrain contour matching
Armament	nuclear or conventional warhead

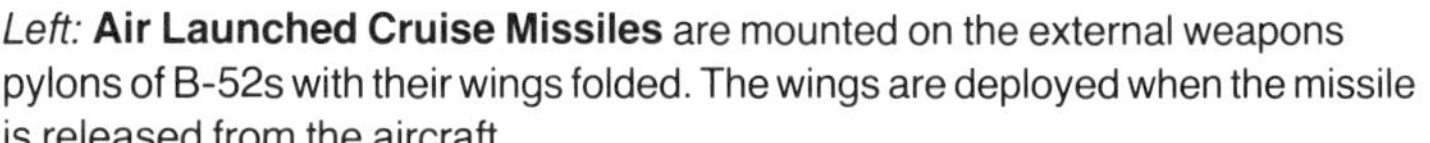

Left: **Air Launched Cruise Missiles** are mounted on the external weapons pylons of B-52s with their wings folded. The wings are deployed when the missile is released from the aircraft.

Below: **ALCMs** under construction on the Boeing Aerospace Company assembly line.

was cancelled. The new missile retained SCAD's shape but assumed a different responsibility: it was stripped of its electronic decoys to become a stealthy attack weapon.

The first ALCM, designated AGM-86A by the Air Force, was about 14 feet long and had a range of about 700 miles. Seven AGM-86As were built during the development and testing phase. Six were launched in 1976 from a B-52 over New Mexico's White Sands desert. The tests demonstrated successfully that the missiles were capable of doing their job. However, the AGM-86A was not put into production, and the seventh was presented to the Smithsonian Air and Space Museum.

Boeing Aerospace Company engineers next produced their Model 641, (Air Force designation AGM-86B). It is six feet longer than its brother, and is capable of traveling up to 1500

Below: A Boeing **AGM-86B** Air Launched Cruise Missile with its wings extended in flight over the Utah Test and Training Range.

miles, a considerable range improvement. It has been designed as an extremely versatile, unmanned, self-guided airplane and is capable of electronically reading the terrain over which it flies. It continuously compares these readings with maps stored in an on-board computer and corrects any deviation from its planned course. Thus, it can guide itself through the enemy defense systems to predetermined targets.

During a test in January 1982, an ALCM was launched from a B-52 over the Pacific Ocean, off California. The missile's inertial navigation system then guided it to the coast, where its contour matching system came into operation. The ALCM continued on a preplanned route across California, Nevada and finally Utah, where it reached its target. The missile, which weighs 3000 pounds, was then recovered by helicopter in mid-air. The ALCM is so accurate that if one were turned loose over Cleveland, it could hit a target between the goal posts in the Pasadena Rose Bowl.

The AGM-86B is an all-weather weapon, as one particularly severe test proved. An AGM-86B was taken up over the Utah Test and Training Range by a B-52. Before launching, a KC-135 Stratotanker drew close and sprayed water on the ALCM where it hung on the B-52's pylon. The result was a coating of ice three-quarters of an inch thick, simulating a condition that could occur on certain kinds of flights. The ALCM was released. It spread its wings and tail surfaces, and streaked through four hours of complex maneuvers before being recovered by helicopter.

Although Boeing makes the ALCM, the go-ahead didn't come by chance, but by competition. The Department of Defense's Joint Cruise Missiles Project Office included General Dynamics in the competition. Each company conducted 10 flights of its missile system. The testing began on 1 August 1979, and ended on 22 January 1980. In their 10 flights, Boeing missiles logged a total of 32 hours of free-flight time, and covered more than 12,000 miles over mountains, deserts, and oceans. All flights were launched from a B-52G. On 25 March 1980, Air Force Secretary Hans Mark announced that Boeing was the winner. It was the biggest single USAF contract since the Vietnam War.

Amid much glitter, the first AGM-86B roll-out was similar to those roll-outs undertaken for Boeing's commercial aircraft, with notables present from both the civilian and military sides. Among the military men present was Lieutenant General Lawrence A Skantze. He praised Boeing for a job well done, and noted that the Air Force would need more than 4000 ALCMs with a price tag of one million each. Boeing's efforts to stay afloat in the highly competitive aerospace business had been successful once again.

In May 1964 Boeing signed a contract with NASA to design five flight test, and three ground test models of a moon-photographing spacecraft called the Lunar Orbiter. Orbiter's task was to obtain detailed photographs of selected areas near the moon's equator to help scientists choose the safest sites for a manned landing. The photos would be of particular significance to the Apollo program.

When completed, the Lunar Orbiter was an 850-pound, open-truss structure, with a 145-pound photographic subsystem, flight programmer, inertial reference unit, transponder and batteries on the lower deck. The upper deck held the 100-pound thrust velocity control engine, fuel, and oxidizer tanks. Not counting solar panels and antennae, the spacecraft was 5 feet wide, and 5

Below: Twelve **ALCMs** can be mounted on the external pylons of the B-52G and H. B-52Gs based at Griffiss AFB in New York were the first to become operational with the ALCM.

Above: An artist's conception of **Lunar Orbiter I**, NASA's first spacecraft to orbit the moon. Launched on 10 August 1966 aboard an Atlas Agena rocket, this spacecraft surveyed nine primary and seven potential Apollo landing sites and the Surveyor I site. Readout from Orbiter I was completed on 13 September and the Orbiter was intentionally impacted to avoid interference with the second mission. Four paddle-shaped solar panels with photo-voltaic sails faced the sun. Internal parts of the Orbiter were protected from temperature extremes by a thermal barrier of aluminized Mylar. In this rendering most of the insulating shroud has been deleted to show the camera system and electronic equipment in the lower module. Oxidizer and fuel tanks are visible on the upper module just below the rocket engine nozzle.

feet 6 inches tall. With the panels and antennae extended, the maximum span was 18 feet. It measured six inches across the antenna booms, and 12 feet 2 inches across the panels.

From August 1966 through August 1967, five Lunar Orbiters photographed nearly all of the moon's surface, more than 14,000,000 square miles. As a result of the Orbiter and Surveyor missions (Surveyor made the first unmanned soft landing on the moon) photographs of eight landing sites were selected from a list of about 30 along the moon's equator. This was the zone of interest for the Apollo landings. Each of the sites was an oval measuring about three by five miles, with an approach path 30 miles long for the Lunar Module.

In addition to their primary photographic missions, the Orbiters were designed to monitor the strength of radiation and the density of meteoroids in the moon's vicinity. During 800 days in lunar orbit, the Orbiter spacecraft reported 18 meteoroid hits. Radiation levels near the moon were generally low. Data from Orbiter findings were correlated with radiation readings from other spacecraft, such as Pioneer.

All five flights of the Lunar Orbiter were successful. Under the terms of NASA's contract, however, penalties could be assessed for late delivery, and a bonus could be granted for outstanding technical performances. Here, a modern irony occurs: Boeing received $6,809,053 in incentive awards for the five flights, but was penalized $130,000 for late delivery of the first two spacecraft. The first launch was made on 10 August 1966, and the last left Cape Kennedy's pad Number 13, the launch pad for all Orbiters, on 1 August 1967.

The Lunar Orbiter program chalked up an impressive list of firsts. The Orbiter was the first US spacecraft to orbit the moon and provided the first photograph of Earth from the moon. The first detailed photographs were taken of the moon's far side, giving complete coverage and better detail than that available of the near side from earth. The first complete coverage of the moon's near side was also made with resolution 10 times better than possible from Earth-based telescopes. Orbiter also produced the first close-up photos of major lunar features, providing details which scientists could use to determine how the moon was formed. The first definitive information about the moon's gravitational field was made available as were the first vertical views of the moon's North and South Poles, and the eastern and western edges (right and left edges as seen from earth).

The entire highly successful program was completed in about 40 months.

Specifications: Lunar Orbiter Boeing Model Number 939

Span (across antenna booms)	18 ft 6 in
Length (across the panels)	12 ft 2 in
Weight*	850 pounds
Photographic Subsystem Weight*	145 pounds
Cruising Speed	2666.66 mph
Range	800 days
Min/Max Orbital Distance from Lunar Surface	Orbiter I-III: 28-1150 miles Orbiter IV: 1650-3800 miles Orbiter V: 125-3700 miles

*weights given are for earth gravity

In September 1965 the Air Force had awarded Boeing Aerospace a contract for the development of an upper stage rocket called Burner II (Boeing model number 946). The object was to create a highly reliable, low-cost 'kick' stage for placing small and medium payloads into precise orbit. The Burner II was also used as the main retromotor for the Surveyor spacecraft, the vehicle that made the first unmanned soft landing on the moon.

The basic Burner II upper stage had a diameter of 65 inches, a height of 68 inches without the nose shroud. It weighed approximately 1780 pounds at ignition, and approximately 315 pounds after payload separation. The motor generated 10,000 pounds of thrust.

Boeing's designers created Burner II so that it could be easily maintained and launched. Components could be serviced, adjusted and even replaced while the vehicle was on the pad. Its guidance system could accurately position the vehicle in high Earth orbit, transfer orbit or parking orbit with its altitude limited only by the power of the lower stage. It was applicable to wide varieties of payloads including scientific experiments,

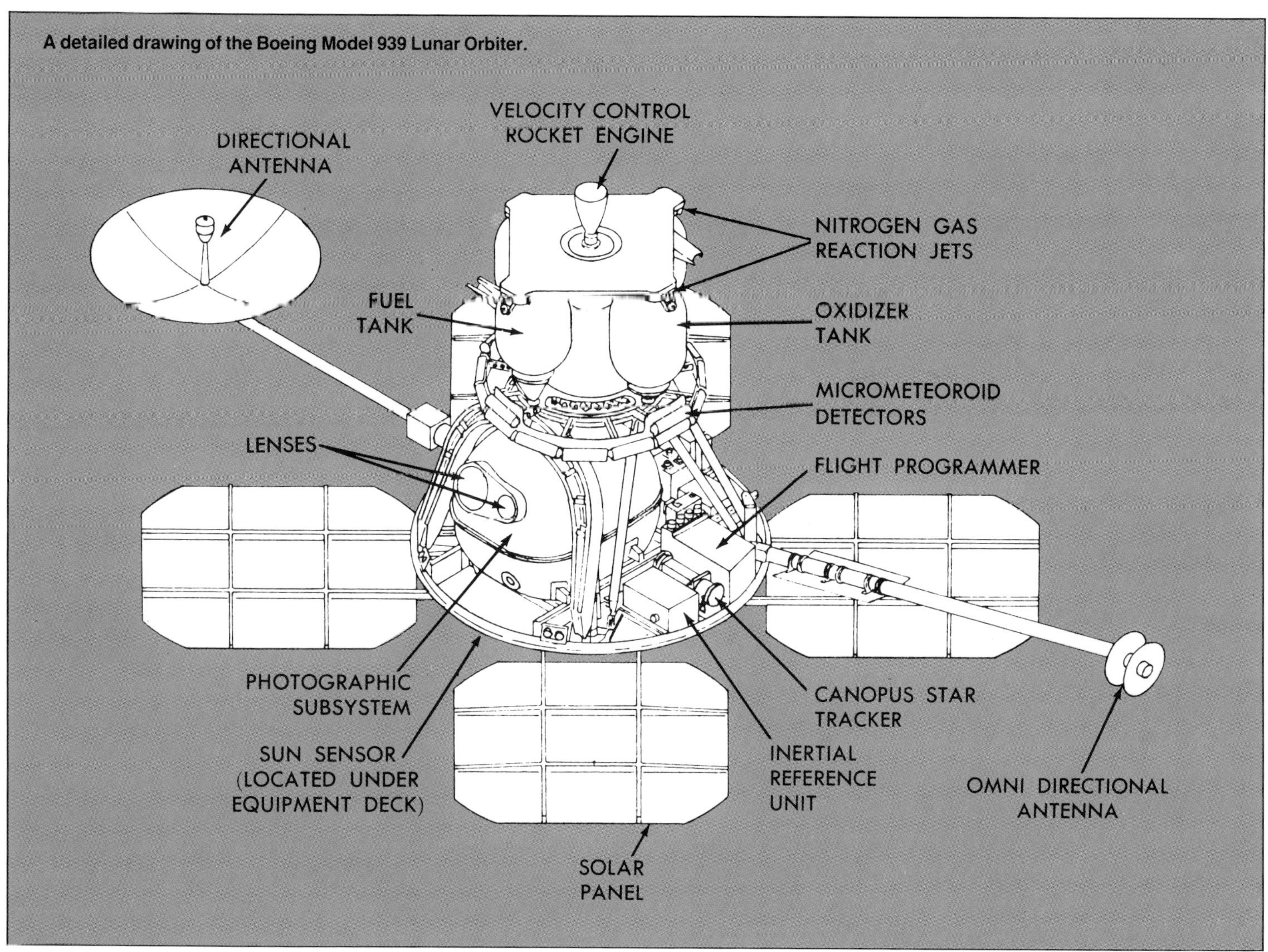

A detailed drawing of the Boeing Model 939 Lunar Orbiter.

weather, navigation or communications satellites. It could be used as an upper stage on almost the entire range of standard launch vehicles. Included were Thor, Atlas and various configurations of Titan.

In August 1969 the Air Force's Space and Missile Systems Organization awarded Boeing another contract to develop and manufacture a two-stage version of Burner II. The modified upper stage was known as Burner IIA. A second stage solid fuel motor with 524 pounds of propellant, furnishing 8800 pounds of thrust, was added to Burner II's 10,000 pound thrust. As with Burner II, Burner IIA had the ability to be used with virtually the entire family of Air Force boosters.

In all, Boeing built 14 basic Burner IIs, and eight Burner IIAs for the Air Force. None of them failed, though two of the overall missions were unsuccessful. In one, a shroud failed to separate from the booster, and in the other the first-stage launch vehicle failed to achieve the desired orbit.

Boeing was delivering Space Shuttle concepts long before *Columbia*'s first launch in 1981. 'The choice of flight paths available to the Dyna-Soar pilot will be almost infinite,' said George H Stoner, Boeing Dyna-Soar program manager on 22 September 1963, at the Air Force Association convention in San Francisco. The Air Force was letting the public know about X-20, its designation for the new spaceship.

The name Dyna-Soar was derived from a combination of 'dynamic' and 'soaring.' It was to be a manned, boost-glide spacecraft, a winged vehicle, designed for maneuverable re-entry through the atmosphere. It would be boosted into space by a Titan III rocket. After entry into space, Dyna-Soar would orbit Earth, then re-enter when its task had been completed.

The project began not long after that fateful day in the fall of 1957, when Russia launched Sputnik I. By March the following year, the Air Force had issued directives to the aerospace industry about Dyna-Soar, inviting response. In June the Air Force selected two major teams to prepare competitive studies. Boeing headed one team, and the Martin Company, combined with Bell Aircraft, headed the other.

The unknowns that faced Boeing in 1958 were typical of those facing all members of the fledgling space industry. Dyna-Soar, for example, would be required to fly at high Mach numbers, and there were few people in the country who had much knowledge of hypersonic flight. Boeing had experience in supersonic flight and related fields, but hypersonic was something else.

One of the first steps Boeing took toward the solutions to those problems was to select preliminary design engineers from its own staff. Among them were people who had worked on an earlier 'paper study' for ROBO, a rocket bomber design. ROBO was designed to shoot high above earth by rocket power and once in space, the bomber would attain hypersonic speed in a glide. Because of its speed, it would generate great heat once it re-entered the atmosphere. To cool off, ROBO would skip in and out of the atmosphere, like a flat rock thrown across the surface of a pond.

The 'skip-glide' concept had been advanced by a University of Vienna professor, Dr Eugen Saenger, in 1933. However, Dyna-Soar's designers set Dr Saenger's ideas aside. They would make Dyna-Soar a 'boost glide' spacecraft. Heat resistant materials

Above: The ill-fated Apollo 13 spacecraft aboard the **Saturn V** with Boeing first stage during rollout on 15 December 1969.

Opposite: James Irwin, Apollo 15 lunar-module pilot, with Boeing's **Lunar Rover** parked near Hadley Rille on 26 July 1971. Apollo 15 was the third from last moon mission and the first to be accompanied by the Rover.

Specifications: Saturn V First Stage Boeing Model Number S-1C

Diameter	33 ft
Length	138 ft
Gross Weight	5,000,000 pounds (fuelled)
Velocity	6000 mph at burnout
Altitude at Burnout	38 miles
Powerplant	five 1,500,000 pound thrust F-1 rocket engines

were tested, and it was felt that Dyna-Soar could effect re-entry in a lengthy glide, instead of skipping in and out of the atmosphere. Though temperatures would reach a mighty 4000 degrees Fahrenheit, the heat-resistant metal sheath would protect both pilot and craft. Though Dyna-Soar's surface would look like 'An old-fashioned wood stove,' on landing, 'It would be no major project to prepare this glider for relaunch,' claimed George Stoner.

There was every reason to believe that Dyna-Soar would succeed. The booster had been chosen and technical problems were finding solutions. Confidence in the outcome of the program was such that gliders, let loose from the wings of B-52s at high altitudes, were showing pilots the special techniques needed for landing this type of aircraft. A wooden mock-up of the Dyna-Soar configuration had been built for study and by 1963, $400 million had been spent on its development. That was a breath-taking figure in 1963, one that even government spendthrifts regarded with respect.

In spite of technological advances and the huge amount of money spent, Secretary of Defense Robert McNamara announced on 10 December 1963, that the Dyna-Soar project had been cancelled. There had been a change in the space program plans. The cancellation brought gloom to Boeing. Good men would have to be laid off, people with special skills. It was a sad end for a noble project.

But there were rays of light in this darkened vale. The Apollo space program was under way, and Boeing was at the center of it. Boeing's knowledge of what it took to conquer space had been considerably enriched by the Dyna-Soar project.

The Saturn/Apollo program of NASA was one of the largest peacetime industrial engineering and scientific efforts of modern times. Everything about the Saturn/Apollo undertaking could be described as big. At its peak in the mid-1960s, more than 250,000 people were directly involved including almost 10,000 Boeing management, engineering, manufacturing and administrative personnel.

NASA made the announcement on 15 December 1961 that Boeing would build the first stage (S-1C) booster for the Saturn V launch vehicle. The three-stage Saturn V, which weighed more than six million pounds at liftoff, could put a 120-ton payload into Earth orbit, or a 45-ton payload in the vicinity of the moon. It was being produced under the direction of NASA's Marshall Space Flight Center, Alabama. The Saturn's three rocket stages were put together at one of the nation's largest buildings at the John F Kennedy Space Center, Florida. Boeing produced 13 flight stages and two test stages under this contract, which ran over one billion dollars by the time it expired in September 1973.

The Saturn V with all three stages and with Apollo command, service and lunar modules on top was 363 feet tall. The first stage, Boeing's S-1C, the largest rocket booster ever produced in the US, stood 138 feet tall and was 33 feet in diameter. It had a dry weight of approximately 300,000 pounds, and a fueled weight of about five million pounds. Five engines were mounted at the base of the S-1C, four in a square, with a fifth in the center. They burned 331,000 gallons of liquid oxygen (LOX), and 203,000 gallons of refined kerosene. The combination produced a prodigious 7.5 million pounds of thrust, which took $2\frac{1}{2}$ minutes to reach burn-out. By then Saturn V would be at an altitude of 38 miles and have attained a speed of 6000mph.

The second stage of Saturn V (S-II) was produced by Space and Information Systems of North American Rockwell. It provided one million pounds of thrust, and was 81.5 feet tall, 33 feet in diameter. It also was powered by five engines. The third stage,

Above: The **Saturn V** rocket with the Boeing-built first stage boosts Apollo 11 skyward from launchpad 39A at Cape Kennedy, carrying the first manned lunar mission in 1969.

Opposite: A **Saturn V** first stage under construction.

Saturn S-1C Program

Flight	Date	Vehicle	Seconds fired
Apollo 4(1)	9 November 1967	S-1C-1(2)	140.9
Apollo 6(1)	4 April 1968	S-1C-2(2)	148.0
Apollo 8	21 December 1968	S-1C-3	153.8
Apollo 9	3 March 1969	S-1C-4	162.7
Apollo 10	18 May 1969	S-1C-5	161.6
Apollo 11	16 July 1969	S-1C-6	161.6
Apollo 12	14 November 1969	S-1C-7	161.1
Apollo 13	11 April 1970	S-1C-8	163.8
Apollo 14	31 January 1971	S-1C-9	164.1
Apollo 15	26 July 1971	S-1C-10	158.8
Apollo 16	16 April 1972	S-1C-11	161.8
Apollo 17	7 December 1972	S-1C-12	160.9
Skylab 1	14 May 1973	S-1C-13	158.2
		Total	2067.3

(1) Unmanned
(2) Assembled by the NASA Space Flight Center. Remainder built by Boeing.

(S-IVB), was built by the McDonnell Douglas Corporation. It was 58.7 feet tall and 21.7 feet in diameter. It carried only one engine which produced 200,000 pounds of thrust.

Twelve of the 15 S-1C stages were flown on Saturn V/Apollo missions. Each performed in nearly flawless fashion during its 2½ minute flight, and each lifted more than 3000 tons of Saturn V rocket off the launch pad and pushed it toward earth orbit.

The Boeing-built S-1C-3 launched Apollo 8 on 21 December 1968, the first flight around the moon. Apollo 11, launched by S-1C-6 on 16 July 1969, carried Neil Armstrong, the first man to set foot on the moon. And S-1C-10, launched Apollo 15, which carried the first of three Boeing Lunar Roving Vehicles (LRV), or moon cars. These moon cars were to expand the astronauts' range of exploration on the moon dramatically. The final moon mission, Apollo 17, was launched by S-1C-12. However, one of the most daring events was still to come, the launching of Skylab.

The Saturn V rocket that carried Skylab into space looked familiar, but it was a new model specially designed for a scientific role. The Boeing S-1C-13 first stage thrusters carried a very different bird into the sky. Much of the difference was apparent only to an engineer's eyes. The S-4B upper stage no longer contained the more than 100 tons of fuel and rocketry needed to boost the vehicle out of the earth's gravitational pull. Instead, it contained a lighter and more spacious workshop in which astronauts conducted experiments.

Skylab was unmanned, so the command and service modules which previously perched atop the S-4B were not used. In their

place was an aerodynamic shroud which housed a solar telescope, an airlock and an adapter to which astronauts docked their spacecraft after rendezvous in Earth orbit.

The changes shortened the Saturn V to 346 feet, and when completely fueled for takeoff it was 219,929 pounds lighter than the Saturn V which sent Apollo 17 to the moon.

This loss of weight gave Skylab added speed. The S-1C-13 was a bit hotter than its brothers, producing 7.8 million pounds of thrust, rather than the usual 7.5 or 7.6 million pounds. After blastoff on 14 May 1973 it took just 160 seconds for the S-1C-13 thrusters to burn their fuel. Skylab had attained an altitude of 45 miles, and was 46.6 miles downrange. This compares to the 35 mile height and 50 mile range attained by Apollo 17 in the same flying time with the same 4,721,000 pound fuel load.

The S-1C was a faithful workhorse, which served well, but its day has come and gone. Thirteen of them saw service, but two were not used. One of these, S-1C-14, is on display at NASA's Michoud Assembly Facility in New Orleans. The last one, S-1C-15, can be seen at the Kennedy Space Center.

In order to give Apollo astronauts more flexibility while on the moon, NASA invited competition from the aerospace industry, leading to a practical Lunar Roving Vehicle (LRV), also known as a moon buggy. Boeing and the Bendix Corporation were finalists, and Boeing was eventually awarded the contract.

Both companies had already conducted studies on several types of vehicles for traveling on the moon's surface. The most important Boeing studies were MOLAB (Mobile Lunar Laboratory), conducted in 1964–65, and LSSM (Local Scientific Survey Module), 1966–67. The MOLAB study yielded a fat-wheeled vehicle, a traveling laboratory, complete with atmosphere, food and equipment. Each of its six wheels was individually powered, and top speed was 10mph. It was electrically powered, and could support two men for trips of up to two weeks, with a total of 250 miles of running.

LSSM was an open spacecraft designed from the standpoint of weight saving and dependability. Also electrically powered, it was little more than a frame seat, tucked between six wheels with woven-wire tires (which eventually appeared on the LRV's final design). It also could travel at 10mph, but was designed to carry only one astronaut (two in emergency) on exploration trips. It weighed 985 pounds, and could range over 200 miles of the moon's surface.

Eight test units in all were developed leading to the manufacture of the first LRV flight model. Program management and engineering work was performed at the Boeing Company's Space Center, Kent, Washington, and at Boeing's facilities in Huntsville, Alabama. The first flight-model LRV was delivered to NASA on 15 March 1971, less than 17 months from the formal signing of the contract. This was the shortest development, design, qualification and manufacture cycle of any major item of equipment for the Apollo program.

The LRV was deceptive in appearance. It looked like a simple, familiar vehicle, perhaps a dune buggy. In reality, it was a specialized spacecraft that had been designed to function safely in the space conditions of vacuum, temperatures ranging from

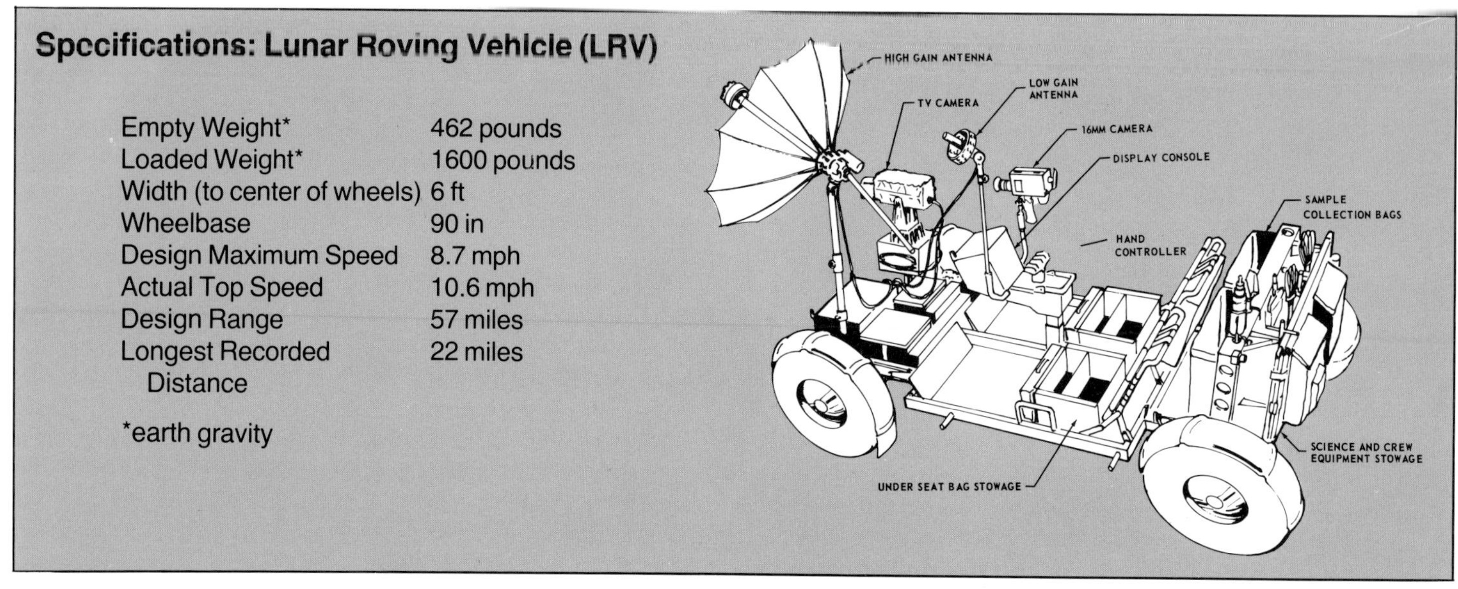

Specifications: Lunar Roving Vehicle (LRV)

Empty Weight*	462 pounds
Loaded Weight*	1600 pounds
Width (to center of wheels)	6 ft
Wheelbase	90 in
Design Maximum Speed	8.7 mph
Actual Top Speed	10.6 mph
Design Range	57 miles
Longest Recorded Distance	22 miles

*earth gravity

plus 200 degrees Fahrenheit to 200 degrees below, and to venture over rough terrain. Among its unique features were wheels specially designed for moon use. Delco Electronics, after studying reports from Apollo 11 and 12, designed a wheel with a spun aluminum hub and a titanium bump stop inside a woven tire. The tire was woven of zinc-coated piano-wire. Each wheel weighed 12 pounds on Earth, two on the moon. Their design saved well over 100 pounds over conventional wheels and rubber tires in a venture where every ounce saved was important.

The vehicles were powered by two 36 volt silver-zinc batteries, developed by Eagle Picher Industries of Joplin, Missouri. They were non-rechargeable batteries of plexiglass monoblock construction. Silver-zinc plates operating in potassium hydroxide electrolyte were used. Each battery was designed for a capacity of 121 ampere hours, and contained 25 cells. The case material was magnesium.

Each vehicle weighed 462 pounds, and the total loaded weight was 1600 pounds. They were 122 inches long, 6 feet wide to the center of the wheels. Maximum speed was 8.7mph, and they had a range of 57 miles.

Use of the first LRV took place on the Apollo 15 trip in July and August 1971. Astronauts Dave Scott and John Irwin more than doubled the amount of work accomplished by previous moon-landings. The ability to carry heavy loads and a television camera greatly expanded the scientific effectiveness of the mission. Ground controllers became part of the exploration team and participated with directions and assistance. The weight of Lunar samples returned with LRV assistance on Apollo 15 was 170 pounds, nearly double the 94 pound record of Apollo 14.

The Boeing-built navigation system on Rover 1 proved to be accurate and reliable. Astronaut Irwin reported the explorers did not hesitate to vary from their planned route, since they had confidence the system would guide them home. Accuracy was within 0.06 miles, which would enable the Rover to return to within 320 fcct of its starting point. The Apollo crew found they could precisely locate their landing site by reporting the distance to the lunar module from known lunar craters as calculated by the navigation system.

On 21–23 April 1972 astronauts John Young and Charles Duke of Apollo 16 explored areas near Descartes Crater aboard Lunar Rover 2. They gathered samples of moon rocks, some of them of a different kind than seen before. More and better data was received as a result of this mission than any before it, including Apollo 15. As the astronauts grew more accustomed to their missions in space, they were able to utilize the equipment more

Below: The inflight configuration of the Boeing-built **Mariner X** spacecraft with its paddle-like solar panels deployed. The spacecraft was launched on 3 November 1973 on NASA's first dual-planet mission and the first to explore Mercury (see diagram, page 238).

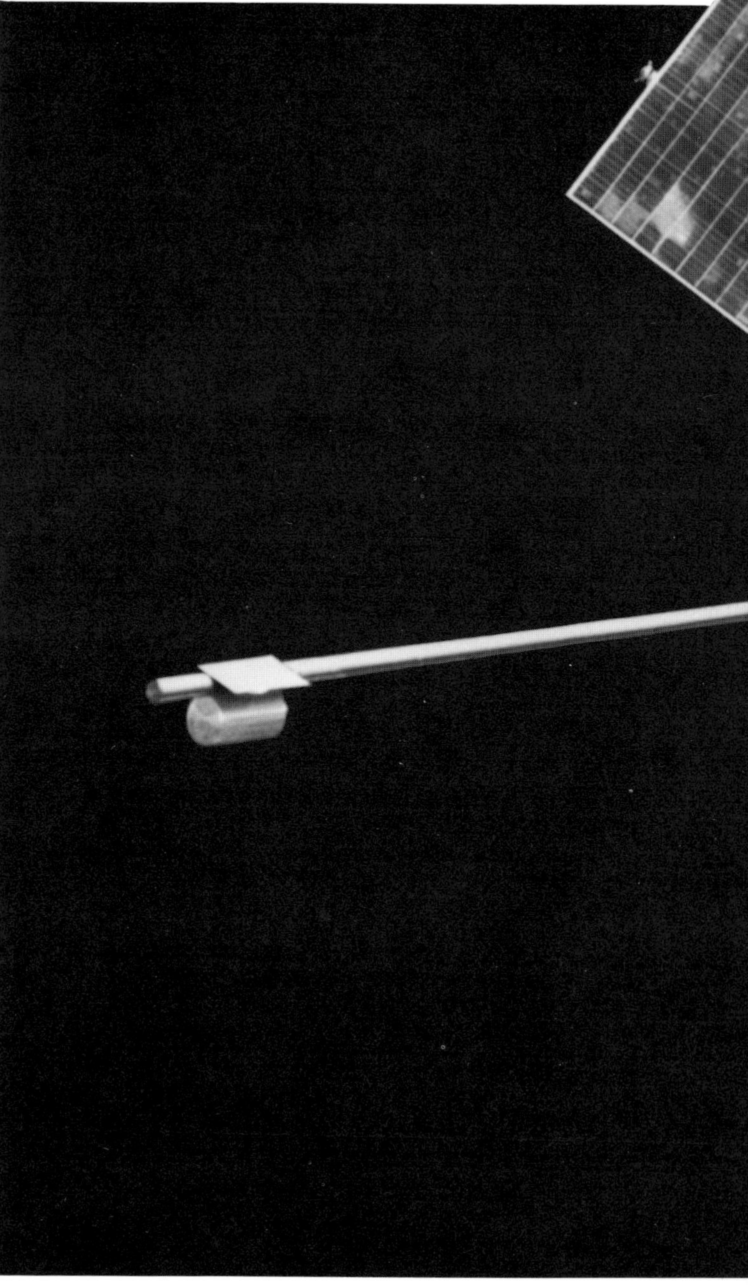

fully. Astronauts Young and Duke reported they set a 'new lunar speed record,' when their moon buggy hit 10.6mph going downhill. Rover 1 had averaged a speed of 5.7mph.

When Apollo 17 reached the moon, after a spectacular night launch on 7 December 1972, Lunar Rover 3 was unloaded from the Lunar Module near Taurus-Littrow. From start to finish, this last Apollo expedition was nearly flawless. Astronauts Gene Cernan and Jack Schmidt, who operated Rover 3, were enthusiastic about their moon buggy. Mission Commander Cernan radioed to earth, after parking Rover 3 for the last time, 'It was the finest machine I've ever had the pleasure to drive.'

On the three Apollo missions on which it was carried, the LRV went everywhere it was programmed to go. It accomplished everything expected of it. Boeing was rightfully proud of its record: three missions, three successes. By now, Boeing was well into the space programs of the United States. The Boeing experience in the technology was invaluable, and growing.

On 29 April 1971, Jet Propulsion Laboratory (JPL), at Pasadena, California, announced the selection of the Boeing Aerospace Company to design a variant of the standard Mariner spacecraft. Boeing would also build the spacecraft and test it at their Space Center in Kent, Washington. JPL had been the prime contractor for moon probe space vehicles such as Lunik, Pioneer, Prospector and Ranger. Unlike its fellows, Mariner was called a 'planet probe.'

The vehicle that Boeing contracted to manufacture was called Mariner 10. Its mission included a flyby of the planet Venus, using the gravity pull of that body to provide energy to continue on to the solar system's innermost planet, Mercury. The spacecraft had to withstand the terrific temperatures predicted at Mercury, and was to be ready for launch in the last quarter of 1973. This was the only time there would be such a launch opportunity for many years because of the changing positions of the planets and the trajectory planned.

The 1160 pound spacecraft that evolved carried a 170 pound science package that included two television cameras, an X-band radio transmitter, a scanning electron spectrometer and a scanning electrostatic analyzer. In addition, Mariner 10 carried two magnetometers, an infra-red radiometer, a charged particle telescope and two ultraviolet spectrometers. To accomplish this, the standard Mariner spacecraft design was modified by Boeing to fit the demands of the mission. Two solar panels were utilized instead of the four which Mariner 9 carried when it photographed Mars in November 1971. The two panels were mounted so they could be rotated into an off-Sun position to protect them from the

Below: Boeing's conception of an initial **Space Operations Center (SOC)** which would be used for servicing satellites and vehicles based in outer space. This space port is being studied by Boeing Aerospace for NASA's Johnson Space Center in Houston. The initial station would include a living and command control module for a crew of four; a logistics module containing food, water and other supplies; a service module containing batteries, oxygen and nitrogen with solar arrays to provide power for the center. SOC is designed to be transported and assembled in low-earth orbit by the space shuttle.

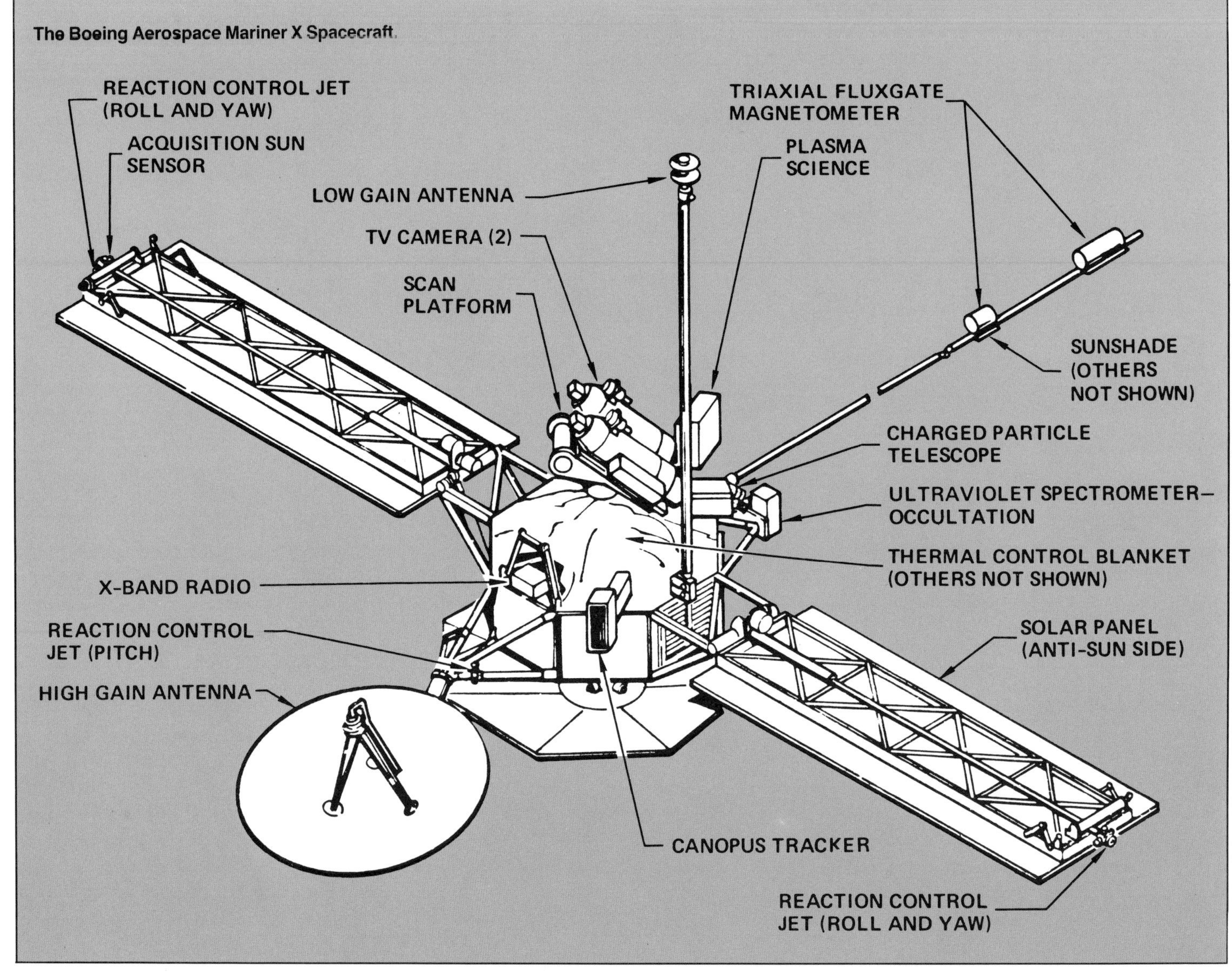

The Boeing Aerospace Mariner X Spacecraft.

Sun's heat. A passive thermal protection system was developed, utilizing state-of-the-art techniques and materials to provide protection from the high temperatures expected during the Mercury flyby.

Shortly after launch on 3 November 1973, Mariner 10's television cameras were activated, and a series of photos was returned of both Earth and Moon.

On 5 February 1974 Mariner 10 swung by Venus returning the first space photos of the planet. Then on 29 March the Mariner 10 cameras were turned on Mercury. On 29 March the craft passed within about 450 miles of Mercury's surface, and the photos revealed incredibly rough terrain. Temperatures ranging from 370 degrees Fahrenheit on the day side to minus 280 degrees on the night side of the planet were reported. Thermal data obtained with the infra-red equipment indicated a total temperature range of 1000 degrees Fahrenheit. There was evidence of helium, argon, neon and, possibly, xenon.

Following what was called Encounter I, the craft swung back into an orbit around the Sun. This brought it back to Mercury in six months. Through the use of a technique of solar sailing, spacecraft controllers at the Jet Propulsion Laboratory were able to conserve control gas supplies aboard. This enabled it to remain operative for subsequent flybys. In solar sailing, the twin solar panels were moved to provide a slight push from the solar wind. This was enough to guide the spacecraft. Rotation of the high gain antenna was also used to impart energy to the craft to keep it stabilized.

Over a six day period, Mariner 10 returned over 500 pictures of the surface of Mercury. The closest approach occured on 21 September 1974 at an altitude of 30,000 miles. Nearly 17 months after Earth launch, and after logging close to a billion miles of spaceflight, Mariner 10 completed its third and final flyby of Mercury in 1975. Following the third encounter, JPL engineers started a series of tests of the spacecraft to diagnose its condition after so long a time in space. On 24 March 1975, controllers estimated stabilization gases were nearly exhausted, and signals were sent to Mariner 10 turning off all equipment and silencing its radios. The spacecraft is now in permanent Sun orbit, and will remain there indefinitely.

As another credit in Boeing's long list, Mariner 10 was selected by the US National Society of Professional Engineers as one of the engineering achievements of 1974. The Society high commended the accomplishment as 'an outstanding example of systems engineering.'

Though The Boeing Company's practical experience and engineering skill have kept it in the front lines of space technology, the company has also become involved in other aspects. Its subsidiary, Boeing Services International, was formed in 1972, and employs thousands of people worldwide.

BSI's involvement with the Space Shuttle program began in 1977. Skilled technicians have been busy at the Kennedy Space Center, providing NASA with a variety of ground systems operations and maintenance service. BSI also installs and modifies launch systems ground support equipment for space flights. Its responsibilities range from operations management through institutional maintenance, including carpentry, plumbing, sandblasting, floor and ceiling care and even bridge repair. The company's people also operate cranes, forklifts and elevators. BSI employees operate the mobile launcher platform on which the Shuttle is stacked and launched.

Where there is a responsibility, mundane or highly critical, BSI is involved. At Edwards AFB, where *Columbia* has landed after orbiting Earth, BSI is primarily responsible for the life support systems used by the orbiter servicing crew. This includes outfitting technicians exposed to hazardous environments. These outfits are self-contained atmosphere-protective ensembles, better known by their typically colorful anacronym as SCAPE suits. They are designed to protect the technicians from toxic chemicals. BSI suits 27 people for duty when *Columbia* or one of its successors touches down. In addition to the 27, two teams of five each provide stand-by service for eight hours in case of hazardous propellant leaks or other emergency situations. Those white suits seen on television after a Shuttle landing are SCAPE suits. If the Shuttle is forced to land at another base because of weather or some kind of emergency such as it had at White Sands, New Mexico, a BSI life-support group, already pre-positioned at Edwards, will begin preparing all systems for shipment.

After landing at Edwards detailed inspections are made of the spacecraft and a mate/demate device is used to lift the Orbiter atop the specially fitted Boeing 747 for transport back to Kennedy Space Center. There are two mate/demate devices, one at Edwards, the other at Kennedy. BSI has total operations and maintenance responsibility for the equipment. Should the Orbiter land on an alternate site overseas, everything needed to ship the space ship back to the US is sent by C-5 cargo planes. It is a big operation, requiring up to 20 aircraft. BSI's Deployed Operation Team is trained and ready to help bring Orbiter back from any location in the world.

Compass Cope (Boeing Model 901) is the largest airplane designed as a remotely piloted vehicle (RPV). Two of the 40 foot long, 90 foot wingspan planes demonstrated the feasibility of performing surveillance and reconnaissance missions from a high-altitude, long-endurance airplane. The Boeing Aerospace Compass Cope, designated YQM-94A by the Air Force, was primarily of fiberglass, the wings having a fiberglass honeycomb core and aluminum skin. The airplane weighed 13,000 pounds and was powered by a single General Electric J-97 turbojet engine.

The initial flight of the first vehicle was in July 1973, from Edwards AFB in California. It was a successful flight, but the craft was destroyed in a landing accident on the second flight. The number two plane completed the entire flight test program, during which it remained aloft for 17 hours.

Compass Cope was operated from a ground station, equipped with standard airplane instruments and controls. The plane and station were connected by digital radio communications, and the pilot saw through a television display relayed from a camera in the vehicle's nose.

Though satisfactory in performance, Boeing was asked to extend the program in 1976. This effort would make Compass Cope fully automatic from takeoff to landing. There would be a station pilot following the airplane's course in case it needed a human hand. However, the Air Force cancelled its contract the following year, and the second series was never finished. A Compass Cope is on display at the Air Force Museum near Dayton, Ohio for those wishing a closer look at this unique airplane.

The Boeing Aerospace Company has become involved in such projects as the 'Thin Film Solar Cell Development.' Under contract to the Department of Energy's Solar Energy Research Institute, Boeing research scientists have been working on low-cost, high efficiency thin-film solar cells. These would be capable of meeting the DOE's goal of an energy conversion efficiency of 10 percent. This means that one-tenth of all available sunlight hitting the cells could be directly converted into energy. For an age threatened with an energy crisis, this is important work.

In November 1975 the Boeing Aerospace Company's Space Division was selected to design, fabricate and test two Applications Explorer Missions (AEM) base modules. The purpose of the AEM, designated AEM-1, and AEM-2, was to study the Earth and its atmosphere. AEM-1, a heat capacity mapping mission, was launched from the Western Test Range, California, under the auspices of NASA, on 26 April 1978. Equipped with a radiometer with which it sensed the Earth's surface temperatures at the hottest and coolest times of the day, AEM-1 provided data which allowed the determination of thermal inertia, or heat capacity, of various segments of the surface. Accurate mapping of these temperatures can lead to: discrimination of rock types and mineral resource locations; measurements of plant canopy temperatures to determine the transpiration of water, which is an early indicator of plant stress; mapping of thermal effluents, both natural and man-made; and the prediction of water runoff from snowfields. Placed into a 373 mile circular sun-synchronous orbit, AEM-1 remained operational until 30 September 1980.

AEM-2 was launched from Wallops Island, Virginia, and its purpose was to establish baseline data on aerosol propellant and ozone concentrations; to understand better the effect of transient phenomena on these concentrations; gain insights concerning the effects of stratospheric aerosol and ozone on the global climate and the implications of this in terms of the availability of solar energy on the Earth's surface. Once again, important work. It was during this period that the aerosol scare began. People were using too many cans of things under aerosol pressure, and too much was escaping into the upper atmosphere. The predicted results were dire. AEM-2 studied what was really happening. Aerosols are still in use.

In addition to all of this, the Boeing Aerospace Company has become involved with developing a space telescope structure. It will hold a telescope out in space, which will enable man to see deeply into the universe. Boeing developed a new material from graphite fibers and epoxy which will keep the telescope structure from feeling the influence of either extreme heat or extreme cold. It will neither contract nor expand, thus providing a stable platform for the extremely sensitive telescope and prevent distortion.

Our knowledge of Space is just beginning, though science fiction has long been with us. But science fiction escapism and space technology are drawing closer together. A 'Space Operations Center' is being studied by BAC, for which a future space shuttle would bring supplies. There would be living quarters in the space operations center as well as food warehouses, service areas, spacecraft hangars and solar panels to provide power. In order to expand the Center and make it more efficient, there would be an area for construction materials.

Some Boeing engineers feel that a space colony would live in an Earth-like atmosphere, have forests and fields – in fact an entire man-made 'outdoors.' Picture windows would give colonists a view of Earth and the stars, and solar collectors would supply energy needs.

The way the Boeing Company and its subsidiaries have been progressing in the past, nothing seems too far-fetched.

A NEW ERA

A new era for Boeing dawned on 4 August 1981 when the prototype of the first new Boeing aircraft design since the 747 rolled out of the world's largest building in Everett, Washington. The world of commercial aviation that the 767 and its sister ship the 757 (which was to make its debut on 13 January 1982) looked out on in the early 1980s was much changed in the dozen years since the 747 first took to the air.

In the world of the early 70s there were six major firms engaged in the commercial jetliner business, five American and one British. Three of these firms, Boeing, McDonnell Douglas and Lockheed were manufacturers of airframes, and the other three, Pratt & Whitney, Rolls-Royce and General Electric were in the business of building the engines for them.

By the end of the decade, Boeing had emerged in the dominant position among the airframe manufacturers, after McDonnell Douglas and Lockheed had neutralized one another through the costly war fought between their rival DC-10 and L-1011. It had been the most vicious fight that anyone in the industry could remember. Among the engine manufacturers, both Pratt & Whitney and General Electric (both being part of larger corporations, United Technologies in the case of P&W, and the larger General Electric Corporation in the case of the GE engine division) remained strong. Meanwhile, Rolls-Royce, fighting its way back from the brink of bankruptcy, was running a poor third.

In the early 80s, the lineup of engine makers, though it has seen some convulsions, was the same as it had been a decade earlier. With the airframe builders, however, the lineup had changed. Boeing was the acknowledged industry leader, running a strong number one with nearly 4000 planes in the air. Lockheed was out, having announced the closing of the L-1011 assembly line, and McDonnell-Douglas was on the ropes in the commercial field. Both had been eclipsed by a newcomer – Airbus Industrie, a European consortium based in Toulouse, France.

The 70s were a bad decade for the Douglas Division of McDonnell-Douglas. For decades Douglas had been one of the premier builders of airliners. Even with the advent of the 707 and Boeing's ascendancy in the jetliner field, Douglas ran a strong second with its DC-8. Then came the 70s, and with them near-bankruptcy and a shotgun marriage to McDonnell. Douglas had seen a strong market for a short range 100-seat aircraft, and introduced its DC-9. Boeing had seen the same market and rushed in with the 737 (which derived many systems from the 727). Because Boeing could build and deliver planes much faster than Douglas, it was able to grab a large market share even though the DC-9 had been there first. The DC-8 fell victim to McDonnel Douglas's desire to produce too many versions, thus driving up unit cost. Finally there was the trouble-plagued DC-10 with some horrible crashes and the costly war with the L-1011.

Enter Airbus Industrie. There had been European jetliners from the start, indeed the British Comet was first, but none had ever been a real commercial success. The Anglo-French Concorde is a good example of such a commercial failure. As late as 1978, it looked as though the big white Airbus A-300 was just another white elephant of the same sort.

Airbus was turning out to be a well-managed company. Beyond that, the A-300 was gradually taking the lead in the worldwide market for a jetliner in the over 250-seat category.

Above: The **757s** for Eastern Airlines are detailed with the same style '757' tail marking as Boeing's 757 prototype.

The territory over which the battle that had ruined the commercial viability of the DC-10 and L-1011 had been fought was slowly being captured by the A-300. The point was made painfully clear to Boeing when Eastern Airlines abandoned American manufacturers to buy A-300s from Airbus.

In the late 70s, the short range market (around 100 seats) was divided between the 737, the DC-9 and, to a lesser degree, planes such as the British Aerospace BAC-111 and the Fokker (Holland) F-28. On the high end of the scale in the over 350-seat long-range category, the 747 was the only contender for a market that it had created. Below the 747, the next rung down (250+) was crowded with the L-1011, DC-10 and A-300. Between this rung and the 100 seat/short range aircraft are two rungs which are generally referred to in the industry as medium range. On the lower of these two (150+) rests the most successful jetliner of all time (over 1800 sold), Boeing's 727. It might be pointed out that the 727 is successful not only because it is an excellent airplane, but also because it is designed to serve the most densely traveled routes in the world. There was no aircraft serving on the other (200+) medium range rung.

If the glamor of wide bodies attracted airframe builders in the 70s, then the pragmatic approach of tailoring aircraft to the most heavily traveled routes with strict attention to fuel efficiency and seat cost per mile marked their thinking in the 80s. The worldwide oil crisis and airline deregulation in the United States and elsewhere were changing the thinking of both the airlines and the airplane makers.

Enter three aircraft builders with an eye on that empty rung. McDonnell Douglas was the first to drop out. They had made extensive engineering studies for what they called their Advanced Technology Medium Range (ATMR) aircraft which had been designated DC-11. The DC-11 was much sought after by the airlines, but recognition of the condition of McDonnell-Douglas caused the airlines to gravitate elsewhere. Airbus was coming along with its contender, the A-310, a double-aisle wide-body like their larger A-300. Boeing followed with not one but *three* new aircraft.

The 767 (another double-aisle wide-body) was designed for the 200+ market, while the 757, originally designed for the 150+ market (it was to have been the 727's successor) gradually grew on the drawing board to close to (and in some seating arrangements beyond 200.) The 777 was a derivative of the 767 idea with about the same seating capacity but with a longer, intercontinental range. It was to have been a tri-jet, with the third engine mounted in the tail in a fashion similar to the DC-10 or L-1011. Marketing studies indicated that the market for the 777 was weaker than for the 757 and 767, so the project was shelved. When the Model 777 designation does appear, and it will, it will probably be attached to a very different sort of plane.

Above: A **757** wind-tunnel model.

Below: The first prototype **767** in Boeing markings during its first flight in September 1981.

The 757 is a short to medium range jetliner which combines the single-aisle/six-across seating typical of the 707, 727 and 737 with a new technology wing and engines. The 757 is capable of carrying about 186 passengers in a typical first class/tourist configuration, and up to 220 in an all-tourist configuration. Boeing offers the 757 in either a 3-door or 4-door model. It is the 3-door model (both have two additional mid-fuselage emergency exits) that permits the higher passenger density.

Fuel efficiency was an important goal for the 757, and the goal was met. On a 500-mile flight it will burn up to 42 percent less fuel per seat than the aircraft it was designed to replace. A ten-plane fleet of 757s, replacing 727-100s, is estimated to be able to save up to $25 million per year in fuel costs as well as additional labor cost savings due to higher productivity.

The new wing, fitted with double-slotted trailing-edge flaps and full-span leading-edge slats, makes possible takeoffs with a full passenger load using about 1250 feet less runway than an Advanced 727 taking off on an equal 1200 mile flight. With its new wing and high-thrust engines, the 757 will be able to cruise 6000 feet higher than the advanced 727-200, thus contributing to fuel efficiency, as well as allowing the aircraft to use higher flight lanes. The four-wheel main landing gear units will allow operations from runways previously unusable by commercial aircraft of equivalent size. Its pavement loading, in fact, will be about the same as the much smaller 737.

Eastern Airlines and British Airways were the first customers for the 757, ordering 40 airplanes between them on 31 August 1978. The formal contract, calling for Rolls-Royce engines, was signed on 23 March 1979 and production began. One year less two days later, Boeing announced that it intended to certify the 757 for two-crew operation, and revealed the new 757/767 flight-deck.

Orders were rolling in, with Transbrasil, Air Florida and Monarch all buying 757s, when Tex Boullioun went down to Atlanta to see Delta. E H 'Tex' Boullioun is the parent Boeing Company's Senior Vice President for Commercial Airplanes and a member of the seven-member executive council that includes the President and the Chairman of the Board of Directors. The President of the Boeing Commercial Airplane Company reports to Tex Boullioun. Boullioun is also the most successful commercial aircraft salesman in the world. On 11 November 1980, Boeing's 'super salesman' closed the biggest commercial airplane deal in history, selling sixty 757s to Delta Airlines for $3,000,000,000. A month later, Delta announced that it wanted its 757s equipped with Pratt & Whitney PW 2037 turbofans, giving the new jet two engine options.

The first wing was complete on 29 May 1981 and attached to the fuselage on 25 August. The first Rolls-Royce engine was mounted on 28 October. Rollout came on 13 January 1982, followed by the first flight on 19 February from Boeing's Renton field.

Specifications: Boeing Model 757

Span	124 ft 6 in
Length	155 ft 3 in
Wing Area	1951 sq ft
Tail Height	44 ft 6 in
Gross Weight	220,000 pounds
Cruising Speed	600 mph
Service Ceiling	38,400-48,000 ft
Range	2867 miles
Powerplant	two 37,400 pound thrust Rolls Royce RB211-535C or two 40,100 pound thrust Rolls Royce RB211-535E4 or two 38,200 pound thrust Pratt & Whitney PW2037 Turbofans
Capacity	178-224 passengers

The Boeing 767 is, as we have noted, an entirely new commercial jetliner designed like the 757 to make use of the latest technology to provide maximum efficiency in the face of rising costs, while extending twin aisle passenger cabin convenience to routes never before served by wide-body airliners. Production of the 767 began with an order for 30 announced by United Airlines on 14 July 1978. The first 767 (destined to be a Boeing-owned test aircraft) was completed and rolled out of the big 747/767 plant at Everett on 4 August 1981 and made its first flight on 26 September. Flight testing and certification were complete in the fall of 1982, and the first 767s went into service in September of that year.

The development of the 767 was an intensive effort aimed at refining the design to give maximum fuel performance, operational flexibility, low noise levels, advanced aircraft systems (including digital electronics) in the most advanced airliner flight deck and finally, growth potential. New structural materials included an improved aluminum alloy, a graphite composite material and a hybrid Kevlar/graphite composite.

The 767's two-aisle passenger cabin follows the tradition Boeing established in the 747 which was the original wide-body jetliner. Extensive passenger research has shown the seven-abreast seating concept to be preferred by the great majority of those surveyed. It allows for six out of seven people in every row to have either an aisle or window seat.

The 767 cabin is more than four feet wider than the six-abreast Boeing jetliners and seats about 211 passenger in a typical mixed-class configuration (six-abreast in first class, seven-abreast in tourist). Many other arrangements are possible, with passenger capacity increasing to 290 in an eight-abreast charter configuration option.

With its advanced-design wing, the 767 will require a 5900 foot runway for take-off at a maximum gross weight of 282,000 pounds, 6700 feet at 300,000 pounds and 7200 feet at 310,000 pounds. The wing, a Boeing advanced technology airfoil, is, like the 757 wing, thicker, longer and less swept back than the wings of earlier Boeing jetliners.

Below: The Rolls-Royce powered **757 first prototype** during its maiden flight. Eastern Airlines and British Airways, the two 757 launch customers, both requested the Rolls-Royce engines.

The performance of the new jet will make possible such non-stop routes as San Francisco-Cleveland, Los Angeles-Miami, Mexico City-Chicago or London-Cairo. In the US transcontinental version, the 767 will be able to operate between New York and San Francisco.

As we have noted, 767 production began on 14 July 1978. One month later, Boeing and Aeritalia, Italy's largest aircraft firm, signed a contract under which Aeritalia became a risk-sharing major participant in the 767 development and production program. It was this deal, some believe, that kept Italy from opting

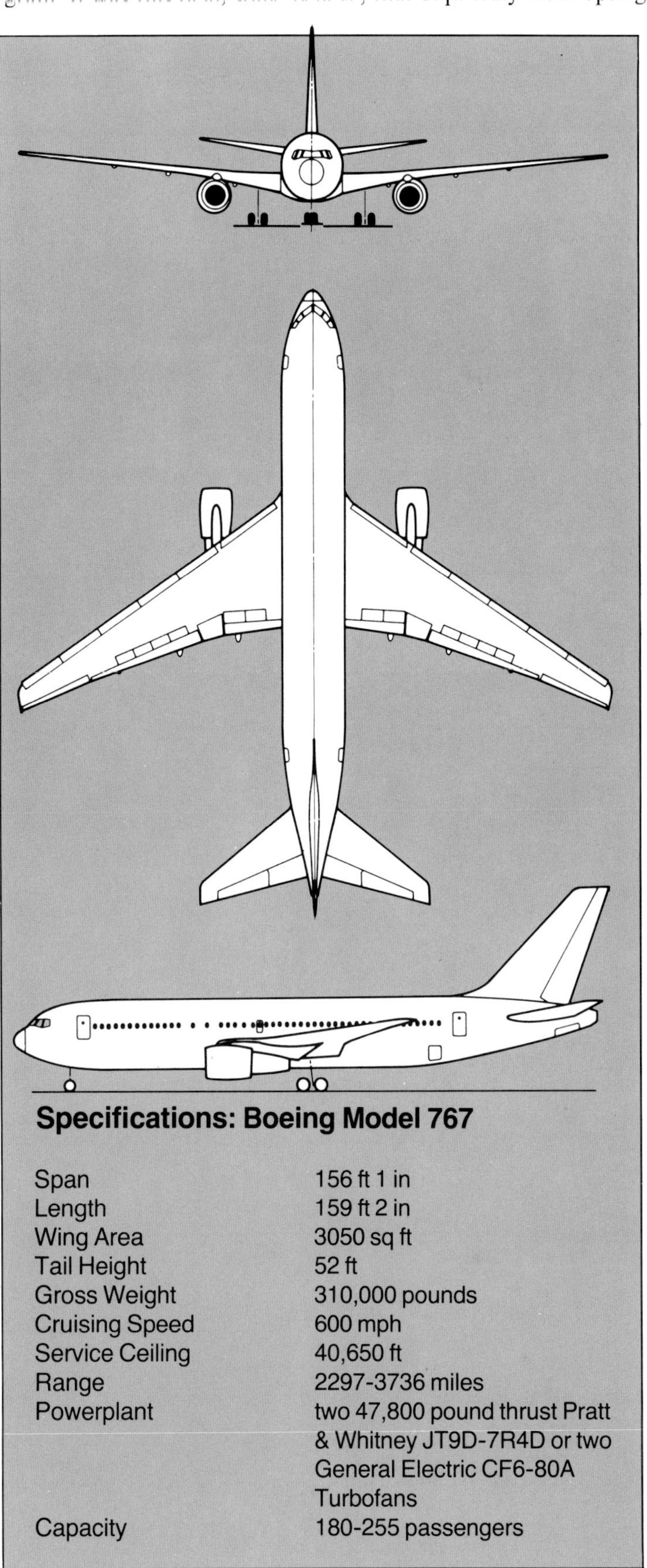

Specifications: Boeing Model 767

Span	156 ft 1 in
Length	159 ft 2 in
Wing Area	3050 sq ft
Tail Height	52 ft
Gross Weight	310,000 pounds
Cruising Speed	600 mph
Service Ceiling	40,650 ft
Range	2297-3736 miles
Powerplant	two 47,800 pound thrust Pratt & Whitney JT9D-7R4D or two General Electric CF6-80A Turbofans
Capacity	180-255 passengers

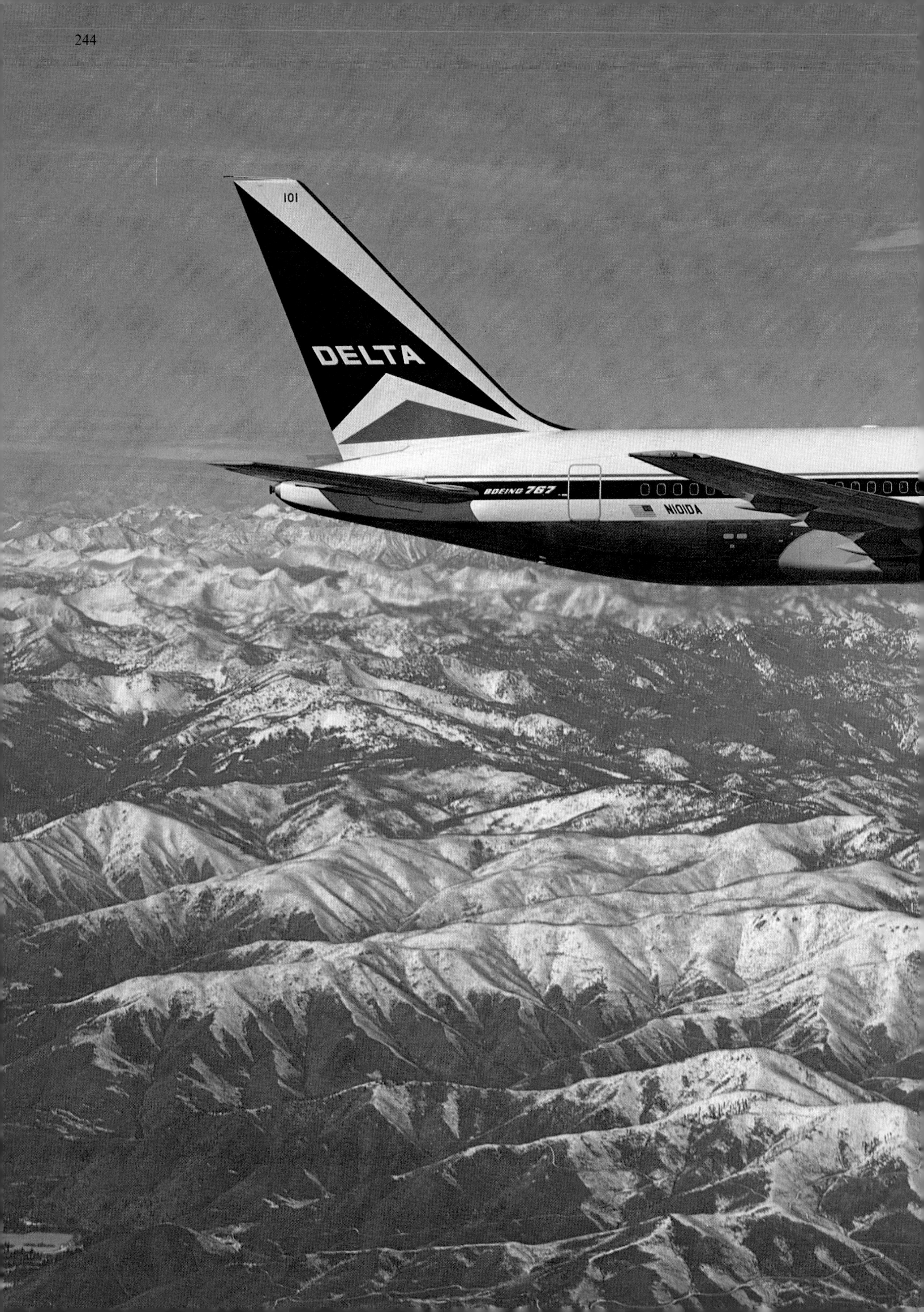
101
DELTA
BOEING 767
N101DA

Below: A Delta **767-200** powered with General Electric engines crosses the Rocky Mountains. In 1984 the 767-300 will be available, offering greater passenger capacity in a fuselage that is 18.3 feet longer than that of the 767-200. The long-range version, 767-200ER, which became available in 1982, offers a 5600-mile range with full passenger load, making possible nonstop 767 service on such routes as New York to Beirut or London to Bombay.

Left: **Thornton Arnold 'T' Wilson** was fascinated by airplanes as a schoolboy, and in 1943 he graduated from Iowa State University with a degree in aeronautical engineering. His plans to join the Army Air Force during his last year in college were thwarted by an injury, and he began working as a draftsman for Boeing.

After a two-year break teaching and studying at Iowa State and Caltech, Wilson rejoined Boeing. Four years later Boeing sent him to MIT as a Sloan Fellow to study industrial management. In 1958 Wilson was given the job of running the Minuteman missile project, and in 1964 he was made head of corporate operations and planning.

Wilson succeeded William Allen as president of Boeing in 1968, a time when the airline industry was at its lowest ebb and when Boeing was extended to the breaking point. The company coffers were stretched to the limit to cover the huge startup costs of the 727, 737 and 747 programs. New problems arose with the 747, and the SST program was cancelled. Wilson faced the crisis and to save Boeing he made drastic cuts in personnel and reorganized the company. By the early 1970s the bitter medicine was beginning to work, and in 1972 Wilson succeeded Allen as chairman of the board.

For a decade Boeing had failed to win significant military contracts, having lost the C-5 and the TFX. During his tenure as president, the company reasserted itself with the $4 billion cruise missile program and the E-4 airborne command post, and T Wilson presided over the birth of the 757 and 767, the aircraft of the 1980s.

Right: **E H 'Tex' Bouillioun**, Boeing's affable senior vice-president for commercial airplanes, is the most successful airplane salesman in the world. The world is Bouillion's turf and he is on the move most of the year, flying from world capital to world capital clinching deals and promoting Boeing's products. An energetic man in his mid-sixties, Bouillioun once sold three billion dollars worth of airplanes in a single deal.

His position as senior vice-president places Bouillioun in the company's inner circle as a member, along with the president and chairman of the board, of the seven-man executive council. On this level, Bouillioun has the president of the Commercial Airplane Company under him.

to join the Airbus consortium. On 22 September Civil Transport Development Corporation of Japan became a second risk-sharing participant in the 767 Program. CTDC is a consortium of Japanese aircraft manufacturers and component suppliers that includes Mitsubishi, Kawasaki and Fuji Heavy Industries.

Under these contracts, Aeritalia is responsible for all the vertical tail surfaces and all the horizontal tail surfaces except the horizontal stabilizer which is produced by Vought. Aeritalia also produces the wing flaps and the wing leading edge, while Japan's CTDC is responsible principally for fuselage sections.

The 757 and 767 share more than just having made their first flights a few months apart. They also have many features in common. Having features in common is an important selling point for airlines that must stock parts for their fleets. Interchangeable parts mean easier and less costly maintenance. Commonality, as this quality is known, is an important factor in Boeing's success in keeping customers. A customer who owns 727s has at least one good reason to come back for 737s. As noted earlier the 707, 727 and 737 have considerable commonality, especially in their fuselages.

The 757 and 767 were designed with commonality in mind, not only to streamline future maintenance, but production as well. While the 757 is all new by comparison to earlier Boeing jetliners. Boeing figures that the 767 is 42.8 percent identical to the 757, and 19.7 percent similar.

The most important feature that the two aircraft have in common is the flight deck. The new two-crewmember flight deck is highly automated so that the pilot and co-pilot can perform all of their own functions plus those that the flight engineer would have performed in the old three-crewmember flight deck. Commonality provides that crew members trained and qualified on the 757 can work on the 767 and vice versa. This provides the airline with training benefits and improved crew productivity.

The new flight deck features digital electronics including an Engine Indicating and Crew Alerting System (EICAS). By graphics and alphanumerics displayed on the center instrument panel (on color cathode-ray tubes), the EICAS provides engine operating parameters, caution and warning alerts and systems status information before takeoff, and for ground personnel, a readout of electronic systems discrepancies to indicate maintenance requirements. The system centralizes all engine displays for two-crew operation, replacing electromechanical instruments with high-technology digital electronic equipment and providing automatic monitoring of engine operation.

The flight deck is based on concepts developed over many years by Boeing and leading electronics firms. Input from major airlines and airline pilots was taken into account in its design. Calling on the experience gained from operations of the two-crewmember 737, of which nearly 900 are operated by 126 airlines worldwide, the new flight deck has all systems within reach of either pilot. Human engineering studies helped designers determine optimum design and positioning of all controls and instruments. Separation of systems controls and indicators required for flight operations from those used to determine airplane dispatch status and maintenance requirements, has resulted in simplified systems panels.

The flight decks include an inertial reference system making use of laser gyroscopes which are rigidly fixed to the airliner

structure, rather than gyros mounted in gimbals as in earlier airliners. This key system also provides information to other flight deck systems, such as the vertical speed indicator and the fuel quantity indicators.

An Electronic Attitude Director Indicator (EADI) is included to provide a multi-color cathode-ray tube display of information such as that found on earlier attitude director indicators. This gives attitude information using an artificial horizon and flight path information showing the airplane's position in relation to the instrument landing system (ILS) beams or VHF Omni-range (VOR) station. In addition, the EADI indicates the mode in which the automatic flight control system is operating and presents the readout from the radio altimeter. Groundspeed is continuously displayed digitally in a position near the airspeed indicator to allow detection of wind-shear.

An Electronic Horizontal Situation Indicator (EHSI) is included to provide an integrated multicolor map of the aircraft's position relative to VHF Omni Range (VOR) stations, way-points, and the Instrument Landing System (ILS) beams. A color radar display can be superimposed on the map to show the location of severe weather. The scale desired for the radar and map can be selected by the pilots. Wind direction and velocity for the airliner's present position and altitude, provided by the Inertial Reference System, are shown at all times. The horizontal situation, both present and predicted, and the aircraft's deviation from a planned vertical path is provided, thus making the system a multi-dimensional indicator.

A flight management computer system integrates navigation, guidance and performance data functions. When coupled with the automatic flight control system ('automatic pilot'), the flight management system provides accurate engine thrust settings and flight path guidance during all phases of flight from immediately after takeoff to final approach and landing. The system can predict the speeds and altitudes that will result in the best fuel economy, and direct the aircraft to follow the most fuel-efficient, or the 'least time' flight path. Depending on the computer programs included, flight planning, ground procedures and airline route information can be stored for use as required.

The flight deck, like the rest of the aircraft, features redundancy, which provides that if a system fails, another can assume its place.

The airline business is cyclical. It was, to employ a pun, flying high in the late 60s, but took a nose dive in the early 70s with the recession and the oil crisis. By the late 70s the industry had rebounded. With airline deregulation, the lines were able to discontinue unprofitable routes. When the number of carriers that could compete on the profitable ones was no longer regulated, the number of airlines on those routes went up, as did their business. The number of airlines serving the popular New York to California route leaped from three to seven. Fares went down for a time but eventually the cycle turned.

By the time the 757 and 767 came on line, times were hard again. Braniff and Laker had folded and others such as Pan American were on the skids. An order for the 757 was cancelled, and some deliveries for it and the 767 were delayed, but most remained solid.

With Lockheed gone, and the possibility of a DC-11 unlikely, Boeing faced off against its new rival Airbus Industrie. As the battle lines were drawn, Boeing found itself in a good position in the American market, but facing tough competition abroad. One field where American exports have remained strong is that of commercial jetliners, particularly Boeing jetliners. Two-thirds of the 737s and 747s and one-third of the 727s are now sold abroad.

With most American airlines buying fewer jetliners, Boeing needed foreign sales more than ever. Though they seemed ready to concede Boeing its first place slot, Airbus was nevertheless prepared to give the giant some serious competition.

Boeing has jetliners in service in nearly every country in the world that has an airline. It has a solid base around the world, built on dependable service and on the performance of the 727, 737 and 747, but foreign sales of the 757 and 767 have been very soft. Airbus is building a solid clientele in Europe, Africa and the Middle East, where the earlier Boeing planes had done well. The serious marketing struggle between Boeing and Airbus is likely to take place along what the industry sometimes calls 'the silk route,' which is composed of those countries between the Middle East and East Asia where strong economic growth is predicted.

As Boeing and Airbus face off, another big question is what will Japan do! The question may more rightly be *when* they will do it. Japan's aircraft industry has concentrated on smaller aircraft and has yet to indicate a willingness to tackle a major jetliner project. It may be only a matter of time. The companies that are part of the Japanese consortium working on the 767 are learning a lot about Boeing, a company they respect and emulate. Meanwhile, a deal has been struck between the Japanese and Rolls-Royce to share development of a new engine. Overtures have been made to the major airframe manufacturers, as well, about the possibility of a jointly produced aircraft. While Airbus and Boeing are likely to say no, McDonnell Douglas is in a position where such a deal might look pretty good.

Below: The Boeing **Model 907** flying wing dwarfs a 747 and a Ford Trimotor. Though aerodynamically functional, the 907 would require, among other things, some air-traffic-control juggling at existing airports because it would need two parallel runways (one for each set of landing gear) for takeoffs and landings.

What of the future of Boeing Aircraft in the late 1980s, the 1990s and beyond? The 757 and 767 will still be in service, as will the new advanced 737-300. The 747 with the expanded upper deck is another aircraft that is being designed for the future. There have also been thoughts given to stretching the entire aircraft by as much as 40 feet and expanding the upper deck the entire length of the aircraft, or a combination of both. Revising the 747 wing incorporating the technology developed on the newer 757 and 767 would give the 747 increased fuel efficiency and allow it to carry a greater payload. It has been estimated that a stretched 747 could carry up to 630 passengers, therefore a stretched 747 with a full length upper deck could probably accommodate 1000 passengers.

With the 777 trijet on the shelf, the most likely follow on to the 757/767 program is a design study with the working designation 7-7. It would employ all of the technological advances of the 757/767 and more. The primary structure would incorporate more and more new materials such as graphite and epoxy composites and improved aluminum and titanium alloys. Eventually, there may be an aircraft composed entirely of graphite and hybrid composites. Laminar Flow Control (LFC), when applied to long range transports, will offer a large potential for fuel savings over that provided by turbulent flow though it is not currently a practical proposition.

Quiet STOL aircraft, such as Boeing's YC-14 and Quiet Short-Haul Research Aircraft (QSRA) are another type of air-

Above: Incorporating 757/767 technology, the 150-passenger **7-7** is a likely candidate to be Boeing's next jetliner.

craft that will probably be seen more and more. STOL aircraft become increasingly attractive as air traffic congestion at airports exceeds available runway and terminal capacity. Quiet STOL aircraft could significantly increase airport capacity, while reducing congestion on main runways. With shorter runways and less noise, airports could be located closer to city centers.

Since the early 70s, Boeing has been working off and on toward a giant flying wing with a wingspan of around 550 feet. Designated Model 907, the big wing was originally planned as a cargo plane. In such a configuration, the 907 would have an astronomical cargo capacity, perhaps as much as eight times that of a 747 or C-5. The passenger capacity of such a plane would be in the thousands, enough to overwhelm the world's existing airport terminals.

The flying wing concept becomes viable for aircraft like the 907, whose takeoff weight would be measured in millions of pounds. The size of wing required is so thick that all the payload can be accommodated within it, eliminating the need for a fuselage. Cargo would be distributed along the span of the flying wing, reducing the net wing bending moment and thereby allowing the use of lightweight structure. The resultant payload to gross weight ratio for this type of aircraft would indeed be very attractive.

Placement of the engines above the wing would help provide STOL characteristics as well as permit a low cargo floor height for easy loading and unloading from platforms or ramps. Flight control surfaces would be located in the trailing edge of the wing and at the wingtips. The wingtips would be hinged to permit access to the cargo compartment within the wing.

Since the cancellation of the Model 2707 supersonic transport in 1971, very promising advances have been made in supersonic transport technology. Efforts funded by NASA, the Department of Transportation and the aircraft industry have been very productive in the four most important areas of concern: propulsion, environment, structures and aerodynamics. With respect to propulsion, for example, effective jet noise reduction features have been incorporated in the proposed variable-cycle engines (VCE). Both Pratt & Whitney and General Electric are conducting aeromechanical and acoustic demonstration tests of VCE designs.

The use of a relatively low-velocity hot-gas shield between the engine and the person on the ground has been demonstrated to be an effective means of reducing noise. Significant improvements can be expected with respect to range, fuel consumption and environmental impact in a future supersonic transport incorporating advanced technologies.

Boeing has developed what may be a practical concept for a family of SST aircraft. Payload capacity of a fuselage that was 'blended' into the wing could be changed by altering its width according to payload need. A family of three airplanes of varying width could be developed with a high degree of commonality and thus a favorable impact on production costs.

Beyond simply supersonic, a hypersonic transport could be a reality in the mid-21st century. It would have roughly the same size and weight as a contemporary 747, but would be capable of transporting its 300 passengers at around 7000mph, making possible a 90 minute flight from New York to Tokyo.

Hypersonics, liquid hydrogen propulsion systems and commuter rockets to the moon have always been the stuff of far-fetched dreams, and the far fetched and the dreams always have a way of yielding to the practical and the attainable. On the other hand, we have seen more than once in Boeing's history that the dreams have become attainable.

OWNERS & OPERATORS OF BOEING JETLINERS (Models 707 through 767)

COMMERCIAL PROGRAMS (Boeing Delivered)

(Dates refer to date of first delivery)

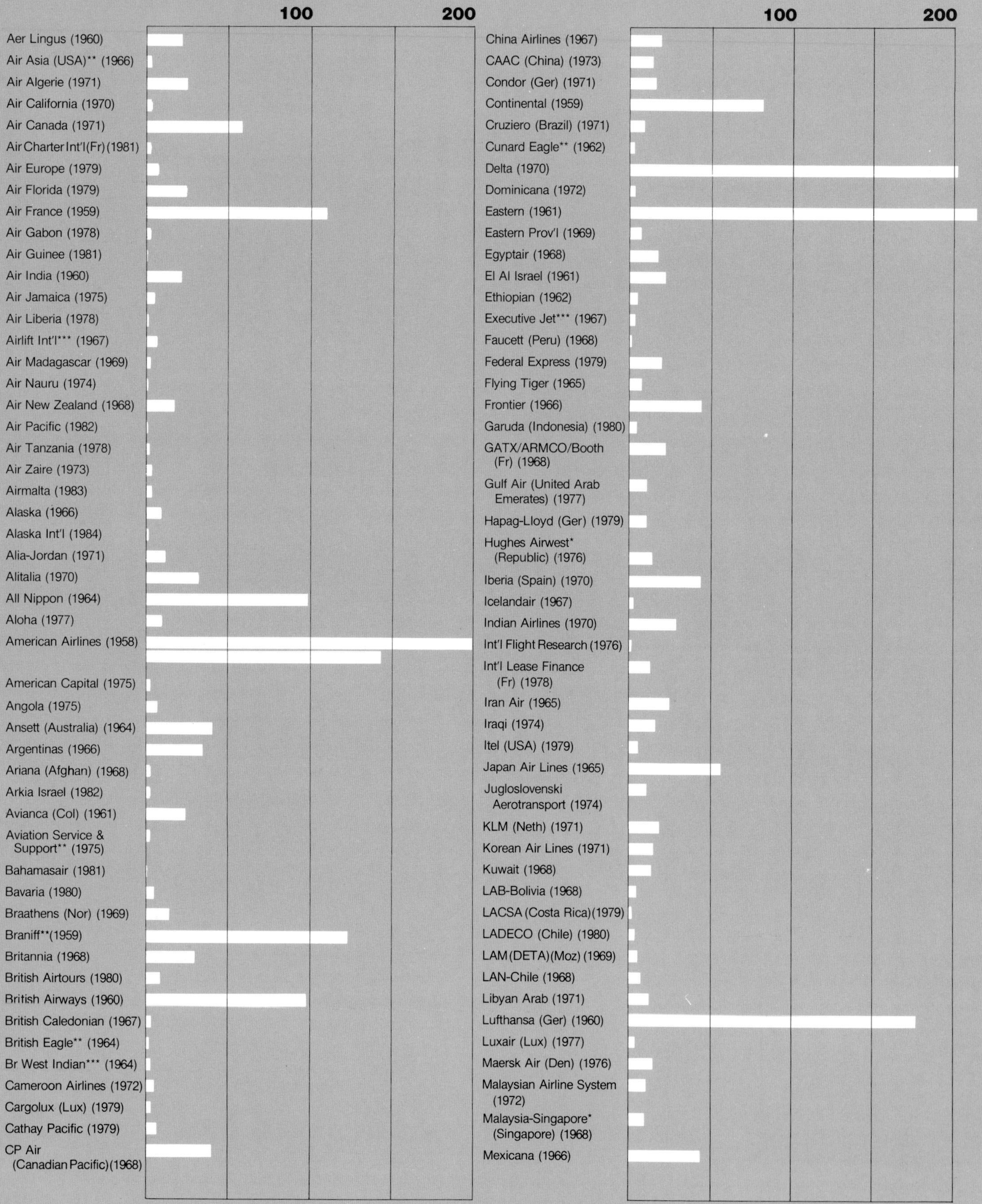

100 200

Aer Lingus (1960)
Air Asia (USA)** (1966)
Air Algerie (1971)
Air California (1970)
Air Canada (1971)
Air Charter Int'l (Fr) (1981)
Air Europe (1979)
Air Florida (1979)
Air France (1959)
Air Gabon (1978)
Air Guinee (1981)
Air India (1960)
Air Jamaica (1975)
Air Liberia (1978)
Airlift Int'l*** (1967)
Air Madagascar (1969)
Air Nauru (1974)
Air New Zealand (1968)
Air Pacific (1982)
Air Tanzania (1978)
Air Zaire (1973)
Airmalta (1983)
Alaska (1966)
Alaska Int'l (1984)
Alia-Jordan (1971)
Alitalia (1970)
All Nippon (1964)
Aloha (1977)
American Airlines (1958)
American Capital (1975)
Angola (1975)
Ansett (Australia) (1964)
Argentinas (1966)
Ariana (Afghan) (1968)
Arkia Israel (1982)
Avianca (Col) (1961)
Aviation Service & Support** (1975)
Bahamasair (1981)
Bavaria (1980)
Braathens (Nor) (1969)
Braniff** (1959)
Britannia (1968)
British Airtours (1980)
British Airways (1960)
British Caledonian (1967)
British Eagle** (1964)
Br West Indian*** (1964)
Cameroon Airlines (1972)
Cargolux (Lux) (1979)
Cathay Pacific (1979)
CP Air (Canadian Pacific) (1968)

100 200

China Airlines (1967)
CAAC (China) (1973)
Condor (Ger) (1971)
Continental (1959)
Cruziero (Brazil) (1971)
Cunard Eagle** (1962)
Delta (1970)
Dominicana (1972)
Eastern (1961)
Eastern Prov'l (1969)
Egyptair (1968)
El Al Israel (1961)
Ethiopian (1962)
Executive Jet*** (1967)
Faucett (Peru) (1968)
Federal Express (1979)
Flying Tiger (1965)
Frontier (1966)
Garuda (Indonesia) (1980)
GATX/ARMCO/Booth (Fr) (1968)
Gulf Air (United Arab Emerates) (1977)
Hapag-Lloyd (Ger) (1979)
Hughes Airwest* (Republic) (1976)
Iberia (Spain) (1970)
Icelandair (1967)
Indian Airlines (1970)
Int'l Flight Research (1976)
Int'l Lease Finance (Fr) (1978)
Iran Air (1965)
Iraqi (1974)
Itel (USA) (1979)
Japan Air Lines (1965)
Jugloslovenski Aerotransport (1974)
KLM (Neth) (1971)
Korean Air Lines (1971)
Kuwait (1968)
LAB-Bolivia (1968)
LACSA (Costa Rica) (1979)
LADECO (Chile) (1980)
LAM (DETA) (Moz) (1969)
LAN-Chile (1968)
Libyan Arab (1971)
Lufthansa (Ger) (1960)
Luxair (Lux) (1977)
Maersk Air (Den) (1976)
Malaysian Airline System (1972)
Malaysia-Singapore* (Singapore) (1968)
Mexicana (1966)

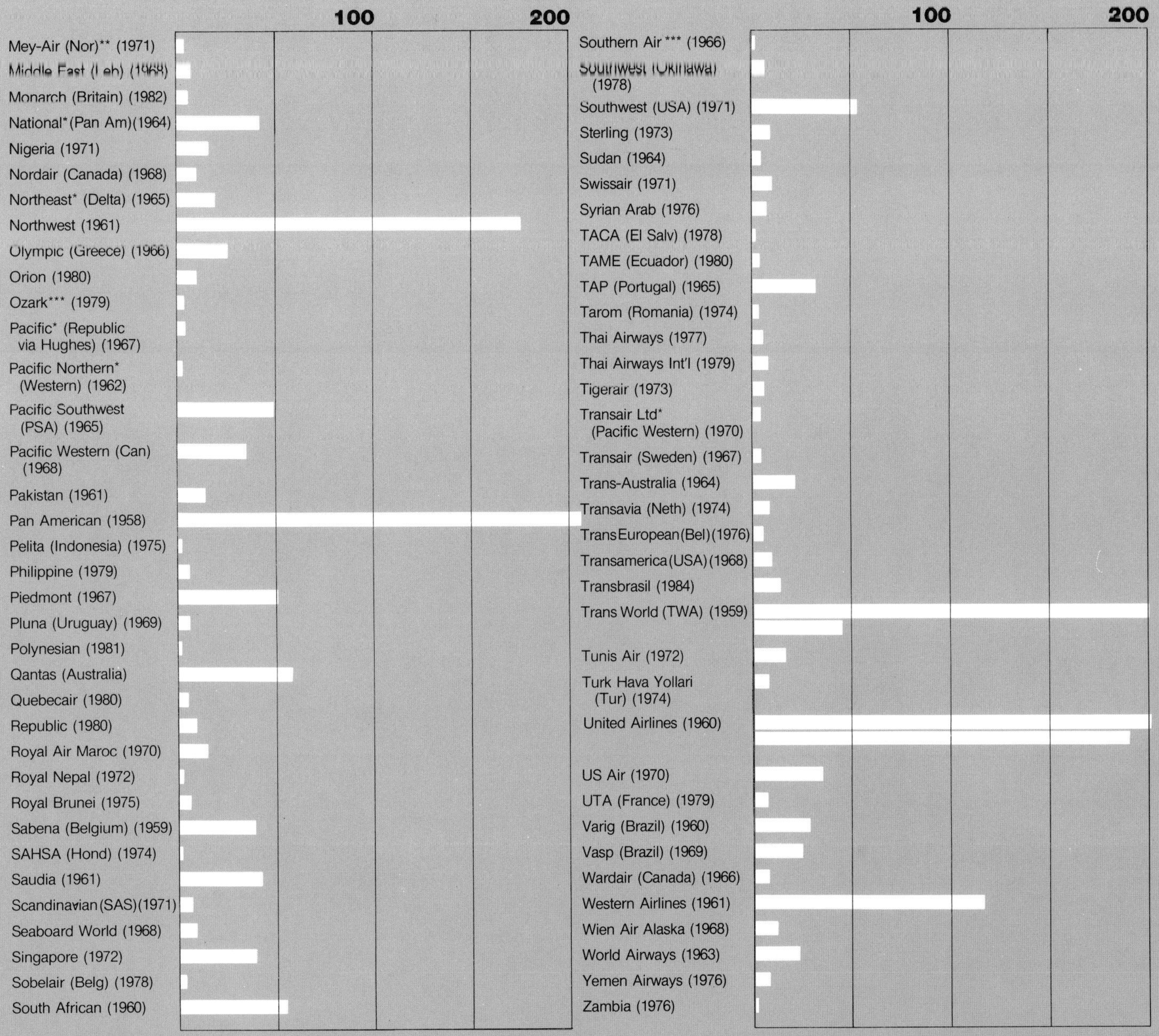

100
200
Mey-Air (Nor)** (1971)
Middle East (Leb) (1968)
Monarch (Britain) (1982)
National*(Pan Am)(1964)
Nigeria (1971)
Nordair (Canada) (1968)
Northeast* (Delta) (1965)
Northwest (1961)
Olympic (Greece) (1966)
Orion (1980)
Ozark*** (1979)
Pacific* (Republic via Hughes) (1967)
Pacific Northern* (Western) (1962)
Pacific Southwest (PSA) (1965)
Pacific Western (Can) (1968)
Pakistan (1961)
Pan American (1958)
Pelita (Indonesia) (1975)
Philippine (1979)
Piedmont (1967)
Pluna (Uruguay) (1969)
Polynesian (1981)
Qantas (Australia)
Quebecair (1980)
Republic (1980)
Royal Air Maroc (1970)
Royal Nepal (1972)
Royal Brunei (1975)
Sabena (Belgium) (1959)
SAHSA (Hond) (1974)
Saudia (1961)
Scandinavian (SAS) (1971)
Seaboard World (1968)
Singapore (1972)
Sobelair (Belg) (1978)
South African (1960)
100
200
Southern Air*** (1966)
Southwest (Okinawa) (1978)
Southwest (USA) (1971)
Sterling (1973)
Sudan (1964)
Swissair (1971)
Syrian Arab (1976)
TACA (El Salv) (1978)
TAME (Ecuador) (1980)
TAP (Portugal) (1965)
Tarom (Romania) (1974)
Thai Airways (1977)
Thai Airways Int'l (1979)
Tigerair (1973)
Transair Ltd* (Pacific Western) (1970)
Transair (Sweden) (1967)
Trans-Australia (1964)
Transavia (Neth) (1974)
Trans European (Bel) (1976)
Transamerica (USA) (1968)
Transbrasil (1984)
Trans World (TWA) (1959)
Tunis Air (1972)
Turk Hava Yollari (Tur) (1974)
United Airlines (1960)
US Air (1970)
UTA (France) (1979)
Varig (Brazil) (1960)
Vasp (Brazil) (1969)
Wardair (Canada) (1966)
Western Airlines (1961)
Wien Air Alaska (1968)
World Airways (1963)
Yemen Airways (1976)
Zambia (1976)

(Dates refer to date of first delivery)

* Airline no longer in operation, aircraft transferred to airline referred to in parentheses
** Airline no longer in operation
*** Airline no longer operating Boeing jetliners

GOVERNMENTAL AND NON-COMMERCIAL PROGRAMS (Boeing Delivered)

30
60
Boeing (1954)
Brazilian AF (1976)
Busy Bee (Norway) (1979)
Canadian AF (1970)
Cameroon Gov't (1978)
Dome (1980)
Eldorado (1980)
Essex* (1969)
FAA (1961)
Indonesian AF (1982)
IT&T (1971)
Iran Gov't (Incl AF) (1974)
Jordan Gov't (1980)
Luftwaffe (1968)
30
60
Maritime Invesm't (1979)
Moroccan Gov't (1982)
NATO**** (1982)
Niger Gov't (1978)
NOGA (1981)
Petrolair Services (1981)
Portuguese Gov't* (1971)
Saudi Gov't (1979)**
Romanian Gov't (1979)
Senegal Gov't (1976)
US Air Force*** (1959)
Venezuela Gov't (1976)
Wedge (1981)
Unidentified

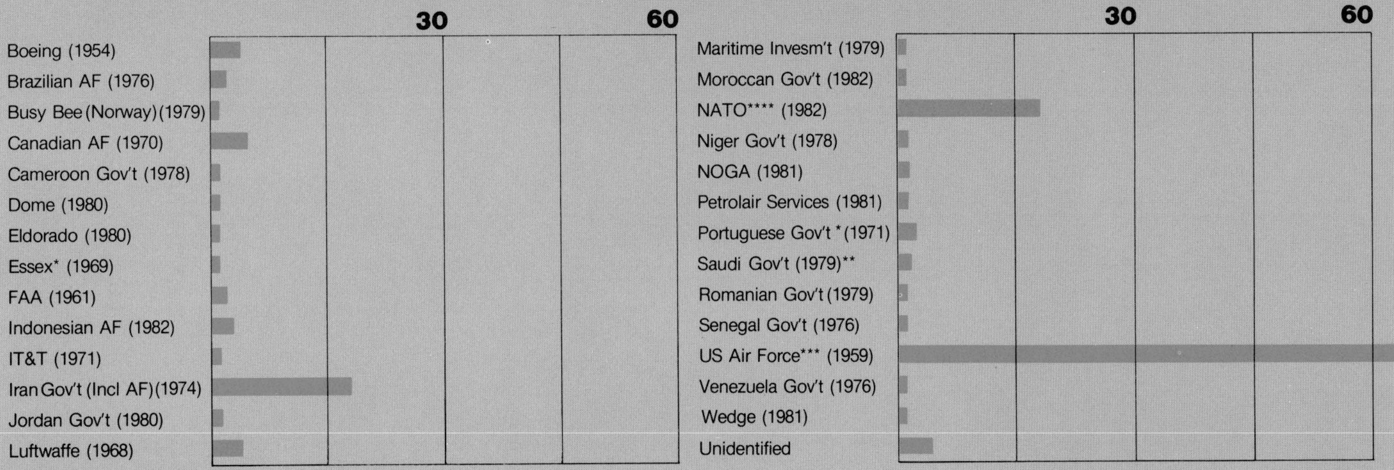

* Service no longer operating Boeing jetliners
** Excludes E-3A AWACS
*** Includes 32 E-3A AWACS (707 airframe), 19 T-43A Trainers (737 airframe). Excludes C-135 transports & tankers (717 airframe)
**** All E-3A AWACS/(707 airframe)

The modern **two-crew-member cockpit** shared by the 757 and 767.

N757A
AB-CF
MAP FAIL
APU
R

Copyright.
Woodburytype.
COLONEL W. F. CODY.
"Buffalo Bill."

CONTENTS

Preceding pages:

Chief Joseph, Nez Percé

Westerners (clockwise from top left):
Texas Ranger;
Hispanic woman, California, 1856;
San Francisco peace officer and his daughter;
Sarah Smith Griffin, Mormon pioneer

Sam Houston, 1851

The family of Don Vicente Lugo, California, 1870

Chinese immigrant, 1851

Texas cowboys in Denver, 1901

William F. "Buffalo Bill" Cody

Pretty Nose, Cheyenne, 1878

Mormon children, about 1900

Lumberjacks, Pacific Northwest, 1907

Following page:

July Fourth, Fort Belknap, Montana, 1906

PREFACE

The Dreaming Place

In a conversation with us several years ago, the Kiowa poet N. Scott Momaday remarked that the American West is "a dream. It is what people who have come here from the beginning of time have dreamed. . . . It is a landscape that has to be seen to be believed, and may have to be believed in order to be seen."

For five years we have traveled that landscape, photographed its vistas, talked to its people, sought out its history, all as part of our production of *The West,* an eight-part documentary series for public television. Now — 100,000 air-miles, 72 filmed interviews, 74 visits to archives and collections, and more than 250 hours of film later — we have begun to understand at least something of what Momaday meant. In the West, everything seems somehow larger than life, and we now can see why so many different peoples have come to consider their own innermost lives inextricably linked with it. Over the centuries, the West has been the repository of the dreams of an astonishing variety of people — and it has been on the long, dusty roads of the West that those dreams have crisscrossed and collided, transforming all who traveled along them, rewarding some while disappointing others.

The story of the West was once told as an unbroken series of triumphs — the victory of "civilization" over "barbarism," a relentlessly inspirational epic in which greed and cruelty were often glossed over as enterprise and courage. Later, that epic would be turned upside down by some, so that the story of the West became another — equally misleading — morality tale, one in which the crimes of conquest and dispossession were allowed to overshadow everything else that ever happened beyond the Mississippi. The truth about the West is far more complicated, and much more compelling.

America without the West is unthinkable now. Yet there was nothing inevitable about our taking of it. Others had prior claim to its vastness, after all, and we could quite easily have remained forever huddled east of the Mississippi. In resolving to move west and become a continental nation we would exact a fearful price from those already living on the land. But we also became a different people, and it is no accident that that turbulent history — and the myths that have grown up around it — has made the West the most potent symbol of the nation as a whole, overseas as well as in our own hearts.

Of course, no film series, no book — no library of books, for that matter — can ever encompass the whole story of the West. There are as many valid approaches to telling it as there are able historians willing to try. We believe that history really is biography, and in this volume — and in the script for the twelve-hour film series upon which it is based — we have chosen to focus on the experiences of individual men and women, many of whom tell their own stories in their own words, through diaries and letters and autobiographical accounts.

Our cast is deliberately diverse — there are explorers and soldiers and Indian warriors, settlers and railroad builders and gaudy showmen, but there are also a Chinese ditch digger and a rich Mexican American landowner, a forty-niner from Chile and a Texas cowboy born in Britain, a woman missionary to the Indians who loathed the West and a Wellesley graduate who loved it in spite of everything it did to her and her family. Some of our subjects are celebrated figures. Others will be new to most readers. None plays the stereotyped part one or another of the West's contradictory myths dictates. All were selected because they seemed to us both to illuminate the times through which they lived and to tell us something important about the West, as well.

Our subjects were chosen, too, to demonstrate that in the often stirring story of the West, a human price was paid for every gain. The stories we've tried to tell in these pages and on the television screen at least suggest, we hope, the outlines of a more inclusive story of the West than is conventionally told; a story that is more frank about our failures and more clear-eyed about the cost of even our greatest successes than the old one, but also a story in which each of us can find a place and all can take pardonable pride.

The story of the American West, we believe, is at once the story of a unique part of the country and a metaphor for the country as a whole. With all its heroism and inequity, exploitation and adventure, sober realities and bright myths, it is the story of all of us, no matter where on the continent we happen to live, no matter how recently our ancestors arrived on its shores.

Stephen Ives and Ken Burns

By the time this Blackfoot village was photographed around the turn of the twentieth century, the Indian world had already changed forever.

CHAPTER ONE

THE NORTHERN MYSTERY

The native peoples of the West were far more varied than were the Europeans who, out of ignorance, would one day call them all "Indians." Each group had its own distinctive story of how it came to exist, and its own special name, which most often translated simply as "the people." And each had proved its ability to adapt to change — shifts in climate, new terrain, pressure from neighboring peoples. But nothing could have prepared any of them for what was about to happen to their world.

Most of the men, women, and children of the Cocos Indian village on Galveston Island were away from their homes, setting traps for fish and gathering roots, one early November day in 1528, and so they did not see the pale, half-naked man with hair on his face slip in among their huts. Moving warily, he stole an earthen cooking pot from one dwelling, grabbed fish from the rack on which they had been drying in the sun, tucked a squirming puppy under his arm. Then he fled toward the beach.

Three warriors did spot him and followed at a distance. When they reached the beach they were astonished to see nearly forty strangers much like the one they'd followed, huddled around a driftwood fire. Some were eagerly tearing at the half-dried fish, others were preparing to roast the stolen dog. Still others were simply sprawled on the beach, apparently too weak to move.

The Cocos were accustomed to trading with other native peoples living far inland, but none of them had ever seen men like these before: most of them were pale and hairy, a few were dark skinned, all spoke a barbarous, incomprehensible tongue. The Indians hurried off for reinforcements. Soon, some one hundred warriors — tall men who pierced their ears and lower lips with reeds and were armed with bows and arrows — had gathered to see the curious newcomers.

One of the strangers tottered toward them, holding out a handful of beads and tiny bells. The warriors accepted them, delighting in the tinkling sound they had never heard before, and they offered arrows in return as a sign of friendship. By hand signals they made it clear that they would bring food and water in the morning.

The grateful, desperate strangers were Spanish soldiers and Moorish slaves, all that survived of a land expedition of some three hundred men that had sailed north from Cuba a year earlier with orders to conquer all of "Florida" — the whole fifteen-hundred-mile Gulf coast from the Florida peninsula to the Panuco River in what is now Mexico. The expedition's commander, a one-eyed conquistador named Panfilo de Narvaez, had proved a disaster in the field. In his overeagerness to find treasure, he had led his army too far inland from their landing place near Tampa Bay for it to be resupplied by sea, then lost touch entirely with the vessels that might have rescued him. His high-handed dealings with the Apalachee Indians of the Tallahassee region had finally led their skilled archers to open fire. Without hope of rescue and in terror of Apalachee arrows, suffering from malaria and reduced to eating his horses and stealing parched corn from Indian towns simply to survive, Narvaez had finally abandoned any thought of further exploration and ordered his men to fashion barges

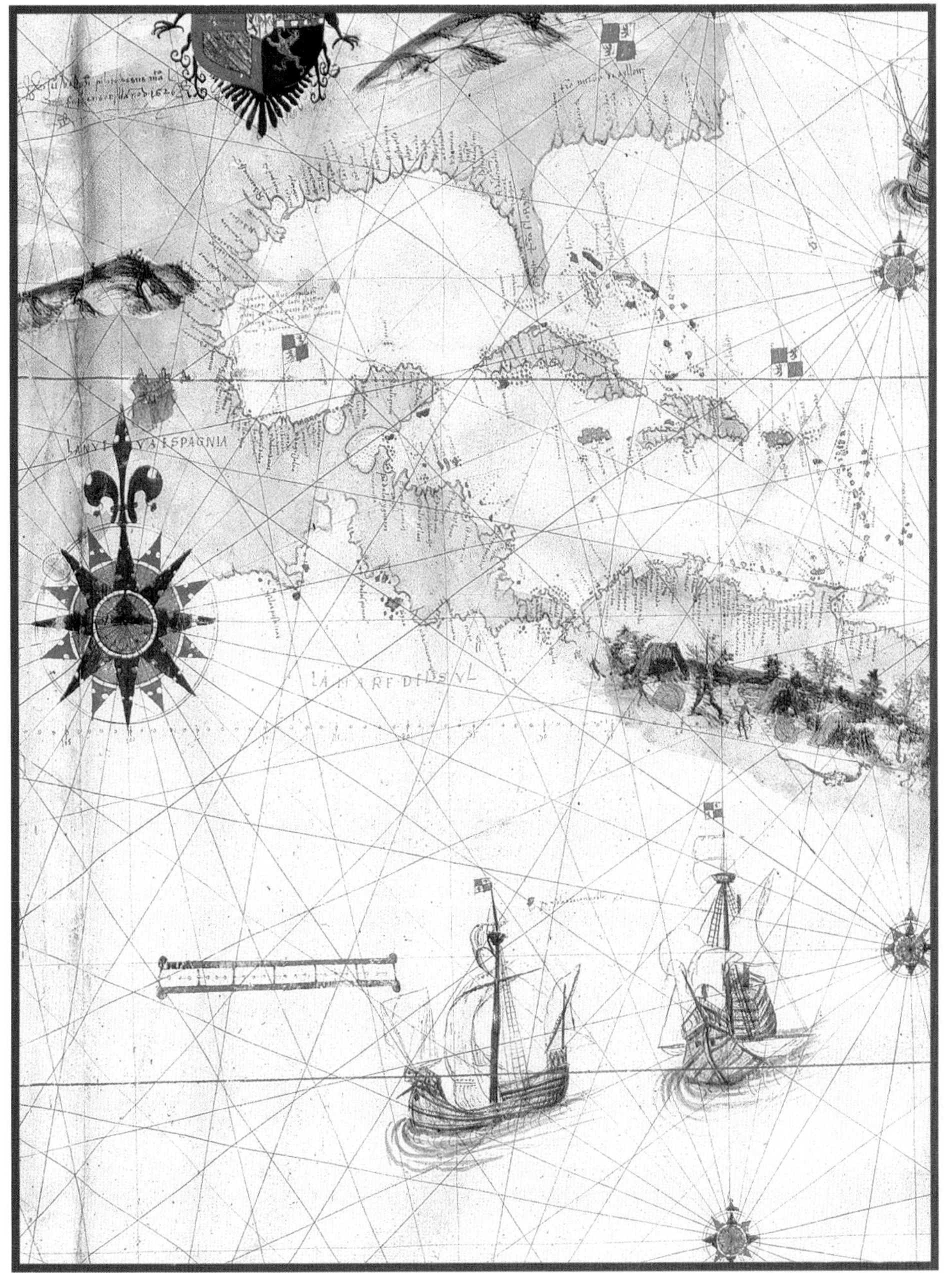

Throughout all this country we went naked, and as we were unaccustomed to being so, twice a year we cast our skins like serpents. The sun and air produced great sores on our breasts and shoulders, giving us sharp pain; and the large load we had . . . caused the cords to cut into our arms. . . . The country is so broken and thickly set, that . . . thorns and shrubs tore our flesh wherever we went.

Alvar Nuñez Cabeza de Vaca

from hollowed-out trees in which to flee. With sails sewn together from the men's shirts, they had set out from Apalachicola Bay and tried to sail their way west to Mexico. They had been on the water for more than a month, subsisting on half a fistful of corn a day as fierce winds shredded their sails. Only hours before the wind blew them onto the beach at Galveston Island, the survivors had watched it overturn a second vessel, drowning more than forty of their friends.

When the Cocos returned to the beach the next day they brought with them so much food that the man now in command of the strangers, a veteran of half a dozen wars in Europe named Alvar Nuñez Cabeza de Vaca, thought he and his men might still be able to continue their journey. They clawed their log boat out of the sand and pushed it back out into the water, then climbed in and began again to row. But the wind came up once more, a big wave tore the oars from their weakened hands, and a

The New World as seen by a Spanish cartographer in 1526, two years before Cabeza de Vaca and his companions were washed up on the Texas coast to begin their extraordinary journey across the Southwest

Encounters: Three engravings of life among the Timucuan people of Florida — based on the firsthand observations of Jacques Le Moyne de Morgues, who visited them with a French expedition in 1564 — suggest something of the complexity of the Indian world Cabeza de Vaca and his contemporaries knew. At left, the Timucuan "king" shows his visitors a pillar, set up by an earlier French party, to which his people continue to make obeisance as a sign of friendship with the exotic strangers. In the center, he leads his men into battle. At right, he comforts the widows of those slain by his enemies.

second turned the barge over. Three men were pulled under and drowned. The rest scrambled to shore and collapsed again on the sand.

Watching from shore, the Cocos were so moved by the strangers' plight, Cabeza de Vaca remembered, that "they sat down and lamented for half an hour so loudly they could have been heard a long way off." Then they motioned for the newcomers to follow them to their camp. The Spanish feared the Indians planned to kill them; instead, they offered only sympathy and hospitality: "Supporting us under our arms, they hurried us from one to another of four big fires they had built along the path [to their village]. At each fire, when we regained a little warmth and strength, they took us on so swiftly our feet hardly touched ground."

These men — their bodies now "so emaciated," Cabeza de Vaca remembered, "we could easily count every bone and looked the very picture of death" — were the first Europeans ever to set foot in the vast region that would one day be called the West.

It was not an auspicious beginning, and all but four of them would soon die. But the adventures that befell those four over the next seven years, and the accounts they gave when they finally reached safety in Mexico, would help to fuel more than two centuries of Spanish adventuring in the region. Their experiences hinted, too, at what the history of the whole West might have been had European assumptions about the people already living there not been so circumscribed, had humility and respect not so often been outweighed by greed and arrogance.

Fourteen ninety-two had marked two great milestones for Ferdinand of Aragon and Isabella of Castile, the rulers of Spain: nearly eight centuries of warfare between Christians and Moorish Muslims on the Iberian Peninsula had ended in victory for the Cross that year, and Christopher Columbus had stumbled upon a whole New World. Surely, the Spanish argued, two such momentous events in a single year were proof that God favored their cause. The following year, Pope Alexander VI, himself a Spaniard, lent that belief his official approval; citing the "authority of the mighty God," he solemnly awarded to his homeland the right to claim the entire New World so that all of its inhabitants could be brought to Christ — by kindness and exhortation if possible, by force of arms if necessary. The same religious zeal that had finally

driven the Moors from Spain would now be loosed upon a whole host of new nonbelievers.

Conquest promised material rewards as well as spiritual ones. To persuade them to finance their holy war against the Moors, the kings of Castile had offered soldiers licenses, entitling them to a handsome share in the spoils. Now, the Spanish king made the same offer to entice adventurers to try their luck across the Atlantic. As Christianity's fortunes improved, so would the fortunes of its soldiers.

The conquistadors seized the island of Española first, then Puerto Rico, Jamaica, Cuba. Hernán Cortés conquered the Aztecs, taking Mexico and with it almost unimaginable riches. Francisco Pizarro crushed the Incas of Peru and commandeered their still richer treasure. By the time Cabeza de Vaca had set out for Florida in 1527, Spain laid claim to the Caribbean and Central America and most of South America, and was eager to probe still farther northward. "We came here to serve God and his Majesty," one conquistador said, "to give light to those who were in the darkness and to get rich, as all men desire to do."

Cabeza de Vaca and his companions shared that desire, and had expected to come as conquerors. Instead, they soon entered the Indian world as supplicants and slaves. The Cocos fed and housed them willingly at first, and Cabeza de Vaca was struck by their tender feelings and generosity: "These people love their offspring more than any in the world and treat them very kindly. If a son dies, the whole village joins the parents and kindred in weeping. The parents set off the wails each day before dawn, again at noon, and at sunset for one year. . . . The people are generous to each other with what little they have."

But when cholera, carried by the Europeans, swept through the Indians' camp, killing all but fifteen of the strangers and almost half the Cocos' own number, the status of the newcomers changed. The surviving Spaniards and Moors scattered, Cabeza de Vaca recalled, and "my life [became] unbearable. In addition to much other work, I had to grub roots in the water or from underground in the canebrakes. My fingers got so raw that if a straw touched them they would bleed. The broken canes often slashed my flesh. I had to work amidst them without benefit of clothes."

In February of 1530, Cabeza de Vaca escaped from his first masters and became a trader instead of a slave, carrying shells and mesquite beans from the coast to the tribes of the interior, and bringing back in exchange flint for arrowheads and red ochre and deer-hair tassels for decoration. "The various Indians would beg me to go from one quarter to another for things they needed," he recalled. "Their incessant hostilities made it impossible for them to travel cross-country. . . . This served my main purpose, which all the while was to determine an eventual road out."

He kept servicing his customers and learning all that he could about the countryside until the summer of 1532, when he came upon three other survivors of his expedition: two soldiers, Alonso del Castillo and Andres Dorantes, and a Moorish slave named Estevanico, who belonged to Dorantes. They were living among a hard-living Tonkawa people called the Mariames, of whom Cabeza de Vaca wrote:

> They cast away their daughters at birth; the dogs eat them. They [say they] do this because all the nations of the region are their enemies, with whom they war ceaselessly; and that if they were to marry off their daughters, the daughters would multiply their enemies. . . . We asked why they did not themselves marry these girls. They said that marrying relatives would be a disgusting thing; it was far better to kill them than give them to either kin or foe.

On September 22, 1534, the four men determined to make a break for the Spanish settlements in Mexico, hundreds of miles away. They had been gone for seven years now and would wander for nearly two more, through present-day Texas, northward along the Rio Grande, then south again into what would become northern Mexico, moving from one tribe to the next.

The hardships I endured in this journeying business were long to tell — peril and privation, storms and frost, which often overtook me when alone in the wilderness. By the unfailing Grace of God our Lord I came forth from all.

Alvar Nuñez Cabeza de Vaca

"They all differ," Cabeza de Vaca wrote of the peoples he and his companions met, "in their habitations, villages and tongues." Some menaced the strangers. Others greeted them as honored guests. Still others asked for their help: "Surely extraordinary men like us, [they said,] embodied . . . powers over nature. . . . Some Indians came [begging us] to cure them of terrible headaches. . . . Our method . . . was to bless the sick, breathe upon them, recite a *Pater Noster* and *Ave Maria* and pray earnestly to God our Lord for their recovery. When we concluded with the sign of the cross, He willed that our patients should directly spread the news that they have been restored to health."

In the end, both Cabeza de Vaca and his companions and their Indian patients came to believe in the travelers' healing powers. They were hailed as the Children of the Sun, showered with food and gifts:

> At sunset we reached a village of a hundred huts. All the people who lived in them were awaiting us at the village outskirts with terrific yelling and violent slapping of their hands against their thighs. They had with them their precious perforated gourd rattles (pebbles inside) which they produce only at such important occasions. . . . This people hysterically crowded upon us, everyone competing to touch us first; we were nearly killed in the crush. Without letting our feet touch ground, they carried us to the huts they had made for us.

In the Valley of the Sonora they were received by the people of the Ures pueblo, who gave them turquoises and arrowheads fashioned from other green stones that resembled emeralds and which they said came from somewhere far to the north.

By the spring of 1536, some six hundred Pima Indian admirers were escorting them from one settlement to the next. Then they entered the valley of the Rio Sinaloa. Here no crowds turned out to greet them. Indian villages stood empty. "With heavy hearts we looked out over the lavishly watered, fertile and beautiful land," Cabeza de Vaca noted, "now abandoned and burned, and the people thin and weak, scattering and hiding in fright. . . . All along the way we could see the tracks of the Christians and traces of their camps." The "Christians" were Spanish slavers who had already managed to seize "half the men and all the women and boys" to work their gold and copper mines.

Cabeza de Vaca sought out the Spanish commander, a conquistador named Diego de Alcaraz. He was "dumbfounded by the sight of me," Cabeza de Vaca recalled,

THE ANASAZI

Several great peoples — remembered collectively as the Anasazi, the Navajo word for "the Old Ones" — once ruled the high country where the present states of New Mexico, Colorado, Utah, and Arizona come together. For centuries, their civilization thrived, trading turquoise with other cultures to the north and south, east and west. They felled trees to make way for fields of corn and beans and squash, dammed streams to water their crops, laid out hundreds of miles of broad, straight roads across the desert, and built towns where thousands lived in houses several stories high.

But by A.D. 1300 — most likely because years of drought had simply made life untenable — they abandoned it all and moved south to establish new towns along the Rio Grande. (The present-day Pueblos, Zuni, and Hopi are believed to be their descendants.) Meanwhile, newcomers — ancestors of the Navajo and Ute and Apache — eventually took over much of the region the Anasazi had occupied. The Old Ones were not the first people to be displaced by others in the West, nor would they be the last.

Anasazi ruins in Canyon de Chelly, New Mexico, photographed by Timothy O'Sullivan in 1873

"strangely undressed and in company with friends." But the commander was frankly delighted by the sight of Cabeza de Vaca's Indian companions, six hundred men, women, and children, ripe for the taking. There were precious few potential slaves in the picked-over region, he explained, and "he was completely undone, having been unable to catch any Indians in a long time; he did not know which way to turn; his men were getting too hungry and exhausted." Seizing Cabeza de Vaca's Indian escort would make the whole expedition worthwhile.

But Cabeza de Vaca refused to cooperate. If Indians were to be converted to Christianity, his travels had now taught him, "they must be won by kindness, the only certain way." He urged his followers to return to their homes as quickly as possible. The Indians hesitated at first, fearful of leaving their healer among such barbaric strangers. They could not believe that these brutal slavers and the men who had healed them could be the same sort of people:

> Conferring among themselves, they replied that the Christians lied: We had come from the sunrise, they from the sunset; we healed the sick, they killed the [healthy]; we came naked and barefoot, they, clothed, horsed, and lanced; we coveted nothing but gave whatever we were given, while they robbed whomsoever they found and bestowed nothing on anyone.

Cabeza de Vaca persisted in urging them to go home, and the Pimas finally agreed. The slavers waited till he and his companions were on their way to the nearest Spanish settlement under escort, then seized the Indians anyway.

By appealing to the Spanish authorities when he got to Mexico City, Cabeza de Vaca managed to win freedom for all of his former followers, but the viceroy was far less interested in his views on how Indians should be treated than he was in the possibility of new treasure. The returned wanderer was careful not to exaggerate. Most of the lands through which he had passed, he said, were "remote and malign, devoid of resources." But he also reported that the Indians had told him of "populous towns and very large houses . . . and many turquoise stones" farther to the north than he had gone.

There had long been rumors in Europe of Seven Cities of Gold, said to have been established by seven fugitive bishops from Portugal and now believed to lie somewhere north of Mexico. Cabeza de Vaca's account was all the would-be treasure-hunters needed. The Seven Cities did exist; here was proof of it. In 1539, the slave Estevanico was asked to guide a priest, Fray Marcos de Niza, and a large scouting party in hopes of finding them somewhere in the region the Spanish called the Northern Mystery.

THE SEVEN CITIES OF GOLD

In the spring of that year, the one hundred Zuni families who made Hawikuh pueblo in what is now Arizona their home were preparing to begin their planting ritual, as they had done for centuries. Their sacred spirits — *katsinas* — were to be evoked to ensure fertility and bring the rain that made life in that arid land possible.

But just as the ceremonies got under way, a lookout spotted a jostling crowd of some three hundred Indians approaching. They were escorting a man unlike anyone they had ever seen before — tall and dark skinned, dressed in pelts and wearing bits of turquoise, walking two greyhounds on a leash. His escorts said he was a great healer, but the people of Hawikuh tried to bar his entry by pouring a line of sacred cornmeal across his path.

The stranger stepped right over it. Declaring himself a Child of the Sun, he demanded turquoise and women, and warned that more of the Sun's children were on their way. As a token of his unearthly power he had sent ahead of him a decorated gourd rattle.

The chief of the pueblo was not impressed. He recognized the rattle as having been fashioned by a people far to the south, with whom his people had no friendly rela-

Dancers assembled to invoke rain as part of the annual summer solstice ceremony at Zuni pueblo, 1899

THE PEOPLE

It stretches from the Pacific Ocean to the Mississippi River, from the Rio Grande to what is now the border of Canada — 2,168,930 square miles of the most extraordinary landscape on earth.

To the Spanish priests and soldiers who rode into it from Mexico, it was the North. To the Russians and British who first sailed along its coast in search of furs to sell to China, it was the East. And to the French and British trappers who wandered into it from Canada, it was the South.

To the Native Americans it was simply home. Yet because its most recent conquerors came from the east, it has come to be called the West.

Its terrain has always beckoned — and repelled. It is a land of grasslands and deserts and mountain barriers: the Rockies and Wasatch, the Bitterroots and Bighorns, the Sierra Nevada and Sangre de Cristo, the Confusions, the Crazies, and the Black Hills.

It is a land of rivers: the Colorado and Columbia and Missouri; the Carson, the Humboldt, and the Dismal; the Big Sandy and the Little Sandy; Sand Creek and the Greasy Grass; the River That Scolds All Others and the River of No Return.

And it is also a land of too little water.

The West exists on a scale virtually unknown elsewhere. It is a land of unimaginable distances and infinite horizons.

But it was never empty. No one knows how many hundreds of thousands of native people occupied it before the coming of the first Europeans, perhaps as many as 3 million. But they had lived there for a thousand generations since their arrival by land from the Asian mainland across the Bering Strait.

Counterclockwise from left: Many Horns, Teton Lakota, 1872; Navajo boy, 1905; Mattie Tom, Apache, 1899

The photographs on these and the following pages, made in the late nineteenth and early twentieth centuries, can only hint at the richness and variety of the Indian world before the coming of the conquistadors.

Devils Tower in Wyoming, sacred to several Indian peoples

Right: Modisi, Hopi, 1879; Chief Washakie, Shoshone

There were those among them who lived in isolated shelters fashioned from brush, and others who occupied large houses made from the tallest trees on earth. Some knew only skin teepees that could be put up and pulled down in minutes; others dwelt in elaborate cliff-top cities that had stood for centuries.

Some prayed to the spirits of the animals they hunted and did not dare alter the earth they believed to be their mother. Others transformed the landscape, burning valleys and hillsides to increase the grasslands — and the deer that fed upon them. Still others built dams and diverted streams to irrigate their crops.

In some tribes, war was considered the highest calling, and wealth was measured in slaves. In others, women owned all the property, and when a couple married, the man joined his wife's family.

Pawnee earth lodge village in present-day Nebraska

Cheyenne painted for a sun dance

Havasupai dwelling made of brush, Southwest

Spokane village, Washington

Two Whistles, Crow

Hopi dancer

Zuni snake priest

Webs of ancient trading trails stretched in every direction and covered every corner of the West. Precious sea-shells from the Pacific Northwest were harvested by people who rode the seas in immense canoes and traded the shells for elk hides with a people who flattened their babies' heads as a sign of beauty and prestige. From tribe to tribe, the shells were passed inland — exchanged for salmon with a merchant people who held a yearly trading fair on the Columbia River.

Kwakiutl wearing mask, Northwest coast

Skidegate village of the Haida tribe, Queen Charlotte Island, British Columbia, 1878

Haida shamans

Umatilla woman, Columbia Basin

Nez Percé woman

Gros Ventre woman drying meat,
Fort Belknap reservation, 1906

Omaha village

Lakota women decorated with
porcupine quills and dentalium shells

The shells were also traded for powerful bows fashioned from the horns of mountain sheep by a tribe who called themselves the Namipu but who would one day be called the Nez Percé, who each year climbed through the Bitterroots to hunt; for buffalo meat provided by people who followed the great herds across the Plains on foot and depended on dogs to haul their few belongings; for corn, grown along the Missouri River by the Mandan people, who lived in large towns of rounded earth lodges; and for wild rice and deerskins, brought from the woodlands east of the Mississippi by the Lakota, a people who would one day migrate west themselves and be renamed the Sioux by their enemies.

And so, people who worshiped different gods, inhabited entirely different worlds, and were sometimes unaware of one another's existence were linked together nonetheless: buffalo robes warmed people who had never seen a buffalo; cornmeal was eaten by people who had never planted corn; and ocean shells decorated the clothing of people who lived a thousand miles from the sea.

Kutenai duck hunter, Montana

Lakota woman and dog travois of the kind used before the coming of the horse, Rosebud reservation

Sia buffalo mask, Southwest

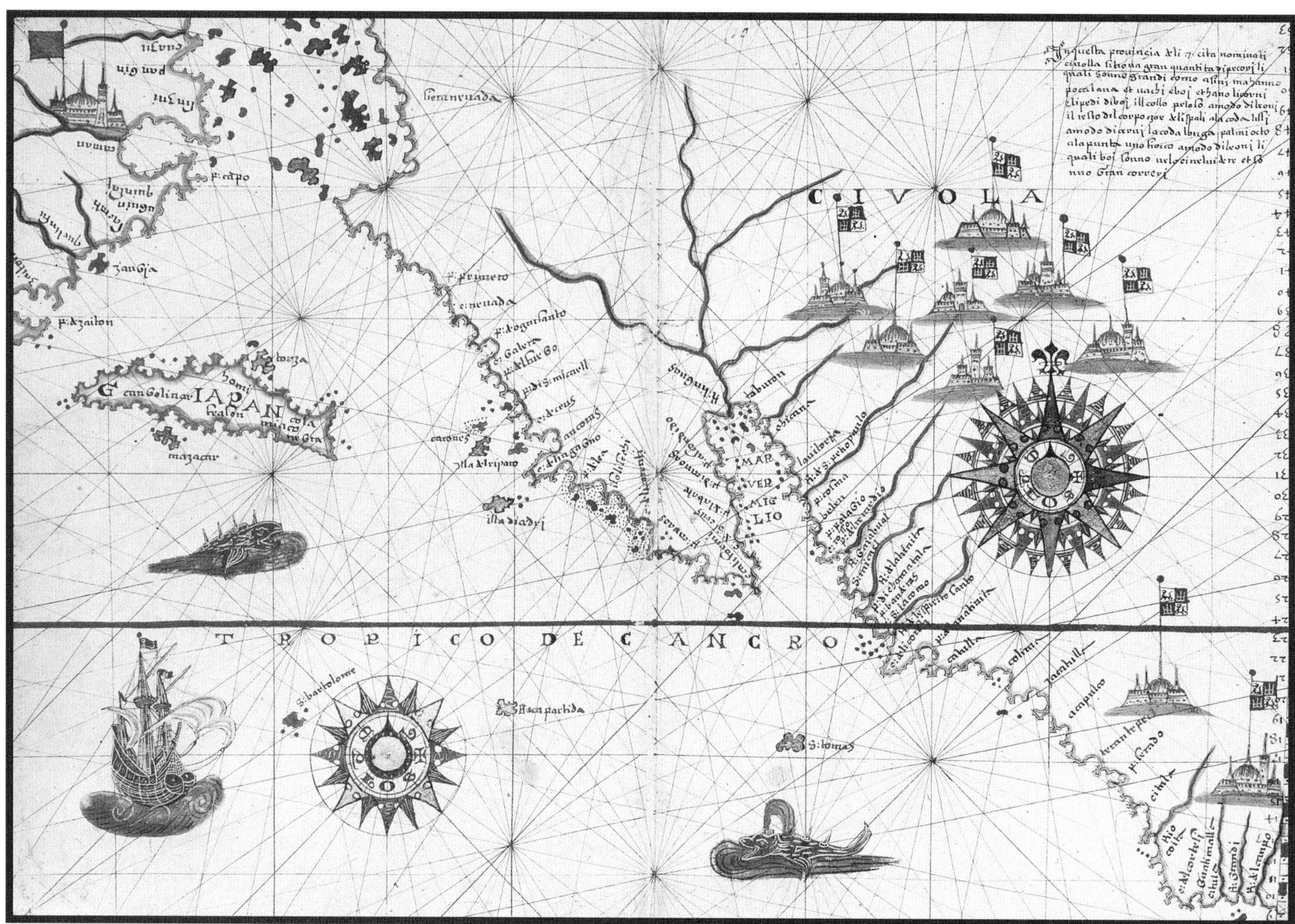

The Seven Cities of Gold were still optimistically included in this detail of a Spanish map showing the Southwest in 1578, nearly four decades after Coronado had failed to find them.

tions. Now believing the stranger either a spy, a madman, or a witch, the chief ordered him killed. Afterward, some of the people of the pueblo wondered if they had done the right thing, whether the dead man's warning of more mysterious strangers on the way would come true. They would have to wait just a little over a year for their answer. They could not have known it then, but nothing in their lives — or the lives of the other peoples who occupied the lands newcomers would one day call the West — would ever be the same again.

The dark-skinned stranger the Zuni of Hawikuh had killed was the Moorish slave Estevanico, and when Fray Marcos got word of his guide's fate, he determined to return to Mexico as fast as he could. But before he fled, he slipped up close enough to have at least a glimpse of Hawikuh, or so he would later claim:

> It had a very fine appearance. . . . The houses, as the Indians have told me, are all of stone, built in stories and with flat roofs. Judging by what I could see from the height where I placed myself to observe it, the settlement is larger than the city of Mexico. . . . It appears to me that this land is the best and largest of all those that have been discovered.

Hawikuh, he assured the authorities in Mexico City, was indeed one of the Seven Cities of Gold and satisfyingly filled with treasure: "I was told that there is much gold there and the natives make it into little vessels and jewels for their ears, and into little blades with which they wipe away their sweat."

The friar's gaudy stories grew with the telling — he confided to a fellow priest that he had also seen a temple filled with idols, its walls covered "inside and outside with precious stones" — and in February of 1540, the Spanish viceroy sent Fray Marcos north again, escorted this time by 292 Spanish soldiers, 3 priests, more than a thousand Indians, and big hungry herds of sheep and cattle and horses. In command was the thirty-year-old governor of a Mexican province who had married a woman of great wealth and was now eager to amass a fortune of his own — Francisco Vásquez de Coronado.

It took Coronado's expedition four months, following Indian trails across deserts and through the mountains, but he finally reached Hawikuh in July.

The Zuni saw them coming, the sun slanting off their helmets. The black stranger had been right: they *were* the Children of the Sun. And this time they came riding on monstrous animals no Native American in the region had ever seen before — horses. The warriors went down to face them, nonetheless. Through an interpreter, Coronado explained that he had come on a sacred mission. He warned that the Indians must submit to the Spanish crown and adopt Christianity. If they did not, "with the help of God we shall forcefully . . . make war against you . . . take you and your wives and children and . . . make slaves of them . . . and shall do to you all the harm and damage that we can."

The Zuni refused to allow the strangers to enter their pueblo, perhaps having heard from their trading partners to the south rumors about the depredations of Spanish slavers. Instead, they began to throw stones and shoot arrows. "They . . . grew so bold," Coronado remembered, "that they came up almost to the heels of our horses to shoot their arrows. On this account, I saw that it was no longer time to hesitate, and as the priests approved the action, I charged them." The Spanish shouted "Santiago!" — St. James — as they went into battle, their war cry invoking the patron saint who they believed had brought them victory over the Moors.

The Indians fled from Spanish lances and from Spanish guns, whose thunderous sound they had never heard before. Several were killed. The rest retreated within the town walls and hurled rocks down on their attackers. Coronado himself was twice knocked to the ground: "If I had not been protected by the very good headpiece," he recalled, "the outcome would have been very bad for me." But the Spanish soon overran the Indians, seized their stores of food, and set up a cross — to which the Zuni began to make frantic offerings.

Christianity had come to the American West.

Coronado renamed Hawikuh "Granada," but quickly realized it was no City of Gold. Instead, one of his disillusioned soldiers remembered, it was "a little crowded village, looking as if

A mestizo artist from Mexico — half-Spanish and half-Tlaxcalan — made this drawing of the Zuni defending their pueblo against Coronado to impress Phillip II of Spain with the part Mexican Indians had played in Spanish efforts to dominate the Southwest.

it had been crumpled all up together. There are ranch houses in New Spain which make a better appearance at a distance."

There was no treasure. Nor did Coronado's men find any in neighboring pueblos. Furious, Coronado sent Fray Marcos back to Mexico for fear one of his frustrated soldiers might kill him if he stayed. "He has not told the truth in a single thing that he said," he wrote to the viceroy, "but everything is the opposite of what he related. . . ."

From Hawikuh, Coronado sent expeditions into the surrounding countryside. One explored the Colorado Plateau and crossed the Painted Desert into the land of the Hopi. Another, with Hopi guides to show them the way, marched for twenty days to the edge of a great gorge — the Grand Canyon of the Colorado. Nothing in the European experience had prepared them for its sheer size. The Spanish determined to cross it, and when the Indians tried to tell them how wide the river and its canyon really were, one member of the party remembered, they refused to believe their guides:

> . . . Captain Melgosa, with Juan Galeras and another companion, . . . undertook to clamber down at a place that appeared to them the least difficult. They kept descending in sight of the men left above until they were lost to view. . . . At four o'clock in the afternoon they returned, without having been able to reach the bottom because of the great obstacles they encountered, for what from above had appeared to be easy, proved to be, on the contrary, rough and difficult. They said they had only been a third of the way down, but from the place they reached, the river looked very large indeed; indeed, judging from what they saw, it must be as wide as the Indians had said. The men who remained above estimated that some rocks jutting out from the canyon must be about as high as a man; but those who went down swore that when they reached them they were found to be taller than the highest tower of Seville.

As winter approached, Coronado sent his army northward toward the Tiwa country on the Rio Grande, halting only long enough to search each pueblo he came upon. His men commandeered the pueblo of Alcanfor, demanded food and clothing, allowed their herds to destroy Indian crops, and molested Indian women. When the nearby pueblo of Arenal rose against them, one of Coronado's lieutenants set it afire, then burned one hundred warriors at the stake and killed many more as they fled in

Strangers: Navajo artists painted these Spanish soldiers and their mounts in Canyon del Muerto in what is now Arizona sometime in the late eighteenth or early nineteenth century.

terror. Twelve villages were destroyed before the Spanish had finished, and many of their occupants driven into the Sangre de Cristo Mountains.

In the spring, Coronado moved still farther north, determined to salvage his reputation, his dream of treasure rekindled by a Pawnee captive of the Pueblos whom the Spanish called "the Turk" because, one Spaniard explained, "he looked like one." The Turk told wondrous tales of his homeland far to the north, a place he called Quivira. "The lord of that land took his siesta under a large tree from which hung numerous golden . . . bells," he promised, and "the common table service of all was generally of wrought silver, and . . . the pitchers, dishes, and bowls, were made of gold."

The country itself is the best I have ever seen for producing all the products of Spain . . . the land itself being very fat and black and . . . very well watered by the rivulets and springs and rivers. . . . [But] what I am sure of is that there is not any gold nor any other metal in all that country, . . . nothing but little villages, and in many of these they do not plant anything and do not have any houses except of skins and sticks, and they wander around with the cows; so that the account [the Indians] gave me was false. . . .

Francisco Vásquez de Coronado

In the spring of 1541, Coronado set out for Quivira. He crossed the panhandle of what would one day become Texas, mostly unimpressed by the nomadic bands of hunters his men encountered; they "have no permanent residence anywhere," wrote the expedition's chronicler, Pedro de Castañeda, and used "troops of dogs" to drag their meager belongings. But the Spanish were astounded by the great herds of buffalo — "cows," Castañeda called them — which parted just long enough to let his columns pass.

Coronado led his men on, through an ocean of grass so vast and featureless they had to navigate with a "sea-compass," onto the great plains of what is now Kansas. Like all the newcomers who arrived in the West after them, these Spanish conquistadors and their Mexican Indian allies were stunned by the grand scale of the landscape through which they passed:

> Who could believe [Castañeda remembered] that 1,000 horses and 500 of our cows and more than 5,000 rams and ewes and more than 1,500 friendly Indians and servants, in traveling over those plains, would leave no more trace when they had passed than if nothing had been there — nothing — so that it was necessary to make piles of bones and cow dung, so that the rear guard could follow the army.

Here, too, the promised treasure failed to materialize. Quivira turned out to be a Wichita village on the bank of the Arkansas River, just another cluster of huts surrounded by corn and bean fields. Under questioning, the Turk admitted it had all been a lie. There had never been any gold or silver. To rid themselves of the Spanish, the Tiwa had evidently urged him to lead the foreigners as far as possible onto the plains — "to take us to a place," one of the soldiers remembered, "where we and our horses would starve to death."

Coronado's men strangled the Turk, then began the long march back to Mexico and safety. There Coronado faced charges of having mismanaged his expedition. "Holy Catholic Caesarian Majesty," he wrote to his sovereign. "I have done all that I possibly could to serve Your Majesty and to discover a country where God Our Lord might be served and the Royal Patrimony increased, as . . . Your Majesty's humble servant and vassal, who would kiss the royal feet and hands." A court of inquiry exonerated Coronado of all charges, but he died in obscurity a dozen years later and his failure to find treasure discouraged further explorations of the Northern Mystery for nearly half a century. Conquest without profit was too costly even for the viceroys of Mexico.

The army passed the great rock of Acoma. As it was at peace, the people entertained us well, giving us provisions and birds. . . . Many soldiers climbed up to the top to see the pueblo. They found it very difficult to climb the steps in the rock, not being used to them. The natives, on the other hand, go up and down so freely that they carry loads of provisions, and the women carry water, and they do not seem to touch the walls with their hands. Our men had to hand their weapons to one another when they tried to make the climb.

Pedro de Castañeda

The ruins of Acoma, photographed in 1904

THE PUEBLO REVOLT

By 1629 — 101 years after Cabeza de Vaca and his companions were washed up on the Gulf coast, 87 years after Coronado returned to Mexico City in disgrace, and 9 years after English Puritans began settling Plymouth and the Massachusetts Bay Colony on the Atlantic coast — the Spanish-speaking presence in the Southwest still numbered well under a thousand persons, most of whom were Indian or part-Indian servants.

The notion of large-scale settlement had been abandoned, but a handful of soldier-settlers had established *haciendas* along the Rio Grande and exacted labor from nearby Pueblos, just as Spanish landowners worked their serfs at home.

New Mexico was now officially a royal colony, ruled from a village on a tributary of the Rio Grande called Santa Fe — the city of "Holy Faith" — and maintained at royal expense to provide protection for a handful of priests who claimed already to have brought some 20,000 Indians to Christ. More than fifty pueblos had churches of their own now, all built by Indian hands.

Then, a new expedition reached Santa Fe from Mexico, a band of thirty Franciscan friars escorted by a handful of soldiers and filled with fresh zeal to see to it that their faith was spread to the farthest reaches of the province. They had come, they told all those they encountered, to liberate them from "the miserable slavery of the demon and from the obscure darkness of their idolatry. . . ."

By now, the people of the pueblos had learned through bitter experience that it was better to tolerate the presence of the Spanish than to defy them openly, simpler to demonstrate exclusive fealty to the friar's god in public, and then, in the privacy of their kivas — the circular, partially underground chambers reached by ladders that symbolized life emerging from Mother Earth — treat "Dios, the Mexican god" as just one of many deities.

There were tense moments between the priests and the people of the pueblos, but there was also continuous conflict between the friars and the secular officials meant to protect them. Settlers charged that the priests took up too much of the Indians' time that might better be spent working their fields. The priests responded that the settlers — and the royal governors who usually sided with them — were interrupting God's work of converting unbelievers. Meanwhile, white man's diseases to which the Indians had no immunities tore through the pueblos — smallpox, measles, tuberculosis, diphtheria. Twenty thousand died in 1638 alone — one-third of the pueblo population. Ten thousand more Indians died in 1640, and those who survived could not help but notice that the prayers of the priests seemed to have no effect on these new enemies that none of them could see.

Then, beginning in 1660, a drought further seared the already parched landscape. It refused to rain, summer after summer. And with the drought came raids by the Pueblos' traditional enemies, nomadic hunting bands who spoke the Athabascan language and whose ancestors had wandered south from Canada. These raiders called themselves *Diné* — "the People" — but the Pueblos called some of them *apachu*, "the enemy," and others *apachu nabahu*, or "enemies of the cultivated fields." Soon, they would be known as the Apache and the Navajo. Driven off the plains and into Pueblo territory by drought, some survived by raiding, sometimes burning crops

Hopi watch a party of strangers approach the stone steps that lead to their mesa-top home at Walpi, Arizona, 1873.

Martyrs: In 1758, Comanche and their Tonkawa and Hasinai allies — armed with French weapons and angry that Spain had forged an alliance with their Apache enemies — attacked the Spanish mission at San Saba in present-day Texas. Eight persons were killed, including two Franciscans, Fray Terreros (left) and Fray Santiestéban, whose deaths are exhaustively commemorated in this anonymous painting made in Mexico City five years later.

and killing the livestock they could not carry off with them. Again, the friars' prayers seemed powerless against these raiders.

All these misfortunes coming at once suggested to some among the Pueblos that by accepting Christianity even in part they had displeased their own divinities, and one Tiwa spiritual leader of the San Juan pueblo began preaching in secret that the Spanish would have to be driven out before life could be made good again. His name was Popé, which means "ripe planting," and his normal ritual duties included blessing crops but not fighting battles. That such a man should have come to advocate violent resistance was evidence of how deeply unhappy his people were. Soon, urged on by Popé and others, young men everywhere were dancing in honor of the *katsinas* that had always brought them prosperity, thumping their feet hard on the earth to awaken the gods who dwelled beneath it.

Meanwhile, the Spanish came to believe they had displeased *their* God. Convinced that their colony's troubles grew out of the lack of Christian unity between priests and governors, the Franciscans redoubled their efforts to blot out the Pueblo religion. Ritual dances were forbidden, religious objects burned.

Twice, the Spanish had Popé flogged publicly, but they could not silence him. The Spanish governor finally ordered him and forty-six others sold into slavery for casting spells. But when a large delegation of armed Tiwa descended upon Santa Fe and demanded the Indians' release, the governor felt he had no choice but to give in. With fewer than a thousand colonists in all New Mexico, he could not risk a full-scale uprising.

That was just what Popé had in mind, and from his post inside the kiva at Taos he began secretly spreading his message from pueblo to pueblo: the people must forget their differences, band together, and finally rid themselves of Spain.

The Christian Indians of this kingdom are convoked, allied and confederated for the purpose of rebelling, abandoning obedience to the crown and apostasizing from the Holy Faith. They plan to kill the priests, and all the Spaniards — even women and children — thus to destroy the total population of this kingdom. . . .

Headmen of three pueblos loyal to Spain, to the Spanish governor of New Mexico, August 9, 1680

On August 10, pueblos all across northern New Mexico rose up and overthrew their priests: at Taos, Santa Clara, Picuris, Santa Cruz, they killed the friars and razed or profaned their churches. Twenty-one of the thirty-three Franciscans in New Mexico were killed. So were 375 settlers and their servants. Terrified colonists and their allies fled to Santa Fe and huddled together inside the adobe-walled Palace of the Governors, where 2,500 warriors surrounded them, cut off their water, burned the rest of the capital, and sang the Catholic liturgy in Latin to mock their captives. After eleven days of siege, the surviving Spaniards fought their way out and set out for the mission of El Paso, far to the south.

The Pueblos let them go. It was enough that New Mexico was theirs again. Popé had inspired the most successful Indian revolt in North American history — but his victory would not last long.

The record of what happened next is only fragmentary. If Spanish sources are to be believed, Popé, like other revolutionaries in other lands, became a despot who ordered all Spanish buildings razed — except for the governors' palace, which he claimed for himself. Determined that everyone should return as swiftly as possible to "the state of their antiquity," he insisted that his followers forget everything they had learned from the Spanish, renounce their baptisms and dissolve their Christian marriages, abandon the metal hoes that made bigger crops possible, even tear up their fruit trees. Some Indians resisted. Others noted that although they had returned to the old ways, the sky still withheld its rain.

In any case, by the time General Diego de Vargas led a detachment of just sixty soldiers and a hundred Indian auxiliaries back to Santa Fe in the summer of 1692, Popé was dead. The Pueblos had fallen out among themselves and were again unable to fend off the Apache and the Navajo. After a bloody battle to wrest the capital from the Tanos — which ended with the execution of seventy warriors and the distribution of their wives and children among the new colonists as slaves — and a second revolt in 1696 in which all but five of the pueblos joined, most of the Indians acquiesced in the restoration of Spanish power.

The Franciscans eventually managed to build a string of new missions in what is now southern Arizona, and the threat of giving up any of the territory Spain claimed to a European rival could still stir Madrid and Mexico City into action: when French traders dared move into what is now Texas from the east, Spain sent expeditions to establish outposts, including the presidio San Antonio de Bexar and its accompanying mission, San Antonio de Valero — whose chapel would one day be remembered as the Alamo.

But Spain had abandoned hope of full-scale colonization: it was too expensive and promised too few rewards. The colonists and the Pueblos needed one another to fend off the Apache and the Navajo, and a brisk trade began in selling one another Indian slaves captured from their mutual enemies. The Pueblos were tacitly permitted to practice their own faith alongside Catholicism: church and kiva, *katsinas* and Christ all came to coexist in relative harmony. Colonists and colonized intermarried. The boundaries between the Indian and Spanish worlds had begun to blur.

SWEET MEDICINE

According to Cheyenne tradition, there was once a prophet named Sweet Medicine who warned that strangers called "Earth Men" would one day appear among them, light skinned, speaking an unknown tongue. And with them would come a strange animal that would change the Cheyenne way of life, forever:

> It has a shaggy neck and a tail almost touching the ground. Its hoofs are round. This animal will carry you on his back and help you in many ways. Those far hills that seem only a blue vision in the distance take many days to reach now; but with this animal you can get there in a short time, so fear him not. Remember what I have said.

A painted buffalo hide memorializes the victory of a party of mounted Pawnee over some horseless Kansa Indians.

The Pueblo Revolt had been confined to one remote corner of the West, but its aftershock would help make that prophecy come true — for the Cheyenne and for most of the other native peoples of the West. It brought them the horse.

Some Spanish horses had already been stolen or illegally traded to other tribes before the revolt began, but when the Spanish were driven out of their lands, the Pueblos, who had little need for the big herds that devoured the grass their sheep required, started trading them off to the Apache and the Navajo, who, in turn, soon began trading them to tribes farther north. And so it went, hunters swapping with farmers, farmers with hunters. By the 1690s, the horse had already reached the Plains tribes of Texas. By 1700, it had reached the Kiowa and Comanche in what is now Colorado.

Opposite, top: A Gros Ventre family demonstrates for the photographer Edward Curtis how households moved from place to place after the coming of the horse, 1904.

Opposite, bottom: Plenty-Coups, Crow, 1880

The Cheyenne had been farmers, dwelling in permanent villages on the banks of rivers in what is now Minnesota, growing corn and beans and squash, until the Lakota began driving them westward. By 1700, they were living in what is now South Dakota, still tending crops and hunting buffalo on foot. Then the horse came. "The first Cheyenne who ever saw horses saw them come to water at a lake . . ." a man named John Stands-in-Timber would remember being told:

> He went down closer to look, and then he thought of the prophecy of Sweet Medicine, that there would be animals with round hoofs and shaggy manes and tails, and men could ride on their backs into the Blue Vision. He went back to the village and told the old Indians and they remembered.
>
> So they fixed a snare, and when a horse stepped into it they ran to him and tied him down. . . . After they got the first horses they learned there were more of them in the South and they went there after them. That was when they began the religion they called the Horse Worship.

Suddenly, a mounted hunter could in one day kill enough buffalo to feed and clothe his family for months. Soon, the Cheyenne were following the buffalo on horseback and raiding other tribes to add to their pony herds. The Great Plains, which had been sparsely occupied mostly by agriculturists, suddenly became a crowded meeting ground for some thirty tribes from every direction. Some, like the Pawnee, would use the horse to move from one campsite to another, hunting buffalo from horseback just twice a year, and otherwise continue to rely on their crops for survival. But others — including the Cheyenne and Crow — abandoned their fields and permanent villages altogether to become nomadic hunters. A Crow chief named Plenty-Coups summed up what his mount meant to him.

> My horse fights with me and fasts with me, because if he is to carry me in battle he must know my heart, and I must know his or we shall never become brothers. I have been told that the white man, who is almost a god, and yet a great fool, does not believe that the horse has a spirit. This cannot be true. I have many times seen my horse's soul in his eyes.

Soon, the horse was so central to the lives of some western peoples that they literally could no longer imagine a time when they had managed to survive without it.

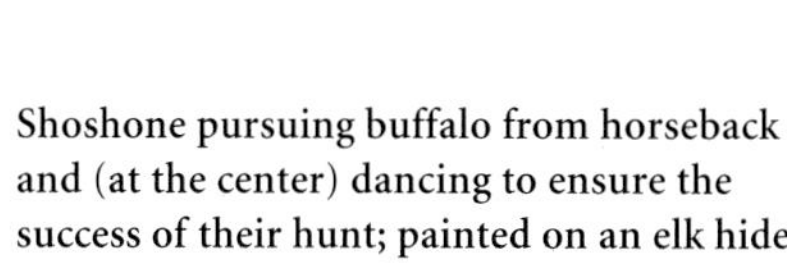

Shoshone pursuing buffalo from horseback and (at the center) dancing to ensure the success of their hunt; painted on an elk hide

Opposite: A Ute warrior and his son, photographed in 1871, some 200 years after the horse and firearms had begun the transformation of their world

There were other signs of white men besides horses. French trappers probed northern lakes and rivers in search of furs, built missions and trading posts down the Mississippi and its tributaries, and armed the tribes with whom they traded. Their rivals, the English, armed and supplied their Indian allies, as well. Guns gave some tribes a sudden, deadly advantage over others, just as European trade goods — blankets, knives, kettles, axes — made some tribes wealthier than others overnight.

But if some Indian peoples were strengthened by the coming of the horse and the gun and trade goods, all were threatened by still another legacy of the Europeans: disease for which they had no immunities. Smallpox swept across the Plains well in advance of the whites who had brought it with them, and reached the Northwest in 1782. There, it may have killed half the Blackfeet — as well as half their sometime enemies, the Nez Percé, occupants of the grassy plateau between the Cascades and the Rockies in what is now Idaho, who had yet even to see one of the white men who had now twice transformed their world; they would not see one for almost another quarter of a century. Some scholars suggest that most of the people who inhabited the West — and the rest of the New World — succumbed to epidemic disease before serious white settlement began.

Sweet Medicine of the Cheyenne had foreseen the coming of the horse. But he also predicted the corrosive impact upon his people of those who had brought the horse with them into the West:

> Some day you will meet a people who are white. They will try always to give you things, but do not take them. At last I think you will take these things that they offer you, and this will bring sickness to you. . . .
>
> Your ways will change. You will leave your religion for something new. You will lose respect for your leaders and start quarreling with one another. . . . You will take the Earth Men's ways and forget good things by which you have lived and in the end become worse than crazy.

THE TERRESTRIAL PARADISE

European legends held that California was an island, a strange and exotic place, the home of beautiful Amazons, each of whom had only a single breast so that she could draw her bow more effectively. In fact, it was the most densely populated region in North America, home to more than 300,000 people, belonging to countless bands, speaking more than eighty mutually unintelligible languages.

In 1769, rumors reached Mexico City that fur traders from Russia were building outposts along California's coast, and the visitor-general of New Spain, alarmed that the Russians and the British might challenge Spain's claim to the region, sent

A man could not even court a girl unless he had proved his courage. That was one reason so many were anxious to win good war records. . . . The women even had a song they would sing about a man whose courage had failed him. The song was: "If you are afraid when you charge, turn back. The Desert Women will eat you." . . . It was hard to go into a fight, and they were often afraid, but it was worse to turn back and face the women.

John Stands-in-Timber, Cheyenne

On May 15, 1769, Father Junipero Serra (below) encountered California Indians (left) for the first time: "I gave praise to the Lord," he remembered, "kissing the ground, and thanking His Majesty for the fact that, after so many years of looking forward to it, He now permitted me to be among the pagans in their own country. . . . I found myself in front of twelve of them, all men and grown up, except two who were boys. . . . I saw something I could not believe. . . . It was this: They were entirely naked as Adam in the garden, before sin. . . . We spoke a long time with them, and not for one moment, while they saw us clothed, could you notice the least sign of shame in them."

an expedition northward to establish missions and garrisons with which to guard them. With them, on what would later be called the "sacred expedition," came Father Junipero Serra.

Serra was a former teacher of philosophy, nearsighted, badly handicapped by an ulcerated leg, and further weakened by his pious habit of scourging his own flesh in atonement for the sins of others. He was so frail at the outset of the journey that he had to be lifted onto his mule, and sometimes had to be carried on a stretcher. But nothing could quell his missionary fervor, and whenever he spotted Indians along the way he rang a little bell to attract them to his side so that he could preach the gospel to them.

Father Serra and his successors would establish twenty missions in all, scattered along five hundred miles of the California coast — including San Diego, San Gabriel, San Luis Obispo, San Antonio de Padua, San Jose, and San Francisco de Asis. Near the mission San Gabriel, where earthquake tremors were so strong they shook the Spanish off their feet, a small town sprang up in 1781, settled by forty-six persons whom the mission fathers considered lazy and corrupt, interested mainly in drinking, gambling, and pursuing women. It was called El Pueblo de Nuestra Senora La Reina de Los Angeles.

The California missions were run very differently from those in New Mexico. There, the priests had attached themselves and their churches to already-established pueblos and often relied on them as allies against raids by other tribes. But in California, the coastal peoples — the Ipais and Tipais, Salinans, Chumash, Constanoans, Gabrielinos, and the rest — lived for the most part in scattered

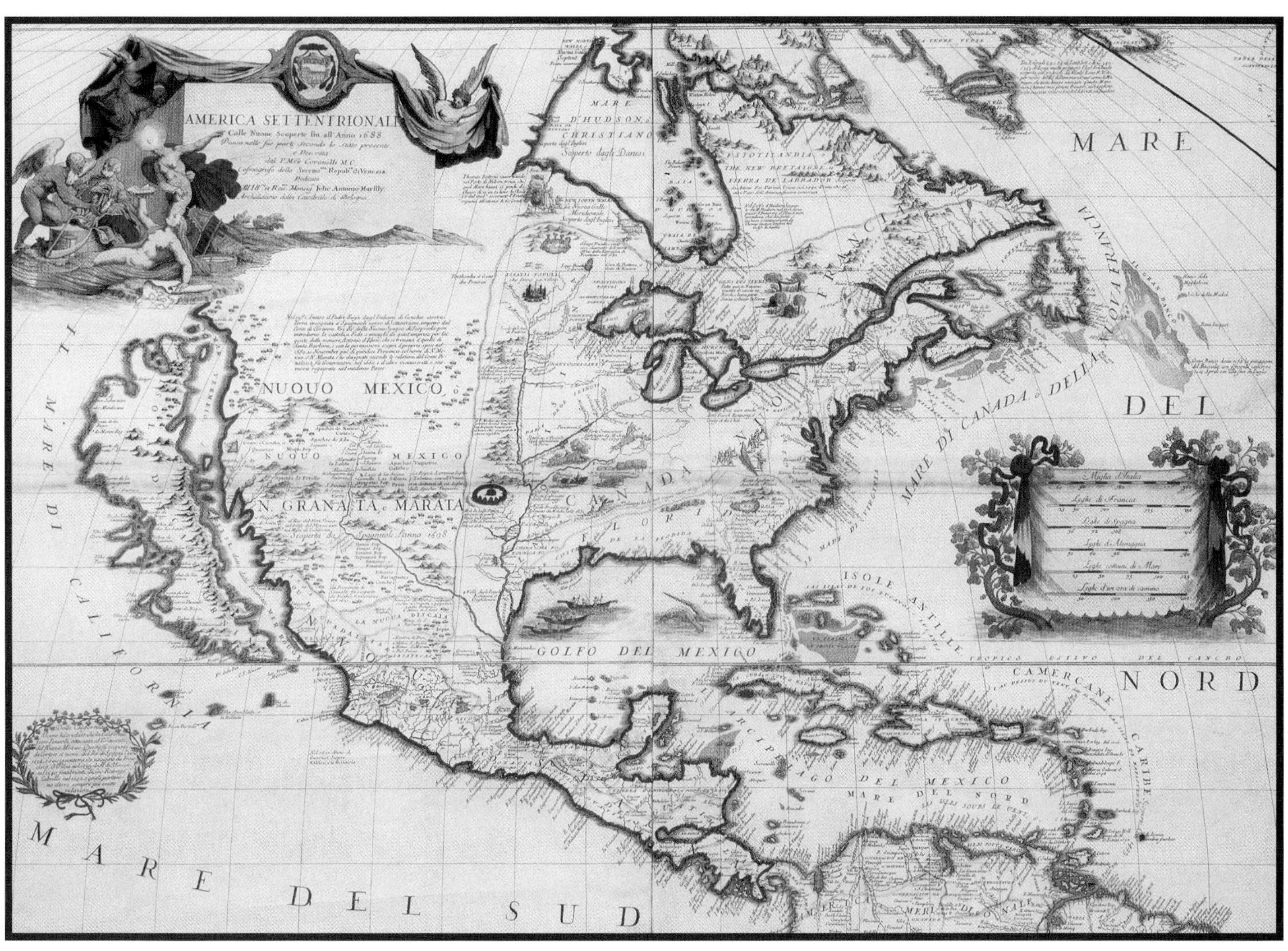

Until Spain sent missionaries north from Mexico, cartographers remained stubbornly convinced that California was an island, as shown in this 1688 rendering.

bands or small villages. To curtail what they called the Indians' "free and undisciplined state," and thereby bring them to Christ, the friars used soldiers to round them up and force them into the missions. There, the Indians — "neopyhtes," the friars called them — had little choice but to do as they were told. They were given new Spanish names, crowded together in sexually segregated barracks, and made to labor without pay or hope of freedom. Those who tried to flee were hunted down and flogged. Such apparent cruelty, the friars held, was really a great kindness because it would lead their converts to Paradise instead of the eternal damnation they were certain awaited all unbelievers.

Those who managed to escape and flee into the hills often joined forces with the Yokuts and other hunting tribes who lived there in raiding the missions, stealing horses, destroying crops, sometimes killing priests.

The fathers managed to baptize some 54,000 California Indians during the mission era, but few survived more than a few years of mission life. The Indian population between San Diego and San Francisco declined from perhaps 72,000 to as few as 18,000, victims of poor food, poor treatment, and European diseases fostered by overcrowding. "They live well free," a puzzled friar said, "but as soon as we reduce them to a Christian and community life . . . they fatten, sicken and die."

The treatment that is shown to the Indians is the most cruel I have ever read in history. For the slightest things they receive heavy floggings, are shackled, and put in the stocks, and treated with so much cruelty that they are kept whole days without a drink of water.

Padré Antonio
de la Concepción Horra,
Mission San Miguel

Christ bearing the cross (top) and being nailed to it, painted by Indian neophytes at Mission San Fernando

THE MISSION

By 1804, white visitors were nothing new to the Mandan, who occupied two great walled towns at the confluence of the Missouri and Knife rivers in what is now North Dakota. When combined with the five nearby villages belonging to their allies, the Hidatsa, theirs was the largest community west of the Mississippi, home to 4,500 people, more than then lived in St. Louis or Washington, D.C. The Mandan had long been the middlemen for trade on the upper Missouri, growing corn for barter and providing neutral ground on which the Cheyenne could trade horses for furs with the Assiniboin and Crow, and the Lakota could swap buffalo meat for French firearms. And ever since the Frenchman Pierre Gaultier de Varennes, Sieur de La Vérendrye, had visited the Mandan in 1738 — under the mistaken impression that they were a mysterious tribe of blue-eyed Welshmen somehow transplanted to the

New World — they had been doing a profitable business with individual traders from England and France.

In fact, a Scottish trapper and several French-Canadians were living in their villages when, on October 15, they looked down from their log ramparts on something they had never seen before — a keelboat so big it took twenty-two men to row it. A red, white, and blue cloth fluttered above a swivel gun that jutted from the bow. No such expedition had ever appeared on the Missouri before, and men, women, and children all hurried down to see it.

The leader of the newcomers — a tall man whose men called him Captain Lewis — distributed gifts and explained that the Mandan's old "Fathers," the Spanish and the French, had recently "gone beyond the great lake toward the rising Sun" and would never return. A new great chief would soon be sending some of his children to live among them:

> The great chief of the Seventeen great nations of America, impelled by his parental regard for his newly adopted children on the troubled waters, has sent us out to clear the road. . . . [He] has commanded us his war chiefs to under-

Mandan women in skin boats skim across the frozen surface of the Missouri in search of firewood during the winter of 1834–35, thirty years after Lewis and Clark wintered with their people. This aquatint was made after a watercolor by the Swiss artist Karl Bodmer.

> take this long journey. You are to live in peace with all the white men, for they are his children. . . . Injure not the person of any trader who may come among you. . . . Do these things which your great father advises and be happy. Avoid the councils of bad birds; turn on your heel from them as you would from the precipice of a high rock . . . lest by one false step you should bring down upon your nation the displeasure of your great father . . . who could consume you as the fire consumes the grass of the plains.

The Mandan were less impressed by what the two American captains had to say than they were by their boat. After all, over the years they had heard from the representatives of many far-off "fathers," and it had not affected business much. They simply added the Americans to their list of potential customers. But they also made them welcome, allowing them to build themselves a palisaded fort on the outskirts of their village in which to spend the winter.

Meriwether Lewis and his second-in-command, William Clark, represented a new country, but they were on what was now a very old mission: trying to find a waterway to the Pacific.

Meriwether Lewis (above) and William Clark, both painted from life by Charles Willson Peale

Of all the myths about North America that fueled Europe's avarice, the one that lasted longest was that there was a Northwest Passage that cut right through the continent, linking the Pacific with the Atlantic. Everyone agreed that the nation that first found it and then controlled its traffic would so dominate trade between the Old World and the New that it would dominate the continent, as well.

John Cabot had been looking for it in 1497 when he touched at Newfoundland and laid claim to all of North America for England, and Sir Francis Drake had been on the same search when he skirted the coast of California in 1578. When the first conquistador marched north to claim New Mexico officially for Spain, he carried with him sails and rigging, just in case the waterway ran through the southwestern desert. Samuel de Champlain fitted out an expedition to find it for France in the vicinity of the Great Lakes in 1634, and La Vérendrye had been trying to locate it when he visited the Mandan.

On July 12, 1776 — just eight days after the thirteen American colonies declared their independence from Great Britain — two British vessels had set out from England with orders to search for the elusive passage along the Northwest coast. In command was England's greatest explorer, Captain James Cook. He proved no more successful than his predecessors — and soon sailed on to the Sandwich Islands, where he was killed — but he anchored long enough off Vancouver Island to stake a British claim to the whole Northwest, and word spread fast of the plentiful furs that his men had obtained there from the Indians.

Soon, Yankee seafarers — "Bostons," the coastal tribes called them — outnumbered British traders along the Northwest coast. To reassert their supremacy in the trade, the British reasoned, they needed to find a passage — a scrics of rivers, if not an actual sea — that would link the coast with their Canadian trading posts. Their American rivals, said the Scottish fur trader Alexander Mackenzie, "would instantly disappear from before [such] a well-regulated trade." Mackenzie himself determined to find the passage that would make that British triumph possible. In 1789, he

too much. His third wife was also a Nez Percé, whom he called Virginia, in honor of his native state. She stayed with him for the rest of his life and bore him eight children.

The summer rendezvous, held in the mountains every year from 1825 to 1840, was the reward for all that he and his fellow trappers had been through, Meek remembered:

> The lonely mountain valley was populated with the different camps. The Rocky Mountain and American Companies with their separate camps; . . . the Nez Perces and Flatheads . . . friends of the whites, had their lodges all along the streams; so that altogether there could not have been less than one thousand souls, and two or three thousand horses and mules. . . .
>
> It was always chosen in some valley where there was grass for the animals and game for the camp. . . . The waving grass of the plain, variegated with wild flowers; the clear summer heavens flecked with white clouds that threw soft shadows; . . . gay laughter and the murmuring of Indian voices, all made up a most spirited and enchanting picture. . . .

Following the trail across South Pass, supply trains from St. Louis arrived at the rendezvous loaded with goods to exchange for beaver pelts. A pound of tobacco, which cost a few cents in Missouri, was worth more at the rendezvous than a pound of beaver fur, which sold for nearly four dollars. Scarlet cloth of the kind favored by Indian women cost six dollars per yard. Whiskey, bought for fifteen cents a gallon in St. Louis, was heavily watered down, then resold for up to four dollars a pint. "The men drank together," one of their employers remembered, "they sang, they laughed, they whooped; they tried to out-brag and out-lie each other. Now and then, familiarity was pushed too far, and would effervesce into a brawl, and a 'rough and tumble' fight; but it all ended in cordial reconciliation and maudlin endearment. . . ."

By the time the annual revels had ended, most of the mountain men were broke again. In later years, they would be romanticized as free spirits, roaming at will and answerable to no man. In fact, most mountain men were "mere slaves," as one of them admitted, hired "to catch beavers for others." But in their frenzied search for furs they did range over much of the West. "Not a hole or corner but has been ransacked by these hardy men," wrote George F. Ruxton a few years later. "From the Mississippi to the mouth of the Colorado of the West, from the forest regions of the North to the Gila in Mexico, the beaver-hunter has set his traps in every creek and stream. All this vast country, but for the daring and enterprise of these men, would be even now a *terra incognita* to geographers." And in pushing and probing beyond the borders of the United States, into California and New Mexico, they also saw firsthand how rich and how thinly defended those regions were.

The 1837 rendezvous on the Green River, painted by Alfred Jacob Miller. "The whole city was a military camp," a nervous eastern visitor remembered, "every little camp had its own guards to protect its occupants from being stolen by its neighbor. The arrow or the ball decided the only disputes that might occur. The only law for horse-stealing was death to the thief. . . ."

By 1840, the mountain men had mostly moved on. Many streams had simply been trapped out. Besides, the stylish gentlemen of London and New York and Paris had finally wearied of beaver hats. They preferred silk now, and so the mountain men had to find other uses for their skills. Jim Bridger began guiding wagon trains through the vast territory he had helped to chart. Jim Beckwourth drifted into the California mountains and became a horse thief.

Joe Meek had had enough of the mountains, too. In 1840, he took his children and his Nez Percé wife, and went all the way west, settling near a British trading post in the disputed Oregon Country, which a handful of American settlers were already talking about making part of the United States. "I was born in Washington County, Virginia, . . ." Meek said. "I want to live long enough to see Oregon securely American, and then I want this section, where I expect to die, to be named Washington County, so I can say that I was born in Washington County, United States, and died in Washington County, United States."

The department of Texas is contiguous to the most avid nation in the world. The North Americans have conquered whatever territory adjoins them. In less than half a century, they have become masters of extensive colonies which formerly belonged to Spain and France, and of even more spacious territories from which have disappeared the former owners, the Indian tribes.

General Manuel de Mier y Teran

TEJAS

Anglo-Americans had kept an eye on the province the Spanish called *Tejas* for a long time. It seemed to have everything — dense forests in the east; rich soil on the central plains, ideal for corn and cotton; vast herds of wild horses and cattle; navigable rivers; natural ports on the Gulf of Mexico. By 1800, the Spanish-speaking populace numbered well under 3,000, most of them living in or around just three towns — San Antonio, Goliad, and Nacogdoches.

American settlers were not welcome, but Spain's grip was weakening everywhere. In 1800, Madrid had turned over the vast Louisiana Territory to France — only to have Napoleon sell it off to the Americans three years later. In Florida, so many Americans had settled illegally that Spain felt it necessary to sell it, too, to the United States. In return, Washington vowed it had no designs on Texas.

Spain did not believe it, and restless frontiersmen in Louisiana, Mississippi, and Tennessee, many of them desperate to get out of debt and eager for new lands on which to make a new start, refused to accept it; the Louisiana Purchase, they claimed, had encompassed all the territory watered by the Mississippi system — including the Red River and each of its tributaries. At a protest meeting in Natchez, Mississippi, three hundred men volunteered to seize Texas for the United States. Their leader was a surgeon with grandiose dreams, Dr. James Long. In July of 1819, he led his army into the border town of Nacogdoches, seized it from its astonished citizens without firing a shot, proclaimed it the capital of the "Republic of Texas" and himself its first president, then hurried off to see if he could persuade the notorious French pirate Jean Lafitte to join forces with him. Lafitte saw no profit in doing so, and while Long was away, Spanish troops took back their town.

Stephen F. Austin

Meanwhile, Moses Austin, a bankrupt Missouri mine owner eager to start over, determined to use persuasion instead of force. He traveled to Mexico City, seeking official permission to bring three hundred American families to Texas. All would be Roman Catholics, he promised, and all would pledge their loyalty to Spain. The Spanish authorities agreed, granting him a vast parcel of land on the Brazos River, but Austin died of pneumonia before he could gather his followers for the journey, and so it was his son, Stephen F. Austin, just twenty-seven, who brought the first handful of American families with him to East Texas in 1821.

Then, shortly after he began laying out his colony, San Felipé de Austin, Mexico won its independence from Spain. Tejas was now a province within the Republic of Mexico and the Austin land grant from Spain was no longer valid. Austin hurried to Mexico City to persuade the new government that it should allow him and his colonists to remain in Texas. "I arrived in Mexico City in April," he remembered,

Carving up the prize: The West in 1821

The names of the early settlers shown in the daugerreotypes on this and the opposite page have long been lost, but they run true to Texas type: all are young, lean, and conspicuously armed.

"without acquaintances, without friends, ignorant of the language, of the laws, the forms, the dispositions and feelings of the government. . . . I found the city in an unsettled state, the whole people and country still agitated by the revolutionary convulsion, public opinion vacillating, party spirit raging."

It took Austin almost a year, but in the end the new government of Mexico proved eager to see its northern frontier settled. Permanent, legal colonies of Anglo-Americans, it reasoned, would help provide protection against Indians and American adventurers alike. To attract still more legitimate settlers, Mexico would exempt Anglo-Americans from taxes for four years, award huge tracts of land to anyone who pledged to settle one hundred new families, pretend not to notice when Protestants as well as Catholics came, even permit settlers to keep their slaves as lifetime "indentured servants" — though the Mexican constitution expressly forbade involuntary servitude.

The lives of Austin's settlers, who called themselves "Texians," were hard at first, and they fought skirmish after skirmish with the Karankawa Indians, who resisted the settlers' intrusion onto their hunting grounds. But the land was fertile, the grasslands seemed "inexhaustible," Austin wrote, "and green, winter and summer," and wildflowers carpeted the clearings. "It does not appear possible," one of the first settlers wrote home, "that there can be a land more lovely."

Soon, there were other American *empresarios* with sprawling colonies of their own. American squatters came, too, carving out homesteads in the Red River country without anyone's permission. Austin dismissed them as "leatherstockings" and "longrifles," unlettered and impatient men likely to make trouble. ". . . [N]o frontiersman who has no other occupation than that of hunter will be received [by me]," he said, "no drunkard, no gambler, no profane swearer, no idler."

They kept turning up, anyway: dirt-poor debtors with dreams of becoming wealthy planters, land speculators, lawyers — and fugitives from the law. "The Sabine River is a greater savior than Jesus Christ," one man wrote. "He only saves men when they die from going to Hell, but this river saves men from prison."

By the end of the decade, there would be some 7,000 American-born Texians and their slaves in Texas — more than twice the Spanish-speaking *Tejano* population. They kept mostly to themselves, and saw themselves as a wholly superior people, sent to conquer a wilderness that the Mexicans and their Spanish forebears had failed to tame over three centuries. Even Stephen Austin privately thought most Mexicans "want nothing but tails to be more brutes than the apes."

Many *Tejanos,* in turn, found the newcomers overbearing, impatient, ignorant even of the language of the country in which they had come to live, and likely to secede from it at the first opportunity.

Stephen Austin never married — "Texas is my mistress," he said — but he saw himself as the father of his colony and took with deadly seriousness his pledge to remain a loyal citizen of Mexico. He barred Protestant clergymen from San Felipé de Austin because he feared they might foment trouble, and when Tejas lost its separate status under the new Mexican constitution of 1824, and was combined with the more populous province of Coahuila to form the new state of Coahuila y Texas, he urged patience rather than angry words and threats of defiance. And when an erratic American *empresario* named Haden Edwards took Nacogdoches in 1826, and proclaimed it the capital of an independent "Republic of Fredonia," Austin sent one hundred American-born militiamen to help quell the rebellion. "I consider that I owe *fidelity and gratitude to Mexico,*" he wrote. "That has been my motto, and I have impressed it upon my colonists."

Other settlers began to develop other ideas. Jim Bowie was a tall, alcoholic Louisianan who, before coming to San Antonio in 1828, had made a fortune selling slaves and land to which he had no title, and had killed several men in duels with a broad-bladed knife said to be of his own design. He converted to Catholicism in Texas, married the wealthy nineteen-year-old daughter of the Mexican lieutenant governor, and hoped to make himself rich once more speculating in land and mining for silver.

William Barrett Travis was quick-tempered, too. A young lawyer who had deserted a wife and child in South Carolina after killing the man he accused of being his wife's lover, he was fond of gambling and women, fiercely ambitious, and so fascinated by himself that he wrote an autobiography at the age of twenty-three.

On December 2, 1832, a tall thirty-nine-year-old Tennesseean stepped aboard the Red River ferry, crossing from Indian Territory into Texas. He was Sam Houston, a former member of Congress and governor of Tennessee who had been spoken of as a possible successor to his friend and political mentor, President Andrew Jackson, until scandal and alcoholism ended his political career. He hoped Texas would provide him with new and glorious opportunities. "An eagle swooped down near my head," he remembered later, "and then, soaring aloft with wildest screams, was lost in the rays of the setting sun. I knew that a great destiny waited for me in the West."

THE ROAD TO SANTA FE

Like the *Tejanos,* the Spanish-speaking people of New Mexico had long felt isolated and neglected by Spain. They were farmers and ranchers, mostly, living in and around small towns scattered along the Rio Grande and its northern tributaries, the Chama and the Pecos. The authorities had been unable to shield them effectively from Comanche and Navajo raiders. All commerce with the United States was barred, and legitimate trade limited to a trickle of pack trains that moved back and forth from Chihuahua, far to the south. When Mexican independence came, only a few had much faith that their lot would greatly improve; the 5,000 citizens of Santa Fe would not get around to celebrating their freedom for a full five months.

On September 1, 1821, a St. Louis trader named William Becknell set out for Santa Fe with some thirty mounted companions, carrying axes, knives, and bolts of bright cotton to swap for horses and mules. They followed the Arkansas River into the Raton Mountains — where they were suddenly surrounded by a squadron of uniformed dragoons. Becknell knew he was deep into Spanish territory and feared the fate that had befallen earlier American smugglers — arrest, confiscation of his goods, imprisonment. Instead, the soldiers smiled and made clear the Americans were to follow them into Santa Fe. There, the governor greeted Becknell warmly and told him everything had changed. The Spanish had been overthrown. He was now in Mexican territory, and Missouri traders henceforth would be welcome at Santa Fe.

The town itself, with its single-story adobe houses, struck one trader as looking "more like a prairie dog village than a capital," but its citizens eagerly bought up all of

Santa Fe: Missouri traders arriving in the capital of New Mexico (above), and the town itself as it looked in 1848 after the Americans had taken over and the Stars and Stripes was raised above the old Palace of the Governors.

The caravan at last hove into sight, and, wagon after wagon, was seen pouring down the last declivity at about a mile's distance from the city. . . . The arrival produced a great bustle and excitement among the natives. "Los Americanos!" — "Los Carros!" — "Le entrada de la caravana!" *were to be heard in every direction; and crowds of women and boys flocked around to see the new-comers. . . . The wagoners were by no means free from excitement. . . . [T]hey were prepared with clean faces, sleek combed hair, and their choicest Sunday suit, to meet the "fair eyes" of glistening black that were sure to stare at them as they passed.*

Josiah Gregg

Becknell's trade goods, and when he and his companions rode home, their saddle-bags were heavy with Mexican silver pesos.

Becknell set out for New Mexico again the next spring, this time bringing three oxcarts laden with goods. Because the wagons couldn't be hauled through the mountains, he blazed a new trail across the Cimarron desert — and almost didn't make it. Comanche harassed his men. They ran out of water, became so desperate that they lopped off their mules' ears to quench their thirst with blood, and were saved only when they shot a buffalo, its stomach still filled with water from the Cimarron.

Still, Becknell already had several Missouri rivals for the Santa Fe trade. In 1824, they joined forces to form one well-defended caravan. The Indians held off, and the traders, who had invested $30,000, brought back $190,000 in gold, silver, and furs.

Thereafter, season after season, the traders made the thousand-mile trek to Santa Fe, sometimes one hundred wagons at a time, bringing with them handkerchiefs and shawls, pots and pans and wallpaper, even window glass. There were rock slides on the mountain route, sudden rainstorms on the Cimarron Cutoff that turned the dusty flatland into a morass of mud and caused flash floods that swept wagons away.

The risks were great. But the rewards were greater, and Mexican traders were soon on the move as well, driving herds of horses, sheep, and mules northward for sale in Missouri. Soon, while the region's cultural and political ties to Mexico remained strong, its economy was increasingly dominated by the Americans, who carried home so many silver pesos that New Mexico virtually ran out of coins by the mid-1820s.

The more the American population of Texas is increased, the more readily will the Mexican Government give it up. A gentle breeze shakes off a ripe peach. Can it be supposed that the violent political convulsions of Mexico will not shake off Texas so soon as it is ripe enough to fall? All that is now wanting is a great immigration of good and efficient families. . . . [Then] . . . the peach will be ripe.

Stephen F. Austin

COME AND TAKE IT

Americans continued to pour into Texas, so many now that when the letters "G.T.T." appeared on the walls of empty cabins throughout the southern United States, everyone knew it meant "Gone to Texas."

Some wealthy *Tejanos* still saw American settlement as the best way to develop the state. "I cannot help seeing advantages," wrote one citizen of San Antonio, "which, to my way of thinking, would result if we admitted honest hard-working people, regardless of what country they come from . . . even hell itself."

But Mexico City soon began to take a very different view and sent the former minister of war, General Manuel de Mier y Teran, north to survey the situation. Riding across the state in a splendidly carved coach inlaid with silver, he was appalled by what he found:

> The whole population here is a mixture of strange and incoherent parts without parallel in our federation: numerous tribes of Indians, now at peace, but armed at any moment ready for war . . . colonists of another people, more progressive and better informed than the Mexican inhabitants, but also more shrewd and unruly; among these foreigners are fugitives from justice, honest laborers, vagabonds and criminals, but honorable and dishonorable alike travel with their political constitution in their pockets, demanding the privileges, authority and officers which such a constitution guarantees.

Land grants (opposite, top) formally given to Stephen Austin and his fellow *empresarios* by Mexico in the years before the Texas Revolution

General Antonio Lopez de Santa Anna (opposite, bottom) served as president of Mexico eleven times over the course of his long and turbulent career, despite his inglorious loss of Texas.

Such people were sure to foment a revolution. "Either the government occupies Texas *now*," the general wrote, "or it is lost forever." Lucas Alaman, the Mexican secretary of state, agreed: "Where others send invading armies," he wrote, ". . . [the Americans] send their colonists." And when President Andrew Jackson sent an emissary to Mexico City, prepared to buy Texas for $5 million, the Mexican government indignantly rejected the offer.

The next year, Anglo-American settlement was barred altogether. Instead of Americans, Mexican citizens and Europeans would now be encouraged to colonize Texas. Convict-soldiers were to be sent north, too, first to enforce the law and then to become settlers themselves. A handful of Irish colonists managed to establish two settlements, Refugio and San Patricio Hibernia — St. Patrick of Ireland. An English settlement was started, too, only to be wiped out by the Comanche.

But the flow of illegal American squatters just increased. Between 1830 and 1834, the population of Texas more than doubled, to better than 20,000. By 1835, 1,000 Americans a month were pushing into Texas at one river crossing alone. The next year, there were 35,000 Anglo-Americans and their slaves in Texas — ten times the number of *Tejanos.* Trying to stop American immigration, Stephen Austin wrote, was "like trying to stop the Mississippi with a dam of straw." Tensions rose. Rumors spread that Mexico intended to insist the Texians' slaves be freed. Mexican troops offered little protection against Indians but insisted on collecting duties, which the colonists resisted paying, and some among the settlers began to compare the Mexican troops newly stationed among them with British redcoats.

The Texians began to divide into two camps: a "war party," headed by impetuous young men like William Travis, who openly urged revolution and independence, and a "peace party," which looked to Stephen Austin for leadership and still hoped for some sort of compromise with Mexico.

Then everything seemed to change. General Antonio Lopez de Santa Anna, the self-styled "Napoleon of the West" who had once destroyed a Spanish army sent to overthrow the Mexican revolution, was elected president of Mexico, promising to restore the old states' rights constitution. Moderate Texans were jubilant, sure their grievances would at last be heard. They drew up a resolution asking that the law against American settlement be repealed, that Texas be allowed to separate itself from Coahuila with a state constitution modeled closely on that of the United States. Austin was appointed to take the petition to Mexico City. Once again, events moved more slowly than he liked, and he wrote an uncharacteristically blunt letter to the mostly *Tejano* city council of San Antonio. "If our application is refused . . ." he said, "I shall be in favor of organizing without it. I see no other way of saving the country from total anarchy and ruin. I am totally done with conciliatory measures and, for the future, shall be uncompromising as to Texas."

Sam Houston, painted by George Catlin in 1840

Santa Anna finally agreed to end the ban on American settlement, at least, but news of Austin's indiscreet letter made its way back to Mexico City. He was arrested and clapped in jail for eighteen months. Meanwhile, Santa Anna betrayed his own revolution and, like his hero, Napoleon Bonaparte, declared himself dictator. Then he sent an army northward under the command of his brother-in-law, General Martin Perfecto de Cos, with orders to crush all resistance to his rule wherever he found it.

Texas-style minutemen began to drill. "Nothing is heard but 'God damn Santa Anna,'" one anxious Mexican official reported. Another warned that Texians would arm "even the children" rather than allow a Mexican army to cross the Rio Grande. Even Stephen Austin's patience had run out. Returning to Texas in the summer of 1835, he declared, "Santa Anna is . . . a base, unprincipled bloody monster. . . . War is our only recourse. No halfway measures, but war in full."

On October 2, as General Cos and his army moved into San Antonio, a detachment of one hundred Mexican cavalrymen was sent to Gonzales to reclaim an aged brass cannon the settlers had borrowed to defend themselves against Indians. The men of Gonzales hung out a banner reading "Come and Take It," and when the Mexicans tried to do just that, they touched it off, sending a load of nails, wire, and horseshoes slashing through the Mexican ranks. The survivors fled.

The Texas Revolution had begun.

At first, it seemed that more easy Texan victories lay in store. They seized the Mexican garrison at Goliad. Stephen Austin himself accompanied a force of 300 to 500 that he called "the Army of the People," bent on besieging General Cos and his army of 800 at San Antonio. Among them were some 160 *Tejanos*, just as eager as the American colonists to restore the Mexican constitution. The Texian army ringed San Antonio and settled in for a siege.

Meanwhile, Austin called for a "general consultation" at San Felipé to map a united defense. The war party called openly for independence, but the moderates were still in the majority: the "consultation" asked only for a return to the Constitution of 1824. Austin was sent east to the United States to rally volunteers and arrange credit with which to finance a war.

Sam Houston was named commander of the Texas forces. He had a distinctly mixed reputation. Some remembered only the bright promise of his youth. Raised by his widowed mother in the Tennessee canebrake and informally adopted by the Cherokee, he survived three serious wounds to distinguish himself in battle against the Creek, then became a general of militia, congressman, and governor, thanks in part to the patronage of his old commander, Andrew Jackson.

But others could not forget the complications of his private life. He had been abandoned by his young wife and had resigned his governorship immediately afterward without explanation: "This is a painful but a private affair," was all he would say.

"I do not recognize the right of the public to interfere." He later beat a congressman senseless with his cane for daring to question his honesty, and drank so heavily that his Cherokee friends nicknamed him "Big Drunk."

No one questioned his courage. But they did worry about his steadiness and some challenged his authority. He had opposed the march on San Antonio as premature, but the forces now shivering in the cold outside the town did not report to him.

On December 5, spurred on by a hot-tempered old settler named Ben Milam, the Texians roared into Goliad. Milam was killed early on, and it took five days of vicious house-to-house fighting, but General Cos and his men were finally driven into an old mission called the Alamo on the far side of the San Antonio River, where they finally surrendered. The Texians gallantly allowed Cos and his defeated soldiers to leave town unmolested after they vowed never to return to Texas — and even gave them powder and shot to ward off any Indians they might meet on their way back to Mexico. The war was over — or so many Texians thought. Most of the volunteers went home.

Sam Houston knew better. The fighting had just begun. Humiliated by his brother-in-law's defeat, General Santa Anna now determined to crush the Texians in person, at the head of an army of 4,000 men. Another 1,500 waited to join forces with him on the Rio Grande.

Davy Crockett, frontiersman and Tennessee politician, painted by John Gadsby Chapman. According to several eyewitnesses, Crockett and five other defenders of the Alamo survived the fighting and surrendered to the enemy, only to be hacked to death at Santa Anna's orders.

Santa Anna's army rode north beneath a black flag that meant no quarter. "The foreigners who wage war against the Mexican Nation have violated all laws and do not deserve any consideration . . ." the general warned. "They have audaciously declared a war of extermination to the Mexicans and should be treated in the same manner."

As Santa Anna's mighty army moved closer, Houston called for more men, from Texas and from the United States. "Let each man," he said, "come with a good rifle and one hundred rounds of ammunition — and come soon." "Texas meetings" were held all over the country. Funds were raised in New York, Mobile, Columbus, Boston. "Texas, Texas," wrote the editor of the Philadelphia *Courier,* "crowded meetings and gun-powder speeches calling down vengeance upon the oppressors of the Texonians is the order of the day." Impetuous young men signed up by the battalion: Captain Duval's Kentucky Mustangs, Captain Shackleford's Red Rovers of Alabama, the New Orleans Greys. "If we succeed," wrote one volunteer, "a fertile region and a grateful people will be for us a home and secure us our reward. If we fail, death in defense of so just and so good a cause need not excite a shudder or a tear."

From Tennessee came Colonel Davy Crockett — hunter, frontiersman, teller of tall tales, and Whig congressman. He had lost his most recent election after announcing that if his constituents didn't reelect him, they could go to hell and he would go to Texas. Now he was on his way.

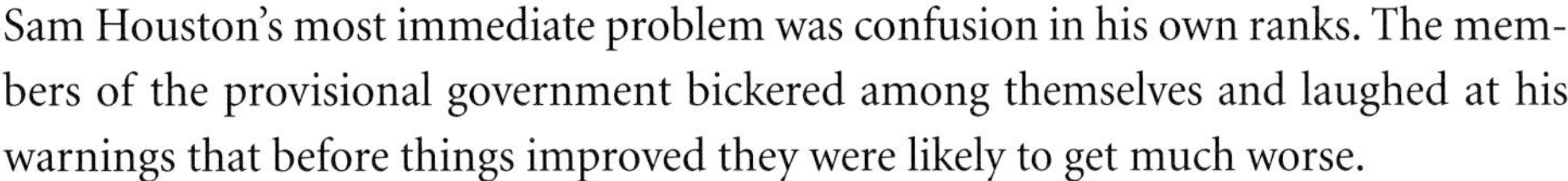

San Antonio de Bejar and the outlying Alamo (top, left), diagrammed by Santa Anna's chief military engineer during the siege, and two of the Alamo's defenders: Jim Bowie (top, right), whose refusal to follow orders and blow up the old mission eventually led to his death and those of almost two hundred of his companions; and Juan Seguín (above), the *Tejano* who slipped through the Mexican lines in search of reinforcements and later distinguished himself at the battle of San Jacinto

Sam Houston's most immediate problem was confusion in his own ranks. The members of the provisional government bickered among themselves and laughed at his warnings that before things improved they were likely to get much worse.

The strategy he favored was simple. He would harass Santa Anna's army from a distance — just as the American revolutionaries had once harassed the British redcoats — stretch the enemy's supply lines, and then hope to defeat him in one climactic battle. "It is better," he said, "to do well . . . *late* . . . than never."

But others refused to see it that way. James Fannin, a former slave runner from Georgia who had once attended West Point and therefore had a dangerously exalted view of his own martial skills, insisted upon starting south with half the army to seize the border town of Matamoros. Houston was violently opposed but powerless to stop him. Halfway to his goal, Fannin himself hesitated and settled in with his army at Goliad.

The Texians were now dangerously divided, and Santa Anna's army was nearing San Antonio, bent on revenge.

Houston knew the Alamo was too isolated, too big, too badly designed and poorly armed to be successfully defended. He sent Jim Bowie to blow it up. But Bowie did not do so. Instead, he and some 123 men prepared to hold the old mission until reinforcements could reach them. There were New Yorkers and Pennsylvanians as well as Kentuckians and Tennesseeans among them, immigrants from England and Ireland and Germany, as well as Davy Crockett and at least six *Tejanos* willing to risk everything for the Texian cause.

William Travis, now a colonel in the Texian army, assumed command, bringing with him some thirty cavalrymen, and on February 24, 1836, when Santa Anna

The battered farmhouse at Washington-on-the-Brazos in which the Texas Declaration of Independence was adopted, photographed many years later

reached San Antonio and demanded that the Alamo's occupants surrender or be annihilated, he answered with a cannon shot.

A steady Mexican shelling began.

Travis scribbled out requests for reinforcements and smuggled them through the gate. One was carried from the Alamo to Gonzales by Juan Seguín, the son of the former mayor of San Antonio, who had organized a force of *Tejano* ranchers to fight for independence. Twenty-nine men responded to Travis's appeals and managed to slip into the Alamo under cover of darkness. Travis now had some 182 men. There would be no more.

The Mexican artillery continued to batter the walls and hurl shells into the courtyard.

On March 2, 1836, fifty-nine Texians gathered in a crude frame building in the tiny settlement of Washington-on-the-Brazos. Cloth was stretched across the windows to keep out the howling wind. It was "a disgusting place," one visitor wrote. "It is laid out in the woods, about a dozen wretched cabins or shanties constitute the city; not one decent house in it, and only one well-defined street, which consists of an opening cut out of the woods, the stumps still standing. A rare place to hold a national convention in."

There, over the course of the next two weeks, the delegates declared Texas an independent republic, hammered out a constitution closely modeled after that of the United States, elected a frail, tubercular planter named David Burnet as interim president, and named Sam Houston commander in chief of the army.

EVEN THE WOLVES WILL SHRINK

The Four Bears, a Mandan chief, shown here in two portraits by Karl Bodmer, was a formidable warrior. He had killed five chiefs of other nations in hand-to-hand combat. Unarmed, he had wrested a knife from a Cheyenne warrior and used it to kill its owner. He also had taken many prisoners, survived an enemy arrow and six gunshot wounds. But he had never shown anything but friendship to the Americans. "Ever since I can remember," he once said, "I have loved the whites. I have lived with them ever since I was a boy and to the best of my knowledge I have never wronged a white man. . . ."

No Indian people had been more cordial to whites than the Mandan. They welcomed traders and trappers of all nations, sheltered Lewis and Clark during the bitter winter of 1805, served as trusted middlemen for the Missouri fur trade.

In the autumn of 1837, they paid a fearful price for their hospitality. When the American Fur Company brought its steamboat filled with supplies to their villages for its annual visit, the smallpox virus was inadvertently harbored among the crew. It raged through the Mandan villages, felling men, women, and children.

"About fifteen days afterward," a trader at Fort Union recalled, "there was such a stench in the fort that it could be smelt at the distance of 300 yards. It was awful — the scene in the fort, where some went crazy, and others were eaten up by maggots before they died; yet, singular to say, not a single bad expression was ever uttered by a sick Indian. Many died, and those who recovered were so much disfigured that one could scarcely recognize them."

When the epidemic had finally run its course, the once-mighty Mandan nation was reduced to barely thirty individuals, huddled together with remnants of the Arikara and Hidatsa, wholly dependent on the U.S. government for their survival.

The Four Bears was among the last to contract the disease. As he was dying, he lamented that he had ever befriended the men who had brought such devastation to his people:

> The Four Bears never saw a white man hungry, but what he gave them to eat, drink and a buffalo skin to sleep on in time of need . . . and how they have repaid it! With ingratitude! I have never called a white man a dog, but today I do pronounce them to be a set of black-hearted dogs. They have deceived me. Them that I always considered as brothers have turned out to be my worst enemies. . . . I do not fear death, my friends, you know it. But to die with my face rotten, that even the wolves will shrink from horror at seeing me, and say to themselves, "That is the Four Bears, the friend of the whites."
>
> Listen well to what I have to say, as it will be the last time you will hear me. Think of your wives, children, brothers, sisters, friends, and in fact all that you hold dear. All are dead or dying, with their faces all rotten, caused by those dogs the whites. Think of all that my friends, and rise together and not leave one of them alive.

Still, the chances for Texian independence now seemed slim. All that stood between the Mexican army and the settlements in East Texas were James Fannin's 420 men, shut up in Goliad, and William Travis's 182 volunteers surrounded inside the Alamo.

There, at five in the morning, March 6, 1836, a Mexican bugler blew the *Deguello,* the signal for death in the bullring, and 2,600 men charged the old mission. The Texians shot them down as they came on, clubbed them as they clambered over the walls, fought them hand-to-hand and room-to-room. At least six hundred Mexican soldiers would fall that morning — many of them shot in the back by their poorly led comrades, coming along behind — though afterward, Santa Anna would officially admit to just seventy deaths among his men. But in the end, the odds proved overwhelming. The Alamo was taken, and Bowie, Crockett, Travis, and all their companions lay dead.

The news galvanized the southern frontier. Many of the dead had been U.S. volunteers and there were calls for revenge up and down the border. New volunteers poured across the Red River and the Sabine.

But Santa Anna was already on the march again, heading straight for the American colonies in East Texas.

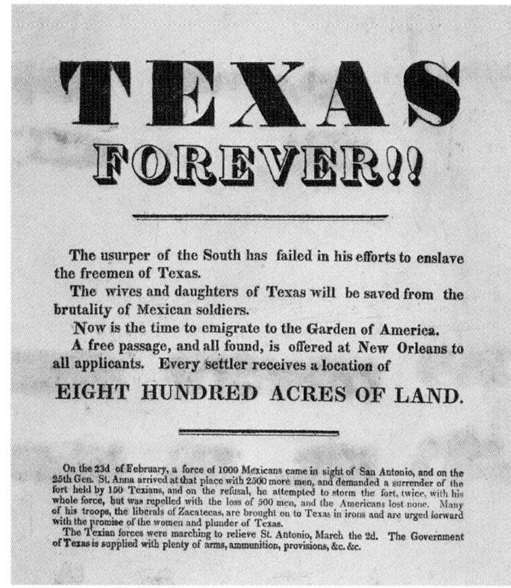

Misinformation: This poster, issued in New Orleans before the Alamo's fall and intended to spur recruitment in Louisiana, alleges that the mission's defenders have fought off Santa Anna's army, killing or wounding five hundred Mexicans, without suffering a single casualty themselves, and that a Texian army is already marching to relieve the siege. None of it was true.

The Texas cause now rested squarely on the shoulders of Sam Houston, who refused to say what he would do. "Had I consulted the wishes of all," he said, "I should have been like the ass between two stacks of hay. I consulted no one — I held no councils of war. If I err, the blame is mine." He began an erratic, zigzagging retreat across Texas, keeping his tiny force just out of range of the advancing Mexicans, in the hope that the winter rains would slow them down enough to let fresh volunteers reach his army before battle was joined.

As Houston fell back, word came of still another disaster. Fannin's force of four hundred men at Goliad had been surrounded and disarmed. They were mostly American volunteers, not Texians, and Santa Anna considered them no better than pirates. At his orders, more than three hundred of them were shot and their corpses set ablaze.

Thousands of frightened settlers and their families began fleeing for the border. "We passed a house with all the doors open," one woman remembered. "The table had been set, all of the victuals on the table, and even the chairs set up in their places. On the table was a plate of biscuits, a plate of potatoes, fried chicken. . . ." Old-timers would remember the exodus as "the Runaway Scrape."

The civilian government panicked, too, retreating to the tiny East Texas town of Harrisburg, then demanding that Houston stand and fight. "Sir: The enemy are laughing you to scorn," President Burnet told Houston. "You must fight them. You must retreat no further. The country expects you to fight. The salvation of the country depends on your doing so." Settlers jeered Houston from the roadside. Rumors spread that alcohol had undercut his courage. Some of his men wept with frustration as they marched. Others deserted in order to escort their families out of harm's way.

Still he kept his own counsel, gnawing on the raw ears of corn with which he filled his saddlebags, poring over Caesar's *Commentaries.* Some soldiers feared he meant simply to flee across the U.S. border and abandon Texas to Santa Anna. Officers threatened to seize command — and Houston threatened to shoot anyone who dared try it.

Then Santa Anna veered off to seize Harrisburg, where he believed the provisional government was hiding. The town was empty when he got there. Santa Anna burned it down, but Houston and his army had now slipped up behind him. The hunter was about to become the hunted.

Late in the afternoon of April 21, 1836, Santa Anna and some 1,250 men were resting in a shady grove of trees near the river crossing at San Jacinto, confident that they had cut off Houston's escape route. It was the moment Houston had been waiting for.

The Texian battle flag, carried into the thick of the fighting by Houston's men and sewn by Kentucky women who sympathized with their cause

Ever since Texas has unfurled the banner of Freedom, and commenced a Warfare of liberty or death, our hearts have been enlisted in her behalf. . . . If we succeed, the country is ours, it is immense in extent and fertile in its soil, and will amply reward all our toil. If we fail, death in the cause of liberty and humanity is not a cause for shuddering.

Daniel Cloud

San Jacinto: Sam Houston (waving his hat at center left, as an aide holds the wounded Saracen) leads his men into battle against the stunned Mexican army, while General Santa Anna (conveniently wearing a white sombrero so the onlooker can't miss him) gallops furiously away at center right. Despite the hand-to-hand heroics rendered here, the real thing was a one-sided slaughter. "I sat there on my horse and shot them until my ammunition gave out," a Texas private recalled. "Then I turned the butt of my musket and started knocking them in the head."

When Alfonso Steele (above), a Kentucky-born volunteer, was photographed at ninety-four, he claimed to be the last living veteran of San Jacinto. His memories included Santa Anna's surrender to Sam Houston, painted by William Huddle in 1866. Houston had been shot in the leg and was unable to stand when the Mexican commander was brought before him by his captors. "I was lying on my left side in a kind of haze," Houston recalled, "when I felt some person clasp my right hand. I looked up as Santa Anna stood before me. He announced his name and rank."

He ordered the bridge behind the Mexicans destroyed. ". . . [I]t cut off all means of escape for either army," he remembered. "There was now no alternative but victory or death." The enemy was cut off by water on three sides and Houston's eight hundred men held the fourth.

Mounted on a white stallion called Saracen, he rallied his troops. "Victory is certain!" he told them. "Trust in God and fear not! The victims of the Alamo and the names of those who were murdered at Goliad cry out for vengeance. Remember the Alamo! Remember Goliad!" Then he led the charge, swinging his saber. When Saracen fell, hit by five musket balls, Houston climbed onto another horse. It, too, was killed, and this time his own right leg was splintered by a ball. But the Mexican army was already in full flight, and the vengeful Texians were right behind them.

The fighting lasted just eighteen minutes, but the slaughter went on for another hour or so. "If Jesus Christ were to come down from Heaven and order me to quit shooting Santanistas," one soldier told an officer, "I wouldn't do it, sir!" A Texian sergeant remembered the special quality of the savagery:

> A young Mexican boy (a drummer I suppose) [was] lying on his face. One of the Volunteers . . . pricked the boy with his bayonet. The boy grasped the man around the legs and cried out in Spanish "Hail Mary, Most Pure! For God's sake, save my life!' I begged the man to spare him, both of his legs being broken already. The man looked at me and put his hand on his pistol, so I passed on. Just as I did so, he blew out the boy's brains.

When it was all over, six hundred Mexican soldiers were dead, nearly seven hundred more had surrendered. The surprise had been so complete, the blow so sudden, that only six Texans died in the battle of San Jacinto. Santa Anna himself was Sam Houston's prisoner and was forced to sign a document ceding Texan independence, which the Mexican legislature indignantly withdrew.

Nonetheless, North America was now divided into five parts — Alaska, claimed by Russia; British Canada; the United States; Mexico; and the brand-new Republic of Texas. "The loss of Texas will inevitably result in the loss of New Mexico and the Californias," warned José Maria Tornel y Mendivil, the Mexican secretary of war. "Little by little our territory will be absorbed until only an insignificant part is left to us. . . . Our national existence, recognized after so many difficulties, [will] end like those weak meteors from time to time, shine fitfully in the firmament and disappear."

IN THE MIDST OF SAVAGE DARKNESS

From the moment Lewis and Clark had first appeared among them, the Nez Percé had been friendly toward the Americans. They trapped with them, attended their rendezvous, even fought alongside them against their rivals, the Blackfeet and Gros Ventre. And they had come to admire their weapons and tools and their ability to communicate with one another over hundreds of miles by making marks on paper.

Clearly, the whites had special medicine, and the Nez Percé began to mimic some of their practices in hopes of sharing in it. Two Nez Percé boys, returning home from a Hudson's Bay school in Canada, explained that the white man's secrets were to be found in a black book called the Bible. Soon, trappers were startled to find that their Nez Percé allies stopped to pray twice a day, said a sort of grace before meals, and would no longer work on Sundays. "They even had a rude calendar of the fasts and festivals of the Romish church," Captain Benjamin L. E. Bonneville remembered, "and some traces of its ceremonials. These have become blended with their own wild rites, and present a strange medley; civilized and barbarous. On the Sabbath men, women and children array themselves in their best style and assemble round a pole erected at the head of the camp. Here they go through a wild fantastic ceremonial, strongly resembling the religious dance of the shaking Quakers."

In 1831, four Indians — three Nez Percé and a member of the Flathead tribe — made their way east to St. Louis, hoping to learn more of the white man's ways and

George Catlin painted the St. Louis waterfront (left), as well as portraits of two of the four Indians — Rabbit's Skin Leggings (top) and No Horn on His Head, both Nez Percé — who came there in 1832 to seek the white man's Black Book.

The Reverend Henry Spalding (top, right) grips both Bible and hoe, twin symbols of his mission to the Indians.

The six-foot-high "learning ladder" (above) was drawn by Spalding's wife, Eliza, and meant to impress upon the Nez Percé the superiority of Presbyterianism over the faith preached by the Spaldings' Roman Catholic rivals. The straight and narrow path on the right represents the one true route to salvation, while a greedy and obese pope blocks the broader thoroughfare. Catholic missionaries countered with ladders of their own, in which Protestants were shown tumbling into hell.

perhaps to see if they could find someone willing to come west to explain to their people the secrets contained in the Black Book. They sought out their old friend William Clark, now the Commissioner for Indians, and spoke with several Catholic priests. Two of the Nez Percé died of disease while still in St. Louis, a third died aboard a steamboat trying to get home. The fourth survived long enough to find a Nez Percé band hunting in Montana and tell them that white men might soon be coming with the Black Book, before he, too, died, at the hands of the Blackfeet.

In St. Louis, a Methodist member of the Wyandot tribe named William Walker heard of the Indians' visit and wrote a highly colored account of it to a friend back East. The friend embellished it still further and published it in the missionary press: the Nez Percé were pleading for salvation, he said. The whole of Oregon lay open to Protestant Christianity if only missionaries could be found to go west and spread the Gospel. "Hear! Hear!" wrote the editor of *The Christian Advocate and Journal.* "Who will respond to the call from beyond the Rocky Mountains? . . . [W]e are for having a mission established there at once. . . . All we want is men. Who will go? Who?"

The Methodists were the first to answer, sending Jason Lee to the Oregon Country in 1834. He set up a mission among the Chinook, but soon proved a disappointment to his church, more interested in colonizing the Willamette Valley with fellow Methodists from New England than saving Indian souls, and was eventually dismissed.

In late 1836, a party of five Presbyterian missionaries from the American Board of Foreign Missions made the 2,000-mile trek from Missouri to Fort Vancouver along the route that would soon be called the Oregon Trail. It was an arduous journey made still more arduous because, while the missionaries agreed on the importance of carrying the Gospel westward, they agreed on very little else. One missionary, William Gray, proved quarrelsome and petulant; trained in carpentry and mechanics and ill-prepared for life among the Indians, he would soon abandon the ministry for farming. Another, the Reverend Henry Spalding, was a rigid and embittered man from upstate New York. Born out of wedlock to a woman who neglected him and a father who would have nothing to do with him, he was newly married to Eliza Gray, but still nursed a grievance against the woman who had turned down his first proposal of marriage, Narcissa Prentiss. That same Narcissa Prentiss and her new husband, Dr. Marcus Whitman, made up the rest of the party, and the two couples were forced to share the same tent all across the continent.

As soon as the party reached Oregon it split up. The Spaldings settled among the Nez Percé. The Whitmans chose to begin their work 120 miles away, at Walla Walla, among the Nez Percé's neighbors, the Cayuse.

Narcissa Whitman was pious and eager and possessed of a fine voice for singing hymns, but, like the rest of her missionary companions, utterly ignorant of the West and of the people she and her husband hoped to convert to Christianity. "Some [of the Indians] feel almost to blame us for telling about eternal realities," she noted. "One said it was good when they knew nothing but to hunt, eat, drink and sleep; now it was bad. [. . . Still,] we long to have them know of a Saviour's pardoning love."

The Cayuse, like the Nez Percé, to whom they were closely related, had hoped to be taught the practical secrets of white civilization — modern weaponry, better tools. Instead, the Whitmans told them they must abandon hunting and fishing and take up the plow, denounced their medicine men as charlatans, and warned that they were doomed if they failed to repent of their sins.

[The Indians] listened to our professions of friendship. We called them brothers and they believed us. They yielded millions of acres to our demands and yet we crave more. We have crowded the tribes upon a few miserable acres of our southern frontier: it is all that is left to them of their once boundless forests; and still, like the horse-leech, our insatiated cupidity cries, give! give! give!

Senator Theodore Frelinghuysen of New Jersey

The Indians came to resent the missionaries' refusal to pay for the land they occupied or to offer gifts, as was the Cayuse custom when visitors came to call. They were insulted when, not long after giving birth to a daughter, Alice, Narcissa barred them from her parlor because, she said, "they would make it so dirty and full of fleas that we could not live in it," and were further baffled when the Whitmans began quarreling with Catholic missionaries over who had a monopoly on religious truth. During their first years in Oregon, the Whitmans managed to convert a Scottish visitor, a French-Canadian Catholic, and several Hawaiian laborers who worked for the mission. But they failed to make a single convert among the Cayuse.

> Never [wrote Narcissa] was I more keenly sensible to the self denials of a missionary life. Even now while I am writing, the drum and the savage yell are sounding in my ears, every sound of which is as far as the east is from the west from vibrating in unison with my feelings. . . . Dear friends will you not sometime think of me almost alone in the midst of savage darkness.

Meanwhile, Henry Spalding did a little better with the Nez Percé. On November 17, 1839 — three years after the Spaldings' arrival in Oregon — he officiated at the baptism of his first two converts. Both were chiefs. He named one Joseph and the other Timothy. The following year, Joseph had a son, whom he named *Hin-mah-too-yah-lat-kekht* — Thunder Rolling from the Mountains. Spalding baptized the infant as Ephraim, but he would one day be known throughout the West as Chief Joseph.

TRAIL OF TEARS

Since Thomas Jefferson's time, Washington had hoped that the Indian peoples of the East might learn the ways of the whites and thus gradually be absorbed among them. But if they could not be absorbed, then they might gradually be moved west of the Mississippi, to a "permanent Indian frontier" carved from the prairies. There, the theory was, they could flourish free from further white encroachment.

Whites disagreed over the degree of kindness or coercion that should be applied to bringing about the Indians' removal, but virtually all agreed that their own wish to expand westward into lands to which they believed the Indian peoples had only the vaguest sort of title should always come first. That, after all, had been how the East was settled; why should the West be any different? "What is the right of a huntsman to the forest of a thousand miles over which he has accidentally ranged in quest of prey?" asked John Quincy Adams. ". . . Shall the field and valley, which a beneficent

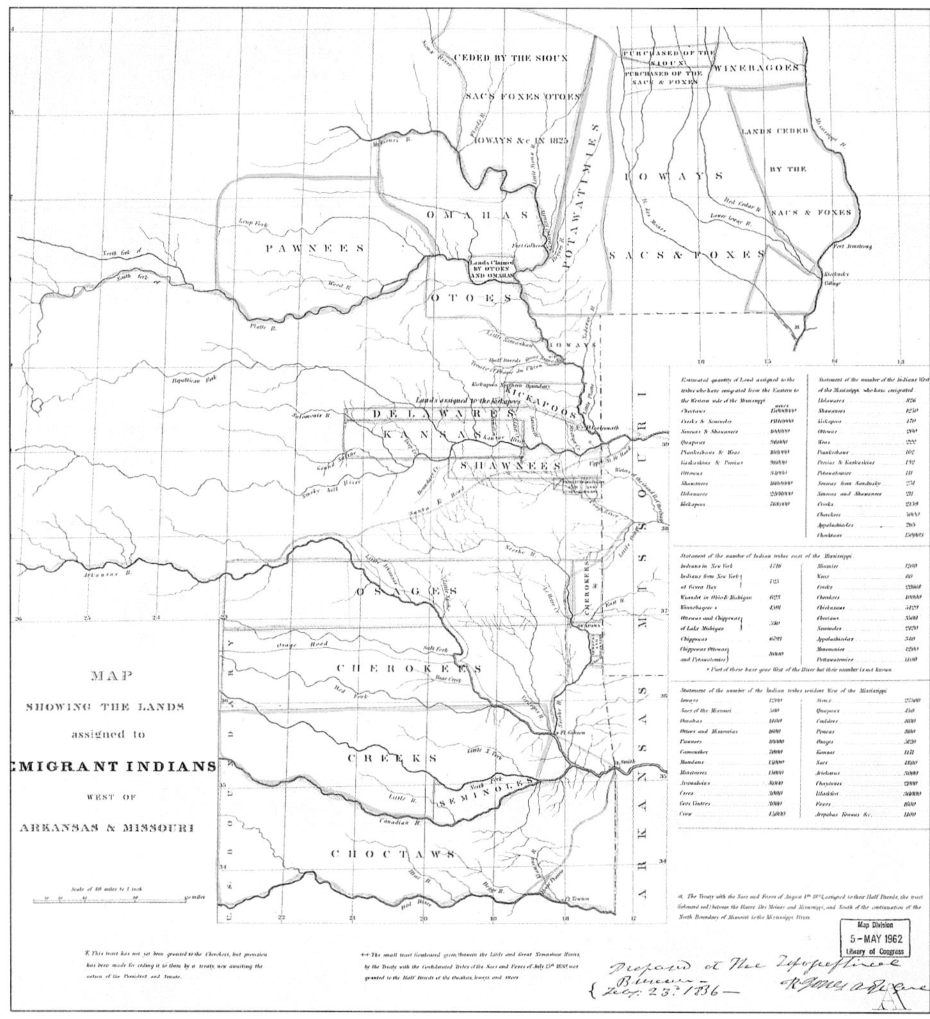

We ask [the President] to protect us, agreeable to treaties. Inclination to remove from this land has no abiding place in our hearts, and when we move we shall move by the course of nature to sleep under this ground which the Great Spirit gave to our ancestors and which now covers them in their undisturbed repose.

Legislative Council of the Cherokee

Indian Territory in 1836, parceled out among euphemistically titled "Emigrant Indians"—actually peoples from eastern and midwestern tribes compelled to leave their homes and move west

God has formed to teem with the life of innumerable multitudes, be condemned to everlasting barrenness?"

On May 28, 1830, President Andrew Jackson had signed the Indian Removal Act, which empowered him to make treaties with all tribes east of the Mississippi to cede their lands in exchange for lands in the West. One by one, Indian bands found themselves forced to move from their old homes — Ottawa, Shawnee, and Potawatomi, Sac and Fox, Miami and Kickapoo.

Indian peoples already living in the West were not consulted about this involuntary invasion. When the newcomers edged too far west in search of buffalo, Kiowa and Comanche attacked them, and federal troops had to be called in to impose a tenuous peace. The Cheyenne and Arapaho also sought to drive the Potawatomi from their hunting grounds but got more than they bargained for; the easterners, trained by the British during the War of 1812, formed ranks, fired organized volleys, and took a terrible toll on their attackers before driving them from the field.

The southern states were home to the peoples whom whites called the "Five Civilized Tribes." The Choctaw were the first to be moved west, followed by the Chickasaw. Some of the Creek had to be driven from their land. So did the Seminoles.

The Cherokee, living on 40,000 acres in the heart of Georgia, sought to resist Removal by legal means. No other Indian people had ever so successfully adopted the white man's ways. Some lived on large plantations worked by black slaves. They had constructed smithies and sawmills and factories for weaving cloth, built public schools and miles of good roads. Many had intermarried with whites. They had their own constitution and government and courts, too, their own written language, their own newspaper.

"Even in our distant state," wrote Ralph Waldo Emerson from Concord, Massachusetts,

> some good rumor of [the Cherokee's] worth and civility has arrived. We have learned with joy of their improvements in the social arts. We have read their newspapers. We have seen some of them in our schools and colleges. . . . [W]e have witnessed with sympathy the painful labors of these red men to redeem their own race from the doom of eternal inferiority and to borrow and domesticate in the tribe the arts and customs of the Caucasian race.

The Cherokee alphabet, introduced in 1821 by Sequoyah, the son of a Cherokee mother and a white trader, had a separate character for each of the eighty-six syllables of the tribal tongue.

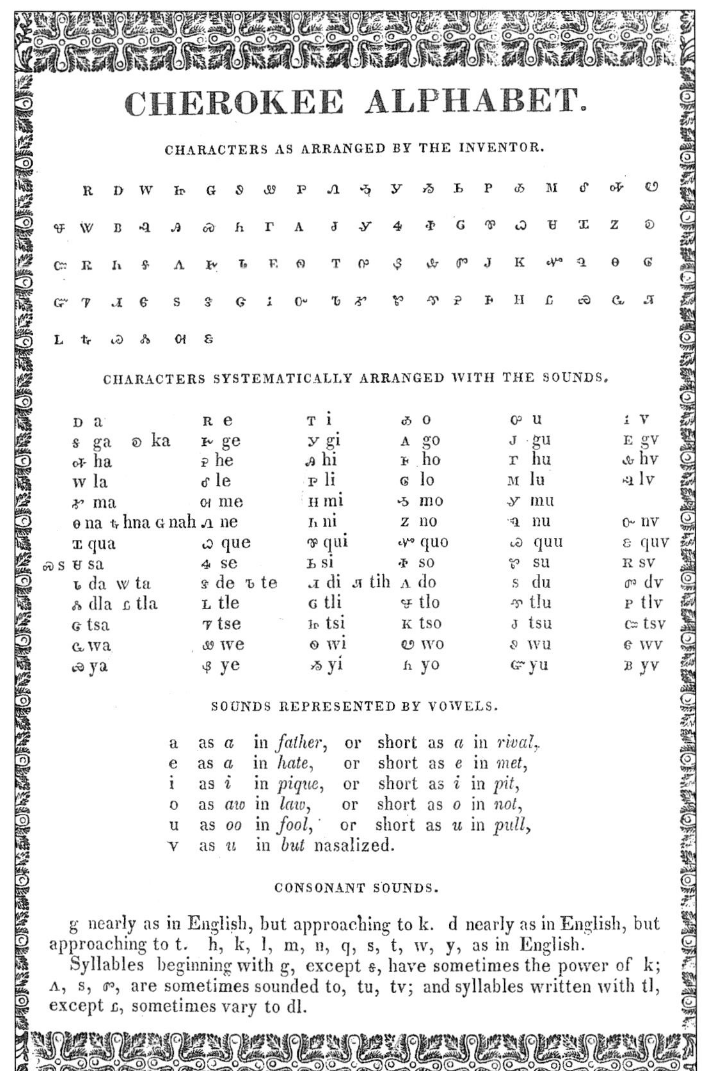

CHEROKEE ALPHABET.

CHARACTERS AS ARRANGED BY THE INVENTOR.

Ꭱ Ꭰ Ꮃ Ꮵ Ꮐ Ꮽ Ꮺ Ꮅ Ꮑ Ꮌ Ꭹ Ᏹ Ꮟ Ꮲ Ꭳ Ꮇ Ꮄ Ꭽ Ꮼ
Ꭾ Ꮤ Ᏼ Ꮈ Ꭿ Ꮝ Ꮒ Ꮁ Ꭺ Ꮷ Ꮍ Ꮞ Ꮠ Ꮆ Ꮘ Ꮗ Ꮜ Ꮖ Ꮓ Ꭷ
Ꮸ Ꮢ Ᏺ Ᏸ Ꮩ Ꭸ Ꮦ Ꮀ Ꮻ Ꭲ Ꭴ Ꭶ Ꮂ Ꮫ Ꭻ Ꮶ Ꮙ Ꮔ Ꮎ Ꮳ
Ᏻ Ꮴ Ꮧ Ꮾ Ꮪ Ꮥ Ꮯ Ꭵ Ꮕ Ꮣ Ꮨ Ꮡ Ꮱ Ꮰ Ꭼ Ꮋ Ꮭ Ꮿ Ꮹ Ꮉ
Ꮮ Ꮏ Ꮚ Ꮬ Ꮊ Ꮛ

CHARACTERS SYSTEMATICALLY ARRANGED WITH THE SOUNDS.

Ꭰ a	Ꭱ e	Ꭲ i	Ꭳ o	Ꭴ u	Ꭵ v
Ꭶ ga Ꭷ ka	Ꭸ ge	Ꭹ gi	Ꭺ go	Ꭻ gu	Ꭼ gv
Ꭽ ha	Ꭾ he	Ꭿ hi	Ꮀ ho	Ꮁ hu	Ꮂ hv
Ꮃ la	Ꮄ le	Ꮅ li	Ꮆ lo	Ꮇ lu	Ꮈ lv
Ꮉ ma	Ꮊ me	Ꮋ mi	Ꮌ mo	Ꮍ mu	
Ꮎ na Ꮏ hna Ꮐ nah	Ꮑ ne	Ꮒ ni	Ꮓ no	Ꮔ nu	Ꮕ nv
Ꮖ qua	Ꮗ que	Ꮘ qui	Ꮙ quo	Ꮚ quu	Ꮛ quv
Ꮝ s Ꮜ sa	Ꮞ se	Ꮟ si	Ꮠ so	Ꮡ su	Ꮢ sv
Ꮣ da Ꮤ ta	Ꮥ de Ꮦ te	Ꮧ di Ꮨ tih	Ꮩ do	Ꮪ du	Ꮫ dv
Ꮬ dla Ꮭ tla	Ꮮ tle	Ꮯ tli	Ꮰ tlo	Ꮱ tlu	Ꮲ tlv
Ꮳ tsa	Ꮴ tse	Ꮵ tsi	Ꮶ tso	Ꮷ tsu	Ꮸ tsv
Ꮹ wa	Ꮺ we	Ꮻ wi	Ꮼ wo	Ꮽ wu	Ꮾ wv
Ꮿ ya	Ᏸ ye	Ᏹ yi	Ᏺ yo	Ᏻ yu	Ᏼ yv

SOUNDS REPRESENTED BY VOWELS.

a as *a* in *father*, or short as *a* in *rival*,
e as *a* in *hate*, or short as *e* in *met*,
i as *i* in *pique*, or short as *i* in *pit*,
o as *aw* in *law*, or short as *o* in *not*,
u as *oo* in *fool*, or short as *u* in *pull*,
v as *u* in *but* nasalized.

CONSONANT SOUNDS.

g nearly as in English, but approaching to k. d nearly as in English, but approaching to t. h, k, l, m, n, q, s, t, w, y, as in English.

Syllables beginning with g, except Ꭶ, have sometimes the power of k; Ꭺ, Ꮪ, Ꮫ, are sometimes sounded to, tu, tv; and syllables written with tl, except Ꮭ, sometimes vary to dl.

None of this mattered to white Georgians. They wanted Cherokee land and methodically went about taking it. Cherokee land titles were declared illegal. Cherokee were forbidden to testify against whites, even to dig for gold on their own lands. Those who resisted were beaten, jailed, killed.

The Cherokee took their case to the U.S. Supreme Court — and won at least a limited victory. The Indians were "domestic dependent nations," wrote Chief Justice John Marshall, subject to the United States, which was responsible for protecting their rights, but not subject to the individual states themselves. Georgia could not simply seize their lands.

But Andrew Jackson refused to intervene. To him, even the Cherokee were an obstacle to American expansion: no matter how hard they had tried to make their civilization match that of the whites who surrounded them, they would have to move. Indians, Jackson believed, had "neither the intelligence, the industry, the moral habits, nor the desire for improvement which are essential to any favorable change in their condition . . . they must necessarily yield to the force of circumstances and ere long disappear."

Some Cherokee, including prosperous mixed-blood planters certain that only disaster awaited them if they resisted, and traditional hunters who hoped to re-create their old lives in new surroundings, had already moved west on their own. The rest of the Cherokee people now began to divide into two camps. A treaty party, led by several members of one influential family — Major Ridge, a wealthy planter and tribal orator, his son, John Ridge, and nephews Elias Boudinot and Stand Watie — had reluctantly come to the conclusion that further resistance would only prolong the tribe's agony: it was time to admit defeat, give up their lands, and move west.

Cherokee rivals: John Ross (far left), who adamantly opposed Removal, and Stand Watie, who reluctantly came to favor it

The Georgians have shown a grasping spirit lately; . . . I know the Indians have an older title than theirs. . . . Yet they are strong and we are weak. We are few, they are many. We cannot remain here in safety and comfort. I know we love the graves of our fathers. . . . We can never forget these homes, I know, but an unbending, iron necessity tells us we must leave them. . . . There is but one path of safety, one road to future existence as a Nation. That path is open before you. Make a treaty of cession. Give up these lands and go over beyond the great Father of Waters.

Major Ridge

But John Ross, the principal chief of the Cherokee, was opposed to any treaty. He was the son of a Scottish immigrant and only one-eighth Indian, and had once served under Andrew Jackson against the Creek. But his followers were mostly full-bloods, generally less well off than the leading members of the treaty party, and adamantly against leaving the land where their ancestors were buried.

On December 29, 1835 — with Ross away in Washington still trying to plead his people's case — the leaders of the treaty party gathered in the parlor of Elias Boudinot's home and signed a treaty ceding all their lands in exchange for $5 million. Fully 80 percent of the tribe — almost 16,000 Cherokee — issued a protest afterward disavowing the treaty: John Ridge and his allies had spoken only for themselves, they said.

Andrew Jackson ignored them. The eastern Cherokee nation, he said, no longer existed. They were given two years to move. Two thousand went voluntarily, including the members of the treaty party. The rest held out to the end. In the spring of 1838, soldiers began to round them up.

> . . . [A]fter all the warning and with soldiers in their midst [an officer remembered], the inevitable day found the Indians at work in their houses and in their fields. . . . Two or three dropped their hoes and ran as fast as they could when they saw the soldiers coming. . . . The men . . . picked them up in the road, in the field anywhere they found them . . . the cows and calves lowing to one another; the poor dogs howling for their owners; the open doors of the cabins as we left them — to have seen it all would have melted to tenderness a heart of stone.

A few Cherokee escaped to the hills and stayed behind. But some 15,000 were kept penned up inside log stockades all summer, subject to measles, whooping cough, and cholera. Then the day came to start west. ". . . [I]n the chill of the drizzling rain on an October morning," one private wrote, "I saw them loaded like cattle or sheep into six hundred and forty-five wagons and started toward the west. . . . Chief Ross led in prayer and when the bugle sounded and the wagons started rolling many of the children . . . waved their little hands good-bye to their mountain homes."

It was 1,200 miles to what is now Oklahoma. Cold autumn rain fell all along the way. Many fell ill and some 4,000 died. The survivors rebuilt their lives, and it is one of the more remarkable ironies of western history that among the first communities to carry the trappings of eastern civilization into the region — churches, schools, slavery, the printing press — were people thought hopelessly "primitive" by their white neighbors.

The only thing we lack here [in California] is a good Government. . . . If we had fifty families here from Missouri, we could do exactly as we pleased without any fear of being troubled. . . . The difficulty of coming here is imaginary.

Dr. John Marsh, 1840

The Cherokee never forgot the Trail of Tears. Nor did those who had never agreed to give up their old lives forget or forgive those they held responsible for their misery. On the morning of June 22, 1839, Cherokee assassins dragged John Ridge from his bed and stabbed him to death. Others stabbed Elias Boudinot and shot Major Ridge.

Still, it was not over. Stand Watie of the treaty party survived. The conflict over Removal would continue to divide the Cherokee for generations. And even before they began their westward march, a small-town blacksmith from Illinois named John Deere had fashioned for a neighbor a new kind of plow, made of steel and capable of turning the rich matted soil of the prairie that had resisted the old wrought-iron plows settlers brought with them from the East. It would take him ten more years to begin mass-producing his invention, but it would transform farming in the West — and one day encourage whites to think of taking over lands the Indians had been assured would be theirs forever. Meanwhile, the permanence of the "permanent Indian frontier" was already being violated as white settlers began to cross it on their way to Oregon and California.

John Bidwell, who went west armed with "nothing more formidable than a pocket knife" and eventually became one of California's richest men

THIS WONDERFUL COUNTRY

John Bidwell was just a twenty-one-year-old schoolteacher in 1840, but he had already moved from New York to Pennsylvania to Ohio to Weston, Missouri — where a claim-jumper stole his land. Unwilling to return to Ohio in disgrace and with nothing much to lose, he heard a French-Canadian trader tell of the wonders he had seen in California and was spellbound:

> At that time when a man moved out West, as soon as he was fairly settled he wanted to move again, and naturally every question imaginable was asked in regard to this wonderful country. Generally, the first question . . . was whether there was any fever and ague. I remember his answer distinctly. He said that there was but one man in California that had ever had a chill there, and it was a matter of so much wonderment to the people of Monterey that they went eighteen miles into the country to see him shake.

A few weeks later, a widely published letter from an American resident of California, Dr. John Marsh, made it seem still more alluring. "The Agricultural capabilities [of California] as yet are but very imperfectly developed," he reported.

> The whole of it is remarkably adapted to the culture of the vine. *Wine & brandy* are made in considerable quantities. Olives, figs & almonds grow well. Apples, pears & peaches are abundant & in the southern part, *oranges. Cotton* . . . suc-

> ceeds well. . . . I think [California] cannot long remain in the hands of its present owners. . . . [A]lthough nominally belonging to Mexico [it] is about as independent of it as Texas and must ere long share the same fate.

California was still only sparsely colonized and poorly defended. Boston-based merchants were making a killing peddling crockery and clothing, coffee and sugar, silks and satins and pins to the *Californios* in exchange for shiploads of tallow and hides. And small numbers of foreigners — Americans, Britons, Europeans, many of whom had married into influential *Californio* families — already dominated commerce from offices in Monterey and Los Angeles.

It all sounded wonderful to John Bidwell. He helped form a "Western Emigration Society." Some five hundred Missourians signed up to go to California the following

Emigrants Crossing the Plains by Alfred Bierstadt, one of the most celebrated of many paintings extolling the pioneer. "The march of emigration is to the West," wrote Alfred Robinson in 1846, "and naught will arrest its advance but the mighty ocean."

spring. But during the winter there were disturbing reports that an American had been imprisoned in California for daring to suggest that the United States might one day seize it, and in the end, of the original five hundred, only Bidwell turned up in the spring, armed and ready to start for the Pacific.

He was undeterred, though it took several weeks to recruit sixty-eight other would-be pioneers, as eager as he to go to California but just as unsure how to get there. "We were ready to start," he recalled, "but no one knew where to go, not even the captain. Our ignorance of the route was complete. We knew that California lay west, and that was the extent of our knowledge."

Then they chanced upon a former mountain man, Thomas Fitzpatrick, whom the Cheyenne called "Broken Hand" because he'd lost three fingers when his rifle blew up, already employed to guide a party that included the Jesuit priest Father Pierre-Jean De Smet to Oregon. He agreed to lead them as far as the point where the trails diverged.

The journey had its share of excitements: a cyclone that dipped down dangerously close to the wagons; buffalo herds so immense the party feared it might be trampled; the death of one man who accidentally shot himself; and an encounter with Cheyenne who turned out to be perfectly friendly but whose sudden appearance so unnerved one of the party's hunters that he stripped off his clothes in terror — and was forever after called "Cheyenne" Dawson.

At Soda Springs, the northernmost bend of the Bear River, the party divided in two: when Fitzpatrick and Father De Smet and their contingent turned north toward Oregon, fully half of Bidwell's original party decided to go with them, frightened of venturing into unknown territory without a guide.

Bidwell and his thirty-one remaining companions determined to struggle south alone. They almost didn't make it. They had to slaughter their oxen for food and abandon their wagons, then ate crows, a wildcat, a coyote, even a pulpy paste, prepared by helpful local Indians, that turned out to be mashed insects. They soldiered on, nonetheless, over the Sierras and down into the San Joaquin Valley, stumbling at last onto the farm of Dr. John Marsh, the same man whose rosy letters had helped lure them to California.

Marsh's enthusiasm for California had been real enough, but he himself turned out to be something of a fraud. A Harvard graduate who practiced medicine without ever having attended medical school, he now asked to be paid for the few rations he allowed the half-starved pioneers to have, then demanded an exorbitant fee for Mexican passports it had cost him nothing to obtain. Bidwell declared him the most "selfish" man he'd ever met.

John Bidwell stayed on, nonetheless, and soon got a job in the Sacramento Valley, a hundred miles to the north, working as chief clerk for John Augustus Sutter, the most important foreigner in California. Sutter had been an utter failure before he got to California, a bankrupt German-Swiss storekeeper on the run from his creditors and from the wife and five children he had left behind in Switzerland. But he was hard to discourage — and persuasive. In 1839, he had arrived at Monterey from Hawaii with a considerable entourage — two Germans and ten Hawaiians, including his mistress — but without any apparent prospects. Nonetheless, he put on a worn French military uniform he had bought for a single beaver skin, asked to see the Mexican governor, and somehow talked him into granting him nearly 50,000 acres at the junc-

tion of the Sacramento and American rivers in the uncolonized Sacramento Valley, where he hoped to establish a colony called Nueva Helvetia — "New Switzerland."

Bidwell's first task for Sutter was to complete the transfer of the contents of Fort Ross, one of two former Russian coastal outposts that Sutter had bought using an unsecured loan that he never managed to repay. The fort was stripped of everything except its apple trees: furniture, tools, lumber, herds of sheep and cattle, military uniforms, and, most important, several French cannons the Russians had captured from Napoleon, which Sutter used to make his new fort impregnable against Indians and suspicious Mexican authorities alike.

John Augustus Sutter and the fortress from which he ruled his California empire

Sutter ran his sprawling domain like a European barony — drilling an army of Indians, dispensing a crude kind of justice, encouraging his workers to plant fields and orchards and harvest timber, and taking very young girls to bed. But he also provided supplies and shelter to the Americans who had begun to follow John Bidwell's footsteps into California. One hundred and twenty-five Americans made it through the next year. In 1845, nearly 3,000 followed. "We find ourselves threatened by hordes of Yankee emigrants, who have already begun to flock into our country, and whose progress we cannot arrest," warned California's governor, Pio Pico. "Already have the wagons of that perfidious people scaled the almost inaccessible summits of the Sierra Nevada, crossed the entire continent and penetrated the fruitful valley of the Sacramento. What that astonishing people will next undertake, I cannot say."

Mariano Guadalupe Vallejo belonged to one of the oldest Spanish families in the Americas. One ancestor had sailed with Columbus, another with Cortés, and his father had been one of the first soldiers to settle in California. The rarified life of the *Californios* that was their legacy to him seemed to him idyllic. "There was never a more peaceful or happy people on the face of the earth than the Spanish, Mexican and Indian population of Alta California," he would write one day. "We were the pioneers of the Pacific coast, building pueblos and missions while General Washington was carrying on the war of the Revolution. . . ."

The Mexican-American War was the first to be photographed. An anonymous daguerreotypist captured Major Lucien B. Webster's battery (above) in the mountains north of Buena Vista, where they had helped smash larger but less well armed Mexican forces. The anonymous portrait opposite is believed to be the only one to show a Texas Ranger in battle dress. No photographs survive of the skirmishing that captured California for the United States, but the flag inset above was carried by the founders of the short-lived Bear Flag Republic, who started it all.

up the governorship. Frémont was an army officer, not a navy man, and should have obeyed. But he liked being governor, hated taking orders from any man, refused to resign. When Kearny sent an intermediary to demand that he surrender his papers, Frémont challenged the man to a duel, with shotguns.

The duel never took place, but Kearny won the political struggle. President Polk had empowered him, not Stockton, to set up a civilian government. Frémont resigned the governorship but refused to apologize for his insubordination. "The younger officers," Lieutenant William Tecumseh Sherman remembered, "had been discussing what the General would do with Frémont, who was supposed to be in a state of mutiny. Some thought he would be tried and shot, some that he would be carried back in irons; and all agreed that if anyone else than Frémont had put on such airs and acted as he had done, Kearny would have shown him no mercy."

Kearny didn't show much: he ordered Frémont's arrest for mutiny. When Kearny left California for the East with part of his victorious army in the summer of 1847, Frémont, facing court-martial, was ordered to ride at the rear of the column, eating his enemy's dust as they made their way back along the trail. Angry and bitter, he found some solace in the praise showered upon him by many of the emigrants who recognized him along the trail. "They were using my maps on the road," he wrote to a friend, "traveling by them, and you may judge how gratified I was to find that they found them perfectly correct. . . ." At Truckee Lake, high in the Sierras, Frémont saw horrific evidence of what could happen to travelers moving through the West without a good map — the bones of California-bound pioneers remembered as the Donner Party, men and women who had taken an untried cutoff and perished in the snow, lay scattered over the countryside, gnawed white by wolves and coyotes.

Meanwhile, the war in Mexico stretched on for another year — a bloody, desperate struggle that cost thousands of Mexican lives and ended only after American troops stormed into Mexico City. On February 2, 1848, Mexico signed the Treaty of Guadalupe Hidalgo, formally ending the war. It had lost nearly half its territory to the invaders from the north.

On July 4, 1848, in Washington, D.C., thousands turned out to see President Polk lay the cornerstone of a new monument — a giant stone shaft modeled after the obelisks of ancient Egypt to honor the nation's first president, George Washington. Washington's America had ended at the Mississippi. But now, as Polk spoke to the crowd, he was the president of a nation three times as large, a continental United States that stretched from sea to sea. In only a generation — by bluff and intimidation, by sacrifice, and by outright conquest — Americans had seized almost all of the West.

Standing near the President at the ceremony was Joe Meek, whose fondest wish had now come true. Born in Washington County, Virginia, the old mountain man was now sheriff of the brand-new Washington County — in Oregon Territory. A month later, even more good news arrived from the newest section of the country. In California — on a stream named the American River — gold had been discovered. Nothing in the West would ever be the same again.

The Mission at Waiilatpu: A Meeting Place for Western Women

Julie Roy Jeffrey

Once, a long time ago, there were two old Cayuse women. While the men went hunting for game, these old women were searching for camas roots. Some they would dry for the winter, but they were using others to make delicious hot mush.

Now at that time, the Snake were on the warpath, and one of the Snake warriors met up with these women. And what do you think the women did? Why, they poured the hot mush all over the enemy's face. The warrior fell back, and these two old women, they just took a knife and scalped him and then escaped to the Walla Walla Valley.

When they got home and told what they had done, all the Cayuse shouted with joy for the feat of these old women, these brave old Cayuse women. Then, they named the creek for them, and that's why it's named Squaw Creek.

In the Cayuse longhouses, each one home to an extended family during the winter months when the tribe camped near the Walla Walla River, you could hear this kind of story and many others during the long dark evenings. Elders, with the wisdom of many years, were the favored storytellers. And while everyone crowded around the fire to listen to them, children and young people were encouraged to pay especially close attention. For it was through stories that Cayuse children were instructed about what was important in life. The story of the two old women, for example, contained many lessons: it taught the importance of heroism, bravery, and quick thinking, defined the character of the Snake, and reflected the power of tribal ties and the people's love for the Walla Walla Valley, their home. Then, too, children could learn to appreciate the critical role women played in sustaining tribal life and to admire female strength and courage.

On cold winter evenings in the mid-1840s, not far from the Indian encampment, quite different scenes of domestic life were taking place in the comfortable mission house. If it were a Thursday night, you could see Narcissa Whitman, the wife of the Presbyterian medical missionary, Marcus Whitman, and an assistant missionary to the Indians herself, leading a religious meeting for her large family of adopted children. She was hoping to alert them to the dangers of their sinful natures and to the promise of God's loving forgiveness. Without a spiritual awakening, they could never experience the conversion she believed necessary for salvation. On other nights, she might lead them in singing, and, when there were guests, show them off a bit, by having them line up according to height as they performed. They were her "family stairway," she said. If she was proud of them for their singing and their neat attire, and if she monitored their spiritual progress very closely, you could hardly blame her. Most of the children had been wild and untutored when she had taken them in, not at all like her own dead child, Alice, who had loved singing hymns and talking of Jesus. The last ones she had adopted, a whole family of children named the Sagers, orphaned during the long overland journey to the West, had been a real challenge — seven of them at once, ignorant and unruly after months of travel. But then, perhaps their dead mother, Naomi Sager, had not taken her obligations as a mother quite so seriously as Narcissa did her own.

These two domestic scenes, so different in character yet unfolding so close to one another in the Walla Walla Valley in eastern Oregon Territory, hint at the diversity of family life and female experience in the nineteenth-century West. While the Whitman mission at Waiilatpu lasted just eleven years, it was a place where Native American, white, and métis women of mixed racial parentage mingled. Even though common experiences like childbirth tied the different women together, were we to visit the mission, we might well have been struck more by the differences than the similarities between them.

Narcissa Whitman's middle-class values, her notions of appropriate roles for women and men, her evangelical background, her education and training in New York State provided the vantage point from which she viewed and judged the Indian women among whom she lived and worked. On the one hand, she pitied Indian women, whom she thought were "slaves to their husbands." Unused to labor outside of the house and garden, Narcissa, like many white women, was horrified at the heavy work that Indian women performed and the many tasks for which they were responsible. On the other hand, she condemned them for being neglectful mothers, bemoaning the fact that she could not see "one savory example" of proper childrearing among the Cayuse. The ease of divorce, the sexual freedom tolerated before marriage, the practice of polygamy all violated her beliefs about morality, female chastity, and marital fidelity.

Frustrated by the Cayuse women's unwillingness to emulate her own domestic habits and routines, believing that she was offering them the comforts of both civilization and salvation, she could only interpret their resistance as either the work of Satan or rival Roman Catholic missionaries. Her exasperation impressed one white observer, who remarked that Narcissa entertained for the "Indians in her charge the feelings of a mother towards ungrateful children." While there were harmonious moments — Narcissa recorded buying berries from Indian women and reading the Bible to them, and she possessed a decorated Indian fan — an underlying current of mutual misunderstanding and frustration simmered below the surface.

A good correspondent, Narcissa has provided us with ample evidence of her own activities and her perceptions of others. But what of the Indian women who left no written record? Although their perspective needs some imaginative effort to recover, there are enough clues to allow us to reconstruct their lives and to speculate about their views. While native women's routines were very different from those of white women like Narcissa, as the story of the two old women suggests, Cayuse women were neither slaves nor drudges. Their activities were crucial to their people's welfare. They were not tribal leaders, but they were eligible to hold important positions within the tribe. Some even became "medicine squaws" and performed the sacred healing rituals that drew out evil spirits from the sick.

The Cayuse were one of several seminomadic Indian tribes living in the plateau area of the Columbia River. Because they were not agriculturalists, hunting and gathering activities determined the tribe's annual movements. During the spring and summer, the tribe was constantly on the move, but in the fall the Cayuse split into small groups of kin and family and erected communal longhouses, where they would spend the winter months. One of these groups had its winter quarters close to the Whitman mission house.

While gender determined the division of labor, men and women had complementary but equally important roles in ensuring that the tribe had enough food for the winter. Men fished for salmon and hunted game. Women dried the fish for future use, butchered game and dried it, cured skins, and, most importantly, gathered and preserved roots, wild plants, and fruits. About half the food the tribe ate came from the plants women obtained. Perhaps in partial recognition of the significance of this female work, Indians attributed to it a sacred dimension. As a Cayuse called Young Chief pointed out, the Great Spirit himself "had named the roots that he should feed the Indians on."

This division of labor stretched back to the days of myth and legend. With the introduction of horses, the character of tribal life had changed, but the basic structure of male and female roles was only modified. Cayuse men became successful horse breeders and traders, able now to join in the great buffalo hunts on the plains and to roam farther in pursuit of their enemies. Cayuse women continued to perform their essential functions in tribal life, but their tasks, too, were made less onerous by the presence of horses. They learned to dry buffalo meat and cure the skins that they decorated with beadwork and shells for their own clothes. As explorers and fur traders made their way into the West in the early decades of the nineteenth century, other changes occurred. New tools and implements became available. But the essential contours of female life remained the same.

Nez Percé women and schoolteachers, Idaho, 1890

By the standards of white middle-class society, Indian culture represented the antithesis of civilization. The Whitmans viewed the Walla Walla Valley as a wilderness and referred to the Cayuse as heathens and occasionally as savages. The missionaries implored the Cayuse to turn away from traditional religious beliefs and attacked their medicine men as Satan's minions. They urged the tribe to abandon their seminomadic life and to settle permanently as farmers around the mission. While the Whitmans argued that settled agricultural life would ensure that the tribe never went hungry during the winter, staying at the mission would obviously eliminate women's work as food providers and the prestige and power that went along with it. The Cayuse soon recognized that the Whitmans' goal was one of transformation. As Narcissa pointed out, "We have come to elevate them and not to suffer ourselves to sink down to their standard."

While none of the Cayuse abandoned their yearly cycle of travel, some took the Whitmans' advice and planted a field or two. But the undertaking was problematic. Some men resisted the whole idea of farming, reminding the Cayuse that the earth was their mother. As a member of a closely related tribe asked, "Shall I take a knife and tear my mother's bosom?" Others regarded working in the fields as unmanly and left the labor to their wives and children or slaves. For the women who tended the crops, the agricultural experiment meant new burdens added to their usual round of work. And unlike their gathering activities, labor in the fields, rejected by men as demeaning and dishonorable, did not bring prestige to the women who did it.

Given the weight of Cayuse cultural values and the importance of traditional female activities, we can understand why many Cayuse women did not respond positively to Narcissa's instruction. Certainly it was hard to view her as a friend. Narcissa's refusal to exchange gifts as was customary in Indian society, and her insistence that the Cayuse must work or pay for goods, symbolized for them her lack of interest in friendship.

Consider some of the implications of her work for the lives of Cayuse women. Like most missionaries, Narcissa was determined to replace polygamy with the nuclear family. As she noted, one of the Cayuse men "thinks he is a Christian, but we fear to the contrary. His mind is somewhat waked up about his living with two women. I would not ease him any, but urged him to do his duty." But what was to happen to the wives who would be so dutifully discarded? What would loss of the labor of several wives mean for a family's diet and health? What would compensate a woman who lost the prestige that accompanied marriage to a chief, one of the men most likely to have more than one wife?

Eager to encourage Indian women to adopt her own construction of womanhood, Narcissa never really considered why Cayuse women might not benefit from the changes she suggested. When they failed to exhibit sufficient interest in acquiring white domestic skills, Narcissa was disgusted. "The Indians do not love to work well enough for us to place any dependence upon them," she remarked. In particular, "the Kayuse ladies are too proud to be seen usefully employed." They even looked askance at having their children perform suitable chores. "The moment they hear of the children doing the least thing," Narcissa reported, "they are panic-stricken and make trouble."

Cayuse women must have wondered where it would all end. Did Narcissa want them to abandon their longhouses, which she obviously found dirty and poorly arranged, for a house like her own? Longhouses provided space for husbands, wives, children, grandparents, cousins, aunts, and uncles to live together as an extended family. They were open and accessible to friends and kin. Narcissa's house had closed doors, windows covered with blinds, and fences to keep people away. Cayuse women knew that they were not welcome there. Why should they want to replicate Narcissa's arrangements and the work that went along with them? Would they even be urged to leave off their familiar clothes in order to wear the kinds of dresses the missionary favored, the ones that needed continual washing? Would she expect them to keep their children close by, as she did her own, forcing them to work and punishing them as no Indian mother would do? (Shaming a child, rather than punishment, was the Indian way of discipline.)

There were a few women who listened and became "good" Indians. But most native women apparently found Narcissa's advice and the manner in which she gave it unappealing. "Firmness in her was natural," observed one white, "and to some, especially the Indians, it was repulsive." In the aftermath of Narcissa's violent death at the hands of the Cayuse, the Indian women played out their hostility to the white missionary who had lived in their midst. One witness recollected the terrible scene, "white women running and screaming, and the Indian women singing and dancing."

The gloomy spiritual lessons both the Whitmans taught also colored the Cayuse perspective of the missionaries. Although many members of the tribe willingly adopted some of the Christian practices introduced at the mission, their religious performances were always judged wanting. The Whitmans continually reminded the Cayuse that they had not experienced the requisite change of heart. They were doomed to hell. Not surprisingly, Indians denounced this "bad talk." "Instead of yielding to the truth," Narcissa wrote, "they oppose it vigourously."

More pliable and positive than the Cayuse women who so frustrated Narcissa was her friend Catherine Pambrun. In the early years of mission life when the sight of white women was a rarity at the mission, Narcissa had depended upon Catherine, the wife of Pierre Pambrun, the factor at the Hudson's Bay Fort Walla Walla, about twenty-five miles distant. At her daughter's birth in 1837, Narcissa had only her husband and Catherine to help her.

Catherine Pambrun was a métis woman, the result of two generations of intermarriage between white fur traders and Indian women. Marriages of this sort were common in the fur trade in the 1820s and 1830s. There were few white women as potential marriage partners in the West, and native and mixed-blood women had family ties and skills that were useful to white traders, who depended on Indians to procure furs and horses, to serve as guides, interpreters, and go-betweens. Marriage with an Indian woman cemented business ties and provided a trader with an ideal racial and cultural intermediary. Mixed marriages were also valued in Indian society, not only for the contacts that a woman possessed in the white world but also for the goods and skills that she could pass along to her Indian relatives.

Catherine Pambrun's material life and habits symbolized her position somewhere between two racial and cultural worlds. The house in which she lived with her husband was "half-native, half-French." When Narcissa met her, Catherine was still washing her clothes in a stream and using cradleboards for her newborn children. Stories suggest she even smoked tobacco. In her household, as was also true at other fur-trading outposts, the men did most of the cooking and housework. Such an arrangement violated Narcissa's understanding of the proper roles for men and women, and she wrote that fur-trade wives were "not first rate housekeepers." While Catherine was fluent in her mother's language and French, she could speak little English.

Narcissa, who was well treated by the head factor of the Hudson's Bay Company and his mixed-blood wife when she arrived in the West, liked Catherine Pambrun and began to teach her English. She taught her other things as well: how to wash her clothes in a bucket instead of in a stream and the importance of not confining a baby in a cradleboard. She felt a great sense of achievement when Catherine abandoned the practice and gave "the blessed privilege of liberty" to her newborn.

Despite the friendship between the women, and the sense that cultural and racial boundaries in the West were permeable, the racial easiness of the métis fur-trade world was fast disappearing as more white women came west and judged métis women by their own standards. Pierre Pambrun sensed, if his wife did not, that times were changing. If women like Catherine were to survive in the white world, they would have to adopt white standards, and even then, they would probably face discrimination. It was Pierre who set the English lessons in motion and tried to persuade Catherine to give up smoking in exchange for diamond earrings. Certainly, Narcissa's own toleration of racial mixing had limits. Although Catherine remained her friend, by 1846 Narcissa was condemning men who were "disposed to degrade themselves" by taking "a native" woman as a spouse.

The uneasiness of Pierre Pambrun, who sensed his world was being undermined by white migration, was matched by that of Indian tribes whose territories lay in the path of the overland wagon trains. The Cayuse, like other tribes, grew restive in the 1840s as the number of white emigrants crossing their lands increased. Some of the whites stopped at the mission station, where the Whitmans gave them supplies for which the Indians had to pay. They even occupied the room that had been set aside as the Indian room. During the winter, emigrants lived at the mission, where the Whitmans organized a school for their children.

Lakota and a missionary

The Cayuse must have sensed how much the attitudes of the missionary couple had shifted. Originally, they had come as missionaries to the Indians. Now they welcomed the emigrants and acted as the white people's trusted friends and defenders. Perhaps some of them even suspected that the Whitmans had consigned them to oblivion. As Marcus wrote candidly in an 1844 letter, "I am fully convinced that when a people refuse or neglect to fill the designs of Providence, they ought not to complain at the results; and so it is equally useless for Christians to be anxious on their account. The Indians have in no case obeyed the command to multiply and replenish the earth, and they cannot stand in the way of others doing so." While Narcissa continued to refer to the "poor Indians" dutifully in her letters, she busied herself with her large family of children and all but removed herself from contact with them.

For Narcissa, the emigration pointed to a hopeful future. She had never felt comfortable in her missionary work, and when her daughter had accidentally drowned, she had gone into a deep depression. A long visit in the more settled Willamette Valley had only made her more aware of the real character of the mission station. Upon her return to Waiilatpu, she had written to a friend despairingly. "What sounds fall upon my ears and what savage sights do I behold every day around me. . . . [E]ven now . . . the drum and the savage yell are sounding in my ears." Now, it seemed possible that civilization as she understood it could be established in the West.

While Narcissa's original missionary vocation marked her as exceptional, her understanding of the female sphere and its obligations was shared by other white women moving west. Although there were few female missionaries, many women, especially those from a middle-class eastern background, agreed with Narcissa that a woman had a duty to reform the world. They would judge western society and find it wanting. In 1856, nine years after Narcissa's death, Kate Blaine, who had come from Seneca Falls, New York, to Portland, Oregon, proclaimed, "This is an awfully wicked country and if it doesn't meet with the fate of Sodom and Gomorrah or Pompeii, it won't be because the people don't deserve it."

The importance Narcissa attached to the domestic sphere and the re-creation of a genteel lifestyle would also be shared by other middle-class emigrants. Narcissa's first home had been a simple adobe building with a log lean-to. Even in these modest surroundings, Narcissa managed to provide some domestic comforts. She put glass in her windows, made feather beds for the bedsteads, for which there were also sheets — a rarity in the West at that time — and had separate pots for brewing coffee and tea. Her washtub, which she believed one of only two west of the Rockies, symbolized her intention to uphold familiar housekeeping standards. She objected to the Cayuse partly because "they are so filthy they make a great deal of cleaning wherever they go." The work they created "wears out a woman very fast." Her attitude toward cleanliness could hardly have escaped Cayuse notice, for she refused to let her daughter Alice crawl on the floor and carried the child around in her arms for the first year of her life.

As the mission became a successful farming operation, a new house was constructed. One of the Sager orphans was amazed at her first sight of it. "We expected to see log houses, occupied by Indians and such people as we had seen about the forts. Instead we saw a large white house surrounded with palisades." Inside Narcissa had both a parlor and a dining room. Floors were tastefully painted yellow and trim was slate gray. Furniture included settees, clothes presses, and rocking chairs. There was even a cabinet for Narcissa's curiosities, English china for the dining table, and, of course, books. Most of the appurtenances for genteel living were now present.

Despite the fact travelers and other missionaries were occasional visitors, this home was, as the Indians recognized, a private space set aside for family life. Like other middle-class women, Narcissa saw her house as a haven from the bustle and confusion of public life that, in the mission setting, the Indians represented. Soon after the Whitmans' arrival, Narcissa had decided that "as soon as we are able [we will] . . . prepare a separate room" for the Cayuse. "They will not be allowed to come in any part of the house at all," she declared. Her insistence on family privacy, so different from the relaxed attitudes of her Indian neighbors, led inevitably to conflict. The Cayuse insisted on access to the house, which the Whitmans refused. In 1841, the Indians hacked in the mission house's door and broke windows but failed to sway the Whitmans. "We told them," reported Narcissa, "that . . . we should order our doors."

Her house was the setting for all the domestic activities that normally were part of a white middle-class woman's domain: cooking on the cookstove (a "luxury in those days"), sewing, spinning, knitting, washing clothes, cleaning, and caring for the garden. Although she had hired help when she could, Narcissa insisted that her adopted children take on domestic chores. She considered it part of her responsibility to teach her girls the housewifely skills that would be expected of them when they married.

The house was also the place where Narcissa exercised her authority as mother and moral guide. By the time she came west in the mid-1830s, there were specific cultural expectations for middle-class motherhood. Unlike her Cayuse neighbors, who spread childrearing responsibilities among members of the extended family, Narcissa believed that training the children was a mother's duty. How well she did the job would determine the future health and welfare of the nation and of the West.

Approaching her task with all the seriousness it required, Narcissa sought help from periodicals like *Mother's Magazine* and shared her challenges and triumphs in letters with family and close friends. The children she adopted had all suffered from neglect or inadequate maternal supervision. Several came to her filthy and in poor health. The youngest Sager child, only a few months old, arrived malnourished and weak. Her brothers and sisters had had little discipline and often appeared willful.

Narcissa established a strict regime that included stringent standards for personal cleanliness (a cold bath daily) and for behavior. Some of the children needed "long and tedious" efforts to be trained properly although others were "easily governed." She expected obedience. "There was no danger of any of us being spoiled," wrote Matilda Sager. "She would point to one of us, then point to the dishes or the broom, and we would instantly get busy." "Any deviation from the laid down rule," remembered Matilda's sister, Catherine, "met with instant and severe punishment." When they looked back on their childhood, the Sager children used the word "puritan" to describe Narcissa's approach, very different, in their opinion, "from the way of the plains" and presumably of their own parents.

Most emigrants who came to the Whitman mission saw only the couple's graciousness and hospitality. The Whitmans were "fine, friendly people," Joseph Williams wrote, "with all kinds of garden vegetables, which they gave us very freely." Emigrants appreciated not only the supplies (sometimes given outright, sometimes sold) but also the medical care and advice the Whitmans provided. For some, like Sarah Cummins, whose party Marcus Whitman helped out of a threatening encounter with Indians, the doctor, at least, took on heroic proportions. Sarah recollected him rising before the Indians to "almost super-human height."

But both Narcissa and her husband harbored private doubts about the character of most emigrants and the society they were likely to establish in Oregon. As Marcus wrote to the missionary board, the Whitmans wanted good men (and women), especially from New England, to "hold a good influence over the Indians & sustain religious institutions as a nucleus for society." Only if the right sort of people came to Oregon, Narcissa asserted in 1844, could the country "be saved from becoming a sink of wickedness and prostitution."

While Narcissa certainly did not judge emigrants as harshly as she judged Indians, many violated the norms and values that were a product of her class, religious commitment, and regional background. Narcissa regarded the woman who had cared for the newborn Sager infant after her mother's death on the Oregon Trail as an "old filthy woman" with "a wicked, disobedient family around her to see to." We can imagine what she might have said about Naomi Sager herself. Naomi, perhaps partly as a result of the family's frequent moves, from Ohio to Indiana to eastern and then western Missouri, had never instructed her children in Christianity, nor had she disciplined them effectively. The three oldest could scarcely read when they joined the Whitman family.

Although Naomi never made it to Oregon, she was probably more typical of white women emigrating to the West than Narcissa was. As the Oregon census of 1850 revealed, while many New Englanders could be found in the territory's towns, the majority of settlers did not come from the Northeast but from the Midwest and the Mississippi Valley. Their roots lay in the South, among self-sufficient white yeoman farmers, not plantation owners.

Narcissa saw that the multitudes who were "hastening to this far-distant land to seek their fortune of worldly goods" were coming "regardless of their treasure in heaven." The Gay family, from Kentucky and Virginia via Springfield, Missouri, were just such a family. They had no vision of establishing a godly society in the West. Like most emigrants they were headed to Oregon for material reasons. Martha Gay remembered her father's western fever and his goals. "He had talked about Oregon and the Columbia River for many years and wanted to go there. He wanted to take his nine sons where they could get land." Land to establish a family, perhaps even to replicate the powerful connections between land and family that characterized the plantation South, this was the cherished dream.

Typically, emigrants like the Gays set off to the West with kinfolk and neighbors. When they left Missouri, there were sixteen in their party, "Father, mother, twelve children, one daughter-in-law and one young man who came all the long way with us." Once in Oregon, they searched out family members who had gone ahead or friends from home. The Gays went first to "the home of an old friend who had come out . . . some years before" and had a "joyous meeting" before moving on "to another old neighbor's place who had sent for us to come and stay in their home. . . . Father and his old neighbor were so moved by this meeting that they lost their power of speech."

The women of such migrant families were tough, adaptable, hardworking, and essential partners in the family dream. The trip west could hardly be undertaken without their cooperation. Martha's mother, despite her husband's enthusiasm, was reluctant "to undertake the long and dangerous journey with a large family of small children." Only when she agreed could Martin Gay "set about making arrangements for the journey." Ann Gay gave birth on the trail, but she also did her share of cooking, minding the children, packing and unpacking the wagons, and perhaps even driving on occasion. Her daughter remembered that her father spent much of his time hunting.

An Assiniboin family — Sampson, Frances Louis, and Leah Beaver, 1907

While these women did not differ from Narcissa in their fundamental understanding of what was proper for women to do, they did not share her reformist and evangelical zeal. Emigrants rarely commented on the spiritual aspect of the missionary operation, suggesting that they had little interest in it. Nor did women share all of Narcissa's demanding middle-class standards. Her comment that those who stopped for any length of time at the mission had "a disposition not to work, at any rate, not more than they can help" may have had more to do with a disagreement with the Whitmans' exacting requirements than with any disinclination to do for themselves. Many were neither literate nor genteel. They were often unkempt, too, at least in Narcissa's eyes. Even the young woman who worked as a cook for the Whitmans was deficient, "not as neat and tidy in her person and work as I could wish and as would be well for her."

The regional and cultural differences that Narcissa noticed pointed to the creation of a more complicated white society in Oregon than reminiscences of pioneer days might suggest. In the 1850s, Kate Blaine was remarking upon social and cultural distinctions in language similar to Narcissa's. A visit with "a poor family from Missouri" prompted Kate to write to friends at home, "I often think when we are with people of this class . . . [that] I wish you could hear them talk. I know you would laugh to hear their negro and western phrases." But Kate herself did not always feel like laughing. At the home of a family from Iowa, the woman of the house asked Kate whether she slept in sheets. "Many of the people from the west sleep between these Indian blankets without any sheets, but I would about as soon have caterpillars on me as to have those blankets touch me."

The circle of female life on the early Oregon rural frontier encompassed family, friends, and neighbors and was intensely local in character. Social and religious activities centered in homes and nearby schoolhouses. While female associational life was weak, interest in religion was not. Although Narcissa had decried the religious credentials of most of Oregon's future settlers, many women were not so much irreligious as weakly connected to any particular denomination. Indeed, women often supported family religious observances and encouraged the visits of itinerant preachers. Remembering how his mother and a neighbor from Missouri arranged a preaching service, one Oregonian described how "our cabin, being large, was for years the preaching place for the neighborhood."

Both women and their menfolk also attended camp meetings. At one, female behavior shocked George Atkinson, a minister from New England, who was engaged in just the sort of missionary work among settlers in the Willamette Valley that Narcissa and Marcus Whitman thought was so necessary. Comfortable with genteel worship, Atkinson was taken aback by the style of camp meetings and women's participation in them. He recorded that "two [women] screamed very loud and grasped hands, uttering many things incoherently." The hymns were almost unrecognizable. "Old tunes are changed. Very few are sung as nearly correct as in country churches at home. Some are barbarously altered. Other tunes are framed apparently for the occasion. I suppose many sung daily here never were expressed as notes."

Atkinson's shock reminds us that the West was home to diverse peoples. Although the mission at Waiilatpu does not figure in most narratives of western history, it allows us to glimpse women from different groups and to see the similarities and contrasts between them. It also shows us the ways in which culture, social and regional loyalties, and, of course, race shaped the perspectives and interactions of the women whose paths crossed at the Whitman mission station. And while following the women in their daily and seasonal routines reveals the misunderstandings and tensions they experienced as they dealt with one another, perhaps there are also lessons we can learn from them about the ways in which groups can and do coexist despite the strains between them.

An entrepreneur named R. Lowe opened this impromptu store in the California diggings. The surest way to riches in gold rush California was not to pan or dig for gold but to cater to the needs of those who did.

CHAPTER THREE

Seeing the Elephant

1848–1855

By 1848, the United States claimed almost all of the West. The Louisiana Purchase, the annexation of Texas and Oregon, and the war with Mexico had stretched the nation's boundaries all the way to the Pacific. But the West was still American in name only. Few people east of the Mississippi were anxious to venture into its forbidding interior. It still seemed too distant, too dangerous. Then gold was discovered at Sutter's Mill and everything changed — for California, for the West, and for the country. "It revolutionized America," wrote one man who had seen it all. "It was the beginning of our national madness, our insanity of greed."

According to the legend written on the back of this hand-tinted daguerreotype, "This nugget of pure gold was mined in the early 1850's by the man holding it: James Warner Woolsey. His mine was near Nevada City, California. [The nugget] was worth $1900.00. It weighed over eight pounds."

John Sutter was never satisfied. He had created an empire for himself in California — 50,000 acres of land, fields, and orchards, a fort and an Indian army to defend his holdings, and a sloop for sailing the Sacramento River. Now he wanted a sawmill with which to produce lumber for still more projects, and sent his foreman, James Marshall, forty-five miles north to build it at a bend of the South Fork of the American River.

On the morning of January 24, 1848, Marshall and his crew were deepening the millrace to speed up the wheel that was to drive the new saw when his eye noticed something out of the ordinary. "My eye was caught by something shining in the bottom of the ditch . . ." he recalled. "I reached my hand down and picked it up; it made my heart thump, for I was certain it was gold. The piece was about half the size and shape of a pea. Then I saw another. . . ." He rode off to Sutter's Fort to show his employer what he had found.

Together, they quietly consulted an encyclopedia, performed tests it suggested, and proved to their private satisfaction that the nugget was almost pure gold. Meanwhile, Marshall's men found more and more of it. Sutter tried to keep it all a secret — he wanted his mill finished and he didn't want anyone else digging for gold until he got clear title to the land on which it had been found — but rumors about the discovery began to spread in spite of him. His workers laid down their tools to look for gold. Gold-seekers began filtering in from others parts of California, as well — too many for Sutter to drive away.

One of them was Sam Brannan, the acquisitive Mormon whom Brigham Young had sent to California by sea with 238 fellow believers. Brannan already owned a flour mill and California's first newspaper, the *Star.* He found gold all right, but he also saw a surer path to further riches: he opened a store right next to Sutter's sawmill, fully stocked with picks and pans and shovels to cater to the needs of the treasure-seekers he was sure would follow him into the goldfields once word got out.

Then he made sure word did get out. He returned to San Francisco and on May 12 walked through the streets waving a quinine bottle filled with gold dust and shouting, "Gold! Gold! Gold from the American River!"

The gold rush was on. By the middle of June, three-quarters of the men living in San Francisco had left for the American River to look for gold. "The great rush from San Francisco arrived at the fort . . ." Sutter remembered. "My cook left me, like everybody else. The merchants, doctors, lawyers, sea captains, . . . all left their wives and families in San Francisco and those which had none locked their doors, abandoned their houses [or] offered them for sale, cheap. . . . The recently opened school had to be closed: teacher and pupils had gone off to the mines."

Gold seemed to be everywhere, lodged among rocks, glittering in sandbars, swirling in pools and eddies. Some made fortunes using nothing but spoons or jackknives to scoop it up. Others brought in crude machinery and hired Indians to do the work: seven men employing fifty Indians dug out 273 pounds of gold in just two months. "My little girls can make from 5 to 25 dollars per day washing gold in pans," a miner wrote home to Missouri. "My average income this winter will be about 150 dollars a day." And there seemed to be new discoveries every day — at Bidwell's Bar on the Feather River, on the Trinity River, on tributaries of the Sacramento, and along the streams that flowed through the foothills of the Sierra Nevada.

Lieutenant William Tecumseh Sherman, just twenty-eight, accompanied Colonel R. B. Mason, the military governor of California, on an official tour of the new goldfields. Four thousand men were already at work, they reported, and they were pulling out $30,000 to $50,000 worth of gold every day.

Soldiers began to desert for the goldfields. So did sailors from ships that docked at San Francisco. Two-thirds of the American men living in Oregon raced south in search of gold. Hawaiians and Chinese came to work the streams. So did gold-seekers from Peru, Mexico, Chile.

Sherman and Mason were stunned by what they saw. "I have no hesitation now," Mason wrote, "in saying there is more gold in the country drained by the Sacramento and San Joaquin rivers than will pay the cost of the war with Mexico a hundred times over." In August, the report Mason and Sherman had written was sent to Washington by ship, along with a tea caddy packed with gold dust.

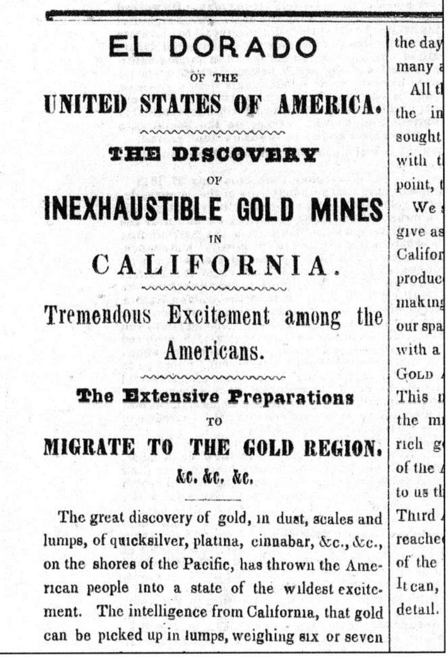

EL DORADO
OF THE
UNITED STATES OF AMERICA.

THE DISCOVERY
OF
INEXHAUSTIBLE GOLD MINES
IN
CALIFORNIA.

Tremendous Excitement among the Americans.

The Extensive Preparations
TO
MIGRATE TO THE GOLD REGION.
&c. &c. &c.

The great discovery of gold, in dust, scales and lumps, of quicksilver, platina, cinnabar, &c., &c., on the shores of the Pacific, has thrown the American people into a state of the wildest excitement. The intelligence from California, that gold can be picked up in lumps, weighing six or seven

James Marshall (left) and the sawmill on the American River where he spotted the first particle of California gold. "It made my heart thump," he remembered, and he began to dream of getting rich quick. But newspaper headlines like those above quickly spread the word of what he'd found, an international stampede began, and in the end Marshall never earned a cent from his discovery.

It was put on display at the War Department. "The accounts of the abundance of gold in that territory [California]," President Polk told Congress, "are of such extraordinary character as would scarcely command belief were they not corroborated by authentic reports of officers in the public service."

Thousands of young men — and a handful of young women — now wanted to get to California right away. The only question was how best to get there. It was impossible to travel overland until spring thawed the prairies and mountain passes, so the most impatient argonauts started off by sea. There were two water routes. The longest — 18,000 nautical miles — went all the way around South America and took so much time that when one captain made the voyage in seventy-six days he asked that his record be engraved on his tombstone. The other route took less time but involved sailing aboard one vessel to Panama, risking death from tropical diseases while crossing the isthmus by mule-back and canoe, then boarding another ship for San Francisco.

Some 25,000 gold-seekers took one sea route or the other in 1849, and most were subjected to the same storms, seasickness, stale water, and worse food. "The passengers [on the steamer] were fed like hogs . . ." a gold-seeker named Isaac Lord remembered. "Some of the hard bread was of good quality, some moldy, and much of it was infested with black bugs burrowing into it like woodchucks in a sand bank."

The vessels were often unsafe, as well as uncomfortable and unhealthy: one woman and her husband were forced to climb aboard four different ships before they

A frenzy seized my soul. . . . Piles of gold rose up before me . . . castles of marble, thousands of slaves . . . myriads of fair virgins contending with each other for my love — were among the fancies of my fevered imagination. The Rothschilds, Girards, and Astors appeared to be but poor people; in short, I had a very violent attack of the gold fever.

Hubert Howe Bancroft

Getting there: In the 1849 lithograph opposite, top, a cartoonist working for the printmaker Nathaniel Currier proposes a "Grand Patent India-Rubber Air Line" to hurl eager gold-seekers all the way across the continent by air. The reality was only slightly less daunting — an arduous overland trek or the long, uncom fortable, sometimes dangerous journey by sea advertised cheerfully opposite, bottom, and rendered more realistically above.

finally reached San Francisco; the first three had to be scuttled after, one by one, their cargoes of coal burst into flame.

Vicente Pérez Rosales and his three younger brothers, members of a landed Chilean family that had fallen on hard times, set out from Valparaiso by sea that winter. "All told," Rosales noted, "we are 149 — 90 men, plus 4 cows, 8 pigs, 12 sheep, a few dozen chickens, 3 dogs, 7 sailors, the captain and the mate. We are a mixed lot in this little tower of babel: Frenchmen, Englishmen, Germans, Italians, Chileans; nabobs and beggars. . . . Seasickness is widespread. . . . The sides of the ships are covered with dripping vomit, and the cabin and the ladders, as well. Everywhere you see green faces and hear the sounds of men retching." Rosales had tried everything he could think of to restore his family's fortunes — ranching, distilling whiskey, making barrels, glass, pottery, even smuggling. Nothing had worked. Now he had staked everything on California gold.

DETERMINED TO HAVE MY SHARE

In April of 1849, some 30,000 Americans started for the goldfields by land. Among them was William Swain, a twenty-seven-year-old farmer's son from Youngstown, New York, and a graduate of Lewiston Academy. His wife, Sabrina, was against it. She did not know if she and her infant daughter, Eliza, could bear to be apart from him so long. His widowed mother refused to intercede — it was his decision, she said, his alone — and his older brother, George, was for his going. If pickings were as easy as the newspapers said they were, George would go west, too, the following spring.

Swain carried with him a guidebook to the Overland Trail, a Bible, and a diary.

> April 11, 1849. All my things being ready last night, I rose early and commenced packing my trunk, preparatory to leaving home on my long journey, leaving for

the first time my home and my dear friends with the prospect of absence from them for many months and perhaps for years. . . .

I had fortified my mind by previous reflection to suppress my emotions, as is my custom in all cases where emotion is expected. But this morning I learned by experience that I am not master of my feelings in all cases. I parted from my family completely unable to restrain my emotions and left them all bathed in tears, even my brother, whose energy of mind I never saw fail before.

The next day, as Swain and his friends boarded a lake steamer from Buffalo for Detroit, his wife began her first letter to him:

Dear, dear William,
I want very much to describe my feelings as near as I can, but in doing so I hope not to crucify yours. I feel as though I was alone in the world. The night you left home I did not, nor could not, close my eyes to sleep. Sis [their daughter] slept very well, awoke in the morning, and looked over at me seeming to welcome a spree with her father, but to her disappointment the looked for one was absent. She appears very lonesome, and seems to miss you very much. . . .

I received your daguerrian. . . . I think I never saw anything but life look more natural. I showed it to little Cub, and to my astonishment and pleasure she appeared to recognize it. She put her finger on it, looked up at me and laughed, put her face down on yours, and kissed it several times in succession. Every time it comes in her sight she will cry after it.

William, if I had known that I could not be more reconciled to your absence than I am, I never could have consented to your going. However, I will try to reconcile myself as well as I can, believing God will order all things for the best. . . .

From Detroit, Swain took the train, then a canal boat, and finally river steamers down the Illinois and on to Independence, Missouri, where he and his friends planned to outfit themselves for the journey.

May 6, 1849. We came up from St. Louis with a company of Californians from Marshall, Michigan. They are got up on the joint stock principle and are going with ox teams. On learning that we are going on oxen, they proposed that we should join them by paying $100 each into the fund, furnishing a wagon and thus becoming members of their company, having one equal share in the company, which we have done.

This company was got up last January. We now consist of sixty-three members, Americans, mostly eastern and some western men, but mostly smart and intelligent. There are among them two ministers and two doctors, one of whom is said to be well educated and very successful in his practice. There are also blacksmiths, carpenters, tailors, shoemakers and many other mechanics. They are men of good habits and are governed by the regulations of civilized life. They are not to travel on the Sabbath and are to have preaching on that day.

The members of Swain's company printed "Wolverine Rangers" on their wagons with axle grease. Other emigrants, one remembered, printed slogans — "Wild Yankee," "Rough and Ready," "Live Hoosier," "Never Say Die," and "Have You Seen the

William and Sabrina Swain (left) in daguerreotype portraits they carefully had made in the spring of 1849 just before he left for California in case they never saw one another again. On April 12, Swain and his companions boarded the side-wheeler *Arrow* (above) at Buffalo, New York. "At half past two o'clock we took passage for Detroit," he wrote. "The lake is very smooth, — the boat shoots along like an arrow, and as she leaves far in the distance objects familiar to me and bears me on to those that are strange, I feel that she bears me to my destiny."

Elephant?" Those who set out for the California goldfields had a phrase for what they were about to experience: they called it "seeing the elephant." It may have come from an old joke. When an eastern farmer heard a circus was coming, he loaded his farm wagon with produce and hurried to town. On the way, he met the circus parade, led by an elephant. His horses bolted at the strange sight, tipping over the wagon and spilling vegetables all over the road. "I don't give a hang," the farmer said, "for I have seen the elephant."

The long road ahead of them had been charted by the mountain men, by Kit Carson and John Frémont, and by the pioneers who carved out the Oregon and California trails. The first leg — thirty days and 320 miles across the rolling prairie to Fort Kearny — passed through Oto, Potawatomi, and Shawnee lands whose fertile soil did not escape the notice of the onetime farmers on their way to the goldfields. "This land . . . will soon be on the market," one noted. "It is inevitable. . . . Some of these Indians do a little farming, but they will never develop the resources of a great state that might lie directly west of Missouri."

"It is said by alarmists that different tribes intend opposing the emigrants," another traveler wrote. "They might as well oppose the whirlwind." In fact, few Indians were seen. They kept away from the wagon trains, fearing that the cholera raging through them might spread to their camps as well. No one knew it then, but cholera, with its soaring fevers, chronic diarrhea, and ghastly death from dehydration, is spread by contaminated water and by flies attracted to raw sewage and the fouled bedding of the dead and dying. It was rampant all across the United States that year, but so virulent among the men and women who now proudly called themselves forty-niners that more than fifteen hundred of those who set out that spring are thought to have died of it.

It tore through Swain's company, too:

> Sabbath. May 27, 1849. In violation of our principle, we travel today on account of the sickness on the route. The health of our company is improving, and it is thought advisable to keep the company in active operation to keep their minds from getting engaged on cholera. I hope we may not have to break the Sabbath again.
>
> May 31. I was attacked at noon by dysentery very badly. I . . . got Reverend Hobart to make me a composition tea. . . .
>
> June 1. Still taking medicine, opium and astringent powders. . . . Today I have thought much of home and of my little girl, who is today one year old.
>
> June 4. This morning I am very unwell. I am very weak. . . . The mess fixed a good bed for me in the wagon, where I rode all day. . . .
>
> June 7. I am . . . on the gain, but very weak. . . . My appetite is good but I cannot eat hearty for fear of the consequences.

Swain and his companions reached Fort Kearny on June 13. Some gold-seekers had already had enough and turned around. "They had seen the *tail* of the Elephant," one more determined traveler wrote, "and can't bear to look any farther. Poor, forsaken beings they are." Most pressed on.

On June 20, Swain's company saw its first buffalo:

The whole emigration is wild and frantic with a desire to be pressing forward. . . . Whenever a wagon unluckily gets stuck in the mud in crossing some little rut, the other trains behind make a universal rush to try to pass that wagon and to get ahead of each other. Amid the yelling, popping of whips and cursing, perhaps a wagon wheel is broken, two or three men knocked down in a fight, and twenty guns drawn out of the wagons. All of this occasioned by a delay of perhaps two minutes and a half.

James Evans, 1849

Most gold-seekers who set out overland to California rode in wagons drawn by oxen, like those advertised on the opposite page, but the two men from Michigan above, Charles W. Cox and Walter Brewster, chose to chance it in the handsome conveyance drawn by two teams of horses with which they posed for a daguerreotypist at Battle Creek in March 1849. Both men — and all the horses — would make it through.

> About eight o'clock the cry "buffalo" ran along the line. . . . [A] drove of nine . . . [were sighted] coursing along the flat. . . . Every man who could gave them his fire as they passed. . . . Some thirty shots aimed at the head of the first one finally brought him to the ground and [another] was soon dispatched.
>
> All returned to the train loaded with buffalo meat, which we cut into pieces and hung along the sides of our wagons, on the reach, and along the tops of the covers. In such a fix we look like living.
>
> We stopped to noon early and all hands struck a fire and had a fine buffalo steak dinner, which certainly is the sweetest and tenderest meat I have ever eaten.

Before the day was over Swain's companions had slaughtered more than fifty animals, though only three were needed for food. "Such wanton destruction of buffalo, the main dependence of the Indians for food, is certainly reprehensible," one of Swain's company recalled. "But, the desire by the emigrant of engaging once at least in a buffalo chase can scarcely be repressed."

July 4th 1849 In camp for Celebration 8 m. below Ft. Larramie

Dear Sabrina

I have just left the celebration dinner table, where the co. now are drinking toasts to every thing & every body & cheering at no small rate; to enjoy myself better in conversing with you through the medium of the pen. It is now some time since I wrote home, or at least, since I wrote at any length; having written to you a line by a returning emigrant as I met him on the road & had just time to say we were well, but there is no certainty in sending letters by such conveyance & you may & may not have received some of the many letters I have sent you by traders & others on many of which I have paid a postage of 25 cts

I wrote to Geo. from Ft. Kerney last & I will give you a sketch of our journey from that point. We left that post on the 14th June & traveled up the platte to the mouth of the forks through a prairie Co. generly called the buffalow country. The River is very strait in its course, has a swift current muddy but good water, is filled with many beautiful Islands which have a little scrubby timber, being the only timber in the country. Our road lay along the river flats, which afford a good level road, & pasture enough for the "Million." they generly average a width of from 3 to 4 m. with bluffs from 60. to 600 ft high broken picturesk & affording plenty of buffalo & antelope, which we had lots of sport in hunting; for a discription of which I must refer you to my journal when I have the joy of presenting it to you. The "Flora" of the platte was of the most splendid & varied discription. The prickely pear was growing all along our road in large patches in full bloom, many of the leaves, carrying as many as 5 or 6 blossoms on. The ball Cactus also was frequently found in bloom & many other flowery specimens of which I have placed in my flower book

But the greatest of all our adventures was a terrable hail storm on the 20th which had well nigh distroyed our train. We had had an

That same afternoon, Swain noted, black clouds swept out of the west:

> The men all clad themselves in India-rubber or oil-cloth . . . all things looked likely for a cooling thunder-storm. But as the clouds advanced, . . . the whole air resounded with a noise resembling a shower of stones falling on a floor of boards. . . . In a moment after the first hail fell, the air was literally *filled* with balls of ice from the size of a *walnut* to that of a *goose egg*, . . . rebounding from whatever they struck. . . . When the storm had subsided sufficiently to permit investigation, it was found that the damage done . . . consisted of . . . one wagon upset, two [wagon] tongues broken, and one wheel smashed, with sundry bruises and gashed heads, black eyes, pounded and swollen backs, shoulders and arms. . . . "No great evil without some good" was our motto, so we filled our pails and kettles with hail and had icewater the rest of the day, a luxury we little expected on this route.

Communications: When William Swain wrote to Sabrina from Fort Laramie on July Fourth, he worried that she might never get the letter: "You may or may not have received some of the many letters I have sent you by traders and others, on many of which I have paid a postage of 25 cents." Sabrina had no address for William in California and so had to send her replies to him (above, right) care of "Sutter's Fort on the American River" and hope that they would somehow be passed on to him. Somehow they were.

On Independence Day, Swain wrote home again.

> Dear Sabrina,
> I have just left the celebration dinner table, where the company are now drinking toasts to everything and everybody and cheering at no small rate. I enjoy myself better in conversing with you through the medium of the pen. . . . I often think of home and all the dear objects of affection there. . . . I am hearty and well, far more so than when I left home. . . . I am also more fleshy. . . .
> Your affectionate husband till death

Fort Laramie was the last stop before the Rockies, and the forty-niners paused there to lighten their loads before they began to climb. Some switched from wagons to mule-back, anxious that there might no longer be grass enough for oxen ahead. Others jettisoned everything they no longer thought they'd need. The trail was lined with boxes, barrels, anvils, cast-iron stoves, sidesaddles, India-rubber boats, rancid slabs of bacon.

DESERET

At Salt Lake City, John D. Lee smelled opportunity in the air. He had joined the Church of Jesus Christ of Latter-day Saints during the troubles in Missouri, had followed them to Nauvoo, where he had displayed such devotion that Brigham Young himself had adopted him as his spiritual son, and was still settling his family in the new Zion. The Mormons were planning a celebration for July 24, 1849, marking two years since they had first entered the Salt Lake Valley. But instead of attending it, Lee hitched one of his wagons and set out on the trail — traveling against the tide of forty-niners heading toward California. He was amazed at what he saw.

John D. Lee,
photographed toward the end of his life

> . . . [T]he road was so lined with wagons . . . that one would be scarcely ever out of sight of some train. Dust very disagreeable but not to compare with the stench from dead carcasses which lie along the road, having died from fatigue and hunger. Destruction of property along the road was beyond description, consisting of wagons, harness, tools of every description, provisions, clothings, stoves, cooking vessels, powder, lead, & almost everything, etc. that could be mentioned.
>
> Very frequently some 20 or 30 persons would surround [my] wagon and plead for a moment's instructions, some of them with consternation depicted on their countenances, their teams worn out, women & children on foot & some packing their provision[s], trying to reach some point of refuge. The general cry was, "Are you from the Mormon city or valley? Yes. What is the distance? Is there any feed by the way? What will be the chance to get some fresh animals, provisions, vegetables, butter, cheese, &c. & could we winter in the valley? Do pray tell us all you can that will benefit us, for we are in great distress. . . . We will pay you all you ask."
>
> Apples, peaches, coffee, sugar, tea, rice, flour, bacon, &c., was often brought & presented. The writer here observes truly what one of the ancients said that the love of money was the root of all evil. It was the love of it that has caused thousands to leave their pleasant homes & comfortable firesides & thus plunge themselves into unnecessary suffering & distress.

Farther on, Lee met the foreman in charge of a Mormon ferry on the North Platte, hurrying back to Brigham Young with $10,000 his crew had earned from forty-niners desperate to get across the swollen river. Near Devil's Gate, Lee turned around for home himself, picking up discarded items as he traveled.

> [I] found an excellent Premium stove No. 3 worth about $50 dollars. . . . Commenced loading up with powder, lead, cooking utensils, tobacco, nails, sacks, tools, bacon, coffee, sugar, clothing, small irons, some trunks, bootlegs, axes, harness, etc. . . . Surely the Lord is mindful of His people, and they that trust in Him will not be forsaken, neither will their seed be found begging bread.

By the time he returned to Salt Lake City, Lee had been gone a month and had missed the anniversary celebration. But the booty in his wagon was worth more than he could have earned in two years of work.

Brigham Young had led the Mormons west to get away from the Americans who had persecuted them in Missouri and Illinois, and they had hung on in the Valley of the Great Salt Lake during the terrible winter of 1848–49, shivering in tents and wagons and dugouts, surviving on roots and thistles and soup made from boiling old ox hides. "Glue soup," one family called it.

But if the Mormons were to survive and prosper in their new home, Brigham Young decreed, they could only do so as a disciplined and cooperative society. The church became the government and, as its president and prophet, Young himself became the supreme authority in all matters, temporal and spiritual. "An old woman," wrote one visitor, exaggerating only slightly, "will go to the president to know whether she had better change her cloak for a tippet, or the new calf for a pig."

We do not intend to have any trade or commerce with the Gentile world, for so long as we buy of them we are in a degree dependent upon them. . . . I intend to cut every thread of this kind and live free and independent, untrammeled by any of their detestable customs and practices.

Brigham Young

Young seemed everywhere at once, laying out and overseeing the building of his city, parceling out lands according to each settler's needs — five acres for unmarried men, ten for heads of families — dispatching missionaries to England, France, Denmark, and Sweden in search of new converts, establishing a Perpetual Emigrating Fund to lend them money with which they might pay their passage to Utah, and founding new towns all across the landscape.

But the rush of events now threatened to destroy everything Brigham Young had built. The nominally Mexican lands on which he had initially settled now belonged to the United States. Thousands of Americans were passing through Mormon country on their way to California. Young forbade his people to join them. "We are gathered here not to scatter around and go off to the mines or any other place," he said, "but to build up the Kingdom of God. . . . [Salt Lake] is a good place to make Saints and it is a good place for Saints to live. It is the place the Lord has appointed and we shall stay here until He tells us to go somewhere else. . . . If you Elders of Israel want to go to the gold mines, go and be damned."

Surrounded once again by the enemy he had gone so far to flee, Young petitioned Congress to establish a sprawling new provisional state encompassing all of Utah and Nevada, and stretching from San Diego to South Pass, the Gila River to Oregon. He called it "Deseret," the Book of Mormon's word for the honeybee, a symbol of industry and cooperation. Within its boundaries, he hoped, the Mormons could continue to build their Zion unmolested by outsiders. "If the people of the United States will let us alone for ten years," he said, "we'll ask no odds of them."

STAY AT HOME

Beyond the Platte, William Swain and the other forty-niners endured fifty miles of treeless sagebrush dotted with pools of alkaline water fatal to oxen. Dead animals lay everywhere, filling the air with a hideous stench. Then they started through the mountains.

Swain and his companions were late and they knew it. Snow would soon begin to fall, closing the mountain passes. The men began to follow shortcuts that seemed likely to speed them through to the goldfields: Sublette's Cutoff, Hudspeth's Cutoff. Lassen's Cutoff looked likely, too. The original trail plunged south before it went west, and it passed through the Humboldt Sink, a fearsome desert where travelers were known to have died. But Lassen's Cutoff promised a more direct route, and after the middle of August, most forty-niners chose to take it.

More than a decade after the rush to California set the pattern for the whole West, these wagons carried gold-seekers to new finds in Montana and Idaho.

In looking behind over the road just traveled, . . . or forward over that to be taken, for an indefinite number of miles there seemed to be an unending stream of emigrant trains, whilst in the still farther distance along these lines could be seen great clouds of dust, indicating that yet others of these immense caravans were on the move. It was a sight which, once seen, can never be forgotten; it seemed as if the whole family of man had set its face westward.

William G. Johnston, 1849

Senator Benton and other big men may talk and humbug the country . . . about a railroad to the Pacific, but if you and I live a thousand years we will never see the resemblance even of any such thing. . . . Men who could build a railroad to the moon perhaps could build one over these mountains, but I doubt it . . . and it is said the worst is yet to come. But never mind, Gold lies ahead.

William Wilson

Before and after: Charles E. Mitchell (above) as he left Middletown, Connecticut, for the goldfields in 1849, and (right) as he looked — richer in experience than in cash — when he got back eight years later

Opposite: The High Sierra

On September 21, the Wolverine Rangers joined the stream of gold-seekers starting down Lassen's Cutoff. It would prove a bad mistake.

The disappointments came fast. Swain's company avoided the Humboldt Sink but they were forced to cross the Black Rock Desert, where both sides of the trail were lined with abandoned wagons and dead oxen. Then the trail itself, which had begun by going west, started leading them farther and farther north, instead. Days stretched into weeks. Ice began to form on the streams. Winter was very close now. Swain and the Rangers voted to throw away "the blacksmith tools and many other articles which we can do without."

On October 11, they started the steep climb to the pass they were sure would finally lead them to the summit of the Sierra Nevada. "Up we ascended," Swain wrote, "slowly but surely, by the toilsome climbing of the teams and by the lifting of the members of the mess at the wheels. Dreadful was the lashing our poor teams received. . . ." When they finally staggered to the summit and looked down, expecting to see spread out before them the comforting green of the Sacramento Valley, they saw only more miles of mountains. A little band of horsemen was waiting for them, sent from Sacramento to provide food and urge the travelers to keep moving as fast as they could. "We should hurry on for our lives," one of the Wolverine Rangers wrote. "[I]t is useless for us to try to get our teams through."

The Rangers agreed to split up into small groups. It would be every man for himself. Some now carried only backpacks. Others still tried to drive their oxen. The roads were made up of almost equal parts mud and boulders. Wagons broke down. Then, on the night of November 1, it began to snow. Oxen and mules collapsed. Then a steady, icy rain soaked the emigrants and flooded the trail. Swain now had no time for writing, but later he would recall his journey's end.

> November 6. Morning came and all but nine men, who were selected to stay with the teams, bade farewell to everything but a small pack of clothes and three or four days' rations, which each packed on his back. . . . I carried a change of underclothes, both of flannel and of cotton, two pairs of socks, one coat, one pants, one neck handkerchief, my journal, pocket Bible, pocketbook and a few day's provisions.
>
> We commenced, our way in ten inches of snow. . . . The storm increased as the day advanced. Had manhood in its strength been doomed to surmount these dangers alone human suffering would have been less. But there were the infirm and aged, for even here were gray heads. Many of the emigrants were palsied by that terrible disease scurvy. Here too were females and children of every age. Here might be seen a mother wading through the snow and in her arms an infant child. . . . There might be seen a mother, sister or a wife, winding along the mountain path. . . .
>
> At dawn we arrived at Antelope Creek, eight miles from [Lassen's Ranch, which had become an unofficial receiving station for gold-seekers] and found it not fordable. The sky cleared. We kindled a rousing fire, dried and rested ourselves till noon when [two other men and] myself — with our clothes lashed to our shoulders — forded the stream with setting poles. None of the others would attempt it. It was the hardest job I ever had. When I stepped onto the opposite shore I thought my flesh would drop from by bones as high as the water came to my waist.
>
> We arrived at Lassen's at sundown, tired and worn with toil and exposure.

"There was some talk between us of your coming to this country," Swain wrote to his brother.

> For God's sake think not of it. Stay at home. Tell all whom you know that are thinking of coming that they have to sacrifice everything and face danger in all forms, for George, thousands have laid and will lay their bones along the routes to and in this country. Tell all that "death is in the pot" if they attempt to cross the plains and hellish mountains. Say to Playter never to think of the journey; and as for you, STAY AT HOME, for if my health is spared, I can get enough for both of us.

An unidentified miner with the tools of his trade and (opposite) just some of the gold-seekers gathered at one camp, each hoping to strike it rich. "Bought a pick for $6.50, — wood for a handle for .50. Made the handle myself," wrote one man. "Got a second hand wash bowl or pan for $1.00, — the selling price of new tin bowls being from $4 to $7.50. Had not money enough left to buy a shovel. I borrowed one . . . [s]elected a spot on the creek bank . . . filled the bowl once to pan out just for an experiment. I did not expect I had reached any gold, yet I was surprised to find when I 'panned out' at twilight, nearly a dollar's worth of gold in the pan. . . ."

THE DIGGINGS

By then, Swain was already at Long's Bar, the nearest diggings on the Feather River, eager to begin gathering gold at last. "It seemed that every rock had a yellow tinge," a fellow miner recalled, "and even our camp kettle, that I thought the most filthy . . . I had ever seen, now appeared to be gilded. . . . During the night, yellow was the prevailing color in my dreams."

In the diggings: A woman — a great rarity in the goldfields — brings lunch to miners in Auburn Ravine, 1852; an unidentified miner (left) shows off his prize — a nugge big enough to balance on the handle of his shovel — while another (below) has done well enough to buy himself a shi emblazoned with picks and shovels.

Men at work: "You can scarcely form any conception of what a dirty business this gold digging is and of the mode of life which a miner is compelled to lead," one man wrote home. "We all live more like brutes than humans."

In their frenzy to get at the gold, these men slept packed together in the brush shelter behind them.

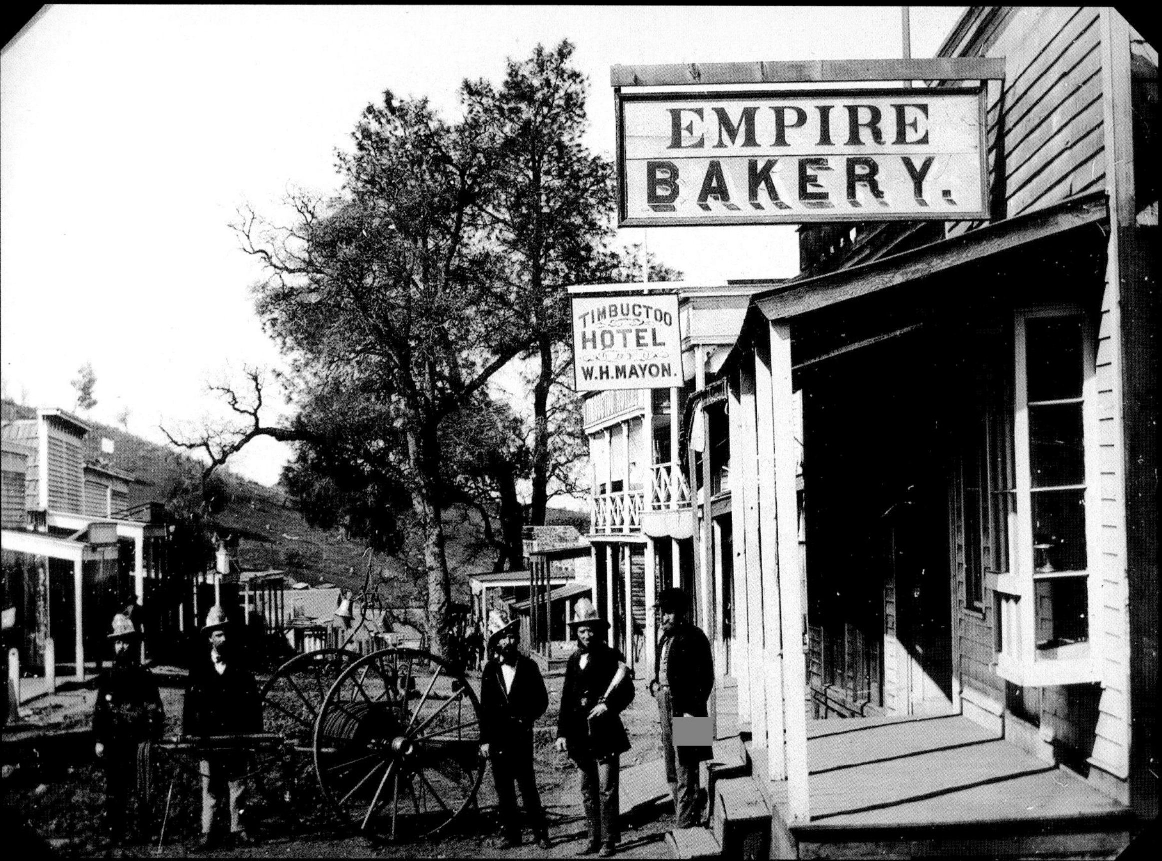

Gold camps were born overnight and sometimes died just as fast: Yuba, the site of A. J. Preston's Livery Stable (above) survived the gold rush to become today's Yuba City, but Timbuctoo, shown here about 1857, burned to the ground the following year.

Orlando Balou of Illinois came west in 1852 and stayed five years in the goldfields.

The name of the miner above and those of the bearded men below, who look enough alike to have been brothers, have been lost, but their determination is unmistakable. "Our object here is to get rich and stay that way," said one of their fellow forty-niners.

Not one man in a hundred . . . ever puts a razor to his phiz. The truth is, something looks wrong to see a white shirt or a shaven face. . . . With the help of shears to keep the road open to our mouths and a little trimming to keep our faces a little shipshape, we are at the top of fashion. Barbers are about as useful here as would be a penny whistle under the falls of Niagara.

Henry Page, 1849

An unidentified but obviously contented argonaut, hung with a gold chain perhaps fashioned from ore he'd mined himself.

Mail from home: "Dear Husband. This is only the 25th of August," Sabrina Swain wrote William in 1849. "What a long summer. O!! how I want to see you. Sometimes I almost imagine myself with you, but alas it is only the dream of fancy. . . . O! William, if I could see you this morning, I would hug and kiss you till you would blush."

The Louisiana Hotel in Jackson, California, ca. 1851. The minimally clad woman lounging near the staircase at the right at least suggests that more than board and room may have been available inside.

Charles McNight hurried west in 1849, only to die in the diggings three years later. He was only thirty-five, and his wife begged his mother for this daguerreotype — "it is the only good one that has ever been taken" — so that she could at least remember how he had looked.

Your advice, Father, is in good time, for here a boy is truly in the very gates of destruction, as all kinds of vices hold unlimited sway in the cities and mines. But I hope and trust I shall be able to leave this country as pure and innocent as I came in — and that ain't anything to brag on, is it?

Lucius Fairchild, 1850

Oh, Matilda, oft is the night when laying alone on the hard ground with a blanket under me and one over me that my thoughts go back to Ohio and I think of you and wish myself with you. But I am willing to stand it all to make enough to get us a home and so I can be independent of some of the darned sonabitches that felt themselves above me because I was poor. Cuss them, I say. I understand they prophesy that I will never come back. Darn their stinking hides. If God spares my life, I will show them to be false prophets, for as sure as I live we will shake hands and give a warm embrace by spring anyhow, and before if you say so.

Captain David Dewolf
July 30, 1850

A lone miner fills the time with music, 1851.

But there were already 40,000 miners at work in the goldfields, and the surface gold that had made so many men rich the year before was harder and harder for newcomers like Swain to find.

> January 6, 1850. South Fork of Feather River. After prospecting two days, we located a spot favorable for damming and draining the river. We made our claim and then built a house as soon as possible to shelter our heads from the soaking rains. So here we are, snug as schoolmarms, working at our race and dam. Whenever the rain will permit, a fall of the river will enable us to get into the bed of the river and know what is there. If there is no gold, we shall be off to another place, for there is an abundance of gold here, and if we are blessed with health, we are determined to have a share of it.

Some 80,000 men swarmed into California in 1849. More than half of them in their twenties — "a grey beard was almost as rare as a petticoat," one man remembered — and most hurried to one or another of the small, single-street settlements that grew up almost overnight wherever gold was found — Jimtown and Jesus Maria, Coyote Diggings and Grizzly Flats and Mad Mule Gulch, Angels Camp and Murderer's Bar, Whiskey Diggings and Delirium Tremens, Slumgullion, Shirt Tail Canyon, Bedbug, and You Bet.

Gold-seekers were delighted by the weather and dazzled by the landscape — "It's a glorious country," one miner remembered hearing over and over again. But everything cost too much: a dollar a pound for potatoes, eggs at fifty cents apiece; twenty dollars for a bottle of rum; two dollars to the expressman for every letter brought from San Francisco.

Digging for gold was hard, monotonous — and mostly unrewarding. It combined, one miner said, "the various arts of canal-digging, ditching, laying stone walls, ploughing and hoeing potatoes. . . ."

Roughly two-thirds of the forty-niners came from the United States and two-thirds of *them* were from New England. They included whites, free blacks, African-American slaves, and Indians. The rest, one wrote, "came from every hole and corner in the world." So many Mexican miners and their families were trooping into the southernmost goldfields, an American officer noted, that it seemed as if "the whole state of Sonora is on the move, passing us in gangs daily." Some 30,000 Frenchmen made it to California. There were Germans, Irishmen, Russians, Italians, West Indians, ex-convicts from Aus-

This stretch of a California stream was worked by a mixed crew that included two men who may have been either black or Indian and — possibly — a woman (center), whose name, "Mary Mc . . . ," is scratched into the back of the plate. The card that gleams in the right foreground advertises the daguerreotypist, "Sterrett & Company."

Opposite: Three panels from a wry broadsheet titled "The Miner's Ten Commandments," popular among the forty-niners. Top to bottom: The elephant, which every miner who made it through to California could claim he'd seen; just one of the dangers the men faced in getting there; miners entertain themselves as best they can while dreaming of womenfolk back home.

tralia. California now had more immigrants than any other part of the United States. Nine out of ten of them were men.

One of the first foreign gold-seekers to head for Sutter's Mill had been a young man from Canton named Chun Ming. He struck it rich and wrote home to say so. Soon young Chinese were setting sail for the land they called "Gold Mountain": 323 in 1849, 450 in 1850. In 1852, 20,000 came, 2,000 of them in a single day, striding ashore "bearing long bamboo poles across their shoulders," a newspaperman noted, and "wearing new cotton blouses and baggy breeches . . . slippers or shoes with heavy wooden soles [and] broad-brimmed hats of split bamboo."

The Chinese were mostly farmers from Guangdong Province and deeply in debt to Chinese credit merchants from whom they had borrowed their passage. They were tough, disciplined, and far more accustomed to backbreaking toil than most of their American counterparts. Working from dawn to dusk in bands of fifty or more, they often managed to sift gold from sites American miners had abandoned as played out.

Others never made it to the diggings, preferring to make money in San Francisco and Sacramento, instead. "The best eating houses in San Francisco are those kept by Celestials and conducted Chinese fashion," one miner recalled. "The dishes are mostly curries, hashes and fricassees served up in small dishes and as they are exceedingly palatable I was not curious enough to enquire as to the ingredients."

Chinese and American miners at work

A man named Wah Lee opened the first large hand-laundry at the corner of Washington and Grant in 1851. There were few laundresses in the gold camps and the wealthiest San Franciscans were said to be sending their best shirts all the way to Hong Kong and Honolulu to have them washed and ironed for rates that ran as high as twelve dollars a dozen. Wah Lee charged just five — and made himself a rich man.

THE CIVILIZING AND DOMINANT RACE

Gold rush Californians were a "percussion people," one of them wrote, "living in a percussive country." They were impatient, energetic, eager to grow. With their rich gold deposits and an "instant" population of 90,000 American citizens, they demanded immediate statehood. A convention at Monterey drew up a proposed state constitution that prohibited slavery, not because most forty-niners were sympathetic to African-Americans, but because they did not want to compete with slaves in the diggings. Blacks in California would be forbidden to vote, serve on juries, and attend school with white children, just as they were in many northern states back East. Also included in the constitution was the nation's first provision for married women to own property — both because that was the Mexican tradition and because, it was argued, it might attract prosperous prospective wives to California.

But Congress itself was split over the question of slavery, and California's statehood threatened that balance. Congress had once hoped that the issue of slavery's extension had been settled forever by the Missouri Compromise of 1820, which barred slavery in most of the West. But the defeat of Mexico — and the sudden acquisition of so many hundreds of thousands of square miles — had changed everything.

Again, Congress sought to settle the issue through a complex bargain that came to be called the Compromise of 1850. It would not restrict slavery in the new territories of New Mexico and Utah, whose citizens would be allowed to decide the question for themselves in the future, and a new, stringent fugitive slave law allowed southerners to retrieve runaway slaves even from free states. In return, California was admitted to the Union without the usual territorial waiting period.

The American newcomers were not satisfied with statehood alone. "Indians, Spaniards of many provinces, Hawaiians, Japanese, Chinese, Malays, Tartars, and Russians," said the *Annals of California,* "must all give place to the resistless flood of Anglo-Saxons [and] American progress. These peoples need not, and most of them probably cannot, be swept from the face of the earth; but undoubtedly their national characteristics and opposing qualities and customs must be materially modified, and closely assimilated to those of the civilizing and dominant race."

One by one, the Americans saw to it that their rivals were driven out or stripped of their power. "The ill will of the Yankee rabble . . . against sons of other nations was rising," the Chilean Vicente Pérez Rosales remembered. "This mutual bad feeling explains the bloody hostilities and atrocities we witnessed every day in this land of gold and hope." It began in 1850, when American miners pressured the California legislature into enacting a monthly tax of twenty dollars on all miners who were not United States citizens, far more than most could possibly pay. The bill was aimed at Mexicans, and most of them left the goldfields. But many Chileans and Peruvians were driven out, too, and when a group of French miners dared display their flag, they in turn were forced to abandon their claims. "The Yankee regarded every man but an . . . American as an interloper," Rosales wrote, "who had no right to come to California and pick up the gold of 'free and enlightened citizens.'" Despite discriminatory taxes and intimidation, Rosales and his brothers hung on in the goldfields.

Chinese working abandoned tailings

Even the Chinese, whom the Americans had once welcomed, came under attack. "The manners and habits of the Chinese are very repugnant to Americans in California," said a San Francisco newspaper. "Of different language, blood, religion, and character, and inferior in most mental and bodily qualities, the Chinaman is looked upon by some as only a little superior to the Negro, and by others as somewhat inferior. . . ." The Chinese kept to themselves, cooked their own kind of food, practiced their own religion, rarely learned English. When they paid the tax and continued to stay on in the goldfields, whites resorted to intimidation to drive them out. They hacked off the Chinese miners' queues, burned down their shacks, beat and flogged and murdered them.

Mexicans, too, felt the Americans' wrath. At Downieville, a Mexican woman — remembered only as Josepha — awoke to find a drunken American in her bedroom. She reached for a

One of the volunteer fire companies that tried — without much success — to keep San Francisco safe: large sections of it burned down several times. "You have heard of our fires," a local lawyer wrote. "They throw light on our character. We burn down a city in a night and build it in a day. Contracts for new buildings are signed by the light of the fire that is consuming the old."

A resident surveys the San Francisco waterfront in the early 1850s. In the fall of 1849 San Francisco had had just over 2,000 citizens. Barely one year later, it was home to nearly 35,000 — including about 2,000 women — and had become the West's first full-fledged city. It would soon have a dozen daily newspapers, 15 fire companies, 16 hotels, 20 bathhouses, 3 hospitals, 18 churches, and an orphanage. There were also 537 drinking establishments, including 48 brothels and 46 gambling dens. Everything was brought in by sea at first — whiskey, shovels, lumber carried all the way from the forests of Maine, prefabricated houses ready to be banged together, even a cargo of cats, ferried in to take on the rats that ruled the waterfront.

knife and stabbed him to death. A mob immediately seized her and, when she failed to express regret for what she had done, watched as she was hanged. "Had this woman been an American instead of a Mexican," one newspaper wrote, "instead of being hung for the deed, she would have been lauded for it. It was not her guilt which condemned this unfortunate woman, but her Mexican blood."

A few displaced Mexican miners took to the hills, returning just long enough to raid the goldfields and ride away again. Somehow, these raiders became fused in the American mind into one daring — and perhaps mythical — bandit named Joaquin Murietta. The governor offered a thousand-dollar reward for Murietta's head, and the legislature outfitted an armed posse of twenty men to hunt him down. They hunted somebody down, cut off his head, pickled it in whiskey, and took it on a tour of the gold camps.

The Treaty of Guadalupe Hidalgo had pledged the United States to honor the land grants awarded by Spain and Mexico, but the titles of the *Californios* were often challenged in court and sometimes simply ignored by avaricious newcomers. They lie "prostrate before the conqueror," one wrote,

> and ask for the protection of the few possessions which remain to them in the bad luck to which they [have] fallen. . . . They are unfamiliar with the prevalent language now spoken in their country. . . . I have seen old men of sixty and seventy years of age weeping because they have been cast out of their ancestral home. They have been humiliated and insulted. They have been refused the privilege of cutting their own firewood. . . .

No *Californio* had been more accommodating to the Americans than Mariano Guadalupe Vallejo. The descendant of Spanish soldiers who had conquered Mexico and colonized California, he had built himself a vast empire on Indian labor, and had welcomed the first American settlers in his homeland, provided hospitality to the first gold-seekers, even served in the first state senate. But his new allies soon abandoned him, nonetheless: lawsuits and an invasion of squatters eventually reduced his sprawling estate from a quarter of a million acres to fewer than three hundred.

> Australia sent us a swarm of bandits [he wrote] who . . . dedicated themselves exclusively to robbery and assault. . . . France, desiring to be rid of several thousand lying men and corrupt women [sent them] to San Francisco. . . . China poured upon our shores clouds and more clouds of Asiatics . . . [who are] very harmful to the moral and material development of the country. . . . But all these evils became negligible with the swollen torrents of shysters who came from Missouri and other states of the Union. . . . These legal thieves, clothed in the robes of the law, took from us our lands and our houses, and without the least scruple enthroned themselves in our homes like so many powerful kings. For them existed no law but their own will and caprice that recognized its right by that of force.

Like other *Californios,* Vallejo was now viewed as an alien in his own land. He remained a realist: "He who calls the bull," he said, "must endure the horn wound."

Since the white man has made a road across our land and killed off our game, we are hungry, and there is nothing for us to eat. Our women and children cry for food, and we have no food to give them.

Chief Washakie, Shoshone

Father Pierre-Jean De Smet, a Belgian-born Catholic missionary who accompanied Assiniboin, Arikara, Crow, and Hidatsa delegations to the great convocation of Indians held at Fort Laramie in 1851, drew this map to help work out a tidy division of the Plains among the tribes. What he remembered most about the talks, however, was not the negotiations but the ceremonial feasting, which, he said, brought about "the greatest massacre of the canine race" in history.

THIS GROUND DOES NOT BELONG TO YOU NOW

The permanence of the "Permanent Indian Frontier" had not lasted long, as the lines of wagons headed for California and Oregon cut broad rutted trails through tribal lands. Some Indian peoples made a good thing of the invasion, at least at first. They acted as guides, sold the gold-seekers horses, mules, and firewood. The Sac and Fox collected fifty cents for every wagon that passed through their land, and the Pawnee did the same for every wagon that traveled over their bridge across the Shell River.

But the gold rush proved a disaster for many peoples of the Plains. The Pawnee's crops were devoured by the emigrants' livestock, and when they went off to hunt buffalo they found that the herds along the main trail had been scared off. Some Pawnee starved to death on the way back to their villages. The Lakota, who had only recently driven the Pawnee from the fork of the Platte, were growing increasingly angry to see the whites cutting down the groves of trees beneath which they liked to shelter in summer; their oxen and horses and mules devouring the grass; their hunters shooting buffalo, taking only the best meat and leaving the rest to rot in the sun.

White diseases took a fierce toll, too. A party of Cheyenne came upon an encampment of forty-niners, several of whom were clearly dying from cholera. They rode away as fast as they could, but several had contracted the disease and died before they reached their villages. They called the sickness the Big Cramps. Several bands gathered for the sun dance on Smoky Hill River in Kansas in the summer of 1849 — Cheyenne, Arapaho, Comanche, Kiowa, Osage, prairie Apache. On the last day of the ceremonies, a Kiowa sun dancer suddenly collapsed and died. Then an Osage fell to the ground. The Cheyenne fled for the Cimarron River but it was too late. Scores died. A celebrated warrior named Little Old Man tried to make war upon the sickness. He put on his scalp shirt and sacred war bonnet, decorated his horse, and rode through the camp shouting, "If I could see this thing, if I knew where it was, I would go there and kill it!" Then the sickness found him; the first cramps hit him as he got down from his horse, and he was dead before nightfall.

Fearing that growing Indian resentment of the emigrants might burst out into open warfare against them, and that intensified conflicts between the tribes over ever-scarcer resources might engulf the wagon trains, the Department of Indian Affairs had begun to talk of dividing up Indian lands into small, well-defined tribal "colonies" or "territories" — the term "reservations" would come later — where they would be safe from whites and where they could be slowly but steadily persuaded to abandon their ways of life in favor of farming and Christianity. "There should be assigned to each tribe, for a permanent home," said the commissioner of Indian affairs in 1850,

> a country adapted to agriculture, of limited extent and well-defined boundaries; within which all, with occasional exceptions, should be compelled constantly to remain. . . . In the meantime, the government should cause them to be supplied with stock, agricultural implements, and useful material for clothing, encourage and assist them in the erection of comfortable dwellings, and secure to them the means and facilities of education, intellectual, moral and religious.

A great issue of government presents was made to the Cheyennes. . . . We were given beef, but we did not care for this kind of meat. Great piles of bacon were stacked up on the prairie and distributed to us, but we used it only to make fires or to grease robes for tanning. . . . We liked the sugar presented to us. They gave us plenty of it, some of it light brown and some dark brown.

Iron Teeth

The first step on the Plains was to persuade Indian peoples — accustomed to a life of nomadism, whose culture was built on the display of courage in combat — that they should forthwith end their wanderings and give up warfare.

The U.S. Indian agent for the Upper Platte and Arkansas Agency was the former mountain man Tom "Broken Hand" Fitzpatrick. He knew and liked Indians and privately thought the effort to pen them up doomed; they did not fully understand what was really being proposed, he complained; and there was no way to get them to comply without the presence of an armed force far larger than any Congress was likely to send west. But he nonetheless summoned as many bands as would come to Fort Laramie on the North Platte in September of 1851.

They camped together in a grassy valley near the fort under the wary eyes of just 270 nervous soldiers — more than 10,000 Lakota, Cheyenne, Arapaho, Crow, Gros Ventre, Blackfeet, Shoshone, and a handful of Assiniboin, Mandan, and Hidatsa, all dressed in their ceremonial finery. (It was one of the largest gatherings in Indian history and would have been still larger had the Pawnee not refused to attend because they were afraid the Lakota would kill them all. The Comanche and Kiowa also stayed away; they had too many horses, one chief said, to risk "among such notorious horse thieves as the Sioux and Crows.")

The government gave those who attended a mountain of gifts and the promise of a total of $50,000 worth of supplies every year for fifty years, plus the promise of swift punishment for any white who trespassed on Indian land. In return, the Indians were to promise not to harass the wagons and grant the government the right to build forts (something it had already begun to do in any case). And each people must agree to stay within the territory assigned to it and stop warring against its neighbors. With the help of a crude map sketched by Jim Bridger, Fitzpatrick explained how the Plains were to be divided up.

The Lakota seem to have understood more fully than most what was being asked of them, and they would have none of it. They, like the Americans, were a restless, aggressive people who had spilled onto other peoples' lands, taken them over, and then saw no reason to give them up. "You have split my land and I don't like it," a Lakota leader named Black Hawk told the government negotiators when he first saw Bridger's map. "These lands once belonged to the Kiowas and the Crows, but we whipped these nations out of them, and in this we did what the white men do when they want the lands of the Indians." Faced with Lakota intransigence, the Americans backed down. The Lakota were allowed to hunt south of the Platte and were given rights to sole occupancy of the rolling country between the Bighorn Mountains and the Black Hills, until recently the home of the Crow, which the Lakota had come to see as their most sacred ground.

To conclude the treaty, each tribe was asked to name a head chief who could sign for his people. None of them acknowledged a single leader, so the Americans picked chiefs for them. A Brulé warrior named Conquering Bear was chosen to represent the Lakota.

For two years the treaty with his people held. Then, in August of 1854, the Brulé came to Fort Laramie to collect their supplies and a calf strayed from a Mormon wagon train and wandered into their camp. A warrior shot it with an arrow. Its owner complained to the commander. Conquering Bear apologized and promised to pay the owner more than the animal was worth. The army brushed him aside and a young lieutenant named John L. Grattan, with twenty-nine soldiers and two howitzers, marched off to the Lakota camp to arrest the man who had shot the calf.

The warrior resisted. Forty-five anxious minutes went by. Finally, Grattan panicked and ordered his men to open fire. Conquering Bear was the first to fall. The outraged Lakota turned on the soldiers. Only one managed to crawl back to Fort Laramie before he died. Jefferson Davis, the secretary of war, declared the tragedy "the result of a deliberately formed plan" and ordered the army to exact revenge. Troops under General William S. Harney attacked the band that Conquering Bear had led at Blue Water Creek, killing eighty-six and carrying off seventy women and children. Half a century of peace between the Lakota and the Americans had come to an end; nothing between them would ever be the same again.

THE WOLF AND THE LAMB

"The Natives of these mountains," wrote William Swain from California,

> are wild, live in small huts made of brush and go naked as when they are born. They are small in stature, and . . . when they visit the camps of the miners, they evince the most timid and friendly nature. The miners . . . are sometimes guilty of the most brutal acts [against them], such as killing squaws and papooses. Such incidents have fallen under my notice that would make humanity weep and men disown their race.

Exploitation was nothing new for the Indian peoples of California. The Spanish had forced the coastal tribes to labor at their missions, and the *Californios* had used them as servants on their ranchos. But the Indians of the interior had never seen any-

By the time these photographs were made near San Bernardino in southern California by the photographer for a government survey in 1863, the once-plentiful Indians of the region had been reduced to a handful of scattered bands dependent on whites for their survival.

thing like this sudden onslaught of whites. They "formerly subsisted on game, fish, acorns, etc.," an Indian agent wrote,

> but it is now impossible for them to make a living by hunting or fishing, for nearly all the game has been driven from the mining region or has been killed by the thousands of our people who now occupy the once quiet home of these children of the forest. . . . The rivers of tributaries of the Sacramento formerly were clear as crystal and abounded with the finest salmon. . . . But the miners have turned the streams from their beds and conveyed the water to the dry diggings and after being used it is so thick with mud that it will scarcely run.

On the night of 19th February 1857 two men (one named Lewis, commonly called "Squire" and the other Lawson, generally known as "Texas") came to an Indian ranch about a mile above this camp. . . . They commenced abusing the Indian squaws, and one squaw, while endeavoring to protect her daughter, was stabbed by Lewis very severely in the back and shoulder, who also stabbed the father of the girl twice in the arm. They then seized two other squaws whom they forced to remain with them all night. . . . [Later,] Lewis seized a club and without provocation, attacked and brutally beat an Indian boy named Tom, so that it is doubtful he will recover. I immediately stationed a guard to protect the Indians from future outrage. The man Lawson was subsequently shot by Captain Young, and Lewis has been bound over for trial. . . . He is, I believe, the first white man who has ever been arrested for anything of this kind in this neighborhood, though his offense, compared with others that have taken place on this river is a mere trivial matter. . . .

C. H. Rundell, Lieutenant 4th Infantry
Klamath, California

Desperate for food, Indians began raiding the diggings, stealing horses and cattle, and angering the miners, who retaliated in a variety of ways. Slavery had officially been outlawed by California's constitution, but California law now made it legal to declare any jobless Indian a vagrant, then auction off his or her services for up to four months. And it permitted whites to force Indian children to work for them, provided the permission of a parent or a "friend" was obtained first. Enterprising whites hunted down adult Indians in the mountains, kidnapped their children, and sold them as "apprentices." "Indians seven or eight years old are worth $100," one Californian noted. "It is a damn poor Indian that's not worth $50."

"If ever an Indian was fully and honestly paid for his labor," another settler remembered, "it was not my luck to hear of it." Indians could not complain in court because by another California statute "no Indian or black or mulatto person" was "permitted to give evidence in favor of or against a white person." When the federal government negotiated treaties that would have provided sanctuary for eighteen tribes, California's congressional delegation blocked their ratification in the Senate. There was no longer room in California for the first Californians.

Thousands of Indians died from diseases the white man had inadvertently introduced among them, but thousands more were killed deliberately. A group of men from Cottonwood who called themselves the Squaw Hunters spent their weekends assaulting Indian women — and killing any men who objected. The towns of Marysville and Honey Lake paid bounties for Indian scalps. Shasta City offered five dollars for every Indian head brought to city hall.

"The Indians . . . had been living at a place called Roff's Ranch," a reporter wrote after covering an incident in the Pitt River valley in January of 1860. "There the 'bold' volunteers crept on them before day, . . . [and] killed about nine men, the balance escaping. The women and children remained, trusting [that an American] would not murder women and children. In this they were mistaken. . . . [T]hey searched around among the haystacks with the hatchet and split the children's heads open. In this way there were over forty women and children butchered. . . ."

Before the forty-niners came there were some 150,000 Indians in California. By 1870, there would be fewer than 30,000. It was the worst slaughter of Indian people in United States history.

Gathering in the Saints: Mormons break ground for their new temple at Salt Lake City, April 6, 1853.

Opposite, top: Brigham Young with Margaret Pierce, one of five women he married in 1846 and the eleventh to bear him a child

Opposite, bottom: an 1897 parade through the streets of Salt Lake City by survivors of the handcart brigades who walked all the way to Utah to people the Mormon kingdom

BE FAITHFUL AND TRUE

The Mormons had asked for immediate statehood for the vast territory they called Deseret because they thought it the best way to ensure that they would be left alone. They were confident, in fact, that if they waited long enough the American government itself would be destroyed, since it had failed to prevent the martyrdom of Joseph Smith. "God Almighty will give the United States a pill that will puke them to death," said Brigham Young. "I am prophet enough to prophesy the downfall of the government that has driven us out. . . . Woe to the United States! . . . I see them greedy after death and destruction."

But Congress was not inclined to grant statehood to an empire so distant and so huge, ruled by a leader whose religion — and loyalty — many of its members questioned. Instead, it reduced the size of Deseret by more than three-quarters, changed its name to Utah — after the Ute Indians — and assigned it the lesser status of territory. Brigham Young was bitterly disappointed, though President Millard Fillmore named him territorial governor and superintendent of Indian affairs.

His policy toward the Goshute, Ute, Paiute, Shoshone, and other native peoples of his region was mixed. When they resisted giving up lands for Mormon settlements he ordered in the Nauvoo Legion to crush them, and he later tried to persuade Congress to remove all Indians from the territory. But Joseph Smith had taught that the Indians were "Lamanites," a lost tribe of Israelites ripe for conversion, and so Young also sent missionaries among them and urged his people to be forbearing when Indians raided their livestock: "The loss of a few cattle does not justify a retaliation sufficient

My soul feels hallelujah, it exults in God, that He has planted this people in a place that is not desired by the wicked. . . . I want hard times, so that every person that does not wish to stay, for the sake of his religion will leave. This is a good place to make Saints, and it is a good place for Saints to live. It is the place the Lord has appointed, and we shall stay here until He tells us to go somewhere else.

Brigham Young, 1849

for White men to kill the offenders." Such orders were eminently practical: "It's cheaper to feed 'em than fight 'em," Young said. And he hoped that if the Americans — the "Mericats," the Paiute called them — ever assaulted his desert stronghold, he could count on them to help him resist.

With a population of 10,000, Salt Lake City was now the second-largest city west of Missouri — eclipsed only by gold-rush San Francisco — and the nearby canyons of the Wasatch Range were stripped of trees because of the growing city's insatiable demand for lumber, fence posts, and firewood. At the city's center, ground was broken in 1853 for a new Mormon temple. Young wanted it built for the ages — far grander than the temple sacked by the gentile mobs in Nauvoo — with footings sixteen feet wide and eight feet deep, and walls eight feet thick.

The Mormons were proud of their growing prosperity. But in the West, as in the East, many gentiles resented it. The emigrants who passed through Utah complained of the high prices the Saints charged them for supplies. Non-Mormons who sought to settle complained of being frozen out by their Mormon neighbors. And there was growing opposition back East to the Mormons' doctrine of plural marriage. Joseph Smith had secretly preached polygamy since 1831, and revelations about his practice of it had helped bring about his murder at Nauvoo, but at Salt Lake City in 1852, Brigham Young publicly announced it as an integral part of Mormon doctrine. Young himself had 27 wives — he was eventually "sealed" to some 50 more women, to whom he expected to be joined in Heaven — and he had 56 children. His chief lieutenant, Heber Kimball — known as America's "most-married" man — had 43 wives, including five sets of sisters, 20 daughters, and 45 sons (16 of whom were named Heber, for their father). They lived in a dozen different households — "twelve teapots," he called them, "each holding different quantities of good tea, yet differing in form."

Despite the example set by some Mormon leaders, four out of five married Mormon men remained monogamous, and even most polygamists had no more than two wives. Still, the practice turned many Americans against them. Polygamy and slavery, reformers charged, were equally wicked; both needed to be expunged from American soil.

By 1855, so many Mormons had been helped to travel from the States and Europe to Utah that the Perpetual Emigrating Fund had run dangerously low. Brigham Young was undaunted: "Let them come on foot with handcarts or wheelbarrows," he said, "let them gird up their loins and walk through and nothing shall hinder them."

The Mormons took him literally at his word. In the spring of 1856, thirteen hundred Britons — Welsh coal miners, Scottish crofters, paupers from big English cities — volunteered to sail to America, take the train to Iowa City, and then simply start walking westward to Salt Lake City, nearly fourteen hundred miles away. "The fire of emigration blazes throughout the Pastorate," one British observer noted, "to such an extent that the folks are willing to part with all their effects, and toddle off with a few things in a pocket handkerchief."

They were an unlikely band of pioneers; most were either very young or past middle age, city dwellers, ill-prepared for carving a new life in the outdoors: bookbinders, bakers, butchers, dollmakers, even an expert in the rigging of sailboats.

The first three companies made it through to Salt Lake City, but two other companies — four hundred men, women, and children, from England, Scotland, Germany, and Scandinavia — started late and half of them didn't make it at all. Brigham Young wept when he saw the condition of the survivors, but he blamed others for what had befallen them — and then called for more handcart companies — seven in all, by 1860. Nothing was to slow the peopling of his Zion, for he knew he would need all the followers he could get for the struggle that seemed about to begin.

Pressure was building back East to remove him from the governorship. In 1855, three new federal judges were appointed for the Utah Territory. Two were apostate Mormons, eager to wreak vengeance on those who had remained true to their former faith. The third, W. W. Drummond, was a political appointee so enamored of his mistress that he liked to have her sit next to him as he presided from the bench. Young ordered his followers simply to ignore Drummond's presence and continue to bring their cases before the county probate courts — controlled by the church — just as they always had. "We have got a territorial government," he said, "and I am and will be Governor, and no power can hinder it, until the Lord Almighty says, 'Brigham, you need not be Governor any longer,' and then I am willing to yield to another Governor."

THE DAYS OF '49

Everything had gone wrong for William Swain in California. He'd spent the whole cold, rainy winter of 1849–50 in a claustrophobic cabin on the Feather River. In the spring, he and his partners moved to Foster's Bar on the Yuba River, only to be kept from panning by a heavy spring snowmelt that turned the clear stream into a roaring brown river. "Five months' rain," he wrote, "four months' high water, and three months . . . almost too hot to work."

The miners shown at work here may have come to California hoping to strike it rich on their own, but they ended up working for a weekly paycheck, pushing wheelbarrows of sand up to water-powered trommels (screen drums) that sifted out the gold and dropped it into flumes waiting below.

From present accounts from California there is much suffering, little success, and great chagrin. . . . I am convinced that digging is not the way to make money there. It is to trade. There, as here, the trader makes the money.

George Swain, 1850

In the end, it was men like these unidentified San Francisco investors who reaped most of the profits from California's streams and gulches; only they had the kind of money needed to pay for the large-scale machinery needed to extract ore once the surface gold was gone.

Day after day without success taxed him. But so did his fear of returning home a failure, and when his brother, George, wrote to ask how he was doing, it was hard for him to admit the truth for fear that those back home would think ill of him: "My specific answer to your kind question is that my expectations are not realized. We have been unlucky — or rather, by being inexperienced, we selected a poor spot for a location and staked all on it, and it has proved worth nothing. . . . I mostly regret the necessity of staying here longer."

And now, my dear, allow me to ask, are your most sanguine expectations realized or at least being so? Or do you find things very much exaggerated? Would you advise anyone to go to California? There are many anxious to hear from you and learn the prospects. . . .

Sabrina Swain

His brother proved understanding:

> Dear William,
>
> . . . Keep your courage up. If you fail there, you are not to blame. You have tried your best to do well, and if you can't do it there, you are better off than many who have gone there with their all and left nothing behind to fall back on. You have something, and friends who will meet you just as cordially unsuccessful as successful. . . . To tell the plain truth, I wish most sincerely you were out of that (if you are alive) and at home, no matter if you haven't got a single mill.

By November of 1850, Swain had been away from home for more than eighteen months. Then, reassured by his brother's letter, he headed for San Francisco. He had just five hundred dollars to show for all his hard work, and by the time he'd paid for his passage home by sea, he had no more cash in his pockets than he'd had when he left Youngstown. "I have got enough of California," he wrote his wife just before boarding his ship, "and am coming home as fast as I can."

By 1852, the surface gold in California was all but gone. Most of what gold remained could no longer be retrieved by a single miner with pick or shovel or pan, no matter how hard he worked. It lay at the bottom of rivers, in veins of quartz that could only be reached by deep shafts, or hidden in hillsides from which it had to be blasted by powerful streams of water.

Big machinery required big money. California's goldfields were soon controlled by investors with headquarters in San Francisco, and worked by miners who labored for a weekly paycheck. Meanwhile, discouraged forty-niners began to head home, some pausing to pan for gold in areas they had bypassed in their hurry to California. They made their biggest strike in the Colorado Rockies, and nearly 100,000 hopeful prospectors, many in wagons painted with the slogan "Pike's Peak or Bust," swarmed in. They founded Denver and soon organized the territory of Colorado, with 35,000 citizens. By treaty, it was Cheyenne land, but with only 4,000 people, the Cheyenne could do little to stop the invasion. There were strikes in other parts of the West, as well: in Montana, Oregon, New Mexico, Arizona, Nevada. And following a pattern set in California that would be repeated again and again all over the West, wherever gold was discovered, Indian peoples suddenly found themselves outnumbered in their own land.

John Bidwell, who had helped lead the American emigrants to California back in 1841, struck it rich in the goldfields and got out fast, then used his fortune to buy himself a 20,000-acre plantation he called Rancho Chico on which he raised every-

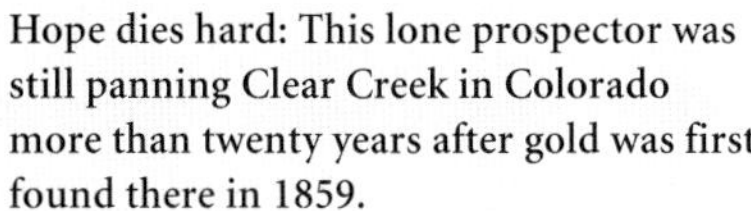

Hope dies hard: This lone prospector was still panning Clear Creek in Colorado more than twenty years after gold was first found there in 1859.

miners continued to scour the western landscape for gold and silver as though there were no Civil War back East, as if no treaties with the tribes had ever been signed to keep them out of Indian lands.

In April of 1862, six miners who had wandered into southwestern Montana in search of gold were captured by the Crow and then let off with a stern warning. Even that did not discourage them. They paused to prospect in a shallow creek that ran through a ravine they called Alder Gulch and found five dollars' worth of gold glinting in the bottom of a single pan. One of the partners, a man named Barney Hughes, was sworn to secrecy and sent to Bannack, the nearest town, to pick up supplies. He kept quiet, but somehow, other miners detected the excitement underlying his silence, and when he started back to the site, some two hundred men were strung out along the trail behind him. Hughes called a halt and said he would not take another step until his pursuers agreed that he and his partners were each to have exclusive rights to two hundred feet of land along the creek bed. By the end of June, full-fledged towns lined both sides of the trickling creek, and miners were moving out into the surrounding countryside in search of more likely sites.

Sam Clemens spent six months with three partners in a ten-by-twelve-foot cabin, panning, digging, drinking, going more and more heavily into debt. Then, he would claim later, he became a multimillionaire — for just ten days. One of his partners discovered a "blind lead" — a subterranean vein of silver on public land — and claimed it for himself and his friends. They stayed up all night talking about what they would do with the money:

> What kind of house are *you* going to build?
>
> Brick.
>
> Bosh!
>
> Why? What is your idea?
>
> Brown stone front — French plate glass — billiard room off the dining room — statuary and paintings — shrubbery and two-acre grass plat — greenhouse — iron dog on the front stoop — gray horses — landau and a coachman with a bug on his hat!
>
> The news was all over town. . . . I walked the streets serene and happy. Higbie said the foreman had been offered two hundred thousand dollars for his third of the mine. I said I would like to see myself selling for any such price. My ideas were lofty. My figure was a million.

The law required that work begin within ten days of filing a claim. Otherwise, anyone else could claim it as his own. Clemens was called away to tend a sick friend. Each of his partners somehow thought the other had started work. No one so much as scratched the surface of the earth, and when Clemens returned he found fourteen armed men had taken over the claim — or so he later liked to say.

"I had been a private secretary," he wrote, "a silver miner and a silver mine operative, and amounted to less than nothing in each, and now what to do next?"

Virginia City would provide the answer. It stood astride the Comstock Lode, the richest body of ore yet discovered in America, and it had grown from a tiny town to a city in less than two years. Fifteen thousand people now lived there. They had put

in gaslights, built stock exchanges, three theaters, four churches — and forty-two saloons. And there was a newspaper, the *Territorial Enterprise.* Sam talked himself into a job as a reporter, then wrote his mother:

> . . . I have just heard five pistol shots down the street — as such things are in my line, I will go and see about it. . . . PS — 5 AM — The pistol did its work well — one man, a Jackson County, Missourian, shot two of my friends (police officers) through the heart — both died within three minutes. Murderer's name is John Campbell.

Soon, Sam was covering everything from candy pulls to shootings, Indian attacks to theatrical performances. He was also writing light pieces — "I have had a 'call' to literature of a low order — i.e. *humorous,*" he told his mother. "It is nothing to be proud of but it is my strongest suit." He had begun to sign his articles "Mark Twain."

ON TO SAN FRANCISCO

Texas had seceded from the Union before the inauguration of Abraham Lincoln, and federal forts and supplies there had been meekly turned over to the Confederates. Now, some within the Confederacy dreamed of stretching their new republic far beyond Texas, north to the Colorado goldfields, and all the way west to California.

In early July of 1861, Confederate colonel John R. Baylor, who had learned his warfare fighting Comanche on the Texas plains, made the first move, sending a Texan force north to seize Fort Bliss without firing a shot and to declare New Mexico's southern half the Confederate Territory of Arizona. The Confederate conquest of the Southwest was off to an early and promising start. Next, the Confederates had to rid the rest of New Mexico Territory of federal troops and seize control of the Rio Grande. Brigadier General Henry H. Sibley eagerly accepted the assignment. A Louisianan who fought almost as hard as he drank — one soldier called him a "walking keg of whiskey" — he drew up a straightforward plan: starting out from El Paso, he would follow the winding river northward all the way to Santa Fe, take the Colorado goldfields, then head west for California. He moved out at the head of four regiments — 3,700 Texans who had coveted the mostly Mexican American settlements of New Mexico for years — on January 4, 1862. Their motto was "on to San Francisco."

Private Simeon Jasper Crews of the 7th Texas Mounted Volunteers, who took part in the Confederate invasion of New Mexico. "The country is worthless," wrote one of his fellow soldiers. "Think this country never was intended for white folks. The first man that ever came . . . ought to have been killed by the Indians."

Mining the Comstock Lode (opposite): In two of the first flashlit photographs ever made, Timothy O'Sullivan caught six miners on their way down a mine shaft belonging to the Savage Silver Mining Works at Virginia City in 1868, as well as one of their comrades at work deep beneath the earth. "It was as if a wondrous battle raged," wrote one visitor to Virginia City, "in which the combatants were man and earth. Myriads of swarthy, dust-covered men are piercing into the grim old mountains, ripping them open, thrusting murderous holes through their naked bodies. . . ."

Within the adobe walls of Fort Craig, Lieutenant Colonel Edward R. S. Canby and some 4,000 poorly trained Union volunteers waited nervously for Sibley and his army to arrive. Canby and Sibley had been classmates at West Point; Canby had been Sibley's best man, had married Sibley's wife's first cousin, had fought alongside him against the Navajo. Now, it was up to Canby to stop his old friend. He sent messages to the governors of the California, Utah, and Colorado territories, pleading for reinforcements, then settled in to wait.

The first Confederate regiment appeared across the river on February 19, and the federal commander, fearful that Sibley meant simply to bypass his fort and plunge on toward Santa Fe, reluctantly left the protection of its walls to attack him near a mesa called Valverde.

The Confederate commander could not believe his luck. At the end of two bloody days of what one soldier remembered as fighting "terrific beyond description" that left the surface of the Rio Grande littered with the bobbing corpses of men and horses, the Texans drove Canby and what was left of his force back inside their fort.

Sibley continued his march. Supplies were growing scarce now, and federal troops destroyed the depots from which the rebels had hoped to replenish them. The pro-Confederate volunteers Sibley had assumed would rally to him failed to materialize — the mostly Spanish-speaking people of the region had little affection for Texans.

Still, the Confederate conquest of the Southwest seemed to be moving forward. Sibley took Albuquerque and plundered Santa Fe. All that now stood between him and the Colorado goldfields was Fort Union. He sent an advance force to the mouth of Apache Canyon to hold it until his whole army was in place and they could pour through together to crush federal resistance forever. But he had not reckoned on the last-minute arrival of the 1st Colorado Volunteers, mostly miners from the goldfields, hastily trained and hard drinking but itching for a fight. They had marched

Sergeant Alexander Coker (above), 2nd Texas Mounted Rifles. "We heeded not their great renown," one Confederate volunteer remembered of the rebel triumph at Valverde. "We charged them with a yell,/We turned their tactics upside down,/And gave the regulars hell."

Costume change: General Henry H. Sibley (center), wearing the Confederate uniform he put on after leaving the Union army, and the Reverend John M. Chivington, dressed as he customarily was before transforming himself into a Union soldier

forty miles a day to get there, through ice and snow and freezing winds. Now, four hundred of them started through the narrow canyon toward the waiting Texans.

In the lead was Colonel John M. Chivington, a big, bearish Methodist parson, the presiding elder of the Rocky Mountain District of his church and as famous for his flamboyance as for his fiery sermons. He sometimes preached with a revolver resting on the pulpit and had refused to serve as regimental chaplain, demanding a "fighting commission" instead, because he thought it would serve better to boost the career in politics he now wished to pursue.

Now, he would get his chance to show what he could do. The Confederates opened fire as soon as they saw Chivington's men, and the Union volunteers fell back for a moment. But then they regrouped and Chivington sent some of his men scurrying up the canyon sides so that they could fire down on the enemy. "They were up on the walls on both sides of us," one Texan remembered, "shooting us down like sheep." Then, Chivington, waving two revolvers, ordered in his cavalry. He "chawed his lips with only less energy than he gave his orders," one of his men recalled. "He seemed burdened with a new responsibility, the extent of which he had never before realized, and to have no thought of danger. Of commanding presence, dressed in full regimentals, he was a conspicuous mark for the Texan sharp sharpshooters. . . . As if possessed of a charmed life, he galloped unhurt through the storm of bullets. . . ."

A Confederate who saw the Coloradans charge was impressed, too:

> On they came to what I supposed certain destruction, but nothing like lead or iron seemed to stop them, for we were pouring it into them from every side like hail in a storm. In a moment these devils had run the gauntlet for a half mile and were fighting hand to hand with our men in the road.

The Texans withdrew. Sibley's success no longer seemed quite so assured.

The two main armies met the following day at Glorieta Pass, "a terrible place for an engagement," a federal officer remembered, "a deep gorge with a narrow wagon-track running along the bottom, the ground rising precipitously on each side, with huge boulders and clumps of stunted cedars interspersed." They slammed at each other amid the rocks for five hours, neither side willing to give an inch to the other, until the Texans suddenly called a truce.

Behind their lines, Chivington and his Coloradans had dealt the Texans a fatal blow. With a Mexican guide to show them the way, they had marched sixteen miles through the mountains to a cliff that overlooked the Texans' supply wagons. There, they lowered themselves by ropes, drove off the guards, set eighty-five wagons filled with provisions on fire, bayoneted five hundred horses and mules. Sibley's Confederate army, so close to victory only a few days before, now suddenly faced starvation and thirst as well as a hostile enemy.

The Confederate invasion had been halted. The battle of Glorieta Pass came to be called "the Gettysburg of the West" and Colonel Chivington — "the Fighting Parson" — and his Coloradans emerged as its heroes.

Sibley now just wanted to get his battered army back to Texas. On April 12, he ordered his men to begin the long retreat. Canby and his army followed at a discreet distance, content for the most part to let the weather and terrain do their deadly work.

Columns got lost. Boots wore out. Men had to stagger through burning sand in bare feet. There was little to eat, still less to drink. There were sandstorms, mountain blizzards. Some Texans mutinied. Others abandoned their weapons, collapsed from exhaustion, dehydration, sunstroke. Thirty-seven hundred Texans had marched north with Sibley. Fifteen hundred of them never returned.

The dream of a Confederate Southwest was dead.

Private Bates of the Texas Mounted Volunteers. He and his comrades vowed to "fight as long as [General] Sibley said fight," one of them declared after their defeat at Glorieta Pass, "but the moment he said surrender, they were going . . . into the mountains and make their way to Texas."

THE WATER RISING ALL AROUND

By 1861, the so-called Five Civilized Tribes that had been forced to crowd together onto Indian Territory had rebuilt much of the world they had left behind: schools, churches, newspapers, plantations worked by slaves. But they were still divided between those who had agreed to come west and those who had opposed it, and now they faced another bitter choice — whether to side with the North or the South.

No people were more deeply split than the Cherokee. John Ross, their principal chief, had fought the Removal treaty, and when in 1861 a Confederate agent called upon him to support the Confederacy, he refused. He wished to remain neutral in this white man's war; he owned slaves himself and had little love for the federal government that had driven his people west, but it still owed them a million dollars and he did not want to forfeit it. "I am — the Cherokees are — your friends," he told two Confederate agents sent to win him to their cause, "but we do not wish to be brought into the feuds between yourselves and your northern brethren. Our wish is for peace. Peace at home and peace among you."

Meanwhile, his ancient enemy Stand Watie, the only prominent signer of the treaty that had ceded the Cherokee lands in Georgia to have escaped assassination by those who had opposed it, pledged his loyalty to the South, and began raising a regi-

White man's war: A Union recruiter swears in recruits somewhere in Indian Territory, while an unidentified Native American (above) displays his loyalty to the Confederacy.

ment of mixed-bloods. Other tribes were signing on with the Confederacy, too — the Chickasaw, Choctaw, Seminoles. The Creek split into two factions, one pro-Union, the other pro-Confederacy. Then came word of Southern triumphs at Bull Run, and again at Wilson's Creek in southwest Missouri, where Stand Watie's Cherokee followers helped turn the tide against the Union. With neighboring Missouri in rebel hands, neutrality no longer seemed practical.

Ross reluctantly forged an alliance with the South in return for a Confederate pledge to honor the Union debt to the tribe and provide white troops, should northern soldiers invade Indian Territory. He prayed he'd chosen the winning side. "We are in the situation of a man standing upon a low naked spot of ground," he wrote, "with the water rising all around him. . . . The tide carries by him, in its mad course, a drifting log. . . . By refusing it he is a doomed man. By seizing hold of it he has a chance for his life."

Indians from all over the country fought in the Civil War. These Union veterans, all members of the Menominee tribe, belonged to the Joseph Lederberger Post No. 267 of the G.A.R.

There soon broke out a bloody civil war within Indian Territory itself that cost the region proportionately more men than any state, North or South. Settlements were burned, crops ravaged. White intruders carried off thousands of head of livestock. John Ross was captured early and spent most of the war as a prisoner in Washington. His nemesis, Stand Watie, took time out from fighting an invading Union force to destroy Tahlequah, the Cherokee capital, and burn Ross's house to the ground.

In the end, the Cherokee and their neighbors would gain nothing by their involvement in the Civil War. After the fighting finally ended, Congress would punish rebel and loyal Indians alike by forcing them to give up still more of their land.

LAWRENCE

No Civil War fighting was more savage than that between pro-slavery and antislavery settlers along the Kansas-Missouri border — and none had a more lasting impact on its region.

The most notorious leader of the Union guerrillas — called Jayhawkers by their enemies — was James H. Lane, a cadaverous former senator from Kansas who thought Missourians "wolves, snakes, devils" whom he wanted to see "cast into a burning hell." He did his best to cast them there, haunting the trail of rebel armies, first to ravage the homes of anyone who had dared help them, then sacking and burning whole towns.

Confederate guerrillas — called Bushwhackers because they hid in the bush — responded in kind. Their most celebrated leader was William Clarke Quantrill, a former schoolteacher from Ohio with little interest in slavery but limitless enthusiasm

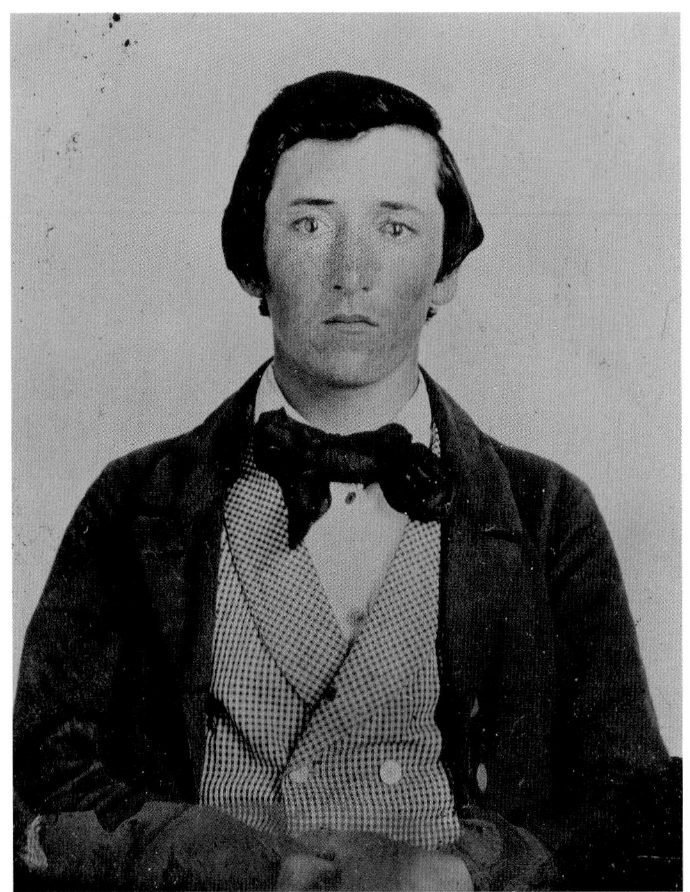

Appearances: William Quantrill (left), in a previously unpublished daguerreotype made when he was fifteen, seems incapable of hurting anyone, while Bloody Bill Anderson (right) seems eager for the carnage to begin.

for looting and killing. He came to Kansas before the war, seemed to favor the abolition of slavery, even helped plan a raid into Missouri to free some slaves, then — for reasons never satisfactorily explained — he betrayed his co-conspirators, led them into a fatal ambush, and went over to the enemy. For helping Confederate regulars take Springfield in 1861, he was made a captain, then raised a loosely knit army of wild young men — some as young as seventeen — and went to war on his own, swearing he would burn Jim Lane at the stake. Union farmers, he warned that autumn, should not bother to plant crops the following spring; they would not live to harvest them.

Quantrill's raiders so angered the local Union commander, Thomas Ewing, that he proposed to exile their families to the South in the hope that the guerrillas would follow them there. "About two thirds of the families on the occupied farms," Ewing reported, "are of kin to the guerrillas and are actively and heartily engaged in feeding, clothing and sustaining them. . . . The families of several hundred of the worst of these men should be sent, with their clothes and bedding, to some rebel district south. . . . The men will follow. . . ."

Ewing arrested several of the wives and sisters of Quantrill's men. Somehow, the old brick building in which some of them were locked up in Kansas City collapsed. Five women died; several others were badly injured. One had been the cousin of Cole Younger, a young Bushwhacker already eager for revenge against the Jayhawkers, who had burned his family home. Another was the sister of an accused horse thief named Bill Anderson, who had already proved himself an adept killer and would soon earn

Unidentified but heavily armed settlers, thought to have been photographed near Lawrence in 1855. No one knows whether these men favored slavery or free soil, but their like could be seen all across the region. "The prairies are ablaze," one Kansas newspaper said. "There is nothing talked about here except war."

himself the nickname "Bloody Bill." His sister's death in federal custody seems to have driven him to madness: he began wearing a garland of Yankee scalps into battle, laughed as he and his followers gunned down unarmed prisoners, then ordered his men to scalp and mutilate their corpses. "I will kill you," he wrote to the readers of one antislavery newspaper. "I will hunt you down like wolves and murder you."

William Quantrill, too, was eager for revenge. "Blood and revenge are hammering in my heart," he said. And Lawrence, Kansas, seemed the ideal target: it had always been a free-soil stronghold and was the headquarters of the hated Jayhawkers. Runaway slaves had found sanctuary there, too, and it was the home of Jim Lane. "Let's go to Lawrence," Quantrill said. "We can get more money and more revenge there than anywhere else in the state of Kansas."

On the morning of August 21, 1863, Quantrill and some 450 men drew up just outside Lawrence. Riding with them were Bloody Bill Anderson, Cole Younger, and a distant cousin of his, Frank James. Along the way, Quantrill had kidnapped ten farmers, forced them to show him the way to town, then murdered them all. And he had just begun to kill.

Quantrill's massacre at Lawrence is almost enough to curdle the blood with horror. In the history of the war thus far, full as it has been of dreadful scenes, there has been no such diabolical work as this indiscriminate slaughter of peaceful villagers. . . .

New York *Daily Times*

The expedition to Lawrence was a gallant and perfectly fair blow at the enemy . . . as the population of Kansas is malignant and scoundrely beyond description.

Richmond *Examiner*

Free-soil citizens of Lawrence: John F. Griswald (top, left) was killed in Quantrill's raid. As an agent of the Emigrant Aid Company, Charles Robinson (top, right) helped pick the site for the town and was later arrested and put on trial for treason by pro-slavery forces at their capital of Lecompton. James and Annie Gleason helped publish the *Kansas Herald of Freedom,* whose weekly antislavery message helped bring the wrath of the Confederate guerrillas down upon their village.

The Bushwhackers surrounded a downtown hotel. A guest hung a white sheet from the window and asked Quantrill what he wanted. "Plunder!" he answered. The guests were ordered out and robbed. The hotel was set afire. Waving two of the six pistols he carried, Quantrill rose in his stirrups and shouted, "Kill! Kill! Lawrence must be cleansed, and the only way to cleanse it is to kill!" Then, while he ordered the terrified staff of another hotel to cook him a big breakfast, his men carried out his orders. Unarmed men were shot down as they ran. Some were dragged from their houses and murdered in front of their families; others were smothered or burned alive inside their homes. Two wounded men who had managed to crawl out of the flames were thrown back in.

"One lady threw her arms around her husband," Julia Lovejoy was told, and begged of them to spare his life. They rested the pistol on her arm as it was around his body, and shot him dead, and the fire from the pistol burnt the sleeve of her dress. Mrs. Reed put out the fire six times to save her house, and they would fire it anew, but she by almost superhuman exertions saved it. Mrs. Fisher, wife of the Rev. H. D. Fisher, of the Kansas Conference, . . . a spunky little Dutch-Irish woman from Pennsylvania, by her own exertion saved the L part of her house, whilst the front, a splendid new brick establishment, was burnt, worth $2,000 probably. All the business houses, banks, stores, &c., in the city were robbed and burned save one, and most of the business men killed. It is estimated that half a million in money has been carried off.

Quantrill's men, many of them drunk from commandeered whiskey, rode up and down the streets with American flags dragging in the dust behind their horses. Jim Lane, the principal target of the raid, had managed to escape through a cornfield in his nightshirt, but 183 men and boys were killed — fewer than 20 of whom had been soldiers — and 185 homes were burned before Quantrill and his men rode out of town, leaving behind 80 widows, 250 fatherless children.

To avenge the Lawrence Massacre and to crush Confederate resistance in Missouri once and for all, General Ewing now issued Order Number 11, which forced from their homes every man, woman, and child living in three Missouri border counties, and half of a fourth. Federal troops drove thousands of people onto the open prairie, while Jayhawkers followed in their wake, burning and looting the empty houses they left behind, raiding the refugee columns, stealing even wedding rings. For years, the region would be known as the "Burnt District." "The very air seems charged with blood and death," a newspaperman wrote. "Pandemonium itself seems to have broken loose, and robbery, murder, . . . and death runs riot over the country."

Seeking vengeance: In October 1864 — just a little over a year after Quantrill's raid — volunteers from Lawrence march north on Massachusetts Street to join federal forces near Kansas City. A few weeks later they would help destroy a rebel army at the battle of Westport.

Now, it was the Confederates' turn to seek revenge. General Sterling Price returned to Missouri with 12,000 regulars. With him rode Quantrill and many of his raiders, whom Price had complimented for their "gallant struggle" at Lawrence. Union forces stopped them at the battles of Pilot's Knob and Westport. Quantrill fled to Texas and was later fatally wounded during a raid into Kentucky; his raiders broke up into small, savage outlaw bands. Bloody Bill Anderson was hunted down by federal troops and shot in the back of the head after charging through their lines. Organized Confederate resistance eventually ended, but the bitterness the bloodshed had produced would persist for generations.

THE WORK OF GOD

In the spring of 1863, a delegation of sixteen Plains Indian leaders was invited to Washington. They were photographed with Mrs. Abraham Lincoln, and the President himself received them in the White House. He hoped to persuade them not to be tempted to side with the Confederacy or take advantage of the Civil War to drive out white settlers.

A Cheyenne named Lean Bear addressed Lincoln. "He wished to live in peace for the balance of his life," a reporter for the Washington *Evening Star* remembered his saying, "on the buffalo, as his fathers had done, . . . and again urged the President to counsel his white children, who were annually encroaching more and more upon

Kiowa and Cheyenne leaders gather in the conservatory of the Executive Mansion in Washington, March 27, 1863, to be photographed with Mary Todd Lincoln (standing, far right). The four Cheyenne leaders seated in the front row all had less than eighteen months to live. Yellow Wolf (right) died of tuberculosis, but the rest were killed by whites: Lean Bear (second from right) would be shot down by regulars as he protested his peaceful intentions; War Bonnet (far left) and Standing in the Water were killed by Colorado volunteers at Sand Creek.

their tribes, to abstain from acts of violence and wrong towards them. He deplored, he said, the war between the whites, now being waged, and expressed the determination of the tribes not to take part or sides in it, and said that its end would be hailed with joy by them."

The President replied that

> the palefaced people are numerous and prosperous because they cultivate the earth, produce bread, and depend upon the products of the earth rather than wild game for subsistence. This is the chief reason of the difference [between the numbers of the two races]; but there is another. Although we are now engaged in a great war between one another, we are not, as a race, so much disposed to fight and kill one another as our red brethren.
>
> You have asked for my advice. I really am not capable of advising you whether, in the providence of the Great Spirit, who is the great Father of us all, it is for you to maintain the habits and customs of your race, or adopt a new mode of life. I can only say that I can see no way in which your race is to become as numerous and prosperous as the white race except by living as they do, by the cultivation of the earth.

Lincoln presented Lean Bear with a medal, which he wore proudly from that day forward as a token of his friendship with the White Father at Washington.

Lean Bear was a peace chief, one of forty-four who worked for the benefit of all the Cheyenne bands, settling internal quarrels, working for the general welfare, urging the younger warriors to avoid war with the whites. So was his friend Black Kettle. He had once led raids against the Kiowa and Ute, had been entrusted with the tribes' sacred arrows in battle against the Delaware when they strayed too far west from their new home in Indian Territory, and had fought white soldiers on the Solomon River in 1858. But he had watched white settlers and gold-seekers crowd onto the lands between the North Platte and the Arkansas that had been promised to the Cheyenne by the Fort Laramie Treaty, and realized that there were too many whites to fight, that some way must be found to live with them. "The whole force of his nature was concentrated in the one idea of how best to act for the good of his race," a regular army officer remembered; "he knew the power of the white man, and was aware that thence might spring most of the evils that could befall his people, and consequently the whole of his powers were directed toward conciliating the whites, and his utmost endeavors used to preserve peace and friendship between his race and their oppressors."

And so, when a new treaty was hastily drawn up at Fort Wise in 1861, ceding all the Cheyenne and Arapaho lands except for a small reservation along Sand Creek southeast of Denver, Black Kettle was one of just six Cheyenne chiefs to sign. "The whites presumed to treat these six chiefs as the head chiefs of the tribe," the trader George Bent recalled, "and as this was against custom the Cheyennes refused to abide by the treaty. They called the signers of this treaty the 'Six Chiefs,' as a sort of nickname. The whites also wished to consider Black Kettle as head chief, and this too, was against custom. . . . The whites had the wrong idea about Indian chiefs." In any case, the treaty proved a bad bargain: the reservation was small, sandy, barren, empty of game, unsuited to agriculture. Whites were not kept out, as the commissioners had

THE FEARING TIME

In the Southwest, Indians saw the withdrawal of regular troops as a signal to drive out all outsiders. Mescalero Apache and Navajo bands stole livestock, attacked settlements, raided mining camps, even ambushed a column of California volunteers that had been sent against Henry Sibley's Confederates. Ute, Zuni, and Mexican Americans joined white settlers in demanding that the government do something.

The commander of the Department of New Mexico, Brigadier General James Carleton, launched a campaign to restore federal control of the region. He had little patience with Indians. A decorated hero of the Mexican War, grim and demanding, he had fought them for nearly two decades before the war and saw nothing to be gained from negotiations. They must surrender and agree to stay on a reservation of his choosing — an arid stretch of land along the Pecos River called Bosque Redondo — or they would be killed, he said.

Kit Carson, now a colonel of the New Mexico Cavalry, was named to carry out his orders. He began with a grueling but successful campaign against the Mescalero, then turned his attention to the Navajo, some 12,000 of them, scattered across thousands of square miles of rugged country. Riding back and forth across Navajo country for six exhausting months, Carson had poor luck hunting down the elusive Navajo themselves, but he burned their homes, blankets, and grain, rounded up their sheep, hacked down their peach orchards. The Navajo began to starve.

Winter came. The cold began to kill the old people and the children. Carson was ordered to pursue the Navajo into their sacred stronghold, Canyon de Chelly.

There, the Indians stood helplessly on the cliffs, hurling curses and stones, as Carson's men methodically destroyed everything they owned on the canyon floor.

Unable to find food, shivering with cold but afraid to build fires for fear the smoke would give them away, the Navajo began to surrender to Carson, in small groups at first, then by the hundreds, convinced that at least he would not murder them if they put themselves in his hands.

Four thousand Navajo held out for two more years in the remote western reaches of their lands before surrendering. But most of the tribe — more than 8,000 men, women, and children — gave themselves up and were made to march three hundred miles across New Mexico to Bosque Redondo. Carleton was not prepared for such numbers of desperate people. There was not enough food, no clothes or other supplies. Hundreds died along the way. Ute and New Mexicans shadowing the slow-moving columns seized stragglers and sold them as slaves.

Despite the hardships of getting there, Carleton was confident that Bosque Redondo would soon become "the happiest and most delightfully located pueblo of Indians in New Mexico — perhaps in the United States."

Instead, it was a disaster. There was no game, not enough fertile land for farming, too little grass even for goats. The meager crops that did grow fell victim to cutworms and sudden downpours. Thin government clothing kept no one warm in winter. Bickering between the army and the Indian bureau meant supplies often arrived late, or not at all. There was constant fighting, too, between the Navajo and the outnumbered Mescalero — who finally fled the reservation and returned to the hills from which Kit Carson had driven them.

Carleton insisted that the Navajo live in adobe houses, but they refused, preferring even holes in the ground because their religion forbade them to continue to live in a structure in which someone had died — and they were dying fast.

The Navajo would remain at Bosque Redondo for four ghastly years — they called them *Nahonzod,* "the Fearing Time." In 1868, a new policy would permit them to return to their homeland. By then, more than one-quarter of them had died.

Kit Carson (above) and some of the Navajo he brought to Bosque Redondo

An American flag — blurred by the slow shutter of the camera — marks the wagon in which Arapaho and Cheyenne chiefs, including Black Kettle, ride into Camp Weld, near Denver, to talk peace in September of 1864.

promised they would be. Annuities and goods often failed to arrive. Some Cheyenne were reduced to begging for food from white settlers. Soon, even Black Kettle had moved his lodges back to the old hunting grounds. Despite the best efforts of the peace chiefs, young men from the warrior societies began raiding settlers.

Governor John Evans of Colorado Territory was an ambitious man: he wanted to be Colorado's first senator and saw a winning issue in ridding his region of its Indians. He warned that any Indian found outside the reservation would henceforth be considered hostile, and called upon the federal government for troops to back up his threat. When they did not come — Washington now had no soldiers to spare — Evans called for volunteers. Hundreds signed up.

Parson John Chivington — now Colonel Chivington after his triumph at Glorieta Pass — continued to preach to big appreciative congregations. But he, too, had his sights set on bigger things. One victory had made him a Colorado hero; two might

Peace talks: At Fort Weld, Major Edward W. Wynkoop kneels at the feet of Black Kettle (partially obscured by Wynkoop's big hat). At the time, war seemed to have been averted.

make him a congressman once Colorado entered the Union. But first he needed a war, and, as military commander in the territory, he was perfectly situated to start one. He ordered his men to burn every Indian village and kill every Indian they came upon.

In May, Black Kettle, Lean Bear, and their bands were hunting buffalo in Kansas. A column of troops appeared near their camp. Lean Bear and another peace chief named Star rode out to meet them. Lean Bear wore the peace medal Lincoln had given him as a sign of his friendship and he held up papers attesting to his loyalty, signed by the President. When the two chiefs were within twenty feet of the soldiers the commanding officer ordered his men to fire. Lean Bear and Star tumbled from their horses; a second volley killed them where they lay.

The younger men wanted to attack the soldiers, but Black Kettle managed to stop them. Even now, there must be no war with the white men, he said; there was no way to win. They held off. But soon, other warriors were seeking revenge. They plundered wagon trains, burned ranches, raped and kidnapped women, and killed some two hundred settlers.

One family was butchered just outside Denver, one city resident recalled:

> . . . About 100 yards from the ranch they discovered the body of the murdered woman and her two dead children, one of which was a little girl of four years and the other an infant. The woman had been stabbed in several places and scalped, and the body bore evidence of having been violated. The two children had their throats cut, their heads being nearly severed from their bodies. [The bodies were brought to Denver and] placed in a box, side by side, the two children between their parents, and shown to the people from a shed where the City Hall now stands. Everybody saw them and anger and revenge mounted all day long as the people filed past or remained to talk over Indian outrages and means of protection and reprisal.

Colonel John M. Chivington

The old trader William Bent, married to a Cheyenne woman and the father of three half-Cheyenne sons, feared what was coming and tried to stop it. He warned Chivington that what had already happened was bad enough, but that if the Indians were further provoked they would unite among themselves — Cheyenne and Kiowa, Arapaho and Lakota — and then no power on earth could protect the whites from their anger. "In reply," Bent remembered,

> [Chivington] said he was not authorized to make peace, and that he was then on the warpath. . . . I then stated to him that there was great risk to run in keeping up the war; that there were a great many government trains traveling to New Mexico and other points; also a great many citizens, and that I did not think there was sufficient force to protect the travelers, and the citizens and the settlers of the country would have to suffer. He said the citizens would have to protect themselves.

In September of 1864, Black Kettle and six other Cheyenne chiefs came to Fort Weld, near Denver, wanting to talk peace, and bringing with them four white captives they had ransomed from other bands as evidence of their good faith. "We have come with our eyes shut . . ." Black Kettle told the fort's commander, "like coming through the fire. All we ask is that we may have peace with the whites; we want to hold you by the hand. You are our father; we have been traveling through a cloud; the sky has been dark ever since the war began. . . . I want you to give all the chiefs of the soldiers here to understand that we are for peace, and that we have made peace, that we may not be mistaken for enemies."

This did not fit well with the war plans Evans and Chivington had already made. ". . . [W]hat shall I do with the Third Colorado Regiment if I make peace?" the governor asked privately. "They have been raised to kill Indians and they must kill Indians."

Some of Black Kettle's own young men had been among the raiders, the chief admitted, but he remained determined not to have a war. He brought his band back to the reservation in November, and reported to Major Edward Wynkoop at Fort Lyon.

Wynkoop, also eager to avoid conflict, promised him protection as well as food and supplies, for which he had no authorization. The Indians would have to be

Blackfoot winter camp, Montana Territory, ca. 1890. It was during the winter that the Plains peoples were most vulnerable to attack.

made "to suffer more" before they could have peace, his superiors said. Wynkoop was replaced.

The new commander, Major Scott Anthony, cooperated with Evans and Chivington. He told Black Kettle to move his band twenty-five miles away, to a bend in Sand Creek. They would be safe there, he said. Then he waited for reinforcements from Denver.

Chivington and some seven hundred volunteers arrived at Fort Lyon on November 26, 1864, eager for a fight before their hundred-day term of enlistment ran out. Some officers protested that to attack the peaceable encampment would betray the army's pledge of safety. "Damn any man that sympathizes with Indians," Chivington said. "I have come to kill Indians and believe it right and honorable to use any means under God's heaven. . . ."

At dawn on November 29, 1864, Chivington and seven hundred men, many of them full of the whiskey they had swallowed to keep them warm during the icy all-night ride, reached the edge of Black Kettle's sleeping camp. "Kill and scalp all," Chivington told his men, "big and little; nits make lice." His men needed little encouragement.

One of William Bent's sons, Robert, was riding with them, commandeered against his will to show the way to the Cheyenne camp. Three of Bent's other children — Charles, Julia, and George — were staying in it. George Bent watched the soldiers come:

> From down the creek a large body of troops was advancing at a rapid trot . . . more soldiers could be seen making for the Indian pony herds to the south of the camp; in the camps themselves all was confusion and noise — men, women, and children rushing out of the lodges partly dressed; women and children screaming at the sight of the troops; men running back into the lodges for their arms. . . . Black Kettle had a large American flag tied to the end of a long lodgepole and was standing in front of his lodge, holding the pole, with the flag fluttering in the gray light of the winter dawn. . . .
>
> All the time Black Kettle kept calling out not to be frightened; that the camp was under protection and there was no danger.

Robert Bent was watching, too:

> I saw the American flag waving and heard Black Kettle tell the Indians to stand around the flag, and there they were huddled — men, women, and children. This was when we were within fifty yards of the Indians. I also saw a white flag raised. These flags were in so conspicuous a position that they must have been seen. . . . I think there were six hundred Indians in all. I think there were thirty-five braves and some old men, about sixty in all. . . . [T]he rest of the men were away from camp hunting. . . .

The volunteers began firing into the lodges. Warriors did all they could to defend their families. "I never saw more bravery displayed by any set of people on the face of the earth than by these Indians," a regular soldier recalled. "They would charge on the whole company singly, determined to kill someone before being killed themselves. . . . We, of course, took no prisoners."

"After the firing," Robert Bent remembered,

> the warriors put the squaws and children together, and surrounded them to protect them. I saw five squaws under a bank for shelter. When the troops came up to them they ran out and showed their persons to let the soldiers know they were squaws and begged for mercy, but the soldiers shot them all. I saw one squaw lying on the bank whose leg had been broken by a shell; a soldier came up to her with a drawn saber; she raised her arm to protect herself, when he struck, breaking her arm; she rolled over and raised her other arm, when he struck, breaking it, and then he left her without killing her. There seemed to be indiscriminate slaughter of men, women and children. There were some thirty or forty squaws collected in a hole for protection; they sent out a little girl about six years old with a white flag on a stick; she had not proceeded a few steps when she was shot and killed. All the squaws in that hole were afterwards killed. . . .

"In going over the battleground the next day," a regular army lieutenant testified later,

> I did not see a body of a man, woman, or child but was scalped, and in many instances their bodies were mutilated in the most horrible manner. . . . I heard one man say that he had cut out a woman's private parts and had them for exhibition on a stick; I heard another man say that he had cut the fingers off an Indian to get the rings on his hand; according to the best of my knowledge and belief these atrocities that were committed were with the knowledge of J. M. Chivington, and I do not know of his taking any measures to prevent them; I heard of one instance of a child a few months old being thrown in the feedbox of a wagon, and after being carried some distance left on the ground to perish; I also heard of numerous instances in which men had cut out the private parts of females and stretched them over the saddle-bows and wore them over their hats while riding in ranks.

Chivington and his men returned to Denver in triumph, claiming to have killed five hundred warriors — instead of ninety-eight women and children and a handful of mostly old men. The *Rocky Mountain News* pronounced it a "brilliant feat of arms." "All did nobly," Chivington said, and one evening during intermission at the Denver opera house, one hundred Cheyenne scalps were put on display while the orchestra played patriotic airs and the audience stood to applaud the men who had taken them.

Regular army officers were appalled by Sand Creek. General Ulysses S. Grant himself privately declared it nothing more nor less than murder. There were separate investigations by Congress and the army. "As to Colonel Chivington," said the official report of the Senate Committee on the Conduct of the War, "your committee can hardly find fitting terms to describe his conduct. Wearing the uniform of the United States, which should be the emblem of justice and humanity . . . he deliberately planned and executed a foul and dastardly massacre which would have disgraced the veriest savage among those who were the victims of his cruelty." But by the time the tribunals reached their verdicts, Chivington was a civilian again and beyond the reach of military justice. In the end, no one was ever punished for the slaughter of Black Kettle's

Lawrence reborn: the south-southwestern side of town, photographed by Alexander Gardner in 1867 from a gentle rise the townspeople had grandly named Mount Oread

Cheyenne. Nor did Chivington ever admit he had done anything wrong. Speaking before a reunion of Pike's Peak pioneers nearly twenty years later, he would declare, "I stand by Sand Creek."

Word of what had happened there spread fast. Cheyenne runners carried war pipes to all the Lakota, Arapaho, and Cheyenne bands. Soon, the whole region was at war: stagecoaches were burned, telegraph wires pulled down. Denver was cut off from the outside world. Cheyenne sacked the little town of Julesburg, Colorado, twice. Soldiers who tried to stop them were killed or driven off. "Since this . . . horrible murder by Chivington," said Major Wynkoop, "the country presents a scene of desolation; all communication is cut off with the States, except by sending bodies of troops, and already over one hundred whites have fallen as victims to this fearful vengeance of these betrayed Indians. All this country is ruined; there can be no such thing as peace in the future."

Still, Black Kettle wanted no part of further fighting. "Although wrongs have been done me," he said, "I live in hopes. I have not got two hearts. . . . I once thought that I was the only man that persevered to be the friend of the white man, but since they have come and cleaned out our lodges, horses, and everything else, it is hard for me to believe white men any more." He took the survivors of Sand Creek south, instead of north, as far from the fighting as he could get.

On April 9, 1865, Robert E. Lee at last surrendered his army at Appomattox Court House in Virginia. The transcontinental telegraph now brought the news west to San Francisco instantaneously, and fireworks were launched from Fisherman's Wharf in celebration. In Los Angeles, there was a parade, and Denver celebrated with a two-hundred-gun salute. All over the West, lives interrupted by war resumed again.

Julia Louisa Lovejoy, now living with her family in the town of Baldwin City in what she proudly called "the *State* of Kansas," expressed her pleasure and pride in another letter to her old New England paper:

> Towns are starting up as by magic all along the valley. . . . Things now look quite city-like, and the sound of the hammer is heard on every hand. . . . I wish to say to our friends in New Hampshire, one and all, we have never regretted coming to Kansas. . . . We have never wavered — never flinched — not even when three times in twenty four hours we were compelled to flee from our house. . . . I tell you all, though we have felt the horrors of war, if we were not in Kansas already, we would come as soon as steam could bring us.

Believing in the American West

Patricia Nelson Limerick

GROWING UP POST-MORMON

My father and I are not Mormons. This fact is true of many other people in the American West, but it is particularly true of us. My father was raised Mormon in Brigham City, Utah. Although it is common for fallen-away members of the Church of Jesus Christ of Latter-day Saints to become fervent believers in other churches, my father took a different path. When he cut his ties to the Mormon Church and moved to California, he turned away from all organized religion.

My sisters and I thus grew up with a particular opportunity to drive our father batty. Here was our distinctive and very gratifying channel of rebellion: we could insist on our First Amendment right to freedom of religion, get dressed up for church, and demand that Father drive us there. The peak of this soul-satisfying mutiny came in asking him for money to put in the collection plate. And, since Mother was (and is) a non–church-attending Congregationalist and thus nearly as vulnerable as Father to the abrasive powers of our piety, there was also considerable pleasure to be gained from coming home from church, sitting down to Sunday dinner, and delivering an earnest prayer on behalf of our parents' redemption.

Such rebellion, however, came at a cost. For me, the cost was repeated exposure to the misery of the unbaptized heathen. Churched or not, our parents had installed into our thinking a great devotion to justice and fairness. And so the dilemma of the poor souls in Africa and Asia, living and dying and heading off to hell without the opportunity to hear the Christian gospel, weighed heavily on me. If God really had decided to let salvation hinge on the basis of the arbitrary facts of place of birth (a fact that He, in His omnipotence, had determined), then God seemed to be following rather questionable values Himself, showing a pretty tenuous understanding of the concept of fairness.

The pleasures of bugging my father were, therefore, already wearing thin on a memorable day in 1962 at the First Baptist Church in Banning, the day on which my rebellion ended. The membership of the First Baptist Church was entirely white. On this Sunday, a black woman, new in town, came to church. I happened to be behind her in the line, waiting to shake hands with the minister. We had spent some time, in Sunday school, singing about Jesus' transcendence of racial prejudice:

> Red and yellow, black and white,
> They're all sacred in His sight.
> Jesus loves the little children of the world.

This little song was not easy to reconcile with the dilemma of the unbaptized heathen, and our minister had, himself, not gotten very far in reconciling Jesus' sentiments with his own. When the black woman shook hands with him, the minister told her that *her* church was on the other side of town.

Since that Sunday, I have learned more about the ways in which race relations in the American West came to bear an unhappy resemblance to race relations in the rest of the country. In religious terms, it was not simply a matter of segregation in western churches, it was often a matter of the active use of the church as a social institution to maintain racial separation and inequality. The minister of the First Baptist Church not only gave me a memorable introduction to this topic, he also persuaded me that my rebellion against my father had gone far enough. Since then I have taken the path leading away from organized religion and toward what I will call disorganized religion. My father and I remain post-Mormon and unchurched, but nonetheless driven by convictions about right and wrong.

For decades, I thought that Father and I had placed ourselves on the margins of conventional religious behavior. But, like so many other westerners who treasured a picture of themselves as odd birds, we have turned out to be birds positioned right at the center of the flock. "[P]oor church attendance is characteristic of westerners generally," the historian Michael Quinn has written. This is the West's principal claim to distinctiveness in religious terms: it is the region with the lowest rates of church participation, in both the nineteenth and the twentieth centuries. In the nation as a whole, "the West as a region has the lowest attendance (36 percent) in church or synagogue." The West thus holds the status of the nation's "Unchurched Belt." In this region, participants in disorganized religion have held and hold a considerable numerical advantage over participants in organized religion.

My father and I turn out to be not rebels and eccentrics, but representative westerners. Still, without official papers of membership, we and our many disaffiliated comrades are not likely to register in the records of western religious history. Contemplating the prospect of one's invisibility, one finds good reason to question how much the fact of church membership reveals about a matter as subjective and private as religious belief. Churches are, of course, the places where *records* of official religious performance accumulate. Historians of religion, oriented to written documents, have had good reason to place churches and their members at the center of their inquiry, in the manner of labor historians who, for a time, hinged their history of the working class on the much more narrow topic of membership in unions.

"In comparison with Whites in the United States today," the anthropologist Harold Driver once wrote, "the Indians [of the past] were at least ten times as religious." Of all the improbable proclamations of academics made over the last forty years, this one is my personal favorite, an example of confident, social-scientific thinking at its goofiest. And yet, whatever Harold Driver meant by this memorable assertion, one suspects that he did *not* mean that Indians were ten times as religious because they were ten times more likely to join formally chartered and organized churches. On the contrary, Driver thought (and he shared this conviction with many others) that Indian people were more religious because they unmistakably and consistently demonstrated their faith, observing little separation between the secular and the spiritual. They did not need to join churches and attend formal services, because they lived virtually every moment in a religious way. By contrast, in Driver's equally widely shared but considerably more questionable assumption, modern white American people have been a very secular group, driven primarily by economic motives. For a group of people holding their souls on such a tight leash, religious conviction could only appear in official membership in an institutional church, with even that level of religious commitment often confined to attendance at Sunday services, cresting at Easter and Christmas.

Kansas baptism

Consider, by contrast, the state of affairs in mid-nineteenth-century rural Oregon. True to the western pattern, church membership there was very limited. But a low percentage of church attendance, historian Dean May has argued, "does not imply . . . an absence of religious sentiment and feelings." The settlers' religious activity was, emphatically, local, often practiced within households, "involving them rarely, if at all, in any broader community." They had Bibles in their homes, and recorded significant family events in those Bibles. "Blessings on food, prayers, prayer meetings, hymn singing, and exhortation were held in home and schoolhouse for gatherings of families and close neighbors." Preachers sent by home missionary societies found Oregon's "seeming incoherence of religious organization" both puzzling and frustrating. In a curious convergence of opinion, historians would come to share the judgment of the preachers: "religion in any setting other than an established congregation was to them hardly religion at all."

Few of the people of the Oregon settlements were joining churches, but they gave many other signs of religiousness. The pattern of Oregon may well be the pattern of the western United States. "[E]xcept in Mormon territory, the majority of far westerners have cared little about traditional religious institutions and practices," the historian Eldon G. Ernst put it. "They form the most secular society in the United States if gauged by church membership statistics, yet when questioned they claim to be religiously concerned and find religion to be important in their personal lives."

We return to the common difficulty faced by anyone exploring this topic: in its subjectivity and privacy, religious belief is very hard to track. A few groups — Indians, missionaries, and Mormons — have made the task easier: for all their differences, these groups were believers who consistently and visibly demonstrated their faith in frequent public rituals, steering by religious principles in everyday activities. Whether the ritual was a dance, a hymn, or a ward-house meeting, whether the consecrated activity was hunting, teaching, or irrigated farming, Indians, missionaries, and Mormons placed their faith front and center, where no one could miss it. Thus, western historians fell into a perfectly logical habit of confining the explicit discussion of religion to topics where it simply could not be avoided. For all the other westerners — for the sizable numbers who were *not* Indians, *not* missionaries, and *not* Mormons — the most resolutely secular history is all they seemed to deserve, and generally all they got.

The fact that American westward expansion was so strongly governed by economic motives reinforced the apparent wisdom of this strategy of reserving religious history for the few, and leaving secular history for the majority. The daily experience of overland travel during the gold rush had many of the qualities of a sacred pilgrimage, testing determination and persistence in a thousand ways. But a journey undertaken as a tribute to Mammon surrendered its credentials as pilgrimage. Fervent participation in mineral rushes and land rushes, in timber booms and cattle speculation deepened the impression that the determination of white Americans to develop the West's natural resources left very little room for the development of their souls. Often invoked in support of these expanding commercial enterprises, God's name looked as if it had become little more than another product endorsement.

Consider, as a striking example of this linkage of religion with commerce, the memorable song "The Cowboy's Prayer":

Lord, please help me, lend me Thine ear,
The prayer of a troubled cowman to hear.
No doubt my prayer to you may seem strange,
But I want you to bless my cattle range. . . .

As you O Lord my fine herds behold,
They represent a sack of pure gold.
I think that at least five cents on the pound
Would be a good price for beef the year round.

When God was asked to intervene on behalf of rising cattle prices, the theological seemed to have made a full surrender to the secular. But then again, when whites asked God to bless their economic undertakings, was this *entirely* different from an Indian hunter's hope that the right gestures of respect would recruit the spirits as the sponsors of a successful hunt? Didn't both practices serve as examples of a people's refusal to draw a hard line between the spiritual and the worldly? If God wanted the best for His Chosen People, wouldn't He *want* them to prosper in the cattle market?

In 1973, my husband and I were driving west, crossing the country on yet another secular pilgrimage. Through the journey, we had invested a great deal in the services of auto mechanics, purchasing, among other things, an entire replacement engine for our VW Bug. We were not entirely sure that we had enough money left to get to California. On a Sunday morning, we turned on the radio and found an evangelist in the middle of a prayer that spoke directly to our dilemma: "Lord," the evangelist asked, "heal our families; heal our hearts; and heal our finances." When my father wired us money in Laramie, we felt that prayer had been heard.

WESTWARD THE COURSE OF CHAOS TAKES ITS WAY

The year after I parted with the First Baptist Church, a remarkable event occurred in the demography of Banning, California. A bunch of kids appeared out of nowhere. Banning was a town of eight or nine thousand people, and I thought I knew most of them; I certainly knew the ones around my own age. But when we left the sixth grade at Central Elementary School and moved on to the seventh grade at Susan B. Coombs Junior High School, some fifteen or twenty strangers joined us. Had a large caravan of families all moved to town over the summer? On the contrary, and very mysteriously, the strangers claimed that they had lived in Banning most, in some cases all, of their lives. But where had they been? How had they stayed hidden all those years?

The strangers were, it turned out, Catholics. They had been hidden in parochial school, but parochial school — whatever that was — ended in sixth grade, and so now they were out of hiding. The term "Mormon" I understood, but "Catholic"? Or, even more puzzling, "Jew"? In the First Baptist Sunday School, our education on that particular topic had been *very* brief. One of the children had said to the Sunday school teacher, "We keep seeing the word 'Jew' in the Bible, but we don't know what it means." The teacher looked unhappy, and then seized on her way out. "You all know Jeff," she said, pointing to one member of the class. "Jeff used to be a Jew, but now he's a Baptist."

The extent of my Sunday school teacher's — and my — ignorance in these matters was at a cosmic scale, and quite surprising, given the West's great history of religious diversity. This diversity represented the realization of the worst fears of many Protestants in the nineteenth-century West. Protestant clergymen in the West confronted a region in which every moment in daily life told them that they were working against a great disadvantage. White American Protestants in the nineteenth-century West knew that they were outnumbered. They knew that they had before them a long struggle to find a permanent place in a society in which neither Episcopalians nor Baptists, Presbyterians nor Congregationalists could dominate. In many western areas, Catholics and Mormons had gotten the jump in timing, as well as in membership, on Protestants of any denomination. Jews were early arrivals in many western settlements. At the same time, American Indian religions and the Buddhism, Taoism, and Confucianism of Asian immigrants stretched the categories of faith along an extraordinarily wide continuum. In the nineteenth-century West, as historian Ferenc Szasz has written, the mainline Protestant groups "confronted the greatest challenge of their day: dealing with religious diversity." Several decades before their counterparts in the eastern United States would come to face a comparable challenge, western Protestant ministers "dealt with pluralism on a daily basis." In religious terms, the West was the American future.

For many of those getting an advance look at this future, religious pluralism proved to be fruitful soil for discomfort and doubt. Where we might see an extraordinary and fascinating mosaic of religious practice, the Protestant ministers were more inclined to see chaos, and dangerous chaos at that. Take the concerns and worries recorded by the Reverend Josiah Strong. After two years' service as a Congregationalist minister in Cheyenne, Wyoming, the reverend came down with a pronounced case of western Protestant anxiety. The West, he wrote in his book *Our Country* (1886), was "peculiarly exposed" to the principal "dangers" of the times: "Mammonism, materialism, luxuriousness, and the centralization of wealth." The region was particularly burdened, as well, with the threats posed by socialism, the saloon, Mormonism, Catholicism, and foreign immigration. Not only were the dangers greatest in the West, the Protestant churches were at their weakest, ill-equipped to respond to any of these challenges.

If this was a region in which all its enemies ganged up on Protestant Christianity, might the good news be that the region's sparse population rendered its religious condition irrelevant to the nation's well-being? On the contrary: in Rev. Josiah Strong's judgment, the West determined the national future. With its vast resources, ready to support an equally sizable population, the West "is to dominate the East"; in the near future, "the West will direct the policy of the Government, and by virtue of her preponderating population and influence will determine our national character and, therefore, destiny."

If Protestant Christianity could not save the West, then nothing could save the nation. And the stakes went considerably beyond the national. In the reverend's vision, the settling of the American West would be only one test of the Anglo-Saxon's "instinct or genius for colonizing," a genius that would finally work its way around the entire planet in *"the final competition of races, for which the Anglo-Saxon is being schooled* [his emphasis]." Through the religious challenge posed by the American West, "God was training the Anglo-Saxon race for an hour sure to come in the world's future."

Full of distrust for European immigrants, for Mormons, and for New Mexican Hispanics, Rev. Josiah Strong nonetheless reserved his greatest distrust for the actions and beliefs of his fellow Anglo-Saxons, those "church-members who seem to have left their religion behind when they crossed the Missouri." Of course, the reverend would worry about all those "others," but it is, at first, a surprise to see how doubtful he was about the religious reliability of his fellow whites. Given the continued status of the West as the nation's unchurched region, he was right to be worried. My father and I, and our many disaffiliated fellow westerners, are the reverend's worst nightmare come true.

In the intervening century, few writers have been able to produce texts that can match *Our Country* in its remarkable mixture of confidence and doubt. In the space of a few pages, Rev. Josiah Strong could shift from a cosmic confidence in Anglo-Saxon destiny to rule the world and to install God's kingdom in the process to a dark vision of a West soon to collapse before the pressures of evil and disorder. How could he be at once so confident and so anxious? The paradox here was a great one. On the ground level the American West had the greatest religious diversity of any part of the nation, and the heightened anxiety of the nineteenth-century Protestant clergy testified to the challenge posed by that diversity. And yet, in the broader sweep of history, expansion into the American West seemed to have shown white American religious belief at its most homogeneous, combining a Christian sense of mission with patriotism to form a virtual state religion. Faith in the United States' Manifest Destiny had long ago melted the division between the sacred and the secular. And yet, by a considerable irony, when Protestant fervor merged into national policy, it ended up producing the region in which Protestant denominations had their weakest hold.

Whites had an indisputable claim on the West, Senator Thomas Hart Benton had said, because they used the land "according to the intentions of the CREATOR." As historian Albert Weinberg observed, "[T]heological literature was scarcely more abundant in reference to Providence than was the literature of expansionism." To one typical expansionist during the Mexican-American War, war was "the religious execution of our country's glorious mission, under the direction of Divine Providence, to civilize and christianize, and raise up from anarchy and degradation a most ignorant, indolent, wicked and unhappy people." And yet one outcome of this enterprise was not the redemption of the Mexican people, but the slide into religious "anarchy and degradation" of many of the Americans who were supposed to be the agents of the West's redemption. As William Jennings Bryan put it after the start of the Philippine insurrection, "'Destiny' is not as manifest as it was" a while ago.

THE *KIVA* IN MY SOUL

In New Mexico, it was never possible to draw a firm border between the secular and the sacred. For centuries, Indian religious belief erased any line between faith and worldly activity. In the Spanish colonization of the sixteenth and seventeenth centuries, missionaries played a role in conquest as important as, if not more important than, the role of soldiers. For the Spanish, religious motives came interwoven with economic and political motives; even when governors fought with friars for the control of colonies, those struggles dramatized the central role that religion played in the whole undertaking. In the nineteenth century, when white Americans entered the scene, Protestant disapproval of Catholicism added to the contest over land and labor and to the frictions of nationality and race. In the history unrolling in New Mexico, religious belief had been everywhere, shaping and being shaped by even the most secular elements of human thought and behavior.

In the summer of 1992, Santa Fe — the town called "Holy Faith" — permitted me a memorable visit to the blurred border between the secular and the sacred. I was meeting with a group of international scholars studying American regionalism. From Senegal to Thailand, from Belgium to the Philippines, all of my companions had grown up watching western movies, and watching them with feelings that bordered on reverence. No conventionally religious mission society, one could learn from the testimony of these visitors, has ever come close to matching the achievements of the Hollywood western in global proselytizing and conversion.

On our last day of class, the participants were having a competition to see who had been the most influenced or tainted by the Wild West myth. We had heard a number of eloquent statements from men whose childhoods had included frequent visits to "Old West" tourist towns in Germany and Austria, where they had cheerfully fired away at the Indian targets in shooting galleries. Then a woman from Poland suddenly and urgently announced her candidacy as the most mythically influenced. "The first thing I can remember," she told us, "is my father reading to me from Karl May's western novels. As soon as I could read, I read them for myself. I loved old Shatterhand, and even after I saw a movie with a fat Frenchman playing his part, my love for him did not change. You may tell me they are factually wrong, but Karl May's novels are . . ." Here she paused and searched for the right word, seizing on a term she had learned the day before during a tour of a pueblo. "Karl May's novels," she ended, with the right word firmly grasped, "are the *kiva* in my soul."

Here was yet another piece of testimony from Santa Fe, reminding me of the hopelessness of trying to separate faith from worldly fact in western America. Once again, Santa Fe offered a reminder that of all the places on the planet where the sacred and the secular meet, the American West is one of the hot spots. One could argue (as indeed one had, and at length) that the vision of the West as a romantic place, where strong and good men went down to Main Street or out to the wilderness to take their courageous stands, held little connection to historical fact. And yet, if Karl May's western fantasies had provided a spiritual and emotional sanctuary for a young woman growing up in Poland in tough times, then we were clearly talking about a realm of belief out of reach of historical fact checking.

Episcopal worshipers, Wichita, Kansas

Trained in movie theaters in Senegal or Thailand, New York City or Denver, the human spirit has developed the conditioned response of soaring when it confronts certain images: horses galloping across open spaces; wagon trains moving through a landscape of mesas and mountains; cruel enemies and agents of disorder defeated by handsome white men with nerves of steel and tremendous — and justified — self-esteem. And when the human spirit undertakes to soar, it is not necessarily the obligation of the historian to act as air traffic controller and force the spirit down for a landing. Improbable as it may seem to the prosaic historian, an imagined and factually unsubstantiated version of western American history has become, for many believers, a sacred story. For those believers, a challenge to that story can count as sacrilege.

In American life today, lots of groups have made a heavy emotional investment in the proposition that history is a sacred, not a secular, tale. The best and clearest example of this comes from the Mormons. In the last few years, historians who are Mormon believers but who try to write searchingly and critically about Mormon history have had a rough time. Some of them have been excommunicated for their failure to write what the church's General Authorities call faith-affirming history. But the pattern seen among the Mormons appears everywhere. Consider, for instance, how similar the Mormon call for faith-affirming history is to the Afro-centric call for a history of African-American people that consistently praises their accomplishments and affirms their self-esteem. Or consider the desire, on the part of some American Indian people, for a writing of Indian history that enshrines Indian people as ecological and environmental saints and traces an unbroken line of nobility and solidarity among tribal people. When white politicians condemn "revisionist" or "multicultural" history and call for a narrative of the past that affirms the achievements and virtues of white Americans, those politicians show a striking kinship to the Afro-centric intellectuals and to the General Authorities of the Mormon Church. *Everyone* wants faith-affirming history; the disagreement is just a question of which faith any particular individual wants to see affirmed. Each group wants history to provide guidance, legitimacy, justification, and direction for its particular chosen people.

These contests over history, often focused on the West, resemble and echo more familiar contests over religious faith. Different versions of history have become creation stories or origin stories for the people who treasure them, and, with so much feeling at stake, the clash between these sacred tales grows increasingly bitter. And yet, while these separate and contesting claims on history proliferate, more and more evidence emerges from the historical record to counter these assertions of exclusivity. Explorations of western American history reveal many examples of unexpected kinship, mixed heritage, cultural trading, syncretism, and borrowing. It is not simply a matter of the blending of the West's people through intermarriage, though this is certainly an enormous part of the region's story. It is also a matter of reciprocal influence and mutual assimilation. The various peoples of the American West have been bumping into each other for an awfully long time, and it cannot be a surprise to discover that their habits and beliefs have rubbed off on each other.

Indian religious movements — from the ghost dance to the Native American Church with its use of peyote — show many Christian elements. Perhaps the best example of this complexity in religious identity is the Lakota religious leader Black Elk. Thanks to the writer John G. Neihardt's telling of his life story in *Black Elk Speaks,* Black Elk came to stand for the most traditional practice of Indian religion, a practice brought to a tragic end by conquest. But his daughter, Lucy Black Elk Looks Twice, hoped to correct and deepen the standing image of her father, and, working with the anthropologist Michael Steltencamp, Lucy told the post-conquest story of Nicholas Black Elk, who became a leading Catholic convert and cathechist on his reservation. This was not a matter of Black Elk "selling out" or betraying his traditional beliefs; this was a matter of sincere religious conviction responding to new beliefs in new times.

In the nineteenth-century West, white Americans had denounced the religions of the "others," labeling other systems of belief as paganism, heathenism, superstition, barbarism, or savagery, and struggling to convert American Indians and Asian immigrants to Protestant Christianity. In the late-twentieth-century West, the tide seems to be reversing, as a number of white Americans have developed an enthusiasm for tribal religions, as well as for the varieties of Asian Buddhism. Particularly well represented in the West, "New Age" religion has appropriated pieces and parts of American Indian religions, with both Indian and white claimants to enlightenment, in the familiar area of overlap between commerce and religion, cashing in on the opportunities so presented. Rev. Josiah Strong and his colleagues were presumably tossing in their graves, but all over the West, the lines dividing the vision quest from communion, the *kiva* from the church, were shifting and wavering.

DREAM OTHER DREAMS, AND BETTER

To many white Americans in our times, belief in the mythic Old West has come to resemble belief in more conventional religious doctrines. For these believers, the Old Frontier is the nation's creation story, the place where the virtues and values of the nation were formed. And yet, for all the faith now invested in it, the mythic version of the Old West had little room for ministers and pastors, congregations and parishes. In a story full of cowboys, sheriffs, saloon girls, outlaws, gunfighters, prospectors, and stagecoach drivers, the church was, at best, the place where the frightened townspeople gathered to sing hymns and await rescue by the all-too-worldly hero. The church, after all, was aligned with the forces of respectability, the forces that would eventually tame the Wild West and end all the fun and adventure of the glory days. If one went in search of the classic heroes in the mythic turf of the Old West, one would not bother to look among the clergy.

In the quest for western heroes, there is good reason now to look in unexpected, less explored places. The old heroes are a pretty battered and discredited lot, with their character flaws on permanent display. The examples they provide often affirm the wrong faith entirely — the faith in guns and violence — or serve solely as individual examples of courage and determination, attached to no particular principle. Driven by the values of conquest and domination, or purely by the goal of personal fortune-seeking, the old heroes are looking pretty tired — depleted, exhausted, and ready for retirement. In truth, they deserve a rest.

Chinese American congregation, California

And yet, when the critics of academic historians say that we have discredited the old heroes and failed to replace them with any new ones, they are right. But this is not because we lack the resources. We have all the material we need to put forward a better team, people whose examples affirm a faith of considerably greater promise. It is time for a different kind of western hero: the sustainable hero who can replace the old, exhausted, and depleted western heroes. As Wallace Stegner said of the old western myths, "dream other dreams, and better."

Sustainability in a hero means, very concretely, providing inspiration that sustains the spirit and the soul. While inconsistency can disqualify a conventional hero, a degree of inconsistency is one of the essential qualifications of a sustainable hero. Models of sustainable heroism are drawn from the record of people doing the right thing *some of the time* — people practicing heroism at a level that we can actually aspire to match. The fact that these people fell, periodically, off the high ground of heroism but then determinedly climbed back, even if only in order to fall again, is exactly what makes their heroism sustainable. Because it is uneven and broken, this kind of heroism is resilient, credible, possible, reachable. Sustainable heroism comes only in moments and glimpses, but they are moments and glimpses in which the universe lights up.

Assigned in 1867 to preside over the vast district of Montana, Idaho, and Utah, Bishop Daniel Tuttle "traveled more than forty thousand miles" by stagecoach. "Most times I enjoyed that mode of traveling," he remembered, "many times I grimly endured it, a few times I was rendered miserable by it." Think about what it meant to ride with strangers for hours and hours, jammed into an inflexible, jostling container, and the fact that Bishop Tuttle kept his temper and most of the time enjoyed the ride is its own measure of sustainable heroism.

While misery most often derived from the rough road conditions or the inadequacy of stagecoach shock-protection, fellow passengers could sometimes match the bumps in the road in their power to annoy. In one case, a fellow passenger "by manner and act was insulting to a colored woman in the coach." Bishop Tuttle firmly "reproved him." When words proved insufficient and the passenger "repeated the offense," Tuttle reported, "I shook him soundly." If this demonstration of muscular Christianity failed to produce a conversion, it still made for a happier ride. "At the next station," the offender "got out and slunk entirely away from our sight."

Bishop Tuttle was a complicated man, full of self-righteous disapproval in his appraisal of Mormon belief and earnestly committed to the growth of his denomination. But when Bishop Tuttle took his stand on behalf of the right of African-American women to travel with dignity, he offered a memorable demonstration of sustainable heroism, an episode in faith-affirming history for those trying to hold on to a belief in an American commitment to justice and fairness.

And then there is the remarkable example of heroism set by Rev. Howard Thurman. An African-American who was the chaplain at Howard University, he headed west to team up with a white man as co-pastor of a new and courageous church. As a young child, he had attended his father's funeral and listened to a preacher condemn his father as an example of an unredeemed, unchurched sinner. Ever since then, Thurman had been on a campaign against exclusivity in Christian practice, fighting the exclusivity of the smugly saved as persistently as he fought the exclusivity of race. When he learned of an effort to form a church in San Francisco uniting people of all races and backgrounds, he felt called. The year was 1943, more than ten years before the Montgomery, Alabama, bus boycott.

The location and the timing were both crucial. "Segregation of the races," Thurman wrote, "was a part of the mores, and of the social behavior of the country." "San Francisco with its varied nationalities, its rich intercultural heritages, and its face resolutely fixed toward the Orient" was the ideal place to undertake a trial run toward a better future in American race relations. War work had brought a much increased black population to San Francisco and heightened the prospects of community friction. Responding to these challenges, an interracial group had decided to form the Church for the Fellowship of All Peoples, and Thurman joined them, following his quest to find out "whether or not it is true that experiences of spiritual unity and fellowship are more compelling than the fears and dogmas and prejudices that separate men." There was considerable risk, financial and otherwise, in the "mission" that brought him and his family "three thousand miles across the continent." And there were constant tests of the spirit, as the Fellowship Church and its founder faced the prospects of sponsoring interracial marriages and other challenges to the social order. Simply visiting a member of the congregation in the hospital could prove to be a test of Thurman's spirit; hospital staffs repeatedly stumbled over and resisted the notion that a white believer could be in the care of a black pastor.

Fellowship Church under Rev. Howard Thurman's leadership proved to be a great success, navigating its way through the difficult divisions between denominations as well as those between races. In God's presence, Thurman always insisted, "the worshiper is neither male nor female, black nor white, Protestant nor Catholic nor Buddhist nor Hindu, but a human spirit laid bare." "Religious experience," he believed — and he had lived this gospel — "must unite rather than divide men."

The examples set by heroes like Bishop Tuttle and Reverend Thurman encourage me to believe in the real American West, a place — in the past and in the present — of dazzling human and natural possibility. Believing in the other West, the mythic and imagined West, has never been much of an option for me. Instead, the very notion of investing any faith in a simple, romantic, glorified West always brought to mind the verse that I learned from my father when I was very young:

> With this bright, believing band,
> I have no claim to be.
> What seems so true to them,
> Seems fantasy to me.

This verse has kept me on course in the company of those who have fallen head over heels in love with a western illusion; and yet, in the presence of more traditional religious believers, it gives me much less comfort. The company of people secure in their faith, whether that faith is a tribal religion, Catholicism, Judaism, Mormonism, or a Protestant denomination, can make me melt with envy. But then the verse — "With this bright, believing band, I have no claim to be" — comes to mind and interrupts the melting. I remain a member of a battered, disorganized, but still pretty bright, believing band of my own, churched and unchurched, composed of all races and backgrounds — people who hold on to a faith that fairness and justice might someday prevail in this region and in this nation. That faith, the faith of my father and my mother, of Bishop Tuttle and Reverend Thurman, is the *kiva* in my soul.

The Union Pacific works its way past Citadel Rock on the Green River in Wyoming Territory, 1868. Work trains like the one shown here ran over a temporary wooden bridge until the permanent one under construction below could be completed.

CHAPTER FIVE

THE GRANDEST ENTERPRISE UNDER GOD

1865–1874

With North and South reunited, Americans were free to move west as they never had been before. Settlers from around the world would soon be stepping off at Red Cloud and Lone Tree and Broken Bow and starting to sow foreign strains of wheat in rich, matted prairie soil that had never known anything but grass. Hundreds of thousands of lean, long-horned cattle would be driven north from Texas and shipped to eastern markets — and the dusty, saddle-sore men who herded them would be transformed into the idols of every eastern schoolchild. Isolated outposts would change overnight into raucous boomtowns, and buffalo hunters would swarm onto the Great Plains and drive the animal that sustained its native peoples to the brink of extinction. The railroads would make it all possible. But first, someone had to build them.

The dreamer: Theodore Judah, photographed when he still believed the transcontinental railroad would one day make him rich. "I have always had to pit my brains . . . against other men's money . . . ," he boasted to his wife. But in the end, other men's money would win.

Railroads had already transformed life in the East, but at the end of the Civil War the rails still stopped at the Missouri. Without them, the development of the West could proceed only slowly. To make the region's mines and forests, farms and ranches pay, westerners needed a transportation system that could dependably haul great loads over long distances.

Americans had been calling for a line all the way across the continent for half a century. In 1817 — eleven years before the first mile of American track was laid — a New Yorker named Robert Mills was already urging that a railroad be built between the headwaters of the Mississippi and Oregon Territory. Thomas Hart Benton, Stephen A. Douglas, and other western politicians had built whole careers on the bright promise of linking the coasts by rail. It would help people the West, they argued, and it would provide a direct route to the Orient, ending Europe's domination of trade with the Far East. "America will be between Asia and Europe," wrote John C. Frémont, "the golden vein which runs through the history of the world will follow the track to San Francisco, and the Asiatic trade will finally fall into its last and permanent road."

But no lines could be built without congressional permission to cross federal land, and no man — or combination of men — was rich enough to undertake such a vast enterprise without massive federal loans and grants of land. Before the war, Secretary of War Jefferson Davis had dispatched teams of topographical engineers to survey five possible routes, but bitter sectional quarrels over which one should be followed had kept Congress from choosing one, let alone voting for either land or loans with which actual construction could begin. Now, the South could no longer block legislation, and in 1862 lobbyists descended on Washington with valises full of schemes.

None had more of them than a California railroad man named Theodore Judah. For more than a decade, he had talked about building a transcontinental railroad with such obsessive fervor that behind his back people called him "Crazy Judah." Born in New England and mad about trains since boyhood, he had laid tracks through the Niagara River gorge in New York State and persuaded himself that laying them through the western mountains would be only a little more difficult. He built California's first line, the Sacramento Valley Railroad, hoping that it might become the first leg of a transcontinental railway, and when that dream died for lack of funds, refused to be discouraged. He made twenty-four lonely mule-back forays into the Sierras in search of a likely route through the mountains before settling on the Donner and Emigrant passes that had first brought Americans into California. Then he set up a paper line called the Central Pacific with himself as chief engineer, and began stumping the state in search of investors.

He found no takers in San Francisco, the financial capital of the West. No such thing as a transcontinental railroad had ever been attempted anywhere — some 1,780 miles of track would have to be laid from Sacramento to Omaha. Fifteen tunnels would have to be cut through mountains higher than any railroad builder had ever faced, while, beyond the Sierras, a roadbed would have to be made across deserts where there was no water for the crews and treeless prairies where Indians were sure to resist their passage.

Then, one June evening in 1861, Judah finally found four Sacramento merchants willing to put up enough money to get started at least. They were Leland Stanford, a grocer with political ambitions (he would be elected California's first Republican governor that November), Charles Crocker, a dry goods merchant and sometime Republican legislator, and Mark Hopkins and Collis P. Huntington, who together owned the hardware store above which the businessmen met.

With their backing — and armed with $100,000 in company stock earmarked for distribution among pliant legislators — Judah hurried to Washington to do all he could to influence the nonpartisan Pacific Railroad Act about to emerge from Congress at last. Few lobbyists in American history can have been more effective: he managed to make himself clerk to both the House and Senate committees that were to

The Sacramento hardware store at 54 K Street above which, just a few weeks after the Civil War began, Theodore Judah talked four storekeepers into investing in his Central Pacific Railroad

The great Pacific Railway is commenced. . . . Immigration will soon pour into these valleys. Ten millions of emigrants will settle in this golden land in twenty years. . . . This is the grandest enterprise under God!

George Francis Train

Labor and management: Union Pacific surveyors (opposite) claw their way up a Wyoming rock face in search of the best line along which the track gangs would lay the rails, while the directors of their railroad (above) confer in the quiet comfort of their private car. Seated, from left to right: Silas Seymour, Sidney Dillon, Thomas C. Durant (who oversaw the financing of the road's construction), and John Duff.

draft the final bill, and not surprisingly, his Central Pacific was awarded the contract to build through the Sierras when it was enacted on June 20, 1862. Meanwhile, an eastern-based line, the Union Pacific, was to start from the one hundredth meridian in Missouri, cross the Great Plains, and cut through the Rockies.

The point at which the two lines were to meet was not designated; from the first, the two companies would be in a race to see who could lay the most track — and therefore make the most money. Each railroad was to receive 6,400 acres of federal land laid out in checkerboard parcels on either side of the tracks for every mile completed, plus vast loans from the treasury as they went along — $16,000 per mile of level track, $32,000 across the plateaus, $48,000 per mile in the mountains.

Both lines resorted to some singularly creative financing in order to get going. The officers of the Union Pacific set up a holding company, the *Crédit Mobilier* of America, through which they siphoned into their own pockets the funds for building their line, and then bought congressmen wholesale to ensure that no one objected. The *Crédit Mobilier*, wrote the reformer Charles Francis Adams, Jr., "is another name for the Pacific Railroad Ring. The members of it are in Congress; they are trustees of the bondholders; they are contractors; in Washington they vote the subsidies, in New

York they receive them, upon the plains they expend them. . . . Ever-shifting characters, they are ubiquitous; they receive money into one hand and pay it into the other. . . ."

Meanwhile, the Big Four made sure that not a penny of potential profits would escape them by awarding the Central Pacific construction contract to one of their number, Charles Crocker, despite the fact that he had no experience whatsoever building railroads and had never managed anything larger than a small Indiana iron foundry. (In the end, the partners would pay themselves some $90 million for work estimated actually to have cost about a third of that.) Using all of their political influence, they then persuaded a malleable state geologist named Josiah Whitney officially to declare the gently sloping Sacramento Valley a mountainous region so that the Central Pacific could collect the highest possible rate for laying track across it; Whitney dutifully ruled that the Sierras began abruptly to rise just seven miles from Sacramento, when the real distance was at least twenty-two miles.

Theodore Judah, who had proved himself a master manipulator in Washington, now objected to the way the Big Four were doing business, and in October of 1863 set out for New York by sea, determined to find enough Wall Street investors to buy them out. But he contracted yellow fever in Panama and was dying when his ship finally docked at New York on November 2, the same day construction began at Sacramento on the railroad that he had championed for so long.

That same year, the Union Pacific staged an elaborate ground-breaking ceremony at Omaha, meant to impress potential investors. Cannons were fired. Nebraska's governor spoke. A telegram from Abraham Lincoln was read. A shovelful of earth was turned. But the East was still preoccupied with the war. The Union Pacific managed to lay just forty miles of track before Appomattox.

But once the shooting stopped, the race began in earnest. Each line faced unique problems. The endless miles of prairie across which the Union Pacific had to lay its tracks provided neither timber for ties nor iron nor provisions, and at first, everything had to be shipped up the Missouri by boat, then hauled overland to the crews. And there was an understandable reluctance to venture too far too fast into the valley of the Platte, which vengeful Cheyenne and Arapaho and Lakota had virtually swept clean of white settlement after the massacre at Sand Creek. A newspaperman who traveled along just thirty miles of the proposed roadbed through Nebraska claimed to have counted "ninety-three graves; no less than twenty-seven of which contain the bodies of settlers killed within the past six weeks. Dead bodies have been seen floating down the Platte."

Indians were soon attacking railroad men, as well — picking off surveyors, graders, whole section gangs. Many years later, a Cheyenne warrior named Porcupine recalled an encounter near the town of Plum Creek in Nebraska Territory:

General Grenville Dodge (above), chief engineer and surveyor of the Union Pacific, and some of the Shoshone and Pawnee (opposite) he hired to help guard his crews against their common enemies, the Cheyenne and the Arapaho, 1868

> We were feeling angry. . . . We looked at [the train] from a high ridge. Far off it was very small, but it kept coming and growing larger all the time, puffing out smoke and steam; and as it came on, we said to each other that it looked like a white man's pipe when he was smoking. . . . After we had seen this train and watched it come near us and grow large and pass by and then disappear . . . we went down . . . to see what sort of trail it made. . . .
>
> . . . [W]e said among ourselves: "Now the white people have taken all we had and have made us poor and we ought to do something. In these big wagons that go on this metal road, there must be things that are valuable — perhaps clothing. If we could throw these wagons off the iron they run on and break them open, we should find out what was in them and could take whatever might be useful to us."
>
> Red Wolf and I tried to do this. We got a big stick, and just before sundown one day tied it to the rails and sat down to watch and see what would happen. Close by the track we built a big fire. Quite a long time after it got dark we heard a rumbling sound.

A handcar was approaching in the dark. Six men were aboard, returning from a day spent repairing telegraph wires. They began pumping furiously when they saw the fire and the shadowy figures of the Cheyenne waiting alongside the track. They never saw the log.

"When the car struck the stick it jumped high in the air," Porcupine remembered. "The men got up from where they had fallen and ran away." The Cheyenne killed five of them instantly. The sixth man, a Briton named William Thompson, got a bullet through his arm before a warrior rode him down, stabbed him in the neck, then began methodically to saw off his scalp while Thompson, fully conscious, did his best to seem dead.

The Cheyenne, delighted with their success, then spied the distant light of an approaching freight. They pried up the rails and waited. The train, too, jumped the track. Two crewmen were killed. As the warriors began to loot and burn the boxcars, Thompson managed to stagger to his feet and set out along the tracks for the nearest railhead, pausing just long enough to pick up his own scalp, evidently mislaid in the excitement of derailing the train by the warrior who'd taken it.

Thompson eventually made it to safety and was carried to Omaha by rail, along with the charred bodies of the derailed train's engineer and fireman. His scalp rode beside him in a bucket of water; a reporter who saw it said it somewhat resembled "a drowned rat, as it floated, curled up. . . ."

HELL ON WHEELS

General Grenville M. Dodge was in overall command of getting the Union Pacific rolling. He was an ideal choice for the job, tough, resourceful, implacable. He had built railroads before the Civil War, rebuilt railroad bridges and southern lines to aid the northern army during it, and then had come west to fight Plains Indians. He armed his crews, hired Pawnee and Shoshone to help drive off their enemies, the Lakota and Cheyenne, and called for military protection; eventually, 5,000 troops would guard the line as it inched its way west.

He picked two tough red-bearded ex-soldiers, General Jack Casement and his brother, Dan, to be the construction bosses. Their crews were mostly Irish — immigrants from eastern slums, many of whom had fought for the Union in the Civil War and were eager for a second new start in the West — but they also included ex–Confederate soldiers, Mexicans and Germans, Englishmen and former slaves. There were some 10,000 men in all, an army of workmen moving across the plains with soldierly precision. First came the surveying parties — each with a chief engineer and his assistant, as well as rodmen, flagmen, chainmen, axmen, teamsters, hunters, and a military escort. Then came the location men, whose task it was to stake out the grades and curves, followed by the big grading crews, who worked well ahead of the tracklayers, getting everything ready.

Finally, the tracklaying could begin. A twenty-two-car work train housed and fed the men, who rose at dawn. A supply train nosed up behind it, carrying all the supplies needed that day — rails, ties, spikes, rods, fishplates — all of which had to be loaded onto flatcars and run up to the railhead where the "iron men" were already waiting.

Each rail weighed seven hundred pounds. Five men were needed to lift it off the flatcar and into place. Then, even before the men with the hammers drove the spikes all the way home, the flatcar rolled forward over the new rails so that the next ones could be unloaded and dropped into place. "It is a grand anvil chorus that these sturdy sledges are playing across the Plains," wrote an awed newspaperman. "It is in triple time, three strokes to a spike, four hundred rails to a mile, eighteen hundred miles to [California] — twenty-one million times are they to come down with their sharp punctuation before the great work of modern America is complete."

"The time is coming, and fast, too," one Union Pacific engineer noted in his diary, "when, in the sense it is now understood, THERE WILL BE NO WEST."

As the crews moved across the prairie, a movable city followed right along behind — hundreds of prostitutes, pimps, gamblers, saloon keepers, gunmen — "a carnivorous horde," one man recalled, "hungrier than the native grasshoppers" and eager to devour the men's weekly pay. The succession of base camps the Union Pacific built

Jack Casement, the ex-soldier who drove the Union Pacific crews, and one of his construction trains. Prefabricated parts of the portable town he carried with him are piled on top of the cars, ready to be set up farther down the track. The crews shown inset below are digging a tunnel near Echo Canyon (left) and constructing the footings for a permanent bridge across the Green River.

A light car, drawn by a single horse, gallops up to the front with its load of rails. Two men seize the end of a rail and start forward, the rest of the gang taking hold by twos until it is clear of the car. They come forward at a run. At the word of command, the rail is dropped into its place, right side up, with care, while the same process goes on on the other side of the car. Less than thirty seconds to a rail for each gang, and so four rails go down to the minute. . . .

William A. Bell

The steady progress Grenville Dodge (far left) hoped to make suffered every kind of interruption, including time-consuming visits by dignitaries. Here, at Fort Sanders in Dakota Territory, Generals Philip Sheridan (third from left), Ulysses Grant (at center, wearing straw hat), and William Tecumseh Sherman (framed by the doorway) and their entourages have all come to see how the great work is going. Grant, about to become the Republican nominee for president, also helped resolve a dispute between Dodge and Thomas Durant (sixth from right), who wanted to lengthen the line unnecessarily to augment company profits. Grant sided with Dodge.

roughly seventy miles apart each had a different name — Elk Horn, Fremont, Columbus, Grand Island, Kearney, Plum Creek, North Platte, O'Fallon's, Oglala, Julesburg, Sidney, Cheyenne, Sherman, Laramie, Rawlins, Bitter Creek, Green River — but the men called them all "Hell on Wheels."

Hundreds of workers contracted venereal disease. There were drunken brawls, shootings, knifings. The journalist Henry Morton Stanley took an after-dinner stroll through Julesburg in August of 1867:

> . . . At night new aspects are presented in this city of premature growth. Watch-fires gleam over the sea-like expanse of ground outside the city, while inside soldiers, herdsmen, teamsters, women, railroad men, are dancing, singing, or gambling. I verily believe that there are men here who would murder a fellow-creature for five dollars. Nay, there are men who have already done it, and who stalk abroad in daylight unwhipped of justice. Not a day passes but a dead body is found somewhere in the vicinity with pockets rifled of their contents. . . .

When things got too bad, Dodge dispatched Jack Casement and a band of two hundred armed men to clean things up. This, Dodge remembered, "was fun for Casement," and after a shoot-out in Julesburg he proudly showed his employer through the town's burgeoning cemetery: "General," he said, "they all died in their boots and Julesburg has been quiet ever since." Julesburg did quiet down. But the next base camp was already being banged together up ahead, and when the crews finally reached it, they would find Hell on Wheels waiting for them all over again.

I WANT THE GREAT FATHER TO MAKE NO ROADS

Red Cloud of the Oglala Lakota was no stranger to war. He had counted eighty coups in battle against the Crow, Pawnee, and Ute, and had earned himself a reputation for both daring and ferocity: his followers liked to recall the time he chased a Ute on a wounded horse into a river; when his quarry fell off his mount, Red Cloud rode into the fast-moving current, hauled him out by the hair, hacked off his scalp, then scornfully let the terrified warrior drop back into the water.

Now, he watched with growing anger as whites surveyed a wagon road through the Lakota country. It was meant to link the Oregon Trail with the new Montana mining towns of Bozeman and Virginia City, but it also threatened one of his people's favorite hunting grounds, the rolling foothills of the Bighorn Mountains along the Powder River. For him, the matter was simple:

> Whose voice was first sounded on this land? The voice of the red people who had but bows and arrows. . . . What has been done in my country I did not want, did not ask for it; white people going through my country. . . . When the white man comes in my country he leaves a trail of blood behind him. . . . I have two mountains in that country — the Black Hills and the Big Horn Mountain. I want the Great Father to make no roads through them.

When two whites seeking to map a route ventured too far into the hills, Red Cloud's warriors surrounded them, demanded their clothes and tools, then sent them running, naked, back toward the fort from which they'd come.

The Dale Creek Bridge on the western slope of the Black Hills epitomized the Union Pacific's somewhat casual attitude toward construction. A company engineer blithely suggested that "when the bridges shall decay," iron or rock should be substituted. "It strikes me," wrote a federal investigator, "that waiting for the bridge to decay would be rather hazardous. Its decay might . . . be discovered by its giving way under a train. . . . [It] is so fixed now that the unsuspecting passengers will not see their danger, nor know that the yawning chasm, granite-bottomed, into which they are plunging is one hundred and twenty feet deep!"

In the ripeness of time the hope of humanity is realized. . . . [This] continental railway . . . will bind the two seaboards to this one continental union like ears to the human head; [to plant] the foundation of the Union so broad and deep . . . that no possible force or stratagem can shake its permanence.

William Gilpin

Handsomely decorated and highly polished by its proud crew, Engine No. 23 waits at a short-lived Union Pacific depot called Wyoming Station, 1868.

Nº 23.

In June of 1866, Red Cloud and several other Lakota leaders were called to Fort Laramie to discuss a new treaty aimed at persuading the Sioux to permit the road to be built. If they would permit safe passage along it, the commissioners promised, the Indians would be given presents and permitted to hunt in peace, as they always had. The talks went cordially enough until a battalion of seven hundred infantrymen arrived unexpectedly under Colonel Henry R. Carrington; he already had orders to protect whites traveling along a road that had not yet officially been begun. Red Cloud felt betrayed: the government clearly planned to have its road, whether or not the Lakota agreed. He angrily denounced the commissioners for "treating the assembled chiefs as children," an eyewitness recalled. The whites were "pretending to negotiate for a country which they had already taken by Conquest. . . .

> [H]e told them that the white men had crowded the Indians back year by year and forced them to live in a small country north of the Platte and now their last hunting ground, the home of their people was to be taken from them. This meant that they and their women and children were to starve, and for his part he preferred to die fighting rather than by starvation. . . . [If] the combined tribes would defend their homes they would be able to drive the soldiers out of their country.

Hear me, Lakotas . . . before the ashes of the council fire are cold, the Great Father is building his forts among us. You have heard the sound of the white soldiers' ax upon the Little Piney. His presence here is an insult and a threat. It is an insult to the spirits of our ancestors. Are we to give up their sacred grounds to be plowed for corn? Lakotas, I am for war.

Red Cloud

Some Lakota leaders who thought resistance futile or who lived south of the Platte and therefore had little interest in the Powder River country signed the treaty anyway, in exchange for annuities of $70,000 every year for twenty years. Some Cheyenne signed, too.

But many Lakota, led by Red Cloud and Man-Afraid-of-His-Horses, refused to sign and rode off to the Powder River, determined to make life impossible for travelers and the soldiers sent to protect them. Cheyenne who had dared favor peace were made to suffer, too: when a band of Lakota chiefs came upon a group of warriors who had agreed to abandon the road to the soldiers, they beat them with the flat of their bows as a sign of their contempt.

Colonel Carrington succeeded in completing three forts along the proposed route before winter set in — Fort C. F. Smith on the Bighorn River in southern Montana, and Forts Reno and Phil Kearny in Wyoming. But Lakota and Cheyenne warriors raided his small, scattered force again and again, picking off stragglers, seizing supply wagons, driving off stock, attacking the men when they ventured out to cut hay or firewood.

Even inside Carrington's headquarters at Fort Phil Kearny some feared for their lives, an officer's wife named Mrs. Frances Grummond remembered:

> More than once the Sioux crawled up to the stockade covered with wolf skins and imitating the wolf cry, and on one occasion actually shot a sentry from his platform with an arrow that noiselessly pierced his heart.
>
> The organs of sight and hearing grew to be extremely acute in that dry and rarefied atmosphere, involving an almost overpowering sense of stillness, especially at night. . . . The sight of the daily wood-party leaving for their accustomed duty, the interval of anxious waiting, and the reassuring bugle notes signalizing their safe return. . . . No less [gratefully received] was the sentry's call at night, "All's well."

Red Cloud

But thirty-three-year-old Lt. Col. William J. Fetterman, a Civil War veteran, claimed to be unafraid. "Give me 80 good men," he said, "and I can ride through the whole Sioux nation." Four days before Christmas, a daring young Oglala named Crazy Horse led an attack on wagons bringing firewood back to the fort. Fetterman saw his chance: he asked Colonel Carrington for permission to ride to the rescue. His commander agreed, but carefully warned him not to allow himself to be drawn out of sight of the fort: "Support the wood train. Relieve it and report to me. Do not engage or pursue Indians at its expense. Under no circumstances pursue over Lodge Trail Ridge."

But not long after Fetterman led his men through the gate, Crazy Horse and a handful of companions appeared in the distance and began taunting the soldiers, waving blankets, shouting curses, even getting off their ponies and ostentatiously adjusting the bridles despite the army bullets that pattered all around them. Then they remounted and raced over the ridge. Fetterman galloped after them. On the far side, nearly 2,000 warriors were waiting for him — Lakota, Cheyenne, and a handful of Santee exiles from Minnesota.

Mrs. Grummond and the other women in the fort could not see the brief, furious battle that followed, but they could hear it: "A few shots were heard, followed up by increasing rapidity . . . a desperate fight was going on in the valley below the ridge . . . in the very place where the command was forbidden to go. Then followed a few quick volleys, then scattering shots, and then, dead silence. Less than half an hour had passed, and the silence was dreadful."

A nervous search party edged over the ridge late that afternoon and found Fetterman and his whole command dead, their bodies mutilated. Fetterman and his second-in-command lay close together. Each had been shot through the temple at close range. They had evidently killed one another rather than fall into Indian hands.

Private John Guthrie was among those who gathered up the dead:

> [We found] all the Fetterman boys huddled together on the small hill. . . . We packed them . . . on top of [the ammunition boxes in the wagons]. Terrible cuts left by Indians. Could not tell Cavalry from the Infantry. All dead bodies stripped naked, crushed skulls, with war clubs, ears, nose and legs had been cut off, scalps torn away and the bodies pierced with bullets and arrows, wrists, feet and ankles leaving each attached by a tendon. . . . Sergeant Baker of Company C 2nd Cavalry, a gunny sack over his head, not scalped, little finger cut off for a gold ring; Lee Bontee, the guide, body full of arrows which had to be broken off to load him. . . . We walked on their internals and did not know it in the high grass. Picked them up, that is their internals, did not know the soldier they belonged to, so you see the cavalry man got an infantry man's guts and an infantry man got a cavalry man's guts. . . .

Back at the fort, Mrs. Grummond remembered,

> [t]he ladies clustered in Mrs. Wand's cabin as night drew on, all speechless from absolute stagnation and terror. Then the crunching of wagon wheels startled us to our feet. The gates opened. Wagons were slowly driven within, bearing their dead but precious harvest from the field of blood and carrying . . . lifeless

One half of the headquarters building, which was my temporary home, was unfinished, and this part was utilized by carpenters for making pine cases for the dead. I knew that my husband's coffin was being made, and the sound of hammers and the grating of saws was torture. . . . My husband had a picture of myself in a choice setting that he always wore, and I have often wondered what Indian . . . has it now in his possession to wear as a trophy. . . .

Mrs. Frances Grummond

bodies to the hospital, with the heart-rending news, almost tenderly whispered by the soldiers themselves, that "*no more were to come in. . . .*"

On the central Plains, the celebrated soldiers who only recently had defeated the Confederacy weren't doing much better. Winfield Scott Hancock — "Hancock the superb," who had broken Pickett's charge at Gettysburg — was in overall command with orders to drive the Cheyenne from Kansas and Nebraska. He was a tenacious soldier, but he knew nothing about Indian warfare. In four months of frustrating patrolling, his men managed to kill precisely two Indians. Meanwhile, the Cheyenne they were trying to find killed better than two hundred white settlers.

Conspicuous among Hancock's commanders was another hero of the Civil War, George Armstrong Custer. An Ohio blacksmith's son, impulsive and high-spirited, charming but self-absorbed, he had just scraped through West Point, accumulating 726 demerits and graduating last in his class. "It was all right with him," a classmate remembered, "whether he knew his lessons or not; he did not allow it to trouble him." And he was an unlikely-looking soldier: his hair swept to his shoulders in golden ringlets, he carried a toothbrush in his jacket pocket so that, no matter what was going on around him, he could polish his gleaming teeth after every meal, and he had worn into battle a gaudy uniform of his own design — Confederate hat, red kerchief, velveteen jacket, and trousers decorated with gold lace.

But he was born for war. His judgment would often be called into question, but no one ever questioned his headlong courage. Again and again, he led the charge — at Bull Run, Gettysburg, Yellow Tavern, Winchester, Fisher's Hill, Five Forks — as though no bullet or saber could touch him. Eleven horses were shot from under Custer, and at twenty-three, he became the youngest general in the Union army, and perhaps its best-known divisional commander. Abraham Lincoln himself called Custer the man who "goes into a charge with a whoop and a shout," and his men — many of whom admired him so much that they, too, wore red kerchiefs into battle — also suffered some of the Union army's highest losses. And when, at the Grand Review, the great Washington parade that celebrated the war's end, three hundred admiring girls all dressed in blue showered him with blossoms and his horse bolted, he became the only man in the Union army to ride past the reviewing stand twice. "In the sunshine," a newspaperman wrote, "his locks, unskeined, stream[ed] a foot behind him. . . . It was like the charge of a Sioux chieftain."

His wife, Elizabeth — "Libbie" — was his match in charm and spirit and ambition. Lovely, well-educated, adoring but strong-minded, she was the daughter of an Ohio judge who took a dim view of soldiers in general and Custer in particular, and she had refused to marry him until he swore that he

George and Libbie Custer and their cook, Eliza, for whom the colonel would bring home a Cheyenne blanket as a souvenir of the battle of the Washita in 1868

would never drink — a promise he kept — and that he would never curse or gamble, either — pledges he largely ignored. She had stayed as close to his side as she could throughout the war, living in tents, farmhouses, boardinghouses just to be near him, and when he decided to stay in the army and go west to take command of the Seventh Cavalry afterward, she came, too, bringing with her to Fort Riley, Kansas, Custer's worshipful brother, Tom, a black cook, a serving boy, a pack of staghounds, and three blooded horses.

At first, Custer professed to love the West, and he designed for himself a new distinctively western costume, meant to catch the eye of visiting newspapermen. Indians especially admired it and, marveling at his curls, began to call him "Yellow Hair." And when he had important visitors he loved to put his men through their paces on the parade ground. One dazzled onlooker, Libbie Custer recalled, "kept turning to take in the rare sight, declaring that nothing in our prosaic nineteenth century was so like the days of chivalry, when some feudal lord went out to war or to the chase, followed by his retainers."

But the glory Custer assumed would once again be his as soon as he faced Indians in battle proved maddeningly elusive. Out hunting one day with his hounds, far from his column and in the heart of Indian country, he galloped after a buffalo, aimed his revolver — and somehow shot his own horse through the head. On foot, bruised and totally lost, he had to be rescued by his own men. Catching Indians was no easier. A Lakota warrior named Pawnee Killer and his band attacked Custer's column, stole several horses, and got away clean. After weeks of fruitless campaigning, forage and supplies failed to materialize. There were endless delays: "The inaction to which I am subjected now . . ." Custer wrote Libbie, "is almost unendurable." The pitiless prairie sun took a heavy toll on Custer's men and horses, and they began to desert in ones, twos, and threes. Then, thirteen troopers left camp together. Custer ordered them hunted down and shot. One was killed outright, two more were brought back wounded. For two days, Custer refused them medical attention. One subsequently died. Custer, Captain Albert Barnitz told his wife, was "the most complete example of a petty tyrant that I have ever seen. You would be filled with utter amazement, if I were to give you a few instances of his cruelty to the men and discourtesy to the officers."

Custer had been on the march for nearly two months with precious little to show for it when, inexplicably, he left most of his command behind and with a personal escort set off at a furious pace for Fort Riley, 275 miles away. When a favorite horse fell behind, he sent six men on worn-out mounts back to find it. Indians attacked them. One trooper was killed, another wounded and left for dead. Custer refused to go back for their bodies — and later blamed them for bringing about their own deaths. He would offer a number of contradictory excuses for this strange forced march, but the real reason seems to have been nothing more than a desperate desire to see his wife.

Custer was arrested, found guilty of "conduct prejudicial to good order and military discipline," and suspended from the service for a year. Libbie dismissed the verdict as "nothing but a plan of persecution" of her husband, the act of envious officers seeking to cover up the shortcomings of the Hancock campaign. The couple moved back East, to Michigan, where Custer did his best to forget his current disgrace by recalling earlier triumphs on other battlefields. "I am like Mr. Micawber," he wrote to a friend, "waiting for something to 'turn up,' meanwhile I am preparing . . . a memoir of my experiences from West Point to Appomattox. Arrangements for this are concluded with Messrs Harper & Brothers."

Sand Creek. The loss of Fetterman's whole command. Hancock's failed campaign. Clearly, something had gone terribly wrong with United States policy toward the Indians. General William Tecumseh Sherman, now in overall command of the army between Canada and Texas, the Mississippi and the Rockies, was neither a patient nor a sentimental man. Wars were to be won, enemies conquered, he believed, before there could ever be peace. He had helped destroy the Confederacy by acting upon those beliefs, and the blackened chimneys of hundreds of homes between Atlanta and the sea attested to his effectiveness against civilians of his own race. The peoples of the Plains could expect no gentler treatment. "I do not understand," he wrote to his friend General Ulysses S. Grant, "how the massacre of Colonel Fetterman's party could have been so complete. We must act with vindictive earnestness against the Sioux, even to their extermination, men, women and children. Nothing less will ever reach the root of the case."

Sherman took up his new duties with a deceptively simple plan: the Lakota were to be confined north of the Platte; the Arapaho, Cheyenne, and Comanche pushed south of the Arkansas. "This," he explained, "would leave for our people exclusively the use of the wide belt, east and west, between the Platte and the Arkansas, in which lie the two great railroads, and over which pass the bulk of travel to the mountain territories."

But Indian policy remained in the hands of the Interior Department, and for the moment, the advocates of less harsh treatment of the Indians seemed to have the upper hand. Memories of the Civil War were still fresh. Many voters found the soaring cost of hunting Indians without catching them absurd. Accordingly, in the late summer of 1867, a peace delegation headed west, empowered by Congress to remove the causes of war with the tribes, and pursue "the hitherto untried policy of conquering with kindness."

At Medicine Lodge Creek in Kansas, a new agreement was outlined to leaders of the southern Plains peoples — Cheyenne, Arapaho, Kiowa, Comanche. The Great Plains were no longer to be considered one great reservation through which they could roam and hunt as they always had. In exchange for agreeing to move out of the way of white settlement and onto reservations in what is now western Oklahoma, the tribes were to receive food and supplies for thirty years, as well as schools to teach them the white man's language and resident farmers to show them how to work the land.

One by one, the chiefs agreed to sign the treaty — Satank and Kicking Bird, Woman's Heart and Standing Bear of the Kiowa; Ten Bears, Silver Brooch, Horse Back, and Iron Mountain of the Comanche; Little Raven of the Arapaho; and the Cheyenne leaders, Bull Bear, Tall Bull, White Horse, Black Kettle. All were eager for a halt to years of sporadic violence and pleased by the gifts the commissioners distributed among them. But few fully understood what was being asked of them, and

Parley at Fort Laramie: Peace commissioners (left), including Generals William S. Harney (white beard) and William Tecumseh Sherman (seated next to Harney), came west in 1868 to seek an end to hostilities with the Cheyenne and the Lakota. Among the Indian leaders attending (opposite, from left) were Spotted Tail, Brulé Lakota; Roman Nose, Cheyenne; and Man-Afraid-of-His-Horses, Oglala Lakota, who is also shown above, smoking a ceremonial pipe.

fewer still could imagine abandoning their old ways. "I remember in particular one Indian who looked disdainfully on the white man's gifts," one officer recalled:

> There was apparently nothing among the paraphernalia of the white man that Kick-a-Bird wanted. Nothing until his eye chanced upon a high silk hat that seemingly delighted him. Setting his symbol of a conquering civilization firmly on his oiled hair he strutted for hours up and down for the amusement of his grinning companions. But presently he grew tired of his selection, and the last we saw of the glossy, high silk hat, Kick-a-Bird and his companions were contemptuously using it for a football.

Farther north, at Fort Laramie on the Platte, the commissioners also signed a treaty with a number of Brulé, Oglala, and Miniconjou Lakota bands. They agreed to remain within a vast Sioux reservation that encompassed all of present-day South Dakota and much of North Dakota and Nebraska, west of the Missouri. In turn, the government recognized their right to hunt buffalo on lands north of the Platte and on the Republican River "so long as buffalo may range there in numbers sufficient to justify the chase."

Red Cloud refused even to meet with the commissioners, but he sent word that all three forts in the Powder River country would have to be abandoned before he touched the pen. "If the Great Father kept white men out of my country," he said, "then peace would last forever. The Great Spirit has raised me in this land and has raised you in another land. What I have said I mean. I mean to keep this land." The commission yielded. The soldiers marched away. Gleeful Lakota burned all three

forts — only cemeteries remained to mark where they once had stood — and the Bozeman Trail was closed. Still, Red Cloud disdainfully stayed away from Fort Laramie all summer and into the autumn, preferring to hunt buffalo as he always had rather than meet with the soldiers. It was not until November 6, 1868, that he and some 125 other chiefs and headmen finally rode in to sign the treaty. Even then, he was ambivalent as to whether he would really agree to live on the reservation, submit to being fed and housed by white men, or be taught how to farm.

By 1872, when this portrait was made in Washington, D.C., by Alexander Gardner, Red Cloud had become a national celebrity and whites vied with one another to be photographed with him. His companion here is an Englishman named William Henry Blackmore.

In the spring of 1870, to convince Red Cloud of the futility of further resistance, he and a delegation of twenty-one Lakota were escorted to Washington, to meet with the new Great Father, President Grant. Everything was arranged to awe the Indians with American might, but none of it seemed to impress them much. A huge cannon that lobbed a shell four miles down the Potomac made a satisfying noise, but the Lakota pointed out that they could simply ride around it while it was being laboriously reloaded; they were quickly bored by the debate on the Senate floor and brightened only when they saw the busts of two Indian chiefs in the Capitol; and an elaborate meal served at the Executive Mansion only demonstrated, one of the chiefs said, that whites had not been sending them the best of their food and drink.

And when Jacob Cox, the secretary of the interior, told his visitors that because of what they had been shown, "Red Cloud and his people . . . will now know that what the President does is not because he is afraid but because he wants to do that which is right and good," the Lakota leader remained unmoved: "The white people have surrounded me," he said through an interpreter, "and left me nothing but an island. When we first had this land we were strong. Now we are melting like snow on the hillside while you are growing like spring grass. . . ." Still, he claimed he had never understood what he had signed at Fort Laramie; the paper was "all lies"; the interpreters had misrepresented everything to him. His people would never go to the agency on the Missouri to collect their gifts; it was an unhealthy place. He would trade only at Fort Laramie.

[Past Indian policy has] driven an independent and lordly race into the condition of dependents and beggars. . . . This Nation cannot evade its Christian duty to save them from destruction and elevate them from their degraded barbarous state. . . . This evil can only be remedied by the selection of some country that shall be set apart for and devoted exclusively to the use and benefit of the Indians.

The Reverend Nathaniel Taylor
Commissioner of Indian Affairs

One goal of the treaty had been to move the Lakota away from the Platte, but the government, anxious to hold on to the fragile peace, again relented: Red Cloud's people would not have to go to the agency to collect their gifts. Instead, a new agency would be built especially for Red Cloud and the Oglala in northwestern Nebraska.

Given the chance to visit New York in order to buy presents before returning home, Red Cloud at first scornfully turned it down: "The whites are the same everywhere," he said. "I see them every day." But in the end he did go, even agreed to parade with his friends on horseback through Central Park past cheering, dazzled crowds, and on the afternoon of June 14, 1869, stood on the stage of Cooper Union, where Abraham Lincoln had delivered the address that first brought him to national attention, and spoke for his people:

> We came to Washington to see our Great Father that peace might be continued. The Great Father that made us both wishes peace to be kept; we want to keep peace. Will you help us? In 1868, men came out and brought papers. We could not read them, and they did not tell us truly what was in them. We thought the treaty was to remove the forts. . . . [We] did not want to go to the Missouri, but wanted traders where we were. . . .
>
> Look at me. I am poor and naked but I am the Chief of the Nation. . . . The riches that we have in this world, Secretary Cox said truly, we cannot take with us to the next world. I wish to know why the Commissioners are sent out to us who do nothing but rob us and get the riches of this world away from us? I was brought up among the traders . . . and I had a good time with them. But by and by, the Great Father sent out a different kind of men; men who cheated and drank whiskey; men who were so bad the Great Father could not keep them at home. . . . I have sent a great many words to the Great Father but they never reached him. They were drowned on the way, and I was afraid the words I spoke lately . . . would not reach you [either], so I came to speak to you myself and now I am going away to my home.

The abuses about which Red Cloud spoke at Cooper Union were all too familiar to members of the Grant administration, and at the time he spoke it had already begun to try to do something about them. Even the Indians' most unyielding enemies knew that the reservation system was profoundly corrupt. Unscrupulous agents, appointed purely because of their political connections, wielded near-absolute power over their charges' lives. Some sold off Indian timber and mineral rights for their own profit; others skimmed off funds meant for buying supplies and food for their charges — or stole them wholesale. "The Indian agent they have sent us is so mean," said one Plains chief, "that he carries around in his pocket a . . . rag into which he blows his nose, for fear he will blow away something of value."

Grant would seek to end the worst abuses of the old patronage system by turning over at least some of the agencies to the churches — Quakers, Presbyterians, Methodists, Catholics, Lutherans, Congregationalists, Episcopalians, Baptists. Some of the agents sent west under this so-called "peace policy" would prove genuinely dedicated to Indian welfare (though they were also almost always woefully ignorant of Indian ways). But the sects quarreled with one another, some of the agents they chose were no more honest than their predecessors, and three heads of the Indian bureau were forced from office under the shadow of scandal. Conditions for agency Indians showed little improvement.

Above all things, the plainsman had to have a sense — an instinct for direction. . . . Few men have this instinct. Yet in the few it is to be trusted as absolutely as the homing instinct of a wild goose. . . . I never had a compass in my life. I was never lost.

Charles Goodnight

Red Cloud had dictated terms to the United States and understandably saw himself as the victor in the war over the Bozeman Trail. But by the time he agreed to end his war the advancing Union Pacific had already made the hated road superfluous. Trains now carried more and more settlers west; they could also haul the soldiers and supplies General Sherman already planned to use against the scattered peoples of the Plains. The Peace Policy, Sherman believed, was doomed to failure, and the Peace Commission responsible for the treaties with Red Cloud and others, he said privately, had been merely "killing time" before the inevitable, final conquest of the Lakota and Cheyenne and their allies could begin. "We will be kind to you if you keep the peace," he warned at one treaty council. "But if you won't listen to reason, we are ordered to make war upon you in a different manner from what we have done before."

Sherman was not alone in his skepticism about the new agreements. Captain Barnitz, who had acted as secretary during the talks at Medicine Lodge Creek, also thought them largely a waste of time:

> [T]he Cheyennes were with great difficulty persuaded to sign the treaty. They were superstitious in regard to touching the pen, or perhaps they supposed that by doing so they would be "signing away their rights" — which is doubtless the true state of affairs, as *they have no idea* they are giving up, or that they have ever given up, the country which they claim as their own, the country north of the Arkansas. The treaty all amounts to nothing, and we will certainly have another war sooner or later with the Cheyennes, at least, and probably with the other Indians, in consequence of misunderstanding of the terms of present and previous treaties.

Barnitz was right. The treaty with the southern tribes proved just another piece of paper. Congress, caught up in politics, failed to ratify the document so that no funds were available to sustain the people in their new homes. Some bands left the reservations in search of food. Others never bothered to go there at all. And in the late summer of 1868, when the Indian agent at Fort Larned refused to hand over arms and ammunition used for hunting, to which the Cheyenne believed themselves entitled by the treaty, warriors began raiding settlers along the Saline and Solomon rivers again, burning cabins and running off stock. Fifteen men were killed. Five women were carried off and raped. More raids and more killing followed. Kansas settlements lived in fear.

Charles Goodnight when he was still a young, threadbare cattleman. Before his long career ended, he would be the master of some 20 million acres of Texas rangeland.

LAID AWAY IN A FOREIGN COUNTRY

Charles Goodnight was twenty-eight when the Civil War ended, and used to tough times. A dirt farmer's son, he had ridden bareback all the way from Illinois to Texas at the age of nine, and had been working full-time to support his widowed mother since he was eleven. At nineteen, he and his stepbrother went into the beef business. Cattle had come north with Coronado in 1540, and the Spanish and Mexican ranchos had established the cattle business and most of its distinctive customs — from the roundup to branding irons, the boots on a vaquero's feet to the wide-brimmed sombrero on his head — long before the United States expanded beyond the Mississippi.

But by the 1850s, Americans were taking over, and the largest herds were in South Texas, in the region around San Antonio, Corpus Christi, and Laredo. Eastern markets were thought too far away to be reached by land, so most ranchers drove cattle south, to ports on the Gulf of Mexico, where hides and tallow were shipped to eastern manufacturers. During the gold rush, more than half a million Texas cattle were herded west, to the mining camps of California. (A roughly equal number of sheep were driven to the goldfields from New Mexico by Mexican American herdsmen.)

Still too poor to buy their own herd, Goodnight and his stepbrother agreed to watch over someone else's — receiving every fourth calf as pay — and had managed to collect 180 head before Texas left the Union and Texas cattlemen found themselves cut off from their markets by the Union blockade of southern ports. Goodnight served as a scout for the Texas Rangers during the war, fighting Comanche and learning lessons about surviving in inhospitable country that would serve him well for the rest of his life. Most important was reading the signs of nearby water: the presence of mesquite bushes, he discovered, meant there was likely to be water within three miles; a swallow flying low, with an empty beak, was headed toward water; one with mud in its beak was coming straight from it.

When he returned to his small ranch at war's end, he found the cattle business in ruins. Texas herds had multiplied wildly — from 3.5 million head to perhaps 6 million. Rustlers were everywhere. "It looked like everything worth living for was gone," he remembered. "The entire country was depressed — there was no hope. . . . In a year or two's time, stealing or so-called mavericking became public. You could count the honest ones on your fingers and still have one hand left."

Goodnight prized honesty and hard work. "Only the weak steal," he once said, and the only way to make an honest profit in cattle was to try to take them north to better markets. He needed a partner and enlisted the help of Oliver Loving, twenty-five years older than he, who had taken Texas herds all the way to Chicago before the war, something no other cattleman had ever done. What Goodnight now proposed was a new, seven-hundred-mile route to new destinations — the Indian reservation at Bosque Redondo, the mining camps of Colorado, and finally the Union Pacific crews working their way across Wyoming. Loving agreed to try it: Goodnight's plan, which required that herds be driven across Comanche hunting grounds, was full of risk, but also possibility.

In 1866, with 2,000 cattle and eighteen cowboys, the two men set out along what would soon be called the Goodnight-Loving Trail. To avoid the Comanche of the panhandle, they first went southwest, across an arid eighty-mile plain toward the Pecos River — "the most desolate country," Goodnight remembered, "that I ever

The danger of swimming rivers is that the cattle will get to milling, and the first you know they will start to jump up and ride one another, trying to climb out, and down they will go and you will lose a lot of them. You have to keep them pointed for the opposite bank, which means that in the water each man has to hold his place alongside the herd, just like on the trail.

Teddy Blue Abbott

Cattle drive, ca. 1900

Right: An army officer distributes rations to Navajo captives at Bosque Redondo.

explored." It took three days and three nights in choking dust without stopping to cross. Newborn calves slowed down the herd, so Goodnight had them killed each morning. (On subsequent drives he would bring along an extra wagon just to carry the calves — each one wrapped in a burlap bag, so that it kept its own scent and its mother could find it when the calves were turned loose to feed at night.) Three hundred cattle died in the heat; a hundred more drowned when the thirst-crazed herd finally smelled the Pecos River and stampeded over its banks into quicksand and swirling waters.

Goodnight and Loving pointed the survivors north, into New Mexico Territory, and at last reached Bosque Redondo, where some 8,000 Navajo were on the verge of starvation and government agents gladly paid top dollar for Texas beef to feed them. The partners now had a $12,000 profit and half the herd still in their possession. They drove them even farther north, into Colorado, fattening their animals on range grasses as they traveled, then sold them in Denver. There, Loving learned that good grazing extended all the way to Montana, where other Indian agencies and military outposts were paying high prices. Excited about their prospects and $24,000 richer, the partners returned to Texas, bought more cattle, and hurried back up the trail they'd blazed.

"Loving was a man of religious instincts and one of the coolest and bravest men I have ever known," Goodnight recalled, "but devoid of caution." This time he insisted on pushing ahead to get in the partners' bid for new government beef contracts at Bosque Redondo before rival ranchers got there. Comanche caught him on the open plain, shot him in the wrist and side, and chased him to the riverbank, where he held them off for several days, then managed to crawl to safety in the night. He was picked up by a passing wagon and taken to the military hospital at Bosque Redondo.

Loving refused an amputation until he could talk to his partner. By the time Goodnight finally reached his bedside, gangrene had set in. The operation was too late to save him. The night Loving died, "his mind turned back to Texas," Goodnight recalled, "and at last he said: 'I regret to have to be laid away in a foreign country.' I assured him that he need have no fears; that I would see that his remains were laid in the cemetery at home. He felt this would be impossible, but I told him it would be done."

Goodnight had his men fashion a tin casket out of flattened cans. They put Loving's wooden coffin inside, covered it with charcoal, sealed the top, and placed it in a wagon. Flanked by a cowboy escort, Goodnight started back south for Texas. Word of the profits Goodnight and Loving had cleared had spread throughout cattle country, and other outfits were already streaming north, headed now for the nearest railheads from which cattle could be shipped east. But in February of 1868, Charles Goodnight, the man who had helped start it all, was headed in the other direction. Keeping his promise to his dead partner, he was taking Oliver Loving home.

THE WHOLE ARTILLERY OF HEAVEN

While the Union Pacific worked its way west across the Great Plains, the Central Pacific, after a fast start, had gotten stuck in the Sierra Nevada. The mountains still looked impenetrable, and Charles Crocker, whose job it was to break through them, could not seem to hold on to his workers: three out of five stuck with him just long enough to get a free ride to the railhead, then set out on their own for the Nevada goldfields. His plans called for a workforce of 10,000. He had fewer than 600 upon whom he could depend.

Desperate, he suggested to his superintendent of construction, James Strobridge, that he try the Chinese, many of whom who were eking out a living working California gold tailings abandoned by others. Strobridge was an ex–forty-niner, loud and profane, accustomed to carrying a pick handle as what he called his "persuader," and unaccustomed to having his judgment questioned. "I will not boss Chinese," he said; they were too small, too frail; they had no training as railroad builders.

Crocker insisted the Chinese be given a chance; their ancestors had, after all, built the Great Wall. Strobridge was to try fifty of them for a month to see how they stood up. They did fine.

Before long, 11,000 of them were at work on the Central Pacific, and Crocker was advertising for still more in China. "They do not drink or fight or strike," wrote the journalist Charles Nordhoff, ". . . and it is always said of them that they are very cleanly in their habits. It is the custom among them, after they have had their suppers every evening, to bathe with the help of small tubs. I doubt if the white laborers do as much."

The Chinese had other advantages over their white counterparts. They arrived at the work site already divided into smoothly efficient work gangs, usually from the same province and speaking the same dialect. They fell ill less often, too, because they drank only tea made from boiled water, and consumed a varied diet instead of the daily ration of beef and potatoes washed down with river water that sustained their white counterparts.

Chinese workers and their white foreman. "Systematic workers these Chinese," said the *Alta California*, "competent and wonderfully effective, tireless and unremitting in their industry."

Before the Central Pacific could get through the Sierras the crews had to carve and gouge and blast fifteen tunnels out of solid granite. It sometimes took them twenty-four hours and five hundred kegs of explosives to move ahead eight inches; in an average week they used more explosives than were heard at Antietam. Then they came up against a face they called Cape Horn: solid rock, nearly straight up and down, more than 3,000 feet above the tumbling American River. There were no

The greater proportion of the laborers employed by us are Chinese who constitute a large element in the population of California. Without them it would be impossible to complete the western portion of this great national enterprise within the time required by the Acts of Congress.

Leland Stanford

End of the line: Union Pacific crews at work and encamped along the newly laid track

The mouth of Tunnel No. 10 in the High Sierra

footholds, but the Chinese still somehow managed to blast and carve out a ledge along the cliff wide enough for a train to pass. To do it, Chinese workers were swung down over the rock face in wicker baskets to gouge holes, pack them with explosives, set the fuses, then hope the explosives did not go off before their comrades above could haul them up and out of harm's way.

A reporter remembered watching the pyrotechnics above Donner Lake:

> Through the gathering shades of night, immense volumes of fire and dense clouds of smoke from the mountainside, as if a mighty volcano was rending it to atoms. Huge masses of rocks and debris were rent and heaved up in the commotion; then . . . came the thunders of explosion like a lightning stroke, reverberating along the hills and canyons, as if the whole artillery of Heaven was in play. Huge masses of rock rolled far down the steep declivity, and pieces weighing two hundred pounds were thrown a distance of a mile. Sometimes the peo-

There was a dance at Donner Lake at a hotel and a sleigh-load of us went up from Truckee and on our return, about 9 a.m. next morning, we saw something under a tree by the side of the road, its shape resembling that of a man. We stopped and found a frozen Chinese. As a consequence, we threw him in the sleigh, with the rest of us and took him into town and laid him out by the side of a shed and covered him with a rice mat, the most appropriate thing for the laying out of a Celestial.

A. P. Partridge

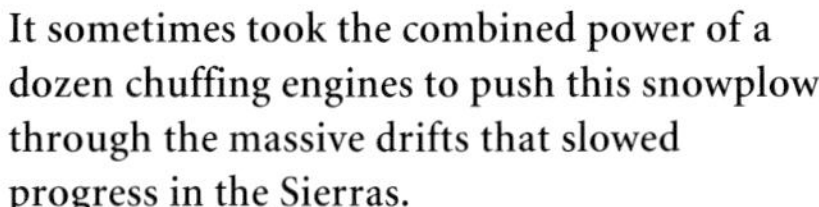

It sometimes took the combined power of a dozen chuffing engines to push this snowplow through the massive drifts that slowed progress in the Sierras.

ple at the hotel, a mile from the scene of destruction, were obliged to retire to avoid the . . . falling fragments.

The crews kept at it right through two of the worst winters in memory. "Snow storms, forty-four in number," remembered a railroad official in 1866, "varied in length from a short . . . squall to a two-week gale. . . . [T]he heaviest storm of the winter, began February 18th, at 2 p.m., and snowed steadily until 10 p.m. of the 22nd, during which time six feet fell. . . ." The Chinese tunneled beneath sixty-foot drifts, working by lamplight, breathing through air shafts. ". . . [S]now slides carried away our camps and we lost a good many men in those slides," another official recalled. "[M]any of them we did not find until the next season when the snow melted." No one kept a precise count, but more than twelve hundred Chinese are believed to have died building the Central Pacific.

In the spring of 1867, some 3,000 Chinese workers struck, demanding an eight-hour day and the same terms as the whites who took fewer risks than they did. (Whites were fed by the railroad, for example; Chinese workers had to feed themselves.) Charles Crocker would not hear of it. He let it be known that he was looking into the possibility of bringing in freed slaves from the South to replace any Chinese who would not go back to work, charged that the whole strike had been inspired by agents of the rival Union Pacific, and cut off the strikers' food supply. But in the end, it was Crocker, not his Chinese workers, who retreated at least a little: his men still had to work a twelve-hour day and got no free food, but he raised their pay two dollars to thirty-five dollars a month.

By the side of the grade are the camp fires of the blue-clad laborers waiting for the signal to start work. These are the Chinese, and the job of this particular contingent is to clear a level roadbed for the track. They are the vanguard of the construction forces. Miles back is the camp of the rear guard — the Chinese who follow the track gang, ballasting and finishing the roadbed.

Alta California
November 9, 1868

Some of the first Chinese to work for the Central Pacific, laboring to complete the Secret Town Trestle on the western slope of the Sierras in the summer of 1866

Finally, in September of 1868, after three long years of backbreaking, dangerous labor, the Central Pacific crews did what few had believed even they could accomplish — they broke out of the High Sierra and onto the Nevada desert. The *Territorial Enterprise* paid heartfelt if patronizing tribute to the men who had made it possible: "John [Chinaman], with his patient toil, directed by American energy and backed by American capital, has broken down the great barrier at last and opened over it the greatest highway yet created for the march of commerce and civilization around the globe."

The hardest part was now behind them. The Central Pacific was back in the race.

I have always done my best to keep my young men quiet, but some will not listen, and since the fighting began I have not been able to keep them all at home. But we want peace, and I would be glad to move all my people down this way; I could then keep them all quietly near camp.

Black Kettle

NOTHING BUT THEIR EYES TO WEEP WITH

General Philip Henry Sheridan — "Fighting Phil" — had now assumed command of the Department of the Missouri, which included Kansas, Oklahoma, New Mexico, and Colorado. The diminutive son of an Irish tenant farmer and trained at West Point — from which he had been suspended for a year for trying to stab another cadet with his bayonet — he was hard, hot-tempered, and still less sentimental about the soldier's task than was his friend Sherman. "The proper strategy," he once said, "consists in the first place in inflicting as telling blows as possible upon the enemy's army, and then causing the inhabitants so much suffering that they must long for peace, and force their government to demand it. The people must be left nothing but their eyes to weep with over the war."

During the Civil War, he had applied his grim theory to the Shenandoah Valley, stripping its people of so much, he boasted, that a crow wishing to fly over the valley had to carry its own rations. Now Sherman asked him to apply similar tactics in the West, wherever Indians continued to resist. They would begin with the Cheyenne, and would attack them in the winter, when they were most vulnerable. "In taking the offensive," Sheridan assured Sherman, "I have to select that season when I can catch the fiends; and if a village is attacked and women and children killed, the responsibility is not with the soldiers, but with the people whose crimes necessitated the attack."

Sherman heartily approved:

> Go ahead in your own way and I will back you with my whole authority. . . . I will say nothing and do nothing to restrain our troops from doing what they deem proper on the spot, and will allow no mere vague general charges of cruelty and inhumanity to tie their hands, but will use all the powers confided to me to the end that these Indians, the enemies of our race and of our civilization, shall not again be able to begin and carry out their barbarous warfare on any kind of pretext they may choose to allege.

To lead his winter campaign, Sheridan sent for Custer. It was all the younger man had hoped for — a chance to redeem himself, erase the bitter memory of the Hancock campaign, and win a great victory. Three separate columns were to force the Cheyenne back onto their reservation, but Sheridan meant for Custer to do the real fighting, attacking the Cheyenne villages when they least expected it. "I rely in everything upon you," he told Custer, "and shall send you on this expedition without giving you any orders, leaving you to act entirely on your own judgment."

Custer drove his men relentlessly through the snow. An old Osage scout asked him what he would do if they were to find "more Indians than we can handle."

"All I am afraid of is we won't find half enough," Custer answered. "There are not Indians enough in the country to whip the Seventh Cavalry."

Then, his scouts reported they had found a Cheyenne village of some fifty lodges. Custer ordered his men to prepare for a dawn attack. Though he didn't know it at the time, Custer had come upon Black Kettle's band, encamped along the Washita River, well within the Cheyenne reservation. A white flag flew above the peace chief's teepee. But some of his young men had slipped away to steal livestock and raid settlers. It was their pony tracks that had led Custer's scouts to the edge of the camp, and four white hostages, women and children, were being held by the Indians.

At dawn on November 27, 1868, just two days short of the fourth anniversary of the Sand Creek massacre, Custer's buglers sounded a somewhat muffled charge — their lips froze to the mouthpieces of their instruments in the fierce cold — and six hundred mounted men started toward the village, firing as they came.

Black Kettle mounted his pony, pulled his wife up behind him, and tried to ride away. A volley of fire hurled him, his wife, and the pony into the river. The soldiers rode over their bodies and on into the camp. The killing went on for half an hour.

Custer (seated at center, in profile) and his officers enjoy the autumn sun at the beginning of the 1868 campaign that ended at the Washita.

The survivors hid in the tall grass. "The soldiers would pass back and forth near the spot where I lay," one Cheyenne girl remembered. "As I turned sideways and looked, one soldier saw us, and rode toward where we lay. He stopped his horse and stared at us. He did not say a word, and we wondered what would happen. But he left and no one showed up after that. I suppose he pitied us, and left us alone."

The surprise had been complete, but Custer had failed to realize that Black Kettle was not alone on the Washita. Some 6,000 Cheyenne and Arapaho, Kiowa and Comanche were camped just downriver, and warriors soon began to swarm out to attack him. Under cover of darkness that evening, Custer managed to escape with some prisoners — including a Cheyenne woman whom he would soon take as his mistress — but not before a foolhardy young major charged headlong into the Indians and was cut down with eighteen volunteers. Custer never even tried to rescue them.

He sent a boastful report to his superiors, nonetheless:

> The Indians left on the ground 103 warriors, including Black Kettle, whose scalp was taken by an Osage guide. 875 horses and mules were captured, 241 saddles . . . 573 buffalo robes, 390 buffalo skins, 160 untanned robes. . . . [All] the winter supply of dried buffalo meat, all the meal, flour and other provisions; in fact, all they possessed was captured, as the warriors escaped with little or no clothing. Everything of value [to them] was destroyed.

Cheyenne survivors said only eleven warriors were killed. The rest of the dead were women and children and old men. Two of the white hostages were dead, too, stabbed to death by Cheyenne women as soon as the shooting began.

"If we can get in one or two more [such] blows," said Sheridan, "there will be no more Indian troubles in my department." The blows were eventually struck, and by the autumn of 1869 Indians had been driven off the plains between the Platte and the Arkansas. But many of Custer's own officers and men never forgave him for abandoning their comrades on the Washita battlefield. "The honor of his country weighed lightly in the scale against the 'glorious' name of 'Geo. A. Custer,'" wrote a private who

Lieutenant-General Sherman,
St. Louis, Mo.
War Department,
Washington City,
December 2, 1868
I congratulate you, Sheridan, and Custer on the splendid success with which your campaign is begun. Ask Sheridan to send forward the names of officers and men deserving of special mention.

J. M. Schofield
Secretary of War

Cheyenne survivors of the Washita, mostly women and children, under guard at Camp Supply in Indian Territory, 1868

served under him, "the hardships and danger to his men, as well as the probable loss of life were worthy of but little consideration when dim visions of an 'eagle' or even a 'star' floated before [his] excited mind. . . ."

May God continue the unity of our country as this railroad unites the two great oceans of the world.

Engraved on a ceremonial spike

The following spring, the last Cheyenne holdouts from the unremitting winter campaign began to come in. One band was led by a chief named Rock Forehead. He held two white women as captives, so Custer decided to talk him into giving up, rather than risk having them killed in another attack.

Custer entered the village with only an interpreter, and was taken to the chief's teepee. He told the Cheyenne that if they released their captives and returned to the reservation, no one would be harmed and peace could be restored.

Eventually, Rock Forehead would agree to give up. But on that day he was not convinced that Custer was trustworthy. He tapped out the pipe's ashes on the general's boots, to bring Custer bad luck and to drive home a warning. "They told him," a Cheyenne woman named Kate Big Head recalled, ". . . that if ever afterward he should break that peace promise and should fight the Cheyennes, the Everywhere Spirit would cause him to be killed."

DONE!

By the spring of 1869, the Central Pacific and the Union Pacific were converging at last in Utah. Speed and distance were still everything: "I would build the road in the cheapest possible manner," Collis P. Huntington told Charles Crocker, "then go back and improve it . . . , because the Union Pacific have built the cheapest kind of road." (Huntington was right about the Union Pacific, which was forced to come up with an extra $7 million for repairs even before the line was completed; by 1887, Grenville Dodge admitted, the original tracks of the line he'd built were "two dirt tracks ballasted with streaks of rust.")

Rival armies of railroad men vied to cover the most ground — and earn the most money for their employers — before the two lines finally met. Still, no fixed rendezvous point had been established, so grading crews, working far ahead of the men who laid the track, passed each other in opposite directions and pushed on for miles, sometimes working so close to one another, the Deseret *Evening News* reported, that blasts set off by one work gang often spattered its rival with dirt:

> [W]hen Sharp & Young's men first began to work for the Central Pacific, [they] would give [the Union Pacific crews] no warning when they lit the fuse. Jim Livingston, Sharp's able foreman, said nothing, but went to work and loaded a point of rock with nitroglycerine, and without saying anything to the Central Pacific "let 'er rip." The explosion was terrific. The report was heard in the Dry Tortugas, and the foreman of the Central Pacific came down to confer . . . about the necessity of each party notifying the other when ready for a blast. The matter was speedily arranged to the satisfaction of both parties.

Finally, government engineers intervened and picked Promontory Summit, fifty-six miles west of Ogden, as the place where the two lines would finally meet.

By May 8, 1869, the rails were at last ready to be joined. Leland Stanford of the Central Pacific had already arrived for the ceremony in his private railroad car. But

Climax at Promontory Summit, May 10, 1869. Above, left: With the final spike driven at last, Leland Stanford (center) brandishes the silver-headed maul with which he managed to hit it the second time he tried.

Above, right: Two stereographic views have been combined to capture in one image both the locomotives that were the focus of the celebration — the Central Pacific's Jupiter (left) and Engine No. 119, pride of the Union Pacific.

Vice President Thomas C. Durant of the Union Pacific was nowhere to be seen. His train had been halted in Wyoming by a crew of angry tie cutters who had not been paid for five months. They chained the wheels of his car to the tracks and would not let him pass until the cash was in their hands.

The Union Pacific sent a special train with the payroll, Durant was released, and on May 10 everything was finally ready at Promontory Summit. The last two lengths of rail were brought up — one by the Union Pacific's Irishmen, the other by the Central Pacific's Chinese. A telegrapher stood by to signal the driving of the final spike to both coasts and all points in between:

> TO EVERYBODY, KEEP QUIET. WHEN THE LAST SPIKE IS DRIVEN AT PROMONTORY POINT, WE WILL SAY "DONE!" DON'T BREAK THE CIRCUIT, BUT WATCH FOR THE SIGNALS OF THE BLOWS OF THE HAMMER.

Four spikes — two gold, one silver, and the fourth a blend of gold, silver, and iron — were to be gently tapped into position to mark the occasion, and then a fifth and final spike — an ordinary one but wired to the telegrapher's key — was to be hammered into the ground.

> ALMOST READY. HATS OFF PRAYER IS BEING OFFERED.

A clergyman intoned what seemed to be an interminable prayer:

> . . . O Father, God of our fathers, we desire to acknowledge Thy handiwork in this great work, and ask Thy blessing upon us here assembled, upon the rulers of our government, and upon Thy people everywhere; that peace may flow

unto them as a gentle stream, and that mighty enterprise may be unto us as the Atlantic of Thy strength, and the Pacific of Thy love, through Jesus the Redeemer, Amen.

ALL READY NOW; THE SPIKE WILL SOON BE DRIVEN.

WE UNDERSTAND; ALL ARE READY IN THE EAST.

WE HAVE GOT DONE PRAYING; THE SPIKE IS ABOUT TO BE PRESENTED.

The final spike was slid into place. Leland Stanford was to have the honor of driving it home, with a special silver-headed maul.

THE SIGNAL WILL BE THREE DOTS FOR THE COMMENCEMENT OF THE BLOWS.

Stanford swung the hammer high above his head, brought it down — and missed. The telegrapher closed the circuit anyway: "DONE!"

In Washington, a great cheer went up from the big crowd in front of the telegraph office and an illuminated ball dropped from the dome of the Capitol. At Independence Hall in Philadelphia, the Liberty Bell was gingerly rung so that its crack would not worsen. And in San Francisco a huge banner was unfurled that proclaimed, "California Annexes the United States."

MAPPING THE WEST

The Hayden Survey moves into the Yellowstone Valley, 1871.

Clarence King at work (above) and Ferdinand Hayden in the saddle

Lewis and Clark had begun the business of charting the region for the government, and John Charles Frémont and other army topographical engineers had continued their work.

In the 1860s and 1870s, a series of four Great Surveys, all but one of them led by civilians, would continue the job — and employ the camera to bring home to their fellow citizens back East the look of the vast region that still had not been conquered.

First Lt. George Montague Wheeler was the last of the great army surveyors. A modest soldier who believed science more important than heroics — "The day of the pathfinder has sensibly ended," he said — he managed to chart some 175,000 square miles of territory from Mexico all the way to Oregon. But his dream of completing a comprehensive map of the whole West by 1900 was dashed by the creation of the civilian United States Geological Survey in 1879.

Its first director was Clarence King, brought up as the pampered son of an old but threadbare Newport family, who nonetheless helped map the path followed by the transcontinental railroad, discovered three American glaciers overlooked even by Frémont, and survived being struck by lightning atop a Utah peak before taking up his new duties in Washington.

His successor was Major John Wesley Powell, an abolitionist minister's son from upstate New York, who volunteered for service in the Union army, lost an arm at Shiloh but stayed in the war until slavery was crushed, then taught geology at Illinois Wesleyan University before undertaking two trips down the Colorado River.

Geologist Ferdinand Hayden was small and voluble, so energetic that Indians called him "Man-Who-Picks-Up-Stones-Running," and so determinedly optimistic that when he discovered a small vein of brown coal near the little town of Laramie, he confidently announced that Wyoming would soon become a second Pennsylvania. In July of 1871, he led an expedition into the Yellowstone Valley. For more than sixty years, trappers and travelers had been returning from there with tales so wondrous that no one believed them. But the photographer William Henry Jackson accompanied Hayden, and his work made all the difference. On March 1, 1872, after viewing Jackson's pictures, Congress voted to create Yellowstone National Park, the first national park in the history of the world.

Canyon de Chelly, photographed by John Hillers for a survey led by John Wesley Powell (right) in 1869. The photographer's wagon and team are in the foreground.

The Grand Canyon of the Colorado (opposite), as seen by John Hillers's assistant during the Powell expedition. Hillers himself perches at the edge of the cliff.

Shoshone Falls on the Snake River in Idaho Territory (above), photographed by Timothy O'Sullivan during the Wheeler Survey, 1874

WALKING GOLD PIECES

At one time, 30 million buffalo may have blanketed the Plains. But by the late 1860s, their numbers had already drastically declined — reduced by competition for winter fodder with the horse, by diseases carried by the emigrants' oxen and loss of grasslands to the overland trails, by hunting that had provided meat first to fur trappers and then to railroad crews, and by the buffalo-robe trade that encouraged Indians to kill more than they needed.

Still, buffalo roamed in herds beyond counting — millions upon millions of animals that to the Plains peoples represented existence itself. "Everything the Kiowas had came from the buffalo," a woman named Old Lady Horse recalled. "Their tipis were made of buffalo hides, so were their clothes and moccasins. They ate buffalo meat. Their containers were made of hide, or of bladders or stomachs. . . . Most of all the buffalo was part of the Kiowa religion. . . . The buffalo were the life of the Kiowas."

Following the lead of the Union Pacific and Central Pacific, other rail lines would soon spread across the West — the Kansas Pacific, Northern Pacific, Denver Pacific, Texas and Pacific; the Burlington and Missouri River, Denver and Rio Grande, Atchison, Topeka and Santa Fe. And as the new railroads began to move onto the Great Plains, the buffalo began to die. Now, almost anyone could shoot one: to raise money for their church, one congregation in Lawrence, Kansas, organized a buffalo excursion; three hundred people signed up for the two-day trip, blasting away from the windows of their chair car.

Foreign sportsmen came, too, including the son of the czar of all the Russias, Grand Duke Alexis Alexandrovitch. Bored with hunting in Europe, he hired an opulently furnished private train and set out for the tiny settlement of North Platte in Nebraska Territory. General Sheridan, in charge of every detail of the arrangements, selected Custer as grand marshal of the hunt and appointed the flamboyant, hard-drinking William F. Cody as his guide. Just twenty-five but already a legend in the East, where dime novels and stage melodramas exaggerating his adventures had earned him the nickname "Buffalo Bill," Cody had killed by his own count more than 4,000 buffalo as a meat hunter for the Union Pacific; his job now was to make sure Alexis got at least one.

It wasn't easy. The first kill was reserved for the grand duke, mounted on Cody's favorite horse, Buckskin Joe, and armed with an engraved revolver, made especially for him by Smith and Wesson. He fired six shots at one buffalo without hitting it, then emptied his revolver at another with the same result. Buffalo Bill handed him his own rifle, "Lucretia," then whipped the prince's horse to get him within ten feet of his target. Alexis fired at point-blank range, and a buffalo tottered and fell dead. Champagne was ordered up, a bottle for each hunter, and after it was downed the chase resumed. When the grand duke shot another buffalo, out came a second round of champagne. "I was in hopes that he would kill five or six more before we reached camp," Buffalo Bill remembered.

Alexis's last day on the Plains was especially memorable. Custer spotted a herd in the distance, and decided it would be fun to pretend the animals were Indians and lead a charge into their midst. "Boys," he shouted, "here's a chance for a great victory over that bunch of redskins on the other side of the hill!" Before they were through,

I have been on a train when the black, moving mass of buffaloes before us looked as if it stretched on down to the horizon. Everyone went armed in those days, and . . . [it] was the greatest wonder that more people were not killed, as the wild rush for the windows, and the reckless discharge of rifles and pistols, put every passenger's life in jeopardy. . . . I could not for the life of me avoid a shudder when a long line of guns leaning on the backs of seats met my eye as I entered a car. When the sharp shrieks of the train whistle announced a herd of buffaloes the rifles were snatched, and in the struggle to twist around for a good aim out of the narrow window the barrel of the muzzle of the firearm passed dangerously near the ear of any scared woman who had the temerity to travel in those tempestuous days. . . . Elizabeth Custer

Student and teacher: Grand Duke Alexis Alexandrovich of Russia (with puppy) and the splashy soldier assigned to bring him success in the hunt, George Armstrong Custer

some fifty buffalo lay dead on the frozen prairie. Alexis had personally killed a dozen and was so excited he grabbed Custer and kissed him.

Newspapermen reported every detail of the prince's hunt, and public interest in the gaudy show Buffalo Bill had orchestrated for his imperial guest helped persuade him to go east and try his hand at show business. If money was being made playing him onstage, Cody reasoned, he might as well get some of it himself. And the final assault on the buffalo herd would prove to be the last time George Armstrong Custer led a headlong charge "to the other side of the hill" — and survived.

Now, a different kind of buffalo hunter was heading for the Plains. Eastern manufacturers had developed new techniques for turning stiff buffalo hides into soft leather — ideal for shoes, cushions, carriage tops, and the belts that turned machinery in eastern factories. The new rail lines still spreading across the Plains meant that buffalo robes and buffalo meat could be shipped to eastern markets in much greater numbers, at far lower costs.

Plans for a railroad stop at the Arkansas River, near Fort Dodge in the heart of buffalo country, had been drawn up in July 1872, and some settlers had started moving in the next month. The first business in town was a tent saloon; an empty boxcar served as the first depot. The first train that pulled up to it in September was two hours late; it had been delayed by a buffalo herd three miles wide and ten miles long crossing the track. The residents christened their town Buffalo City, but the postmaster general in Washington vetoed their choice: Kansas already had towns named Buffalo and Buffalo Station. So, in honor of the fort nearby, they renamed it Dodge City.

"Hardly had the railroad reached there . . ." one citizen remembered, "[than the buffalo-hunting] business began; and such a business! The streets were lined with wagons, bringing in hides and meat and getting supplies from early morning to late at night. I have been to several mining camps where rich strikes have been made, but I never saw any town equal to Dodge." In just its first three months of existence, the town shipped east 43,029 buffalo hides and 1.4 million pounds of buffalo meat. That winter, more than a hundred buffalo hunters froze to death along the Arkansas River, and the Fort Dodge surgeon performed seventy amputations for frostbite.

But still more hunters turned up in the spring of 1873. In the midst of a national economic depression, buffalo hunting looked like a good thing.

Frank H. Mayer, a twenty-two-year-old Louisianan who had been a rebel bugler in the Civil War, was hanging around Dodge City that spring looking for work and excitement when he met two hunters who offered to show him their trade. "I was young. . . . I could shoot. . . . I liked to hunt. . . . I needed adventure," he remembered. "Here was it." Mayer sank everything he owned into a hunting outfit — wagons, mules, camp equipment, and firearms — and headed out onto the Plains. The buffalo didn't belong to anybody," he wrote. "If you could kill them, what they brought was yours. They were walking gold pieces."

> When I went into the business, I sat down and figured that I was indeed one of fortune's children. Just think. There were 20 million buffalo, each worth at least \$3 — \$60 million. At the very outside, cartridges cost 25 cents each, so every time I fired one I got my investment back twelve times over. I could kill a hun-

Shooting buffalo from trains proved so easy and so popular with passengers that the Kansas Pacific found it profitable to operate its own taxidermist's department just to mount their trophies.

A gigantic buffalo rifle reminds hide-hunters working out of Dodge City in 1872 that they will always find a welcome at Zimmerman's Hardware.

The Swedish immigrants, opposite, settled in Greeley County, Kansas, in the 1870s, confident that they would not have to worry about getting enough rain.

dred a day. . . . [T]hat would be $6,000 a month — or three times what was paid, it seems to me, the President of the United States, and a hundred times what a man with a good job could be expected to earn. Was I not lucky that I discovered this quick and easy way to fortune? I thought I was. . . .

Before long, Frank Mayer was competing with some 2,000 other marksmen to kill the buffalo of Kansas.

RAIN FOLLOWS THE PLOW

It had at first been thought that no settlers could survive anywhere on the semiarid, mostly treeless Great Plains that rolled all the way from Montana and the Dakotas south into Texas. Back in 1820, Major Stephen Harriman Long had led an exploring party across the Great Plains region of Nebraska and Colorado to the Rockies and pronounced all of it unfit for white people: "uninhabitable by a people depending on agriculture" and useful to the United States in the future only as "a barrier against too great an expansion of our population westward." Mapmakers called it "the Great American Desert," and for forty-odd years pioneers had carefully avoided settling on it.

With a logic that cannot rest we are forced to this conclusion, that the agencies of civilization now in action are such as will secure a complete victory over the wilderness and waste places of western territory. The plow will go forward. God speed the plow. By this wonderful provision, which is only man's mastery over nature, the clouds are dispensing copious rains. . . . [The plow is] more powerful in peace than the sword in war, the instrument which separates civilization from savagery; and converts a desert into a farm or garden. To be more concise, Rain follows the plow.

Charles Dana Wilber, 1879

But the Homestead Act of 1862 began to change all that. It promised 160 acres of public land to any person who filed a claim, paid a ten-dollar fee, and agreed to work the property for five years. As it happened, the 1870s and early 1880s were unusually wet years in the West, and the prairies, plowed and planted for the first time, yielded bumper crops. Promoters made the most of it. The Plains might once have been desertlike, they admitted, but no longer. The climate itself, they promised, had changed for good. Some believed the presence of railroads had brought rain: "The increase of railroads," said one Colorado newspaper, "and also the increase of activity on the roads has the . . . effect of producing more showers. . . . The concussion of the air and rapid movement produced by railroad trains and engines affects the electrical conditions of the atmosphere." Others believed that the change in climate had been caused by farming itself: rain was said somehow to follow the plow.

Then, too, just a few days after the Union Pacific and Central Pacific lines met at Promontory Summit in 1869, word had come that another of the great engineering feats of the nineteenth century had been completed — the Suez Canal, linking Africa and Asia. Much of the trade between Europe and the Orient that the new western lines had hoped to carry would now never reach the United States at all, and American railroads would have to depend on domestic business to keep from going under. The competition intensified to see which lines could lure the most settlers to live along their tracks, providing business for their freight trains and buying up the 181 million public domain acres Congress had provided to the railroad corporations to encourage construction. "You can lay track to the garden of Eden," said the head of the Northern Pacific, "but what good is it if the only inhabitants are Adam and Eve?"

At the same time, as territories became states, they, too, were given federal land, and used the proceeds from selling or renting it to support their schools. Most set up promotional bureaus to lure in new settlers. "No crop to be harvested by the farmers of Kansas next summer," said the Kansas Bureau of Immigration, "will be equal in value [to] the harvest of people that may be gathered. . . . It [is] our desire to fill,

Newcomers: Members of the tennis club at Runnymede, a British colony in the middle of Kansas (left), and a flatcar filled with European immigrants being shown likely sites for farming

upon the map of Kansas, the blank space heretofore allotted to the 'Great American Desert' — that myth of the old geographers."

Most of those who came west were farmers from the midwestern states. But when the financial panic of 1873 threw thousands out of work in the East, worried industrialists hoped the promise of free land in the West would also drain off the unemployed — and with them, social unrest in the cities. One businessman suggested that factory owners without jobs to offer simply tack a copy of the Homestead Act to their plant gates: "There can be no excuse for begging in a country which offers every pauper a quarter-section of as rich land as the sun shines upon. It is more profitable to raise farmers than convicts." Others contributed to organizations — the Co-Operative Colony Aid Association of New York; the Cosmo-American Colonization and General Improvement Bureau of Philadelphia — that promised to direct the newly jobless poor from the crowded eastern cities to the open spaces of the West.

Most of these efforts came to nothing. Factory workers weren't farmers, and even those who might have wanted to try it could only rarely afford it. Land itself was cheap, but getting to it, getting started, and surviving for the five years required to get title to a homestead cost money most of them didn't have.

Prospects seemed better overseas. The Hebrew Emigrant Aid Society recruited Jewish immigrants from eastern Europe to establish farming communes in Oregon, Colorado, Kansas, and the Dakotas. The First Swedish Agricultural and Galesburg Colonization Companies started the towns of Salemsborg and Lindsborg in Kansas. Small groups of Dutch, French, Bohemian, English, and Irish families scattered across the Plains. Two hundred Scottish families settled together on the Kansas-Nebraska border. By 1875, more than half of Nebraska's 123,000 settlers were members of families headed by foreign immigrants.

The expanding railroad companies and the young western states dispatched agents to Europe to recruit settlers. In just three weeks, an agent for the Burlington railroad boasted, he had entirely filled a boat with immigrants from Liverpool, all destined for company land in the West. Nebraska's agent in Scandinavia would claim that he personally had persuaded 10,000 Swedes, Danes, and Norwegians to move to his state.

But the undisputed champion of foreign immigration agents was C. B. Schmidt of the Sante Fe Railroad in Kansas, a tireless, imaginative salesman, successful throughout Europe but especially so in Germany because he spoke the language and seemed to know by instinct just where to show up when political unrest had farmers ready to consider moving. Because of Schmidt, one person said, Kansas was "as familiar to the households of the German peasant as that of Canaan was to the Israelites in bondage." Through his efforts alone, 60,000 Germans settled along the Santa Fe route.

Then Schmidt was dispatched for the biggest prize of all — the German-Russian Mennonites. They were pacifists who had fled Prussia rather than serve in its army three-quarters of a century earlier. Promising them military exemption, the freedom to speak their own language and run their own schools, plus 175 acres of land, Catherine the Great had lured them to the Russian steppes, where they had become the best wheat farmers in the world. But in 1870, a new czar withdrew their religious privileges, and they were looking for a new home.

Armed with encouraging letters from Mennonites already in Kansas taped to his body to escape notice by the border guards, Schmidt entered Russia. As he toured the prosperous Mennonite communities, he handed out the letters, sang the praises of Kansas, and offered incentives for them to relocate — until the czar's officers chased him out.

There was plenty of competition for these able and prosperous farmers. After Canada offered them immunity from military service and free transportation if they would settle there, Kansas, Nebraska, and Minnesota all also solemnly offered to exempt them from militia duty — although they had no legal authority to do so. Everyone promised them the right to govern themselves in their own communities, to speak German in their schools, plenty of land at good prices, and easy credit.

Mennonite emissaries were taken to Washington to meet President Grant, as one of them remembered:

> In Russia, we associated a government official with a uniform and lots of lace and trimmings, and the higher ones would always have guards of soldiers at the entrances of their quarters. . . . Imagine our surprise when we reached the White House to find the portals guarded by a single colored man who did not even display a sword.
>
> Our admission and introduction to President Grant was equally simple. . . . He told us that in his younger years he had been in the habit of milking twenty cows, mornings and evenings. President Grant also told us of his early experiences on the farm and said that he could hitch up and drive a team of horses as well as ever. You who never knew life in Europe, and especially in Russia, can hardly imagine our surprise when [he] gave us the impression that it was the usual thing for the highest official of the United States . . . to do manual labor.

Secretary of State Hamilton Fish personally assured them the United States would not go to war again for at least fifty years.

In the end, although Nebraska boosters deliberately delayed the Mennonite emissaries' luggage in Lincoln so that they could be taken on a last-minute tour of their state, most of their followers finally chose to settle in Kansas, where Schmidt's Santa Fe Railroad sold them 100,000 acres in 1874 alone. Tens of thousands of other German-Russians — Catholics, Hutterites, Amish — also came to the Plains in the 1870s.

"They seem well pleased with the country," reported the Kansas *Daily State Journal.* "They wear the simple garb of the German peasant, but have well-filled wallets. The men are sturdy, healthy looking fellows. The women all wear calico gowns, with a blue handkerchief thrown over their heads, and no signs of ribbons or ear rings, or brooches, or even of wedding rings. Those articles are considered too worldly. Both men and women are very stoop shouldered which we are informed comes from hard work."

They arrived in the midst of a drought and one of the worst grasshopper plagues in Kansas history: ". . . They devoured every green thing but the prairie grass," one American-born woman homesteader remembered. "Water troughs and loosely covered wells were foul with drowned 'hoppers," another man recalled.

All honor and reverence to good men; but they and their attentions are not the only source of happiness on the earth and need not fill up every thought of woman. And when men see that women can exist without their being constantly at hand it will perhaps take a little of the conceit out of some of them.

Emmeline Wells

THE FOUNTAIN OF ALL TRUTH

Brigham Young had brought his Mormon people west in search of sanctuary from the rest of the United States. But the new transcontinental railroad now ran right through Utah and began bringing thousands of new settlers into Young's kingdom — nonbelievers who threatened his authority and deplored the Mormon practice of plural marriage. (By 1880, one out of every five citizens of Utah would be a non-Mormon.)

In 1870, some three thousand Mormon women held an "Indignation Meeting" in the Salt Lake Tabernacle, to protest against those nonbelievers who had dared criticize polygamy. One of the speakers was Emmeline Wells. "The world says polygamy makes women inferior to men — we think differently," she told the cheering crowd. "Polygamy gives women more time for thought, for mental culture, more freedom of action, a broader field of labor, . . . [and] leads women more directly to God, the fountain of all truth. . . ."

Born in Massachusetts and graduated from a select girls school, Wells had converted to Mormonism and moved to Nauvoo, where she lost her first child and was abandoned by her husband — all before the age of sixteen. She made the exodus to Utah with her second husband, a church bishop, and bore him two daughters before he died; then became the seventh wife of Daniel H. Wells, the mayor of Salt Lake City, whom she bore three more daughters. Now, she lived in her own small house with her five children, and was expected to help make up the difference whenever her husband's finances suffered. But nothing could shake her belief in plural marriage — or in giving women the vote, the other cause for which she campaigned in a newspaper for Mormon women she somehow found the time to edit.

In her push for the vote, Wells soon found a most unlikely ally. Brigham Young remained anxious about his people eventually being outnumbered — and outvoted in their own land. In Washington, a congressman urged that Utah women be given the vote, certain that they would use it to outlaw polygamy themselves.

Young needed no such urging: he knew that by adding Mormon women to the Utah voters' rolls he would strengthen his hold on the territory. On February 14, 1870, with Young's backing, the Utah territorial legislature granted women the vote. A few days later, for the first time ever in a United States territory, women cast ballots in a municipal election. Young's niece voted first, followed by one of his daughters.

Emmeline Wells never stopped urging the rest of the United States to follow the West's example. (Wyoming Territory, too, had enfranchised its women.) But she never stopped lobbying, either, on behalf of the right of every woman to remain a plural wife.

Emmeline Wells and (below) her newspaper

The polygamous family of Aaron Johnson of Springville, Utah, 1870

WOMAN'S EXPONENT.

Vol. 7. SALT LAKE CITY, UTAH, DEC. 1, 1878. No. 13.

> Neighbors passing spoke of strange happenings. A young wife awaiting her first baby, in the absence of her husband . . . had gone insane from fright, all alone in that sun-baked shanty on the bald prairie. Eggs and milk tasted of the 'hoppers and cows were drying up, somebody said. . . . A train had stalled on a curve coming out of Leavenworth on the narrow-gauge because the crushed grasshoppers greased the track so that the wheels couldn't take hold. Some of the farmers here and there began plowing their denuded corn lands for wheat, turning up the 'hopper eggs to the sun and harrowing the ground thoroughly in hope of destroying the pests as they hatched. Others said that it was wasted effort. . . . If winter didn't kill them off, it was all up with the people, there'd never be another harvest in Kansas.

To many new settlers, unaccustomed to life on the open prairie and already battered by icy winters, howling winds, and desolation, the ravenous insects were the last straw. But not for the Mennonites. "The Mennonites are not afraid of the grasshopper," the Newton *Kansan* assured its anxious readers. "He is an old acquaintance of theirs; and they kill him at once without holding mass meetings or writing complaining letters to the newspapers. With the Mennonites every year is a good year, and adds to their wealth."

Grit and patience and religious faith kept the Mennonites going. Winter wheat made them prosper. The strains of seed they brought with them from Russia flourished as no other domestic crops ever had before on the semiarid western Plains, and would soon transform them into the most productive wheat-growing region in the world. And mixed in with the wheat from Russia came weeds that adapted just as successfully as did the immigrants who brought them — corn cockle, cheatgrass, Russian pigweed, Russian knapweed, and a plant that spread so fast and ranged so widely that it became a symbol of the American West, the Russian thistle, better known as tumbleweed.

For a man to be stove up at thirty may sound strange to some people, but many a cowboy has been so bunged up that he has to quit riding that early in life. . . . My advice to any young man or boy is to stay at home and not be a rambler, as it won't buy you anything. And above everything stay away from a cow ranch, as not many cowpunchers ever save any money and 'tis a dangerous life to live.

James Emmit McCauley

WHOA, BLUE!

The era of the Texas trail drive, ushered in by Charles Goodnight and others, would last just a little over two decades, but by the time it was over and cattle ranching had mostly moved onto the central and northern Plains, it rivaled mining as the West's dominant industry. Some 10 million head of sinewy Texas longhorns were driven north between the end of the Civil War and 1890; so many, one trail driver said, that in places the dust was knee-deep to the cattle. From the southernmost tip of Texas, the trails all pointed north — the Shawnee Trail, the Chisholm, the Stimson, the Goodnight-Loving, the Eastern, and the Western — but their destinations shifted with the market. At first, the herds were driven to mining towns in New Mexico and Colorado, and to reservations and military forts, where the government bought beef to feed its troops and the Indian peoples they were steadily subduing. But in the end, most Texas cattle were taken to the new railheads in Kansas and Nebraska, then shipped east by rail to feed the hungry workers of the cities.

For all the romance that grew up around the cattle drives almost as soon as they began, it was a distinctly unromantic business, and the workingmen who made the cattleman's profits possible labored for wages so low and under conditions so

Teddy Blue Abbott (above), dressed up and slicked down after a successful trail drive in 1879, and a flash-lit photograph (right) of the changing of the cowboy guard at night, made during the 1880s. "When you add it all up," Abbott remembered, "the worst hardship we had on the trail was loss of sleep. There was never enough sleep. . . . I would get maybe five hours' sleep when the weather was nice and everything smooth and pretty, with cowboys singing under the stars. If it wasn't so nice, you'd be lucky to sleep an hour. But the wagon rolled on in the morning just the same. Sometimes we would rub tobacco juice in our eyes to keep awake. It was rubbing them with fire. I have done that a few times, and I have often sat in my saddle sound asleep for just a few minutes."

difficult and so dangerous that only a third of them were willing to undergo them more than once.

Cowboys liked nicknames — Pinnacle Jake, Mesquite Bill, Bronco Jim, Buckskin Joe, Wyoming Pete. Edward C. Abbott was known to his friends as "Teddy Blue" because, while drunk and lurching after a prostitute at a theater in Miles City, Montana, in 1881, he somehow found himself onstage. There, to cover his embarrassment and entertain his fellow cowboys in the audience, he commandeered a chair from a startled musician, straddled it as if it were his horse, and shouted, "Whoa, Blue! Whoa, Blue!" The men in the audience, not entirely sober themselves, loved it. "When I went out of that theatre that night," he remembered as an old man, "I was Blue, and Teddy Blue I have been for fifty-five years."

He was born in England and brought to Nebraska by his parents as a boy. His father let him accompany a trail drive when he was just ten years old, hoping the open air would improve the boy's frail health. "The experience," he said later, "made a cowboy out of me. Nothing could have changed me after that. . . . My family and I went separate ways, and they stayed separate forever after. My father was all for farming . . . and all my brothers turned out farmers except one, and he ended up the worst of the lot — a sheepman and a Republican." Teddy Blue made his first trail drive in 1871 and his last one — still before his twenty-fourth birthday — in 1883, going all the way from San Antonio to Montana. By that time, no one could have suspected that he was not a Texan, born as well as bred.

Like most cowboys, Teddy Blue was young (the average age was twenty-four), and slightly built — big men were too hard on the horses. Most cowboys were Texans, and many were ex–Confederate soldiers whose feelings about northerners had not improved since the Civil War. But there were Mexicans among them too, and blacks,

Riding herd in the 1880s

All in all, my years on the trail were the happiest I ever lived. There were many hardships and dangers, of course, that called on all a man had of endurance and bravery; but when all went well there was no other life so pleasant. Most of the time we were solitary adventurers in a great land as fresh and new as a spring morning, and we were free and full of the zest of darers.

Charles Goodnight

either former Texas slaves or refugees from other parts of the old Confederacy. Whatever their background, almost all the cowboys were poor — willing to work seventeen-hour days, seven days a week for up to four months, at thirty to forty-five dollars a month — and most were uncomplaining. "They had very little grub [on the trail] and they usually run out of that and lived on straight beef," one recalled. "[T]hey had only three or four horses to the man, mostly with sore backs; . . . they had no tents, no tarps, and damn few slickers. They never kicked, because those boys was raised under just the same conditions as there was on the trail — corn meal and bacon for grub, dirt floors in the houses, and no luxuries."

No harder life is lived by any working man. Our comfort was nothing; men were cheap, but cattle cost money.

Andy Adams

A drive's success depended on discipline and planning. According to Teddy Blue, most Texas herds numbered about 2,000 head with a trail boss and about a dozen men in charge — though herds as large as 15,000 were also driven north with far larger escorts. The most experienced men rode "point" and "swing," at the head and sides of the long herd; the least experienced brought up the rear, riding "drag" and eating dust. At the end of the day, Teddy Blue remembered, they "would go to the water barrel . . . and rinse their mouths and cough and spit up . . . black stuff. But you couldn't get it up out of your lungs."

They had to learn to work as a team, keeping the herd moving during the day, resting peacefully at night. Twelve to fifteen miles a day was a good pace. But such steady progress could be interrupted at any time. A cowboy had to know how to gauge the temperament of his cattle, how to chase down a stray without alarming the rest of the herd, how to lasso a steer using the horn of his saddle as a tying post. His saddle was his most prized possession; it served as his chair, his workbench, his pillow at night. Being dragged to death was the most common death for a cowboy, and so the most feared occurrence on the trail was the nighttime stampede. As Teddy Blue recalled, a sound, a smell, or simply the sudden movement of a jittery cow could set off a whole herd.

> If . . . the cattle started running — you'd hear that low rumbling noise along the ground and the men on herd wouldn't need to come in and tell you, you'd know — then you'd jump for your horse and get out there in the lead, trying to head them and get them into a mill before they scattered to hell and gone. It was riding at a dead run in the dark, with cut banks and prairie dog holes all around you, not knowing if the next jump would land you in a shallow grave.

Most cowboys had guns, but rarely used them on the trail. Some outfits made them keep their weapons in the chuck wagon to eliminate any chance of gunplay. Charles Goodnight was still more emphatic: "Before starting on a trail drive, I made it a rule to draw up an article of agreement, setting forth what each man was to do. The main clause stipulated that if one shot another he was to be tried by the outfit and hanged on the spot, if found guilty. I never had a man shot on the trail."

Regardless of its ultimate destination, every herd had to ford a series of rivers — the Nueces, the Guadalupe, the Brazos, the Wichita, the Red. A big herd of longhorns swimming across a river, Goodnight remembered, "looked like a million floating rocking chairs," and crossing those rivers one after another, a cowboy recalled, was like climbing the rungs of a long ladder reaching north.

“After you crossed the Red River and got out on the open plains,” Teddy Blue remembered, “it was sure a pretty sight to see them strung out for almost a mile, the sun shining on their horns.” Initially, the land immediately north of the Red River was Indian territory, and some tribes charged tolls for herds crossing their land — payable in money or beef. But Teddy Blue remembered that the homesteaders, now pouring onto the Plains by railroad, were far more nettlesome:

Isom Dart, like a good many Texas cowboys — black, white, and Hispanic — was not overly particular as to whose cattle he drove to market. He was shot dead as a rustler in 1903.

> There was no love lost between settlers and cowboys on the trail. Those jay-hawkers would take up a claim right where the herds watered and charge us for water. They would plant a crop alongside the trail and plow a furrow around it for a fence, and then when the cattle got into their wheat or their garden patch, they would come cussing and waving a shotgun and yelling for damages. And the cattle had been coming through there when they were still raising punkins in Illinois.

The settlers’ hostility was entirely understandable. The big herds ruined their crops, and they carried with them a disease, spread by ticks and called “Texas fever,” that devastated domestic livestock. Kansas and other territories along the route soon established quarantine lines, called “deadlines,” at the western fringe of settlement, and insisted that trail drives not cross them. Each year, as settlers continued to move in, those deadlines moved farther west.

Sometimes, farmers tried to enforce their own, as John Rumans, one of Charles Goodnight’s hands, recalled:

> Some men met us at the trail near Canyon City, and said we couldn’t come in. There were fifteen or twenty of them, and they were not going to let us cross the Arkansas River. We didn’t even stop. . . . Old Man [Goodnight] had a shotgun loaded with buckshot and led the way, saying: “John, get over on that point with

Getting comfortable: Hungry cowboys remove a thicket of spurs before settling down to dinner, 1903.

> your Winchester and point these cattle in behind me." He slid his shotgun across the saddle in front of him and we did the same with our Winchesters. He rode right across, and as he rode up to them, he said: "I've monkeyed as long as I want to with you sons of bitches," and they fell back to the sides, and went home after we had passed.

There were few diversions on the trail. Most trail bosses banned liquor. Goodnight prohibited gambling, too. Even the songs for which cowboys became famous grew directly out of doing a job, remembered Teddy Blue:

> The singing was supposed to soothe [the cattle] and it did; I don't know why, unless it was that a sound they was used to would keep them from spooking at other noises. I know that if you wasn't singing, any little sound in the night — it might be just a horse shaking himself — could make them leave the country; but if you were singing, they wouldn't notice it.
>
> The two men on guard would circle around with their horses on a walk, if it was a clear night and the cattle was bedded down and quiet, and one man would sing a verse of a song, and his partner on the other side of the herd would sing another verse; and you'd go through a whole song that way. . . . "Bury Me Not on the Lone Prairie" was [a] great song for awhile, but . . . they sung it to death. It was a saying on the range that even the horses nickered it and the coyotes howled it; it got so they'd throw you in the creek if you sang it.

The number of cattle on the move was sometimes staggering: once, Teddy Blue rode to the top of a rise from which he could see seven herds strung out behind him; eight more up ahead; and the dust from an additional thirteen moving parallel to his. "All the cattle in the world," he remembered, "seemed to be coming up from Texas."

At last, the herds neared their destinations. After months in the saddle — often wearing the same clothes every day, eating nothing but biscuits and beef stew at the chuck wagon, drinking only water and coffee, his sole companions his fellow cowboys, his herd, and his horse — the cowboy was about to be paid for his work, and turned loose in town.

Several Kansas communities eventually qualified as cow towns — Abilene, Chetopa, Coffeyville, Ellsworth, Hays, Wichita, Great Bend, Caldwell, and Dodge City (after hunters destroyed the buffalo herds). Some flourished for only a season or two before the shifting quarantine line cut them off from the bawling herds and the big profits they brought to Main Street merchants. Others reaped the benefits — and endured the annual cowboy invasion — for more than a decade.

Cowboys were big spenders, and the shelves of the town stores were carefully stocked with items they especially liked. Teddy Blue remembered his arrival at one cow town:

> [T]hey paid us off, and [I] bought some new clothes and got [my] picture taken. . . . I had a new white Stetson hat that I paid ten dollars for and new pants that cost twelve dollars, and a good shirt and fancy boots. Lord, I was proud of those clothes! They were the kind of clothes top hands wore, and I thought that I was dressed right for the first time in my life. . . . [When] my

Washing up, somewhere in the Oklahoma panhandle, about 1880

sister saw me, she said: "Take your pants out of your boots and put your coat on. You look like an outlaw." I told her to go to hell. And I never did like her after that.

> . . . After packing away our plunder, we sauntered around town . . . visiting the various saloons and gambling houses.

All the cow towns were wilder than their permanent residents liked. "Morally, as a class," said the Cheyenne *Daily Leader,* "[cowboys] are foulmouthed, blasphemous, drunken, lecherous, utterly corrupt. Usually harmless on the plains when sober, they are dreaded in towns, for then liquor has an ascendancy over them." The *Annals of Kansas* agreed: "When he feels well (and he always does when full of what he calls 'Kansas sheep-dip') the average cowboy is a bad man to handle. Armed to the teeth, well mounted, and full of their favorite beverage, the cowboys will dash through the principal streets of town yelling like Comanches. This they call 'cleaning out a town.'"

Bad feelings between townspeople and cowboys, Teddy Blue remembered, were exacerbated by memories of the Civil War.

> Most of them that came up with the trail herds, being from Texas and Southerners to start with, was on the side of the South, and oh, but they were bitter. That was how a lot of them got killed, because they were filled full of the old dope about the war and they wouldn't let an abolitionist arrest them. The marshals in those cow towns . . . were usually Northern men and the Southerners wouldn't go back to Texas and hear people say: "He's a hell of a fellow. He let a Yankee lock him up." . . . I couldn't even guess how many was killed that way on the trail.

Dodge City is a wicked little town. Indeed, its character is so clearly and egregiously bad that one might conclude . . . it was marked for special Providential punishment. Here those nomads in regions remote from the restraints of moral, civil, social and law enforcing life, the Texas cattle drovers, . . . the embodiment of waywardness and wantonness, end the journey with their herds, and here they loiter and dissipate, sometimes for months, and share the boughten dalliances of fallen women.

Washington *Evening Star*
January 1, 1878

WILD BILL

No town had worked harder to attract the trail drives than Abilene. It had been just a cluster of a dozen log huts 140 miles west of Kansas City in the spring of 1867, when a sharp-eyed entrepreneur from Illinois named Joseph McCoy picked it to promote as the best possible shipping point for Texas cattle. He ordered a shipping yard built next to the Kansas Pacific tracks, put up a barn and a small office building, then sent an employee pounding south on horseback to intercept the herds and tell the trail bosses about the brand-new Abilene yards. Just twenty boxcars filled with cattle headed west from there that year, but the following spring Abilene shipped 75,000 head east. In 1869 and 1870 the number was 350,000, and in 1871 the total reached 700,000.

But by then, the railroads had pushed farther west, developing new cow towns, and the land around Abilene was being worked by farmers who deplored the annual influx of longhorns and the rowdy men who tore up their town each spring. In early 1871, the members of the town council, too, were weary of the cowboy horde, and saddened by the recent death of Marshal "Bear River" Tom Smith, who had refused to use his revolvers and had paid with his life for his pacifism when an angry homesteader killed him with an ax.

Sterner measures were needed, and the council voted unanimously to hire a new town marshal with no such compunctions — James Butler Hickok, or "Wild Bill." He

James Butler Hickok in his earliest-known photograph, a tintype made at Lawrence, Kansas, in 1859, and as he looked in his dangerous prime (opposite)

was the most flamboyant and among the most feared of all the gunmen who drifted from mining camps to cow towns and back again after the Civil War. He was also the teller of the tallest tales, rarely disappointing eastern newspapermen who sought him out for stories.

"I say, Mr. Hickok," the journalist Henry Morton Stanley asked him early in his career, "how many white men have you killed to your certain knowledge?"

Hickok pretended to think for a moment, then answered, "I suppose I have killed considerably more than a hundred . . . [and not] one without good cause!" The actual number he killed seems to have been fewer than ten, and his motives for killing them did not always bear close scrutiny. But he was formidable enough with a pistol that few thought it wise to challenge his claims. He was born in Troy Grove, Illinois, in 1837 and moved to Kansas in 1855, hoping to become a farmer. But he was thought tough enough to be made a town constable before he was twenty-one. He didn't stay at it — or any job — for long. In 1858, he was working at a Nebraska freight station when he shot and killed from ambush his first man, an indignant but unarmed customer who had dared demand money owed to him. Somehow, Hickok got off, claiming self-defense.

He served as a Union scout along the Missouri border during the Civil War, then became a professional gambler. Over the next few years, local newspapers chronicled events that earned him a reputation as a man it was best not to cross: "David Tutt. of Yellville, Arkansas, was shot on the public square at 6 o'clock P.M. on Friday last," reported the Springfield, Missouri, *Weekly Patriot* on July 27, 1865, "by James B. Hickok, better known in southwest Missouri as 'Wild Bill.' The difficulty occurred from a game of cards."

Four years later, on August 26, 1869, the Leavenworth, Kansas, *Times and Conservative* noted that "J. B. Hickok . . . shot one Mulrey at Hays Tuesday. Mulrey died yesterday morning. Bill has been elected sheriff of Ellis County."

"On Monday last 'Wild Bill' killed a soldier and seriously wounded another at Hays City," the Topeka *Daily Commonwealth* reported on July 22, 1870. "Five soldiers attacked Bill, and two got used up. . . . The sentiment of the community is with 'Bill,' as it is claimed he but acted in self-defense."

Hickok had already been a lawman at Hays, Kansas, when he came to Abilene. There were those who took a dim view of his private life: he roomed with a succession of prostitutes and he drank too much. "If the enthusiastic admirers of this . . . 'plainsman' could see him on one of his periodical drunks," wrote a reporter for the St. Joseph *Union,* "they would have considerable romance knocked out of them."

Wild Bill may not always have been sober, and he ran his town from the card tables inside the Long Branch Saloon, but he earned his $150 a month, nonetheless, keeping a tight lid on unruly cowboys and clearing dead dogs and horses from the streets during more tranquil times. Hickok's presence alone — along with a glimpse of his twin revolvers, pearl handles reversed to speed up his draw — was enough to intimidate all but the most drunken cowboy. "When I came along the street," one recalled, "he was standing there with his back to the wall and his thumbs hooked in his red sash. He stood there and rolled his head from side to side looking at everything and everybody from under his eyebrows — just like a mad old bull. I decided then and there I didn't want any part of him."

Abilene citizens were delighted. Hickok, said the Abilene *Chronicle,* "has posted up printed notices, informing all persons that the ordinance against carrying fire arms or other weapons in Abilene, will be enforced. That's right. There's no bravery in carrying revolvers in a civilized community. Such a practice is well enough and perhaps necessary when among Indians or other barbarians, but among white people it ought to be discountenanced."

With gun control strictly applied, the town enjoyed a somewhat nervous peace for eight months. Then, a gambler named Phil Coe, who may earlier have quarreled with Hickok over the affections of a woman, let off a couple of shots in front of the Alamo Saloon; he said he was shooting at a stray dog.

Hickok rushed to the scene, saw Coe with his revolver in his hand, and drew his own. Both men began firing. A special deputy named Mike Williams hurried round the corner to help the marshal — and ran into two of Hickok's bullets. "The whole affair was the work of an instant," the *Chronicle* reported. "The Marshal, surrounded by the crowd and standing in the light, did not recognize Williams whose death he deeply regrets. Coe was shot through the stomach, the ball coming out his back; he lived in great agony until Sunday evening; he was a gambler, but a man of natural good impulses, in his better moments."

Public sentiment was generally with Hickok, but the shooting had shocked the town, and the city council decided not to renew his contract. "He acted only too ready to shoot down, to kill outright," one citizen wrote, "instead of avoiding assassination when possible, as is the higher duty of a marshal. Such a policy of taking over justice into his own hands exemplified, of course, but a form of lawlessness."

Pressured by farmers and ordinary citizens, the Abilene town council also now voted to declare their town off-limits to the cattle drives. "Business is not as brisk as it used to be during the cattle season," the *Chronicle* admitted the next summer, "but the citizens have the satisfaction of knowing that 'hell' is more than 60 miles away."

Jobless and increasingly unsteady now with drink, Hickok began to ghost from town to town, playing cards, sometimes serving as a colorful tour guide for wealthy easterners who wanted to see something of the Wild West before it vanished.

In 1873, his old friend Buffalo Bill invited him to come east with him and tour in a melodrama, *The Scouts of the Plains.* It didn't go well. Hickok was often drunk and unable to remember his lines. He had a high girlish voice that was hard to hear, and whenever the spotlight failed to follow him closely enough, he would step out of character and threaten to shoot the stagehands. Buffalo Bill finally had to let him go when he could not be dissuaded from firing blank cartridges at the bare legs of the actors playing Indians, just to see them hop.

Soon, he was back in the West, unable to find work, drifting from cow town to mining camp, still drinking too much, and doing his best to disguise the worsening eyesight that now made his reputation as a gunfighter more and more precarious. He tried gold mining, but when it failed to make him rich he settled back into his old routine — drinking and playing poker.

He was at the Number Ten Saloon in a Dakota mining town called Deadwood one August afternoon in 1876, uncharacteristically seated with his back to the door, when a demented little man named Jack McCall slipped up behind him. McCall had evi-

Fact and fiction: The two dead cavalrymen above may have run afoul of Wild Bill Hickok at Hays City in 1870. Exaggerated reports of this and similar violent encounters helped launch him on a brief show business career as one of three stars of an 1873 melodrama, *The Scouts of the Plains* (above, right): Hickok is second from the left, his weapon unaccountably upside down. Buffalo Bill Cody is at the center, and, next to him, another showman-scout, Texas Jack Crawford. The other two buckskin-clad men in this studio photograph made in Rochester, New York, not long before Hickok left the show were friends of the players.

dently persuaded himself that Hickok was responsible for the death of a brother at Hays City, though no evidence of such a crime was ever found. He stood watching the game for a moment, then drew his revolver and fired it into the back of Wild Bill's head. Hickok died instantly, scattering his cards as he fell.

The editor of the Cheyenne *Daily Leader* offered a grudging obituary that showed how rapidly life in the West was changing:

> "Wild Bill" . . . was one of those characters developed by the onward strides of the iron horse when the "Great American Desert" was spanned by the Pacific railways. Seven or eight years ago his name was prominent in the . . . border press and if we could believe the half of what was written concerning his daring deeds, he must certainly have been one of the bravest and most scrupulous characters of those lawless times. Contact with the man, however, dispelled all these illusions, and of late, Wild Bill seems to have been a very tame and worthless loafer. . . . Years ago, before wine and women had ruined his constitution and impaired his faculties, he was more worthy of the fame which he attained on the border.

BUSINESSMEN WITH RIFLES

Frank Mayer and his competitors called themselves buffalo "runners," not hunters, but they avoided running — or even riding — after buffalo as much as possible. For efficiency's sake, the mounted chase had long since given way to a technique called "the stand," Mayer remembered:

> The thing we had to have, we businessmen with rifles, was one-shot-kills. We based our success on . . . the overwhelming stupidity of the buffalo, unquestionably the stupidest game animal in the world. . . . If you wounded the leader, didn't kill her outright, the rest of her herd, whether it was three or thirty,

> would gather around her and stupidly "mill." . . . [A]ll you had to do . . . was pick them off one by one, making sure you made a dropping kill at every shot, until you wiped out the entire herd. . . . I once took 269 hides with 300 cartridges. . . .

In the East, improved rifles were specially manufactured for the trade, capable of bringing down a buffalo at better than six hundred yards. It "shoots today," one astonished bystander said, "and kills tomorrow." Individual hunters recorded kills of one hundred, then two hundred, from a single stand, pausing only to cool their overheated rifle barrels with canteens of water. When the water ran out, they urinated down the barrel and kept shooting. Orlando A. Bond, nicknamed "Brick" by his friends, killed 300 animals in a single day and 5,855 in one two-month outing, so many that he was permanently deafened by the sound of his own rifle.

Frank H. Mayer, about the time he began shooting buffalo for a living

Frank Mayer's favorite rifle, a Sharps, cost him $125, secondhand. It weighed twelve pounds, its barrel was nearly three feet long, and its telescopic sight was manufactured in Germany. "I was proud of that first Sharps of mine," he said. "It killed quicker . . . and it added 10 to 30 percent efficiency to my shooting." On a bet, he fired at a buffalo a half a mile away with it, and when it dropped from the shot, won a three-gallon keg of "Three Roses" whiskey.

"Where there were myriads of buffalo the year before," the commander at Fort Dodge remembered, "there were now myriads of carcasses. The air was foul with a sickening stench, and the vast plain, which only a short twelvemonth before teemed with animal life, was a dead, solitary, putrid desert." The buffalo hunters themselves, working day after day with rotting flesh, were distinctly gamey. They "didn't wash," Teddy Blue Abbott remembered, "and looked like animals. They dressed in strong, heavy warm clothes and never changed them. You would see three or four of them walk up to a bar, reach down inside their clothes and see who could catch the first louse for the drinks. They were lousy and proud of it."

All across western Kansas, the slaughter went on — an estimated 1.5 to 3 million buffalo killed in a little over two years. Buffalo skeletons, bleached by the sun, soon covered the prairies — and started still more industries. Newly arrived homesteaders augmented their income by harvesting bones. Crews of professional "bone pickers" gathered the skeletons and brought them by wagon to railroad sidings. Buffalo horns were turned into buttons, combs, knife handles. Hooves became glue. Bones were ground into fertilizer. Thirty-two million pounds of buffalo bones made their way from the Plains to eastern factories in just three years.

Some Americans grew alarmed at the extent of the slaughter, and Congress passed a bill in 1874 making it illegal for anyone to kill more buffalo than could be used for food. But President Grant allowed the law to die without his signature. Meanwhile, hunters began to talk of moving south of Kansas, onto hunting grounds reserved for the Indians. What would the government do if they shifted there? a delegation asked the commander at Fort Dodge.

"Boys," he answered, "if I were a buffalo hunter, I would hunt where the buffaloes are."

They swarmed into the Texas panhandle to harvest the southern herd, where the Indians sensed, Frank Mayer remembered, "that we were taking away their birthright

As the skinners began at the edge, they would have to roll each carcass out of the way to make room for the next. In the end the bodies would be rolled up as thick as saw logs around a mill.

Skelton Glenn

Cheyenne women dressing buffalo hides in 1878 (above) and a hide-hunter's camp on Evans Creek in Texas, 1874

and that with every boom of a buffalo rifle their tenure on their homeland became weakened and that eventually they would have no homeland and no buffalo. So they did what you and I would do if our existence were jeopardized: they fought. . . . They fought by stealth. They fought openly. They murdered if they had a chance. They stole whenever they could." In the summer of 1874, the Kiowa, Comanche, Arapaho, and southern Cheyenne rose up and drove out the hunters — and any other whites they came across. In response, Sheridan ordered a massive campaign against them, deploying five columns of troops to pursue the Indians relentlessly, depriving them of rest, or the opportunity to hunt. By the next spring, virtually all of the resisting bands on the southern Plains — desperate now for food — had come in to the agencies.

The buffalo hunters went back to work until both the northern and the southern herds had all but disappeared. Then, "one by one," Frank Mayer recalled, "we runners put up our buffalo rifles, sold them, gave them away, or kept them for other hunting, and left the ranges. And there settled over them a vast quiet. . . . The buffalo was gone." For his years as a buffalo runner, Frank Mayer had his wagon and outfit free and clear, and several thousand dollars in the bank. He left the Plains, married a girl in Denver, and took a job in the Rocky Mountains — hunting game to feed the miners of Leadville.

"Maybe," he recalled,

> we runners served our purpose in helping abolish the buffalo; maybe it was our ruthless harvesting of him which telescoped the control of the Indian by a decade or maybe more. Or maybe I am just rationalizing. Maybe we were just a

Golgotha: buffalo skulls heaped at trackside in Detroit, Michigan, ready to be hauled to the Michigan Carbon Works, 1880s

> greedy lot who wanted to get ours, and to hell with posterity, the buffalo, or anyone else, just so we kept our scalps on and our money pouches filled. I think maybe that is the way it was.

The buffalo had provided both material and spiritual sustenance to the people of the Plains. Life without it seemed inconceivable, and some began to seek some explanation for what had befallen them. Old Lady Horse remembered a story that circulated among her desperate people, the Kiowa:

> The buffalo saw that their day was over. They could protect their people no longer. Sadly, the last remnant of the great herd gathered in council, and decided what they would do.
>
> The Kiowas were camped on the north side of Mount Scott, those of them who were still free to camp. One young woman got up very early . . . and . . . peering through the haze, saw the last buffalo herd appear like in a spirit dream.
>
> Straight to Mount Scott the leader of the herd walked. Behind him came the cows and their calves, and the few young males who had survived. As the woman watched, the face of the mountain opened. Inside Mount Scott the world was green and fresh, as it had been when she was a small girl. The rivers ran clear, not red. The wild plums were in blossom, chasing the red buds up the inside slopes. Into this world of beauty the buffalo walked, never to be seen again.

Great Migrations: The Pioneer in the American West

John Mack Faragher

One of the greatest mass migrations in American history began in 1815. With Indian resistance in the Mississippi Valley broken by the victories of American forces during the War of 1812, thousands of families in Pennsylvania and Virginia, Kentucky and Tennessee packed their goods and poured west into Alabama, Missouri, and Illinois. There was "good land dog-cheap everywhere," wrote English settler George Flower, "and for nothing, if you will go far enough for it." From his porch in southern Illinois, Baptist preacher John Mason Peck watched a steady westward procession of wagons, carriages, and two-wheeled carts, and fancied that "Kentucky and Tennessee were breaking up and moving to the 'Far West.'" Within five years the population of Missouri nearly tripled, and there was comparable growth all along the frontier. From 1810 to 1820 the proportion of Americans living west of the Appalachians rose from 15 to 27 percent.

Contemporaries christened this mass movement "the Great Migration," a phrase rich with historical associations. It was the name the Puritans of Massachusetts Bay gave to their Atlantic crossing of the 1630s, the name claimed by pioneers headed overland for the Far West in the 1840s, and the name historians apply to the migration of tens of thousands of black people from the rural South to the industrial North in the twentieth century.

We Americans have always had itching feet. The movement of people from one place to another is one of the most important factors in our history. Even in colonial New England, where there was a strong commitment to the value of community, high levels of migration became notable within the first fifty years of settlement. "That they might keep themselves together," Increase Mather wrote in 1676, the first Puritan colonists had been "satisfied with one Acre for each person." But "how have Men since coveted the earth," he lamented; "they that profess themselves Christians have forsaken Churches, and Ordinances, all for land and elbow-room." That pressing American need for elbowroom was so strong that by the time of the Revolution, in typical American communities in all regions of the country, at least four of every ten households packed up and left every ten years. High rates of geographic mobility have continued to characterize our national life ever since. In the world, only New Zealanders exceed Americans in their rate of mobility. We have always been a people in motion, right up to the present shift of population away from the Northeast and toward the metropolitan centers of the Sun Belt.

Mobility was particularly important in the settlement of the American West. Rates of migration in western and frontier communities were probably as high as they ever got in American experience. In one backcountry Virginia county on the eve of the American Revolution, about two in ten families departed each year, only to be replaced by three new arrivals. Perhaps the most extreme turnover in population occurred in the mining towns of gold rush California, where only 10 or 15 percent of the people listed in the federal census of 1850 persisted to the next one ten years later. More typical western communities experienced ten-year rates of persistence of about 20 or 30 percent. Transience was one of the most important facts of pioneer life.

To bring some order to this great swirl and rush of people it helps to remember that this movement was largely of families. It is true that many single, unattached men moved west (very few single, unattached women did so). But with the exception of the gold rush and other mining booms, they tended to travel with family parties as hired hands or teamsters. These emigrating families frequently had prodigious histories of migration. "Many of our neighbors are true backwoodsmen, always fond of moving," John Woods of southern Illinois noted in 1820. Among these "extensive travelers," he wrote, "to have resided in three or four states, and several places in each state, is not uncommon." His observation is borne out by a close study of the family histories of the pioneers of the community of Sugar Creek in central Illinois, first settled during the Great Migration of 1815–20. Eight in ten families had moved from another state at least once before, and 35 percent had moved two or more times. Similarly, 78 percent of the families who participated in the Great Migration on the Overland Trail to Oregon and California in the mid-nineteenth century had made at least one previous move, many had moved several times, and a substantial minority had been almost continuously in motion.

For most moves westward, the process of decision making was not documented. The Overland Trail migration, however, provides a unique opportunity for examining the way families made those choices, for literally hundreds of men and women left journals and recollections in which they discussed, among other things, the decision to move. "Oh let us not go," Mary Jones cried when her husband John told her of his decision to relocate the family; but, she lamented, "it made no difference." Lucy Deady, daughter of an emigrant family, wrote that her despairing mother knew "nothing of his move until father had decided to go." A close study of women's overland diaries finds not a single wife who initiated the idea of moving, while nearly a third actively objected. One emigrant wife told a hired hand that "the journey for which she was bending all her energies in preparation was not in her judgment a wise business movement. But

'Wilson' wished to go, and that settled the question with her." The decision to emigrate, in short, seems to have been an example of the exercise of husbands' power.

Consider the number of "gold rush widows" left behind when tens of thousands of fevered men left their homes for western mines after 1849. "My old man has left me & has gon to Californa and took my wagon and left me and my Children in a bad situation." So Elizabeth Cress of Illinois wrote to her parents appealing for a loan to see her through the winter. But some wives simply forbade their husbands' going. "The Rolling Stone," a song popular throughout the Midwest during the 1850s, recounted such a struggle:

Since times are so hard, I'll tell you, my wife
I've a mind for to shake off this trouble and strife,
And to California my journey pursue
To double my fortunes as other men do.
For here we may labor each day in the field
And the winters consume all that summers doth yield.

Dear husband, remember your land is to clear,
It will cost you the labor of many a year.
Your horses, sheep and cattle will all be to buy,
And before you have got them you are ready to die.
So stick to your farming; you'll suffer no loss,
For the stone that keeps rolling can gather no moss.

The wife of the song, like thousands of uncounted women, succeeded in keeping her feverish husband on the farm. Other women took a different approach. When Gay Hayden came down with gold fever in early 1850, he announced to his wife, Mary Jane, that he was leaving her behind. "I was nearly heartbroken at the thought of the separation," she remembered, but she wisely adopted an aggressive defense. "We were married to live together," she declared, "and I am willing to go with you to any part of *God's foot stool* where you think you can do best, and under these circumstances you have no right to go where I cannot, and if you do you need never return for I shall look upon you as dead." And so, she concluded, "it was settled that *we* should go the next year."

Historians of the American frontier have tended to celebrate the legacy of the people called "the movers" by their contemporaries. Migration offered Americans "a gate of escape from the bondage of the past," wrote Frederick Jackson Turner, the influential historian of the American frontier. "The advance of the frontier has meant a steady growth of independence on American lines. And to study this advance, the men who grew up under these conditions and the political, economic and social result of it, is to study the *really American* part of our history." In Turner's judgment, the process of migration and resettlement, and the cultural attitudes and character they engendered, were peculiarly American, dramatically contrasting with the conservatism and persistence of traditional European societies.

In American folklore, the figure of Daniel Boone — the heroic pioneer leader of the settlement of trans-Appalachia — became the personification of this sense of possibility. "Boone used to say to me," claimed a resident of the Carolina hills, "that when he could not fall the top of a tree near enough his door for fire-wood, it was time to move to a new place." In a folktale that refers to Boone's last remove, from Kentucky to the frontier of Missouri, the old pioneer declares to a traveler, "I wanted to go where I would not be around so much by neabors," but complains that even in Missouri, "I am too much crowded." Well, how close *are* your neighbors, the man asks, and is incredulous at Boone's reply. Only twenty miles away! This sentiment was well expressed by the American poet Arthur Guiterman, whose verses were memorized by several generations of schoolchildren.

. . . Daniel Boone was ill at ease
When he saw the smoke in his forest trees.
There'll be no game in the country soon.
Elbow room! cried Daniel Boone.

. . . Ever he dreamed of new domains
With vaster woods and wider plains;
Ever he dreamed of a world-to-be
Where there are no bounds and the soul is free.
At fourscore-five, still stout and hale,
He heard a call to a farther trail;
So he turned his face where the stars are strewn;
Elbow room! sighed Daniel Boone.

Down the Milky Way in its banks of blue
Far he has paddled his white canoe.
To the splendid quest of the tameless soul
He has reached the goal where there is no goal. . . .
East of the sun and west of the moon,
Elbow room! laughs Daniel Boone.

During Boone's own lifetime his movements westward, and his lifelong love of solitude, became the stuff of folklore. But tales of his supposed wanderlust angered Boone the old man. "Nothing embitters my old age," he told a visitor a few years before his death, "like the circulation of absurd stories that I retire as civilization advances, that I shun the white men and seek the Indians, and that now even when old, I wish to retire beyond the second Alleghenies." Indeed, there was a double edge to the folklore of Boone's wanderlust, for while it celebrated migration, the very essence of American pioneering, it also raised questions about his social commitments. Boone "did not stay [in] one plase long [enough] to get acquainted," complained one of his former Kentucky neighbors; he "always lived in a world of his own." Settlers depended upon mutual assistance for survival and mistrusted men who refused to be neighborly.

Many conservative commentators likewise feared the consequences of high levels of mobility. Yale clergyman Timothy Dwight lamented in 1819 that the pioneers, "impatient of the restraints of law, religion, and morality," were "too idle, too talkative, too passionate, too prodigal, and too shiftless to acquire either property or character." On the frontier "everything shifts under your eye," wrote Timothy Flint, another Yankee, but one who had moved west. "The present occupants sell, pack, depart. Strangers replace them. Before they have gained the confidence of their neighbors, they hear of a better place, pack up, and follow their precursors. This circumstance adds to the instability of connexions."

These perspectives call attention to the riddle of community life in the American West. What kind of communities could form with so many men and women moving in and moving out, with people constantly passing through, with the faces in the neighborhood changing so frequently? Again, a family perspective is useful. Looking at communities as collections not of individuals but of households and families reveals considerably more social continuity than suggested by the raw data of the persistence statistics. In the community of Sugar Creek in central Illinois, for example, a quarter of the original settler families laid down roots deep enough to persist through the nineteenth century. Three-quarters of the children and grandchildren of this group chose to begin households and raise children of their own in the local community. Over time kinship ties became increasingly important. In 1830 about one in five heads of household shared his surname with the heads of at least two other households; thirty years later that proportion had doubled.

By marrying locally and building family alliances, these generations of "stickers," as the western historian Wallace Stegner called them, strengthened their influence within the local community. Seven in ten children and better than half the grandchildren of those original families found spouses among others who had lived in the community for ten years or more. Although in part these were the choices forced upon people by life in a small and relatively isolated community, the practice of what some have called "sibling-exchange marriage" suggests that there was considerable deliberation at work here. A significant minority of marriages among the descendants of original families took place among sibling sets, the brothers and sisters of one family marrying the brothers and sisters of another. Such marriage patterns seem strange today, but were commonplace in the nineteenth-century countryside, and are still a fact of life in some regions. "My three daughters married Ed's three sons," one Appalachian woman told a sociologist in the 1960s; "ain't nothing that brings a family together like that." Sibling exchange accounted for nearly one in five of the marriages within the group of original families in Sugar Creek.

The J. H. Byington family, Utah, 1870

Families practicing intermarriage stood a much better chance of retaining their original grants by combining their resources with others, facilitating the concentration of real property. In 1838 members of these families controlled nearly 90 percent of the local arable land. Twenty years later, although their proportional strength in the community had greatly declined, they continued to hold over half the land. Today, more than a century and a half after the area was first settled during the Great Migration, the descendants of some two dozen of those original families continue to live in the Sugar Creek area, and control at least 10 percent of the land.

The riddle of community in the American West is resolved, then, by recognizing the coexistence of both the "movers" — the transient majority who farmed for a time before pushing on — and the "stickers" — the men and women who persisted on the land and rooted themselves in the community during the first decades of settlement, intermarried with each other, and passed their farms on to their children. The westward movement is the story of the choices of families in both groups. Long ago this was recognized by the early-nineteenth-century Illinois writer James Hall. "The settlers are not always in motion," Hall wrote. "They remain for years in one spot, forming the mass of the settled population, and giving a tone to the institutions of the country; and at each remove, a few are left behind, who cling permanently to the soil, and bequeath their landed possessions to their posterity." As much as mobility, posterity and landed possessions, family, and land shaped the character of western communities.

During the second half of the nineteenth century the direction of American expansion shifted from the countryside to the city. The West was popularly known as the land of wide-open spaces, but by the 1890s the typical westerner lived in an urban oasis like Omaha, Denver, or San Francisco. The American West included the fastest-growing cities in the nation, and by 1890 had become more heavily urban than any other region except the Northeast. When we think of the astounding growth of nineteenth-century American cities, most of us think of the flood of immigration from abroad; yet the single most important source of the expanding population of western cities came from the countryside. With the expansion of the commercial economy, farming and ranching became a significantly more capital-intensive business. After the Civil War a western settler needed an average of a thousand dollars to purchase land, the equipment necessary to work it, and the transportation to get the family there. Although railroads and land speculators continued to promote the West as a safety valve for the urban working class, as the "free range" disappeared and the number of tenant farmers and hired hands grew larger, it is more accurate to say that it was the cities that provided the safety valve for *rural discontent.* As one historian has put it, for every industrial worker who became a farmer, twenty farm boys moved to the city.

This is relatively well known. Less so is the fact that for every twenty farm boys, there were in the late nineteenth century perhaps twenty-five or thirty farm girls moving from the rural to the urban West. The prominent place of young, unattached women in the migration from farm to city marks it as significantly different from the process that settled the countryside. While a great many families came to the city from American farms, the great majority of the migrants were unmarried young people, and there seem to have been many more migrating women than migrating men. Many studies of short-distance migrations from country to city, throughout the world, confirm that young women predominate in these movements. Throughout the West they left home at a considerably greater rate than their brothers. One study of rural households found that among middling to poor farmers, only four in ten daughters as compared to seven in ten sons remained on the land. Apparently, when the resources of the family were not sufficient to provide for all the children, daughters were the most likely to migrate. Another study found a persistence rate of only 31 percent among the daughters of Minnesota farmers, compared to 46 percent for sons. Evidence of the greater movement of young women also exists at the other end of the trail. In Chicago, which was the Mecca for young people from Indiana to Kansas and beyond, native-born young women began to outnumber native-born young men during the 1880s, and over the next forty years the female proportion of this group continued to rise. As the westward movement shifted from country to city, young women were prominent among the new urban pioneers.

What accounted for the greater number of women choosing the city over the country? In the opinion of many contemporaries, a lack of opportunity pushed them out. "I hate farm-life," says a young wife in Hamlin Garland's *Main-Travelled Roads,* published during the 1890s. "It's nothing but fret, fret, and work the whole time, never going any place, never seeing anybody but a lot of neighbors just as big fools as you are. I spend my time fighting flies and washing dishes and churning. I'm sick of it." Farm and ranch women themselves added to the chorus of complaint. "Isolation, stagnation, ignorance, loss of ambition, the incessant grind of labor, and the lack of time for improvement by reading, by social intercourse, or by recreation of some sort are all working against the farm woman's happiness and will ultimately spell disaster for the Nation," one wife wrote. "In my opinion," declared another, "the worst feature of farm work is too much work and too little pleasure. No wonder young folks leave the farm." Rural women generally agreed that they suffered from the drudgery of household and outside labor, that male attitudes kept them from full participation in public and community life, and that lack of educational and vocational opportunity bound them to the fate of their mothers.

A letter from a rural woman, published in *The Farmer's Voice* in 1912, warned of the growing dissatisfactions of the country daughter: "She isn't going to 'stay put,' but will get out where she can earn some money of her very own, to buy the little things so dear to the hearts of girls; and she will not be questioned and scolded over every little expenditure." The progressive reformer Martha Foote Crow, in a 1915 study, *The American Country Girl,* warned that "if the home cannot be made happy and the work in the farmhouse cannot be made interesting, if her fair share of incentive as a human being in the common round of life cannot be assigned to her, if her part in the complex structure of the farmstead cannot be put upon an equitable basis, if the universal happy fortune of woman cannot be seen to shine as a goal in the long service of the farmstead, why, she will have none of it!" Another reformer lamented that practically the only alternatives to marriage for country girls were teaching district school and leaving home to go to the city. The emancipation of women still had far to go in the country. In the view of most contemporaries, it was the lingering tradition of rural patriarchy that pushed young women from the farm.

But perhaps even more compelling than the push of the country was the pull of the city, which represented the hope of a better life for many women. "It is the girl with ability," one observer noted, "who dares to migrate to the city." The conditions of country life, echoed another, "tend to create gradually a strong revolt on the part of girls of vigorous personality." Many contemporaries emphasized the hopes of women migrants. "Women find in cities greater opportunities for partial or entire self-support," wrote a social scientist in 1895, "while the scope for employment afforded them by country life is much less." In the city a new sense of possibility could develop from the freedom afforded by wage work outside the household. Abraham Bisno, a union organizer among Chicago's women cloak makers, found that women fresh from the rural family "appreciated the opportunity of working a limited number of hours and earning money. Though their wage was small, they considered it large." It was, Bisno declared, "a historic revolution in their lives." With work in the public world, wrote one observer, the perspective of the young rural migrant changes: "the world is bigger than she knew and there are other ways of living than those she has been taught to accept. A new attitude toward life begins to develop, manifested in a little more self-assertion and a desire 'to do as other girls do.' Gradually she comes into her own world of hopes and ambitions in which the parents have little part."

One of the important dimensions of urban work was the extent to which it allowed young migrant women money of their own, a means to determine their own affairs. Many of the working women who continued to live with their families, and brought their wages home to their mothers, attempted to squeeze out a small allowance for their own needs. A federal study of 1909 found that working girls often kept the extra income they earned from tips or overtime. One young woman, asked in her mother's presence how much she could save each week for herself in this way, replied, "Oh, about $1.50." Surprised, the mother exclaimed, "Why, Nellie, you don't do any such thing." "Yes, I do," Nellie answered, "but I never told you." This pattern encouraged girls doing piecework to speed up their own routines so they could earn a little something for themselves. "As there is often a difference of two or three dollars a week between what she accepts as her limit and what she can do 'on a spurt,'" reported one social worker, "the temptation to earn more money may be accepted at a frightful cost of nervous energy."

As early as the 1880s, young working girls in San Francisco, Denver, and cities all over America were spending relatively substantial sums on clothes, makeup, and amusements. After the working day, wrote one investigator, girls sought excitement at the dance halls and the theater, later at the movies, or simply by strolling the streets with their companions and enjoying the scene. "Those who faithfully hold to a difficult and uncongenial occupation, bringing home the entire wage to the family and submitting to an almost patriarchal control in other matters," she wrote, "will demand a freedom in the use of the evening before which their parents are helpless."

Most unmarried working women in western cities resided with families, but the number living on their own increased greatly as the nineteenth turned to the twentieth century. In Chicago about 20 percent of white working women lived on their own in the early 1890s; by 1909, according to one survey, nearly half of them were living on their own. Many country women in western cities for the first time found rooms in the "newcomer" homes of charitable organizations like the YWCA, but few of them chose to live there for long. Social workers often held suspicious attitudes about working girls, and regulations about visitors, "lock-up," and "lights-out" alienated many young women, who stayed only until they could find other accommodations. If she had her way, a worker in one of the organized homes told a reporter, the women in her care would be more closely supervised, but, she admitted, this was impossible because of the freedom demanded by young business girls. From the 1880s to the 1950s the Harvey chain of restaurants along the Santa Fe line in Kansas, Colorado, and New Mexico hired thousands of single women to serve hungry travelers and tourists. Harvey Girls lived in company dormitories, but were free to do as they pleased after work. In the words of a popular tune of 1907:

> O the pretty Harvey Girl beside my chair,
> A fairer maiden I shall never see.
> She was winsome, she was neat, she was gloriously sweet
> And she was certainly good to me.

Few single working women could afford their own apartments. Most settled for furnished rooms, in the words of one young Los Angeles migrant of the 1920s, "a place where we can unpack our trunk, anchor our electric iron, and hang our other blouse over the chair." The demand for rooms, for freedom and independence in living arrangements by young people living and working in the city, led to the growth of rooming house districts in all the major cities of the West. In San Francisco, Portland, Denver, and Chicago such districts became little bohemias, dominated by young people interested in culture and politics. According to one study of Chicago, the West Side rooming house district was filled with "genuine Americans, most of them men and girls under thirty, who have come to Chicago from towns and country districts of Illinois, and from Wisconsin, Michigan, and other neighboring states, most of whom lead irregular lives and very few of whom are found in families."

As this last line suggests, there was considerable fear that naive and innocent young country girls would be ruined by their urban experience. The migrating girl, warned Martha Foote Crow, "exchanged the safe and kindly surroundings of the rural home for the dangerous conditions of the city, its unregulated contacts, its promiscuity and its perils, and its loneliness in the midst of strangers." Were these the same young women that Crow described as understanding the limitations of country life and acting hopefully to create new opportunities of their own? Somehow the contradiction between the two images got lost in the anxiety of social change. Surely young working women faced challenges. "A girl has to be some sport to work in this joint," said a Portland waitress who told of sexual harassment by customers and fellow workers. But things may have been worse down on the farm; according to a recent study of late-nineteenth-century migrating women, many reported fleeing sexual abuse at home. Certainly few women drifted into sin in the cities. Most worked for a time, then married and raised children. But into those marriages they carried a set of expectations very different from those of their mothers, the result of their several years of independence.

These young migrating women were the urban pioneers of the West. Historians of the changing manners and morals of women have generally focused on the middle and upper classes. But close attention to the choices of migrating country girls suggests that it was they who took the lead in creating new opportunities for twentieth-century women. Jane Addams, the founder of Hull House in Chicago, and a sensitive observer of the city, wrote in 1909 that "through the huge hat, with its wilderness of bedraggled feathers, the girl announces to the world that she is here. She demands attention to the fact of her existence, she states that she is ready to live, to take her place in the world." Let us give these young urban pioneers their appropriate place, side by side with the forty-niners and the migrating family in the drama of the Great Migrations.

Mammoth Hot Springs,
Yellowstone Valley

CHAPTER SIX

RIVERS RUN BACKWARD

1874–1877

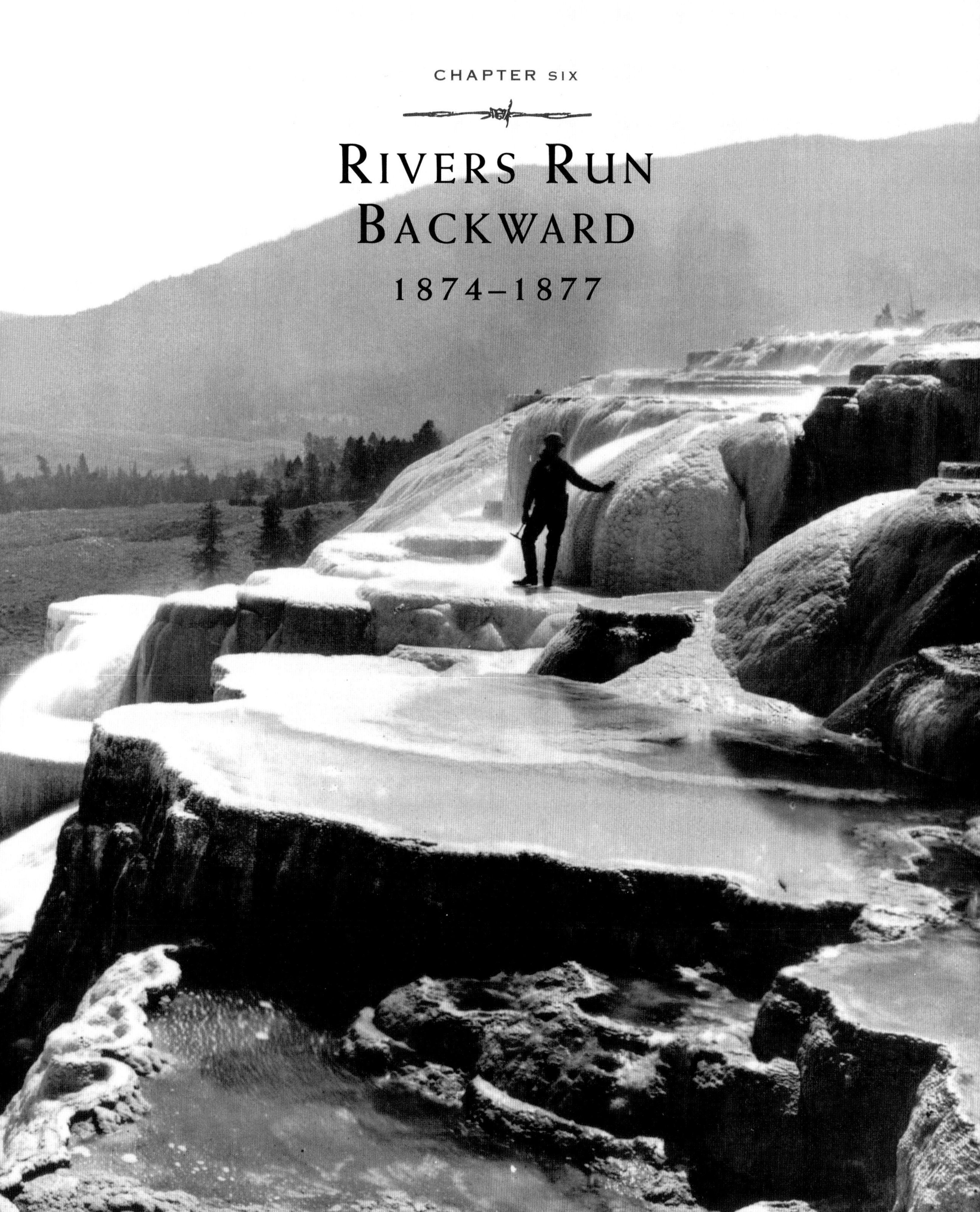

By 1874, the railroads had changed much of the West forever, opening whole regions to settlement, transforming the lives of those who already lived there, helping the United States to consolidate its authority. But some stubbornly held out against the American transformation. In their desert stronghold, the Mormons found themselves again besieged and sought to survive by sacrificing one of their own for the greater good, while two great Indian leaders refused to abandon lands they believed should be theirs alone, scored astonishing triumphs, and then discovered that there was no way to get away from the Americans.

George Armstrong Custer with the Black Hills bear he claimed as his own. "I have reached the highest rung on the hunter's ladder of fame," he wrote his wife. "I have killed my grizzly." In reality, he had had a good deal of help from backup bullets fired into the animal by his Cree scout Bloody Knife (left) and Captain William Ludlow (right).

In the summer of 1874, two long columns — more than a thousand soldiers, a hundred wagons, sixty-one Arikara scouts, and three newspapermen — marched out of Fort Abraham Lincoln on the Missouri and started southwest across the Great Sioux Reservation. They were officially looking for a site on which to build a fort from which the army could keep an eye on the Lakota who lived around the Red Cloud and Spotted Tail agencies.

But they were also looking for gold. For half a century now, Americans had scoured the West in frantic search of it. California, Oregon, Washington, Nevada, Montana, Colorado, Arizona, New Mexico — all had already been made to yield up much of their treasure. Now, rumors held that the Black Hills, too, were full of gold. But they were technically off-limits to gold-seekers, part of the Great Sioux Reservation promised to the Lakota in perpetuity in the treaty of Fort Laramie of 1868.

That was no longer going to matter. "As the Christian looks forward with hope and faith to that land of pure delight," said the editor of the Bismarck *Tribune,* "so the miner looks forward to the Black Hills, a region of fabulous wealth, where the rills repose on beds of gold and the rocks are studded with precious metal. . . . [T]he time has come when the entire army could not much longer keep the country from being over-run by the invincible white man — by the hardy pioneer."

George Armstrong Custer rode at the head of the expedition. His destruction of Black Kettle's Cheyenne on the Washita in 1868 — and his own colorful published accounts of this and other exploits — had made him the army's most celebrated Indian fighter. Now, the Black Hills expedition promised Custer still more of the excitement and adventure he craved. "We have discovered a rich and beautiful country," he wrote to his wife. "I have been Commanding Officer and everything else, especially guide." Custer helped blaze the trail, shot at the deer and pronghorn antelope that stopped to watch him pass, and wrote it all up for the New York *World.* And in French Creek, a narrow stream that wound through a glade, which one of his topographical engineers named "Custer Park," his men found gold — not a real bonanza, but enough to persuade his troopers to line up shoulder to shoulder along the creek to try their luck at panning, more than enough to inspire wild-eyed stories in the local press of pay dirt "from the grass roots down."

"This immense section," wrote the editor of the Bismarck *Times,* "bids fair to become the new El Dorado of America." Gold-hungry whites would soon swarm in and begin banging together a dozen mining camps — Lead City, Washington, Blacktail, Golden Gate, Deadwood — and Custer City. Whites now called the path Custer's columns had followed the "Freedom Trail."

The Lakota called it the "thieves' road." They kept their distance as Custer's columns invaded their sanctuary, but they were deeply disturbed. They professed a spiritual attachment to the Black Hills and considered them uniquely sacred to their tribe, though they had only relatively recently wrested them from other Indian peoples. But the Black Hills also had practical meaning for them: the Hunkpapa holy man Sitting Bull called them a "food pack," by which he meant that their valleys were alive with small game, their slopes covered with trees for fuel, ideal for winter camp. Once the Black Hills were lost to the white man, he believed, it would no longer be possible to sustain the old ways any longer. And as far as Sitting Bull was concerned, those ways were the only ones by which a true Lakota could live. "I will remain what I am until I die," he said, "a hunter, and when there are no buffalo or other game I will send my children to hunt and live on prairie mice, for where an Indian is shut up in one place his body becomes weak."

If I were an Indian, I often think that I would greatly prefer to cast my lot among those . . . who adhered to the free open plains, rather than submit to the confined limits of a reservation, there to be the recipient of the blessed benefits of civilization, with its vices thrown in without stint or measure.

George Armstrong Custer

Some 30,000 Lakota, Arapaho, and Northern Cheyenne now drew rations at the five agencies. But another 3,000 Lakota, along with some 400 Cheyenne — whites called them all "Non-Treaties" — spent much of the year in the unceded hunting grounds that extended west, beyond the reservation, to the Bighorn Mountains.

Custer's columns advancing into Castle Creek valley in the Black Hills, 1874

Gall, Hunkpapa Lakota, who would fight with special fervor at the Little Bighorn armed only with a hatchet because, he remembered, army bullets had killed his two wives and three of his children and "my heart was bad that day"

Custer's camp at Hiddenwood Creek in the Black Hills, not far from the spot where his men found gold

Some of them wandered still farther, to raid white settlements in Montana Territory and to harass their old enemies, the Crow. And when in 1872 surveying parties for the Northern Pacific tried to chart a route through the Yellowstone Valley, they had been attacked by them, again and again.

They had many leaders — Black Moon, Four Horns, Gall, Crow King, Black Eagle, Rain-in-the-Face, American Horse, and Crazy Horse, the daring Oglala who had helped lure Captain Fetterman and seventy-nine of his men to their death back in 1866. But the man to whom even these veteran fighters often looked for guidance was Sitting Bull. He was born about 1831 on the Grand River at a place the Lakota called Many Caches because of the pits for storing food they had dug there, and he would devote much of his life simply to ensuring that his people had enough to eat.

He counted his first coup at fourteen during a raid on the Crow, and led the Strong Heart warrior society, whose members ascribed their triumphs in battle against the Crow, Assiniboin, and Shoshone to the extraordinary power of his visions. No one had earned a greater reputation for bravery. Once, in the midst of a fight with soldiers guarding a railroad crew on the Yellowstone, he strolled out between the lines with two warriors and calmly sat down. Then, with bullets whizzing all around him, he filled his pipe, smoked it slowly, passed it back and forth to his companions until the bowl was empty, then reamed it out and walked away from the fighting.

Crow King, who would lead his own Hunkpapa Lakota band in the Custer fight

Rain-in-the-Face, Oglala Lakota, whom Custer had once arrested for the murder of three men on the Yellowstone River. After escaping from his captors, he too would battle Custer at the Little Bighorn.

He was an implacable opponent of accommodation. "Look at me!" he once shouted to a group of Assiniboin who had made their peace with whites. "See if *I* am poor, or my people, either. The whites may get me at last, as you say, but I will have good times till then. You are fools to make yourselves slaves to a piece of fat bacon, some hard-tack, and a little sugar and coffee."

Sitting Bull's name was meant to describe an intractable buffalo bull, on its haunches but still resolute in the face of danger. That resolution would soon be tested.

By the winter of 1875, some 15,000 miners had crowded into the Black Hills, in violation of the treaty with the Lakota. It was the army's task to drive them out. But there were far too many. "I have been captured and sent out of the Hills four times," one resolute prospector said. "I guess I can stand it as long as they can." "We owe the Indians justice and fair play," said the Chicago *Inter-Ocean,* "but we owe it to civilization that such a garden of mineral wealth be brought into occupation and use."

Another solution had to be found. A Senate commission was sent west, prepared either to lease the Black Hills from the Lakota or to pay $6 million for them if the Indians were willing to sell them outright. Twenty thousand Lakota came to meet with the commissioners, but Sitting Bull, Crazy Horse, and other defiant bands stayed away entirely, unwilling even to discuss selling their most sacred place. They sent a messenger named Little Big Man to express their scorn. He rode into the council on horseback, with three hundred warriors, all painted for battle and chanting a new song:

> Black Hills is my land and I love it
> And whoever interferes
> will hear this gun.

Little Big Man waved his Winchester at the commissioners and shouted, "I will kill the first chief who speaks for selling the Black Hills," then wheeled his horse and led his warriors away.

The senators plunged ahead, regardless. "You should bow to the wishes of the Government which supports you," their chairman told the assembled chiefs. "Gold is useless to you, and there will be fighting unless you give it up."

Chief Spotted Tail of the Brulé responded first. He evidently saw the sale as inevitable — there were too many whites to be resisted — but he wanted to set the highest possible price. "As long as we live on this earth, we expect pay . . ." he said. "The amount must be so large that the interest will support us. . . . If even only two Indians remain, so long as they live they will want to be fed, as they are now."

Red Cloud gave more specifics. He was proving as formidable in negotiation as he had been skilled at war.

> . . . I want seven generations ahead to be fed. . . . These hills out here to the northwest we look upon as the head chief of the land. My intention was that my children should depend on these hills for the future. I hoped that we should live that way always. . . . I want to put the money that we get for the Black Hills at interest among the whites, to buy with the interest wagons and cattle. . . . For

Two brand-new mining camps — Custer City (above, left), named in honor of the man whose expedition discovered gold, and Deadwood — sprawl across the Lakota hunting grounds. "I want to hunt in this place," Sitting Bull warned whites. "I want you to turn back from here. If you don't, I'll fight you."

Opposite: Sitting Bull, 1884

I will remain what I am until I die, a hunter, and when there are no buffalo or other game I will send my children to hunt and live on prairie mice, for where an Indian is shut up in one place his body becomes weak.

Sitting Bull

seven generations to come I want our Great Father to give us Texas steers for our meat. I want the Government to issue for me hereafter, flour and coffee, and sugar and tea, and bacon, the very best kind, and cracked corn and beans and rice and dried apples . . . and tobacco, and soap and salt and pepper for the old people. . . . I want a sow and a boar, and a cow and a bull, and a hen and cock, for each family. I am Indian and you want to make a white man out of me. I want some white men's houses at this agency to be built for the Indians. I have been into white people's houses, and I have seen nice black bedsteads and chairs and I want that kind of furniture . . . a saw-mill, . . . a mower and a scythe. Maybe you white people think that I ask too much . . . but I think those hills extend clear to the sky — maybe they go above the sky, and that is the reason I ask so much. . . .

For three full days, as other chiefs echoed Red Cloud's demands and then added to them, the commissioners grew more and more disheartened — the Lakota's speeches were "of so extraordinary a character," they wrote later, "as to make it manifest that it was useless to continue the negotiations. . . . The Indians place a value on the hills far beyond any sum that could possibly be considered by the Government." Congress should therefore simply "fix a fair equivalent . . . taking into account all the circumstances surrounding them, and the value of the Hills to the United States," and then present that arrangement to the Lakota as a "finality."

To increase the pressure, Congress threatened to withhold food until the Lakota capitulated. President Grant secretly ordered the army to ignore the miners' intrusions. The Interior Department demanded that the non-treaty bands be compelled to abandon the unceded hunting grounds and come into the agencies by January 31, 1876. Sitting Bull, Crazy Horse, and the others refused.

A GOOD DAY TO DIE

Sometime in the early spring of 1876, Sitting Bull had climbed to a hilltop to commune with the spirits. In his vision, a great dust storm swirled down upon a small white cloud that resembled a Lakota village. Through the whirlwind, Sitting Bull could see soldiers marching. There was a great storm and the cloud was swallowed up for a time, but it emerged intact and the dust storm disappeared. It was an encouraging vision.

In the spring of 1876 the Lakota needed encouragement — the United States Army was about to move against them. In his far-off Chicago headquarters, General Philip Sheridan had already drawn up a plan that would send three columns of soldiers to drive the Lakota into the agencies, a plan that had worked against the Cheyenne eight years earlier and in the Red River campaign against the southern Plains tribes. One column, led by Brigadier General George Crook, was to move north from Fort Fetterman; another, under Colonel John Gibbon, would march east from western Montana, while Custer and the Seventh Cavalry drove west from Fort Abraham Lincoln.

General George Crook, a veteran Indian fighter, was first assigned the hopeless task of clearing prospectors from the Black Hills, then fared poorly against the Lakota and the Cheyenne at the battle of the Rosebud. Later, he would redeem himself subduing the Apache in the Southwest.

Custer was in his element: "General George A. Custer, dressed in a dashing suit of buckskin, is prominent everywhere . . ." a correspondent for the New York *Herald* reported. "The General is full of perfect readiness for a fray with the hostile red devils, and woe to the body of scalp-lifters that comes within reach of himself and brave companions in arms."

His command included 566 enlisted men and 31 officers. Some venerated their commander, among them three of his own brothers, a nephew, and a reporter for a New York newspaper who could be counted on to issue admiring progress reports. But others loathed him, including his second-in-command, Major Marcus A. Reno, who had once schemed to supplant Custer as commander, and Captain Frederick W. Benteen, an alcoholic whose hostility extended beyond Custer to most of the other officers in the Seventh Cavalry.

None of the commanders knew precisely where Sitting Bull and his followers were, but they believed one column or another would find and destroy them. "I have given no instructions . . ." wrote General Sheridan. "Each column will be able to take care of itself [while] chastising the Indians, should it have the opportunity."

A private in Custer's Seventh left a letter behind for his sister:

> Dear Sister,
>
> . . . The Indians are getting bad again. I think we will have some hard times this summer. The old chief Sitting Bull says that he will not make peace with the whites as long as he has a man to fight. . . . As soon as I get back [from] the campaign I will write you. That is, if I do not get my hair lifted by some Indian.
>
> From your loving brother,
> T. P. Eagan

On June 6, some 3,000 Lakota and Cheyenne were camped along Rosebud Creek. There they held their most sacred ritual — the sun dance. Sitting Bull slashed his arm a hundred times as a sign of sacrifice, then had a new vision. In it, the soldiers came again to attack his people — "as many as grasshoppers," he said — but this time they were upside down, their horse's hooves in the air, their hats tumbling to the ground as they rode into the Lakota camp. The soldiers were coming again. He was sure of it. But this time, his people would be ready for them.

Eleven days later, on the morning of June 17, General Crook's column stopped to brew coffee on the bank of the Rosebud. Crook and his officers began a leisurely game of whist. Suddenly, some five hundred Sioux and Cheyenne warriors attacked Crook's force, which was twice the size of their own. Sitting Bull was too weak from the sun dance to fight, but he urged the young men into battle.

In a fierce, desperate fight that boiled on for more than six hours, Crook was saved in part by his Crow and Shoshone allies, who twice scattered the attackers by riding through their ranks. The general declared the battle of the Rosebud a victory because the Indians withdrew from the battlefield, but it had really been a standoff, and it had signaled something new in Plains warfare. Until now, Indian fighting had largely been a matter of pursuit and surprise. This time, the Lakota and Cheyenne had been the first to attack and had more than held their own against a far larger force. Crook thought it best to withdraw. The Lakota and Cheyenne moved north onto Crow lands and set up a new camp along a winding stream they called the Greasy Grass. Whites called it the Little Bighorn.

Six troopers from the Seventh Cavalry, photographed at Fort Lincoln, before Custer's last campaign began

On June 21, Custer met on the Yellowstone River with Gibbon and their superior, Brigadier General Alfred Terry. They knew nothing of Crook's retreat.

Terry's Arikara scouts told him that Sitting Bull was now camped somewhere in the valley of the Little Bighorn. He ordered Gibbon to march up the Yellowstone and Bighorn to block its mouth. Meanwhile, Custer and the Seventh Cavalry were to hurry up the Rosebud, where, if they could locate the Indians, they would attack them from the south and drive them toward Gibbon and annihilation.

As Custer began his march, Terry called out to him, "Now Custer, don't be greedy, but wait for us."

"No," Custer said, laughing as he rode off, "I will not."

Custer's scouts were Crow, eager to defend their lands against the Lakota, and he was delighted with them. "They are magnificent-looking men," he wrote to his wife, "so much handsomer and more Indian-like than any we have ever seen, and jolly and sportive; nothing of the gloomy, silent red-man about them. . . . [T]hey said they had heard that I never abandoned a trail; that when my food gave out I ate mule. That was the kind of man they wanted to fight under; they were willing to eat mule, too."

Fearful Sitting Bull would elude him, Custer pushed his column hard under a merciless prairie sun — twelve miles the first day, thirty-three the second, twenty-eight the third. The men began to grumble about the man they privately called "Hard Ass." They found the Indians' trail, but evidently did not grasp the full meaning of the fresh layers of pony and travois tracks that crossed and recrossed it.

In fact, during the last few days, 3,000 more Indians — angered by the ongoing white invasion of the Black Hills, eager to return to their old ways — had left their agencies to join Sitting Bull. The encampment now stretched for three miles along the river. In it were more than 6,000 Indians — Hunkpapa, Oglala, Miniconjou, Sans Arc, as well as Blackfoot Sioux and Northern Cheyenne. Almost 2,000 of them were

Curly, one of Custer's Crow scouts, said to have been the first man to bring news of what had happened at the Little Bighorn to the outside world

warriors. "There were more Indians . . ." a Cheyenne woman named Kate Big Head recalled, "than I ever saw anywhere together. . . . The chiefs from all the camps decided we should move down the Little Bighorn River to its mouth . . . and kill antelope in the great herds they had seen there. The plan was to stay at this camp but one night, and go on down the valley the next day."

On the evening of June 24, Sitting Bull made his way to a ridge that overlooked the camp and the Bighorn Valley beyond. There, he made offerings to the Creator and prayed for the protection of his people.

> *Wakantanka,* pity me. In the name of the [people] I offer you this peace-pipe. Wherever the sun, the moon, the earth, the four points of the wind, there you are always. Father save the [people], I beg you. . . . We want to live. Guard us against all misfortune. . . . Pity me.

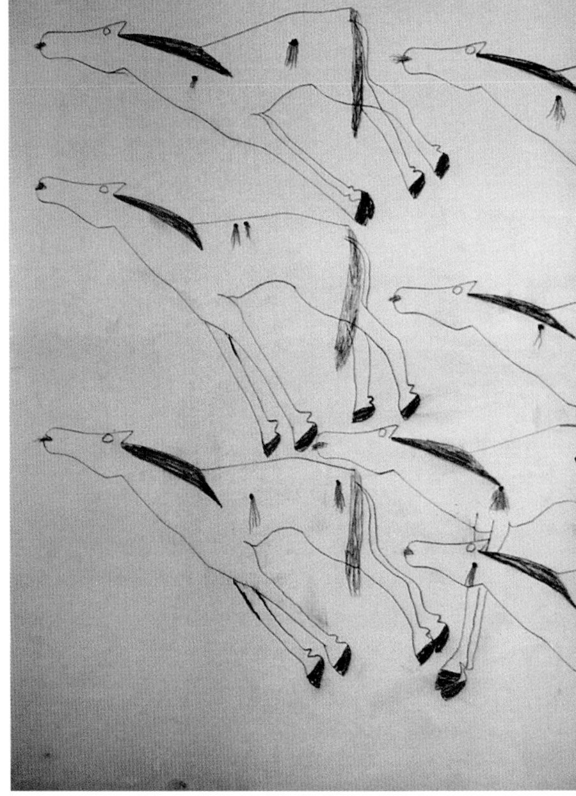

The next day was June 25, a Sunday, cloudless and hot. Custer's Crow scouts spotted the village from a distant hilltop and called Custer up to have a look. Even with a telescope, he was unable to see much more than a white blur on the valley floor, but the Crow warned him that there were enough Indians to fight for many days.

Custer just laughed: "I guess we'll get through them in one day," he said. His only concern was that he had already been spotted, that unless he attacked right away, the Indians would split up and flee in so many different bands that he could never stop them. There was no time to send men ahead to reconnoiter. He knew nothing of the terrain, could not tell how many Indians awaited him, but he was evidently not worried. It had been a surprise attack that had allowed him to destroy Black Kettle's Cheyenne on the Washita nine years earlier, after all, and a victory here seemed just as likely.

He ordered Captain Benteen, with 125 men, south to seek out a ridgeline from which to survey the valley and make sure no hostiles were behind him. Then, he hurried toward the Little Bighorn. When he saw dust rising over a ridge just ahead of him he was sure it meant that the Indians were already on the move.

It was now or never. Some forty warriors appeared, then began racing back toward their camp. Custer ordered Major Marcus Reno and three companies — 140 men — to pursue them, promising he would be right behind.

"It was somewhere past the middle of the afternoon," Kate Big Head recalled, "and all of us were having a good time. We found our women friends bathing in the river and we joined them. Other groups . . . were playing in the water. . . . Two Sioux boys came running toward us. They were shouting, 'Soldiers are coming!' We heard shooting. We hid in the brush."

Reno's men crossed the river, formed a thin skirmish line, and began firing into one edge of the village, assuming that Custer would quickly reinforce them. But he did not come and they were soon outnumbered. Reno's men held until a Lakota bullet struck the head of Bloody Knife, an Arikara scout, splattering his brains over Reno's face. Then, he shouted to his men to fall back into a grove of cottonwoods.

From her hiding place in the brush near the river Kate Big Head could see little. But she could hear what was happening:

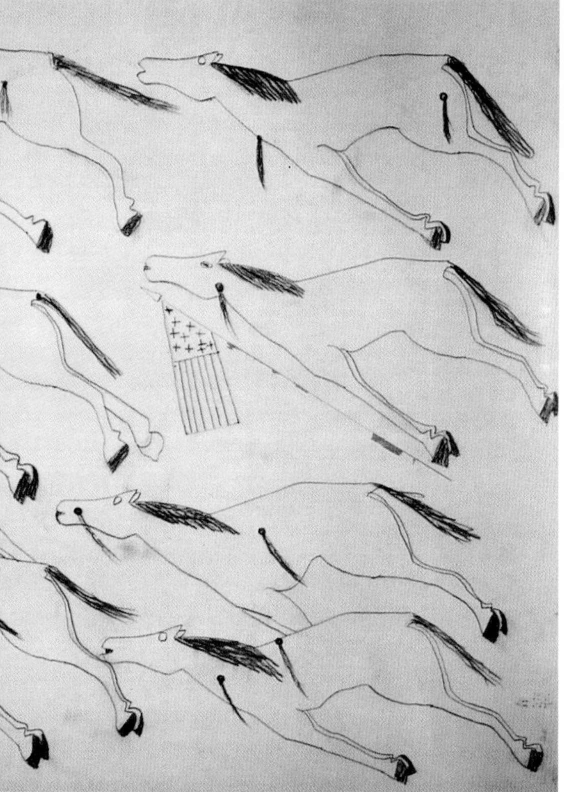

The Custer fight, as remembered by Red Horse, Miniconjou Lakota

> The sounds of the shooting multiplied. . . . We heard women and children screaming. Old men were calling the young warriors to battle. Young men were singing their war songs. . . . We heard the sounds of battle change from place to place. It seemed the white men were going away, with the Indians following them . . . shooting and beating them.

More warriors swarmed out of the village. Reno ordered his men to retreat. The soldiers were falling into the village, just as Sitting Bull's dream had suggested they would. "Indians covered the flat," the Cheyenne Two Moons remembered. "They began to drive the soldiers, all mixed up — Lakota, then soldiers, then more Lakota, and all shooting."

The soldiers struggled across the swift-running river and tried to clamber up the riverbank. Those who made it did their best to find cover in the thick grass, and began to fire back. And still there was no sign of Custer. He had changed his plan, turning northwest and leading his five companies of 210 men toward a ridge that overlooked the village, apparently convinced the Indians were fleeing from Reno and that by charging down into it, he could cut them off. But when he got to the crest and saw for the first time the size of the village spread out below, a Crow scout named White-Man-Runs-Him remembered, he "looked whiter than ever."

Custer's Crow scouts began to sing their death songs. Custer told them they could go. They had found Sitting Bull's camp for him; that was enough.

He scribbled a note in pencil and sent his bugler back to deliver it to Benteen, in charge of the ammunition train: "Come on, Big Village. Be Quick. Bring packs. Hurry." Then he waved his hat to rally his troops and led them down toward the encampment, firing as they rode.

Kate Big Head left the brush and ran toward her teepee, but "[b]efore I got to my home lodge all [the warriors] were riding wildly back . . . through the camps. It appeared they had been beaten and were running away. But I soon learned what had happened. I heard a Cheyenne old man calling out: 'Other soldiers are coming! Warriors, go and fight them!'" Cheyenne warriors led by Lame White Man, Hunkpapa Lakota under Gall, and Oglala under Crazy Horse rode out together to turn back these new attackers.

"It appeared there would be no end to the rushing procession of warriors," Kate Big Head remembered. "They kept going, going, going. I wanted to go, too. . . . I had seen other battles in past times. I always liked to watch the men fighting."

The soldiers stopped at the sight of the advancing line of warriors, milled around for a moment, then began a headlong retreat toward the summit of a long, high ridge. The Indians noticed that the legs of the men and the horses trembled as they staggered onward. Some were simply exhausted. Others seemed terrified.

"I called to my men," Low Dog remembered. "'This is a good day to die: follow me.' We massed our men, and that no man should fall back, every man whipped another man's horse and we rushed right upon them."

"Little Bird and I were after one certain soldier . . ." a Cheyenne named Wooden Leg recalled. "We were lashing him and his horse with our pony whips. It seemed not brave to shoot him. . . . He pointed back his revolver, though, and sent a bullet into

Little Bird's thigh. . . . I whacked the white man . . . on his head with the heavy elk-horn handle of my pony whip. The blow dazed him. I seized the rifle strapped on his back . . . he fell to the ground. I did not harm him further. I do not know what became of him. The jam of oncoming Indians swept me on."

Scattered across the slope, Custer and his men dismounted and tried to defend themselves as best they could, firing into the swirl of ponies and warriors. Then, Crazy Horse and his Oglala rode down upon them. One by one, Custer's companies were wiped out. "As we rushed upon them the [soldiers] dismounted to fire," Low Dog recalled, "but they did very poor shooting. They held their horse's reins on one arm while they were shooting, but their horses were so frightened that they pulled the men all around and a great many of their shots went up into the air and did us no harm."

Another Lakota warrior, White Bull, remembered the fury of the fighting — and the pleasure he took in it:

> I charged in. A tall, well-built soldier . . . saw me coming. . . . [W]hen I rushed him, he threw his rifle at me without shooting.
>
> We grabbed each other and wrestled there in the dust and smoke. He hit me with his fists on the jaw and shoulders, then grabbed my long braids with both hands, pulled my face close and tried to bite my nose off. I yelled as loud as I could to scare my enemy, but he would not let go. Finally, I broke free.
>
> He drew his pistol. I wrenched it out of his hand and struck him with it three or four times on the head, knocked him over, shot him in the head and fired at his heart. . . .
>
> *Ho hechetu!* That was a fight, a hard fight. But it was a glorious battle, I enjoyed it. . . .

After a little while, "[t]he shots quit coming from the soldiers," Wooden Leg recalled. "Warriors who had crept close to them began to call out that all of the white men were dead. . . . All of the Indians were saying these soldiers . . . went crazy and killed themselves. I do not know. I could not see them. But I believe they did so. . . ."

And Kate Big Head, watching from the hillside, "saw several different ones of the soldiers not yet quite dead. The Indians cut off arms or legs or feet of these, the same as was done for the entirely dead. . . . Some of the women mourning for their own dead, beat and cut the dead bodies of the white men."

The fighting, one warrior remembered, had lasted no longer than a hungry man needed to eat his dinner. Almost one-third of Major Reno's command were killed before Benteen and his men finally arrived to relieve them. But all of the men in Custer's command now lay dead — 209 soldiers, along with the newspaper reporter whom Custer had brought along to write up his exploits. Only his Crow scouts had managed to get away. It was the greatest Indian victory of the Plains wars.

According to Kate Big Head, two Cheyenne woman found Custer's body:

> The women . . . pushed the point of an awl into each of his ears, into his head. This was done to improve his hearing, as it seemed he had not heard what our chiefs in the South had said when he smoked the pipe with them. They told him

then that if ever afterward he should break that peace promise and should fight the Cheyennes the Everywhere Spirit surely would cause him to be killed. . . . I often have wondered if, when I was riding among the dead where he was lying, my pony may have kicked dirt upon his body.

The next day the great encampment broke up. The Indians set the grass afire to mask their passage with smoke. Some 8,000 Lakota and Cheyenne separated into bands and started for the Bighorn Mountains. They had won the Custer fight, had killed the man who had invaded the Black Hills and most of his command. It had been his last stand, but it would prove to be their last stand, as well.

The Custer fight, as recalled by Amos Bad Heart Bull, Oglala Lakota

At Fort Abraham Lincoln, the wives of the officers of the Seventh Cavalry knew nothing of what had happened to their husbands. Their chief concern was the steady, wearying heat:

Our only pleasure after the torrid day [one remembered] was to gather on someone's porch in the long twilight, enjoy what little music we could muster, and try to forget our worries and the devilish mosquitoes. Many among us had sweet voices, and while I played the guitar everyone sang. . . . Then, glancing across the parade ground, we noticed small groups of soldiers talking excitedly together, and several people came running toward us, faces set and wild-eyed. One was Horn Toad, the Indian scout, who gasped in short, sharp sentences, "Custer killed. Whole command killed."

The guitar slipped from my knees to the floor, the pink ball of knitting fell out of Charlotte Moylan's hands, the letter lying idly in Mrs. Benteen's lap fluttered over the rail and onto the . . . lawn. . . .

Americans were celebrating their centennial that summer, proud of one hundred years of independence, and the news that George Armstrong Custer and 263 men of his command had been killed by Indians was greeted with simple disbelief. How could such a thing possibly have happened? they asked. How could mere Indians with names that sounded absurd to eastern ears — Low Dog, Crazy Horse, Sitting Bull — have defeated so celebrated a soldier?

General Philip Sheridan, the architect of the plan that had ended in disaster, was so humiliated that he denied for a time that there really was a "Sitting Bull," assuring the press that the alleged name was just a Sioux phrase that meant "hostile Indians."

Sitting Bull had not joined the fighting at the Little Bighorn, but across the nation, he was now believed to be the Indian who had beaten the army. Others were convinced Sitting Bull couldn't really be an Indian at all — since no Indian could outgeneral a white man. Or that he was an Indian dropout from West Point, "the red Napoleon."

"Who slew Custer?" asked the New York *Herald.* "The celebrated peace policy of General Grant, which feeds, clothes, and takes care of their noncombatant force while men are killing our troops . . . [and] the Indian Bureau, with its thriving agents and favorites as Indian traders, and its mock humanity and pretense at piety — *that* is what killed Custer."

Price 25 Cents.

MASSACRED

GEN. CUSTER AND 261 MEN THE VICTIMS.

NO OFFICER OR MAN OF 5 COMPANIES LEFT TO TELL THE TALE.

3 Days Desperate Fighting by Maj. Reno and the Remainder of the Seventh.

Full Details of the Battle.

LIST OF KILLED AND WOUNDED.

THE BISMARCK TRIBUNE'S SPECIAL CORRESPONDENT SLAIN.

Squaws Mutilate and Rob the Dead

Victims Captured Alive Tortured in a Most Fiendish Manner.

What Will Congress Do About It?

Shall This Be the Beginning of the End?

It will be remembered the the Bismarck Tribune sent a special correspondent with Gen. Terry, who was the

Aftermath: news of the Custer disaster as it first appeared in the Bismarck *Tribune* on July 6, 1876, and (above, right) three of Custer's Crow scouts photographed among the gravestones of Custer's men, many years after the battle.

Sheridan promised Custer would be avenged, and fresh blue columns were soon crisscrossing the Powder River country in pursuit of the bands that had split up after the Custer fight. One by one, they were forced to surrender. There were simply too many soldiers to fight, too few buffalo left to feed their women and children. In the spring of 1877, even Crazy Horse came in with fifteen hundred Oglala, laying down his rifle as a token of peace. By September, he would be dead, bayoneted in the back while under guard.

Congress took away the Black Hills and another 40 million acres of land from the Lakota by obtaining the signatures of non-hostile chiefs and headmen and ignoring the provision of the 1868 Fort Laramie Treaty that required the vote of three-quarters of all adult males before any changes could be made. Indians who had had nothing to do with the warfare were disarmed.

Sitting Bull alone held out. He and his followers were now beyond the reach of American troops, across the border in Canada, which he called the "Land of the Grandmother," in honor of Queen Victoria. When General Alfred Terry traveled north to offer him a full pardon on the condition that he settle at an agency, Sitting Bull angrily sent him away again. "This country is my country now," he told the general, "and I intend to stay here and raise people to fill it. We did not give our country to you; you stole it. You come here to tell lies; when you go home, take them with you."

For thirty years, Brigham Young had attended to every possible detail of life in Mormon Utah. "I feel like a father with a great family of children around me, in a winter storm," he once told his people, "and I am looking with calmness, confidence and patience, for the clouds to break and the sun to shine, so that I can run out . . . and say, 'Children, come home. . . . I am ready to kill the fatted calf and make a joyful feast to all who will come and partake.'"

But now he felt besieged. Congress was trying once again to assert control over Utah. A new law gave federal courts, not local ones, jurisdiction over criminal cases in the territory, and one of the first actions of the federal prosecutors was to arrest Young's devoted follower John D. Lee for murder in the matter of the Mountain Meadows Massacre, twenty years earlier. He and the other Mormon participants had taken a blood oath that they would never reveal what had really happened, church officials blamed the Paiute for the massacre, and for nearly twenty years non-Mormons had struggled in vain to force a full accounting.

But the memory of the massacre continued to haunt Utah, and even among some of the faithful pressure had slowly grown to find and prosecute the guilty so that the church as a whole might be exonerated. In 1870, Brigham Young excommunicated John D. Lee, and in 1872 he urged him to disappear into the wilderness. Lee gave up his home and business. With one of his eleven wives, he fled deep into Arizona, where the Mormons were starting new colonies. Then, he settled with another wife at the mouth of the remote Paria River, just north of the Grand Canyon, and started a ferry business across the Colorado. Church officials always sent him warning if lawmen were in the area, so that he could hide out until they were safely gone. With the exception of a few Mormons headed to Arizona, his only visitors were Indians, outlaws, and explorers.

Still, he remained steadfast in his devotion to Brigham Young. "It is told around for a fact that I could tell great confessions and bring in Brigham Young and the heads of the church . . ." he wrote. "[But] I will not be the means of bringing troubles on my

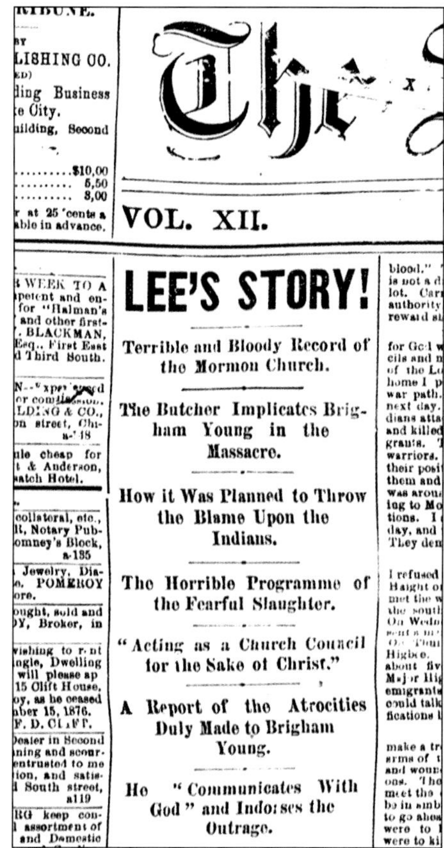

VOL. XII.

LEE'S STORY!

Terrible and Bloody Record of the Mormon Church.

The Butcher Implicates Brigham Young in the Massacre.

How it Was Planned to Throw the Blame Upon the Indians.

The Horrible Programme of the Fearful Slaughter.

"Acting as a Church Council for the Sake of Christ."

A Report of the Atrocities Duly Made to Brigham Young.

He "Communicates With God" and Indorses the Outrage.

Exile's return: "Lonely Dell" (left), the home at Jacob's Pool in Arizona Territory to which Brigham Young banished John D. Lee after the Mountain Meadows Massacre, and Lee's confession issued after he was sentenced to death in 1877

Last look: John D. Lee (seated on coffin, left) just before his execution and (above) after the firing squad had done its work

people, for . . . this people is a misrepresented and cried-down community. Yes, a people scattered and peeled . . . and if at last they did rise up and shed the blood of their enemies, I won't consent to give 'em up."

As Lee awaited trial federal prosecutors offered him money and leniency if he would implicate others, including Young. Lee refused: "I chose to die like a man," he said later, "rather than to live as a villain." Orders went out from Salt Lake City that no Mormon should testify against him. None did, and when the four gentiles on the jury found Lee guilty, the eight Mormons were unanimous for acquittal. Across the nation, the case became a symbol for everything Americans despised about Mormonism, and pressure mounted for the government to strip Brigham Young and the church of its authority in Utah.

In the second trial everything changed. This time, since the prosecutors concentrated their attack on John D. Lee alone, Brigham Young ordered Mormons to cooperate: all the blame for the tragedy was to be placed on the shoulders of one man. Witnesses now testified that the killing had been Lee's idea and Lee's alone.

All the members of the jury were Mormons. All now voted to convict. Under Utah law, Lee was allowed to choose whether he wished to be shot, hanged, or beheaded. He chose a firing squad.

On March 23, 1877, he was escorted to the site of the massacre and seated on a coffin so that he might be photographed. He made arrangements for each of the two wives who remained true to him to get a copy of the picture, then rose and spoke to the little crowd that had turned out to see him die:

> I am ready to die. . . . I do not fear death, I shall never go to a worse place than I am now in. . . . I do not believe everything that is now being taught and practiced by Brigham Young. I do not care who hears it. . . . I studied to make this man's will my pleasure for thirty years. See, now, what I have come to this day! I have been sacrificed in a cowardly, dastardly manner. . . . Sacrifice a man that has waited upon them, that has wandered and endured with them in the days of adversity, true from the beginnings of the Church! And I am now singled out and am sacrificed in this manner! What confidence can I have in such a man! I have none, and I don't think my Father in heaven has any. . . .

> I regret leaving my family; they are near and dear to me. These are things which touch my sympathy, even when I think of those poor orphaned children.
>
> I declare I did nothing designedly wrong in this unfortunate affair. . . . I do not fear death, I shall never go to a worse place than I am now in. . . .
>
> Having said this, I feel resigned. I ask the Lord, my God, if my labors are done, to receive my spirit.

Then Lee shook hands with his executioners, and handed his hat and overcoat to a friend. His last words were to the firing squad: "Center my heart, boys. Don't mangle my body."

No one else was ever indicted for the Mountain Meadows Massacre.

Brigham Young toward the end of his life. "He has been the brain, the eye, the ear, the mouth and hand for the entire people of the Church," said one of the eulogists at his funeral. "Nothing was too small for his mind; nothing was too large."

Brigham Young was failing badly now. Rheumatism had so crippled him that he had to be carried on a chair during his ceaseless inspection tours. Then, while passing through the town of Ephraim, a Scandinavian convert darted into the street and berated him for having sacrificed John D. Lee: "Oh, you Cheat!" he shouted, shaking his fist. "Oh Church Fraud! You coward to forsake your tools! You are the man that they should have hung instead of Lee!" The man was pulled away. Young said nothing, but his hands gripped the seat of his coach until his knuckles turned white.

On August 23, 1877, he was seized by sudden terrible stomach pains. For six days, surrounded by his huge family, he floated in and out of consciousness. Then, on August 29, 1877, he called out the name of Joseph Smith, his predecessor as prophet of the church, and died. It would be nearly three decades before his people were rewarded with the statehood he had sought, and to get it they had to forswear the policy of plural marriage he had defended so hard.

Even in death, Brigham Young remained in charge. He was laid in a redwood coffin of his own precise design, fashioned "two or three inches wider than is commonly made for a person of my breadth and size . . . to have the appearance that if I wanted to turn a little to the right or left I should have plenty of room to do so. . . ." Twenty-five thousand Mormons filed past his bier inside the still-unfinished Salt Lake Tabernacle before his remains were placed in a stone vault overlooking his desert city. Jedediah Grant, one of Young's closest advisers, tried to convey to the readers of the New York *Herald* something of what Brigham Young had meant to his people:

> I can't undertake to explain Brigham Young to your Atlantic citizens, or expect you to put him at his value. Your great men Eastward are to me like your ivory and pearl handled table knives, balance[d] handles, more shiny than the inside of my watch case; but, with only edge enough to slice bread and cheese or help spoon victuals, and all alike by the dozen, one with another.
>
> Brigham is the article that sells out West with us — between a Roman cutlass and a beef butcher knife, the thing to cut up a deer or cut down an enemy, and that will save your life or carve your dinner every bit as well, though the handpiece is buckhorn and the case a hogskin hanging in the breech of your pantaloons.
>
> You, that judge men by the handle and the sheath, how can I make you know a good *Blade?*

A TOUGH BUNCH

A regular army private named Comfort had this formal portrait made on a rare trip to town.

"I was a boy during the Civil War," one rueful western regular remembered, "and there was an army camp near and I guess I soaked in some of the game, for later, every time I got Spiflicated I wanted to enlist. . . . [I] . . . thought it would be like the volunteers during the Civil War . . . but I found out the mistake. The Regular Army was a tough bunch in those days."

The western army had an impossible job — policing some two and half million square miles of land between the Missouri and the eastern slope of the Sierras. There were never more than 15,000 men, scattered among one hundred forts and outposts, yet they were somehow expected to defend settlers, ranchers, miners, railroad crews; keep thousands of Indians confined to their reservations — and keep tens of thousands of whites out of Indian lands.

But even though army pay was low — just thirteen dollars a month — steady jobs were scarce during the economic slump that followed the Civil War, and army ranks were soon filled with immigrants, some of whom could speak almost no English. There were drifters, too: men with assumed names; men escaping bad marriages — or the law. "Some of the recruits [I joined with]," one recalled, "had no doubt served in some penitentiary before enlisting, and I shouldn't wonder that some went back to their old prisons as a haven of rest and decent treatment."

Promotions were rare, and riddled with politics. Discipline was severe; men were flogged for minor infractions, locked up in log stockades, suspended by their thumbs, made to sit for hours on a wooden horse.

The climate added to the soldiers' woes. "Everything dries," one man wrote during a tour of duty at Fort Yuma in Arizona Territory. "Men dry; chickens dry; there is not juice left in anything. living or dead, by the close of summer. . . .

The parade ground at Old Camp Grant, Arizona Territory. "Some of what are called military posts," General William Tecumseh Sherman wrote, "are mere collections of huts made of logs, adobes or mere holes in the ground, and are about as much forts as prairie dog villages might be called forts."

Sleeping it off: Whiskey was the soldier's curse. Forty men out of every thousand were hospitalized for alcoholism — and that was only those whose drinking had actually rendered them unfit for service.

Victuals: Army food was almost always unpalatable, sometimes inedible. Hardtack — flour-and-water biscuits — delivered to the Seventh Cavalry at Fort Hays was six years old and had to be shattered with a hammer.

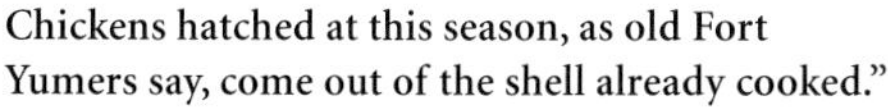

Chickens hatched at this season, as old Fort Yumers say, come out of the shell already cooked."

Winter on the northern Plains was just as bad: "I am now wearing two flannel and a buckskin shirt," one soldier reported, "one pair of drawers, trousers of buckskin and a pair of army trousers, two pairs woolen socks, a pair of buffalo overshoes and big boots, a heavy pair of blanket leggins, a thick blouse and heavy overcoat, a heavy woolen cap that completely covers my head, face and neck except nose and eyes — and still I am not happy."

Most regulars never met an Indian in battle. Some never saw any Indians at all. Boredom was all the men could depend upon, three to five years of it. They quarreled, drank, pitted red ants against black ants just to stir things up.

Disease was the worst killer. In one two-year period, the Seventh Cavalry lost thirty-six men to Indians — and fifty-one to cholera. And desertion rates were understandably high. "I want to get out of the army honorable,"one soldier wrote home, "but if I can't get out otherwise I will give the cursed outfit the 'Grand bounce.' I can not endure them much longer. None but a menial cur could stand the usage of a soldier of the army today in America."

Officers tent, Seventh Infantry, somewhere on the Plains

Troopers in buffalo coats struggle to keep warm at Fort Keogh in Montana Territory, 1879.

Officers and their wives and children take time out from croquet at Fort Bridger in Wyoming Territory, 1873.

FIGHT NO MORE, FOREVER

Of all the Indian tribes in the West, none had a longer record of unbroken friendship with the United States than the Nez Percé. They had saved Lewis and Clark and their companions from starvation in the autumn of 1805, and when their neighbors, the Cayuse, had risen up against Marcus and Narcissa Whitman and other whites in 1847, they had refused to join them. During the early 1860s, when thousands of whites in search of gold crowded onto land that was theirs by a treaty signed in 1855, they had remained resolutely peaceful. And when in 1863 the government sought to purchase all but about 10 percent of their land and persuade them to move onto what was left, a narrow strip of land along the Clearwater in Idaho, most had reluctantly agreed. Many converted to Christianity, wore white men's clothes, and took up farming and stock raising.

But several bands resisted. One had its home in the beautiful Wallowa Valley of eastern Oregon and was led by a chief called Old Joseph. He had been the first Nez Percé to be baptized by the missionary Henry Spalding, but had soon grown so disillusioned with the white man's faith and with his incessant demands for Indian lands that he refused to sign the new treaty and tore up his copy of the Gospel of Saint Matthew, which Spalding had translated for him. His people had signed no agreement to sell their land, he maintained, and he saw no reason to give it up. The Nez Percé were now split in two: Christians versus non-Christians, treaty supporters versus treaty opponents. "It was these Christian Nez Perces who made with the government a thief treaty," a man from Old Joseph's band named Yellow Wolf remembered. "Sold to the government all this land. . . . Sold what did not belong to them. We got nothing for our country. None of our chiefs signed that land-stealing treaty. . . . Only Christian Indians and government men."

President Grant himself agreed that Joseph's band could not legally be moved and by executive order even set aside part of the valley for them in 1873, but local whites were so exercised by this action that it was rescinded. Whites poured into the valley. Killings of Indians went unpunished. Still, the Nez Percé refused to retaliate. Old Joseph died and leadership of his band fell to his sons, *Ollokot,* known for his bravery and skill at buffalo hunting, and *Hin-mah-too-yah-lat-kekht* — Thunder Rolling from the Mountains — known to whites as Young Joseph and responsible for the daily welfare of his people.

Faced with increasing tension between the Nez Percé and the invading whites, the government finally decided in 1876 to compensate the Wallowa Nez Percé for their lands and then make sure they, and all the other non-treaty bands, moved. General Oliver Otis Howard was dispatched to get the job done. He had lost an arm at the Civil War battle of Seven Pines and won the Medal of Honor; after the war, he ran the Freedmen's Bureau to help emancipated slaves, founded Howard University for African-Americans, and negotiated a peace between the United States and the Apache leader Cochise in Arizona. He was as pious as he was unyielding.

Joseph tried to explain to the general what the valley meant to him. It was the place where his ancestors were buried, he said. He had promised his late father never to abandon it. "Do not misunderstand me . . . [and] my affection for the land. I never said the land was mine to do with as I chose. The one who has the right to dispose of

My father was the first to see through the schemes of the white men. He said, "My son . . . [w]hen I am gone . . . [y]ou are the chief of these people. Always remember that your father never sold his country. You must stop your ears whenever you are asked to sign a treaty selling your home. . . . My son, never forget my dying words. This country holds your father's body. Never sell the bones of your father and mother." I pressed my father's hand and told him I would protect his grave with my life. . . . A man who would not love his father's grave is worse than a wild animal.

Chief Joseph

Chief Joseph, photographed in 1877 at the end of his astonishing journey

it is the one who has created it. I claim a right to live on my land, and accord you the privilege to live on yours."

Howard, whose sympathies were with the Nez Percé and who was ordinarily a patient man, soon wearied of Joseph's protests: "We do not wish to interfere with your religion," he told the chiefs, "but must talk about practicable things. Twenty times over you repeat that the earth is your mother. . . . Let us hear no more, but come to business at once."

Howard gave all the non-treaty bands an ultimatum: accept compensation for their lands and move to a reservation at Lapwai, in Idaho, or his soldiers would force them in. They had just thirty days to comply. To avoid war, the non-treaty chiefs reluctantly began moving their people to the reservation. "I knew I had never sold my country," Joseph remembered, "and that I had no land in Lapwai; but I did not want bloodshed. I did not want my people killed. I did not want anybody killed. . . . I said in my heart that, rather than have war, I would give up my country. I would give up my father's grave. I would give up everything rather than have the blood of white men upon the hands of my people."

Our fathers gave us many laws, which they had learned from their fathers. . . . They told us to treat all men as they treated us; that we should never be the first to break a bargain; that it was a disgrace to tell a lie; that we should speak only the truth. . . . We were taught to believe that the Great Spirit sees and hears everything, and that he never forgets. This I believe, and all my people believe the same.

Chief Joseph

It was slow going. There were cattle and horses to round up. The Snake River was still swollen by melted snows. The young men particularly resented giving up their homeland without resisting, and when Joseph's band met up with those led by White Bird and Toohoolhoolzote, three young warriors, full of whiskey and eager for revenge, slipped away and murdered four whites whom they believed guilty of crimes against their people.

Joseph and the other chiefs realized immediately what the killings meant: soldiers would be coming, and for the first time in their history, the Nez Percé and the United States would be at war. Joseph still wanted to talk with Howard: the actions by the young men had not been sanctioned by anyone. "I would have given my own life if I could have undone the killing of white men by my people . . ." Joseph said. "I saw that war could not then be prevented. . . . I knew we were too weak to fight the United States. We had many grievances, but I knew that war would bring more." But the other chiefs overruled him and another unsanctioned raid in which seventeen settlers were killed made further talks irrelevant. The non-treaty bands headed for the Salmon River.

Howard sent Captain David Perry and the Mount Idaho Volunteers after them, and confidently wired his superiors: "Think we will make short work of it." When the volunteers neared the Nez Percé encampment at White Bird Canyon on the Salmon, the Indians sent out a party under a white flag, still hoping somehow to avoid bloodshed. The volunteers opened fire, anyway. It was a bad mistake. "It was just like two bulldogs meeting," Yellow Wolf recalled. "Those soldiers did not hold their position ten minutes. Some soldiers . . . were quickly on the run. Then the entire enemy force gave way. . . . We counted 33 dead soldiers. We did no scalping. We did not hurt the dead. Only let them lie."

Just three Nez Percé warriors had been wounded in the battle, and their companions had captured sixty-three rifles and stores of ammunition. "I have been in lots of scrapes," one army scout remembered, but "I never went up against anything like the Nez Percés in all my life." News of the stunning defeat at White Bird Canyon, less than

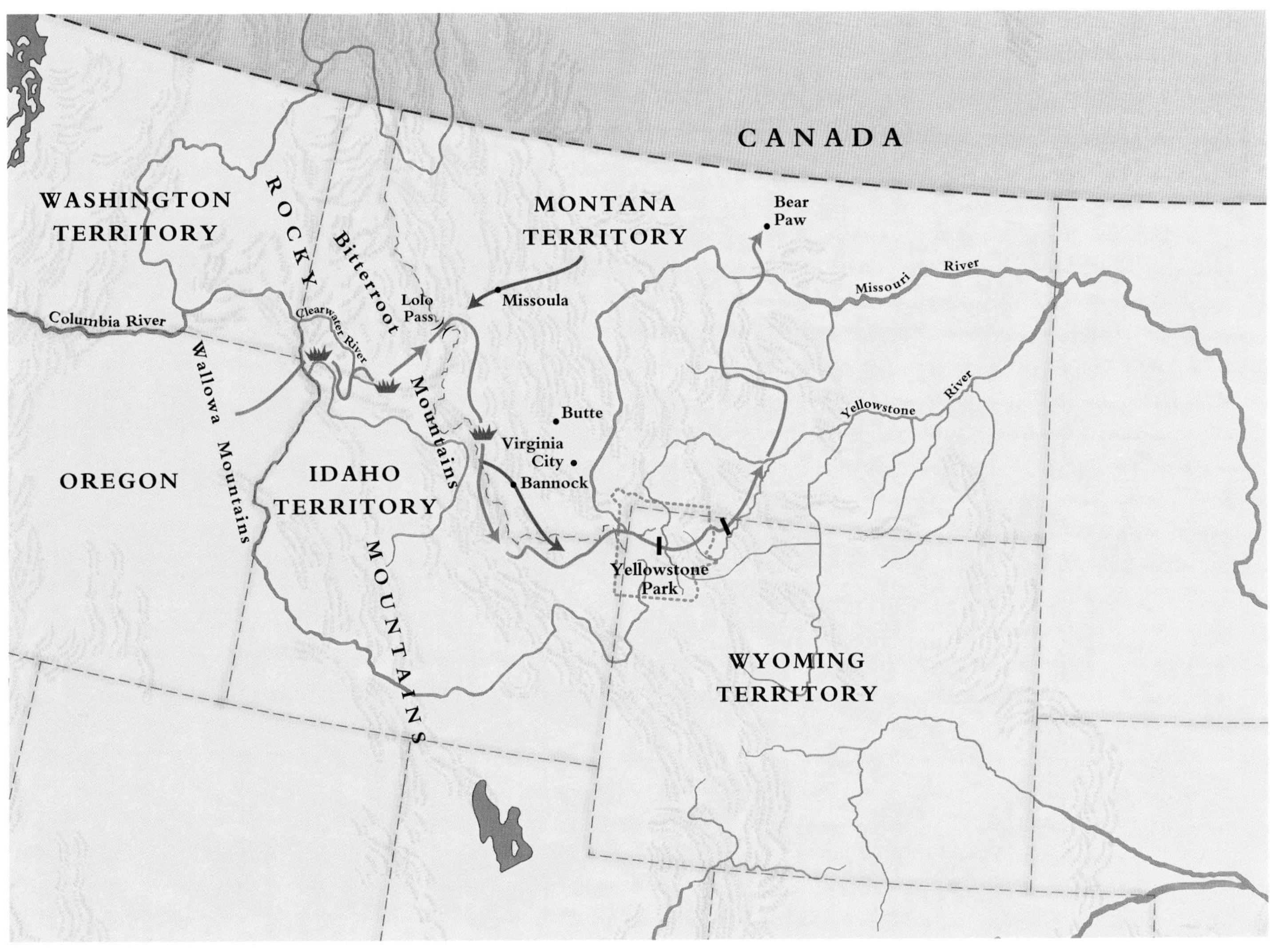

The flight of the Nez Percé and some of the battles and skirmishes they survived along the way

a year after Custer's death at the Little Bighorn, shocked the country. Howard called for more troops and set out in pursuit of the Indians.

Meanwhile, the Nez Percé leaders debated what to do next, finally agreeing with a war chief named Looking Glass to head east, out of Idaho. In Montana, he said, the white people would not bother them. And the Nez Percé's Indian allies, the Salish and the Crow, would surely shelter them along the way. They could hunt buffalo until a peace was negotiated for their return. As they began moving east, there were about seven hundred of them — only two hundred were warriors, the rest were women, children, and old people, with their horse herd and belongings, all in Joseph's care. For the next three months, the Nez Percé would lead the United States Army on one of the most remarkable pursuits in American military history.

On July 3, they wiped out an army scouting party of thirteen men that got too close. The next day, Independence Day, they fought off an attack at an old stage stop called Cottonwood. A week later on the Clearwater River they killed thirteen more of Howard's men. "They fought as well as any troops I ever saw," Howard said. Then, the Indians began climbing the Bitterroots, following the same trail that had brought Lewis and Clark to them three-quarters of a century earlier.

Howard also wired ahead to Montana so that troops would be sent to block their exit from the mountains. "There are high mountains and a narrow pass where the [Montana] soldiers were camped," Yellow Wolf remembered:

> They had built a long log barricade across the trail. That was the trail we had thought to travel. I saw Salish Indians at the soldiers' fort. They seemed quite a bunch. All had white cloths tied on arm and head . . . so as not to shoot each other. So the soldiers would know they were not Nez Perces. They were helping the soldiers. Always friends before, we now got no help from them. . . . No help any time. Here, another body of soldiers came upon us and demanded our surrender. We refused. They said, "You can not get by us." We answered, "We are going by you without fighting if you will let us, but we are going by you, anyhow."

The outnumbered soldiers let the Indians pass without firing a shot. Local citizens derided their strongpoint as "Fort Fizzle."

The Nez Percé turned south, along the Bitterroot River, meticulously paying for all the food and supplies they obtained from the settlers they happened upon. "We bought provisions and traded stock with white men there," Joseph remembered. "We understood that there was to be no more war. We intended to go peaceably to the buffalo country, and leave the question of returning to our country to be settled afterward." But in the towns of Missoula, Butte, Bannack, and Virginia City terrified citizens demanded army protection.

On an elevated plateau ringed by mountains, called the Big Hole, the war chief Looking Glass convinced the weary Indians they could rest for several days. Howard, he said, was now too far behind for them to worry about. But Colonel John Gibbon, who had pursued Sitting Bull's Lakota the year before, had meanwhile assembled all the available soldiers in western Montana — 163 regular infantrymen and 34 volunteers — and begun to track the unsuspecting Nez Percé. "The trail led us along the bluffs overlooking the brush-covered valley . . ." Gibbon recalled, "and as we moved stealthily forward I could hear a cautious whisper, 'there they are — look!' . . . and the main camp of our enemies was as plainly in sight as the dim starlight permitted. . . . The troops attacked at dawn."

"It must have been about three o'clock in the morning, just before daylight, when I heard it — a gun — two guns! . . ." Yellow Wolf remembered. "I lay with my eyes closed. Maybe I was dreaming? I did not [know] what to do! Then I was awake. . . . Then came three volleys from many rifles, followed by shouting of soldiers." In the first moments, between sixty and ninety Indians were cut down — more than half of them women and children, many killed before they could kick free of their blankets. "It was not good to see women and children lying dead and wounded," Yellow Wolf recalled:

> Wounded children screaming with pain. Women and men crying, wailing for their scattered dead! The air was heavy with sorrow I would not want to hear, I would not want to see, again. About ten warriors had been killed when the tepees were fired on before anyone was armed. All this was seen. The chiefs now called to the warriors to renew the fighting where the soldiers had hidden themselves.

Independent Extra

Big Hole Battle.

Gibbon Makes a Desperate Fight and is Overpowered.

LOGAN & BRADLEY KILLED

Gibbon and three Lieutenants Wounded.

" Help! Help!! Send us all the Relief you. We are Cut off from Supplies."

FIRST DISPATCH.

BIG HOLE, August 9; 1877.

To Governor Potts –

Had a hard fight with the Nez Perces, killing a number and losing a number of officers and men. We need a doctor and

A breathless dispatch in the Helena *Independent* gives the first news of the battle at the Big Hole and suggests a Nez Percé victory over Colonel John Gibbon's forces.

Looking Glass, the war chief who helped direct the Nez Percé retreat, photographed by William Henry Jackson in 1871, six years before the tribe was driven to desperation

The furious warriors regrouped and drove the soldiers from the camp. Gibbon suddenly found himself on the defensive, digging in on a wooded hillside while the Nez Percé pinned his men down with their fire. Twenty-nine soldiers were killed, forty more were wounded, including Gibbon himself. Lieutenant James H. Bradley, the first soldier to discover the bodies of Custer and his men a year earlier after the Little Bighorn battle, was among the dead.

The Nez Percé moved south now, back into Idaho, then turned east again. Angered over the loss of women and children at the Big Hole, some of the younger warriors began to disregard their leaders' urgings of restraint. Ranches along the way were raided, and some civilians murdered.

Howard — now ridiculed daily in the press for his inability to stop the Nez Percé — continued his dogged pursuit, and nearly caught up to them at Camas

The Grand River in the heart of Yellowstone National Park, through which the Nez Percé retreat passed in 1877. This view was made during the Hayden Survey six years earlier by William Henry Jackson.

Meadows, just west of the Wyoming border. But Nez Percé raiders stole his mule herd, and stalled him once again. He and General Sherman exchanged heated telegrams:

> [To General William T. Sherman. From General Oliver O. Howard. Sir:] My command is so much worn by over fatigue that I cannot push it much further. . . . I think I may stop near where I am, and in a few days work my way back to Fort Boise slowly.
>
> [To General Oliver O. Howard. From General William T. Sherman.] That force of yours should pursue the Nez Perces to the death, lead where they may. . . . If you are tired, give the command to some young energetic officer, and let him follow them. . . . No time should be lost.
>
> [To General William T. Sherman. From General Oliver O. Howard.] Sir: You misunderstood me. I never flag. . . . You need not fear for the campaign. Neither you nor General McDowell can doubt my pluck and energy. My Indian scouts are on the heels of the enemy. . . . We will move in the morning and will continue to the end.

It gave us no pleasure to see our wagons overhauled, ransacked and destroyed. . . . We did not appreciate the fact that the Indians seemed to enjoy the confiscated property. One young chap dashed past us with several yards of pink mosquito bar tied to his horse's tail. A fine strip of swansdown, a trophy from Henry Lake, which an ugly old Indian had wrapped around his head turban fashion, did not please me either.

Emma Cowan

While the soldiers bickered, the Nez Percé slipped back into Idaho, then turned east again, toward the Yellowstone plateau, which only five years earlier had been set aside as a national park. William Tecumseh Sherman himself had assured tourists they were in no danger: Indians, he said, were too superstitious to venture near the geysers.

The women were not insulted. Can the white soldiers tell me of one time when Indian women were taken prisoners, and held three days and then released without being insulted?

Chief Joseph

"I was camped in the Lower Geyser Basin," a visitor named John Shively remembered. "I was eating my supper, and on hearing a slight noise, looked up, and to my astonishment, four Indians, in war paint, were standing within ten feet of me, and twenty or thirty more had surrounded me. . . ."

The Nez Percé swept into the park without a pause. On August 24, a scouting party came upon a party of ten tourists from Montana. The chiefs ordered them released, but some of the warriors wanted to avenge the killing at the Big Hole. "A pistol shot rang out," a woman named Emma Cowan remembered, "my husband's head fell back, and a red stream trickled down his face from beneath his hat. The warm sunshine, the smell of blood, the horror of it all, a faint feeling and all was blank."

"Emma fainted, then," another woman recalled, "and I jumped and screamed and ran in and out among the Indians and horses. The Indians ran after me, and one caught me by the throat and choked me. I bore the prints of his fingers on my neck for two weeks. As he loosened his hold I had the satisfaction of biting his fingers."

Before things could get any worse, a war leader named Red Scout intervened: "I had not the heart to see those women abused. I thought we had done them enough wrong. . . . Poker Joe and I prevented other injuries being done the party."

The Indians moved on, still hoping to find sanctuary among their longtime friends, the Crow.

The army, meanwhile, now believed it had the Nez Percé surrounded. Six companies of soldiers under Colonel Samuel D. Sturgis blocked the Clark's Fork River. Five

The Nez Percé had hoped that Crow warriors like these men, photographed in 1890, would help shelter them from the whites. When they failed to do so and turned up fighting alongside their pursuers, the Nez Percé leaders feared that the end was near.

more guarded the Shoshone River. Still more troops were positioned north of the park, and Howard, with the largest force, was slowly coming through it from the west.

Somehow, the Nez Percé eluded them all. Sturgis finally caught up with them at Canyon Creek on the Yellowstone River, but couldn't stop them. His Crow scouts, however, engaged them in running skirmishes, killing some stragglers and stealing horses. This was an especially bitter blow for the Nez Percé. "Crows! . . ." Yellow Wolf remembered:

> Many snows the Crows had been our friends. But now . . . [they had] turned enemies. My heart was just like fire. . . . I do not understand how the Crows could think to help the soldiers. They were fighting against their best friends! Some Nez Perces in our band had helped them whip the Sioux who came against them only a few snows before. This was why Chief Looking Glass had advised going to the Crows, to the buffalo country. He thought Crows would help us, if there was more fighting.

The Nez Percé were alone. With the hope of finding friends and sanctuary on the northern Plains gone, they fastened on one last chance for escape. Sitting Bull had found safety in Canada. They would head north across Montana to join him. At first it seemed nothing could stop them. They crossed the Yellowstone River, then the Musselshell, and finally, in late September, the Missouri, where they easily drove off a detachment of troops at Cow Island and helped themselves to an army supply depot.

They had now come more than seventeen hundred miles across some of the most rugged terrain in North America; fought in seventeen engagements against more than two thousand soldiers and Indian scouts; suffered hardships, disappointments, and the loss of loved ones. But they had beaten or eluded every army sent against them, and Canada — and freedom — were now only forty miles away. Howard, they knew, was more than two days' march behind them, and so before crossing the border the Nez Percé stopped to camp on Snake Creek near the Bear Paw Mountains.

"No white men were seen by scouts ahead," Yellow Wolf remembered:

> We guarded the back trail, but saw no signs of soldiers. We knew the distance to the Canadian line. Knew how long it would take to travel there. But there was no hurrying. . . . With horses' feet mostly sick and lots of grass, the chiefs ordered, "We camp here until tomorrow forenoon." . . . We knew General Howard was more than two suns back on our trail. It was nothing hard to keep ahead of him. . . .

But for nearly two weeks, Colonel Nelson A. Miles, who had taken over Custer's old command, had mercilessly pushed the Seventh Cavalry all the way from eastern Montana to intercept the Nez Percé. With him rode Lakota and Cheyenne warriors, who just a year before had defeated the Seventh at the Little Bighorn but had little affection for the Nez Percé. Now, they rode into the Nez Percé camp at a full gallop. "The Nez Percés were quietly slumbering in their tents," Miles remembered, "evidently without a thought of danger. . . . When the charge was made . . . [t]he tramp of at least 600 horses over the prairie fairly shook the ground, and, although a complete surprise to the Indians in the main, it must have given them a few minutes' notice, for as the troops charged against the village the Indians opened a hot fire upon them."

Despite the complete surprise, the Nez Percé warriors repulsed one attack — then a second, and a third. They killed or wounded fifty-three of the soldiers, but all their horses had been driven off. Both sides dug rifle pits. The weather turned colder. Snow started falling. Looking Glass was killed. Then, night fell, Yellow Wolf remembered:

> Most of our few warriors left from the Big Hole had been swept as leaves before the storm. Chief Ollokot, Lone Bird, and Lean Elk were gone. . . . A young warrior, wounded, lay on a buffalo robe dying without complaint. Children crying with cold. No fire. There could be no light. Everywhere the crying, the death wail. . . . I felt the coming end. All for which we had suffered lost! Thoughts came of the Wallowa where I grew up. Of my own country when only Indians were there. Of tepees along the bending river. Of the blue, clear lake, wide meadows with horse and cattle herds. From the mountain forests, voices seemed calling. I felt as dreaming. Not my living self.

Sunday, September 30th, 1877. Reveille at 2 o'clock a.m. The moon and stars shine in a clear sky, the air is chilly. We march as soon as we can see to move. A wolf serenades us at our first halt by the side of a stream. We soon come upon the broad Indian trail. Our Cheyenne and Sioux undergo a sudden transformation: they are painted, stripped for a fight, on their favorite chargers. . . . They are bounding over the plain on either side of the column, which is now in rapid motion. To be astride a good horse, on the open prairie, rifle in hand . . . [as] one of four hundred horsemen, galloping on a hot trail, sends a thrill through the body which is seldom experienced.

Major Henry Remsen Tilton
Seventh Cavalry

For five more days, the siege went on. A few Nez Percé slipped behind the lines and straggled into Canada. Sitting Bull welcomed them, but would send no force to help the others. Their last hope of rescue was gone.

Under a white flag, Miles opened negotiations. Since most of their chiefs were dead, Joseph was selected to talk with him. The general told Joseph that if he and his men turned over their weapons, they would be allowed to return home in the spring.

> I knew that we were near Sitting Bull's camp [Joseph remembered,] and I thought maybe the Nez Percés who had escaped would return with assistance. . . . My people were divided about surrendering. We could have escaped from Bear Paw Mountain if we had left our wounded, old women and children behind. We were unwilling to do this. We had never heard of a wounded Indian recovering while in the hands of white men. . . . I could not bear to see my wounded men and women suffer any longer; we had lost enough already. General Miles had promised that we might return to our own country with what stock we had left. I thought we could start again. I believed General Miles, or I never would have surrendered.

On the afternoon of October 5, Joseph rode out to the foot of a bluff on the prairie. Miles and General Howard were waiting for him. "Joseph threw himself off his horse," an officer noted, "draped his blanket about him . . . and with a quiet pride, not exactly defiance, advanced toward General Howard and held out his rifle in token of submission. Howard gestured for him to hand it over to General Miles."

"I am tired of fighting," Joseph told Howard, through an interpreter:

> Tell General Howard I know his heart. What he told me before, I have in my heart. I am tired of fighting. Our chiefs are killed. Looking Glass is dead. Toohoolhoolzote is dead. The old men are all dead. It is the young men who say "Yes" or "No." He who led the young men is dead. It is cold, and we have no blankets. The little children are freezing to death. My people, some of them, have run away to the hills, and have no blankets, no food. No one knows where they are — perhaps freezing to death. I want to have time to look for my children, and see how many of them I can find. Maybe I shall find them among the dead. Hear me, my chiefs! I am tired. My heart is sick and sad. From where the sun now stands I will fight no more, forever.

Joseph and his people were loaded onto a riverboat and sent down the Missouri River toward Fort Abraham Lincoln in Dakota Territory, where they expected to spend the winter. But while they were on the way, the promise that Miles and Howard had made, that the Nez Percé would be allowed to return to their home country, had been overruled by General Sherman:

> [The war with the Nez Percé] was one of the most extraordinary Indian wars of which there is any record. The Indians throughout displayed a courage and skill that elicited universal praise. They abstained from scalping; let captive women go free; did not commit indiscriminate murder of peaceful families, which is usual, and fought with almost scientific skill. . . . Nevertheless, they would not settle down on lands set apart for them . . . and when commanded by proper

A Presbyterian missionary (back row, second from right) and some of her Nez Percé charges on the Lapwai reservation to which Joseph and his band had refused to go

> authority, they began resistance by murdering persons in no manner connected with their alleged grievances. . . . They should never again be allowed to return to Oregon.

When the Nez Percé arrived at the fort, its cannon boomed a greeting, and the steam engine of a Northern Pacific train blasted its whistle three times. They had never seen a train before and began a mournful song. It sounded, one onlooker said, like a "death chant." Then they were loaded onto the train.

They were not going home, they were now told, but far away, into exile in Oklahoma's Indian Territory. "We were not asked if we were willing to go," Chief Joseph remembered. "We were ordered to get into railroad cars."

Joseph and 337 others were taken to the northeast corner of Indian Territory in Oklahoma. There, they soon began to fall sick. Sixty-eight died in the first year alone. Soon, they had a cemetery set aside solely for infants, with one hundred graves. They called the place of their exile *Eeikish Pah,* which meant both "the hot place" and "hell."

General Miles continued to promote the exiles' cause. But white settlers in Joseph's homeland in the Wallowa Valley adamantly opposed his return. Even some of the Nez Percé on the Idaho reservation considered Joseph and his band troublemakers who should be kept away.

To plead for his people, Chief Joseph went to Washington. He met with President Rutherford B. Hayes, and in Lincoln Hall, near the Capitol, spoke to a gathering of congressmen, cabinet members, and businessmen.

> I have shaken hands with a great many friends, but there are some things I want to know which no one seems able to explain. I cannot understand how the Government sends a man out to fight us, as it did General Miles, and then breaks his

What I heard those generals and chiefs say, I have always remembered. But those generals soon forgot their promises. Chief Joseph and his people were not permitted to return to their own homes. We were not captured. It was a draw battle. . . . We expected to be returned to our own homes. This was promised us by General Miles. That was how he got our rifles from us. It was the only way he could get them.

Yellow Wolf

Joseph and members of his family, photographed during their confinement in Oklahoma

word. Such a Government has something wrong with it. . . . If the white man wants to live in peace with the Indian he can live in peace. There need be no trouble. Treat all men alike. Give them all the same law. Give them all an even chance to live and grow. All men were made by the same Great Spirit Chief. They are all brothers. The earth is the mother of all people, and all people should have equal rights upon it.

The speech prompted praise and sympathy all across the nation, but nothing changed. Joseph and his band still could not go home.

Wilderness and the West

T. H. Watkins

In the late summer of 1861, a young man sat in a rowboat and watched in awe while much of an entire western forest went up in flames. His name was Samuel Clemens, a tramp newspaperman and sometime riverboat pilot who had come west earlier that summer as companion to his brother, Orion, the newly appointed secretary to the governor of Nevada Territory (carved off from Utah Territory earlier that year, after the discovery of huge deposits of silver in the mountains north of Carson City had given Nevada a claim to its own identity). Before wandering up to the mining region to see what they could see, Sam and a companion decided to spend the rest of the summer of 1861 loitering about the shores of Lake Tahoe up in the Sierra Nevada. It was an interlude of splendid isolation in the heart of one of the most compellingly beautiful wild areas on the planet, and the two young men embraced it gratefully. "The forest about us was dense and cool," Clemens remembered in *Roughing It* (1872), writing now as Mark Twain,

> the sky above us was cloudless and brilliant with sunshine, the broad lake before us was glassy and clear, or rippled and breezy, or black and storm-tossed, according to Nature's mood; and its circling border of mountain domes, clothed with forests, scarred with land-slides, cloven by cañons and valleys, and helmeted with glittering snow, fitly framed and finished the noble picture. The view was always fascinating, bewitching, entrancing.

Listen now to what the young nature lover soon did to the beauty he had described so elegantly. He left a cook fire unattended briefly one evening, and before he could get back to it a vagrant gust of wind had sent sparks into the tinderlike pine needles of the forest floor. When the resulting flames reached a stand of summer-dry manzanita, the resulting explosion of heat sent the two young men into their rowboat and out onto the lake. "Within half an hour," Twain wrote,

> all before us was a tossing, blinding tempest of flame! It went surging up adjacent ridges — surmounted them and disappeared in the cañons beyond — burst into view upon higher and farther ridges, presently — shed a grander illumination abroad, and dove again — flamed out again, directly, higher and still higher up the mountain-side — threw out skirmishing parties of fire here and there, and sent them trailing their crimson spirals away among remote ramparts and ribs and gorges. . . .
>
> Every feature of the spectacle was repeated in the glowing mirror of the lake! Both pictures were sublime, both were beautiful; but that in the lake had a bewildering richness about it that enchanted the eye and held it with the strongest fascination.

It is not Twain's carelessness that we find startling today; many forest fires still begin with some camper's runaway cookfire. It is his attitude toward the whole business that mystifies us. Smokey the Bear would weep large ursine tears over such a spectacle, and even the most hidebound fire ecologist probably would offer some barbed observations regarding human stupidity as being an unnatural and inappropriate substitute for lightning as the prime cause of environmentally correct forest fires. But in Twain's eyes, for all his infatuation with the scenery of the forested mountains, the fire was a grand entertainment, remembered without so much as a passing phrase of remorse for all that he had sent to perdition. His description of the event was the raucous celebration of a Hannibal-indoctrinated frontier mentality that sees even the most beautiful land essentially as something subservient to human needs, no quarter given, no regrets expressed.

That mentality represents the oldest and most dominant philosophical strain in the history of the settlement of the West. It is a perception that sees the land mainly as a resource, a commodity to be used to fuel national dreams of progress and an ever-growing gross national product, as well as personal dreams of security, wealth, and power. The perception hardly was confined to the West, of course; it already had flamed through most of the land east of the Big River, with consequences (erosion-caused flooding in the timber-stripped Appalachians, for example, or farmed-out soils in New England) that were beginning to be understood, though fitfully. But there seemed to be so *much* beyond the wide Missouri — so *much* land, so *many* forests, so *many* rivers, so *enormous* a population of wild creatures, so *thick* a crust of treasure-laden rock formations — that for sensibilities already profligate with hope it seemed it all would last forever. It could not last, and much of it did not last, and most of what was lost will never be reclaimed: native prairie grasses plowed under and replaced by millions of acres of wheat and corn and other commercial species; forests scythed off the slopes of scores of mountains in nearly every major range in the West; grasslands in the deserts of the Southwest and the High Plains of the Dakotas and mountain meadows everywhere eaten down to their nubby roots by millions of cattle and sheep; wild rivers converted into plumbing systems by dams and poisoned by runoff from smoking industrial mining complexes and agribusiness farms the size of Balkan nations; urban conurbations oozing everywhere, linked by habitat-fragmenting highway systems and kept alive by rapidly dwindling supplies of water, while plant and animal species are eased ever closer to the abyss of extinction.

A familiar litany, and usually an angry one, as if most of those who created this imperfect world west of the Mississippi had been nothing more than bands of wild-eyed Visigoths laying waste with ax, plow, and cement, dancing, like Twain, before the flames of their vandalism, then moving on. It leaves out of the equation those whom Wallace Stegner has called "the stickers," the men and women who came to make a life in the West, not to take what they could from it and leave it the poorer for their passage. It was the stickers who gave the region the best that was in it, after all: resiliency, community, humor, and hope, all of it forged in that difficult arena where human character is tested.

Still, there were Visigoths enough, opportunists and entrepreneurs who used both the land and the people in it with such arrogant disregard that historian Vernon L. Parrington would call their era the time of "the Great Barbecue" and Bernard DeVoto would describe the West as the "Plundered Province." Like the story of what our culture did to the Native American cultures that lay in its path, the story of what happened to the land provides a dark counterpoint to the brimming excitement of the western adventure. But even as the driving force of settlement was puncturing and peopling and plundering the land, there was another, paradoxical sensitivity developing — more slowly and never so completely as that which shaped the essential history of the West, to be sure, but one that nevertheless was not without its own excitements, its own shades of color, its own heroes and heroines. It was an idea, as one of its historians has characterized it, and it was called wilderness.

In March of 1862, just about seven months after Mark Twain set fire to much of the Tahoe Basin in the Sierra Nevada, a seriously ill Henry David Thoreau sat at the writing desk of his house in Concord, Massachusetts, and gave the final polish to an essay called "Walking." When done, he sent it off to *The Atlantic Monthly,* where it was accepted immediately. On May 6, he died, and "Walking," appearing in the June 1862 issue of the magazine, became the first posthumously published work produced by the nineteenth century's most recognized natural philosopher. It is a pity Thoreau did not live to see the essay given the luminosity of print, for it proved to be one of the most enduring pieces he ever wrote, one whose insights into the natural order of things carry a special weight when applied to the West.

Not that Thoreau ever saw anything of the land that lay beyond the wild Missouri. Red Wing, Minnesota, was as far west as he ever got, and that only briefly a few months before his final illness. But if he had not seen the West, he somehow knew it in his New England bones, and it spoke to him of something crucial to the spiritual and physical well-being of the human species. When he went out of the house for a walk, he wrote, he instinctively turned in a westerly direction.

> The future lies that way to me, and the earth seems more unexhausted and richer on that side. . . . Eastward I go only by force; but westward I go free. . . . I believe that the forest which I see in the western horizon stretches uninterruptedly toward the setting sun. . . . Let me live where I will, on this side is the city, on that the wilderness, and ever I am leaving the city more and more and withdrawing into the wilderness. I should not lay so much stress on this fact if I did not believe that something like this is the prevailing tendency of my countrymen. I must walk toward Oregon, and not toward Europe.

But there was more to this instinct than just a vague cultural yearning to escape Europe's intellectual and psychological bonds, Thoreau believed. The movement was like that of a compass's arrow trembling always in the direction of magnetic north; he turned west, toward the wilderness, he thought, because he was drawn there by a connection that was as irresistible as it was poorly understood. "The West of which I speak," he went on, "is but another name for the Wild; and what I have been preparing to say is that in Wildness is the preservation of the World." The presence of uncorrupted wildness, he believed, enriched both the physical and spiritual needs of the human societies that pocketed and threatened to overwhelm it, and to ignore or destroy that connection would be to diminish not merely the character of human life, but its chances of survival. And, as he had suggested even before "Walking" was published, it might be as necessary as it was desirable to save some of the wild. Why not, he had asked in an 1858 essay, set aside "national preserves" in which "the bear and panther, and some even of the hunter race [by which he meant Indians], may still exist, and not be 'civilized off the face of the earth' . . . ?" In "Walking," he had attempted to set forth some of the compelling reasons for such preservation.

For the most part, Thoreau's posthumous thesis fell upon uncomprehending ears, and it would be more than another two generations before his message would be understood in its deeper meanings. Still, there already was concern about what the engines of progress had so far accomplished in the way of environmental damage, and some worry about consequences. If few were yet talking about the preservation of wilderness as an abstract aesthetic or ethical notion, some people, at least, were beginning to see the links between a healthy, productive natural world and the continuing survival of American civilization. The polymathic George Perkins Marsh — linguist, architect, historian, folklorist, former Vermont fish commissioner, and U.S. ambassador to Italy — for example, pointed back in time to lost civilizations and found in them cautionary tales. In *Man and Nature; or, Physical Geography as Modified by Human Action* (1864), he declared that "man has too long forgotten that the earth was given to him for usufruct alone, not for consumption, still less for profligate waste." The systematic disregard of that responsibility, he said, had made of the ancient Fertile Crescent "an assemblage of bald mountains, barren, treeless hills and Swampy and malarious plains," while the marbled relics of vanished Greek and Roman civilizations were surrounded by "a desolation almost as complete as the moon." And here in the United States, he feared, we were in all ignorance repeating the same mistakes, "breaking up the floor and wainscoting and doors and window frames of our dwelling, for fuel to warm our bodies and seethe our pottage. . . ." He called for stewardship based on the lessons of the past and, like Thoreau, embraced the idea of setting aside a reserve of "American soil . . . as far as possible, in its primitive condition."

President Theodore Roosevelt and John Muir (fifth and seventh from left) at Yosemite National Park, 1903

Marsh's audience was hardly bigger than that enjoyed by Thoreau even in the East. And as Twain's unenlightened celebration of casual destruction suggests, out in the West, where a lot of pottage already was being seethed to a fare-thee-well, virtually no one was listening. True, Congress had given the Yosemite Valley to the state of California to be used as a park "for public use, resort and recreation," and in 1872 would establish 2.2 million acres of the upper Yellowstone River region as "a public park or pleasuring ground for the benefit and enjoyment of the people" — the first national park in our history, if one does not include Hot Springs, Arkansas, set aside forty years earlier for the presumed medicinal value of its waters. But the Yosemite and Yellowstone reserves were made possible largely because these areas were perceived to have no particular economic value. They were the exceptions that tested the rule, and the rule was still unfettered use.

This was no more true at any time than in the years immediately following the Civil War, when the full surge of settlement began to spill across the Mississippi and Missouri rivers, encouraged by such laws as the Homestead Act of 1862 and the plethora of land laws that followed it, each patterned on assumptions derived from experience in the humid and subhumid lands east of the isohyetal line that divides the portion of the country getting twenty inches or more of rain every year from that which gets less — which includes most of the West, once described by historian Walter Prescott Webb as a "semi-desert with a desert heart." This, Major John Wesley Powell announced in 1878, had been a mistake. The one-armed major, who lost his right arm at the battle of Shiloh, was a largely self-trained scientist and explorer who had reached some considerable fame after leading an expedition down the Green and Colorado rivers and through the Grand Canyon in 1869. With that accomplishment as his portfolio, he was given government support for a survey of the lands of the Colorado Plateau, embracing much of what is now southern Utah and northern Arizona, as well as portions of Nevada, Colorado, and New Mexico.

Powell, for all his experience of wild country, was no Thoreau. He was here to see what resources the plateau might hold and how the land might otherwise be put to human use. But he was a sublimely rational man, and among the things he learned in the nearly seven years of the survey was that because there was so little water available in most of the land west of the Mississippi Valley, the traditions of settlement exemplified by the Homestead Act were simply not appropriate. Land laws would have to be reshaped, he said, with land units drawn larger and water rights guaranteed to all settlers in order to prevent the monopoly of both land and water. The system of rectilinear surveys that had marched across most of the eastern landscape should be scrapped beyond the Mississippi and the boundaries of states and territories be redrawn to conform to geographic, not political, imperatives. All current land laws, including the Homestead Act, should be suspended until surveys were completed to identify all available irrigation sites, as well as whatever timber, mineral, and other resources the land might hold. Above all, if agriculture was to survive here, irrigation was going to be necessary — and even irrigation had its limits.

Powell's *Report on the Lands of the Arid Region of the United States* flew in the face of expectations and was ignored by the Congress that had authorized it, as was a similar public lands commission report that followed it a couple of years later. By the 1890s, however, tens of thousands of Homestead entries had gone bust, done in by the realities of which Powell had warned, while land and water monopoly by a few plagued most of those homesteaders who had not gone under. A great cry for irrigation to supply "a million forty-acre farms" now arose in the West. Can't be done, Powell said. "Gentlemen," he told an Irrigation Congress in 1893 when it showed interest in the Colorado River as one source of water for those million little farms, "you are piling up a heritage of conflict, for there is not enough water to supply the land!" Never mind: then as now, it was the boomers and the boosters who controlled both the economy and the politics of the West, and the boomers wanted irrigation dams. In 1902, Congress passed the Newlands Act, creating the Reclamation Service (later renamed the Bureau of Reclamation), and put the federal government in the dam-building business. An antimonopoly provision in the law stipulated, among other things, that no one could receive water from any federally constructed reservoir for more than 160 acres and that all recipients must live on the land and work it personally. This provision was systematically ignored by the beneficiaries of federal water and never seriously enforced by the Bureau of Reclamation, whose officials knew perfectly well that Congress would rise up and stifle the attempt, and as one western river after another was relentlessly plugged over the next half century, fewer and fewer nonresident individuals and corporate entities ended up in control of more and more land.

Powell died before witnessing the final perversion of his vision for the rational settlement of the West. The ideas of another rational man of the era had better fortune. He was Gifford Pinchot, trained by Germans in the then embryonic field of silviculture and forest management and as early as the beginning of the 1890s recognized as this country's leading — which is to say, nearly only — professional forester. His work as a "consulting forester" was at first confined to private forests, like those owned by George W. Vanderbilt on his Biltmore estate in North Carolina, but his ambitions were capacious enough to include the entire 200 million acres of federally owned forests in the West (including Alaska).

Most of those lands certainly were in need of stewardship. Many had already been mutilated. Even legitimate timber companies had the habit of abusing such laws as the Timber and Stone Act, clear-cutting their federal grant lands and moving on before establishing final title. In 1866, so much damage already had been done in both Washington and Colorado to cause the surveyors general of the two territories to recommend that the government sell the forests that remained while it still had something left to sell.

The government did not sell the forests, but such depredations did enable a small contingent of reformers in Congress to win passage of the Forest Reserve Clause in 1891, a law that gave the president authority to withdraw federal forest regions from land-claim filings. President Benjamin Harrison withdrew 13 million acres immediately, and at the end of his second term President Grover Cleveland withdrew another 21 million. In 1896, Cleveland also formed a National Forest Commission, a body whose members traveled from state to state in the West to determine the condition of the forests. Among the members was young Gifford Pinchot, and he helped to write much of the language for legislation that grew out of the commission's investigations. The legislation, passed in 1897, was called the Forest Organic Act, and it stipulated that the forest reserves had been established "to improve and protect the forest . . . for the purpose of securing favorable conditions of water flow, and to furnish a continuous supply of timber for the use and necessities of citizens of the United States." A Forestry Division was created in the Department of the Interior, the agency then in control of the public forests. Pinchot was appointed to head the division, and eight years later the Progressive-minded President Theodore Roosevelt persuaded Congress to pass the Forest Transfer Act, which took responsibility for the forests out of Interior and put it in the Department of Agriculture. Shortly thereafter, the forest reserves became "national forests," the Forestry Division of the Interior Department became the U.S. Forest Service of the Department of Agriculture, and Gifford Pinchot was appointed chief forester of the United States. By the time a political conflict with President William Howard Taft caused his resignation in 1910, Pinchot had fashioned the Forest Service into one of the most dedicated federal agencies in government, and the National Forest System had grown to 148 million acres (later withdrawals and purchases would bring the total to what it is today: 191 million acres).

What about wilderness in the equation, then? As a concept separate from utilitarian values, it simply did not exist in the minds of Powell, Pinchot, and most of the other Progressive spirits who were striving so hard to give the concept of stewardship political and legal validity. They were, Pinchot would later say, practicing "conservation," a term he always claimed he had invented and that he unquestionably defined more precisely than anyone before or since: "Conservation means the wise use of the earth and its resources for the lasting good of man. Conservation is the foresighted utilization, preservation, and/or renewal of forests, waters, lands, and minerals for the greatest good of the greatest number for the longest time." The concept's unadorned anthropocentrism limited its philosophical scope; it left no room for the notion that at least some enclaves of the natural world might best be left entirely alone.

Still, it should be remembered that without the accomplishments of utilitarian conservation, particularly with regard to the forests, there might have been precious little left to preserve. One of the preservationists who would have been willing to concede that point — indeed, his lobbying of President Theodore Roosevelt had gone a long way toward helping to establish the U.S. Forest Service and put Pinchot at its head — was John Muir, who had met and learned to respect Pinchot while serving with him on the 1896 National Forest Commission. Muir, born in Scotland, raised in Wisconsin, and seduced at an early age by the mysteries of nature, found himself drawn more and more to an almost visceral love of all Creation for its own pure sake and of wilderness as Creation's most joyful trove of fascination and knowledge. "In God's wildness," he would write in 1890 in a deliberate reprise of Thoreau, "lies the hope of the world — the great fresh unblighted, unredeemed wilderness." With that as yet unstated and inchoate love circulating throughout his wiry Scottish being, he had turned his back on a career in manufacturing in the Midwest in 1867, walking a thousand miles to Florida and, after a season of illness, taking a ship bound for California in 1868.

There, he hired on as a herder of sheep ("hooved locusts," he would come to call them) in the Sierra Nevada and soon encountered the Yosemite Valley. He was dumbstruck with awe. Here was nature at its most sublime, wilderness given its greatest celebration, and except for a ten-year stint running his family's farm in the San Joaquin Valley, Muir would spend most of the rest of his life delving into and writing about the secrets of the valley and of the mountains in which it lay, the Sierra Nevada, the "Range of Light," as he called it. Along the way, Muir became the best-known and most articulate spokesman for the necessity of the wilderness, the unofficial leader of a tiny preservation movement whose philosophy combined romantic literary notions of a lost Eden and the ostensibly noble savages who had inhabited it; elaborate aesthetic traditions of natural beauty; a conviction that American history and character had been largely shaped by the wilderness that had challenged the growth of our civilization, and that wildness should be honored as a kind of artifact of our own past; and, among a few like Muir himself, the almost mystical belief that the essence of the wild was in them, that humans were inextricably bound up in its mysteries and enlarged by its power.

Muir's growing fame and mystical certainties were turned to a practical end when it became clear that the State of California, into whose care the valley had been placed in 1864, was allowing it to be degraded by sundry entrepreneurs. Encouraged by eastern nature enthusiast Robert Underwood Johnson, who offered the pages of his influential *Century* magazine, Muir bent his writing talents and his passions to a campaign to have the valley returned to the federal government and declared a national park. That effort succeeded in 1890, and in 1892 the now prototypical environmental activist joined with Johnson and a few like-minded California friends to form the Sierra Club. The organization's general goal was the preservation of the wild country of the Sierra Nevada, but its specific goal soon became to add the meadows and forests in the ring of high country surrounding the Yosemite Valley to Yosemite National Park. That effort, too, succeeded, in 1905. In the meantime, Muir and the club cheered the creation of Sequoia, General Grant, Mount Rainier, and Crater Lake national parks, and would cheer again as Mesa Verde, Petrified Forest, Grand Canyon, Zion, Olympic, and Glacier were added to the National Park System, either as full-fledged parks or as national monuments, each to be preserved, in the words of the 1916 National Parks Organic Act, "unimpaired, for the enjoyment of future generations."

Visitors to Yosemite, 1890

What with the forests finally in the hands of intelligent management and parks being established as never before in American history, the deliberate preservation of the wild might have seemed well on its way toward becoming an accepted part of the country's land policy in the West. Not quite yet. In 1901, the city of San Francisco petitioned Congress for the right to dam the Tuolumne River in the Hetch Hetchy Valley of the Sierra Nevada. Congressional permission was necessary, for the Hetch Hetchy Valley lay in the heart of Yosemite National Park. The city wanted to eliminate its dependence on a private water monopoly by establishing its own supply, an ambition the civic-minded Progressive movement could be expected to support — and indeed, Gifford Pinchot became one of the project's most vigorous champions. Congress granted its permission, but Muir, who considered the Hetch Hetchy Valley to be even more beautiful than the Yosemite Valley, violently opposed its destruction, however worthwhile the cause. Congress and the dam promoters, he wrote President Roosevelt early in the conflict, were demonstrating "the proud sort of confidence that comes of good sound irrefragable ignorance," and for twelve years one secretary of the interior after another refused to authorize the building of the dam, while Congress never followed its permission with enabling legislation. That stalemate ended in 1913 when Franklin K. Lane, former city attorney for San Francisco and an important supporter of Woodrow Wilson's 1912 presidential campaign, was appointed secretary of the interior. As good a Progressive as Gifford Pinchot and an even better friend of San Francisco, Lane promoted the Hetch Hetchy project and in December 1913 Congress passed enabling legislation.

The conflict had split even the Sierra Club, most of whose members, after all, were Progressive San Franciscans who, while they may have loved Yosemite, wanted to see their citizens freed of the dead hand of monopoly. The conflict saddened the last years of the club's founder, and the final defeat in 1913, most believed, broke his heart. The seventy-five-year-old Muir cursed "this dark damn- dam-damnation," and a little over a year later was dead.

In the Hetch Hetchy conflict, Muir and the nascent wilderness movement had come smack up against the fact that while some landscapes might assuredly be saved from exploitation, the dominant view still held that no piece of land, however beautiful, was better than any apparently superior human use that might be made of it. Wilderness preservation was not yet an idea whose time had come, but it was a good deal closer than a despairing Muir might have imagined. Even as the controversy over Hetch Hetchy developed, preservation sentiment began to simmer in the mind of another wilderness philosopher in the making. His name was Aldo Leopold, a dedicated and practical-minded ranger in Pinchot's utilitarian Forest Service, and in 1909 and 1910 he spent a lot of time packing into the wild country of Apache National Forest in New Mexico, surveying the boundaries of the forest, checking on the condition of the land, monitoring the grazing of sheep and cattle, taking stock of the timber "inventory," and chasing game poachers.

And on at least one occasion, killing wolves. He and a crew had stopped to eat lunch on some rimrock in the Blue Range when they noticed an old female wolf below them, surrounded by cavorting pups. Without a second thought, Leopold and his crew whipped out their rifles and began pumping bullets into the little pack. They then clambered down the rocks to see how well they had done their work. The mother was still alive when they approached her, Leopold remembered many years later:

> We reached the old wolf in time to watch a fierce green fire dying in her eyes. I realized then, and have known ever since, that there was something new to me in those eyes — something known only to her and the mountain. I was young then, and full of trigger-itch; I thought that because fewer wolves meant more deer, that no wolves would mean hunters' paradise. But after seeing the green fire die, I sensed that neither the wolf nor the mountain agreed with such a view.

That moment in the Blue Range was an epiphany that would nourish a growing conviction in Leopold that sooner or later a line would have to be drawn between what human beings merely thought they needed to manage and what they truly needed to save: wilderness. Conviction soon became passion, and just ten years after Muir's death Leopold would persuade his superiors in the Forest Service to establish the 500,000-acre Gila Wilderness, the first federal wilderness area in our history. In another eleven years he would join with forester Robert Marshall to help found the Wilderness Society, and even while a gaggle of New Deal planners transformed the river basins of the Tennessee, the Colorado, the Columbia, and the Missouri with concrete, electricity, and irrigation, and the machinery of World War II and the booming postwar years bloated the urban enclaves that pocked the wide-open spaces of the West, a reborn wilderness movement would forge the protocols of preservation and offer them to the Congress and the people with increasing skill and persuasiveness.

And on September 3, 1964, President Lyndon B. Johnson would take pen in fist and in the Rose Garden of the White House sign the Wilderness Act, which, in order "to secure for the American people of present and future generations the benefits of an enduring resource of wilderness," established "a National Wilderness Preservation System to be composed of federally owned areas designated by Congress as 'wilderness areas' . . . administered for the use and enjoyment of the American people in such manner as will leave them unimpaired for future use and enjoyment as wilderness."

This, then, is what we have done with at least some of the best of the land beyond the wide Missouri in the 130 years since Mark Twain celebrated the fiery spectacle he created on the shores of Lake Tahoe: an idea that had been little more than a suspicion then has now been sanctified by law to provide a more durable legacy than the burned-over lands and sensibilities left by all the years of boom and bust.

It has not been a perfect transformation. While the National Wilderness Preservation System has grown to more than 104 million acres, virtually every acre of each new wilderness area has been placed in the system only after years of agitation among wilderness advocates, reluctant land-managing agencies, presidential administrations whose dedication to the wilderness idea has run the gamut from enthusiastic endorsement (Carter) to open opposition (Reagan), national corporations and small-town entrepreneurs who remain unconvinced that the measure of the West should be taken in anything but greenbacks or their equivalent, and the politicians who service their needs and parrot their philosophies.

Still, it is important to listen to the names as they ring on the tongue, for they reverberate triumphantly with an ineffable westernness: Comanche Peak, Lizard Head, Escudilla, Superstition, Gates of the Mountains, Great Bear, Bosque del Apache, Black Canyon, High Uintas, Indian Heaven, Coyote Mountains, Fishhook, Powderhorn, Jedediah Smith — and hundreds more, talismans carved by law to stand forever as testimony to this nation's commitment to turn its back on much of the history of the West, to pause in the midst of careless enthusiasms fired by transient dreams of wealth just long enough to leave for future generations "an enduring resource of wilderness."

Winter roundup

CHAPTER SEVEN

THE GREAT DIE-UP

1877–1887

WILLIE
Son of
H B & J ANDREWS
DIED

By 1877, the American conquest of the West was nearly complete; for every Indian in the West, there were now nearly forty whites, homesteaders had plowed up the plains that had once nourished the buffalo, and, as the Indian wars drew to a close, the last obstacles to complete American domination seemed to drop away. From now on, there would be less and less room for those who didn't conform to American ways. But then, in one savage winter the newcomers would learn just how "wild" the West could really be — and that no matter how many of its native people were subdued, conquest of the western landscape could never be complete.

In the autumn of 1872, a thirty-year-old Union veteran named Uriah Wesley Oblinger left his rented farm in Onward, Indiana, and set out by wagon with his brother and two brothers-in-law for eastern Nebraska. After years of working for other people, all four hoped to rise in the world by establishing homesteads of their own. They were not alone. "There is a heavy emigration this fall," Uriah wrote home. "The wagons are going in our direction by the hundreds, the people tell us. . . . We meet a good many coming east that have been out and located and are going to move permanent in the spring."

Uriah Oblinger was part of one of the greatest migrations in history. Nearly 2 million people moved out onto the prairies and the plains in the 1870s, lured in large part by the theory that rain followed the plow. The populations of Colorado and Nebraska doubled. South Dakota's, Montana's, and Wyoming's tripled. In 1880, North Dakota had 37,000 non-Indians within its borders; by 1890, there would be five times as many more.

Oblinger's wife, Mattie, and infant daughter, Ella, were to wait until he sent for them, but he wrote to them as often as he could:

> Fillmore County, Nebraska. Dear Wife & baby: . . . I can get along well enough through the week, but when Sunday comes I feel a little lonesome without you. . . . I am hunting a home for us where we can enjoy ourselves without . . . being bothered doing as other people says whether it is my interest or not. . . .
>
> Give baby a kiss — yes, 2 of them — and take one yourself.

> Well I suppose the first question you would ask me now would be how do you like Nebraska. [Mattie,] . . . you can see just as far as you please here, and almost every foot in sight can be plowed. . . .
>
> The longer I stay here, the better I like it. There are . . . mostly young families, just starting in life the same as we are and I find them very generous, indeed. We will all be poor here together.

> [Wife,] you must not get out of heart because people try to discourage you. . . . When they tell you we have nothing to live on, just tell them we can raise larger vegetables here than Indiana can grow to save her neck. . . .

It would take Oblinger a while to find the homestead he wanted — "all the good ones are taken up," he told his wife — and he finally settled on a parcel that had been

Uriah and Mattie Oblinger, with their firstborn child, Ella, probably photographed in Indiana before Uriah set out for the West

claimed by another man who had returned to the East without ever working it. "There is not a square inch of it but is as rich as cream and can be plowed," he wrote, "and I can stand almost anywhere on it and see it all."

Throughout the long winter, Uriah hauled ice and railroad ties in Lincoln at three dollars a day to pay the lawyer who did the paperwork that legitimized his claim and to save up for his little family's passage west.

> [W]hen the bachelors in Nebraska all get women it will fill up rapidly . . . or at least it ought to, for there are a number of men here who have homesteads . . . & nearly all have a "bird" in view as soon as they can get a cage ready. As for me I will build my cage soon and then send for my birds to come. I want you to cook, wash, iron, scrub, bake, make & mend — and do many things too numerous to mention. I'm getting tired of sleeping with bachelors, [even] if they are your brothers.

In May, Uriah Oblinger's nine-month wait finally ended. Mattie and Ella, along with a crate containing all their worldly goods and another filled with live chickens, arrived at the Crete depot aboard the morning train. Uriah took them to their new home, built from blocks of prairie sod cut with his own hands.

Soon, Mattie Oblinger and her daughter, too, were sending letters east.

> May 19th, 1873
> Dear Mother and Father,
> At home in our house and a sod at that! . . . We moved in last Wednesday — Uriah's birthday — It is not quite so convenient as a nice frame, but I would as soon live in it as the cabins I have lived in. . . . I ripped our wagon sheet in two, have it around the sides and have several papers up. . . . It looks real well. . . . The only objection I have is that we have no floor yet. . . .

January 26, 1874
Dear Grandpa,
I have learned my letters and can spell. I will be ready for more books pretty soon. I can spell Ax & Cat & Dog & Girl off the book when Pa or Ma give it out to me. I love to spell so well. I bother Pa and Ma considerable to get them to learn me. . . . I am learning "Twinkle, twinkle, Little Star." Grandma, I know you would learn me if I was at your house.

Lots of love and kisses . . .
Ella Oblinger

July 5th, 1874
[W]e have just come in from the truck patch and found the gophers had about cleaned the peas off all the vines. They hull the peas out and leave the pods so it looks as though they were full yet. [But] our squash vines are full of bloom and watermelon too, and we had cucumbers sliced for breakfast. We brought in beets just now that measured one foot in circumference and potatoes almost as large as a goose egg . . . so . . . just step in this fall and see if we don't have enough of the substantial for any Dutch family to eat!

Mattie

November 24th, 1874
. . . Mr. Macbeth [a neighbor] buried their babe yesterday. Died of the whooping cough. Was about nine months old and they have another child that is very poor with it. . . . They are very poor folks and like the rest of us, see pretty hard times, and it seems hard to see their child taken away, but I suppose it is all for the best as it is the Lord will remove those that He sees fit to remove from earth to Heaven.

Mattie

There was no well — the Oblingers hadn't the money to have one dug — and water had to be hauled from a nearby stream. Cooking pots and tin dishes were washed with sand. Twice, grasshoppers swooped down to devour their crops. A prairie fire burned down the nearest schoolhouse and would have destroyed their home, too, if Uriah hadn't plowed a circle around it to keep the flames from reaching the roof. Still, he refused to be defeated: "What a pleasure it is to work one's own farm," he wrote, "for you can feel that it is yours and not for someone else. I would rather live as we do than have to rent and have someone bossing us as we used to do."

August 8th, 1876
. . . Mother, you said in your letter for us to keep a stiff upper lip. . . . Well, that is no trouble for us any more, for we have had to keep a stiff upper lip so much since we have been here that they have about grown stiff. . . . It has kept us scraping and gathering pretty close to keep agoing, but we have managed so far not to go in debt one cent this summer. Uriah is going to town tomorrow afternoon and I want to send a little butter and potatoes and corn and pickles to get some groceries. Credit is pretty hard for anyone to get in Sutton and we have learned he is a poor customer to deal with and the least we have to do with him

The Chrisman sisters of Custer County, Nebraska, four daughters of a wealthy and calculating rancher who built each of them three small shacks like this one in which they took turns living. By so doing he was able to claim title simultaneously to a dozen 160-acre homesteads.

that much better off we are. We will have to get some calico for the girls' dresses or we will have to grease and go naked.

Mattie

September 10, 1876

. . . I suppose you would like to know if we have been grasshoppered again. They were here several days pretty thick and injured the corn considerable. Some fields they stripped the blades all off and other pieces stripped partly. They nibbled the end off most all the ears and ate off all the silks so it will not fill out. Nebraska would have had a splendid crop if the grasshoppers had stayed away a while.

Mattie

Things did not get easier for the Oblingers — or their fellow homesteaders. The series of unusually heavy rains that had fed the notion that rain followed the plow eventually ended. Many places on the High Plains emptied almost as fast as they had filled with farmers. It was becoming clear that the generous-sounding 160 acres of

Solomon D. Butcher, shown above in front of the crumbling dugout in which he rode out his first Nebraska winter, came west to Custer County from Virginia in 1880. He abandoned homesteading after only two weeks, attended medical school but never got a degree, and opened a post office and photographer's studio in the brand-new town of Walworth only to watch the community die as drought drove farmers from the land. Then, he hit upon the scheme that kept him and his family fed and much later made him one of the West's best-remembered photographers: chronicling the history of his county and selling prints of his pictures to its citizens . His photographs — some published here for the first time— constitute an unrivaled record of the fierce odds homesteaders faced and the fierce pride they took in what they'd done.

The family of Ike Bentley (second from right), near Sargent in Custer County, Nebraska, 1887. Bentley's father (third from left) — remembered in Solomon Butcher's records only as "Grandpa Bentley" — had seen a lot of American history: long before heading west, he had fought in the War of 1812.

Mr. and Mrs. L. N. Beager exchange wedding vows on the open prairie north of West Union, August 13, 1889.

The family of Orson Cooley, near Coolytown Post Office, 1887. Mrs. Cooley had been married before back in Wisconsin, lost her husband after bearing him two sons, and then wrote to a Nebraska newspaper asking if a widow could make a living on the prairie. Mr. Cooley, himself a widower, began writing to her, they were eventually married, and she brought her boys west to live. The Cooleys' own child, perched here on Father's lap, did not survive infancy, but the boys grew up to inherit their stepfather's farm.

The home of the Reverend and Mrs. E. Eubank (seated), Clear Creek, 1888. He was the first minister in Custer County, and she was the first schoolteacher.

John Spellmeyer of Sumner offered a special sort of testimony to the fertility of Nebraska. He and his wife (third from left) had sixteen children, including the three sets of twins on the porch, the last of which came into the world at about the same time the family cow produced triplets.

In March, 1884 . . . I took a pre-emption on Spring Creek. I'll never forget that first night out there. After supper I went outdoors and stayed so long that my sister came out to look for me. She found me crying and I told her that it was the worst-looking country I had ever seen and that we had little enough in Iowa but this was worse. She said it wasn't bad, and I would soon get used to it. That was the only time I ever cried in Custer County.

Mrs. Joanna Hickenbottom Jensen

Prairie style: In 1887, the one-room sod structure (above) in Cummings Park served as schoolhouse for twenty-eight pupils of every age and size, while the comparatively elegant soddy (left) in the southwestern section of the county boasted plastered and whitewashed recesses for the doors and windows and a dinner bell attached to the windmill that on a clear day could be heard for miles.

Not everyone in Custer County was comfortable with the pioneer life. When Solomon Butcher visited the David Hilton homestead (far left) south of Weissert in 1887, Mrs. Hilton insisted on having the pump organ that was her most prized possession pulled out into the yard so that no one back East would see that she and her husband were still living in a sod house.

Success stories:
G. W. Farmer of Mena grew 6,000 bushels of corn in 1902, according to Butcher's notes: "No state in the Union but Nebraska has such cribs of corn."

Nothing came easy in Custer County. A veteran farmer named Swain Finch demonstrated how he used a branch to beat the grasshoppers off his crops — and then made sure Butcher drew a suitably daunting swarm of insects onto the glass photographic plate before printing his picture.

A farmer named Gillette and his family (left), dressed in their best clothes, pretend to be on their way way to harvest their wheat, 1886.

John J. Downey (standing at center in the photograph at right) came to Dale Valley in Custer County in 1887 with two mules and twelve dollars. He built his family a sod house, went to work, and seventeen years later was a prosperous farmer and stock-raiser and the owner of the handsome house shown above.

FREE GROUND

In 1877, the last federal troops were withdrawn from the South, Reconstruction collapsed, and new state laws began to restrict the rights of freed slaves. Blacks found themselves once again under the power of their former masters. Black colonization committees were formed all over the South, seeking some means of escape. Some favored emigrating to the African republic of Liberia, or northward into Canada.

To others, the open spaces of the West seemed to offer more immediate hope. Benjamin "Pap" Singleton was an ex-slave from Tennessee who believed himself appointed by God to rescue his people. He had fled from his masters more than a dozen times during slavery, and ran a station on the Underground Railroad. But he had finally become convinced that there was no future for African-Americans unless they left the South and formed their own independent communities in the West. He flooded the South with handbills.

Those who answered his call called themselves "Exodusters" because, like the Old Testament Hebrews, they believed their salvation lay in reaching a promised land. Soon, blacks were scattered all across Kansas, and their hopeful letters home were being read aloud in black churches.

Then, in the spring of 1879, a rumor raced through African-American communities throughout the Deep South. The federal government had set aside all of Kansas for former slaves, the story went, and would provide every black family that could get there with free land and five hundred dollars. It wasn't true, but it was enough to convince some 6,000 people to start west. Some went by riverboat as far as St. Louis. Others, too poor to pay their passage, walked the whole way.

By 1880, more than 15,000 African-Americans had migrated to Kansas, most of them living on farms or in small communities like Juniper Town, Dunlap, and Rattlebone Hollow. Nicodemus, in western Kansas, was the largest settlement, home to 700 settlers from Kentucky. Some whites welcomed the newcomers. Others shunned them, or tried to drive them away. Many Exodusters returned to the South, defeated by the harsh climate of the Plains. But most stayed, or tried again still farther west.

"When I landed on the soil [of Kansas]," one man named John Solomon Lewis remembered, "I looked on the ground and I says, 'This is free ground.' Then I looked on the heavens and I says, 'Them is free and beautiful heavens.' Then I looked within my heart and I says to myself, 'I wonder why I was never free before?' I said, 'Let us hold a little prayer meeting . . . on the river bank.' It was raining but the drops fell from heaven on a free family, and the meeting was just as good as sunshine. We was thankful to God and we prayed for those who could not come.

"I asked my wife did she know the ground she stands on. She said, 'No.'

"I said, 'It is free ground,' and she cried for joy."

Benjamin "Pap" Singleton (below) and some of the Exodusters who answered his call, waiting for a steamboat to carry them westward

The family of Jerry Shores (seated, second from right), a former slave who made his home near Westerville in Custer County, 1887. Not all black newcomers were met with hostility: the Shores family, one white woman who lived nearby remembered, "were as fine neighbors as any one would want."

free land for which the homesteaders had come west was insufficient on the semi-arid plains.

The Oblingers held on, had two more daughters, Stella and Maggie. By early 1880, Mattie was about to give birth to still another baby.

> January 11, 1880
> . . . Uriah is repairing the minutes of the last Literary Society which was held last Saturday night. They have some big times debating. The question for next Saturday night is "Resolved that Intemperance causes more sorrow than war." . . . I go once in a while to hear them spout.
>
> We had rather a nice time [over the holidays]. . . . We had a Christmas tree at the schoolhouse. It was something new for this neighborhood. Every thing went off nice and agreeable. We had a Norway spruce evergreen tree. It looked nice filled with presents for the little ones and some for the old ones. Uriah played Santa Claus but the little ones most all knew him. . . .
>
> Mattie

January 12th, 1880

Dear Grandpa and Grandma: I must tell you how I spent Christmas. We all went to a Christmas tree on Christmas eve and each of us girls got a new red oil calico dress . . . and a doll and Uncle Giles put a book on the tree for Stella and me and each one of us girls got a string with candy and raisins on it.

From your grandchild,
Ella Oblinger

Mattie Oblinger with Ella (right) and Maggie

A Nebraska settler named Harvey Andrews and his wife tend the grave of their infant daughter, Victoria, carefully planted with pine seedlings and protected by a picket fence, 1887.

February 27th, 1880. The Lord called for [my] Sister Mattie this evening at 4:15 o'clock . . . and she is now resting with the angels in Heaven.

She was confined Tuesday evening about 4 o'clock and about 8 o'clock she took a fit very sudden and never spoke after the first one. The doctors were compelled to perform a surgical operation by relieving her of the child. The child is also dead and will be buried with her some time Sunday.

Uriah said he could not stand to write now. I don't know what he will do yet. It's left him and his three little girls in a sad condition — without a Mother.

Giles S. Thomas

Dear Father and Mother: I try to bear the trouble cheerfully, though the task is hard at times. . . . This season has not been a success with me in farming. . . . Crops and prices are so poor that it is making times pretty close here. . . . I hardly know how to manage. . . .

Uriah did everything he could think of to hold on to his farm and what was left of his family. He rented out his land, hired himself out to plow other people's fields, but nothing worked. Finally, he abandoned his homestead and moved back east, to Minnesota, where his family was now living. There, he remarried and had three more daughters, before returning to the Plains to start over in Nebraska, then Kansas, then Nebraska again, where he rented a parcel of land not far from his first homestead and finally broke his health trying once more to make a go of it. He spent the last few months of his life being cared for by his daughter, Ella, the same girl, now grown, he had once been so eager to bring out to Nebraska with her mother.

A HARD TIME I HAVE

By the spring of 1881, the Indians who had occupied the lands that Americans and Europeans were now settling so fast had all but lost their struggle to remain free. The Lakota and Cheyenne bands that had wiped out Custer and his command were now living at or near the agencies. Only Sitting Bull and fewer than two hundred of his followers, many of them members of his own family, remained defiant, in Canada. But the Canadian tribes had wearied of sharing their depleted hunting grounds with Sitting Bull's band, and Canadian officials had come to see his presence as a political embarrassment. "We began to feel homesick for our own country where we used to be happy," a young Lakota named Black Elk recalled. "The old people talked much about it and the good old days before the trouble came. Sometimes I felt like crying when they did that."

Finally, on July 19, 1881, having been promised a full pardon, Sitting Bull led a handful of his hungry people south across the border to Fort Buford and gave up. "I

The life my people want is a life of freedom. I have seen nothing that a white man has, houses or railways or clothing or food, that is as good as the right to move in the open country, and live in our fashion.

Sitting Bull

Lakota who had surrendered to the army going aboard the steamboat that would take them to the Standing Rock agency in the spring of 1881

surrender this rifle to you through my young son," he told the commanding officer, "whom I now desire to teach in this manner that he has become a friend of the Americans. I wish him to learn the habits of the whites and to be educated as their sons are educated. I wish it to be remembered that I was the last man of my tribe to surrender my rifle. This boy has given it to you, and he now wants to know how he is going to make a living."

Sitting Bull still wanted the right to cross back and forth into Canada at will, to have a reservation of his own on the Little Missouri, near the Black Hills, and to hunt wherever he wished. But the Lakota were now surrounded by newcomers — immigrants from Russia, Germany, Denmark, Sweden, as well as the eastern states — who were building homes on what had once been Lakota lands. Whites now filled the Black Hills; cattle grazed on their foothills.

The soldiers granted none of Sitting Bull's requests. They ordered him to go to the Standing Rock reservation hundreds of miles to the east, instead, and to live there as

Lakota receiving government rations

his people lived. There, he was reunited with his daughter, and wept to see again those who had fought alongside him at the Little Bighorn. But he also gave an interview to a reporter in which he breathed some of the old defiance.

> When I came in I did not surrender. I want the government to let me occupy the Little Missouri Country. There is plenty of game there. I want to keep my ponies. I can't hunt without ponies. I want no restraint. I will keep on the reservation, but want to go where I please. I don't want a white man over me. I don't want an agent.

The army was jittery that Sitting Bull might lead another uprising. Soldiers herded him and 167 followers back onto the steamboat at bayonet point, and steamed farther down the river to Fort Randall, where they were to be kept indefinitely as prisoners of war. The army had already broken its promises to him. There, the Lakota were made to pitch their teepees and wait. He asked to be allowed to go to Washington and see the Great Father, demanded to know how long he would have to stay apart from his people, and received no satisfactory answer to either request. To pass the long hours, Sitting Bull painted scenes from his own life as gifts for individual soldiers who had been kind to him, and charged curiosity-seekers for his autograph, one dollar for ladies, five for men. He and his small band spent twenty months in lonely exile at Fort Randall before the army felt secure enough to permit them to return to Standing Rock and start new lives as wards of the government.

Sitting Bull came back to his people on May 10, 1883 — and entered a world unlike any he had ever known. The power of the chiefs had largely been broken. Their fate was now in the hands of an Indian agent, James McLaughlin, who was himself married to a half-Lakota woman but determined to transform the lives of her people.

Antagonists: Sitting Bull (above, at center) and James McLaughlin (the bearded civilian at the table) were at loggerheads almost from the moment the holy man arrived at Standing Rock. Each struck the other as imperious and unyielding. Below, the two men awkwardly flank the rock formation resembling an Indian woman with a child on her back that gave the agency its name. Sitting Bull had opposed moving it to this new site near McLaughlin's headquarters; the agent had done it anyway, and then held a dedication ceremony.

He considered Sitting Bull vain and boastful and was wary of having him under his charge. The leader who whites believed had conquered Custer was to be treated merely as one more mouth to be fed, McLaughlin said; just one more body to be clothed.

The Lakota lived in log cabins now, as well as teepees, and they were expected to farm. Even Sitting Bull eventually found himself at work, hoe in hand.

When a delegation of senators visited the agency in August of 1883, with a plan for opening part of the reservation to white settlement, Sitting Bull protested bitterly.

"Do you know who I am?" he demanded of the commissioners. "I want to tell you that if the Great Spirit has chosen any one to be the chief of this country, it is myself."

The senators had no patience with him. "You were not appointed by the Great Spirit," John Logan of Illinois replied. "Appointments are not made that way . . . you have no following, no power, no control, and no right to any control. . . . If it were not for the Government you would be freezing and starving today in the mountains."

Just across the Grand River from his cabin, Sitting Bull could see the spot where he had been born into an entirely different world. To fill the empty hours, he composed his own song. "A warrior I have been," he sang. "Now it is all over. A hard time I have."

BARBARIANS

In October of 1871, an eager and ambitious young Chinese named Chung Sun arrived in California. He carried six hundred dollars with him, and dreamed of starting a tea plantation in southern California. But in Los Angeles he found himself caught up in a riot. It started as a quarrel between two Chinese factions over a woman, but quickly turned into an armed struggle between the small Chinese community and the rest of the city. "For two days," a reporter wrote,

> that portion of the city cursed by the presence of the Mongols was in a state of war. . . . Chinatown, wholly surrounded, was in a state of siege. Mounted men came galloping from the country — the *vaquero* was in his glory, and the cry was *"Carajo la Chino!"* . . . A young Israelite, heavy-framed and coarse-featured, and a German known as "Dutch Charley" were prominently active and cruel. "Crazy" Johnson seemed to represent all Ireland; while Jacques, a Frenchman, shirtless and hatless and armed with a cleaver . . . was the fire-fiend of the occasion — time and again Chinatown was ablaze — and Jacques with his cleaver was always found pictured in the glare.

Damage done by an anti-Chinese riot in Seattle, Washington

Before it was over, at least twenty-three Chinese immigrants had been hanged or stabbed or dragged or shot to death, and Chung Sun had been beaten and robbed of his savings.

By the time of his arrival, more than 300,000 Chinese had entered the country, the vast majority of them west of the Mississippi. They had begun coming to California during the gold rush of 1849, and now could be found in every corner of the West. They dug irrigation ditches and planted vineyards in Sonoma, operated laundries and restaurants, established fishing fleets up and down the coast.

But in 1877, depression gripped the country. In the East, there were strikes, lockouts, riots that left scores dead, factories and rail yards demolished. Western workmen joined the protests, too, denouncing the railroads and the wealthy men who owned them. But they also came to believe they had

A Democratic cartoonist accuses the Republicans of favoring an all-Chinese California, 1889.

another enemy — the Chinese with whom they were forced to compete for what little work there was.

The San Francisco workers' best-known spokesman was an Irish-born merchant sailor named Denis Kearney, a failure at the cartage business, who blamed what he called "the interests" for all his troubles. He helped found the Workingmen's Party and hoped to use anti-Chinese feeling to win political power. "We intend to try and vote the Chinaman out, to frighten him out, and if this won't do, to kill him out," he boasted, "and when the blow comes we won't leave a fragment for the thieves to pick up. . . . The heathen slaves must leave this coast, if it costs 10,000 lives. . . ."

Kearney was eventually jailed — and later abandoned politics to sell real estate. His party fell apart, but the anti-Chinese feeling it had helped foster only intensified. Anti-Chinese riots erupted throughout the West. In Rock Springs, Wyoming, whites murdered twenty-eight Chinese, and drove out hundreds more. In Tacoma, state militiamen had to be called in to restore order. The Chinese in Seattle were rounded up, pushed onto boats, and forced out to sea.

The Los Angeles riot had left Chung Sun penniless. He made his way north to the little town of Watsonville, where he managed to find a job digging ditches and laying a gas line for $1.50 a day.

> I left the loved and ever-venerated land of my nativity to seek [in the United States] that freedom and security which I could never hope to realize in my own. . . . I hope you will pardon my expressing a painful disappointment. The

> ill treatment of [my] own countrymen may perhaps be excused on the grounds of race, color, language, and religion, but such prejudice can only prevail among the ignorant. . . . [B]eing a man of education and culture I am capable of other work than digging in the streets, but my philosophy teaches me, any useful work is more honorable than idleness. I shall therefore, with patience, continue to dig with an abiding hope for something better. . . .

But when the ditch was finished, Chung Sun could not find another job. No one would hire him. And in 1882, western politicians and labor unions persuaded Congress to pass the Chinese Exclusion Act.

The year before the law was enacted, nearly 40,000 Chinese entered the United States. The next year, just 23 were allowed in.

Even the 1882 act failed to placate anti-Chinese sentiment in the West. "This Oriental octopus [of coolieism] . . . this herculean of all gigantic evils . . . from the shores of Asia . . . embraces within it explosives more deadly than dynamite . . ." said Senator John H. Mitchell of Oregon.

> [It] depresses labor, corrupts morals, debases youth, makes merchandise of personal freedom and female virtue, mocks at justice, defies law, dwarfs enterprise, obstructs development, chains personal liberty, destroys personal freedom, menaces the public peace, invades domestic tranquility, endangers the public welfare, converts whole sections of beautiful American cities . . . into squalid, wretched, crime-smitten, and leperous spotted habitations of the lowest and most debased classes of the pagan mongol. . . .

More discriminatory statutes followed, barring Chinese laborers from entering the country, forbidding even the thousands who had gone home on visits the right to return, requiring longtime Chinese residents to carry certificates of eligibility to remain in the United States.

Meanwhile, Chung Sun moved on to San Francisco, then set sail for home. But before he left he wrote up his stay for a California newspaper:

> [Americans] have no purely national settlement in anything. . . . [T]here is no uniform mode of dress or manner of living; no system, regularity or order . . . but all is a jumble of confusion and a labyrinth of contradictions. . . . [I]n civility, complaisance, and polite manners [Americans] are wholly wanting and are very properly styled barbarians.

THE DUDE

At two in the morning on September 8, 1883, a twenty-four-year-old New York assemblyman stepped down from the train at the Little Missouri River in the heart of Dakota Territory. His name was Theodore Roosevelt and he had already earned a reputation for himself back East as a noisy but energetic reformer. Now, he had come west to shoot a buffalo before the species vanished — and to build himself up after a bout of cholera.

He seemed the quintessential dude — shrill, nearsighted, Harvard-educated, wheezing with asthma, and insistent upon being called "Mr. Roosevelt." Still, despite day after day of rain so cold that even his guide urged him to abandon the chase, he

A LIFE OF TAUT NERVES

[Westerners] value good government and have a remarkable faculty for organizing some kind of government, but they are tolerant of lawlessness which does not directly attack their own interests. Horse-stealing and insults to women are the two unpardonable offenses; all others are often suffered to go unpunished. . . . [The leading newspaper of a considerable western city], commenting on one of the train robberies that had been frequent in the state, observed that so long as the brigands had confined themselves to robbing the railway companies and the express companies of property for whose loss the companies must answer, no one had greatly cared, seeing that these companies themselves robbed the public; but now that private citizens seemed in danger of losing their personal baggage and money . . . something ought to be done.

James Bryce

Frank and Jesse James with tools of their trade, shortly after the Civil War

On January 31, 1874, the Iron Mountain Express rolled into the tiny Missouri hamlet of Gads Hill, where a signal flag at the station brought the train to a halt. Expecting to meet a new passenger, the conductor stepped down — only to be greeted by five men holding cocked pistols and wearing white sheets.

The bandits took over the train, emptied its safe of two thousand dollars, and then demanded money and jewelry from the passengers. They announced theatrically that the poor would be exempt. They would steal only from those who didn't have the calluses of a workingman. But in the end, no one's wallet was spared. Before riding away, one of the robbers handed the conductor a note and asked that it be given to the newspapers. It was a press release, written in advance, with all the details of the robbery filled in, except for a blank space for the amount of money stolen:

> THE MOST DARING ROBBERY ON RECORD.
> The southbound train on the Iron Mountain railroad was boarded here this evening by five heavily armed men and robbed of __ dollars. The robbers arrived at the station a few minutes before the arrival of the train and arrested the station agent and put him under guard, then threw the train on the switch. The robbers were all large men, none of them under six feet tall. They were all masked and started in a southerly direction after they had robbed the express. They were all mounted on fine, blooded horses. There is a hell of an excitement in this part of the country.

The James-Younger gang had struck again.

Frank and Jesse James and the four Younger brothers were all products of the sectional violence that had plagued the Kansas-Missouri border since the 1850s. They had themselves ridden with guerrilla bands during the Civil War, more interested in looting and killing civilians than in fighting Union forces, and their families had felt the full brunt of the Union forces who turned western Missouri into the "Burnt District." Kansas raiders murdered the Youngers' father and burned their home. Federal militia jailed the James boys' mother for spying.

Frank James, who had taken part in William Quantrill's butchery of unarmed men at Lawrence, Kansas, was tall, big boned, and quiet. He enjoyed reading Shakespeare and the essays of Francis Bacon. Because of his book learning, some people suspected he was the gang's strategist.

But it was Frank's younger brother who became the gang's best-known member. He was vain about his looks, rarely drank or smoked, never swore in the presence of women, and was devoted to his mother. He had become a Confederate guerrilla at seventeen, was wounded three times, and in one skirmish personally killed the Union commander — some said by slitting his throat. Jesse James, said his leader, Bloody Bill Anderson, "is the keenest . . . fighter in the command."

After the war, other Confederates had gone home and back to work. The James and Younger brothers kept right on stealing and killing — and used the war's bitter, lingering passions as their excuse. They robbed banks and trains on a regular basis, killed cashiers, engineers, innocent bystanders — then hid out among their Missouri neighbors, who considered railroads and banks hated symbols of northern oppression.

The gang had an influential public defender — John Newman Edwards, a prominent Missouri editor and unreconstructed Confederate in whose florid reports the outlaws were always victims of Yankee mistreatment, not ruthless outlaws but modern Robin Hoods. Theirs, he wrote, was the "Chivalry of Crime."

Having given up hope that local authorities could stop the gang, an association of bankers turned to the nation's most celebrated private investigator, Allan Pinkerton, founder of Pinkerton's National Detective Agency, whose slogan was "We never sleep."

But in the James gang and their protective neighbors, the Pinkertons more than met their match. When one detective disguised himself as an itinerant farmhand and applied for work on the James farm, he was found on the roadside the next

Pinkerton agents acted as Union spies during the Civil War, and afterward helped break up labor unions and chased embezzlers and robbers for the railroads. The term "private eye" was inspired by their symbol.

morning, shot in the head and chest. A few days later, two more Pinkerton agents were gunned down in a shootout that also killed John Younger.

Then, just as local public opinion was beginning to turn against the gang, the Pinkertons reversed it once again. On the night of January 26, 1875, they quietly surrounded the James home in Kearney, Missouri. Believing Frank and Jesse were inside, they tossed a canister through a window — only a flare, the Pinkertons later claimed; a grenade, according to the Jameses. "I was blown against the ceiling and heard a tremendous report," their stepfather said. "Outside I heard several hurrahs, then the groans of my little boy and the agonized cries of my wife, who told me her right arm was blown to pieces."Archie Peyton Samuel, Frank and Jesse's nine-year-old half-brother, was dead. Their mother's arm, shattered by the explosion, had to be amputated later that night.

Newspapers across the nation condemned the Pinkertons for the bombing. The Missouri legislature called for an official investigation and nearly passed a bill giving the James and Younger brothers amnesty. A local grand jury even indicted Allan Pinkerton for murder, though he was never arrested or formally charged.

A few months later, a neighboring farmer suspected of having harbored a Pinkerton man before the raid was shot down at his doorstep. Others were warned that they would share his fate if they cooperated with lawmen.

Around the same time, the first book appeared devoted entirely to the exploits of the James and Younger gang. There would be many more in the years to come.

But by the early 1880s, the gang's fortunes started to sour. An attempted bank robbery in Northfield, Minnesota, ended in disaster when angry townspeople opened fire on the bandits. Three gang members were killed. The three Younger brothers — Cole, Jim, and Bob, all severely wounded — were captured, tried, and sentenced to life imprisonment.

Frank and Jesse James escaped. Then, in the summer of 1881, two trains were robbed in western Missouri. Two men were killed, and two more brutally beaten. For Missouri's governor, Thomas Crittenden, it was the last straw. He spread the word that any gang member who surrendered and turned witness against the brothers would be given clemency. And he offered ten thousand dollars for Frank or Jesse James — dead or alive.

Robert Ford was a new recruit to the gang and had never taken part in a robbery, although his older brother, Charley, had helped hold up a train. On April 3, 1882, the Ford brothers came to Jesse's house in St. Joseph, Missouri, where he was living with his wife and two children under the assumed name of Thomas Howard.

"Between eight and nine o'clock this morning while the three of us were in a room in Jesse's house," Robert Ford would tell a lawman that evening, "Jesse pulled off his coat and also his pistols, two of which he constantly wore, and then got up onto a chair for the purpose of brushing dust off a picture. While Jesse was thus engaged, Charley winked at me, so I knew he meant for me to shoot. So, as quickly as possible, I drew my pistol and aiming at Jesse's head, which was not more than four feet from the muzzle of my weapon, I fired, and Jesse tumbled headlong from the chair on which he was standing and fell on his face. . . ."

The Fords rushed from the house, telegraphed Governor Crittenden that they had killed Jesse James, and turned themselves over to the police. Two weeks later, they pleaded guilty to murder, were sentenced to hang, and were immediately pardoned by the governor. But the Fords never got to enjoy their reward money. Songs glorified Jesse and mocked them as cowards. Former friends shunned them. Charley Ford became despondent and committed suicide. Bob Ford went on tour with a stage show, reenacting the shooting every evening. The big crowds that turned out to see him do it booed as often as they cheered. He began to drink heavily, wandered the West, finally settled down in the mining town of Creede, Colorado, opened a tent saloon, and was shot to death there after a quarrel.

Zerelda James Samuel, Jesse's fiercely protective mother, insisted that his body be buried in the yard at the family home. For twenty-five cents, visitors were allowed to see the tombstone and listen to Mrs. Samuel tell stories glorifying her son and condemning the Fords. For an extra quarter, she would give the tourists a pebble from the grave site, which she kept restocked from a nearby streambed.

Six months after Jesse James's death, his older brother, Frank, turned himself in. "I have known no home," he said. "I have slept in all sorts of places — here today — there tomorrow. . . . I am tired of this life of taut nerves, of night-riding and day-hiding, of constant listening for footfalls, cracking twigs and rustling leaves and creaking doors; tired of seeing Judas on the face of every friend I know — and God knows I have none to spare — tired of the saddle, the revolver and the cartridge belt. . . . I want to see if there is not some way out of it." A sympathetic Missouri jury refused to convict him.

The James-Younger gang lived on in people's imaginations. Rumors spread that Bob Ford had somehow shot someone else, that Jesse James was still alive. In less than a year, a neighboring farmer reported seeing Jesse James in the flesh, and Jesse's son would later count twenty-six imposters. Even while Frank James was alive, a farm worker in Washington claimed to be the real Frank James.

Dime novels about the James gang proliferated, too — and placed them in the most improbable locales: *Jesse James Among the Mormons, Jesse James in New York, Jesse James at Coney Island.* Critics blamed the books for the rising rate of juvenile crime in eastern cities, and for a time the postmaster general refused to deliver them.

For his part, Frank James never again turned to crime. He worked as a race starter at county fairs, as a shoe salesman, a livestock importer, a doorman at a burlesque house, even a department store detective. He eventually returned to the James family farm and carried on his mother's tradition of leading tours for a price. As he grew older, he developed a fear that his corpse would one day be disturbed by grave robbers and left instructions that he was to be cremated and his ashes kept out of the reach of any thief — in a bank vault.

JOHN WESLEY HARDIN

The son of a Methodist minister who named him for the founder of his faith, John Wesley Hardin was bright and personable and articulate enough to have succeeded in the law or politics. Instead, he became the most feared gunfighter in Texas. In the showy autobiography he was working on when he died, he claimed to have killed forty-four men, and he may actually have killed twenty — including one man, shot through the wall of his room at the American Hotel in Abilene, Kansas, whose only offense had been to disturb Hardin's sleep. "They tell lots of lies about me," he said. "They say I killed six or seven men for snoring. Well, it ain't true. I only killed one man for snoring." He had accounted for four men — an ex-slave and three federal troopers sent to arrest him for his murder — before he was sixteen, and would spend ten years on the run from federal authorities, hiding out among relatives scattered across central Texas, before he was finally arrested and sent to jail in 1874 for killing a deputy sheriff. He opened a law office in El Paso after he got out of prison, but was rarely sober enough to practice, and was eventually shot from behind by a policeman whose life he had threatened.

BLACK BART

Charles Boles (below) had lived a full life as a farmer, Union soldier, and prospector before he took to robbing Wells, Fargo stagecoaches in California in 1879. Before he was through, he would hold up twenty-eight stages, wearing a black hood and leaving behind handwritten verse signed "Black Bart" to mock his pursuers.

Here I lay me down to sleep
To wait the coming 'morrow.
Perhaps success, perhaps defeat,
And ever lasting sorrow.
But come what may I'll try it on,
My condition can't be worse,
If there's money in that box,
'Tis money in my purse. . . .

He might have continued stealing and versifying for years had he not dropped a handkerchief, which a shrewd San Francisco detective traced to him by its Chinese laundry mark.

BELLE STARR

Myra Belle Shirley, a farmer's daughter from Scyene, Texas, could not seem to get enough of outlaws or the outlaw life. She was first the mistress of Cole Younger, then of another bank robber, Jim Reed. After he was shot and killed, she helped run a horse- and cattle-stealing ring with a Cherokee named Blue Duck (shown here), then married another Cherokee rustler, Sam Starr, and became notorious as Belle Starr, "the Bandit Queen." She served six months in jail with her husband, and after he was killed in a barroom brawl in 1886, took up with still another Indian outlaw named Jim Tully. Three years later, an unknown gunman shot her from her horse.

THE DALTONS

Hubris: The three Dalton brothers were Coffeyville, Kansas, boys who decided in 1892 to set a new record by simultaneously robbing two banks in their own hometown. It was not a good idea. Townspeople recognized them and opened fire: four local citizens were killed in the crossfire, but so were two of the Daltons — Bob and Grat, whose corpses are being held up here for the photographer — and the third was badly wounded and spent fifteen years in prison.

BILLY THE KID

He was remembered as Billy the Kid, but his real name was Henry McCarty, and he was born in a New York slum, the son of a widowed Irish laundress who moved to New Mexico to try to cure the tuberculosis that quickly killed her. Small and slight, her orphaned son began his life of crime at fifteen, pilfering a tub of butter from a rancher and clothes from a Chinese laundryman; graduated to stealing horses and rustling cattle; broke out of three jails; and in 1877 shot and killed his first man, a bullying blacksmith who had dared make fun of his girlish looks.

A few weeks later, he signed on with one of two rival armies of gunmen about to go to war over just who in Lincoln County should profit from supplying beef and other provisions to army posts and Indian reservations. It was a bloody business that lasted for nearly two years. McCarty — now calling himself William H. Bonney — played a prominent part in it. And his faction lost.

Legend had him killing twenty-one men before his twenty-first birthday. He seems actually to have killed just four, but when the fighting finally ended and Governor Lew Wallace offered a general amnesty to all who had taken part, Billy was exempted from it because a sheriff had been among his victims. He tried to win himself a pardon by turning in old friends for new crimes committed since the shaky peace was established — but then was told he would have to stand trial for murder, anyway.

Between crimes, Billy was evidently amiable and outgoing. "You appear to take it easy," a reporter told him once, as he smiled for the crowd that had come out to see him momentarily locked up.

"Yes," the Kid answered. "What's the use of looking on the gloomy side of everything? The laugh's on me this time." A sympathetic lawman let him get away again, and he returned to his old profession — cattle rustling.

Then, local ranchers, tired of losing cattle to him, helped elect a local bartender named Pat Garrett sheriff (below), with orders to hunt him down. On the night of July 13, 1881, Garrett cornered him in the darkened bedroom of a ranch where he'd taken refuge and shot him dead. He was just twenty-one.

Within a year there were eight novels about him in the bookstores, plus a spurious but best-selling biography written by the man who killed him.

found and shot his buffalo. And he fell in love with the Dakota Badlands — and with the prospect of quick riches its grassy slopes seemed to offer virtually free of charge. Before he returned home that fall, Theodore Roosevelt had invested nearly $14,000 in a herd of cattle.

Roosevelt was just one of hundreds of eager entrepreneurs then hoping to cash in on the beef boom on the northern Plains. Everything seemed to suggest it was a sure thing. "A good-sized steer when it is fit for the butcher market will bring from $45 to $60," boasted the *Breeder's Gazette.* "The same animal at its birth was worth but $5. He has run on the plains and cropped the grass from the public domain for four or five years, and now, with scarcely any expense to its owner, is worth forty dollars more than when he started on his pilgrimage. . . ."

The government was buying more than 50,000 head of western cattle a year, solely to feed the Indian tribes now confined to reservations. Railroads with refrigerated cars could now ship western beef all around the world. By 1881, 110 million pounds were being exported each year to England alone.

And all one needed to do was buy a herd and turn it loose on grasslands that seemed as limitless as the profits they promised. "Cotton was once crowned King," wrote a western newspaper editor, "but *grass* is now." Marshall Field, the Chicago dry goods king, invested. So did William K. Vanderbilt, the railroad magnate, and Joseph Glidden, the manufacturer of barbed wire. Fortune-seekers from England, Scotland, and Europe invested, too, after reading newspaper stories that proclaimed profits of forty cents on the dollar routine. "Rich men's sons from the East were nothing new as far as I was concerned," Teddy Blue Abbott remembered. "The range in the eighties was as full of them as a dog's hair of fleas, and some of them were good fellows and some were damn fools."

But for Theodore Roosevelt, the West was much more than a chance to get rich; it was also a chance to escape the sorrows of his private life. In 1884, after his mother and wife died within hours of one another, he returned to the Badlands to deal with his grief in long, solitary rides:

> Nowhere, not at sea, does a man feel more lonely than when riding over the far-reaching, seemingly never-ending plains. . . . Nowhere else does one feel so far off from mankind; the plains stretch out in deathless and measureless expanse, and as he journeys over them they will for many miles be lacking in all signs of life. . . . Black care rarely sits behind a rider whose pace is fast enough.

Over the course of three summers on his Dakota ranches, Roosevelt hunted, rounded up cattle, and reveled in the rugged landscape and equally rugged life. When a drunken cowboy, a revolver in each hand, cursed and called him "four eyes," he knocked him senseless with his fists. And when three squatters stole his rowboat, he set out with two friends to track them down, carrying copies of *Anna Karenina* and the poetry of Matthew Arnold for campfire reading. Roosevelt captured all three thieves and drove them forty miles on foot to the town of Dickinson to stand trial.

Then, in the autumn of 1886, he decided to return to New York to run for mayor and to court Edith Carow, the childhood sweetheart who would become his second wife. In the West, Roosevelt had transformed himself. "Here," he said later, "the romance of my life began."

FRIENDS OF THE INDIAN

Theodore Roosevelt (opposite) the fledgling ranchman in 1885, and one of the books that made limitless profits in cattle raising seem plausible. "The beef business," its author assured his readers, "cannot be overdone."

Policy for the Indians of the West was largely set in the East, and much of it was made by the self-styled Friends of the Indian, who met annually at the Mohonk Mountain House in upstate New York.

In the autumn of 1883, the same year Sitting Bull was reunited with his people, a group of white people gathered at the Mohonk Mountain House in upstate New York to make decisions that would change his life and the lives of all the Indian peoples of the West. They were clergymen, social workers, lecturers on moral topics, government officials who had fought hard against corruption, and although some of them had never met an Indian, they were convinced they knew how to bring the first Americans into the mainstream of American life.

Indians were "vanishing," they believed, victims of white mistreatment, but also of their own benighted tribal nature. "The Indian," said Merrill Gates, the president of Amherst College, "must be made to be intelligently selfish . . . [got] out of . . . blankets and into trousers — and trousers with a pocket in them, and a pocket that aches to be filled with dollars."

In the classrooms of the Riverside Indian School at Anadarko, Oklahoma Territory, seen here in 1901 — and in scores of other schools backed by eastern reformers at the turn of the century — Native American children were taught to abandon tribal ways.

Indians had first been removed from their lands, then herded onto scattered reservations. Now, if the Friends of the Indian had their way, they were no longer to be Indians at all. The reformers would first see to it that the youngest generation was transformed as rapidly as possible. Indian children as young as five were to be taken from their families and sent halfway across the continent to school, to the United States Indian Training and Industrial School at Carlisle, Pennsylvania. There, Captain Richard Henry Pratt ran a boarding school whose purpose was to teach them useful skills while making them forget their Indian ways. It was his task, he said, to make the Indian a member of a "new social order" and "to do this we must recreate him, to make him a new personality."

Indian children were punished if they dared speak the languages their parents had taught them, were forbidden to dance or to sing their religious songs. "Our belongings were taken from us," remembered a Blackfoot boy who made the journey, "even the little medicine bags our mothers had given us to protect us from harm. Everything was placed in a heap and set afire."

Lakota boys on their arrival at Carlisle (left) and after the process of "civilizing" them had begun

Within twenty years, there were 24 other off-reservation schools like the one at Carlisle — and 81 boarding schools and 147 day schools on the reservations themselves. All shared the same goal. "Education," said one reformer, "should seek the disintegration of the tribes. . . . They should be educated, not as Indians, but as Americans." (In the end, however, the Indian schools taught another lesson, as well: that no matter what tribe they belonged to, they were all Indians and needed to begin thinking of themselves in those terms.)

The assault on tribal culture extended beyond the schools. Even on the reservation, parents and old people were ordered to abandon their faith, put behind them all their religious customs. Men were to give up all but one wife — though what was to be done with those they discarded was never made clear. The Lakota were not even supposed to keep the ritual bundles that allowed the spirits of those who had died to be released. "The white people made war on the Lakotas to keep them from practicing their religion . . ." a warrior named Short Bull recalled. "The white people wish to make us cause the spirits of our dead to be ashamed."

MEDICINE FLOWER

Frank Cushing (top, in the dark clothing), taking part with other Zuni bow chiefs in the War God Ceremony, and (above) wearing a costume of his own creation, part-Navajo, part-Spanish

The Zuni of New Mexico had been among the first Indians of the West to meet a European — the explorer Coronado, who had stormed Hawikuh pueblo in 1540. Three and a half centuries later, they looked out from their mesa top and saw a very different group of explorers approaching. They represented the first expedition of the newly formed U.S. Bureau of Ethnology, sent to survey Indian tribes as quickly as possible, on the belief that Native Americans and their customs were on the verge of disappearing.

With them was a frail but eager twenty-two-year-old named Frank Hamilton Cushing, who had been fascinated by tales of Indians ever since discovering an arrowhead near his home in central New York as a boy. To the shock of his eastern companions — and to the surprise of the Zuni — Cushing immediately moved into one of the Indian's homes and announced he intended to stay. The best way to understand Indians, he said, was to live the way they did. The expedition hurriedly moved on, but Cushing remained.

He learned the Zuni language, cooking and pottery making; grew his hair long and had his ears pierced; adopted Zuni clothing and a Zuni name — Medicine Flower. With the help of his friend Pedro Pino, an aging patriarch of the pueblo, Cushing studied the Zuni's sacred ceremonies, which for centuries they had kept secret from outsiders.

"The Zuni faith . . ." [he wrote,] "is as a drop of oil in water, surrounded and touched at every point, yet in no place penetrated or changed inwardly by the flood of alien belief that descended upon it. . . . [The Zuni] adjusts other beliefs and opinions to his own, but never his own beliefs and opinions to others. . . . In religious culture, the Zuni is almost [the same] as ere his land was discovered."

The Zuni permitted Cushing to learn the rituals of their sacred priesthood of the bow, but only after he went through the lengthy and torturous initiation it required — including days of fasting, sitting motionless on a hill of fire ants, and taking an enemy's scalp.

After word spread in the East that a white man had been initiated into the Zuni tribe, tourists began showing up. They wanted to become members, too, they said, and asked how much they had to pay for the initiation fee.

Cushing was now an influential member of his tribe. He took part in their councils, joined war parties against Apache and Navajo raiders, and justified it all to startled Indian agents:

> Mr. Galen Eastman
> U.S. Indian Agent
> Navajo Indian Agency
> Fort Defiance, Arizona Territory
>
> Sir: It is quite true that I fired, not twice, but three times into two different bands of horses belonging to the Navajo Indians. It is possible that, as I intended, I killed one or two of them, although of this I cannot be certain. . . . Rest assured, sir, that . . . when all of our grievances are set right by the Navajos, we shall be then very ready to say amen, and to act all things aright on our side.
>
> Very respectfully, Your Obedient Servant,
> F. H. Cushing,
> 1st War Chief of Zuni
> U.S. Ass't Ethnologist

Cushing quarreled with missionaries and Indian agents intent on changing their charges. His warrior society tracked down two horse thieves — one a Mexican, one an American — and killed them. And after he exposed a scheme by relatives of a powerful U.S. senator to build a ranch on valuable Zuni land, his superiors finally ordered him back to Washington. He had been sent to study the Zuni, not become one.

Cushing died in 1900. In 1938, fifty years after he left Zuni pueblo, an archaeologist reported that older Zuni people still wondered why their good friend Medicine Flower had never returned.

MONEY OUT OF WIND

To the casual visitor, Los Angeles in the 1870s seemed much as it had always been — a largely Hispanic farming town, with a population of fewer than 10,000. Without either a railroad or an opening to the sea, it seemed likely forever to be dwarfed by San Francisco to the north.

But life for its inhabitants had already begun to change. Political power had long since passed from the old, landed *Californio* families into the hands of the Anglos, who now insisted that the town's original inhabitants remain within barrios. The schools no longer taught Spanish. Bullfights and bear-baiting had been outlawed, replaced by baseball as the city's most popular sport.

Then, the Southern Pacific Railroad was persuaded to build a line right into Los Angeles — and around the town's chief rival, San Diego. The Atchison, Topeka and Santa Fe followed in 1886, and the two lines began a fare war. At its frenzied height, passengers buying excursion tickets could make it all the way to Los Angeles from St. Louis for as little as one dollar.

The pace of change accelerated overnight. Now, easterners and midwesterners, drawn by reports of warm sunshine, fresh air, and cheap land began arriving in larger and larger numbers, 120,000 in 1887 alone. "Hell, we're giving away the land," one promoter said. "We're selling the climate."

"The crazy part of it was started by professional boomers flocking from Kansas City, Chicago, St. Paul, San Francisco . . ." another man recalled, "showing the natives

Hilario Ybarra and his family, Main Street residents of late-nineteenth-century Los Angeles

Mexican American citizens stroll around the plaza that was the heart of the original Los Angeles, 1893.

By the time the costumed Mexican caballeros above paraded down Main Street as part of a fiesta celebration in 1901, their pueblo had been engulfed by a sprawling, mostly Anglo city (below) and they were considered relics of a distant and romantic past.

It has been a sore subject ever since that I did not buy Southern California when I was there last March and sell it out the same month. I should have made enough money to pay my railway fare back . . . and had money left to negotiate for one of the little States on the Atlantic coast.

Charles Dudley Warner

Salesmanship: Thanks to ceaseless advertising, one frustrated San Jose booster wrote in 1885, "the average eastern mind conceives of California as a small tract of country situated in and about Los Angeles. The mines, parks, vineyards, and redwood forests are all thereabouts. . . ."

Los Angeles fields and farms: looking toward the Hollywood Hills, 1900 how to make money out of wind. . . . Farmers began to neglect their farms and go into town-lot speculation. . . . It became far more dignified for the owner of town-lots that were advancing in value by the day to buy his eggs from Iowa, his chickens from Kansas City, his pork from Chicago . . . than to bother with raising them."

Speculators poured in, so many the hotels ran out of beds and rented them bath-tubs to sleep in. They staged picnics and circuses and barbecues to pull in the customers, sometimes offering dubious title to house lots in new communities that existed only on paper. "[N]ot one in ten [buyers] had ever seen the place," one man remembered, "and not one in ten intended to live there."

In just thirty months, sixty new towns were founded in Los Angeles County, including Avalon, Burbank, Glendale, Pasadena, Pomona. Many of the new communities died not long after they were born, but by the end of the decade, Los Angeles's population was five times what it had been in 1880.

Northwest of town, a pious speculator from Ohio named Horace Henderson Wilcox began subdividing ranch land into town lots for what he hoped would be a model community. Liquor and vice would be permanently barred, and Wilcox offered a free plot to any congregation willing to put up a church. His wife named the new town for a friend's country house back home in Ohio — Hollywood.

HELL WITHOUT THE HEAT

By the summer of 1886, the supposedly risk-free cattle business was in trouble on the northern Plains. Seven and a half million hungry cattle were now competing for grasses that every year grew less plentiful from overgrazing. In some places where it had once taken just five acres of land to support a steer, it now took more than ninety. Big herds of voracious sheep were beginning to move across the landscape, too, devouring everything in sight, and farmers were advancing as well, turning the grass-lands into fields, building fences, driving cattle from their crops.

Ranchers formed stockmen's associations to fight back. They bought and sold congressmen, ran down rustlers, slaughtered sheep wholesale — and put up fences of their own, claiming vast areas for themselves, then defending them with armies of hired gunmen.

Meanwhile, beef prices were dropping. The summer of 1886 was hot and dry. On the overgrazed ranges, the cattle grew thin and weak.

Then came winter. "In November we had several snowstorms," Teddy Blue Abbott, who had followed the beef business north from Texas, remembered, "and I saw the first white owls I have ever seen. The Indians said they were a bad sign, 'heap snow coming, very cold.' . . . It got colder and colder. . . . It was hell without the heat."

On the northern Plains it began snowing on November 13, 1886, and did not stop for a month. The cattle struggled to stay alive, nosing through the snow in search of what little grass remained. January 1887 was the coldest month anyone on the northern Plains could recall. The snow fell so hard during one seventy-two-hour blizzard, a survivor wrote, that "it seemed as if all the world's ice from Time's beginnings had come on a wind which howled and screamed with the fury of demons."

Across the Plains, the unsheltered, helpless cattle began to die. Some, too weak to stand, were simply blown over by the savage wind. Others, their feet frozen into the ice, died like statues. Teddy Blue Abbott remembered doing all he could to save them:

> It was all so slow, plunging after them through the deep snow. . . . The horses' feet were cut and bleeding from the heavy crust, and the cattle had the hair and hide wore off their legs to the knees and the hocks. It was surely hell to see big four-year-old steers just able to stagger along. It was the same all over Wyoming, Montana, and Colorado, western Nebraska, and western Kansas.

When the snow and ice finally began to melt, cattlemen understood for the first time the magnitude of what had happened. Dead animals were everywhere, hundreds of thousands of them, sprawled across the hillsides and along fence lines, heaped at the bottom of coulees, where the snow had trapped them, swollen and bobbing in the rushing rivers. "[I saw] a grim freshet pouring down the river valley as no man had ever seen before or would see again . . ." a rancher remembered, "countless carcasses of cattle were going down with the ice, rolling over and over as they went, sometimes with all four stiffened legs pointed skyward. For days on end, tearing down with the grinding ice cakes, went Death's cattle roundup."

Ranchers scoured the prairies for survivors. "The first day I rode out," one remembered, "I never saw a live animal." Cattlemen would remember the winter of 1886–87 as the "Great Die-Up." Many eastern investors now withdrew what was left of their

Aftermath: Snow slowly retreats from a Montana ranch.

funds. Foreign ranchers packed up and went home. In the end, the only men who made much money on the northern cattle ranges that spring were scavengers, gathering bones to sell to fertilizer companies.

Like the homesteaders who had learned that their mere presence could not change the climate of the West, the ranchers who had rushed in during the beef bonanza had learned they could not ignore it. The great days of the open range were coming to an end. From now on, cattlemen would have to feed their herds in winter. Theodore Roosevelt had remarried and was in Europe on his honeymoon when the storm hit. He hurried west as soon as he got back to see how bad the damage was. "The losses are crippling," he wrote.

> For the first time I have been utterly unable to enjoy a visit to my ranch. I shall be glad to get home. In its present form, stock-raising on the plains is doomed and can hardly outlast the century. The great free ranches . . . mark a primitive stage of existence as surely as do the great tracts of primeval forests, and like the latter must pass away before the onward march of our people . . . and we who have felt the charm of the life, and have exulted in its abounding vigor and its bold, restless freedom . . . must also feel real sorrow that those who come after us are not to see, as we have seen, what is perhaps the pleasantest, healthiest and most exciting phase of American existence.

A GUNPOWDER ENTERTAINMENT

Among those who had sought to avenge George Armstrong Custer in the summer of 1876 had been Buffalo Bill Cody, back scouting for the army between theatrical engagements. On July 17, while wearing one of his stage costumes — a black velvet outfit modeled after those worn by Mexican vaqueros, with a scarlet sash, silver embroidery, and lace at the collar and cuffs — he helped lead a troop of cavalry within sight of a small band of Cheyenne warriors.

Buffalo Bill arrives at Chehalis, Washington, aboard his private car in 1915, still the idol of every American schoolchild after nearly half a century on the road.

Vaquero, cowboy, and Indian (left), leading figures in Buffalo Bill's epic of the West

DY

"The most animated equestrian spectacle ever seen." The people eagerly lined up (above) to see the show in 1900 happen to be Chicagoans, but when they passed through the entrance they saw much the same astonishing performance as the people of Omaha (below) drank in two years later. Even members of the show's cast (right) could not seem to get enough of it.

By the time this advertisement went up in France in 1905, Cody's face was so universally recognizable that the only legend the poster maker had to print was "Je Viens" — "I am coming"— to pull in big Parisian crowds.

There was a fight. One chief fell, a bullet through his skull. Cody took his scalp and mailed it to his own sister — who fainted when she opened the parcel. The Cheyenne's name had been Yellow Hair, but a newspaperman reported it as Yellow Hand, and that name stuck. The story grew with the telling until the Cheyenne had challenged Cody to hand-to-hand combat and when the duel was over a triumphant Cody had shouted, "The first Scalp for Custer!"

It was just the latest in a long litany of embroidered tales that attached themselves to Cody, some his own handiwork, most created by others. "There being but little prospect of any more fighting," he wrote later, "I determined to go East as soon as possible to organize a new 'Dramatic Combination,' and have a new drama written for me, based upon the Sioux war. This I knew would be a paying investment, as the Sioux campaign had excited considerable interest."

Cody had done a good many of the things a young man could do in the West — he'd been a wrangler, expressman, gold-seeker, buffalo hunter, ranchman, army scout, winner of the Medal of Honor for valor against the Cheyenne. And he had a natural talent for drawing attention to himself. Teddy Blue Abbott remembered working briefly for him as a cowboy:

The perennial finale of Cody's show (right) and the cast of the 1908 version sitting for a collective portrait in front of Wanamaker's Manhattan department store (below). The Russian Cossack with his shaggy hat at the left was a comparatively late addition to Cody's Congress of Rough Riders of the World.

> Buffalo Bill was a good fellow, and while he was no great shakes as a scout as he made the eastern people believe, still we all liked him, and we had to hand it to him because he was the only one that had brains enough to make that Wild West stuff pay money. I remember one time he came into a saloon in North Platte, and he took off his hat and that long hair of his that he had rolled up under his hat fell down on his shoulders. It always bothered him, so he rolled it back under his hat again and Brady the saloon man, says: "Say, Bill, why the hell don't you cut the damn stuff off?" And Cody says: "If I did, I'd starve to death."

But Cody was also unhappily married to a woman who understandably objected to his fondness for young actresses; he was very often drunk between performances, and he seemed unable to resist dubious investment schemes that kept him perpetually on the brink of bankruptcy.

None of this mattered to the eastern audiences who saw him as the living embodiment of every frontier virtue. The five-act melodrama called "Buffalo Bill's First Scalp for Custer" had no "head or tail," he recalled, "and it made no difference at which act we commenced the performance. . . . It afforded us, however, ample opportunity to give a noisy, rattling, gunpowder entertainment . . . which seemed to give a general satisfaction."

The stage eventually proved too confining for Cody, and in 1883, he launched "Buffalo Bill's Wild West — America's National Entertainment," an outdoor extravaganza that featured live elk and buffalo, genuine cowboys in spotless outfits roping steers and playing music, authentic Indians attacking a real stagecoach, and a deeply affecting — and totally fictional — tableau in which Cody arrived at the Little Bighorn too late to save Custer and his command from disaster. Even Libbie Custer came to see it several times. It ran for three decades, imprinting its own version of the West on the minds of an entire generation, at home and overseas.

Buffalo Bill backstage after a New York appearance toward the end of his long career. When he died in 1917, a procession of 3,000 motorcars would follow the hearse to his tomb high above Denver, Colorado. Even in death, he remained an attraction.

In 1885, Sitting Bull joined Cody's entourage. He was paid $50 a week, a bonus of $125 for signing on, and the right to profit directly from the sale of autographs and pictures of himself. The aging chief was required only to ride around the arena once a show, doing his best to ignore the boos of Custer's admirers, and afterward, to sign his name for the awed visitors who came to peer at him in his teepee. Sitting Bull liked Cody — who presented him with a handsome hat and the gray horse he'd ridden in the show as gifts — and during an appearance in Washington, D.C., he managed to shake hands with President Grover Cleveland, an event that he took to be evidence that he was still considered a great chief.

But he spent just four months with the Wild West show. He had seen enough of whites, and could not understand why beggars were left to drift about the streets of big cities. He gave much of his pay away to newsboys and hoboes he encountered on the tour, and when he got back to Standing Rock, he used the money he had left to provide feasts for his friends, much to the disgust of agent James McLaughlin: "He is . . . too vain and obstinate to be benefitted by what he sees and makes no good use of the money he thus earns."

Now, the aging medicine man was once again back in the land of his birth, living quietly with his two wives, five children, and a nephew named One Bull, whom he had adopted as his son. He refused to give up either of his wives and rejected Christianity, but he sent his children to a Congregational day school run by a woman missionary, convinced that in the future all Lakota children would need to be able to read and write. "We were always good friends personally," she remembered, "but he hated Christianity and found great satisfaction in taking my converts back into heathendom while of course I felt equal satisfaction in converting his heathen friends."

Soon after he returned to his cabin on the Grand River, he had another of his mystical visions about the future. In 1876, one had warned him that white men were pursuing the Lakota. Another had predicted that Custer's soldiers at the Little Bighorn would fall into the village, upside down. His new vision was equally clear. Wandering alone near his home one morning, he watched a meadowlark flutter down onto a hillock. Then the bird spoke to him, saying, "Your own people, Lakotas, will kill you." Sitting Bull had faith in his visions; they had always proved true in the past.

The American West and the Burden of Belief

N. Scott Momaday

I.

> West of Jemez Pueblo there is a great red mesa, and in the folds of the earth at its base there is a canyon, the dark red walls of which are sheer and shadow stained; they rise vertically to a remarkable height. You do not suspect that the canyon is there, but you turn a corner and the walls contain you; you look into a corridor of geologic time. When I went into that place I left my horse outside, for there was a strange light and quiet upon the walls, and the shadows closed upon me. I looked up, straight up, to the serpentine strip of the sky. It was clear and deep, like a river running across the top of the world. The sand in which I stood was deep, and I could feel the cold of it through the soles of my shoes. And when I walked out, the light and heat of the day struck me so hard that I nearly fell. On the side of a hill in the plain of the Hissar I saw my horse grazing among sheep. The land inclined into the distance, to the Pamirs, to the Fedchenko Glacier. The river which I had seen near the sun had run out into the endless ether above the Karakoram range and the Plateau of Tibet.
>
> — *The Names*

When I wrote this passage, some years ago, it did not seem strange to me that two such landscapes as that of northern New Mexico and that of central Asia should become one in the mind's eye and in the confluence of image and imagination. Nor does it seem strange to me now. Even as we look back, the partitions of our experience open and close upon each other; disparate realities coalesce into a single, integrated appearance.

This transformation is perhaps the essence of art and literature. Certainly it is the soul of drama, and historically it is how we have seen the American West. Our human tendency is to concentrate the world upon a stage. We construct proscenium arches and frames in order to contain the thing that is larger than our comprehension, the plane of boundless possibility, that which reaches almost beyond wonder. Sometimes the process of concentration results in something like a burden of belief, a kind of ambiguous exaggeration, as in the paintings of Albert Bierstadt, say, or in the photographs of Ansel Adams, in which an artful grandeur seems superimposed upon a grandeur that is innate. Or music comes to mind, a music that seems to pervade the vast landscape and emanate from it, not the music of wind and rain and birds and beasts, but Virgil Thomson's "The Plow That Broke the Plains," or Aaron Copland's "Rodeo," or perhaps the sound track from *The Alamo* or *She Wore a Yellow Ribbon.* We are speaking of overlays, impositions, a kind of narcissism that locates us within our own field of vision. But if this is a distorted view of the West, it is nonetheless a view that fascinates us.

And more often than not the fascination consists in peril. In *My Life on the Plains,* George Armstrong Custer describes a strange sight:

> I have seen a train of government wagons with white canvas covers moving through a mirage which, by elevating the wagons to treble their height and magnifying the size of the covers, presented the appearance of a line of large sailing vessels under full sail, while the usual appearance of the mirage gave a correct likeness of an immense lake or sea. Sometimes the mirage has been the cause of frightful suffering and death by its deceptive appearance.

He goes on to tell of emigrants to California and Oregon who, suffering terrible thirst, were deflected from their route by a mirage, "like an *ignis fatuus,*" and so perished. Their graves are strewn far and wide over the prairie.

This equation of wonder and peril is for Custer a kind of exhilaration, as indeed it is for most of those adventurers who journeyed westward, and even for those who did not, who escaped into the Wild West show or the dime novel.

For the European who came from a community of congestion and confinement, the West was beyond dreaming; it must have inspired him to formulate an idea of the infinite. There he could walk through geologic time; he could see into eternity. He was surely bewildered, wary, afraid. The landscape was anomalously beautiful and hostile. It was desolate and unforgiving, and yet it was a world of paradisal possibility. Above all, it was wild, definitively wild. And it was inhabited by a people who were to him altogether alien and inscrutable, who were essentially dangerous and deceptive, often invisible, who were savage and unholy — and who were perfectly at home.

This is a crucial point, then: the West was occupied. It was the home of peoples who had come upon the North American continent many thousands of years before, who had in the course of their habitation become the spirit and intelligence of the earth, who had died into the ground again and again and so made it sacred. Those Europeans who ventured into the West must have seen themselves in some wise as latecomers and intruders. In spite of their narcissism, some aspect of their intrusion must have occurred to them as sacrilege, for they were in the unfortunate position of robbing the native peoples of their homeland and the land of its spiritual resources. By virtue of their culture and history — a culture of acquisition and a history of conquest — they were peculiarly prepared to commit sacrilege, the theft of the sacred.

Even the Indians succumbed to the kind of narcissism the Europeans brought to bear on the primeval landscape, the imposition of a belief — essentially alien to both the land and the peoples who inhabited it — that would locate them once again within their own field of vision. For the Indian, the mirage of the ghost dance — to which the concepts of a messiah and immortality, both foreign, European imports, were central — was surely an *ignis fatuus,* and the cause of frightful suffering and death.

II.

George Armstrong Custer had an eye to the country of the Great Plains, and especially to those of its features that constituted a "deceptive appearance." As he stealthily approached Black Kettle's camp on the Washita River, where he was to win his principal acclaim as an Indian fighter, he and his men caught sight of a strange thing. At the first sign of dawn there appeared a bright light ascending slowly from the skyline. Custer describes it sharply, even eloquently:

> Slowly and majestically it continued to rise above the crest of the hill, first appearing as a small brilliant flaming globe of bright golden hue. As it ascended still higher it seemed to increase in size, to move more slowly, while its colors rapidly changed from one to the other, exhibiting in turn the most beautiful combinations of prismatic tints.

Custer and his men took it to be a rocket, some sort of signal, and they assumed that their presence had been detected by the Indians. Here again is the equation of fascination and peril. But at last the reality is discovered:

> Rising above the mystifying influences of the atmosphere, that which had appeared so suddenly before us and excited our greatest apprehensions developed into the brightest and most beautiful of morning stars.

In the ensuing raid upon Black Kettle's camp, Custer and his troopers, charging to the strains of "Garry Owen," killed 103 Cheyenne, including Black Kettle and his wife. Ninety-two of the slain Cheyenne were women, children, and old men. Fifty-three women and children were captured. Custer's casualties totaled one officer killed, one officer severely and two more slightly wounded, and eleven cavalrymen wounded. After the fighting, Custer ordered the herd of Indian ponies slain; the herd numbered 875 animals. "We did not need the ponies, while the Indians did," he wrote.

In the matter of killing women and children, Custer's exculpatory rhetoric seems lame, far beneath his poetic descriptions of mirages and the break of day:

> Before engaging in the fight orders had been given to prevent the killing of any but the fighting strength of the village; but in a struggle of this character it is impossible at all times to discriminate, particularly when, in a hand-to-hand conflict such as the one the troops were then engaged in the squaws are as dangerous adversaries as the warriors, while Indian boys between ten and fifteen years of age were found as expert and determined in the use of the pistol and bow and arrow as the older warriors.

After the fighting, too, Black Kettle's sister, Mah-wis-sa, implored Custer to leave the Cheyenne in peace. Custer reports that she approached him with a young woman, perhaps seventeen years old, and placed the girl's hand in his. Then she proceeded to speak solemnly in her own language, words that Custer took to be a kind of benediction, with appropriate manners and gestures. When the formalities seemed to come to a close, Mah-wis-sa looked reverently to the skies and at the same time drew her hands slowly down over the faces of Custer and the girl. At this point Custer was moved to ask Romeo, his interpreter, what was going on. Romeo replied that Custer and the young woman had just been married to each other.

In one version of the story it is said that Mah-wis-sa told Custer that if he ever again made war on the Cheyenne, he would die. When he was killed at the Little Bighorn, Cheyenne women pierced his eardrums with awls, so that he might hear in the afterlife; he had failed to hear the warning given him at the Washita.

In the final paragraph of *My Life on the Plains,* Custer bids farewell to his readers and announces his intention "to visit a region of country as yet unseen by human eyes, except those of the Indian — a country described by the latter as abounding in game of all varieties, rich in scientific interest, and of surpassing beauty in natural scenery." After rumors of gold had made the Black Hills a name known throughout the country, General (then Lieutenant Colonel) George Armstrong Custer led an expedition from Fort Abraham Lincoln into the Black Hills in July and August 1874. The Custer expedition traveled six hundred miles in sixty days. Custer reported proof of gold, but he had an eye to other things as well. He wrote in his diary:

> Every step of our march that day was amid flowers of the most exquisite colors and perfume. So luxuriant in growth were they that men plucked them without dismounting from the saddle. . . . It was a strange sight to glance back at the advancing columns of cavalry and behold the men with beautiful bouquets in their hands, while the headgear of the horses was decorated with wreaths of flowers fit to crown a queen of May. Deeming it a most fitting appellation, I named this Floral Valley.

In the evening of that same day, sitting at mess in a meadow, the officers competed to see how many different flowers could be picked by each man without leaving his seat. Seven varieties were gathered so. Some fifty different flowers were blooming in Floral Valley.

Imagine that Custer dreamed that night. In his dream he saw a man approaching on horseback, approaching slowly across a meadow full of wildflowers. The man drew very close and stopped, sitting straight up on the horse, holding Custer fast in his gaze. There could be no doubt that he was a warrior, and fearless, though he flourished no scalps and made no signs of fighting. His unbound hair hung below his waist. His body was painted with hail spots, and a white bolt of lightning ran down one of his cheeks, and on his head he wore the feathers of a red-backed hawk. Except for moccasins and breechcloth he was naked.

"I am George Armstrong Custer," Custer said, "called Yellowhair, called Son of the Morning Star."

"I am Curly," the man said, "called Crazy Horse."

And Custer wept for the nobility and dignity and greatness of the man facing him. And through his tears he perceived the brilliance of the meadow. The wildflowers were innumerable and more beautiful than anything he had ever seen or imagined. And when he thought his heart could bear no more, a thousand butterflies rose up, glancing and darting and floating around him, to spangle the sky, to become prisms of the sun. And he awoke serene and refreshed in his soul.

Lakota, ca. 1900

George Armstrong Custer sees the light upon the meadows of the Plains, but he does not see disaster lurking at the Little Bighorn. He hears the bugles and the band, but he does not hear or heed the warning of the Cheyenne women. All about there is deception; the West is other than it seems.

III.

In 1872, William Frederick Cody was awarded the Medal of Honor for his valor in fighting Indians. In 1913, U.S. Army regulations specified that only enlisted men and officers were eligible to receive the Medal of Honor, and Cody's medal was therefore withdrawn and his name removed from the records. In 1916, after deliberation, the army decided to return the medal, having declared that Cody's service to his country was "above and beyond the call of duty."

Ambivalence and ambiguity, like deception, bear upon all definitions of the American West. The real issue of Cody's skill and accomplishment as an Indian fighter is not brought into question in this matter of the Medal of Honor, but it might be. Beyond the countless Indians he "killed" in the arena of the Wild West show, Cody's achievements as an Indian fighter are suspect. Indeed, much of Cody's life is clouded in ambiguity. He claimed that in 1859 he became a pony express rider, but the pony express did not come into being until 1860. Even the sobriquet "Buffalo Bill" belonged to William Mathewson before it belonged to William Frederick Cody.

Buffalo Bill Cody was an icon and an enigma, and he was in some sense his own invention. One of his biographers wrote that he was "a man who was so much more than a western myth." One must doubt it, for the mythic dimension of the American West is an equation much greater than the sum of its parts. It would be more accurate, in this case, to say that the one dissolved into the other, that the man and myth became indivisible. The great fascination and peril of Cody's life was the riddle of who he was. The thing that opposed him, and perhaps betrayed him, was above all else the mirage of his own identity.

If we are to understand the central irony of Buffalo Bill and the Wild West show, we must first understand that William Frederick Cody was an authentic western hero. As a scout, a guide, a marksman, and a buffalo hunter, he was second to none. At a time when horsemanship was at its highest level in America, he was a horseman nearly without peer. He defined the plainsman. The authority of his life on the Plains far surpassed Custer's.

But let us imagine that we are at Omaha, Nebraska, on May 17, 1883, in a crowd of 8,000 people. The spectacle of the "Wild West" unfolds before us. The opening parade is led by a twenty-piece band playing "Garry Owen," perhaps, or "The Girl I Left Behind Me." Then there comes an Indian in full regalia on a paint pony. Next are buffalo, three adults and a calf. Then there is Buffalo Bill, mounted on a fine white horse and resplendent in a great white hat, a fringed buckskin coat, and glossy thigh boots. He stands out in a company of cowboys, Indians, more buffalo, and the Deadwood Stage, drawn by six handsome mules, and the end is brought up by another band, playing "Annie Laurie" or "When Johnny Comes Marching Home." Then we see the acts — the racing of the pony express, exhibitions of shooting, the attack on the Deadwood Stagecoach, and the finale of the great buffalo chase. Buffalo Bill makes a stirring speech, and we are enthralled; the applause is thunderous. But this is only a modest beginning, a mere glimpse of things to come.

What we have in this explosion of color and fanfare is an epic transformation of the American West into a traveling circus and of an American hero into an imitation of himself. Here is a theme with which we have become more than familiar. We have seen the transformation take place numberless times on the stage, on television and movie screens, and on the pages of comic books, dime novels, and literary masterpieces. One function of the American imagination is to reduce the American landscape to size, to fit that great expanse to the confinement of the immigrant mind. It is a way to persist in our cultural being. We photograph ourselves on the rim of Monument Valley or against the wall of the Tetons, and we become our own frame of reference. As long as we can transform the landscape to accommodate our fragile presence, we can be saved. As long as we can see ourselves on the picture plane, we cannot be lost.

Arthur Kopit's play *Indians* is a remarkable treatise on this very subject of transformation. It can and ought to be seen as a tragedy, for its central story is that of Buffalo Bill's fatal passage into myth. He is constrained to translate his real heroism into a false and concentrated reflection of itself. The presence of the Indians is pervasive, but he cannot see them until they are called to his attention.

> BUFFALO BILL: Thank you, thank you! A great show lined up tonight! With all-time favorite Johnny Baker, Texas Jack and his twelve-string guitar, the Dancin' Cavanaughs, Sheriff Brad and the Deadwood Mail Coach, Harry Philamee's Trained Prairie Dogs, the Abilene County Girls' Trick Roping and Lasso Society, Pecos Pete and the —
>
> VOICE: *Bill.*
>
> BUFFALO BILL: (Startled.) Hm?
>
> VOICE: Bring on the Indians.
>
> BUFFALO BILL: What?
>
> VOICE: The *Indians.*
>
> BUFFALO BILL: Ah . . .

Solemnly the Indians appear. In effect they shame Buffalo Bill; they tread upon his conscience. They fascinate and imperil him. By degrees his desperation to justify himself — and by extension the white man's treatment of the Indians in general — grows and becomes a burden too great to bear. In the end he sits trembling while the stage goes completely black. Then all lights up, rodeo music, the glaring and blaring; enter the Rough Riders of the World! Buffalo Bill enters on his white stallion and tours the ring, doffing his hat to the invisible crowd. The Rough Riders exit, the Indians approach, and the lights fade to black again.

At five minutes past noon on January 10, 1917, Buffalo Bill died. Western Union ordered all lines cleared, and, in a state of war, the world was given the news at once. The old scout had passed by. Tributes and condolences came from every quarter, from children, from old soldiers, from heads of state.

In ambivalence and ambiguity, Cody died as he had lived. A week before his death, it was reported that Buffalo Bill had been baptized into the Roman Catholic Church. His wife, Louisa, was, however, said to be an Episcopalian, and his sister Julia, to whom he declared, "Your church suits me," was a Presbyterian. Following his death there was a controversy as to where Cody should be buried. He had often expressed the wish to be buried on Cedar Mountain, Wyoming. Notwithstanding, his final resting place is atop Mount Lookout, above Denver, Colorado, overlooking the urban sprawl.

IV.

DECEMBER 29, 1890

Wounded Knee Creek

In the shine of photographs
are the slain, frozen and black

on a simple field of snow.
They image ceremony:

women and children dancing,
old men prancing, making fun.

In autumn there were songs, long
since muted in the blizzard.

In summer the wild buckwheat
shone like fox fur and quillwork,

and dusk guttered on the creek.
Now in serene attitudes

of dance, the dead in glossy
death are drawn in ancient light.

On December 15, 1890, the great Hunkpapa leader Sitting Bull, who had opposed Custer at the Little Bighorn and who had toured for a time with Buffalo Bill and the Wild West show, was killed on the Standing Rock reservation. In a dream he had foreseen his death at the hands of his own people.

Just two weeks later, on the morning of December 29, 1890, on Wounded Knee Creek near the Pine Ridge agency, the Seventh Cavalry of the U.S. Army opened fire on an encampment of Big Foot's band of Miniconjou Sioux. When the shooting ended, Big Foot and most of his people were dead or dying. It has been estimated that nearly 300 of the original 350 men, women, and children in the camp were slain. Twenty-five soldiers were killed and thirty-nine wounded.

Sitting Bull is reported to have said, "I am the last Indian." In some sense he was right. During his lifetime the world of the Plains Indians had changed forever. The old roving life of the buffalo hunters was over. A terrible disintegration and demoralization had set in. If the death of Sitting Bull marked the end of an age, Wounded Knee marked the end of a culture.

> I did not know then how much was ended. When I look back now from the high hill of my old age, I can still see the butchered women and children lying heaped and scattered all along the crooked gulch as plain as when I saw them with eyes still young. And I can see that something else died there in the bloody mud, and was buried in the blizzard. A people's dream died there. It was a beautiful dream. . . .
>
> —Black Elk

In the following days there were further developments. On January 7, 1891, nine days after the massacre at Wounded Knee, a young

Sioux warrior named Plenty Horses shot and killed a popular army officer, Lieutenant Edward W. Casey, who wanted to enter the Sioux village at No Water for the purpose of talking peace. The killing appeared to be unprovoked. Plenty Horses shot Casey in the back at close quarters.

On January 11, two Sioux families, returning to Pine Ridge from hunting near Bear Butte, were ambushed by white ranchers, three brothers named Culbertson. Few Tails, the head of one of the families, was killed, and his wife was severely wounded. Somehow she made her way in the freezing cold a hundred miles to Pine Ridge. The other family — a man, his wife, and two children, one an infant — managed to reach the Rosebud agency two weeks later. This wife, too, was wounded and weak from the loss of blood. She survived, but the infant child had died of starvation on the way.

On January 15 the Sioux leaders surrendered and established themselves at Pine Ridge. The peace for which General Nelson A. Miles had worked so hard was achieved. The Indians assumed that Plenty Horses would go free, and indeed General Miles was reluctant to disturb the peace. But there were strong feelings among the soldiers. Casey had been shot in cold blood while acting in the interest of peace. On February 19, Plenty Horses was quietly arrested and removed from the reservation to Fort Meade, near Sturgis, South Dakota.

Nachez, son of Cochise, Chiricahua Apache, 1883

On March 27, General Miles ordered Plenty Horses released to stand trial in the federal district court at Sioux Falls. Interest ran high, and the courtroom was filled with onlookers of every description. The Plenty Horses trial was one of the most interesting and unlikely in the history of the West. Eventually the outcome turned upon a question of perception, of whether or not a state of war existed between the Sioux and the United States. If Plenty Horses and Casey were belligerents in a state of war, the defense argued, then the killing could not be considered a criminal offense, subject to trial in the civil courts.

General Nelson A. Miles was sensitive to this question for two reasons in particular. First, his rationale for bringing troops upon the scene — and he had amassed the largest concentration of troops in one place since the Civil War — was predicated upon the existence of a state of war. When the question was put to him directly, he replied, "It was a war. You do not suppose that I am going to reduce my campaign to a dress-parade affair?" Second, Miles had to confront the logically related corollary to the defense argument, that, if no state of war existed, all the soldiers who took part in the Wounded Knee affair were guilty of murder under the law.

Miles sent a staff officer, Captain Frank D. Baldwin, to testify on behalf of Plenty Horses' defense. This testimony proved critical, and decisive. It is a notable irony that Baldwin and the slain Casey were close friends. Surely one of the principal ironies of American history is that Plenty Horses was very likely to have been the only Indian to benefit in any way from the slaughter at Wounded Knee. Plenty Horses was acquitted. So too — a final irony — were the Culbertson brothers; with Plenty Horses' acquittal, there was neither a logical basis for nor a practical possibility of holding them accountable for the ambush of Few Tails and his party.

We might ponder Plenty Horses at trial, a young man sitting silent under the scrutiny of curious onlookers, braving his fate with apparent indifference. Behind the mask of a warrior was a lost and agonized soul.

As a boy Plenty Horses had been sent to Carlisle Indian School in Pennsylvania, the boarding school founded by Richard Henry Pratt, whose obsession was to "kill the Indian and save the man." Carlisle was the model upon which an extensive system of boarding schools for Indians was based. The boarding schools were prisons in effect, where Indian children were exposed to brutalities, sometimes subtle, sometimes not, in the interest of converting them to the white man's way of life. It was a grand experiment in ethnic cleansing and psychological warfare, and it failed. But it exacted a terrible cost upon the mental, physical, and spiritual health of Indian children.

Plenty Horses was for five years a pupil at Carlisle. Of his experience there he said:

> I found that the education I had received was of no benefit to me. There was no chance to get employment, nothing for me to do whereby I could earn my board and clothes, no opportunity to learn more and remain with the whites. It disheartened me and I went back to live as I had before going to school.

But when Plenty Horses returned to his own people, they did not fully accept him. He had lost touch with the old ways; he had lived among whites, and the association had diminished him. He rejected the white world, but he had been exposed to it, and it had left its mark upon him. And in the process he had been dislodged, uprooted from the Indian world. He could not quite get back to it. His very being had become tentative; he lived in a kind of limbo, a state of confusion, depression, and desperation.

At the trial Plenty Horses was remarkably passive. He said nothing, nor did he give any sign of his feelings. It was as if he were not there. It came later to light that he was convinced beyond any question that he would be hanged. He could not understand what was happening around him. But in a strange way he could appreciate it. Indeed he must have been fascinated. Beneath his inscrutable expression, his heart must have been racing. He was the center of a ritual, a sacrificial victim; the white man must dispose of him according to some design in the white man's universe. This was perhaps a ritual of atonement. The whites would take his life, but in the proper way, according to their notion of propriety and the appropriate. Perhaps they were involving him in their very notion of the sacred. He could only accept what was happening, and only in their terms. With silence, patience, and respect he must await the inevitable.

Plenty Horses said later:

> I am an Indian. Five years I attended Carlisle and was educated in the ways of the white man. . . . I was lonely. I shot the lieutenant so I might make a place for myself among my people. Now I am one of them. I shall be hung and the Indians will bury me as a warrior. They will be proud of me. I am satisfied.

But Plenty Horses was not hanged, nor did he make an acceptable place for himself among his people. He was acquitted. Plenty Horses lived out his life between two worlds, without a place in either.

Perhaps the most tragic aspect of Plenty Horses' plight was his silence, the theft of his language and the theft of meaning itself from his ordeal. At Carlisle he had been made to speak English, and his native Lakota was forbidden, thrown away, to use a term that indicates particular misfortune in the Plains oral tradition, where to be "thrown away" is to be negated, excluded, eliminated. After five years Plenty Horses had not only failed to master the English language, he had lost some critical possession of his native tongue as well. He was therefore crippled in his speech, wounded in his intelligence. In him was a terrible urgency to express himself — his anger and hurt, his sorrow and loneliness. But his voice was broken. In terms of his culture and all it held most sacred, Plenty Horses himself was thrown away.

In order to understand the true nature of Plenty Horses' ordeal — and a central reality in the cultural conflict that has defined the way we historically see the American West — we must first understand something about the nature of words, about the way we live our daily lives in the element of language. For in a profound sense our language determines us; it shapes our most fundamental selves; it establishes our identity and confirms our existence, our human being. Without language we are lost, "thrown away." Without names — language is essentially a system of naming — we cannot truly claim to be.

Pacer's Son, Kiowa Apache

To think is to talk to oneself. That is to say, language and thought are practically indivisible. But there is complexity in language, and there are many languages. Indeed, there are hundreds of Native American languages on the North American continent alone, many of them in the American West. As there are different languages, there are different ways of thinking. In terms of what we call "worldview," there are common denominators of experience that unify language communities to some extent. Although the Pueblo peoples of the Rio Grande valley speak different languages, their experience of the land in which they live, and have lived for thousands of years, is by and large the same. And their worldview is the same. There are common denominators that unify all Native Americans in certain ways. This much may be said of other peoples, Europeans, for example. But the difference between Native American and European worldviews is vast. And that difference is crucial to the story of the American West. We are talking about different ways of thinking, deeply different ways of looking at the world.

The oral tradition of the American Indian is a highly developed realization of language. In certain ways it is superior to the written tradition. In the oral tradition words are sacred; they are intrinsically powerful and beautiful. By means of words, by the exertion of language upon the unknown, the best of the possible — and indeed the seemingly impossible — is accomplished. Nothing exists beyond the influence of words. Words are the names of Creation. To give one's word is to give oneself, wholly, to place a name, than which nothing is more sacred, in the balance. One stands for his word; his word stands for him. The oral tradition demands the greatest clarity of speech and hearing, the whole strength of memory, and an absolute faith in the efficacy of language. Every word spoken, every word heard, is the utterance of prayer.

Thus, in the oral tradition, language bears the burden of the sacred, the burden of belief. In a written tradition, the place of language is not so certain.

Those European immigrants who ventured into the Wild West were of a written tradition, even the many who were illiterate. Their way of seeing and thinking was determined by the invention of an alphabet, the advent of the printed word, and the manufacture of books. These were great landmarks of civilization, to be sure, but they were also a radical departure from the oral tradition and an understanding of language that was inestimably older and closer to the origin of words. Although the first Europeans venturing into the continent took with them and held dear the Bible, Bunyan, and Shakespeare, their children ultimately could take words for granted, throw them away. Words, multiplied and diluted to inflation, would be preserved on shelves forever. But in this departure was also the dilution of the sacred, and the loss of a crucial connection with the real, that plane of possibility that is always larger than our comprehension. What follows such loss is overlay, imposition, the distorted view of the West of which we have been speaking.

V.

My children, when at first I liked the whites,
My children, when at first I liked the whites,
I gave them fruits,
I gave them fruits.

— Arapaho

Restore my voice for me.

— Navajo

The landscape of the American West has to be seen to be believed. And perhaps, conversely, it has to be believed in order to be seen. Here is the confluence of image and imagination. I am a writer and a painter. I am therefore interested in what it is to see, how seeing is accomplished, how the physical eye and the mind's eye are related, how the act of seeing is or can be expressed in art and in language, and how these things are sacred in nature, as I believe them to be.

Belief is the burden of seeing. And language bears the burden of belief rightly. To see into the heart of something is to believe in it. In order to see to this extent, to see and to accomplish belief in the seeing, one must be prepared. The preparation is a spiritual exercise.

In order to be perceived in its true character, the landscape of the American West must be seen in terms of its sacred dimension. "Sacred" and "sacrifice" are related. Something is made sacred by means of sacrifice; that which is sacred is earned. I have a friend who wears on a string around his neck a little leather pouch. In the pouch is a pebble from the creek bed at Wounded Knee. Wounded Knee is sacred ground, for it was purchased with blood. It is the site of a terrible human sacrifice. It is appropriate that my friend should keep the pebble close to the center of his being, that he should see the pebble and beyond the pebble to the battlefield and beyond the battlefield to the living earth.

The history of the West, that is, the written story that begins with the record of European intervention, is informed by tensions that arise from a failure to see the West in terms of the sacred. The oral history, the oral tradition that came before the written chronicles, is all too often left out of the equation. Yet one of the essential realities of the West is centered in this still living past. When Europeans came into the West they encountered a people who had been there for untold millennia, for whom the landscape was a kind of cathedral of their spiritual life, the home of their deepest being. It had been earned by sacrifice forever. But the encounter was determined by a distortion of image and imagination and language, by a failure to see and believe.

George Armstrong Custer could see and articulate the beauty of the Plains, but he could not see the people who inhabited them. Or he could see them only as enemies, impediments to the glory for which he hungered. He could not understand the sacred ceremony, the significance of the marriage he was offered, and he could not hear the words of warning, nor comprehend their meaning.

Buffalo Bill was a plainsman, but the place he might have held on the picture plane of the West was severely compromised and ultimately lost to the theatrical pretensions of the Wild West show. Neither did he see the Indians. What he saw at last was a self-fabricated reflection of himself and of the landscape in which he had lived a former life.

The vision of Plenty Horses was that of reunion with his traditional world. He could not realize his vision, for his old way of seeing was stolen from him in the white man's school. Ironically, just like the European emigrants, Plenty Horses attempted by his wordless act of violence to persist in his cultural being, to transform the landscape to accommodate his presence once more, to save himself. He could not do so. I believe that he wanted more than anything to pray, to make a prayer in the old way to the old deities of the world to which he was born. But I believe too that he had lost the words, that without language he could no longer bear the burden of belief.

The sun's beams are running out
The sun's beams are running out
The sun's yellow rays are running out
The sun's yellow rays are running out

We shall live again
We shall live again

— Comanche

They will appear — may you behold them!
They will appear — may you behold them!
A horse nation will appear.
A thunder-being nation will appear.
They will appear, behold!
They will appear, behold!

— Kiowa

Leadville, Colorado, ca. 1890

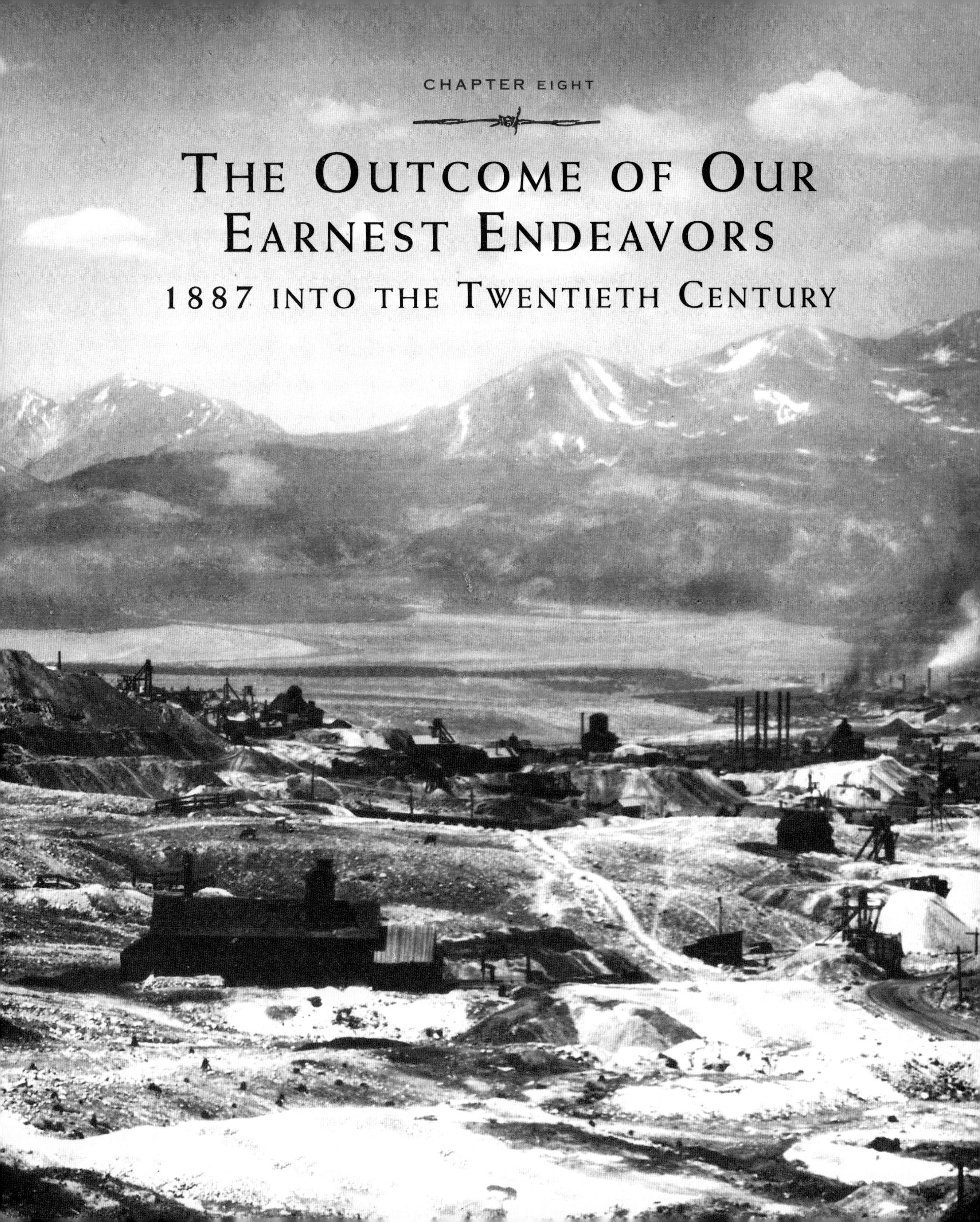

CHAPTER EIGHT

The Outcome of Our Earnest Endeavors

1887 into the Twentieth Century

In 1893, the four hundredth anniversary of the arrival of Columbus in the New World was celebrated in Chicago. The World's Columbian Exposition was so large, so ambitious, so self-congratulatory, that it took an extra year just to get everything ready. There were 63 million Americans in 1893. Twenty-four million tickets to the fair were sold. More people attended it than had ever attended any other single event in the history of the world. Their pride was understandable. In a span of less than fifty years, the United States had stretched its boundaries to the Pacific and altered everything in its path. The conquest of the West that had begun with Coronado at last seemed complete. But beyond the fairgrounds, beyond Chicago, in the real West, for every frontier story that was coming to an end, another one began.

In the spring of 1889, two determined middle-aged women arrived at the Nez Percé reservation in Lapwai, Idaho. They had been active in the temperance and women's rights movements and were now deeply committed to a new cause.

Jane Gay, fifty-nine, from New Hampshire, had nursed Union soldiers during the Civil War, had published a book of poems, and was accustomed to hard work and attention to detail, having been a clerk for seventeen years in the dead letter office of the postal service. To document her time with the Nez Percé, she had learned the art of photography.

Her companion, Alice Fletcher, fifty-one, was the former secretary of the Association for the Advancement of Women and a skilled performer on the lecture circuit. After visits to the Plains to study the ceremonies of the Lakota, Ponca, and Omaha tribes, she had become a pioneer in the emerging field of ethnology. Among the Friends of the Indian, who gathered each summer at Lake Mohonk, Fletcher was one of the relatively few who had ever actually gone west to meet Indians, and so her opinions were given special weight and she had become the group's most visible — and effective — lobbyist in passing the Dawes General Allotment Act of 1887.

It was meant, said the head of the Lake Mohonk Conference, to be "a mighty pulverizing engine for breaking up the tribal mass." The act provided for each reservation to be surveyed, and each head of a family to be given 160 acres of farmland or 320 of grazing land. Then, once each family had its allotment, the remaining tribal lands were to be declared "surplus" and opened up for homesteading. Tribal ownership — and the tribes themselves — were meant simply to disappear.

"The Indian may now become a free man," Alice Fletcher said; "free from the thraldom of the tribe; free from the domination of the reservation system; free to enter into the body of our citizens. [The Allotment Act] may therefore be considered as the Magna Carta of the Indians of our country." She and other reformers favored the new policy because it seemed the fastest way to force Indian peoples to become like other Americans. Land speculators liked it, too. Indians themselves were not consulted.

On behalf of the Bureau of Indian Affairs, Fletcher had already implemented allotments in Nebraska among the Omaha and Winnebago. Now, she would divide up the lands of the Nez Percé, the nation's oldest friends in the West. "If I believe in anything for the Indians, I believe in allotment . . ." she said. "I always help the progressive Indians first. It helps to break the dead monotony of the tribe. . . . [P]erhaps one third will make successful farmers, another third will make a scramble, . . . and the other third will be a miserable worthless lot. But I do not believe in keeping all the others back for this fraction. I have always had to coerce a few, and I rather enjoy it."

Fletcher's strong will — as well as her physical resemblance to Queen Victoria — prompted her companion to refer to her privately as "Her Majesty." The Nez Percé came to call her the "Measuring Woman." She had her work cut out for her at Lapwai. The first Nez Percé she settled among simply refused to cooperate. Fletcher and Gay — along with a surveyor and an interpreter — then relocated to another part of the reservation, nearer a group of Christian Nez Percé more willing to comply.

Even there, Fletcher wrote, it was "the worst struggle of my life." Jane Gay recalled an early meeting with tribal leaders:

> [She] explained what she had called them together to hear: explained the land allotment, the meaning of citizenship and her wish that the whole people would see the wisdom of the great change that she had come to bring upon them. . . .
>
> Still a silence. . . . The Interpreter read the law and then sat down and waited. A little stir arose among the people, . . . and at length one man stood up, a tall, broad-shouldered fellow with . . . an air of authority about him. . . . He said, "We do not want our land cut up in little pieces; we have not told you to do it. . . . We are content to be as we are." And a groan of assent ran along the dark line of Sphinxes as the old man drew his blanket about him. . . .
>
> . . . "Our people are scattered," [said] another. "We must come together and decide whether we will have this law."
>
> [She told] them that there is nothing for them to decide; they have no choice. The law must be obeyed. . . .

Whites — anxious for the "surplus" lands to be opened, and just as anxious that the Indians not be allotted the prime parcels — came to call, hoping to persuade Fletcher to see things their way. "Already we have been called upon by a delegation of cattlemen," Gay wrote,

> who desire to know what the Allotting Agent proposes to do about their "rights" upon the Reservation. They seem to be utterly ignorant of the intent of the Severalty Act. . . . Her Majesty . . . explained that it was her sworn duty to place the Indians upon their best lands. . . . The men are evidently non-plussed, for, as they mounted their horses [I] heard one mutter, "Why in thunder did the Government send a woman to do this work? We could have got a holt on a man."

Chief Joseph and Alice Fletcher, the "Measuring Woman," on the Nez Percé reservation in Idaho, 1890. Joseph was willing to take an allotment, but only if it were granted to him in the Wallowa Valley, where his father was buried. Fletcher could do nothing for him, but she thought him "a most interesting blending of the old and the new."

Chief Joseph came to pay a visit to the "Measuring Woman," too. After his long flight from the army in 1877, he had been exiled to Oklahoma, and then finally allowed to return to a reservation in eastern Washington — but not to his beloved Wallowa Valley. Using a new device — a wax cylinder — Fletcher convinced the old chief to record one of his traditional songs. But she could not talk him into taking an allotment at Lapwai.

> If you tie a horse to a stake, [he asked,] do you expect he will grow fat? If you pen a man on a small spot of earth, and compel him to stay there, he will not be contented, nor will he grow and prosper. I have asked some of the great white chiefs where they get their authority to say to that man that he shall stay in one place, while he sees white men going where they please. They can not tell me.

Jane Gay was impressed by Joseph's dignity and his determination: ". . . He will have none but the Wallowa valley, from which he was driven; he will remain landless and homeless if he cannot have his own again. It was good to see an unsubjugated Indian. One could not help respecting the man who still stood firmly for his rights, after having fought and suffered and been defeated in the struggle for their maintenance." (Joseph remained unsubjugated to the end and died in 1904, without ever seeing his beloved valley again.)

Fletcher went back to work:

> It requires all Her Majesty's tact to avoid open conflict, [Gay continued,] for she is constantly meeting decided opposition . . . old men whose splendid obstinacy is invincible; who refuse to take their quota of land on principle, holding to their tribal right to roam at will all over the Reservation. It is of no use to explain to them that the world is so rapidly filling with people that no tribe can longer hold unused land against the clamor of a multitude of homeless men and women; that the earth, in a sense, belongs to all that are upon it and that no man can be allowed to claim more than he can use for his own benefit or for that of others; that no treaty could be enforced that sought to hold

Between two worlds: Alice Fletcher (top, at work) felt herself caught between "the greed of the whites" and the reluctance of the Nez Percé (shown gathered in council above) to give up any part of their land.

back the living tide that had set in upon this continent; that any tribe of Indians that stood out against that flood would be overwhelmed. . . . Nor is it worthwhile to try persuasion upon the chiefs who, Her Majesty says, "oppose because land in severalty breaks up completely their tribal power and substitutes civilization and law."

Fletcher kept at it for four years, and when she was finished had made over 2,000 Nez Percé allotments — some 175,000 acres. Then she and Jane Gay returned to Cambridge, Massachusetts, where Fletcher had been awarded a lifetime fellowship at Harvard's Peabody Museum. "In the week's journey [home] across the continent,"

SOONERS

By the mid-1880s, the biggest single area in the West suitable for farming and still largely untouched by white settlement was Indian Territory. Representatives of some fifty-five tribes now called it home, but there were large tracts within it upon which no one lived.

One of these — 2 million empty and unassigned acres — was called "the Oklahoma District," and the army was soon kept busy driving from it armed parties of squatters from Kansas who called themselves "Boomers." Furious lobbying eventually succeeded where invasion failed, and Congress finally voted to buy out all Indian claims to the Oklahoma District.

On the morning of April 22, 1889, some 100,000 eager Boomers surrounded it, waiting for the signal to storm in and stake their claims.

At precisely noon, the bugles blew and the Boomers started forward. "The last barrier of savagery in the United States was broken down," said a reporter for *Harper's Weekly.* "Moved by the same impulse each driver lashed his horses furiously; . . . each man on foot caught his breath and started forward."

Some pedaled bicycles. Others jumped aboard special Santa Fe trains that steamed along slowly so as not to give their passengers too great an advantage over those on foot.

Many headed for the sites of new towns about to be born: Oklahoma City, Stillwater, Kingfisher, Norman — and Guthrie, which was to become the provisional territorial capital. There, a wild scramble began to stake claims on parcels of land, but the choicest lots had already been taken by settlers — known as "sooners"— who had illegally slipped through the army lines the night before. "Men who had expected to lay out the town-site were grievously disappointed at their first glimpse of their proposed scene of operations," a reporter noted. "The slope east of the railway at Guthrie station was [already] dotted white with tents and sprinkled thick with men running about in all directions."

Others staked claims in what turned out to be the middle of the streets and had to be driven out later by armed marshals. By nightfall, all 1.92 million acres of land in the district had been claimed, and Guthrie was a tent city with 15,000 residents.

By noon of the following day, the new citizens of Guthrie began choosing their mayor. It wasn't easy. There were two candidates and no ballots. Two lines were formed and each man's vote was tallied, but so many voters ran to the back of the line to vote again that the whole business had to be done over.

Everything was improvised. A blacksmith saw the need for a dentist, declared himself one, and advertised his skills by hanging the teeth he extracted on a string outside his tent. Three men without a cent between them simply exchanged worthless notes for $10,000, declared capitalization of $30,000, and opened a bank. Deposits were kept in a potbellied stove until they could afford to buy a vault. An elderly woman named Button Mary, who had already performed the same function in other western towns, opened for business, sewing buttons back on bachelors' shirts for ten cents each. Within five days, wood-frame buildings were being banged together along Main Street. And by the time Guthrie was five months old, it had a hotel, three newspapers, three general stores — and fifty saloons.

Within a little over a year, the Oklahoma District became Oklahoma Territory. In the next few years, five more "runs" would open up all but a few scattered patches of Indian Territory to settlement. But in the end, when Oklahoma became a state in 1906, it was Oklahoma City that became the state capital. Guthrie was left out in the cold.

The last — and largest — of the Oklahoma land rushes gets under way (above) on September 16, 1893. Within hours some 6 million acres of land — the so-called Cherokee Outlet — had been carved up among nearly 100,000 newcomers.

Guthrie going up: the land office (left), where claims were registered; two armed sooners (opposite, left) whose weapons ensured that no one dared jump their claim to a choice site between the land office and the depot; and Hilarity Roost or Boomers Retreat (opposite, right), to which all of Guthrie's brand-new citizens were cordially invited once they'd completed their onerous paperwork

HILARITY ROOST or
BOOMERS RETREAT.

Gay wrote as they were packing up, "we shall have time to review the outcome of our earnest endeavors, so far as it has been revealed to us. But if it has been well for us, and well for the Indian . . . is not for us to know. We can only leave the question among the unsolvable, whose multitude grows ever greater as life goes on."

In 1895, the remaining half million unallotted acres of Nez Percé tribal land were declared surplus and opened for homesteading. Two thousand whites rushed in to file claims on the first morning alone. By 1910, there would be 30,000 whites within the Nez Percé reservation — and just 1,500 Nez Percé. "It will only be a few generations," the government Indian agent predicted, "before the tribe is extinct." All across the West, the story would be the same. Before the Dawes Act, some 150 million acres still remained in Indian hands. Within twenty years, two-thirds of that land would be gone, too.

If the Californios could all gather together to breathe a lament, it would reach Heaven as a moving sigh which would cause fear and consternation in the Universe! What misery!

Mariano Guadalupe Vallejo

RELICS

During his long life, Mariano Guadalupe Vallejo had fought California Indians on behalf of Spain, commanded *Californio* troops for Mexico, welcomed the Americans to the Pacific coast — and then watched as they dispossessed him of his lands and ignored his culture. While many of his children adjusted well to the new, American California, Vallejo worried that the legacy of his people was being forgotten. His father had been one of the first settlers of San Francisco, yet now the city's schools taught French and German, but not Spanish. Immigrants from other countries, he complained, were "fawned upon while we Californios are despised. . . . If the Californios could all gather together to breathe a lament, it would reach Heaven as a moving sigh which would cause fear and consternation in the Universe! What misery!"

Mexican American mine workers somewhere in the Southwest, 1890s

An agricultural workers' encampment in southern California, ca. 1900. As Mexican Americans left their own village lands to make their homes in cities, many still found themselves in the countryside at harvesttime, gathering crops belonging to others.

He was hounded by lawyers, plagued by debts. "Everyone is money-mad," he said. "Everyone barks, cries, and whines for it." His once vast estate was reduced to fewer than three hundred acres. With his wife, Benicia, Vallejo now lived in a New England–style cottage in Sonoma that he called Lachryma Montis — Tear of the Mountain. But he sometimes visited his old adobe home near Petaluma, now decaying from neglect. "I compare that old relic with myself . . ." he wrote, "ruins and dilapidation. What a difference between then and now. Then, youth, strength and riches; now age, weakness and poverty."

Friends petitioned Congress for a pension for the old man, recognizing "his kindness to immigrants and his noble conduct" during California's transition from Mexican to American rule. But before any action could be taken, Vallejo died on January 21, 1890.

By then, hundreds of Mexicans were crossing the border into the United States every month. Some were escaping political turbulence and crushing poverty. Others were lured by the promise of jobs — working in mines, on the railroads, or in the farm fields and orange and lemon groves made possible by irrigation. Their reasons for coming north were more or less the same as those that drove Americans west:

"My intention is to get a good job and save some money and start out for myself," said one, "for one can make good money and there is always work."

In the next thirty years, 1.5 million men, women, and children — 10 percent of the population of Mexico — would come north in pursuit of that dream, following many of the same routes once taken by Coronado and the conquistadors.

WOUNDED KNEE

In 1890, the United States undertook the last census of the nineteenth century. Back when some of the Americans counted in that census had been born, everything west of the Mississippi lay beyond the boundaries of the nation. Now, after a rush of statehood ceremonies that brought Montana, Washington, North and South Dakota, Idaho, and Wyoming into the Union in the space of two years, only Utah, Arizona, New Mexico, and Oklahoma remained as territories.

Nearly 17 million people lived between the Mississippi and the Pacific — three times the population of the entire nation when Thomas Jefferson completed the Louisiana Purchase in 1803 and propelled his countrymen toward the western sea. "This census completes the history of a century," wrote the man who directed it; "a century of progress and achievement unequaled in the world's history." Nearly 2 million square miles had been "redeemed from wilderness and brought into the service of man."

No Indian people anywhere in the West now lived freely on their own land — and even the lands on which they were now forced to huddle were being broken up under the Allotment Act.

Lakota lands had yet to be allotted, but a commission headed by General George Crook had managed, by playing the chiefs off against one another, to talk them into giving up some 9 million acres, nonetheless.

Sitting Bull had done everything he could to keep his people from signing away their land. "[The whites] will try to gain possession of the last piece of ground we possess," he warned them. "Let us stand as one family as we did before the white people led us astray." In the end, he was ignored. Afterward, a reporter asked him how the Indians felt about losing their lands. "Indians!" he said. "There are no Indians left but me!"

The Lakota had been assured they would continue to receive the rations their previous treaties guaranteed them. But as soon as the commission left for the East, Congress cut appropriations for all reservation Indians everywhere. Rations were drastically reduced. It was a dry summer and the crops failed. Children went hungry. There were epidemics of measles, influenza, and whooping cough. "They made us many promises," one old man said, "more than I can remember, but they never kept but one; they promised to take our land and they took it."

Pawnee ghost dancer's shirt

That same summer, reports began to filter in from reservations all over the Plains of a new religion that seemed to promise a revival of the old ways. Its

Wovoka (top), the Paiute shaman whose message of renewal was entirely peaceful, and Kicking Bear, the Lakota who brought a more militant version of it to Standing Rock

prophet was a Paiute named Wovoka, and the gospel of salvation he proclaimed, filled with Christian as well as Indian elements, was simple:

> My brothers, I bring to you the promise of a day in which there will be no white man to lay his hand on the bridle of the Indians' horse; when the red men of the prairie will rule the world. . . . I bring you word from your fathers the ghosts, that they are marching now to join you, led by the Messiah who came once to live on earth with the white man but was killed by them.

Men and women were first to purify themselves and forswear alcohol and violence. "You must not hurt anybody or do harm to anyone," Wovoka said. "You must not fight. Do right always." Then they were to dance in a large circle, chanting and appealing to the spirits of their ancestors. If their faith was strong enough, Wovoka promised, the old world of their fathers would return, the whites would vanish, the buffalo would cover the earth again.

It was called the "ghost dance," and James Mooney, director of the Bureau of American Ethnology, understood its appeal:

> When the race lies crushed and groaning under an alien yoke, how natural is the dream of a redeemer . . . who shall return from exile or awake from some long sleep to drive out the usurper and win back for his people what they have lost. The hope becomes a faith and the faith becomes the creed of priests and prophets, until the hero is a god and the dream a religion, looking to some great miracle of nature for its culmination and accomplishment.

One day that autumn, a Miniconjou from the Cheyenne River agency came to see Sitting Bull. His name was Kicking Bear and, with his brother-in-law, Short Bull, he had returned from a train trip to the Far West where he had seen the prophet Wovoka and learned from him of the great renewal that was coming the following spring. The dancing had already begun at Cheyenne River and Rosebud and Pine Ridge, Kicking Bear said; Sitting Bull's people at Standing Rock should start dancing, too.

Sitting Bull was concerned that the whites would send soldiers to stop the dancing. Kicking Bear reassured him. If the dancers dressed as Wovoka had told them to dress — in white shirts, painted with special symbols — no bullet could harm them. This was no part of Wovoka's teaching, and Sitting Bull remained skeptical, but he agreed to let Kicking Bear stay and teach the ghost dance to the people of Standing Rock.

They sang as they danced, "Mother, hand me my sharp knife,/Mother, hand me my sharp knife,/Here come the buffalo returning —/Mother, hand me my sharp knife." And they sang, "Mother, do come back!/Mother, do come back!/My little brother is crying for you —/My father says so!"

At all the Lakota agencies, people began to dance. Some moved out of their cabins into teepees, as in the old days. Children abandoned their schoolrooms, one Pine Ridge pupil recalled.

> That part about the dead returning was what appealed to me. To think I should see my dear mother, grandmother, brothers, and sisters, again! . . . Soon fifty of us, little boys, about eight to ten, started out across country . . . almost thirty

The only known photograph of the Lakota ghost dancers at Pine Ridge, made by a small-town photographer, J. E. Meddaugh, in September of 1890, when whites still considered the new ceremony merely a curiosity

> miles. There on the Porcupine Creek thousands of Lakota people were in camp. . . .
>
> The people, wearing the sacred shirts and feathers, . . . formed a ring. We [boys] were in it. All joined hands. Everyone was respectful and quiet, expecting something wonderful to happen. . . . The leaders beat time and sang as the people danced, going round to the left in a sidewise step. Occasionally, someone . . . fell unconscious into the center and lay there "dead." After a while, many lay about in that condition. They were now "dead" and seeing their dear ones. As each one came to, she, or he, slowly sat up and looked about, bewildered, and then began wailing inconsolably.

Although most Indians had nothing to do with the ghost dancers, some Indian agents grew frightened. To them, the mysterious dancing and the boasts about magic shirts that could not be pierced by bullets sounded like warnings of war.

No one was more frightened than Daniel Royer, agent at Pine Ridge. A political appointee, utterly ignorant of his charges and so often alarmed by them that the Lakota called him "Young Man Afraid of Indians," he was sure he was about to be attacked. On November 12, 1890, he wired the army for help: "Indians are dancing in the snow and are wild and crazy. . . . We need protection and we need it now. The leaders should be arrested and confined at some military post until the matter is quieted, and this should be done at once."

General Nelson A. Miles was dispatched with 5,000 troops, including the Seventh Cavalry, the successor to Custer's old command. Scores of reporters came along, too, eager to cover a new Indian war. No one was sure what Miles planned to do. Miles wasn't either. The West had changed since he had last waged war there. "It would be unwise to say anything at this time," he told reporters. "Anything I might say would be telegraphed over the country. Indians now have young men who read English perfectly well, and they no longer depend upon runners to take their news from camp to camp. They utilize the mails, and keep posted with regard to current events affecting their interests."

The ghost dancers at Pine Ridge and Rosebud, frightened that the soldiers had come to attack them, fled to a remote plateau surrounded by cliffs that nervous whites began calling "the Stronghold."

At Standing Rock, Sitting Bull now actively encouraged his people to dance. Nothing that might lead to a return to the old ways should be overlooked — and no one, white or Lakota, was to interfere with the practice of their faith. His old enemy, agent James McLaughlin, now became convinced that Sitting Bull was the "high priest and leading apostle of this latest absurdity." If he were removed from the scene, McLaughlin concluded, the whole business might just blow over. A message from Lieutenant Bull Head of the Oglala police provided him with the excuse he needed to act:

Coup de grâce: Sergeant Red Tomahawk (center) of the Lakota police fired the fatal bullet into Sitting Bull's head.

> Sitting Bull has received a letter from the Pine Ridge outfit asking him to come over there, as God was to appear to them. Sitting Bull's people want him to go, but he has sent a letter to you asking for your permission, and if you do not give it he is going to go anyway; he has been fitting up his horses for a long ride and will go on horseback in case he is pursued. [I] would like to arrest him at once before he has the chance of giving them the slip. . . .

When McLaughlin heard that Sitting Bull was planning to leave Standing Rock to join the ghost dancers in the Pine Ridge stronghold, he determined to stop him. Forty-three Indian policemen were sent to do the job. Two troops of cavalry were to follow along at a distance, so as not to make a bad situation worse. They were to intervene only if the police ran into trouble.

Early in the morning of December 15, 1890, Lakota policemen burst into Sitting Bull's house and ordered him to his feet. His wives began to wail. The police pushed him toward the door. Lieutenant Bull Head and an officer named Shave Head grabbed his arms, and Sergeant Red Tomahawk walked behind as they started toward the wagon that was to carry the prisoner back to the agency.

But Sitting Bull's followers were now awake. They began to taunt the police. One of Sitting Bull's adopted sons urged his father to resist. Sitting Bull slowed, apparently unsure what to do.

The police shoved him toward the wagon. One of his supporters, a man named Catch-the-Bear, raised his rifle and fired into Lieutenant Bull Head's side. As the policeman fell, he fired his revolver into Sitting Bull's chest. At the same time, Red Tomahawk put a bullet through his head. The cavalry rushed in, and when it was all over, Sitting Bull and eight of his followers lay dead. The last of his visions had come true; his own Lakota people had killed him.

Four Indian policemen were also dead, and two more mortally wounded. One of them, Shave Head, later asked agent McLaughlin if he had done well. The agent nodded that he had. Then he asked for a Catholic priest so that he might be married to his wife in the church before he died.

We tried to run but they shot us like we were buffalo. I know there are some good white people, but the soldiers must be mean to shoot children and women.

Louise Weasel Bear

Sitting Bull's grieving followers, fearful now that the soldiers would attack them, hurried toward the Cheyenne River reservation, where they joined a Miniconjou band led by a chief named Big Foot. He had once been an enthusiastic ghost dancer but was now ill with pneumonia, and no longer certain that the world would truly be transformed in the spring. Red Cloud and other chiefs, seeking to avoid further trouble with the soldiers who now seemed to be swarming everywhere, asked him to bring his band in to Pine Ridge and see if there weren't some way to reconcile things before more blood was shed.

General Miles misunderstood what was happening. Convinced that Big Foot's Miniconjou, their numbers swollen by refugees from Sitting Bull's band, intended to make a stand in the stronghold, he ordered his men to intercept them.

Colonel John Forsyth and the Seventh Cavalry caught up with Big Foot near Porcupine Creek three days after Christmas. Big Foot rode in a wagon, too sick even to sit up but with a white flag above his head as evidence that he meant no harm to anyone.

The soldiers transferred him to an army ambulance and then led his band down to a little creek called Wounded Knee for the night. There were 120 men and 230 women and children. The soldiers distributed rations. An army surgeon did what he could for Big Foot. But the soldiers also posted four Hotchkiss guns on the top of a rise overlooking the camp. If there was trouble their shells would tear through the whole length of the encampment. Big Foot and his people could not possibly get away. Both sides were sure of it. The Lakota would be disarmed the next day.

"The following morning there was a bugle call," a Lakota named Dewey Beard remembered. "Then I saw the soldiers mounting their horses and surrounding us. It was announced that all men should come to the center for a talk. . . . Big Foot was brought out of his tent and sat . . . and the older men were gathered around him. . . ."

Colonel Forsyth asked Big Foot if his people had any arms. A few were handed over and placed in a pile. They were old weapons, for the most part.

Forsyth demanded to know where the Indians' repeating Winchesters were hidden. Big Foot denied they had any. Forsyth ordered his men to search the whole village. As his troops began moving from teepee to teepee, confiscating knives and axes from the women, and sometimes seizing a repeating rifle, a reporter named Charles Allen noted something else: ". . . eight or ten Indian boys dressed in the gray school uniforms of that period. The fun they were having as they played 'bucking horse,' 'leap frog,' and similar games, carried the mind for a fleeting moment back to the days of boyhood."

Then, a medicine man began to dance, pausing from time to time to throw pinches of dust into the air. "Do not fear," he shouted to the warriors, "but let your

Three of the four breech-loading Hotchkiss guns that did such deadly work at Wounded Knee

hearts be strong. Many soldiers are about us and have many bullets, but I am assured the bullets cannot penetrate us. . . . If they do come toward us, they will float away like dust in the air."

"He was an orator of the first water," Charles Allen recalled. "Every gesture and body movement flowed rhythmically. . . . Suddenly, scooping up a handful of dirt he tossed it scattering in the air, and with eyes turned toward heaven, implored the Great Spirit to scatter the soldiers likewise. I remarked to some troopers nearby that if the man were an ordained minister of some Christian church he would convert the world."

A soldier spotted a rifle beneath one man's blanket. Forsyth ordered him disarmed. The soldiers did not know the man was deaf and snatched impatiently at his blanket. He pulled away, raising the rifle above his head. "If they had left him alone he was going to put his gun down . . ." Dewey Beard remembered. "They grabbed him and spun him in the east direction. He was still unconcerned even then. . . . They came on and grabbed the gun. Right after there was a report of a gun, quite loud."

Snow blanketed Wounded Knee after the shooting stopped, and 146 dead Lakota were left where they had fallen for three days, then buried in a mass grave on the top of the hill from which the Hotchkiss guns had fired into their camp.

The soldiers opened fire with rifles, revolvers, struggled hand to hand, then the Hotchkiss guns began to hurl exploding shells into the teepees. The Lakota did their best to fight back. "I was badly wounded and pretty weak, too," Dewey Beard recalled. "I looked down the ravine and saw a lot of women coming and crying. . . . I saw soldiers on both sides of the ravine shoot at them until they had killed every one of them. . . . One woman was crying, 'Mother! Mother!' She was wounded under her chin, close to her throat and the bullet passed a braid of her hair and carried some of it into the wound. Her mother had been shot down behind her."

When the shooting finally stopped, perhaps 250 Lakota — men, women, and children — were dead. "It was a thing to melt the heart of a man, if it was stone," said one soldier, "to see those little children with their bodies shot to pieces. . . ."

Charles Allen had watched it all in horror:

> While the officers moved among the bodies, feeling that it might not be in order for a civilian to join them, I walked around east of the guards viewing the sad spectacle. On reaching the corner of the green where the schoolboys had been so happy in their sports but a short time before, there was spread before me the saddest picture I had seen or was to see thereafter, for on that spot of their playful choice were scattered the prostrate bodies of all those fine little Indian boys, cold in death. . . . The gun-fire [had] blazed across their playground in a way that permitted no escape. They must have fallen like grass before the sickle.

Dead, too, were twenty-five soldiers.

Wounded Lakota and wounded troopers alike were loaded onto army wagons and taken to the Holy Cross Episcopal Church at Pine Ridge, its walls still hung with Christmas decorations. "Pews were torn from their fastenings and armsful of hay fetched by Indian helpers," a nurse remembered. "Upon a layer of this we spread quilts and blankets taken from our own beds. The victims were lifted as gently as possible and laid in two long rows on the floor — a pathetic array of young girls and women and babes in arms, little children, and a few men, all pierced with bullets."

"A young girl," another nurse recalled, "who had a ghost shirt on underneath her clothes [said,] 'They told me if I put this on the bullets would not go through and I believed them. Now see where we are.'"

The fighting stuttered on for nearly two weeks. When angry warriors set agency buildings afire in retaliation for the killing at Wounded Knee, Colonel Forsyth led the Seventh Cavalry in pursuit, clumsily failed to secure the surrounding hillsides, and suddenly found himself surrounded by angry Lakota, just as Custer had been fifteen years before. This time, however, troops of the all-black Ninth Cavalry came riding to the rescue.

Some 4,000 ghost dancers remained at large, including 1,000 warriors, all huddled together in one big village. Miles, who blamed Forsyth for the slaughter at Wounded Knee, was determined not to have more such killing if he could help it. He surrounded the village, then drew the noose tight slowly enough to give the Indians plenty of time to think about the folly of further resistance.

Finally, on January 15, 1891, the ghost dancers surrendered. Kicking Bear, the man who had brought news of the ghost dance to the Lakota agencies, was one of the last to turn over his rifle to General Miles.

THE OWENS RIVER IS OURS

Between 1890 and 1904, the population of Los Angeles mushroomed from 50,000 to nearly 200,000. There was already too little water in dry years to keep the city parks green, and it seemed clear that Los Angeles could not grow much further without some new source of supply. But Los Angeles had to grow — its whole economy was based on frenzied boosterism. "If Los Angeles runs out of water for one week," warned the head of its Water Department, William Mulholland, "the city within a year will not have a population of 100,000 people. A city quickly finds its level, and that level is its water supply."

And the water Los Angeles wanted was 250 miles away, across the Sierra Nevada in the Owens River that wound through a high valley 250 miles northeast of Los Angeles. It was home to several thousand small ranchers who had dug canals to irrigate their apple orchards and fields of hay and alfalfa with snowmelt from the Sierras.

In September of 1904, two strangers traveled through the valley. They were careful not to identify themselves, but one was Fred Eaton, a shrewd financial operator and former mayor of Los Angeles.

The other was William Mulholland himself. An Irish immigrant, he'd served briefly as a merchant seaman, tried lumberjacking and panning for gold, then joined the privately owned L.A. Water Company as a lowly ditch-tender. A big man with infinite energy and a remarkable memory — he is said to have committed to memory the location of every pipe and valve and fire hydrant in the city system — he was made superintendent just eight years later, when the city bought the company and began to run it on its own. Mulholland believed rivers existed only to be used: if it were left up to him, he once said, he would have the Yosemite Valley carefully photographed and then "build a dam from one side of that valley to the other and *stop the goddamned waste.*"

The people of the Owens Valley were optimistic that year. The brand-new federal Bureau of Reclamation had promised to improve the irrigation system that made their farms possible. But Mulholland and Eaton had other plans. Mulholland believed he could build a system of aqueducts and siphons and tunnels that would take Owens River water right through the Sierras and on into Los Angeles — provided he got the funds.

Eaton hurried to Washington and quietly helped convince the Bureau of Reclamation to abandon its plan to aid the Owens Valley: the water would benefit many more people if it could be moved to Los Angeles, instead. Then, he went back to the valley and, posing as an eccentric but enormously wealthy rancher, began buying up land and water rights. In cooperation with a clandestine syndicate of investors — unknown even to Mulholland — he also bought up large tracts in the still-dry San Fernando Valley, where plans called for a vast reservoir from which water would one day be sold to farmers.

Mulholland and Eaton then persuaded the city's voters to pass the largest bond issue in the history of the United States up to that time — $23 million. "Owens River is ours," said the Los Angeles *Times*, "and our business now is to hustle and bring it here and make Los Angeles the garden spot of the earth and the home of millions of contented people."

The dreamer and his dream: William Mulholland (above) and some of the mules that outperformed tractors and kept his project moving across the Mojave Desert

At last, William Mulholland could get to work. Neither personal profit nor politics ever interested him: once, asked if he wanted to run for mayor, he answered that he'd sooner give birth to a porcupine — backward. He lived only to build, and now faced an engineering challenge that rivaled those faced by the builders of the transcontinental railroad and the Suez Canal. Fifty-three tunnels had to be blasted through the mountains; 500 miles of trails and roads had to be built; 120 miles of railroad track laid; 170 miles of power lines brought in from two specially built power plants. Five thousand to 6,000 men had to be fed and housed and doctored while they inched their way across the Mojave Desert — immigrant Irishmen, Greeks, Austrians, Serbians, Hungarians, Italians, and grizzled veterans of the West's gold and silver strikes, a few of whom had worked the Comstock Lode before the Civil War. The 110-degree heat spoiled food moments after it was cooked. Blowing sand destroyed twenty-eight Caterpillar tractors that had to be replaced by fifteen hundred mules. Forty-three men died in the six years it took to finish the job.

But finally, on November 5, 1913, before a huge crowd at Exposition Park, valves were turned and Owens River water rushed down the spillway for the first time. "There it is!" said Mulholland. "Take it!" Thanks largely to Mulholland, Los Angeles soon surpassed San Francisco to become the biggest and most powerful city in the West.

The Owens Valley never recovered from its loss. "Ten years ago this was a wonderful valley," Will Rogers wrote in 1923, "with one quarter of a million acres of fruit and alfalfa. But Los Angeles had to have more water for its Chamber of Commerce to drink more toasts to its growth, more water to dilute its orange juice and more water for its geraniums to delight the tourists. . . ."

The first water from the Owens River cascades down the last sluiceway of the Los Angeles aqueduct and into the San Fernando Valley, November 5, 1913.

SEEING EDEN

The first quarter century of the world's first national park, Yellowstone, did not go smoothly. Just five years after the park was established in 1872, Chief Joseph's Nez Percé had raced through Yellowstone, killing several tourists along the way.

In 1882, during an expedition through the park, General Phil Sheridan had discovered the park's minimal management in shambles. Poachers were indiscriminately slaughtering the wildlife — 4,000 elk in one winter alone and buffalo, whose heads were worth three hundred dollars apiece because there were so few left. Sheridan also learned that a company run by the Northern Pacific Railroad was being granted monopoly rights to develop the park at a ridiculously low rent.

Launching a national campaign to protect the wildlife and keep the park under federal control, Sheridan brought President Chester A. Arthur to Yellowstone the next year.

In 1886, the army took over. It supervised Yellowstone for the next thirty-two years, brought poaching under control, and with the help of breeding stock from Charles Goodnight's private herd in Texas, helped save the buffalo from extinction.

Meanwhile, more and more people were coming to view Yellowstone's marvels. By the turn of the century, tourist traffic was increasing throughout the West. Ranchers who for years had freely hosted eastern friends seeking a taste of western life began accepting payment for their hospitality, and the dude ranch was born. Elegant hotels went up, too — on the rim of the Grand Canyon, in the Rockies, in Yellowstone itself. And still the visitors kept coming, eager to see for themselves the West they had only read about till now.

In 1913, after intense lobbying by the new American Automobile Association, cars were permitted for the first time in Yosemite National Park. Two years later, they entered Yellowstone. The number of visitors to both parks immediately doubled. To help cope with them all, Congress created the National Park Service in 1916. Eventually, tourism would become the biggest industry in the West.

Well-shaded hikers at rest on the Minerva Terrace, Yellowstone, 1888

I heard the other day that a question has been raised as to whether automobiles should be admitted in the Yosemite Valley. May a word be permitted on that subject? If Adam had known what harm the Serpent was going to work, he would have tried to prevent him from finding lodgment in Eden; and if you stop to realize what the result of the automobile will be in that wonderful, that incomparable valley, you will keep it out. . . . Do not let the Serpent enter Eden at all.

James Bryce, 1912

Seeing Yosemite from the comfort of one's parlor (opposite, bottom) and from horseback (above)

The first automobiles chug their way into Yosemite, 1913.

WHY IN HEAVEN'S NAME THIS HASTE?

Gentlemen, why in heaven's name this haste? You have time enough. No enemy threatens you. No volcano will rise from beneath you. Ages and ages lie before you. Why sacrifice the present to the future, fancying that you will be happier when your fields teem with wealth and your cities with people? In Europe we have cities wealthier and more populous than yours and we are not happy. You dream of your posterity; but your posterity will look back to yours as the golden age, and envy those who first burst into this silent, splendid Nature, who first lifted up their axes upon these tall trees and lined these waters with busy wharves. Why, then, seek to complete in a few decades what [took] the other nations of the world thousands of years. . . ? Why do things rudely and ill which need to be done well, seeing that the welfare of your descendants may turn upon them? Why, in your hurry to subdue and utilize Nature, squander her splendid gifts? . . . Why hasten the advent of that threatening day when the vacant spaces of the continent shall all have been filled, and the poverty or discontent of the older States shall find no outlet? You have opportunities such as mankind has never had before, and may never have again. Your work is great and noble; it is done for a future longer and vaster than our conceptions can embrace. Why not make its outlines and beginnings worthy of these destinies. . . ?

James Bryce

Smoke belching from the smelters that surrounded Butte, Montana (above), was so thick that one perpetually blanketed neighborhood was called "Seldom Seen."

Undergrowth ablaze after lumbermen clear-cut a slope in Washington State, about 1900

ON THE LONG HORIZON LINE

On October 20, 1905, the Rawlins-to-Lander stagecoach rattled north toward the Sweetwater River in Wyoming. Al Dougherty, a hardened veteran of the lonely trail, held the reins. He had been driving the same route during the terrible winter of 1886–87, when a blizzard stranded him and a young woman passenger. Before help finally arrived, the woman froze to death, and Dougherty was so frostbitten that he lost six fingers, half of one foot, and all of the other. His nickname now was "Peggy."

This day his passenger was twenty-three-year-old Ethel Waxham, daughter of a prominent Denver physician and a recent graduate of Wellesley College, where she had studied classical literature, learned four languages, and earned a Phi Beta Kappa key. She dabbled in poetry, enjoyed amateur theatricals, and was voraciously curious about the world. During one school vacation, she had volunteered for work in the slums of New York City. "I do not want to see one side of life only, but many," she explained to a friend. And she soaked up experience:

> Peggy Dougherty . . . is tall and grizzled. They say that when he goes to dances they make him take the spike out of the bottom of his wooden leg. Our way lay up to Crook's Gap, the coldest part of the road where the night before, the thermometer had registered zero. . . . [Y]e gods, how he could swear. We switched him off to telling stories of the cold winter of '86 and the old times. . . . "The winters have not been so severe lately," he said. "No," said [another passenger], "and we haven't had a blizzard this summer."

Now, she had accepted her first full-time job: as the teacher in a one-room school in the isolated center of Wyoming, in a county named Frémont, in honor of the pathfinder who had first mapped it in the 1840s.

> At last we saw the little school house of logs, fourteen by sixteen with a good [sod] roof, almost flat coming low over the sides. . . . The whole was put up, I believe, at an original expenditure of seventy-five dollars. . . . We soon had the place swept out and arranged, brought in the books that we had carried over,

Miss Ethel Waxham as she looked at Wellesley College shortly before heading west in search of adventure

The Rawlins-to-Lander stage, with Peggy Dougherty holding the reins. "Ye gods," Ethel Waxham noted, "how he could swear."

> and set the traps for the mountain rats that had left traces of themselves over the place. . . . The door has had some passerby's six shooter emptied into it.

She had seven students, ages eight to sixteen, and lived with a ranch family, and so soon became acquainted with the customs of a place where the nearest neighbor lived miles away, and Lander, the closest "city" — population 1,000 — was visited just once a year. She took it all in, with what one friend called "her combination of strength and the gentlest charm — welded by that flashing mind."

> People passing, we call company. Sometimes no one comes by for days. Sometimes many pass. A Mormon boy . . . Old Hanley . . . [and] Ted Abra, one of the roustabouts. . . . He enjoys the reputation of being cattle thief and horse wrangler. Roy McLaughlin is another of the gang. They went by once with about fifty head of horses. . . .
>
> Bill [Bruce] is an Irishman. . . . He has a childlike gentleness and drollery of manner that is either innocence itself or simulated. He came over to this country and found a five-dollar gold piece on the sidewalk. "Come over, Brothers," he wrote home. "It's all true." Later, he got a job of carrying bricks. "Come over, Brothers," he wrote again. "All I have to do is to carry bricks up to the fourth floor in a hod and the man up there does all the work."

Among those who began showing up with considerable regularity, despite the fact that his home was an eleven-hour ride away, was a sheep rancher named John Galloway Love.

Ethel Waxham out riding near her parents' home in Denver

> Mr. Love is a Scotchman about thirty-five years old. At first sight he made me think of a hired man, as he lounged stiffly on the couch, in overalls, his feet covered with enormous red and black-striped stockings edged with blue around the top, that reached to his knees. . . . His face was kindly, with shrewd blue twinkling eyes. A moustache grew over his mouth, like willows bending over a brook. But his voice was most peculiar and characteristic. Close analysis fails to find the charm of it. A little Scotch dialect, a little slow drawl, a little nasal quality, a bit of falsetto once in a while, and a tone as if he were speaking out of doors. There is a kind of twinkle in his voice as well as in his eyes, and he is full of quaint turns of speech, and unusual expressions. For he is not a common sheepherder, [it is said,] but a mutton-aire, or sheep baron.

John Galloway Love

He was born on a Wisconsin farm to Scottish parents. His mother died shortly after his birth, and his father, a professional photographer and lecturer, had taken him back to Scotland, then died when the boy was only ten. After a few years in an orphanage, he joined his four older sisters in Custer County, Nebraska, where they had each taken homesteads and also worked as schoolteachers. He was a bright boy — he could recite by memory Sir Walter Scott's "The Lady of the Lake" in its entirety — but also high-spirited.

Expelled from the University of Nebraska in 1891 for a foolish prank, he invested his savings in two horses and a buggy, and headed for Wyoming. When his horses died after drinking poisoned water, Love walked a hundred miles to the Sweetwater country. There, he had worked as a sheepherder and cowboy, and, some said, had also been a friend of the outlaw Butch Cassidy. In any case, after seven straight years of living on the range, without a roof over his head, Love had decided to start his own ranch on a treeless stretch along Muskrat Creek. Why, a friend asked, had he chosen "that God-forsaken lonesome place"? "Because," Love answered, "it has lots of room and that is what I want." President Theodore Roosevelt had signed Love's papers under the new Desert Land Act, granting him outright ownership of 640 acres and, because of the water on it, effective control of a thousand square miles, as well. He had big dreams for his land — thousands of sheep and cattle, irrigated grain fields, and hay meadows and fruit orchards.

Now he had another dream as well. Nearly from the moment he first saw her, he wanted Ethel Waxham for his wife. But he was not her only suitor, and when he proposed marriage, she refused, and thought no more about it. When the school year ended, she returned home, and entered the University of Colorado for a master's degree. But memories of the seven months she had spent in the wilds of Wyoming were rarely far from her mind.

> I know a land where the gray hills lie
> Eternally still, under the sky,
> Where all the might of suns and moons
> That pass in the quiet of nights and noons
> Leave never a sign of the flight of time
> On the long sublime horizon line —

And a steady stream of letters from John Love kept those memories fresh:

It is a cruel country as well as a beautiful one. Men seem here only on sufferance.

Ethel Waxham

An isolated Wyoming ranch, about 1908

Muskrat, Wyoming.
September 12, 1906
Dear Miss Waxham,

. . . [When I received your letter] I lay awake . . . out in the sagebrush curled up in my buggy robes and thought and studied astronomy. . . . You have no idea how pleased I was to hear from you and it is beyond my pencil to express the satisfaction I felt. Thank you very much for the picture. It does not flatter you any, but at the same time it is very lifelike. . . .

Of course it will cause many a sharp twinge and heartache to have to take "no" for an answer, but I will never blame you for it in the least and I will never be sorry that I met you. . . . I know the folly of hoping that your "no" is not final, but in spite of that knowledge, in spite of my better judgment, and in spite of all I can do to the contrary, I know that I will hope until the day that you are married. Only then I will know that the sentence is irrevocable. . . .

Yours Sincerely,
John G. Love

John Love's sheep wagon (above) and one of his hired hands (opposite) hard at work on one of the two dams Love hoped would turn his ranch into a garden

November 12, 1906
Dear Miss Waxham,

. . . I know that you have not been brought up to cook and labor. I have never been on the lookout for a slave and would not utter a word of censure if you never learned or if you got ambitious and made a "batch" of biscuits that proved fatal to my favorite dog. I honestly believe that I could idolize you to such an extent as to not utter a harsh word. "Little girl," I will do my level best to win you and will be the happiest mortal on earth if I can see the ring that I wear on my watch chain flash on your finger. It has never been worn by or offered to another. . . .

We had one very hard storm and several herders lost their lives but that I think was their own fault.

February 15, 1907
Dear Mr. Love,

I am fortunate in having two letters from you to answer in one. . . . [T]he days have been comparatively dull. . . . I am too busy for dances here, if I care to go, which I do not. They are prosaic affairs in the boys' fraternity houses — not at all like the "Hailey Ball!" . . . The seven months I spent at the ranch I would not exchange for any other seven months in my life. They seem shorter than seven weeks, even seven days, here.

Dear Miss Waxham,

. . . I for one am glad that your curiosity led you to drift up here to Wyoming and now my supreme desire in life is to persuade you to come back. . . .

In 1907, Ethel received her degree in literature, having written her thesis — "The Dramatic Theory and Practice of Maurice Maeterlinck" — in both French and English. She took a job teaching Latin at a private school in Wisconsin for a year; returned home to be in charge of her father's household; then, in 1909, went to Pueblo, Colorado, as a high school teacher.

Everywhere she went, John Love's letters continued to follow her, steadily weakening her defenses, friendship slowly warming into something else:

> April 3, 1909
> Dear Mr. Love —
> There are reasons galore why I should not write so often. I'm a beast to write at all. It makes you — (maybe?) — think that "no" is not "no," but "perhaps," or "yes," or anything else. . . .
> Good wishes for your busy season from E. W.
> P.S. I like you very much.

> October 12th, 1909
> Dear Miss Waxham,
> . . . I am once more in debt, but if my season of bad luck has come to an end and the winter is not too severe, I will come out with flying colors in the spring. . . . Your picture nicely framed now adorns the wagon. . . .

Meanwhile, through unending labor and with the same determination with which he kept at his courtship, Love continued to develop his ranch. Sheep, cattle, and horse herds grew, then declined, then grew again depending on the whims of weather and markets. To water the grain fields, gardens, and fruit orchards that were still only dreams, he began work on two dams and a long irrigation ditch. All the work had to be done by hand and by horse. He had no dam-building experience, so he consulted government bulletins, the *Encyclopaedia Britannica,* and any passerby with advice to give. He scoured the countryside for abandoned buildings, too, dismantled them, and moved them to his ranch. A saloon, an old hotel, and other buildings from two former stage stations became bunkhouses, sheds, barns, a blacksmith shop on Muskrat

Creek. Around what had once been a hotel dining room, he constructed the large main house. For logs, he had to travel a hundred miles to the Wind River Mountains, then haul them back by wagon. Each trip for a load of twenty took two weeks.

After four years, he was finally ready to try again to persuade Ethel to marry him.

> October 25th, 1909
> Dear Miss Waxham,
> . . . There is no use in my fixing up the house anymore, papering, etc., until I know how it should be done and I won't know that until you see it and say how it ought to be fixed. If you never see it, I don't want it fixed, for I won't live here. *We* could live very comfortably in the wagon while *our* house was being fixed up to suit you if you only would say yes.

> January 1, 1910
> Dear Mr. Love,
> . . . Suppose that you lost everything that you have and a little more; and suppose that for the best reason in the world I wanted you to ask me to say "yes."
> What would you do?
>
> E.

> January 11, 1910
> Dear Miss Waxham,
> . . . *Hope* is far far from being dead yet, "little girl." I have lost over twenty thousand dollars in the last forty days. If I lose another twenty thousand, hope will still live and not even be very feeble. . . . If I were with you, I would throw my arms around you and kiss you and wait eagerly for the kiss that I have waited over four years for.

Finally, in the spring of 1910, Ethel Waxham agreed to be John Love's wife. Many years later, their son David remembered family stories of their honeymoon:

> When my father was sure that my mother was going to marry him he had a sheep wagon built especially to his order. And that was to be the honeymoon sheep wagon. . . . They were married on June 20th, 1910 and it was pretty hot, so they started out for the mountains and from then on there is a blank in our knowledge. Mother rarely discussed it except uh, in times of crisis. And my father never discussed it. But apparently it rained a great deal. The horses got away and they were marooned and never got to the mountains. So the honeymoon was not a romantic success.

I AM NOT AFRAID

By 1900, there were 76 million Americans, more than 20 million of them living in the West. But the number of Native Americans had dropped to only 237,000 — the smallest number the continent had held since the coming of the first Europeans.

"The field of research is speedily narrowing," wrote the explorer and pioneer anthropologist John Wesley Powell, "because of the rapid change in the Indian population now in progress; all habits, customs, and opinions are fading away; even languages are disappearing; and in a very few years it will be impossible to study our North American Indians in their primitive condition except from recorded history."

My little son grew up in the white man's school. He can read books, and he owns cattle and has a farm. He is a leader among our Hidatsa people, helping teach them to follow the white man's road.

He is kind to me. We no longer live in an earth lodge, but in a house with chimneys; and my son's wife cooks by a stove.

But for me, I cannot forget our old ways.

Buffalo Bird Woman

Buffalo Bird Woman (left), her hair cut short in mourning for her husband, and her daughter-in-law, Sioux Woman, prepare prairie turnips.

Since the time they had sheltered Lewis and Clark during the winter of 1804, the Mandan and Hidatsa had been forced to move twice, each time farther up the Missouri. Smallpox and the Lakota had first driven them north during the 1830s. Then the federal government insisted they abandon their communal life, centered on earth lodge villages, and spread out onto individual parcels of land. One by one, families left their villages, and as they departed their lodges were dismantled to prevent them from returning.

Among the last to leave was the extended family of *Waheenee-wea,* Buffalo Bird Woman. She had been born in 1840, the granddaughter of an important Hidatsa medicine man named Missouri River, from whom she learned the traditions of her people. "My old grandfather," she remembered, "taught me of the spirits. . . . 'Not all the spirits are good,' he said. 'Some seek to harm us. The good gods send us buffaloes, and rain to make our corn grow. But it is not well to provoke the gods. My little granddaughter should never laugh at them or speak of them lightly.' "

Buffalo Bird Woman never forgot that admonition.

As a gift, her mother had taught her the ceremonies for making an earth lodge — a special skill that earned her many robes from other families. She learned to weave baskets and mats, make pots from clay, decorate robes with paint and porcupine quills, and was rewarded for her work with a beaded belt of which she said she was as proud "as a war leader of his first scalp."

Buffalo Bird Woman's family moved onto land that her brother had selected while fasting for a vision. It was on a hill the Hidatsa called *Awatahesh,* "hill by itself," and came to be known as Independence.

Her people were told to build square cabins. Building a house was now a man's job — and no longer sacred. But as a link with their past, her husband, Son of Star, placed a buffalo skull over the door, and set their stove in the center of the house, where an earth lodge fire would once have been.

For Buffalo Bird Woman it was not the same: "I think our old way of raising corn is better than the new way taught us by white men," she told a visitor. "Last year, our agent held an agricultural fair . . . and we Indians competed for prizes for the best corn. The corn which I sent to the fair took the first prize. . . . I cultivated the corn exactly as in the old times, with a hoe."

She spoke only her native language, shunned the clothing of white people, and when her husband died in 1906, mourned in the traditional way: she cut her hair short and wore it loose, and sliced off the tip of her little finger. "Sometimes at evening I sit," she said,

> looking out on the big Missouri. The sun sets, and dusk steals over the water. In the shadows I seem again to see our Indian village, with smoke curling upward from the earth lodges; and in the river's roar I hear the yells of the warriors, the laughter of little children as of old. It is but an old woman's dream. Again I see but shadows and hear only the roar of the river; and tears come into my eyes. Our Indian life, I know, is gone forever.

As a young man, Buffalo Bird Woman's brother, Wolf C. Chief, had hunted buffalo, become a successful warrior, learned sacred songs, and gone on vision quests — all in hopes of becoming a leader of his people. But unlike his sister, who resisted change, Wolf Chief was quick to adopt new ways, not just to survive, but to succeed. "My people often talk against me," he said, "& laugh & say 'That man wants to be a white man.' . . . [But] I want to be strong & go forward. . . ."

At thirty, he had decided to learn the white man's language: "When Indians come to a white man's store for bacon and think [he] cannot understand them, they make signs like a flat curled up nose for pig and go 'unh-unh' — grunting. But when I go to a store I say 'bacon' and get it right away."

Soon, he opened his own store, but when the reservation agent's brother decided to get into the business, Wolf Chief was pressured to close it. Instead, he wrote to the commissioner of Indian affairs in Washington.

> My Dear Sir:
> . . . The present Agent John S. Murphy bothered me in every way to keep me from keeping a Store. He did not do a single act that will encourage me in this. . . . I think it's [an] honorable way of making my living. . . . I wish you sent me a copy of Reservation laws so that I will read it and be not troublesome to my agent and to this office.
>
> Yours respectfully,
> Mr. Wolf C. Chief

A federal inspector was dispatched. Eventually, the agent's brother had to close his store. Wolf Chief's doors stayed open. He kept writing letters to Washington, more than a hundred before he was through — on his own behalf, and that of his people.

Wolf Chief as he looked when he was a thirty-year-old warrior (above), and, at right, waiting on a customer in the store he successfully insisted he had the right to run

Fort Berthhold, Dakota Territory, March, 1882.
To the Great Father [Chester Arthur]:
My name is Wolf Chief. I am poor. My agent is bad . . . he tells lies. . . . [He] says I am bad bec[a]use I write. . . .

December, 1888.
Dear Great Father [Grover Cleveland]
. . . I want to speak for my people. . . . [T]he frost came and now we have no crop at all and we do not know what we will do this winter for food. . . . We have no more buffalo and very few deer left. If you . . . do not help us we don't know how we [are] going to get along. I wish you would write me and tell me what you are going to do.

April 29th, 1891.
President [Benjamin] Harrison, President of the United States at Washington, D.C.
My Dear Friend Sir: Our school houses [are] very old indeed. No good white man [would] keep children in such bad and dangerous buildings. At a little blow of wind the houses might fall down, killing every child. . . . I wish that the school houses be removed [and new ones built]. . . . I am trying to be like a white man and am learning the best I can. . . . Please, I wish to hear from you soon on this matter. I am your friend.

Wolf Chief eventually converted to Christianity, and donated ten acres of land for a chapel close to his cabin. But in an old earth lodge near his house was the sacred medicine bundle that had belonged to his grandfather, Missouri River. The two human skulls wrapped in a blanket had been passed along for generations, used to invoke the help of spirits in war, in hunting, and especially in bringing rain.

Missionaries and Indian agents had urged Wolf Chief to destroy the sacred bundle. He had refused, out of respect for his ancestors. But no member of the special Waterbuster clan — the Hidatsa group responsible for the bundle's ceremonies — would come forward to take responsibility for it, and Wolf Chief grew worried that neglecting the medicine bundle while he practiced Christianity would anger both his old gods and his new one. In 1907, he sold the relic to an anthropologist who placed it in a New York museum.

Shortly before she died, Buffalo Bird Woman cooperated with an anthropologist, explaining her people's ways so that they might be remembered in the future. Her son, Edward Goodbird, who had converted to Christianity, did the translations:

I have changed my ways and become Christian, but that one way I have not changed. When poor people and hungry old people come for food, I cannot refuse them. I am sure that Jesus fed people when He was on earth.

Wolf Chief

Whenever the white man treats the Indian as they treat each other, then we will have no more wars. We shall all be alike — brothers of one father, and one mother, with one sky above us and one country around us, and one government for all. Then the Great Spirit Chief who rules above will smile upon this land . . . and . . . all people may be one people. Hin-mah-too-yah-lat-kekht has spoken for his people.

Chief Joseph

A mixed world: dinnertime at the home of a Crow family in Montana in 1910

Opposite: Independence Chapel, built in 1910 entirely through the donations and labor of Wolf Chief's Indian friends and neighbors and presided over by his nephew, Edward Goodbird, the son of Buffalo Bird Woman

> White men think it strange that we Indians honored sacred bundles; but I have heard that in Europe men once honored relics, the skull, or a bone, or a bit of hair of some saint, or a nail from Jesus' cross; that they did not pray to the relic, but thought that the spirit of the saint was near; or that he was more willing to hear their prayers when they knelt before the relic. In much the same way, we Indians honored our sacred bundles.

Wolf Chief, meanwhile, kept writing letters to Washington up to his death in 1934. His last one — to President Franklin Roosevelt's commissioner of Indian affairs — described the drought that was turning the plains into a dust bowl. Shortly after his death, the Hidatsa Waterbuster clan petitioned the Museum of the American Indian for the return of the sacred medicine bundle that Wolf Chief had sold. In 1938, in one of the first instances in which sacred Indian objects were returned to the people who revered them, it was sent back to the tribe.

That summer, rain fell again on the plains.

I WILL NEVER LEAVE YOU

After their honeymoon, John and Ethel Love had returned to the ranch on Muskrat Creek. Seventy miles from the schoolhouse where she had once taught, it was more remote, more treeless, more immense than anything Ethel had ever seen before. "We live the ranchiest kind of ranch life . . ." Ethel wrote. "The sheer alone-ness of it is unique — never a light but one's own, at night. No smoke from another's fire in sight. . . ." In an area the size of Rhode Island, the Loves were the only inhabitants.

During their first winter together, John lost 8,000 sheep and 50 cattle. Ethel lost a baby. But they managed to complete one dam near the ranch headquarters, nonetheless, and to begin work on a larger one downstream.

The next winter was the worst since the Great Die-Up of 1887, and Ethel, pregnant again, left John alone and went home to Denver to have the baby under her father's care. She and the infant, a son, had just returned when the spring floods began.

> Black clouds, thunder and lightning showed heavy rains up the creek, although we had only showers about the house. All that afternoon John had been chanting happily, "Roll, Jordan, Roll," in anticipation of water to fill the small reservoirs, already nearly empty, in front of the house, and partly fill the large one down the creek, on which he had had men working for many months. I fed the baby and went to bed about nine o'clock.
>
> Then Jordan rolled. I heard John shout, "The creek's coming down." A suddenly increasing roar of water charged the air, while I pulled my bathrobe around me, stepped into my sandals, and picked up the baby, asleep in his blan-

Life with the Loves: glimpses from a family album

kets. When I reached the back door, water was up to my knees. John lifted the baby and myself in his arms and, water swirling about us, carried us up the slippery hill behind the house.

They tried to sleep that night in the sheep wagon in which they'd spent their honeymoon.

At daylight we returned to the house. Stench, wreckage and debris met us. The flood had gone. Its force had bust open the front door and swept a tub full of rain water into the dining room. Chairs and other furniture were overturned in deep mud. Mattresses had floated. . . . Kitchenware, groceries and silverware were filthy. . . . It rained every day for a week. . . . Later, when John's office desk could be opened, we found the largest drawer full of a tangled mass of roots and sprouts a foot or two long. The envelopes of garden seeds had disintegrated.

Bankers from Lander showed up, surveyed the damage, and brusquely announced that they were foreclosing on Love's livestock loans:

The aftermath came quickly. Buyers arrived to take over the sheep, sheep wagons, dogs and equipment. Cowboys rode to collect the string of saddle

horses. . . . The boys gathered the hundred and fifty head of cattle. John paid his own cowboys, and they departed. Ranch work stopped.

Before he left, the childless banker asked, "What will you do with the baby?"

"I think I'll keep him," I said.

All of John Love's dreams seemed shattered. Everything he'd promised his wife had fallen through; he told her she had every right to leave him. She said, "I will never leave you."

They went back to living in a sheep wagon while they cleaned out the flood wreckage and began rebuilding. A second son, David, was born, and by the next year, the big dam downstream was finished. It was the largest irrigation project ever built in Wyoming without government funds.

"That summer we had a lulling sense of satisfaction and anticipation . . ." Ethel remembered, "awaiting a real test of the dam's strength. The sky in the west was blackened by a hail storm. . . . It filled the dam, overflowing the spillway. Under the pressure the dam burst. . . . John salvaged five loads of rye and more of winter wheat. . . . This was all he had to show for his years of expensive effort on the dam. 'Love's Labor Lost,' was his summary."

John Love was forty-three years old. He still had his land and his family, but that was all. He hired himself out as a common sheepherder for forty dollars a month and started over again. Ethel concentrated on the children — three, now that a daughter had been born. "I have been busy trying to get some raw material in shape for you teachers," she wrote to her Wellesley College newspaper. "And this report is late because the raw material has been teething."

Beside the pleasure of watching the . . . babies' development, I had the contrasting daily struggle with what I thought of to myself as the three damned D's — dirt, dishes, and diapers. . . . We keep open house for all who pass. . . . "When did you eat last?" is the correct greeting.

Their son David remembered one dinner guest:

A chap named Bill Grace. He had been rather lively as a young man and killed somebody and had been sent to the penitentiary for it. But he was a decent sort and, as my father said, the man needed killing anyway.

We little boys — we were about ten or eleven years old — were in a kind of awe to be in the presence of this murderer and it just happened that one day he was at the ranch we had found an enormous rattlesnake. It was five feet nine inches without the head. That's a big rattlesnake and it was beautiful and we skinned it out because we wanted the skin. And we saw all this beautiful meat and we thought, well, it will make a good supper, so we brought it in and mother took the bones out of it and creamed it and served it on toast. And we boys were told not to say anything about this being rattlesnake meat, because it might offend Bill. So, we didn't but we couldn't really quite stay away from the thought and so we were talking about rattlesnake meat and how good it could be. And Bill Grace struck his fist on the table and he said, "If anybody fed me rattlesnake meat I would kill 'em." And there was a dead silence, and then

John Love at seventy-six, photographed in the doorway of his ranch house just before he and his wife left it for the last time

mother passed the plate of rattlesnake meat and said, "Have some more chicken, Bill."

Ethel taught the children their lessons around an old gambling table their father had salvaged from a ghost town. There was no electricity or indoor plumbing, but the house was filled with books to be read by the light of kerosene lamps.

There were still more setbacks. The great Spanish influenza epidemic of 1919 that ravaged eastern cities found its way to the Loves' ranch. John and David very nearly died. Then fire destroyed one of the ranch buildings. Hopes for sudden wealth during a Wyoming oil boom ended in disappointment. One year, shipping cattle to Omaha ended up costing Love twenty-seven dollars more than he received for them in sale. Disease took another herd of sheep. A bank failed, and with it went the family savings.

John and Ethel Love stayed on their ranch for thirty-seven years, and watched their children grow, go off to college, and succeed. One became a chemist, another a design engineer, the third a geologist.

Finally, illness and old age forced them to leave their ranch for good. In the car that drove them away for the last time, Ethel pronounced herself satisfied. "At least," she said, "I left it clean for the next people."

John Love died in 1950. Ethel joined him nine years later.

Looking back many years later, their son David thought that in their determination to endure in spite of everything his mother and father were typical of many of the men and women who settled the West. The winter of 1919 had "pretty much wiped us out," David remembered, and influenza had so weakened him and his father that each had had to teach himself to walk again. "I can still remember us standing together, each leaning on the other, this six-year-old boy and the fifty-year-old man, and his saying, 'Well, laddy, even we can make it.' So, of course, we did."

Monument Valley

Dayton Duncan

A few years ago, I stopped at Monument Valley, a place on the border between Arizona and Utah that I have always considered one of the West's most breathtakingly beautiful spots, and one of its most symbolic. I was near the end of a particularly long and grueling road trip and needed a short rest to gather my thoughts before moving on. A spectacular sunset, I figured, would do the trick, and few places can top Monument Valley when the evening shadows begin to lengthen.

It was a late-fall afternoon, and the desert air was about to be freshened by one of those storms unique to the West — the kind you can see coming toward you for hours, even though it's moving fast, a series of billowy cumulous clouds, each one trailing angled tentacles of rain like some giant Portuguese man-of-war migrating across the sky. I watched in sunlight as the clouds approached, felt the wind change and the temperature drop when the shadows reached my spot, then a spattering of rain and the pungent scent of damp sagebrush, and then sunlight again as the cloud migration floated on indifferently toward the next horizon.

The brief storm settled the dust and cleared the way for an especially stunning sunset. Rising mysteriously from the flat desert floor of Monument Valley are immense buttes of red sandstone. Each monolith is individually distinct, mutely telling its own story of both timelessness and change, in which the rise and fall of human civilizations are subjects too puny and too hurried to consider, compared with the vaster, ceaseless struggle between wind, rock, and water that created the buttes aeons ago. If the gods had a sacred graveyard, this would be it. The buttes would be their tombstones, their etched epitaphs faded over so much time, decipherable only in certain light.

As the sun lowered, the rocks turned to burnt orange, then blood red, then shades of purple that seemed to change by the minute. The slanting sunlight cast shifting shadows across the valley and threw every eroded notch and line on the buttes' sides into sharp relief. There was a remarkable clarity to the light, but it was restless, like a supernatural flashlight moving steadily from point to point to read hieroglyphic inscriptions that spoke of time in millions of years.

Then the colors turned deeper and softer, and the light slowly dimmed until the buttes became coal-black silhouettes against a cobalt sky. The stars popped out. A coyote howled. I was ready to go home.

When I remember that sunset, I see myself alone in Monument Valley, silent and awestruck, just me and the ageless, primal elements. But in truth, I wasn't alone at all.

At least three busloads of tourists — Japanese and Germans mostly — had been there the same afternoon, enjoying the same scenery and listening to tour guides explain Indian customs. On the valley floor, a scattering of cars and RVs moved over dirt roads, stopping occasionally while people in expensive hiking boots got out to snap a photograph. The highway leading into the valley was lined with tents and booths of Navajo offering curios that ranged from expensive pottery and turquoise jewelry to cheap beads and toy tomahawks with rubber blades.

In two locations, commercials were being made with the monuments as a backdrop. One of them featured a shiny new car, the other a gorgeous model who would emerge from a trailer from time to time, have her picture taken in an elegant dress, and then go back inside to change outfits and do it all again. (When I returned home, I started counting the advertisements I saw that were set in Monument Valley: Estée Lauder perfume, Guinness beer, IBM typewriters, specially designed running shoes, two or three automobiles, Marlboro cigarettes, and an 18-karat-gold watch available only in New York, Bal Harbour, and Palm Beach. The cover of a fashion magazine, using high-tech photo-imaging to merge the features of beautiful women to create what it called "today's all-American beauty," displayed her exquisitely morphed face looming in front of three of the valley's distinctive buttes. When I saw a television commercial for Oscar Mayer weiners that showed a vehicle shaped like a hot dog driving across Monument Valley, I quit counting.)

And of course there were Navajo in the valley. Not just those selling tourist curios or leading pony rides over the dunes, but families that tend small herds of sheep, cart their water from wells and streams by hand, and live in hogans tucked away along the bottom of some butte, several strata below the poverty line. Perhaps they had a rusting pickup truck parked outside, a pack of cigarettes and some hot dogs inside — but little else even remotely resembling the multitude of products constantly promoted for sale to the rest of the world using the powerful mystique of Monument Valley, their home, as the come-on.

It was probably only by chance that a Hollywood movie crew wasn't also there with me. In 1938, John Ford came to Monument Valley and filmed *Stagecoach,* a western that won him an Academy Award, made a star out of one its young actors, John Wayne, and turned the valley into the location of choice for Ford and other filmmakers, whether or not their storylines actually matched the locale. Monument Valley has served as Tombstone, Arizona, for *My Darling Clementine* and as Lincoln, New Mexico, for *Billy the Kid* and *Young Guns.* In *Fort Apache,* the cavalry chases Apache through the buttes. In *She Wore a Yellow Ribbon,* it's tribes from the Great Plains they're after, and in one scene a cavalryman crests a dusty sand dune and points to something in the distance, which the next shot reveals to be a huge buffalo herd filmed in some other part of the West. Comanche are the enemy in *The Searchers*, one of my personal favorites, which pretends that Monument Valley is part of the Texas cotton belt. A Swedish settler, whose every other statement seems to be "yumpin' yiminy," complains to John Wayne about how hard it is to get a crop to grow, but Wayne's too busy trying to track down the tribe that captured his niece to point out that the homesteader might have better luck planting cotton in a place that gets more than six inches of rain a year.

John Ford's stagecoach takes one of several on-screen turns around the Mittens in Monument Valley.

In more recent films, Michael J. Fox was transported through time to Monument Valley to reach his past; Thelma and Louise drove a convertible through it in an attempt to escape from theirs. In either case, the valley itself proved inescapable, much like its image in modern times. I have no way to verify this, but I believe that the cumulative result of all the movies and commercials is that Monument Valley is immediately recognizable to virtually everyone in the nation, perhaps much of the world, even though few people could name it and fewer still have actually been there in person. It has become the visual symbol to conjure the West and all it represents. For most people, in fact, it *is* the West, a mythic place that exists as much in the imagination as in reality.

There's nothing particularly new in that. From its beginning, the story of the West has in great part been the story of different people seeing whatever it was they wanted to see there, often to the exclusion of harder truths and messier realities. It's as if the vast canvas of the western spaces has been some epic Rorschach inkblot test, with each people imposing on it their own individual or collective dreams, hopes, and desires. Some have looked at the majestic landscape and seen objects of reverence and worship; some have seen a warehouse with stockpiles of treasure available on a first-come, first-served basis. People have seen the West as the place to lose themselves, or find themselves; to save others' souls, and sometimes risk their own; to get rich, get lucky, or get away; to chase adventure and court danger; to be brave and free or left alone. The West is where the trickster Coyote created the *Nimipu* — the "real people" — and corn crops listened like children to the singing of women. It has been the Seven Cities of Gold or the Great American Desert, Zion or the Heart of Heathen Darkness, Across the Wide Missouri and Home on the Range, that spot just over the horizon where the sunsets are always golden and rain follows the plow. For some the West was (and is) a fresh start and new beginning. For others it is (and was) the last, best place.

The only thing that's changed is that somehow, through the wonders of mass entertainment, mass advertising, and mass media, Monument Valley's image now compresses all those various and contradictory western dreams — and expresses them all in a visual shorthand of, say, thirty seconds.

If I tended to block out the presence of everyone else during my sunset reverie at Monument Valley, then I was also not alone. Those German and Japanese tourists, no doubt, had come with certain expectations, perhaps to see more sand, rock, sky, and horizon than their homelands could ever provide; and they probably focused most of their attention toward whatever it was that they had spent so much money and traveled so far to see. The commercial crews, I'm sure, carefully adjusted their camera angles to make sure that the tourists, vendors, and especially any hogans with rusty pickups were not in their final frames. The Navajo may have viewed the scene with the same combination of nonchalance and complex, deeply freighted emotions that all people have when looking at their home. They may have seen the tourists, camera crews, and people like me as intruders in that home, outsiders chasing — and exploiting — foolish fantasies. But they may also have seen us through the prism of their own dreams of getting ahead, seen us not as individual people but as a resource whose tourist dollars and permit fees might help them improve their lives in those hogans and shacks that most of us so studiously screened from our selective vision of Monument Valley.

An important part of the reality of the West is the dream — or more accurately, the dreams — of the West. Its history can only be understood with that in mind. And the same is true of the present. Separating myth and dream from reality is as impossible now as ever. They are distinguishable, but inseparable.

As a journalist and writer of history, I am by nature most interested in fact. But what I have learned in the West is that facts — reality — are often driven by dreams. I learned this again, in compressed form, at Monument Valley. The tour buses, the shiny car, the rusting pickups were facts. The fuel that made them all go was dreams. I was in the midst of many people that sunset. *And* I was alone in my dream.

All places have their own coordinates of latitude and longitude, their own topographical idiosyncrasies, their own particular look and feel that set them apart from all other locations. With its signature buttes and sweeping vistas, Monument Valley just happens to have this spatial distinctiveness in spades. It cannot be mistaken for any other place.

But I also believe that places exist not only in space, but in time. When I visit a location, I feel that I'm standing not just at an intersection of map lines, but at many intersections from the past as well. I don't mean this in some soft and fuzzy, New Age sense of "channeling" with previous incarnations. I mean that history can be read in books and told in stories, but it can also be read in the land. And in the West, because of the wide-open spaces, the general sparsity of rain, and a variety of other reasons, those marks from history seem more accessible and stark, like the exposed layers of sediment on a butte's cliffside at sunset. They make the past, and its role in shaping the present, more palpable.

Tucked away in corners of Monument Valley are the elaborate ruins of the Anasazi, a civilization that once dominated the Four Corners region. The Anasazi hit their peak of population in the eleventh century, about the same time William the Conqueror invaded England. Three centuries later (still before Columbus "discovered" the New World) their major cities and villages had been abandoned, and the ancestors of the Navajo — believed to have taken over after migrating south from Canada — were already referring to them and their mysterious relics as "the ancient ones." One of the best Anasazi ruins in Monument Valley is called the House of Many Hands, built in the recess of an overhanging cliff. On the cliff walls are hundreds of faded, white-paint handprints, put there more than five centuries ago for reasons no one fully understands. Not far away, in Canyon de Chelly, I've seen more of them on canyon walls, as well as primitive drawings of people and animals. The early Navajo painted the rocks, too. One cave drawing depicts a pitched battle with the Ute. Another shows a man on a horse, bearing a lance and the Christian cross.

No one, it seems, has been immune to the impulse to leave some evidence of their individual passing through the west. Juan de Oñate inscribed his name on El Morro Rock in New Mexico as he searched for a water route to the Pacific in 1605, adding that he — not the king of Spain — was paying for the expedition. In 1743, as the Vérendryes explored South Dakota for the same fabled Northwest Passage on behalf of France, they buried a lead tablet bearing their names. From 1804 to 1806, as Meriwether Lewis and William Clark pursued the same myth and became the first American citizens to see the West, Clark was particularly prone to the inscription habit. He carved his name on cottonwoods along the Missouri River. He left it on evergreens along the Clearwater and Snake and overlooking the mouth of the Columbia. And near the banks of the Yellowstone, in the only inscription of his still visible today, he etched his name in a sandstone outcropping that he named Pompey's Pillar in honor of Sacagawea's infant son, who had accompanied the expedition to the sea. Seventy years later, soldiers under the command of George Armstrong Custer scratched their names on the same outcropping. When I visited Pompey's Pillar in the 1980s, I noticed a family of four sneaking to a secluded nook in the rock, where they added their names to the hundreds already there.

Such sites cover the West: petroglyphs and rock art from people whose names and customs we will never know; Indian paintings telling stories of ancient battles and animals that talked; thousands of names of American pioneers chiseled into the rounded hump of Independence Rock during the Great Migration and gold rush. In a way, they all could be considered graffiti. To me, they're the simplest and most direct thread connecting the succession of human presence over the ages. I've driven hundreds of miles out of my way to see them. They seem somehow endearing and poignant, an understandable and absolutely human response to such an immense and timeless landscape. In their own ways, they seem to say, "I was here. I count for something, too. Remember me." And although I have always resisted the urge to put my own name next to theirs, I have placed my hand on their handprints or rubbed my fingers across their inscriptions, reaching across time to people who once stood at this same precise spot.

At South Pass in Wyoming, and other places along the main Overland Trail, I have seen wagon ruts left more than a hundred years ago. The missionary Narcissa Whitman, the land-hungry Sager family, the scout Kit Carson, the Mormon prophet Brigham Young, and the forty-niner William Swain passed this way. Each one pursued different dreams, yet the dreams led them all — and so many thousands more of their countrymen — in the same direction, west, and through this same gentle saddle in the otherwise impenetrable Rockies. It does not take an overactive imagination to stand in those ruts and seem to hear the creak of ox yokes from wagon after wagon after wagon, to sense a restless nation on the move, or to feel a moment of anticipation knowing that the slope on the other side at last leads to the Pacific.

At Sand Creek in eastern Colorado, one fall afternoon I visited the place where Colonel John Chivington and his volunteers massacred the peaceful Cheyenne village of Black Kettle in 1864. Not surprisingly, the site is not as well marked for travelers as South Pass — it's part of a privately owned ranch, not public land — but after two stops for directions I found it easily enough off a gravel road. I clambered down a steep embankment to the dry creek bed, lined with cottonwoods, and walked across toward the other side, where the Indian village had been. Chivington's men would have come this same way and encountered an old chief named White Antelope, the first of his tribe to have visited Washington, D.C., and received a peace medal from the President. The morning of the attack, he was wearing the medal and flying an American flag over his teepee, and when the shooting started White Antelope had run forward and shouted "Stop, stop!" in English. The soldiers paid no attention. As the rest of the village scattered for their lives, White Antelope stood in the center of camp, his arms folded, singing his death song:

> Nothing lives long,
> Except the earth and the mountains.

Some two hundred Cheyenne were slaughtered that morning, most of them women and children. White Antelope had been one of the first to fall. His ears and nose were cut off by one of the volunteers;

someone took his scalp; his scrotum was removed and put to use as a tobacco pouch. No one knows what became of the presidential peace medal he was wearing.

Poster for *Stagecoach,* 1939

When I crossed Sand Creek, I saw a lone cottonwood towering by itself from the dusty, broken ground. As I approached, an eagle suddenly lifted from one of the middle branches — noiseless, but startling in its emergence. It flapped slowly, up and away, and then, riding an updraft, began circling higher and higher directly above me. The circles got smaller as the eagle gained altitude. He became a tiny dot overhead. I stood motionless the whole time, hardly breathing, squinting in the sun to follow him, knowing that, with his vision, he was looking right in my eye. Then the dot became even smaller, merged with the sky, and disappeared. My breath returned in a gulp, and so did my awareness of sound. A wind swept down the creek, rustling the cottonwood leaves. The cicadas in the trees started rasping, answered by the dry clatter of grasshoppers on the range. It sounded like the shaking of several hundred Indian gourds in a solemn ceremony. Or one very large rattlesnake. I couldn't stay there any longer. By the time I had climbed the creek bank to reach my truck, my heart was pounding, and I immediately drove away.

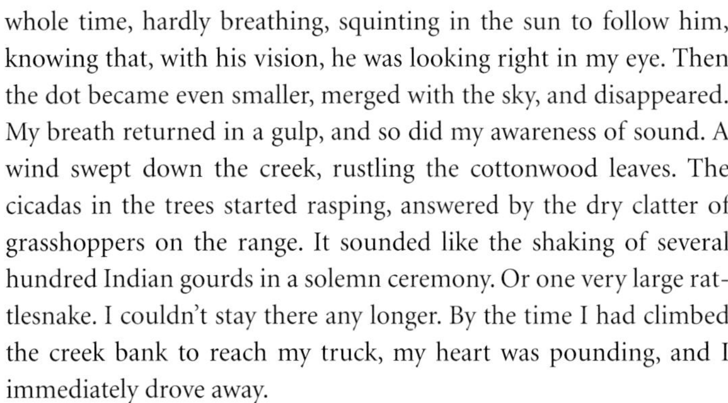

I would have stopped at the nearest town to have a cup of coffee and try to recompose my nerves, but it was one of those places that exist more on the map than in reality — a dying Plains village a half-step away from becoming a ghost town. There were only a few houses standing, most of them unoccupied, no café or gas station. In the center of town stood a big, two-story brick building, the last evidence that someone had once held grand dreams for the place. The building looked as if a bomb had hit it. The windows were all shattered, the roof had collapsed, part of the second story had crumbled into the ground floor, and tumbleweeds had rolled in through a broken door and piled up inside. The town's name was Chivington. I kept on driving, telling myself that nothing lives long, only the earth and the mountains.

In John Ford's movie *Stagecoach,* which first brought the image of Monument Valley to a worldwide audience, the fictional journey begins against the backdrop of the Mittens, one of the valley's most distinctive landmarks. The stage passengers include a salesman and a gambler, a corrupt banker and a drunken doctor, a proper lady and a prostitute, a sheriff and an impulsive, though brave and good-hearted outlaw named Ringo, played by John Wayne. Each one has his or her own private reason for needing to get to Lordsburg, farther west, as quickly as possible. They ford a swirling river, stay at two or three stage stops, narrowly survive an Indian attack, face other hardships and danger together, bicker with one another, and then coalesce as a group (except for the banker). Finally they reach their destination, which a close viewer would recognize as a movie set somewhere near the base of the Mittens in Monument Valley. In reality — though not in the story — they're back where they began.

Ford, I'm sure, had the most practical of reasons for this. He probably had a tight budget, and since he was in this terrific location that nearly *begs* to be filmed, he shot as much footage in the same place as he felt he could get away with. Besides, he probably figured, few people would notice; or, if they're as wrapped up in the story as I always am, even fewer would be bothered by it.

In fact, I've come to enjoy the fact that on one level *Stagecoach*'s journey seems to be a long and arduous straight line, while on another, unintentional level it turns out to be a circle. Like so many other things I associate with Monument Valley, it condenses another lesson I have learned in the West. *Stories* have a definite beginning and an end; *history* doesn't. And yet the way we most vividly remember and tell history — from gathering around campfires in the oldest times to reading a book or watching television in the present — is through stories. Stories are usually linear. But history can be circular, unending, returning to essentially the same place again and again like a song with many verses but the same refrain. Some Native Americans have always contended that history revolves this way, referring to a Sacred Hoop or large Medicine Wheel.

Many of my experiences in the West have turned out to be the pursuit of stories that circled back in time, linking past and present in both direct and oddly dizzying ways. At a place called Hovenweep (a Ute word for "deserted valley"), I once camped in the midst of some Anasazi ruins and marveled at clusters of buildings, some of them several stories high, built in the crevices and alcoves of steep cliffs. It seemed a most unlikely — and difficult — spot in which to erect such complex structures. I wondered which fact would astonish their architects and masons the most: that their work would still be standing after five hundred years, or that their civilization would not be. The next day I went to Tickaboo, Utah, where a uranium-processing plant had been built during a big boom in the nuclear market in the 1980s. Tickaboo had been laid out in eager anticipation of the hundreds of people expected to move in and go to work. But the uranium bubble had burst, the completed plant never opened for business, and no one ever showed up to buy house lots. When I stopped, Tickaboo was a grid of paved streets and sidewalks, some fire hydrants and junction boxes for underground utilities —

and nothing more. A western ghost town without even abandoned buildings, without even ghosts.

On the Nevada-California border, I once watched a modern gold mine in operation. It was not the first mining boom the place had experienced. A century and a half earlier, some forty-niners were in such a rush to reach California that they ventured with their wagon train out onto the scorching alkali flats of the hemisphere's lowest, driest, and hottest spot. When it nearly killed them, they named it Death Valley.

In the early 1900s, another mining boom touched Death Valley. Much of it turned out to be fraudulent — stock sold in nonexistent mines with the knowledge that no one in the East would ever dare come to such a forbidding place to check out his or her investment in person. But there were some legitimate finds. One touched off a human stampede that included a man pushing a wheelbarrow loaded with supplies across seventy-five miles of desert (jackasses, even at the inflated price of five hundred dollars each, had been sold out). It also gave birth to the town of Rhyolite, which in six short months was transformed from a barren patch of rock to the home of twenty-five hundred rainbow-chasers. There were 50 saloons, 16 restaurants, 19 hotels, 6 barbers, and 1 public bath. At four hundred dollars a ton, ice fetched a higher price than gold ore. Rhyolite, like the boom that spawned it, went under in less than a decade.

When I was there in 1990, all that was left of the town were a few shells of buildings, protected from final destruction as a national historic site. But a new gold boom was under way, swelling the population — and driving up the prices — in the nearby town of Beatty. On the outskirts of Rhyolite, a mining company using dynamite, massive bulldozers, and giant trucks was steadily tearing down a small mountain. The low-grade ore is crushed and soaked in cyanide to separate microscopic amounts of gold from the waste rock, which is then piled up like a pyramid where a mountain once stood. Aside from the newer technology — and its capacity to alter the landscape in ways the gold rushes of 1849 and 1900 never dreamed of — history was repeating itself.

History's wheel had also turned full circle in places I visited on the Great Plains portions of Texas, Oklahoma, and Colorado. There I met farmers who had invested heavily in center-pivot irrigation systems to bring up water from the underground Oglala aquifer, so they could grow corn and cotton in places that don't get enough rain for either one. As grasslands were turned into fields of cash crops, money flowed like water, and both seemed endless. They even called the circling sprinklers "Wheels of Fortune." Then the aquifer's water level dropped and the cost of the gasoline running the pumps tripled. Hundreds of farmers went bust, and the small towns that relied on their business dried up.

In the very same places, I talked to old people who had lived through the Dust Bowl of the 1930s. Their parents had moved onto the Plains during a great wheat bonanza during World War One, when good crop prices and a string of wetter-than-usual years had resulted in thousands of acres of grasslands being plowed up. Then drought hit, and the exposed topsoil was lifted into dark clouds stretching from horizon to horizon. People told me of sitting inside their homes with washcloths over their mouths so they could breathe without choking on the dust that engulfed everything. They talked of high noons turned dark, of shoveling paths through sand drifts to reach dying cattle, and of dry winds that eventually swept away two-thirds of their county's population.

And before all *that,* in the 1880s, the same area had experienced homesteaders arriving by the thousands, persuaded by land promoters and even some university professors that their very act of settling the Plains would alter its climate. People who would have considered an Indian performing a rain dance a superstitious savage nonetheless believed that the vibrations of railroad engines, the atmospheric disturbances created by larger concentrations of population, and most of all the simple plowing of virgin prairie brought more rain. Not just an occasional storm, of the kind the medicine man with his chant and his drum might claim credit for, but a permanent change toward a moister Plains. Dry times drove most of them off their land before 1890. Rain, it turns out, does *not* follow the plow. But, as those who followed in their footsteps proved, hope is the West's most reliable crop, a hardy perennial that grows with or without irrigation.

I don't remember the first time I ever saw the endless sweep of the Plains — I was too young at the time — but I'll never forget re-experiencing the moment with my wife, Dianne, a New Englander accustomed to horizons foreshortened by humped mountains, to roads that wind through canopies of trees, and to a scale of landscape in which twenty miles can seem like a considerable distance. On her first trip to the West, she flew out to meet me in Great Falls, Montana, arriving at night. At dawn the next morning, we set out by car. The Plains are absolutely treeless here. On the flattest parts, to the east and north, unfenced wheat fields stretch toward Canada, 120 miles away. If you look in that direction, the only thing that prevents you from seeing the small station at the border crossing is the curvature of the earth. A little to the west, the Plains begin undulating — short-grass rangeland that gently rolls and swells until it crashes into the massive ramparts of the northern Rockies, which you can see from a distance of nearly a hundred miles. Overhead was a clear bowl of azure sky covering a perspective that encompassed in one view a landmass roughly equivalent to Dianne's home state of Vermont. For hours, she rode in rapt silence.

It was a personal exposure to an immensity of sky and land and nature beyond all experience, beyond expectation, almost beyond imagination. But it was nothing new. Coronado's men had felt the same emotion — part awe, part uneasiness — when they marched toward Quivira in the 1540s and entered into a sea of grass they feared might swallow them without a trace. A little emigrant girl, trudging across the Plains in a covered wagon three hundred years later, woke up each morning crying inconsolably. Her parents asked her why. "We will never get to Oregon," she sobbed, "if we come back and camp in the same place every night." Across the centuries, every explorer, every pioneer, every traveler has experienced some variation of the same stunned response. So much sky. Such yawning distances. Such a humbling moment to discover oneself so insignificant compared with such a vast, indifferent landscape. I've read it in diaries, journals, and letters dating back to the start of recorded history in the West. I've heard it at gas stops on the interstate. And I've seen it in my wife's wide-open eyes.

Sometimes, I have encountered places where it seemed the wheel of history had rotated halfway, turning old stories upside down. In southern Utah, I met a man who had moved into a remote canyon in the 1970s, trying to escape modern society and live apart with his multiple wives and expanding family. After an armed confrontation with federal officials over a homesteading claim, he had been forced from his sanctuary, and his houses had been bulldozed. But now he was mayor of a growing, if still tiny town on the main highway — and supplemented his income with government consulting contracts on emergency management. One hundred years earlier, under intense and persistent pressure from the federal government, the Mormon Church had renounced one of its most distinctive features: plural marriage. But this mayor made no secret that he was a polygamist. Everyone in town — in fact, in the state — knew it. And although the Mormons had excommunicated him, no one representing the government seemed inclined to prosecute him, least of all the town attorney, who happened to be one of his nine wives.

Near Monument Valley, I followed a young Navajo political leader who was mounting a campaign to bring electricity, running water, passable roads, telephone service, and other amenities that most of us take for granted to his corner of the reservation. In essence, he was leading an Indian "uprising," but the goal was to catch up with — not slow down — the white man, and the method was ballots instead of bullets. In an old hogan, some tribal elders conferred with a federal mediator, assigned to monitor the upcoming election after some tense incidents between Indians and whites over voter registration. The elders spoke no English so the translations took a long time and the meeting went late into the night, lit by kerosene lamps that hissed as they burned. The next day we went to a gathering of environmental activists, where we listened to a lively discussion about whether merely *hiking* in a wilderness might cause too much damage to it. My friend had come hoping to raise some money for his campaign. Instead, he was asked why his people still cut down cedar trees on a mesa that was being designated as wilderness. For the same reason they had been cutting down those trees for centuries, he answered — for heat.

As we drove one day over the washboard roads he wanted paved, we listened to a tribal radio station broadcasting some campaign commercials in Navajo. During the news reports, the only words I recognized were "George Bush," "Saddam Hussein," "Bureau of Indian Affairs," and then, just before the music started, "Dolly Parton." Later, at a two-day powwow, he handed out leaflets that said *Niha whol zhiizh* ("It's our turn"). They showed a water spigot, a modern house, a road grader, and the symbol of a Democratic ballot being put in a voting box. The powwow featured traditional Native American dancing, a rodeo, and a "mud bog" competition in which souped-up trucks with oversized tires try to speed through a short stretch of desert that has been transformed by fire hoses into a man-made swamp. My friend took a break from campaigning to win the rodeo's bareback riding event. But his two brothers, the reigning all-Indian mud bog champions at the time, lost at the powwow to a white man driving a truck called "Custer's Revenge."

No one disputes that the West has held a unique grip on our nation's and the world's imagination, yet no one knows for certain why. There are as many theories as there are historians and social scientists. But I believe that one of the most important factors is the West's unique landscape. It is the screen onto which so many dreams have been projected, the stage on which so many human dramas have been enacted. Those dreams and dramas, in themselves, are not unique. Greed, folly, inquisitiveness, love, courage, ambition, and hope — these have always been elemental to the human story. They are timeless. Each generation reenacts them anew. The Sacred Hoop whirls, the Wheel of Fortune spins, the stagecoach rolls out — and they all eventually return to where they began and start all over again.

What separates those same stories when they occur in the West is the landscape. It exposes everything to a harsher, clearer light. It, too, seems elemental and timeless. And, as a projection screen for the looping reels of human history, it is, well, *monumental.*

And that is why Monument Valley is one of the most appropriate symbols of the West. I've felt it every time I've been there — and especially during that magic sunset after a storm. In every direction, I could see into the folded layers of time. Through the gullies ran streams of water tinged red from the tiny bits of soft stone that the rain had washed off the buttes, continuing a slow, steady process that began before humans walked the planet. In the House of Many Hands, the Anasazi homes and eerie wall paintings spoke of a past civilization that flowered and withered in the time the buttes might have eroded less than an inch. Some of the Navajo I could see were wearing headbands and bright print skirts and tending sheep the way their ancestors had done in the nineteenth century; others were busy trying to bring their people the basic accoutrements of the twentieth century, hopefully before the onset of the twenty-first. There were buses and cars and RVs, tourists hoping to buy some piece of their own vision of the "Old West." There were advertisers plugging into the same dream, making commercials to sell the West's mystique like a bar of soap. And we were all there together, a mixture of different times and different dreams, united at least in the thought that this particular spot of earth was someplace special.

Monument Valley's story is the West's story, and the West's story is everyone's story. In Monument Valley, the past and the present stand side by side. People come and go, repeating what seem to be arcs on the circle of a never-ending story. But nothing lives forever, only the earth and the mountains.

Camera Club at General Sherman Tree in the Mariposa Grove, California

Acknowledgments

Beginning early in the nineteenth century, Americans dreamed of a railroad that would span the continent, but it could not be undertaken by one individual, or one company — the distances were too vast, the terrain too daunting, the costs prohibitive — and it was only when the government got involved that the dream became a reality. Much the same thing could be said about directing and producing a twelve-and-a-half-hour film series on the history of the West: no individual filmmaker could do it alone, no one company could manage it, and only a partnership between corporations, foundations, and the government enabled it to be "built," hour by hour, shot by shot, frame by frame. Our PBS series *The West*, and this illustrated history that grew out of it, were realized because an extraordinary collection of dedicated men and women invested their heart and soul in telling the western story.

This project would not have happened without the guidance and unwavering support of Ken Burns, our Executive Producer and Senior Creative Consultant. Ken first conceived the series, and throughout the more than five years we worked on the films, he was our principal creative collaborator. He brought his uncompromising standards, intuitive sense of storytelling, and boundless energy to every aspect of the series production. It was because of his pioneering work in the field of historical documentary filmmaking that *The West* came into existence, and it is because of his ongoing support and advice that it exists today.

More than anyone else, my co-producers are responsible for this project's completion. For five years they sustained me through all of its vicissitudes and all of its victories. Jody Abramson oversaw virtually every aspect of *The West*'s production, and in every area brought her competence, composure, and impeccable professionalism to bear. She was one of the first people to come on board, and she never failed me or the rest of the staff. Whether it was a complex technical task or a painful administrative one, Jody met every challenge that was thrown at her head-on, and helped shape the series and make the films stronger. Documentaries such as this one are chaotic by nature, and it was Jody's remarkable good humor, good instincts, and good Yiddish that kept us all together.

Michael Kantor was in many ways *The West*'s trail boss, managing the immense logistical and technical demands of filmmaking with a steadiness and sure-handedness that was extraordinary. In addition to his role as a co-producer, time and again Michael shouldered responsibilities no one else could manage — master of our computers and editing facilities, coordinator of our voice-over sessions, and most remarkable of all, post-production supervisor for twelve and a half hours of film. And yet, while juggling all of these managerial roles, Michael never stopped contributing to the film's creative lifeblood — on location, in the voice-over studio, and in the editing room.

Like the explorers Lewis and Clark, our writers, Geoffrey C. Ward and Dayton Duncan, brought an amazing combination of skills to their endeavor, and like the leaders of the Corps of Discovery, they agreed to "share the command . . . and the hardships." Films like *The West* are filled with words — words from diaries and letters, from newspapers, journals, and editorials — but most of all they are filled with words that form a unifying narration out of an infinite number of possible stories, themes, and ideas. Geoff and Dayton crafted that story, in draft after draft, never flagging in their determination to see the history of the West clearly and honestly, never hesitating to embrace difficult stories and make them work in the dramatic context of a documentary film.

Geoff brought his inexhaustible love of history to our project, but he also brought a keen appreciation of the limitations that filmmaking places on the writer's craft. Time and again he allowed the pictures to tell the story, recognized how little needed to be said to make the message clear. And his words that survived stand as eloquent testimony to his skill as a writer for the screen.

Dayton joined this project over coffee in a café in Norcatur, Kansas (population 189), in the summer of 1991. Since that day, he traveled thousands of miles as our Consulting Producer, sharing with us his innate feel for the western landscape and his sensitive understanding of western people. Like any group of easterners heading west, at the outset of this project we were in need of a guide, and no mountain man or army scout could have served us better than Dayton. He introduced us to the realities of the West's geography, climate, and social customs, and perhaps most important of all, showed us how to find the best rib-eye steak — in Santa Fe or Cheyenne, Durango or Dodge.

Once drafted into service as a co-writer, Dayton became a full partner in the scripting process. For him, perhaps more than for any other member of this project, *The West* has been a labor of love, and throughout the long years of research and writing, editing and reediting, his commitment to see this film through — and his determination to tell the complex history of the West in a new and lasting way — has been a source of inspiration to us all.

Victoria Gohl was the Associate Producer and director of all of the visual research for the series. In all my experience in historical documentaries, I have never seen anyone throw herself into her work with such all-consuming enthusiasm. It is rare for archivists, private collectors, and curators to know, or long remember, an associate producer, even less common for them to actively seek *her* out, ask *her* advice, and see *her* as a kindred spirit, but this was Victoria's reception across the country. The film and this book have been immeasurably enriched by the unpublished, undiscovered, or merely unnoticed collections that have found their way to us because of her research and her reputation.

The West's scripts went through more than twenty complete drafts, and Michelle Ferrari brought her rigorous editor's eye to our scripting process, while qualifying the hundreds of books needed to write the script, uncovering new collections of letters in archives, and managing the historical research that was such an important part of the film's content. She also brought a clear and consistent focus to the arduous task of film research at archives throughout the country.

For nearly two years, Suzanne Seggerman organized our production trips with unfailing energy and skill, and helped initiate the archival film research process. Jeff Dupré not only organized our office with great efficiency and almost unfathomable good cheer, but also served as a fast-learning Production Coordinator during our final year of shooting. Sarah Bingham served with great distinction as our Production Secretary, before heading off to a new career in Great Britain, and our bookkeeper Maureen Dougherty brought an attention to our checkbook that made our funders sleep more soundly. Near the end of the project, photo research assistance was provided by Linda Hattendorf and Allison Ross with such intelligence and efficiency we wished we had discovered them years before.

It is perhaps a truism that documentaries are made in the editing room, but there is truth in truisms. We edited *The West* for more than twenty-eight months, and the team that we assembled deserves a special place in the film's honor roll. The Supervising Editor was Paul Barnes, one of the most accomplished film editors of our generation. A veteran of countless documentary film credits, including the *Civil War* and *Baseball* series, Paul braved an arduous weekly commute from Walpole, New Hampshire, to New York City and brought his calm yet passionate eye to our editing room. Throughout the long schedule, he set a memorable example of the myriad ways in which a talented editor can transform a film, while also providing the guidance and experience that our ever-expanding editing staff required. Most of all, Paul provided me with an unforgettable lesson in the ways an editor can both support a director and challenge him to do his best work.

The three principal editors, Richard Hankin, Michael Levine, and Adam Zucker, made *The West* what it is, chapter by chapter, scene by scene, and they brought to that task an overabundance of enthusiasm and humor, as well as a keen understanding of the editor's craft. Their persistent attention to detail and their keenly observant insights influenced this film profoundly. Their assistant editors — Laura Congleton, George O'Donnell, Keir Pearson, and Jay Pires — tirelessly administered to our AVID editing systems, often working the graveyard shift to meet our ever-shrinking editing deadlines, but still managed to contribute creative ideas to the editing process. In the eye of the storm, Hope Litoff and Vanessa Cochran managed our editing room with energy and inimitable style.

We are also grateful to our sound editors, Ira Spiegel, Marlena Grzaslewicz, Jacob Ribicoff, and Missy Cohen, who brought such subtlety and nuance to our sound design, to Lou Verrico and our friends at A&J Recording in New York, and Scott Greiner at Transmedia in San Francisco, for attending to our voice-over work in the studio, and to Bill Nisselson, Dominick Tavella, and Lee Dichter at Sound One, who made our mix come out so well.

Once again Buddy Squires brought his remarkable skills as a cinematographer to bear on one of our projects, helping us record the many moods of the western landscape. Evocative imagery is what you expect from Buddy, and he always delivers, but what is never included in his job description is the wellspring of creative advice that he willingly shares whenever he is not behind

J. J. Reilly's Stereoscopic View Tent in Yosemite

the camera. His patient wisdom helps you get the most out of every day of shooting. Buddy was joined by another gifted cinematographer, Allen Moore, who journeyed to some of the most remote parts of the West on our behalf (including Devils Tower, Wyoming, for several subzero nights) and always managed to return with images of great beauty and power. Both of our cameramen were often assisted by the irrepressibly good-natured and talented Anthony Savini, who also drove more than 30,000 miles of the West in our trusty Chevy Suburban.

Teese Gohl composed, orchestrated, arranged, and conceived our musical score, and masterfully incorporated a wide variety of musical traditions into a unified whole, while Jay Ungar and Molly Mason, Jacqueline Schwab, Andy Tierstein, Dennis Yerry, Ken Littlehawk, Dane LeBeau, Ellsworth Brown, and Melvin Youngbear played music from those various traditions with precision and pride. And Courtney Little made our recording sessions run smoothly, even in the blizzard of '96.

The West's narration is Peter Coyote's, and for more than twenty days in the studio Peter brought his skill as an actor and keen sense of language to bear on our film. Time and time again he made our narration come alive with his gift for drama and storytelling, and he often caught problems with our script, then helped us fix them. Peter is a person who clearly loves history and loves his work, and he made my job directing the narration a challenge, a learning experience, and a damn good time!

Our maps were painstakingly created by Deborah Freer, of Geosystems Global Corporation, and animated with great technical skill and almost superhuman patience by Rob Issen, of the Tape House, Computer Ink & Paint, Inc. Alex Gatje created our distinctive title design.

Throughout the making of the series, we had the advice and counsel of a panel of academic consultants whose eye for historical detail kept our stories clear and our chronology on track. Four scholars — David Gutiérrez, Patricia Nelson Limerick, N. Scott Momaday, and Richard White — gave us consistent, often sharp criticism for almost four years, and labored hard to understand the peculiarities of historical filmmaking and to serve our project and our subject fairly and honestly. They deserve our special thanks. These four were joined by an admirable group of historians and writers who shared their knowledge of the West with us, including Alan Brinkley, William Cronon, R. David Edmunds, William K. Everson, John M. Faragher, Yvette Huginnie, Alvin Josephy, Clara Sue Kidwell, Howard R. Lamar, Henrietta Mann, Gail Nomura, Joseph Porter, James P. Ronda, Robert M. Utley, T. H. Watkins, James Welch, and Laura Wilson.

The West was a partnership between Insignia Films and two other producing organizations, Florentine Films and WETA-TV, Washington, D.C. Once again we are grateful to the always cheerful and supportive Walpole, New Hampshire, crew of Florentine Films: Pam Baucom, Camilla Rockwell, Suzanna Steisel, Patty Lawlor, Susan Butler, Brenda Heath, Kevin Kertscher, and Shannon Robards. Our thanks as well to the wonderful staff at WETA, our coproduction partner and presenting station to the PBS system, especially Sharon Rockefeller, Phylis Geller, David Thompson, Noel Gunther, Lin Lloyd, Rick Heiman, Jay Phillips, Elise Adde, and Mary Schultz.

This handsome volume exists because of the interest and enthusiasm of our publishers at Little, Brown and Company, especially our insightful editor, Bill Phillips. The elegant design was created by Wendy Byrne, who calmly sifted through our archives and created a book that is a remarkable reflection of the film's spirit and intention. Her quiet skill and taste are visible on every page. She was assisted in the research and photo selection by Victoria Gohl, who tackled her first book project with the same determination she brought to our film. We also relied on the steady hand of Carl Brandt, who was present at this book's creation and helped us see it through to the very end.

The West Film Project was lucky enough to have Jim Kendrick as its attorney and to benefit from his wise counsel. Ed Weisel's careful guidance kept our books balanced and made sure we came out on the right side of the ledger in the end. Every frame of *The West*'s negative was developed and processed by Tim Spitzer, Al Pierce, and Joe Monge at Du Art, and managed with precision by Elliot Gamson at Immaculate Matching. Every frame was cut with steady hands and steadier nerves by Noelle Penraat. John Dowdell made that negative look wonderful transferred to videotape, and Mark Polyocan helped us navigate through the complicated postproduction process with his gifted staff at the Tape House.

Of course, no film of this magnitude could ever arrive on the screen without the support of underwriters who share a commitment to education, the mission of public television, and the importance of promoting and understanding our nation's past. *The West* was made possible by generous grants from The Public Broadcasting System, The Corporation for Public Broadcasting, The National Endowment for the Humanities, the Arthur Vining Davis Foundations, and The General Motors Corporation.

Standing behind these organizations were people whose talent and vision helped bring the series to the screen. Phil Guarascio and Luanna Flocuzio at GM, Skip Roberts and Tricia Kenney at N. W. Ayer & Partners, Sandy Heberer and John Wilson at PBS, Don Marbury at CPB, Jim Dougherty at the NEH, and Max King Morris and Jonathan Howe at the Arthur Vining Davis Foundations.

And I would like to add a special note of thanks to David and Jane Love, whose family story concludes our series and this book. David shared his parents' remarkable letters with us, gave us wonderful photographs of their family's life on their ranch in Wyoming, and provided one of the most emotional and inspiring on-camera interviews I have ever recorded. I am also indebted to his daughters, Frances Love Froidevaux and Barbara Love, who made available to us their own research already collected for their superb memoir about their grandparents, *Lady's Choice*. I believe that the story of this remarkable family, with its combination of endurance, love, and undying hope, profoundly reflects the essence of the western experience.

In the end, five years is a long time to work on any creative endeavor, and inevitably there are individuals whose kindness and generosity are overlooked in the passage of time. I hope the many friends of this project will not forget how much we relied on them for their advice and how grateful we are for their support.

Finally, I would like to thank Anne Symmes, who more than anyone else helped me make it through the last year of this project, and the Board of Directors of Insignia Films — Daniel C. Esty, David O. Ives, John T. Sughrue, and Robert A. Wilson — for their steadfast encouragement and understanding, without which my job would have been impossible.

Stephen Ives

SELECTED BIBLIOGRAPHY

In preparing this book and film series we consulted a great many sources, far too many to list here. But we do want to acknowledge those that meant the most to us. We are grateful to the authors and editors of all of them; any errors uncovered, either onscreen or in these pages, are our own.

Abbott, E. C., and Helena Huntington Smith. *We Pointed Them North: Recollections of a Cowpuncher* (Norman, 1939).

Ambrose, Stephen E. *Crazy Horse and Custer* (New York, 1975).

Arrington, Leonard. *Brigham Young: American Moses* (Urbana, 1986).

———. *The Mormon Experience: A History of the Latter-day Saints* (New York, 1979).

Ballantine, Betty, and Ian Ballantine (editors). *The Native Americans: An Illustrated History* (Atlanta, 1993).

Beilharz, Edwin A., and Carlos V. Lopez (translators and editors). *We Were 49ers!: Chilean Accounts of the California Gold Rush* (Pasadena, 1976).

Billington, Ray Allen, and Martin Ridge. *Westward Expansion* (New York, 1982).

Branch, Edward Marquess, et al. (editors). *Mark Twain's Letters. Volume 1 (1853–1866)* (Berkeley, 1989).

Brooks, Juanita. *The Mountain Meadows Massacre* (Norman, 1950).

Carter, Harvey Lewis. *Dear Old Kit: The Historical Christopher Carson* (Norman, 1968).

Chen, Jack. *The Chinese of America* (New York, 1980).

Connell, Evan S. *Son of the Morning Star* (San Francisco, 1984).

Covey, Cyclone (editor and translator). *Cabeza de Vaca's Adventures in the Unknown Interior of America* (Albuquerque, 1961).

Daniels, Roger. *Asian America: Chinese and Japanese in the United States Since 1850* (Seattle, 1988).

Dary, David A. *The Buffalo Book: The Full Saga of the American Animal* (Chicago, 1974).

———. *Cowboy Culture: A Saga of Five Centuries* (Lawrence, 1981).

De Bruhl, Marshall. *Sword of San Jacinto* (New York, 1993).

Dillinger, William C. *The Gold Discovery: James Marshall and the California Gold Rush* (Sacramento, 1990).

Duncan, Dayton. *Out West: An American Journey Along the Lewis and Clark Trail* (New York, 1987).

Egan, Feral. *Frémont: Explorer of a Restless Nation* (Reno, 1985).

Emmons, David M. *The Butte Irish: Class and Ethnicity in an American Mining Town, 1875–1925* (Urbana, 1990).

———. *Garden in the Grasslands: Boomer Literature of the Central Great Plains* (Lincoln, 1971).

Faragher, John Mack. *Daniel Boone* (New York, 1992).

Gilman, Carolyn, and Mary Jane Schneider. *The Way to Independence: Memories of a Hidatsa Indian Family, 1840–1920* (St. Paul, 1987).

Goodrich, Thomas. *Bloody Dawn: The Story of the Lawrence Massacre* (Kent, Ohio, 1991).

Gutiérrez, Ramon A. *When Jesus Came the Corn Mothers Went Away* (Stamford, 1992).

Haley, J. Evetts. *Charles Goodnight: Cowman and Plainsman* (Boston, 1936).

Hoig, Stan. *The Battle of the Washita: The Sheridan-Custer Indian Campaign of 1867–69* (Lincoln, 1976).

———. *The Sand Creek Massacre* (Norman, 1985).

Holliday, J. S. *The World Rushed In: An Eyewitness Account of a Nation Heading West* (New York, 1981).

Hutton, Paul Andrew (editor). *The Custer Reader* (Lincoln, 1992).

Jackson, Donald (editor). *Letters of the Lewis and Clark Expedition with Related Documents, 1783–1854.* 2 vols. (Urbana, 1978).

Jeffrey, Julie Roy. *Converting the West: A Biography of Narcissa Whitman* (Norman, 1991).

Josephy, Alvin M. *The Nez Perce Indians and the Opening of the Northwest* (Lincoln, 1965).

———. *The Patriot Chiefs* (New York, 1958).

Kraus, George. *High Road to Promontory: Building the Central Pacific Across the High Sierra* (Palo Alto, 1969).

Lamar, Howard R. (editor). *The Reader's Encyclopedia of the American West* (New York, 1977).

Lavender, David. *Let Me Be Free: The Nez Perce Tragedy* (New York, 1992).

Lazarus, Edward. *Black Hills, White Justice* (New York, 1991).

Limerick, Patricia Nelson. *Legacy of Conquest: The Unbroken Past of the American West* (New York, 1987).

Limerick, Patricia Nelson et al. (editors). *Trails: Toward a New Western History* (Lawrence, 1991).

Long, Jeff. *Duel of Eagles: The Mexican and U.S. Fight for the Alamo* (New York, 1990).

Love, Barbara, and Frances Love Froidevaux (editors). *Lady's Choice: Ethel Waxham's Journals and Letters, 1905–1910* (Albuquerque, 1993).

Malone, Michael P. *The Battle for Butte* (Seattle, 1981).

Mark, Joan. *Stranger in Her Native Land: Alice Fletcher and the American Indians* (Lincoln, 1988).

Marks, Paula Mitchell. *Precious Dust: The American Gold Rush Era: 1848–1900* (New York, 1994).

Mayer, Frank H., and Charles B. Roth. *The Buffalo Harvest* (Denver, 1958).

McKittrick, Myrtle M. *Vallejo, Son of California* (San Francisco, 1944).

McPhee, John. *Rising from the Plains* (New York, 1986).

Milner, Clyde A. II et al. (editors). *The Oxford History of the American West* (New York, 1994).

Moulton, Gary E. (editor). *The Journals of the Lewis and Clark Expedition* (Lincoln, 1986).

Nabokov, Peter (editor). *Native American Testimony: A Chronicle of Indian-White Relations from Prophecy to the Present, 1492–1992* (New York, 1991).

Nelson, Howard J. *The Los Angeles Metropolis* (Dubuque, 1983).

Painter, Nell Irvine. *Exodusters: Black Migration to Kansas After Reconstruction* (New York, 1976).

Pitt, Leonard. *The Decline of the Californios* (Stamford, 1961).

Prucha, Francis Paul. *The Great Father: The United States Government and the American Indians* (Lincoln, 1984).

Rawls, James J. *Indians of California: The Changing Image* (Norman, 1984).

Ronda, James P. *Lewis and Clark Among the Indians* (Lincoln, 1984).

Rosenbaum, Robert J. *Mexicano Resistance in the Southwest: The Sacred Right to Self-Preservation* (Austin, 1981).

Russell, Don. *The Lives and Legends of Buffalo Bill* (Norman, 1973).

Sanborn, Margaret. *Mark Twain: The Bachelor Years* (New York, 1990).

Schlissel, Lillian. *Women's Diaries of the Westward Journey* (New York, 1982).

Schlissel, Lillian et al. (editors). *Far from Home: Families of the Westward Journey* (New York, 1989).

Stands in Timber, John, and Margot Liberty. *Cheyenne Memories* (New Haven, 1967).

Stegner, Wallace. *The Gathering of Zion: The Story of the Mormon Trail* (New York, 1964).

Stratton, Joanna L. *Pioneer Women: Voices from the Kansas Frontier* (New York, 1981).

Takaki, Ronald. *A Different Mirror: A History of Multicultural America* (Boston, 1993).

Thompson, Erwin N. *Shallow Grave at Waiilatpu: The Sagers' West* (Portland, 1985).

Twain, Mark. *Roughing It* (New York, 1962).

Unruh, John D., Jr. *The Plains Across: The Overland Emigrants and the Trans-Mississippi West, 1840–60* (Urbana, 1979).

Utley, Robert M. *Cavalier in Buckskin: George Armstrong Custer and the Western Military Frontier* (Norman, 1988).

———. *Frontier Regulars: The United States Army and the Indian, 1866–1891* (New York, 1973).

———. *Frontiersmen in Blue: The United States Army and the Indian, 1848–1865* (New York, 1967).

———. *The Indian Frontier of the American West, 1846–1890* (Albuquerque, 1984).

———. *The Lance and the Shield: The Life and Times of Sitting Bull* (New York, 1993).

———. *The Last Days of the Sioux Nation* (New Haven, 1963).

Vestal, Stanley. *Joe Meek: The Merry Mountain Man* (Lincoln, 1952).

Weber, David J. *The Mexican Frontier, 1821–46: The American Southwest Under Mexico* (Albuquerque, 1982).

Weber, David J. (editor). *Foreigners in Their Native Land* (Albuquerque, 1973).

———. *The Spanish Frontier in North America* (New York, 1992).

Weems, John Edward. *Dreams of Empire* (New York, 1971).

West, Elliott. *Growing Up with the Country: Childhood on the Far Western Frontier* (Albuquerque, 1989).

White, Richard. *It's Your Misfortune and None of My Own: A History of the American West* (Norman, 1991).

———. *The Roots of Dependency: Subsistence, Environment, and Social Change Among the Choctaws, Pawnees and Navajos* (Lincoln, 1983).

Williams, John Hoyt. *A Great and Shining Road* (New York, 1988).

———. *Sam Houston* (New York, 1993).

INDEX

Figures in italic type refer to illustrations.

Mr. and Mrs. O. C. Smith being photographed at Echo Canyon during the building of the Trans-Mississippi Railroad, ca. 1868

Camp Curry Souvenir Shop, Yosemite Valley

ILLUSTRATION CREDITS

Each credit lists source, negative number (when one exists), and photographer/artist last name (where one is known). When there is more than one credit for a page the images will be listed clockwise from top left.

INSTITUTION ABBREVIATIONS

AC	Amon Carter Museum
AHC	American Heritage Center, University of Wyoming
BAL	The Bancroft Library
BBHC	Buffalo Bill Historical Center
BL	Beinecke Rare Book and Manuscript Library, Yale University
BYU	Brigham Young University
CAH	Center for American History, University of Texas at Austin
CAP	Society of California Pioneers
CHS	California Historical Society
CSHS	Colorado State Historical Society
CSL	California State Library
DPL	Denver Public Library, Western History Department
GG	Greg Gibbs Collection
HL	The Henry E. Huntington Library
ISHS	Idaho State Historical Society
JMW	John McWilliams Collection
Joslyn	Joslyn Art Museum
KC	Kansas Collection, University of Kansas Libraries
KSHS	Kansas State Historical Society
LAPL	Los Angeles Public Library
LBHB	Little Big Horn Battlefield National Monument
LDS	Church of Jesus Christ of Latter-day Saints Archives Division
LOC	Library of Congress — Prints and Photographs Division
Loves	J. David Love Family
MHS	Montana Historical Society
MI	Matthew R. Isenburg Collection
MNHS	Minnesota Historical Society
MNM	Museum of New Mexico
MPM	Milwaukee Public Museum
NA	National Archives
NAA	National Anthropological Archives, Smithsonian Institution
NHS	Nebraska State Historical Society
NMAA	National Museum of American Art, Smithsonian Institution
NMAI	National Museum of the American Indian
NP	Nez Perce National Historical Park
NYHS	New-York Historical Society
NYPL	New York Public Library
OH	Oregon Historical Society
OM-A	The Oakland Museum Art Department
OM-H	The Oakland Museum History Department
PP	Peter E. Palmquist Collection
SA	Stephen Anaya Collection

SC Seaver Center for Western History Research, Natural History Museum of Los Angeles County
SL Department of Special Collections, Stanford University Libraries
TXL Archives Division, Texas State Library
UNP University of Nebraska Press
UOK Western History Collections, University of Oklahoma Library
UPRR Union Pacific Museum Collection
USC University of Southern California, Department of Special Collections
USHS Utah State Historical Society
WDC Division of Cultural Resources, Wyoming Department of Commerce
WS William L. Schaeffer

Photographers, artists, and other abbreviations

Abert, James W.; **Anderson**, George Edward; **Anderson**, John A.; **Baker & Johnston**, Charles S. & Eli; **Baker**, Isaac Wallace; **Barry**, David F.; **Bastida**, Ignacio de la; **Beaman**, E.O.; **Bell**, William A.; **Bierstadt**, Albert; **Bodmer**, Karl; **Butcher**, Solomon; **Cameron**, Evelyn; **Carter**, Charles W.; **Catlin**, George; **Chapman**, John Gadsby; **Choate**, John N.; **Choris**, Ludovik; **Compton**, Alma W.; **Currier**, Nathaniel; **Curtis**, Edward Sheriff - most images from **NAI**: *North American Indian*, 20 volumes and 20 **S** supplementary folios. **Deas**, Charles; **DeBry**, Theodor; **D'Heureuse**, R.; **Fennemore**, James; **Fouch**, John H.; **Gardner**, Alexander; **Gay**, Jane; **Goff**, Orlando S.; **Grabill**, John C.H.; **Hart**, Alfred A.; **Haynes**, Frank Jay; **Hillers**, John K.; **Huddle**, William H.; **Huffman**, Layton Alton; **Hunter**, Elliott W.; **Illingworth**, William H; **Jackson**, William H.; **Kane**, Paul; **Kinsey**, Darius; **Kirkland**, Charles D.; **Lamb**, Adrian; **L'Ouvrier**, Paul; **McArdle**, Henry Arthur; **McClintock**, Walter; **McClure**, Lewis; **Martinez**, Juan de; **Matteson**, Sumner; **Meddaugh**, J. E.; **Miller**, Alfred Jacob; **Moon**, Karl; **Morledge**, Charles D.; **Morrow**, Stanley; **O'Sullivan**, Timothy; **Peale**, Charles Wilson; **Prettyman**, William S; **Reilly**, John J.; **Remington**, Frederic; **Rhinehart**, Frank A.; **Robertson**, George; **Russell**, Andrew J.; **Sherman**, F.M.; **Steele**, F.M.; **Stimson**, Joseph E.; **Throssel**, Richard; **Traeger**, George; **Vance**, Robert; **Vespucci**, Juan; **Vollmer**, H. D.; **Vroman**, Adam Clark; **Watkins**, Carlton E.; **Wilson**, Gilbert; **Wittick**, Ben; **Wright**, Jefferson

Endpapers: WS, Russell.
ii-iii: MHS. v: LOC #USZ62-49148, Curtis, NAI-S V8 #256. vi: JMW; OM-A #A-84.2.1; JMW; LDS #P 100 42. vii: Museum Fine Arts Houston #92.444. viii: SC #4670. ix: OM-A #68.94.1, Baker. x: MHS #946-434. xi: BBHC #P.69.2088. xii: MHS #981-096, Huffman. xiii: BYU, Anderson. xiv: Whatcom Museum #7978, Kinsey. xvi: MPM #43953, Matteson.

The Northern Mystery

1: BL #F805, McClintock. 3: Hispanic Society of America #K42, Vespucci. 4-5: BL #Taylor 192, DeBry. 7: AC #P198.27.38, O'Sullivan. 8-9: SC #V-879, Vroman. 10-11: BL #Zc16 T29 +978ga, Gardner; DPL #F20285, Rhinehart; LOC #USZ62-109747, Moon. WDC #457, Stimson; NAA #1784, Hillers; NAA #42,021, Baker & Johnston. 12: NHS I396:1-4; BL #ZZc12 907cua, Curtis NAI-S Vol 2 #72; LOC #USZ62-106280, Curtis NAI Vol 6 P88. 13: LOC #USZ62-113091, Curtis; SC V-648, Vroman; LOC #USZ62-101197; LOC #USZ62-83603, Curtis. 14-15: LOC #USZ62-47017, Curtis NAI Vol 10 P243; National Archives of Canada #PA37756; American Museum of Natural History #32960; LOC #USZ62-111291, Curtis. 16: LOC #USZ62-113085, Curtis; MPM #112055, Matteson; NAA #54663; NHS C951.8:2-9. 17: BL, Curtis NAI-S Vol 7 #249; NHS A:547-222, Anderson; LOC-Rare Books #USZ62-47017, Curtis NAI-S Vol 16, # 563. 18: British Museum Library, Martinez. 19: University of Glasgow Library. 20: Canyon de Chelly National Monument; School for American Research, Karl Kernberger. 22-23: SC #V-947, Vroman. 24: LOC #USZ62-109374, Hillers. 26: New Phoenix Sun Corp. 28: NMAI #1/6745. 29: LOC #USZ62-40310, Curtis; NAA #3404-A, Bell. 30: NMAI #12/2147. 31: NAA #1535, Beaman. 32: BL #EEcd 815d, Choris; Mission Santa Barbara. 33: OM-H, Coronelli. 34: Both Mission San Fernando, Norman Neuerberg. 35: Joslyn Tab. 16, Bodmer. 36: Both Independence National Historical Park by Peale, #40 & #30. 39: BL #WA MSS 303-4. 40: Both BL #Zc10 807 gac. 41: Joslyn #NA 118A, Bodmer. 42: BL #WA MSS S897. 43: Joslyn, Bodmer. 44-45: ISHS #63-221.223B. 46: American Philosophical Society #871. 49: LOC #USZ62-3283, Hennepin. 51: LOC #USZ62-104344. 52: Old Mission Santa Ines, Jim Frank.

The Most Avid Nation

54-55: LDS #C-188, Carter. 57: Charles Terrill. 58: Shelburne Museum #27.1.5-18, Deas. 59: Joslyn, Miller. 60-61: BL #Zc74870vib; AHC, Miller. 62: BL #WA MSS S498 Box 1 File13. 64: Both GG. 65: Both JMW. 66-67: Both BL #Zc50844gr Vol 1 Copy 1, Didier; BL #Zc50848uqa Copy 2, Abert. 69: CAH #Young TX Map; NYHS #1878.3, L'Ouvrier. 70: RW Norton Art Gallery #311, Catlin. 71: San Jacinto Museum of History, Chapman. 72: CAH #CT0004, Bastida; Daughters of the Republic of Texas Library; TXL #1979/86-1, Wright. 73: CAH. 74: Both Joslyn by Bodmer #NA117 & R16. 75: CAH #CT0034. 76-77 Both TXL 1989/154-1 & 1990/139-1, McArdle. 78: UOK Rose #105; TXL 1990/18-1, Huddle. 79: All NMAA #'s 1985.66 145, 146, 311 by Catlin. 80: OH #87847B; Whitman College. 82: LOC Map Div US West Inds 1:2, 625,000. 83: Houghton Library, Harvard University ABC 18.3.2 Vol 1. 84: Philbrook Museum of Art; UOK Phillips #1459. 85: CSL #550-1. 86-87: National Cowboy Hall of Fame, Bierstadt. 88: BAL #1963.2.1536-D; CSL. 89: California Department of Parks & Recreation #70-02; BAL #1963.2.831-D. 91: Both Whitman College. 92-93: NA #57-HS-277. 94: DPL #F3226. 96: OH #11167. 97: Both Museum of Ontario, Kane. 99: Both LOC #USZ62-14734 & #USZ62-31528. 101: National Portrait Gallery #71.43, Lamb; LDS #P145. 102: LDS #P1300/135. 103-104: Both Church of Jesus Christ of Latter-day Saints Museum of Church History and Art. 105-106: Both USHS #917.81. & #917.8 P24. 108: GG; LOC #LC-BH-8201-8. 109: AC #79.33. 110-111: BL Mexican War; CAP; GG. 113: NP #0226. 115: DPL #F29210. 117: Whyte Museum, Banff #V469/2771.

Seeing the Elephant

118-119: SA. 120: Mrs. Philip Kendall Bekeart. 121: BAL, Watkins/Vance; BL #AN.33.N5.C128. 122: OM-A #A68.90.2, Currier; Museum City of New York. 123: Museum City of New York #57.300.31. 124: Both BL WA MSS 96 F Box 2. 125: Great Lakes Maritime. 126: BAL #1963.2.1418Fr. 127: MI. 128: Both BL WA MSS 96 F Box 2. 129: USHS #92.P4. 131: NYHS #67962. 132: PP, Reilly. 133-134: MI. 135: PP. 136-137: MI; CSL; JMW; MI. 138-140: SA. 141: Gary W. Ewer; JMW; Mark Koenigsberg. 142-143: JMW; SA; MI; MI. 144-145: CAP #C002950. 146: Mrs. Philip Kendall Bekeart. 147: MI. 148: CSL. 912149: WS. 150-151: Greg French; BAL Mackay #105. 153: LOC Maps #US-NW-1851. 156: Peter Shearer; BAL Picture Drawer #16894 (36), D'Heureuse. 158-159: All LDS #P100/6, #P914, #P11. 160-161: BAL Mackay #95. 162-163: BAL Mackay #49; CAP #C004282; CHS #6-G. 165: Porter Historical Society. 167: SC #3516. 170: LAPL #S-000-947-120.

A Hell of a Storm

172-174: All KSHS B, Doy, John. 175: Watkins Community Museum #CS3118.288.40.1. 176: KSHS #B Lovejoy. 177: LDS #P574. 178: USHS #979.2P.13.5. 179: Brownsville Historical Association. 180: WS; WS; JMW. 181: UOK, Rose #937; NAA #1746-A-6; GG. 182: CSL. 184: DPL MC1367. 186: Both NA by O'Sullivan #77-KW-140 & #77-KS-1-13. 187: GG. 188: GG; LOC #B8172-1976; AC-Mazzulla Collection. 189: GG. 190: State Historical Society of Wisconsin WHi(X3)33609, LOT 4645; GG. 191: State Historical Society of Wisconsin WHi(X3)33609, LOT 4645. 192: Linda Harper; State Historical Society of Missouri. 193: KSHS #FK2.D4.2X*1. 194: All KC RHPH 87.5, RHPH 18K:108:D, RHPH 18K:51. 195: KSHS #FK2.D4.L53 1865*1. 196: NAA #79,4274. 198: MNM #7151; NA #111-SC-87976. 199: CSHS #F1897. 200: CSHS #WPA 834. 201: MNM #9829. 202-203: AHC #TP566. 204-211: KSHS #44, Gardner, #C.50*1, #FK2 S3W.71 EP1*1. 212: University of California, Santa Cruz.

William Henry Jackson photographing on Glacier Point, Yosemite Valley, 1880s

The Grandest Enterprise Under God

214-215: OM-H #78, Russell. 216: University of Southern Mississippi. 217: Mariners Museum #P820. 218: OM-H #91, Russell. 219: UPRR #H-5-3, Russell. 220: OM-H #234, Russell. 221: UPRR #H-5-61. 223-229: All OM-H by Russell, #59, #S-176, #S-267-A, #37-b, #23, #55. 231: NAA #3237-A, Bell. 233: LBHB #562. 236: NA #111-SC-87316; NAA #7713305. 237: UOK Campbell #78, Gardner. 238: BL #Zc16D1 +872ga, Gardner. 241: Panhandle-Plains Historical Museum #PH 1 1980-251/24. 242-243: AC; NA #111-SC-87978. 244: Mead Kibbey, E&HT Anthony & Co. 245-247: All SL by Hart, #317, #327, #255, #239. 248-249: Charles Schwartz, Watkins. 251: BL #WA MSS S-1294 S 3 B10 F153. 252: BL WA Photos 27. 254-255: All SL by Hart, #356 & #358-359 (composite). 256: NA #57-HS-114, Jackson; DPL #F20301; Eastman House #GEH 9312.29043, O'Sullivan. 257: NA #57-PS-87, Hillers; DPL #F45231. 258: Both NA #57-PS-61, Fennemore, & #106-WB-304, O'Sullivan. 260-261: UOK, Campbell #1667. 262: LOC #USZ62-42305. 263: Charles Schwartz. 264-265: KSHS #FK2.F2.D73 Zim*1, #FK2.G8.2E.SW*3. 266-267: KSHS #FK2.H2.R65.A.1891*1; KC #RH PH P1924.1. 269: LDS #P100/2882; LDS; BYU #4596507, Anderson. 271: University of Oklahoma Press; LOC #USZ62-36143, Steele. 272-273: LOC #USZ62-55222,

Steele. 275: DPL #F21407; DPL #F26839, Sherman. 276-278: KSHS #F596*27 & #B, Hickok*10. 279: BBHC #P.71.659.2. 280-281: KSHS #FK2.E3.H77*22; DPL #F20368. 282: Sage Books, CO. 283: TXL #1/112-6, Robertson; NAA #3701, Morrow. 284: Detroit Public Library. 287: DPL #F12921, Compton.

RIVERS RUN BACKWARD
290-291: CSHS #WHJ 1190 F24157, Jackson. 292: South Dakota State Historical Society, Illingworth. 293: NYPL #NYPG 90-F80, Illingworth. 294: NYPL #NYPG 90-F80, Illingworth; NAA #3189-B-10, Barry. 295: Both DPL by Barry, #B920, #B156. 296: LOC #USZ62-12281, Palmquist & Jergens. 297: Both NHS by Illingworth, #B774-37, #B774-54. 298: HL. 299: BL #Uncat WA MSS US Army 7th Cavalry Box 3, Goff; James S. Brust, MD, Fouch. 300-301: Both NAA by Red Horse, #CT 72.3934 & #CT 72.3940. 302-303: Both UNP by Amos Bad Heart Bull. 304: Bismarck *Tribune;* AHC #TP633, Throssel. 305: LDS; USHS #728.P2. 306: LDS #P1300/648; NHS #R539-39:2. 307: LDS #P1700/4347. 308: NA #111-SC-88717; NA 106-WB-100, Hillers; MHS #H-3067, Haynes. 309: AC #P1989.7.2; NA #111-SC-82497; MHS #981-359; NA #111-SC-88170. 311: James S. Brust, MD, Fouch. 314: MHS - Library. 315: NAA #2953-A, Jackson. 316-317: Huntington Library, Jackson. 319: AHC #T192, Throssel. 322: Schlesinger Library, Radcliffe College. 323: Washington State Historical Society #1.01, 001. 326: Yosemite Museum #RL-13. 724. 328: MHS #H-2080, Hunter.

THE GREAT DIE UP
330-331: BBHC #P67.279. 333: NHS #012:1-2. 335: NHS #B983-1053, Butcher. 336-337 Both NHS, Butcher, #B983-1216 & #B983-2938a. 338: Both NHS, Butcher, #B983-2182 & #B983-1221. 339: Both NHS, Butcher, #B983-1402 & #B983-1906a. 340-341: All NHS, Butcher, #B983-3137, #B983-73 & #B983-1694. 342: All NHS, Butcher, #B983-2026, #B983-3208 & #B983-1007. 343: Both NHS, Butcher, #B983-1552a & #B983-1552. 344: KSHS #B Singleton*3; LOC #USZ62-26365. 345: NHS #B983-1231, Butcher. 346: NHS 012:1-4. 347: NHS #B983-2567, Butcher. 348: MHS, Huffman Stereo Collection. 349: NAA #56630. 350: Both DPL, Barry, #B751 & #B754. 351: University of Washington #1678. 352: BAL #1963.21477. 354: DPL #F27468. 355: Pinkerton's. 356: Charles Terrill Collection; CSL; Oklahoma Historical Society #4631. 357: Oklahoma Historical Society #8957; NA #111-SC-93354; DPL #F24121. 358: Brown Brothers; BL #Zc10 881br. 359: Mohonk Mountain House. 360: UOK Phillips #436. 361: NAA, Choate, #125 & #195. 362: NAA #78-12294 & #22E. 363: SC #3061. 364: SC #2873. 365: HL Pierce #1185; SC #3000. 366-367: SC #4637 & #1109. 369: MHS PaC 90-87 35-8, Cameron. 370: Jack Rannert; BBHC #P.69.750. 372-373: BBHC #MS47; BBHC #P.69.1918; BBHC #1.69.442; WDC #1846, Stimson. 374-376: All BBHC #P.69.54 & #1.69.2165. 376 & #P.6.454. 379: NHS A547:1:81, Anderson. 381: MNM #15901, Wittick. 382: NHS #R539:18-2.

THE OUTCOME OF OUR EARNEST ENDEAVORS:
384-385: DPL #McL934, McLure. 387: ISHS #3771, Gay. 388: ISHS #63-221-24, Gay. 388-389: MHS #955-986, Gay. 390-391: All UOK Cunningham#182, Prettyman; Swearingen #113; Swearingen #103; Cunningham #106. 392: WDC, Stimson. 393: SC #4170. 394: NMAI #2/1133. 395: NAA#1659-A; LOC #USZ62-40973. 396: NHS Private Collection, Meddaugh. 397: DPL #B835, Barry. 399: LOC #USZ62-11974, Grabill. 400-401: NHS #W938-47, Traeger & Morledge. #403: USC #5; Los Angeles Department of Water & Power #121. 404-405: USC #063. 406: MHS #H-1946, Haynes; Ted Orland Collection. 407: LOC #USZ62-97453; Yosemite Museum. 408: LOC #USZ62-113600; Whatcom Museum, Kinsey. 409-411: J. David Love Family. 412-413: WDC #3781, Stimson. 414-415: J. David Love Family. 417: MNHS #42845, Wilson. 419: State Historical Society of North Dakota #8820; MNHS #9562-A, Wilson. 420: MNHS Wilson Album #V-78-1913 9480-A, Wilson. 421: NAA #4644, Throssel. 422-425: J. David Love Family. 427: Museum of Modern Art. 429: Bruce Herschenson, Plains MO.

432: LOC #USZ62-63510. 434: PP, Reilly. 439: OM #S-591, Russell. 442: Ted Orland. 444: DPL #F7527. 445: BBHC #P.69.2054. Endpaper: WDC

CONTRIBUTORS

DAYTON DUNCAN is the cowriter of the script on which this book is based. He is also a journalist and the author of several books, including *Out West: American Journey Along the Lewis and Clark Trail* and *Miles from Nowhere: Tales from America's Contemporary Frontier.*

JOHN MACK FARAGHER is a professor of history at Yale. He is the author of *Women and Men on the Overland Trail,* for which he received the Frederick Jackson Turner Award, and *Daniel Boone: The Life and Legend of an American Pioneer.*

DAVID GUTIÉRREZ is a member of the history faculty at the University of California, San Diego. He is also the author of *Walls and Mirrors: Mexican Americans, Mexican Immigrants, and the Politics of Ethnicity,* and editor of *Between Two Worlds: Mexican Immigrants in the United States.*

JULIE ROY JEFFREY is Elizabeth Connelly Todd Professor of History at Goucher College. She is the author of *Frontier Women: The Trans-mississippi West, 1840–1880,* and *Converting the West: A Biography of Narcissa Whitman.*

PATRICIA NELSON LIMERICK is professor of history at the University of Colorado at Boulder and author of *Legacy of Conquest: The Unbroken Past of the American West.*

N. SCOTT MOMADAY is a poet, playwright, painter, Pulitzer Prize–winning novelist, and professor of English and American literature. He is the author of many books, including *House Made of Dawn, The Way to Rainy Mountain,* and *Circle of Wonder.*

T. H. WATKINS is the editor of *Wilderness* magazine and the author of many books about the human and natural history of the West. His *Righteous Pilgrim: The Life and Times of Harold L. Ickes 1874–1952* won the Los Angeles *Times* book prize in 1991.

RICHARD WHITE is a professor of history at the University of Washington and the author of *It's Your Misfortune and None of My Own: A New History of the American West.*

A NOTE ABOUT THE AUTHOR

GEOFFREY C. WARD, historian, former editor of *American Heritage* magazine, and writer of more than sixty hours of historical documentaries for public television, is coauthor of *The Civil War: An Illustrated History* and *Baseball: An Illustrated History* as well the principal writer for the television series on which they were based. He is also the author of five other books, including *A First-Class Temperament: The Emergence of Franklin Roosevelt,* which won the 1989 National Book Critics Circle Award for biography and the 1990 Francis Parkman Award of the Society of American Historians.

Production still of mock battle scene during the filming of *The Indian Wars,* produced by Buffalo Bill Cody in 1913

FILM CREDITS

THE WEST

A FILM BY
Stephen Ives

WRITTEN BY
Geoffrey C. Ward and
Dayton Duncan

PRODUCED BY
Stephen Ives
Jody Abramson
Michael Kantor

SENIOR PRODUCER
Ken Burns

SUPERVISING EDITOR
Paul Barnes

EDITED BY
Richard Hankin
Michael Levine
Adam Zucker

NARRATED BY
Peter Coyote

VOICES
Victor Aaron, George Aguilar, Adam Arkin, Philip Bosco, Matthew Broderick, Tantoo Cardinal, Keith Carradine, John Cullum, Blythe Danner, Ossie Davis, Laura Dern, Hector Elizando, Peter Gallagher, Gilly Gilchrist, Murphy Guyer, Julie Harris, Derek Jacobi, Cherry Jones, Gene Jones, Stephen Lang, Ben Lin, Becca Lish, John Lithgow, Ken Littlehawk, Amy Madigan, Mary Stuart Masterson, Charlie McDowell, Zahn McLarnon, Walt McPherson, Russell Means, Arthur Miller, Esai Morales, Martin Moran, Tom Nellis, Larry Pine, Tony Plana, George Plimpton, Murray Porter, Michael Potts, Robert Prosky, Pamela Reed, Jason Robards, Tim Sampson, Miguel Sandoval, August Schellenberg, Gary Sinise, Jimmy Smits, Sheila Tousey, John Trudell, Daniel Von Bargen, Terry Waite, Eli Wallach, M. Emmet Walsh, Fred Ward, Andy Weems, B. D. Wong

MUSIC BY
Matthias Gohl

DIRECTOR OF PHOTOGRAPHY
Buddy Squires with
Allen Moore

CONSULTING PRODUCER
Dayton Duncan

ASSOCIATE PRODUCER
Victoria Gohl

SCRIPT AND FILM RESEARCH
Michelle Ferrari

PRODUCTION MANAGER
Suzanne Seggerman

PRODUCTION COORDINATOR
Jeffrey Dupré

PRODUCTION SECRETARY
Sarah Bingham

BOOKKEEPING
Maureen Dougherty

ASSISTANT EDITORS
Laura Congleton, George O'Donnell, Keir Pearson, Jay Pires

APPRENTICE EDITOR
Hope Litoff

SUPERVISING SOUND EDITOR
Ira Spiegel

SOUND EDITORS
Marlena Grzaslewicz
Jacob Ribicoff

MUSIC EDITOR
Missy Cohen

SOUND RECORDISTS
Michael Kantor, Michael Becker, Doug Cameron, Peter Drowne, Steve Longstreth, Dale Lynn, Bruce Pearlman, Bob Silverthorne, Swain Wolfe

ADDITIONAL CINEMATOGRAPHY
Ken Burns, Jon Else, Mead Hunt, Kevin Kertscher, David Pickner, Dyanna Taylor

ANIMATION PHOTOGRAPHY
Rob Issen
Peter Longauer
The Frame Shop, Edward Joyce and Edward Searles

ASSISTANT CAMERA
Steve Bannister, Ulli Bonnekamp, Justin Fonda, Roger Haydock, Molly O'Brien, Rita Roti, Anthony Savini, Brett Wylie

RESEARCH ASSOCIATES
Nick Davis, Bronwyn Emmet, Mia Gallison, Jan Grenci, Linda Hattendorf, Allison Ross

CONSULTANTS
Alan Brinkley, R. David Edmunds, William K. Everson, John M. Faragher, David Gutiérrez, Yvette Huginnie, Alvin Josephy, Clara Sue Kidwell, Howard R. Lamar, Patricia Nelson Limerick, Henrietta Mann, N. Scott Momaday, Gail Nomura, Joseph C. Porter, James P. Ronda, Robert M. Utley, T. H. Watkins, James Welch, Richard White, Laura Wilson

ADDITIONAL RESEARCH
Nancy Bernard, Brian Bibby, Russell Frank, Jane Jordan, Tina Klein, Jack McDermott, Robin Richman

POSTPRODUCTION ASSISTANTS
Vanessa Cochran
Courtney Little

STILL PHOTOGRAPHY
Paul Christensen
Robert Burgess
Peter Palmquist
Brad Townsend

DIGITAL ENHANCEMENT
Christensen Carver Digital

NEGATIVE MATCHING
Immaculate Matching
Noelle Penraat Incorporated

MAPS
Deborah Freer
Geosystems Global Corporation

RERECORDING ENGINEER
Dominick Tavella
Sound One

TITLE DESIGN
Alexandra L. Gatje

VOICE-OVER RECORDING
Lou Verrico, A & J Recording Studios, Inc.
Scott Greiner, Transmedia
Jeff Robeff, Interlock Audio Post

AMERICAN FOLK MUSIC
Jay Ungar
Molly Mason
Andy Stein
John Kirk
L. E. McCullough
Andy Tierstein

SOLO PIANO
Jacqueline Schwab

NATIVE AMERICAN MUSIC
Dennis Yerry
Bernard Cottonwood
Luke Dubray
James Fall
Ken Littlehawk
Louis Moffsie
Sherry Blakey-Smith
Butch Brown
Charlie Smith
Johnny Smith
Larry Swalley
Melvin Youngbear
Darryl Ironwing Zephier

ADDITIONAL MUSIC
Matthias Gohl, Peter Calo, Richard Martinez, Nana Vasconcelos

MUSIC CONSULTANTS
Dennis Yerry
Andy Tierstein

NATIONAL PUBLICITY
Owen Comora Associates

SPECIAL THANKS
Daniel C. Esty
David O. Ives
John T. Sughrue
Robert A. Wilson

THANKS
Celie's Waterfront Bed & Breakfast; Eric Altman, Film Video Denver; Pam Tubridy Baucom; J.S. Canner & Company, Inc.; Custer County Historical Society; Durango and Silverton Railroad; Peggy Frank; J. S. Holliday; Gary Keller, South Dakota Film Commission; Bertha Kucera; Duane Lammers, Triple 7 Ranch; Howard Lay; Bill Lindstrom, Kathy Landau; Wyoming Film Commission; Mike McCone, California Historical Society; Barbara Love; David and Jane Love; Frances Love Froidevaux; Dan Markoff; Nannies Unlimited, Los Angeles; Toby Shimin; Sterling Memorial Library, Yale University; Lonie Stimac, Montana Film Commission; Anne Symmes; University of Oklahoma Press; Annette Windhorn, University of Nebraska Press; Dr. Deward E. Walker, Jr. ; and Lucy

A Coproduction of Insignia Films and
WETA-TV, Washington,
in Association with
Florentine Films
and
Time-Life Video & Television

FOR WETA
Sharon P. Rockefeller, President and CEO
Phylis Geller, Executive-in-Charge
David S. Thompson, Project Director
Mary Schultz and
Cecily Van Praagh, Promotion

SENIOR PROGRAM CONSULTANT
Geoffrey C. Ward

EXECUTIVE PRODUCER
Ken Burns